THE TOURISM SYSTEM

An Introductory Text

Second Edition

Robert Christie Mill

School of Hotel and Restaurant Management
University of Denver

Alastair M. Morrison

Department of Restaurant, Hotel, and Institutional Management
Purdue University

Prentice-Hall International, Inc.

© 1992 by Prentice-Hall, Inc.
A Simon and Schuster Company
Englewood Cliffs, New Jersey 07632

Printed in the United States of America
10 9 8 7 6 5 4 3 2

ISBN 0-13-928094-4

Prentice-Hall International (UK) Limited, *London*
Prentice-Hall of Australia Pty. Limited, *Sydney*
Prentice-Hall Canada Inc., *Toronto*
Prentice-Hall Hispanoamericana, S.A., *Mexico*
Prentice-Hall of India Private Limited, *New Delhi*
Prentice-Hall of Japan, Inc., *Tokyo*
Simon & Schuster Asia Pte. Ltd., *Singapore*
Editora Prentice-Hall do Brasil, Ltda., *Rio de Janeiro*
Prentice-Hall, Inc., *Englewood Cliffs, New Jersey*

To
Patty Mill
Calum and Jessie Morrison

CONTENTS

FOREWORD

SALAH E. A. WAHAB, Ph.D., F.BIM, C.H.A.

Professor of Tourism, University of Alexandria, Egypt
President of Tourismplan, Affiliate Member to WTO
Chairman of the Egyptian Society of Scientific Experts on Tourism
Past Vice-President of IUOTO, forerunner of WTO
Former Chief of Tourism Programmes, ILO Turin Centre, Italy
Former First UnderSecretary of State for Tourism in Egypt

Tourism has become a significant expression of human activity that has contributed and still contributes much to receiving countries' economies, social welfare, and cultural patrimony. In 1988 world tourism generated 12 percent of world gross national product (GNP). International tourism totalled 390 million visits, and tourism spending in destinations reached 195 billion American dollars. Domestic tourism in the four corners of the world is believed to constitute a sizable volume nine times greater than international tourism. Within each country, domestic tourism contributes to an improved economic balance through a redistribution of the national income. It, moreover, stimulates small business expansion and generally promotes activity favorable to the overall economy of the country concerned. In sum, tourism as a human phenomenon of social mobility has surpassed the point of no return.

It is quite a responsibility to accept writing this foreword to the second edition of *The Tourism System,* a book that has already proved in its first edition to be one of the leading textbooks in the English-speaking orbit, notwithstanding the increasing number of these textbooks in the 1980's.

After the appearance of the *General Theory of Tourism* in German in 1942 (the first serious and scientific book on tourism) by Professors Kraph and Walter Hunziker, there was a dearth of serious textbooks for about thirty years. It was the early seventies before some good textbooks were published. The eighties represented another decade of tourism scientific research in which a noticeable advancement was achieved in the number of publications and quality of knowledge. This is deemed necessary as tourism research, like any other scientific discipline, undergoes a fast and ever-evolving development in harmony with the swift-changing structures in the tourism industry.

The Tourism System (Second Edition) represents an orderly argument for renewed scholarly interest in tourism. It offers an important means of comprehending human sociability, motivations for travel, people's encounters with new places, and their cognitive relationship to landscape; development of tourism thus becomes an exercise of challenge for the destination in terms of planning, industry organization, and marketing. As a textbook on the introductory part of tourism, it is a step forward and carries many improvements and changes that cope with and take account of the new challenges and international supervening variables affecting the tourism phenomenon and the tourism industry at various destinations.

Although the whole book is a pleasure to read and study, there are certain chapters which illustrate the focal points of establishing a sound tourism industry, some of which are sometimes overlooked or underestimated by tourism destinations. Such chapters deal with selecting a travel destination, travel motivations, environment for tourism, characteristics of travel segments, tourism policy formulation, tourism planning, tourism development, and tourism marketing.

In sum, this book's uncontested academic value, as well as its practical benefit to those responsible executives dealing with tourism development or those involved in the tourism business at various destinations, make it an indispensable tool for tourism learning, teaching, and practice.

SALAH E.A. WAHAB

PREFACE

In writing this book we set out to do two things: describe how tourism works and indicate how people who are part of tourism can utilize this knowledge to make tourism work for them and their particular business or destination.

Tourism is a difficult phenomenon to describe. We have trouble in thinking of tourism as an industry. Wells defines an industry as a "number of firms that produce similar goods and services and therefore are in competition with each other."[1] In no sense of the word does this describe a *tourism industry*. The businesses that comprise tourism offer complementary rather than competing products and services. The airline, hotel, restaurant, and attractions industries do not compete with each other. They complement each other and come together to offer tourists the services that comprise a vacation. The idea of a *tourism industry* would give some unity to the idea of tourism, and from an image and a political viewpoint it sounds attractive. From an image viewpoint, tourism is presently thought of in ambiguous terms. No definitions of tourism are universally accepted. There is a link between tourism, travel, recreation, and leisure, yet the link is fuzzy. All tourism involves travel, yet not all travel is tourism. All tourism involves recreation, yet not all recreation is tourism. All tourism occurs during leisure time, but not all leisure time is given to tourist pursuits. The definition of tourism as an industry with clearly defined limits would aid both those within and outside of tourism in getting a clear picture of what tourism is all about. With a clear image would come a better understanding.

The idea of a tourism industry is also attractive politically. One of tourism's strengths is the fact that its effect is felt by many businesses, organizations, and people. The tourist dollar finds its way into many pockets. At first glance this might seem ideal as a means of gathering political support for the development, management, and marketing of toursim. However, this apparent strength is a basic weakness for those interested in tourism. Because tourism touches so many people in major or minor ways, the overall effect is difficult to measure or appreciate totally. There is no standard industrial classification number for "tourism." Also, many people whose lives or businesses are touched by tourism are primarily engaged in other activities serving other markets. The

---

[1]Alexander T. Wells, *Air Transportation: A Management Perspective,* Second Edition (Belmont CA., Wadsworth Publishing Company, 1989), p. 162.

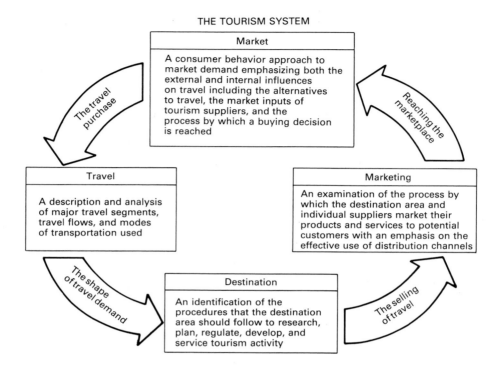

THE TOURISM SYSTEM

Market

A consumer behavior approach to market demand emphasizing both the external and internal influences on travel including the alternatives to travel, the market inputs of tourism suppliers, and the process by which a buying decision is reached

The travel purchase

Reaching the marketplace

Travel

A description and analysis of major travel segments, travel flows, and modes of transportation used

Marketing

An examination of the process by which the destination area and individual suppliers market their products and services to potential customers with an emphasis on the effective use of distribution channels

The shape of travel demand

The selling of travel

Destination

An identification of the procedures that the destination area should follow to research, plan, regulate, develop, and service tourism activity

storekeeper sells to tourists and local people. The museum serves visitors and residents. We may know that tourism affects us. It is often difficult to evaluate the extent of our involvement. Thus, from a political viewpoint, the idea of a tightly defined tourism industry would allow us to demonstrate to everyone's satisfaction the impact and importance of tourism. Political support matched with economic assistance would more readily be forthcoming.

Yet, tourism is not an industry. *Tourism* is an activity. It is an activity that takes place when, in international terms, people cross a border for leisure or business and stay at least twenty-four hours, but less than one year. Those who stay less than twenty-four hours are defined by the World Tourism Organization as *excursionists*. Domestically, the United States has emphasized distance traveled from home. The present definition of a *trip* is a person traveling to a place at least 100 miles from home. The purpose may be for business or pleasure.

The study of tourism is the study of this phenomenon and its effects. The business of tourism is the business of encouraging this kind of activity and taking care of the needs of people while engaged in this kind of activity.

We chose to describe tourism as a system. It is important to see tourism as consisting of interrelated parts. Because of reasons mentioned earlier, businesses and organizations that have been, to some degree, affected by tourism, often do not consider themselves part of tourism. Many people within the hotel industry or the restaurant industry do not feel part of tourism. Their business begins when the customer walks in the front door. This myopic view has meant that those in the industry have ended up *reacting* to changes that have occurred outside their front door, rather than *acting* in anticipation of upcoming changes. The system is like a spider's web—touch one part of it and reverberations will be felt throughout. By showing where the hotelier is linked to the tourist and by further examining the factors that influence the decision to become a tourist, the hotelier at a particular destination can watch for changes in those factors and can anticipate changes in the number and characteristics of tourists that may be induced to stay at his or her hotel.

The Tourism System consists of four parts—Market, Travel, Destination, Marketing. The decision to travel or become a tourist can be understood by an examination of the market segment of the system. The decision to travel is made if the individual has learned in the past that travel satisfies felt needs, if the individual perceives that future travel will satisfy felt needs, and if travel falls within the external constraints of that individual's environment. A consumer behavior model is the mechanism by which these processes are examined. Changes in any of these three processes will affect the individual's travel purchase behavior.

Once a person decides to travel, decisions must then be made as to where, when, and how to go. The second segment of *The Tourism System* describes and analyzes these choices. Trends in the various travel segments are outlined. An examination of tourist flows both internationally and domestically is the first step in understanding present movements; it will also help to predict future travel movements. In conjunction with this, the modes of travel are discussed to determine recent trends and future prospects. The shape of travel, then, is the combination of who is traveling, and where, when, and how she or he is traveling.

The destination is the third major part of the system. The destination mix consists of the attractions and services used by the traveler. If one examines the parts of the mix, it becomes clear that each part is dependent upon the others for success in attracting, servicing, and satisfying the tourist. In order to sell travel, the destination must be aware of the benefits to be gained from tourism and the pitfalls to be avoided. An overall policy towards tourism can then be formulated and development plans drawn up within the context of the regulatory framework affecting tourism.

The destination area reaches people in the market and encourages them to travel through the process of marketing, the fourth part of the system. The development of a marketing plan, the selection of an appropriate marketing mix, and the choice of a distribution channel will spell success or failure for the destination's attempt to encourage tourist travel.

At the conclusion of each section a reading is presented that summarizes the overall theme of the preceding section.

In describing the various parts of the system and their interactions, those who operate within the system can see who they and their businesses or destinations affect and how they are affected by other participants in the system.

The text goes beyond a description of tourism to outline principles to influence tourism. In describing the process by which tourists decide to travel, insight is shared into how that process can be influenced. The segment on travel leads readers to an understanding of how to benefit from existing movements and future changes. The destination chapters give specifics on how those who are part of a destination's attractions and services can optimize tourism's contribution to the destination. The section on marketing lays out ways and means to develop a marketing plan and work through the apropriate channel to reach the target market.

This book will be of assistance to students and practitioners alike in understanding how tourism works and how it can be made to work for them, their business, and their destination.

TOURISM:

An Introduction

"A traveller has the need of a falcon's eye, a monkey's face, a merchant's words, a camel's back, a hog's mouth, a deer's feet. And the traveller to Rome—the back of an ass, the belly of a hog, and a conscience as broad as the king's highway.

Line your doublet with taffetie, taffetie is lice-proof. Never journey without something to eat in your pocket, if only to throw at dogs when attacked by them.

Carry a notebook and red crayon.

When going by coach, avoid women, especially old women; they always want the best places.

At sea, remove your spurs; sailors make a point of stealing them from those who are being seasick, Keep your distance from them in any case; they are covered with vermin.

In an inn-bedroom which contains big pictures, look behind the latter to see they do not conceal a secret door, or a window.

Women should not travel at all and married men not much."

E.S. Bates, *Touring in 1600* (Boston and New York, Houghton Mifflin) pp. 58–59.
Copyright 1911 by E.S. Bates.

HISTORICAL DEVELOPMENT.

For tourism to occur, there must be people who have the *ability* both in terms of *time* and *money*, the *mobility*, and the *motivation* to travel. While the era of mass tourism is a relatively recent one, an individual's propensity and ability to travel has been advanced by numerous developments throughout time.

In preindustrial times much of the motivation for travel was to develop trade. As empires grew, the conditions necessary for travel began to be developed. Egyptian travel was for both business and pleasure. Travel was necessary between the central government and the territories. To accommodate travelers on official business, hospitality centers were built along major routes and in the cities. Egyptians also traveled for pleasure. Public festivals were held several times a year. Travel was also for curiosity—to visit the great tombs and temples of the pharoahs.

Assyria comprised the area now known as Iraq. As the empire expanded from the Mediterranean in the west to the Persian Gulf in the east, mobility was made easier to facilitate moving the military. Roads were improved; markers were established to indicate distances; and posts and wells were developed for safety and nourishment. Even today we see the influence of military construction aiding pleasure travel. The recently completed U.S. Interstate highway system was developed initially to facilitate transportation in the event of a national emergency.

While previous civilizations had set the stage for the development of travel, it took the Greeks and, later, the Romans to bring it all together. In Greek times water was the most important means of moving commercial goods. This combined with the fact that cities grew up along the coast to ensure that travel was primarily by sea. Travel for official business was less important as Greece was divided into city-states that were very independent. Pleasure travel did exist in three areas—for religious festivals, for sporting events (most notably the Olympic games), and to visit cities, especially Athens.

Travel was advanced by two important developments that made travel easier. First, a system of currency exchange was developed. Previously, travelers would pay their way by carrying various goods and selling them at their destinations. The money of Greek city-states was now accepted as international currency, eliminating the need to travel with a cargo of goods. Second, the Greek language spread throughout the Mediterranean area, making it easier to communicate as one traveled.

Travel flourished in Roman times for five reasons. The control of the large empire stimulated trade and led to the growth of a large middle class with the money to travel; Roman coins were all the traveler had to carry to finance the trip; the means of transportation—roads and waterways—were excellent; communication was relatively easy, as Greek and Latin were the principal languages; and the legal system provided protection from foreign courts, thereby ensuring the safety of the traveler.

The sporting games started by the Greeks were copied in the gladiators' fights to the death. Sightseeing was also popular, particularly to Greece. Greece had recently become a part of greater Rome and was now the place to see. Touring was also popular to Egypt, site of the Sphinx and the pyramids, and to Asia Minor, scene of the Trojan War. Aristotle visited Asia Minor before establishing his school for students. A final development was that of second homes and vacations associated with them. Villas spread south to Naples, near the sea, the mountains, or mineral spas.

As the Roman empire collapsed in the fifth century, roads fell into disuse and Barbarians made it unsafe to travel. Whereas a Roman courier could travel up to 100 miles a day, the average daily rate of journey during the Middle Ages was 20 miles. It was not until the twelfth century that the roads became secure again. This was due to the large numbers of travelers going on pilgrimages. Pilgrims traveled to pay homage to a particular site or as an atonement for sin. Those who heard confessions often required the sinner to travel barefoot. In other cases pilgrims journeyed to fulfill a promise made when they were sick.

The next important factor in the history of travel was the Renaissance. As society moved from a rural to an urban base, wealth grew, and more people had the money to travel. Pilgrimages were still important, though journeys to Jerusalem declined due to the growth of Protestantism in Europe. The impetus to travel to learn was aided by the arrival of Renaissance works from Italy. Stable monarchies helped assure travelers' safety.

The beginning of the sixteenth century saw a new age of curiosity and exploration, which culminated in the popularity of the Grand Tour. This was initially a sixteenth century Elizabethan concept, brought about by the need to develop a class of professional statesmen and ambassadors. Young men traveled with ambassadors over Europe to complete their education. The practice continued to develop in the seventeenth and eighteenth centuries until it became the "in" thing. No gentleman's education was complete until he had spent from one to three years traveling around Europe with a tutor.

The Grand Tour began in France, where French was studied, together with dancing, fencing, riding, and drawing. Before Paris could corrupt the morals or ruin the finances, the student would head for Italy to study sculpture, music appreciation, and art. The return was by way of Germany, Switzerland, and the Low Countries (Holland, Belgium, and Luxembourg). The Grand Tour reached its peak of popularity in the 1750's and 1760's but was brought to a sudden end by the French Revolution and the Napoleaonic Wars.

In the late eighteenth century and early nineteenth century two major factors affected the development of tourism. Increased industrialization accounted for both of them. First, the industrial revolution accelerated the movement from rural to urban areas. This produced a large number of people in a relatively small area. The desire or motivation to "escape," even for a brief period, was there. Associated with this was the development of steam engines in the form of trains and steam ships. This allowed the means or mobility to escape.

Because of the proximity of the coast to the major urban areas, it was only natural that train lines extended in these directions. However, the vast majority of visitors to the seaside were day trippers. It was well into the second half of the eighteenth century that the working classes in Britain were able to get regular holidays and sufficient income to use their leisure time to travel.

The desire or motivation to "escape," even for a brief period, was there—yet today's vacation spots often generate a large number of people in a relatively small area.

The development of spas was largely due to the members of the medical profession, who began to recommend the medicinal properties of mineral waters during the seventeenth century. The idea originated, however, with the Greeks. Spas on the continent of Europe were developed two to three hundred years before their growth in England. Development occurred because of three factors—the approval of the medical profession, court patronage, and local entrepreneurship to take advantage of the first two.

Patronage by Court figures helped establish spas as the "in" place to be. Today we talk in tourism about "mass follows class"—the idea that the masses are influenced in their choices of vacation spots by people they consider influential. Today film stars seem to have taken over the role of influencer from royalty.

The number of people who could afford to "take the waters" was rather small. By the end of the seventeenth century the influence of the medical profession had declined, and spas were more for entertainment than for health. Their popularity continued, however, into the nineteenth century. It is still possible today to drink from the mineral waters at Bath in England, while Hot Springs in Arkansas and Glenwood Springs in Colorado still attract many visitors. Additionally, many Eastern European towns proclaim the beneficial effects of mud packs and hydrotherapy.

The medical profession, the British court, and Napoleon all helped popularize the seaside resort. The original motive for sea bathing was for reasons of health. Dr. Richard Russell argued that sea water was effective against such things as cirrhosis, dropsy, gout, gonorrhea, and scurvy and insisted that people drink a pint of it. It is worthy of note that the good Dr. Russell was a physician in Brighton, a resort close to London and on the water! Brighton's fame was assured after the patronage of the Prince Regent, who later became George IV. Similarly, Southend and Cowes are associated with Princess Charlotte and Queen Victoria respectively.

The growth of the seaside resort was stimulated by the French Revolution and the Napoleaonic Wars. It will be recalled that both put an end to the Grand Tour. Those who would have taken the Grand Tour could not travel to the Continent. The now fashionable seaside resorts were the alternative. Towards the end of the nineteenth century, the seaside resorts in Europe became the palaces for the working classes. This was due to the introduction of paid holidays and better wages.

The term *holiday* comes from holy days—days for religious observances. Ancient Rome featured public holidays for great feasting. As Europe became Christian, certain saints' days and religious festivals became holy days when people fasted and prayed and refrained from work. After the Industrial Revolution the religious holidays gradually became secularized, and the week's holiday emerged. The vacation was negotiated between employer and workers and was again due to the economic and social changes brought about by the Industrial Revolution. It made sense to take the holidays during the warmer summer months. For the employer it was advantageous to close the entire factory down for one week rather than face the problems of operating with small groups of people absent over a longer period of time. Still today certain weeks are associated with the general holidays of certain towns.

Prior to World War I the principal mode of domestic transportation was the railway. This meant that development was concentrated at particular points. Regional development occurred with particular resorts growing to serve specific urban areas. Mass production of the car, as will be seen later, allowed the dispersion of destination developments.

Tourism in the United States developed for the same reasons as in Europe. Travel was limited by the need for transportation. The first development of note was that of resorts. With the encouragement of physicians, resorts like Saratoga in New York became very fashionable by the early 1800s. The ocean also became attractive for health reasons initially, although amusements soon sprang up as well.

It took the development of the railway to open up the country to travelers. The completion of the Erie Railroad spurred the development of Niagara Falls as a honeymoon paradise by the 1870s.

The vast river network of the interior of the country allowed the development of steamboat excursions, particularly gambling and amusement trips between New Orleans and St. Louis.

The Industrial Revolution produced a class of wealthy people who had the time to travel. Touring became popular. Many took the Grand Tour while, for most in the South, an American-style ''grand tour'' to the North took a comparable amount of time and money. Three attractions were paramount—Northern cities, historical sites (the American Revolution and the Civil War), and resorts.

By the late 1800's the West was attracting not only Easterners but also Europeans to see the natural beauty and to hunt buffalo. Foreign travelers were also fascinated at this time by travel for religious reasons—to visit the important places where the various religious sects had sprung up.

In the United States the late nineteenth century and early twentieth centuries were characterized as days of "high society." The population was rural and centered in the Northeast and Midwest. The 50 million people lived in typically large families who had a strong puritanical work ethic and a belief in self-denial. A sixty-hour workweek with Sundays off was the norm. Much of the working class' leisure time was centered around the church. For the wealthy, travel was by railroad and ship to luxury hotel resorts and large second homes. Only the wealthy few were able to travel overseas. The twelve-hour workday had been reduced to ten hours by the end of the 1800s. Vacations were beginning to be recognized. While travel had been for the few, now it began to come within the reach of more of the people.

Between the World Wars we began to see the emergence of today's consumer society and an era of mass recreation. The 130 million people in the United States spread increasingly to the West coast and a rural-urban population emerged. Families were smaller, a fifty-hour workweek was common, and more workers were given paid vacations. The development of the automobile allowed the freedom to travel and led to the emergence of the motel. Attractions and facilities became more dispersed as people were not restricted in their movements by the use of public transportation. More middle class people were purchasing second homes and seeing leisure time as something that was a privilege to enjoy. In Europe legislation was passed giving paid vacations.

Mass tourism as we know it today is a post–World War II phenomenon. Women who had to work during the War felt more independent; men and women who traveled overseas to fight wanted to return as visitors; travel overseas was encouraged as part of the U.S. attempt to aid war-torn European economies; the introduction of the passenger jet reduced travel time from the U.S. to Europe from five sailing days or 24 flying hours to eight hours; and surplus propeller airplanes were made available to charter operators to transport tourists, not troops, as airlines rushed to purchase new jet aircraft.

The sixties marked the democratization of travel. In the U.S. the growth of the population—the baby boomers—together with the 40-hour workweek, increasing numbers of three-day weekends, and higher levels of disposable income enabled the large numbers of people with the time and money to indulge themselves. The ease of credit and the development of the "me generation" led to an attitude that travel was a right. A hedonistic—pleasure for the sake of pleasure—attitude increasingly overtook the self-denial of the work ethic.

Temporarily stunned by the oil crises of the seventies, tourism continued to grow. The late seventies and eighties saw the development of single-parent families and two-income families, together with an increased accent on individual awareness and self-improvement. For many, indulgence was replaced by a concern for physical fitness.

Today travel and tourism is a $260 billion endeavor in the United States, with travel receipts accounting for 6.4% of the Gross National Product. Americans spend $748 million a day on travel and tourism. Domestically and internationally for the United States, it generates:

Americans spend $748 million a day on travel and tourism

- Payroll income of $57.8 billion
- 5.21 million jobs directly and an additional 2.2 million indirectly
- Federal tax revenues of $17.9 billion
- States tax revenues of $12.1 billion
- Local tax revenues of $3.6 billion

Travel and tourism is the second largest private employer in the nation, accounting for 8.7% of total nonagricultural payroll employment. Travel and tourism is the first, second, or third largest employer in 39 states—the largest employer in 15 states, the second largest in 12 states, and the third largest in 12 states. For every seven jobs in travel and tourism, three jobs are generated in businesses that supply goods and services to those in travel and tourism.

The major beneficiaries of tourism in terms of dollars spent there are California, Florida, New York, Texas, and New Jersey.

In 1987 foreign visitors to the United States consumed, each *hour*: 3,200 chickens; 68,000 eggs; 27,000 link sausages; 34,000 slices of bacon; 6,600 orders of prime rib; over 4,200 steaks; nearly 6,000 hamburgers; over 3,000 gallons of milk; over 2,700 pounds of cheese; 3,100 gallons of ice cream; over 27,000 pounds of potatoes; 860 cases of beer; and 1,300 bottles of wine!

TOURISM: A DEFINITION.

A variety of definitions exist for what we call tourism. Tourism is not an industry, although tourism gives rise to a variety of industries. Tourism is an *activity* engaged in by people who travel.

In 1963 the United Nations Conference on International Travel and Tourism in Rome recommended a definition of the term *visitor* to include any person who visits a country other than the one in which he or she lives for any purpose other than one which involves pay from the country being visited. Specifically they noted that visits could be for the following reasons:

1. Leisure, recreation, holiday, sport, health, study, religion
2. Business, family, friends, mission, meeting

Persons staying for less than 24 hours would be *excursionists*. Those staying longer would be *tourists*. Under this definition a tourist would be someone who traveled for business or for pleasure, as long as he or she did not receive money from the country visited.

In 1968 the United Nations Statistical Commission accepted this definition but recommended that member nations decide for themselves whether to use the term *excursionist* or *day visitor*. The important point was to distinguish between visitors who did or did not stay overnight.

In 1978 the U.N. Department of Economic and Social Affairs published a set of guidelines which included a definition of the term *international visitor*. The Commission recognized that international visitors were those who visited a given country from abroad (what we might call inbound tourists) and those who went abroad on visits from a given country (outboard tourists). They indicated that the maximum period a person could spend in a country and be called a visitor would be one year.

Most countries at the national level accept the United Nations definition of visitors. Briefly, an international tourist is someone who spends at least one night, but no more than one year, in a country other than his or her own. The tourist can be there for a variety of reasons, but not for pay from the country being visited. A person who meets the above criteria but who does not stay overnight is called an excursionist.

The World Tourism Organization has also proposed a definition for *domestic tourist* that is based on length of stay: Any person residing within a country, irrespective of nationality, travelling to a place within this country other than his usual residence for a period of not less than 24 hours or one night for a purpose other than the exercise of a remunerated activity in the place visited. The motives for such travel may be:

1. Leisure (recreation, holidays, health, studies, religion, sports);
2. Business, family, mission, meeting.

A domestic excursionist is someone who meets the above definition but who does not stay overnight.

The U.S. Census Bureau publishes the National Travel Survey every five years. In the 1963 and 1967 surveys they defined a *trip* as "each time a person goes to a place at least 100 miles away from home and returns or is out-of-town one or more nights." Later surveys omitted the phrase "or is out-of-town one or more nights."

This means that estimates of national tourist travel are understated as, for example, travel for the weekend to spots less than 100 miles away are not counted.

The prestigious Travel Data Center regularly collects, analyzes, and publishes data on travel and tourism in the United States. It has accepted the definition of the U.S. Census Bureau. Travel as part of an operating crew on a train, plane, bus, truck, or ship, commuting to a place of work, or student's trips to and from school are not included in their definition of a trip.

For the purpose of this text travel refers to the act of moving outside of one's home community for business or for pleasure but not for commuting or traveling to or from school.

Tourism is the term given to the activity that occurs when tourists travel. This encompasses everything from the planning of the trip, the travel to the place, the stay itself, the return, and the reminiscences about it afterwards. It includes the activities the traveler undertakes as part of the trip, the purchases made, and the interactions that occur between host and guest. In sum, it is all of the activities and impacts that occur when a visitor travels.

Recreation is what happens during an individual's leisure time.

The term *recreation* overlaps in many ways with tourism. Recreation is what happens during an individual's leisure time. Leisure time is the time people have discretion over. During leisure time people can do what *they* want. The activities that people engage in during leisure time are known as recreation. Some say that to be recreation the activity should be constructive or pleasurable. This might involve either active or passive pursuits, indoor or outdoor activities. There is no time or distance aspect to recreation. A game of tennis or golf two miles from home after work would constitute recreation. If one were to drive 100 miles to a resort for the weekend, the game of tennis would be part of tourism and the golfer would be on a trip.

It is projected that tourism will be the world's largest economic activity by the year 2000. It is hoped that, by applying the principles developed in this text, those involved in the future development of travel and tourism will be able to lead the way into the 21st century.

THE TOURISM SYSTEM

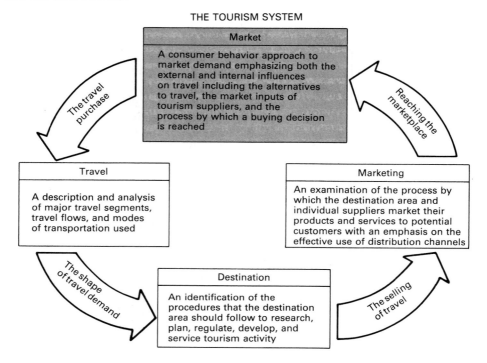

In order to market a destination or a travel product effectively, it is necessary to understand how individuals decide to make a vacation purchase. As Tom Peters said, "Markets don't buy things; people buy things." The first four chapters explain the forces that determine whether or not a vacation will be purchased. Although each part of the model (a consumer-behavior explanation of vacation purchases) is explained in detail, it should be noted that the process is dynamic. Some forces will work towards a decision to purchase, while others will work against it. By understanding how each part influences the overall process, a greater understanding of vacation purchases will be gained. From a practical viewpoint, marketers will be able to influence each part of the process in an attempt to have their tourism product bought.

Individuals are motivated (1) to buy a vacation to satisfy unmet needs and wants. They will go on to buy that vacation if they have learned that vacation purchases tend to gratify an important need. Particular motives are combined with known destination alternatives (2) and the purchase criteria (3) both considered important to arrive at an inclination (4) towards each alternative that may be either positive ("I'm inclined to go there") or negative ("I don't think that's for me"). This inclination will affect the individual's attitude (5) towards that destination at a later

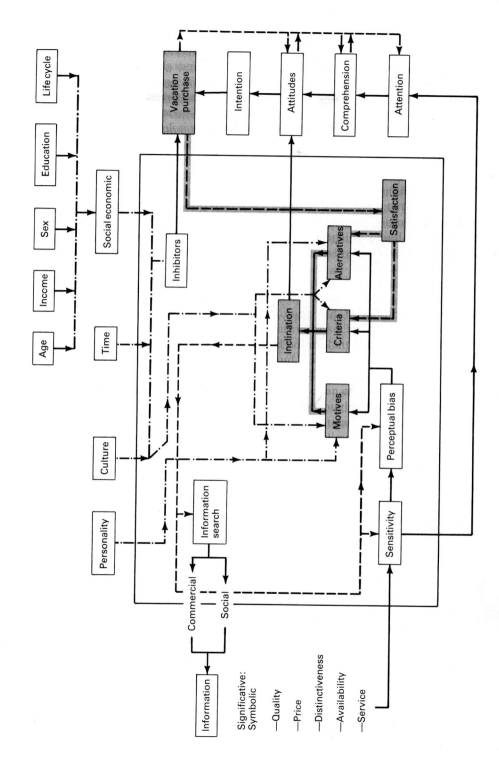

A consumer-behavior explanation of vacation purchases.

11

stage in the process. The level of satisfaction (6) from a prior vacation purchase (7) will impact both alternatives (2) and purchase criteria (3). If a vacation was purchased and the tourist was dissatisfied, that particular destination may be eliminated from future consideration. It may have been that price was very important as a purchase criterion. The returning tourist may now feel that cutting back on price produced an inferior vacation. As such, the purchase criteria (3) may be changed to substitute *price* with *value*. The topics of needs, wants and motives and how tourists learn is covered in Chapter 1.

The vacation purchase is made, not on the actual facts, but on the individual's *perception* of these facts. The perception may be a true reflection of the actual situation, or it may not. The key point is that the buying decision is perceptual. This is the subject of Chapter 2.

Depending upon their inclination (4) to buy, potential travelers will search for information (8) on various vacation alternatives. They seek information from both the commercial environment (9)—advertisements, brochures, and the like—and the social environment (10)—friends and relatives. The available information may be significative (11), or actual, or it may be symbolic (12), or perceptual. A four-ounce hamburger is the *actual* weight of the burger, while a quarter-pounder makes it *seem* larger. Information is generally sought, and travel products can be differentiated on the basis of quality, price, distinctiveness, availability and service (13). Information coming in from the commercial (9) and social (10) environments is taken in, depending upon how sensitive (14) the tourist is to it. This is affected in great part by the inclination (4) to receive the incoming information. If the tourist is not inclined towards a particular vacation opportunity, information on it in the form, for example, of advertisements or personal recommendations will be blocked out—the individual is just not interested. The reverse is also true. This first stage of sensitivity (14) determines the quantity of information that gets the attention. The next stage—perceptual bias (15)—determines the quality of information that gets through. Again, this is affected by the tourist's inclination (4) to the vacation possibility. If the tourist is already positively inclined towards a destination, information on it will be viewed in a more favorable light than if the tourist were initially negative towards it. The information received may be powerful enough to strengthen or weaken either motives (1), alternatives (2), or purchase criteria (3). In the final stage of this part of the process, once the tourist has been sensitized to incoming information, the message has been brought to his or her attention (16).

Even if tourists are motivated to travel, have learned that vacations will satisfy important needs, and perceive that a particular destination is for them, they are constrained by external factors—inhibitors (17) that restrict their travel plans. The culture (18) in which they were raised and the amount of available time (19), in addition to various socio-economic (20) factors such as their age (21), income (22), sex (23), education (24) and stage in the family life cycle (25), all influence, and may inhibit, the purchase decision. An individual's cultural background wll also impact the motives (1) and the purchase criteria (3) he or she considers important as well as the list of alternatives (2) considered. There is also a link between personality (26) and motives

(1) and personality (26) and alternatives (2). A more authoritarian person, for example, will consider fewer alternatives before arriving at a purchase decision. The link between personality and motives is less clearly defined. Conservative people tend to be motivated to make conservative purchases. But which influences which? Is a person conservative because conservative purchases are made or is the fact that conservative purchases have been made reason to label someone "conservative"? The external influences on the purchase decision are explored in Chapter 3.

Attracting the attention of tourists

The final part of the purchase model is covered in Chapter 4. Depending on the individual's sensitivity (14) to incoming information, the sender of the information has attracted the attention (16) of the tourist. The tourist must still, in her or his mind, go through a process before arriving at the decision to buy. After the message attracts the attention (16) of the tourist, he or she must comprehend (27) the advantages of the vacation opportunity. The more the tourist understands the advantages of the travel product, the more attention gets paid to the message. Then a positive attitude (5) towards the vacation has to develop in the tourist's mind. Attitudes towards the vacation are influenced by the tourist's inclination (4) towards or against it. A positive attitude (5) will influence the extent to which the vacation's advantages are comprehended (27). The reverse is also true. Once a positive attitude (5) has developed, the tourist goes through an intention (28) to buy stage before making the actual vacation purchase (7). The vacation purchase (7) will affect future attitudes (5), the amount of effort put into comprehending a message—inhibitors (17)—and even the extent to which information on that particular vacation option will be attended to—attention (16).

To repeat, each part of the process is working at the same time. Some parts work to encourage a particular purchase decision, while others work against it. The system is in a constant state of flux. What we have done in the first four chapters is to stop and explain the effect of each variable on the decision to buy.

REFERENCES

"Interrelationships of Leisure, Recreation and Tourism," *Annals of Tourism Research*, Special Issue, vol. 14, no. 3, 1987.

LUNDGREN, JAN O.J., "The Development of the Tourist Travel Systems," *The Tourist Review*, no. 1, January/March 1973, pp. 2–14.

Tourism Facts: A Resource Kit (Washington, D.C., Travel and Tourism Government Affairs Council, 1988).

VAN DOREN, CARLTON S., "Outdoor Recreation Trends in the 1980's: Implications for Society," *Journal of Travel Research*, vol. 19, no. 3, Winter 1981, p. 4.

1

TO TRAVEL
OR NOT TO TRAVEL

Travel as
a Need/Want Satisfier

Travel is motivated by "going away from" rather than
"going towards" something or somebody. To shake off
the everyday situation is much more important than the
interest in visiting new places and people. . .travellers'
motives and behavior are remarkably self oriented: Now I
decide what is on and what is good for me.'

Jost Krippendorf,
The Holiday Makers

The reasons people give for taking vacations are insufficient to explain their travel motivations. In order to market to potential tourists and to serve them at their destinations, it is essential to understand the underlying needs that tourists wish to satisfy when considering a vacation.

This chapter explores tourism as a satisfier of needs and wants. The relationship between lists in travel literature showing reasons for pleasure travel and Maslow's hierarchy of needs is developed.

Some people hypothesize that tourists travel if they have learned that travel for a particular reason will help satisfy various needs and wants considered important to them, and if they perceive that their needs and wants will be satisfied within the constraints of such things as time, money, and social pressure.

LEARNING OBJECTIVES

Having read this chapter, you should be able to:

1. Explain why surveys of travelers often do not reveal the true reasons for their trips.
2. Explain the difference between a need and a want.
3. Describe and illustrate in a diagram the process through which people are motivated to travel.
4. Explain the role of the travel marketer in motivating people to travel.
5. Explain the difference between general and specific motives.
6. Describe Maslow's Need Theory, listing the five original and two additional needs and explaining the concept of *prepotency*.
7. List the other factors, in addition to motivation, that influence the behavior of travelers.
8. Describe how past experiences with the same or similar vacations influence future vacation decisions.
9. Explain the psychology of simplification concept and how it affects people's travel decisions.
10. Compare and contrast consistency and complexity needs.

IMPORTANCE OF MOTIVATION

Why do people take vacations? To date, studies of tourist motivations have concentrated on developing lists of the reasons people say they travel. A variety of studies report that tourists travel, for example, to view scenery, to learn about other cultures, or to visit friends and relatives. This approach to understanding tourist motivation is insufficient for two reasons. First, the tourists themselves may be unaware of the true reasons behind their travel behavior. Individuals are often unaware of the real reasons for doing certain things. A person leaving for a tennis vacation may see the trip as simply a reason "to play tennis." When questioned, however, the traveler may reveal that a concern for his or her health prompted the trip. Also, the tourist may not wish to divulge the *real* reason or motivation behind a trip. For instance, much of the tourism literature mentions "status" as a tourist motivator, yet many tourists will not feel comfortable admitting that a major reason for taking a vacation is that they will be able to impress their friends upon their return home. A second reason that such lists are insufficient for explaining consumer motivations is that they concentrate on selling the product rather than on satisfying the needs of the market. But the development of such lists is a necessary first step toward establishing a classification system that will enable us to understand and ultimately predict the tourist's decision-making process.

TRAVEL AS A NEED/WANT SATISFIER

The key to understanding tourist motivation is to see vacation travel as a satisfier of needs and wants. Tourists do not take vacations just to relax and have fun, to experience another culture, or to educate themselves and their children. They take vacations in the hope and belief that these vacations will satisfy, either wholly or partially, various needs and wants. This view of tourist motivations is critical. It is the difference between seeing a destination as a collection of palm trees and hotel rooms for the tourist and seeing it as a means for satisfying the needs and wants of tourists. It is the difference between those travel agents who see themselves as sellers of airline seats and those who view themselves as dealers in dreams.

Needs, Wants, and Motives

A description of the process begins with a consideration of the needs of an individual. When an individual takes a trip, buys a cruise, or rents a cabin, the action is done in hopes of satisfying some need of which he or she may be only partially aware. We could provide a better service if we could only be aware of which need or needs the individual is attempting to satisfy.

A business is not interested so much in a person's needs as in how that person seeks to satisfy those needs. The difference between a need and a want is one of awareness. It is the task of the people in marketing to transform needs into wants by making the individual aware of his or her need deficiencies.

A person *needs* affection, but *wants* to visit friends and relatives; *needs* esteem from others, but *wants* a Mediterranean cruise. In these and other situations people can be made aware through advertisements, for example, that the purchase of an airline ticket to visit parents will result in feelings of love and affection for them, thereby helping satisfy that need.

Although a person may want satisfaction for a need or needs, no action will be taken until that person is motivated.

Motivation occurs when an individual wants to satisfy a need. A motive implies action; an individual is moved to *do* something. Motivation theories indicate that an individual constantly strives to achieve a state of stability—a homeostasis. An individual's homeostasis is disrupted when she or he is made aware of a need deficiency. This awareness creates wants. For the individual to be motivated to satisfy a need, an objective must be present. The individual must be aware of a product or service and must perceive the purchase of that product or service as having a positive effect on satisfying the need of which she or he is now aware. Then, and only then, will the individual be motivated to buy. Again, it is the role of marketing to suggest objectives—cruises, flights, or vacations—to satisfy needs, an awareness of which has already been created. (This process is outlined in Figure 1.1.) For example, several years ago an advertisement ran in the Scottish papers showing two little girls with one saying, "Guess what? Next month Grandma and Grandpa are visiting us—from *Scotland*." The advertisement was promoting flights from Scotland to Canada. It managed to say (between the lines), "We know you love your grandchildren [a need].

Needs ————awareness————▶ Wants

creates

satisfy   **Marketing**   motivation

suggests

Objectives

Figure 1.1 Needs, wants, and motives

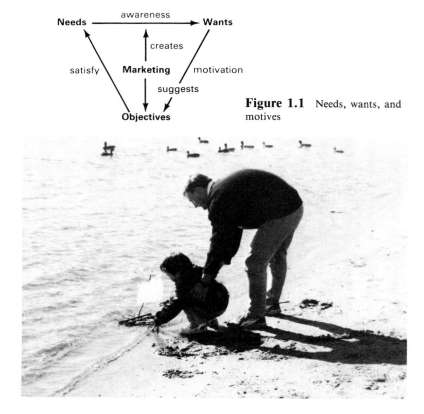

Grandparents and children

By showing you this picture we have made you aware of that [a want]. By visiting them [an objective] you will satisfy that need for love.'' In such a way grandparents are motivated to fly to Canada.

Behavior is influenced by a number of things, with motives being only one. We cannot even specify that an individual is motivated at any one time by only one motive. It is important, as we discuss needs and motives individually, to bear in mind that behavior results from the interaction of various motives, one of which may be dominant at any one time as well as interacting with various other socioeconomic and psychographic factors.

Motives may be specific or general. A general motive would be the end objective, and a specific motive would be a means to reach that end objective. For example, a person may be motivated to take a spa vacation. This, however, may be no more than an indicator of a more general motive, that of good health. Viewed in this way, it can be seen that good health can be achieved by means other than taking a vacation. We are in competition not only with the next destination, but also with other activities for the consumer's time and money. Although a vacation represents a break from routine for many, that same feeling can also be obtained from decorating the house or laying out a garden. The marketing task is to convince an individual that the purchase of whatever we are selling is the best, if not the only, way of satisfying that need. To the extent that we are successful in accomplishing this, an individual will be motivated to buy.

Maslow's need theory and travel motivations. A study of the travel literature indicates that travel motivations can fit into Maslow's hierarchy of needs model. Maslow proposed the following listing of needs arranged in a hierarchy:

1. Survival—hunger, thirst, rest, activity
2. Safety—security, freedom from fear and anxiety
3. Belonging and love—affection, giving and receiving love
4. Esteem—self esteem and esteem from others
5. Self-actualization—personal self-fulfillment

This hierarchy suggests that lower-level needs demand more immediate attention and satisfaction before a person turns to the satisfaction of higher-level needs. It might be better to think of the hierarchy as a series of nested triangles (Figure 1.2). This representation emphasizes the fact that higher-level needs encompass all lower-level needs. It also illustrates the relative value size of each need better.

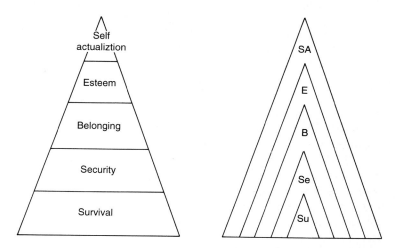

Figure 1.2 Maslow's hierarchy of needs. Source: Arnold Mitchell, "Social change: Implications of Trends in Values and Lifestyles," VALS Report No. 3, January 1979.

Although the first need listed is physical, the other four are psychological. To this original list two intellectual words were added:

To know and understand—acquiring knowledge
Aesthetics—appreciation of beauty

The relationship between the physical, psychological, and intellectual needs is unclear. It is thought that the intellectual needs exist independently of the others.

The relationship between needs, motives, and references from the tourism literature is shown in Table 1.1. Those who say they travel "to escape" or "to relieve tension" can be seen as seeking to satisfy the basic survival or physiological need. Such motivation may be for physical or mental relaxation. Vacationers often return from a trip physically exhausted but mentally refreshed. Although there seems to be a difference between those people who take an active vacation and those who opt for a passive vacation, both are motivated by a need for tension reduction. Passive

TABLE 1.1   MASLOW'S NEEDS AND MOTIVATIONS LISTED IN TRAVEL LITERATURE

Need	Motive	Tourism Literature References
Physiological	Relaxation	Escape
		Relaxation
		Relief of tension
		Sunlust
		Physical
		Mental relaxation of tension
Safety	Security	Health
		Recreation
		Keep oneself active and healthy for the future
Belonging	Love	Family togetherness
		Enhancement of kinship relationships
		Companionship
		Facilitation of social interaction
		Maintenance of personal ties
		Interpersonal relations
		Roots
		Ethnic
		Show one's affection for family members
		Maintain social contacts
Esteem	Achievement	Convince oneself of one's achievements
	Status	Show one's importance to others
		Prestige
		Social recognition
		Ego-enhancement
		Professional/business
		Personal development
		Status and prestige
Self-actualization	Be true to one's own nature	Exploration and evaluation of self
		Self-discovery
		Satisfaction of inner desires
To know and understand	Knowledge	Cultural
		Education
		Wanderlust
		Interest in foreign areas
Aesthetics	Appreciation of beauty	Environmental
		Scenery

vacationers are seen as achieving tension relief by giving in or submitting to the surrounding environment. From this submission comes the very relief of tension that will result in their returning refreshed and renewed. The overworked factory worker may relax by lying on a beach for two weeks. The active vacationer achieves tension reduction through physical activity. The activity can also be seen as being related to achievement and mastery of the environment and, as such, being related to the need for self-esteem. Some people who have jobs that are not physically demanding compensate by engaging in physical activity when on vacation. This illustrates the point made earlier that, at any one time, one may be motivated to satisfy more than one need.

Traveling for reasons of health can be interpreted as a way of attempting to satisfy one's safety needs. By taking care of the body and/or mind, we are "protecting" ourselves and helping assure our own longevity. Visits to spas can be seen in this light. Several references specifically link recreation and health, implying a relationship between the two.

The need for belonging and love relates to the desire for affection, for both giving and receiving love. The organized tour is often mentioned as a method of encouraging and satisfying this need for companionship and social interaction.

Visiting friends and relatives

This motivation is frequently referred to as the "VFR" market—"visit friends and relatives." Part of this is the ethnic or roots market—the desire to revisit the homeland or previous residence of oneself or one's ancestors. This segment of the market tends to fall into two groups. First, there are those who were born somewhere else and desire to return to their own homeland. Second, there are those in later generations who wish to experience the land of their ancestors. For the people in the first segment of the market, the desire is to see people and things and to relive experiences as they are remembered. This desire to recapture previous experiences means that these tourists are willing to adjust to the conditions of the destination visited. They are there, after all, to enjoy again what they remembered from their past. Inconveniences of the homeland can be tolerated. At the same time, however, people in this market segment may have little economic impact on the destination because of the tendency to stay with friends and relatives. Later generations will have the slightly different desire to experience vicariously the land of one's ancestors; however, because the personal experience of one's roots is missing and has been replaced by standards of living learned in one's country of birth, it is these accustomed standards of living that are taken on the journey for one's roots. Therefore, living standards are expected to be comparable to those experienced at home. At the same time, however, this segment of the market tends to have a greater impact on the economy if lodging and meals are taken in hotels instead of with family.

Maslow's concept of the need for esteem breaks down into two components—that of self-esteem and that of esteem from others. The idea of self-esteem is embodied in such ideas as the need to exhibit strength, achievement, mastery, competence, and independence. This might explain why people take whitewater rafting trips. Esteem from others is explained by such concepts as reputation, prestige, status, and recognition. Travel can certainly boost one's ego, both at the destination and upon one's return. It may be that as people grow older, their status in society declines. Travel is one way to enhance that status.

Self-actualization can, in fact, be considered the end or goal of leisure. Leisure is the state of being free from the urgent demands of lower-level needs. Vacations offer an opportunity to reevaluate and discover more about the self, to act out one's self-image as a way of modifying or correcting it.

The need to know and understand can be viewed in light of the desire for knowledge. Many people travel to learn of others' cultures. It is also true that contact with people of another culture offers an opportunity to discover one's own culture. This same concept has also been expressed as a motivation for education, wanderlust, and interest in foreign parts.

The need for aesthetics is seen in those who travel for environmental reasons—to view the scenery.

The traveler, then, is better understood and better appealed to if he or she is recognized as a person consuming products and services. Seeing the traveler in this manner will result in a change of attitude on the part of the observer and enable the marketer to provide a better product or service to the traveler. A second more tangible benefit to be gained from this approach relates to the idea of prepotency. If one accepts Maslow's idea of prepotency—that lower-level needs should be satisfied to some extent before the satisfaction of higher-level needs becomes a concern—we would expect that products and services, including vacations, which are targeted towards the satisfaction of lower-level needs, would be regarded as more of a necessity than a luxury and would, as such, be more resilient to external pressures of time and money.

The need to escape and getaway vacations are particularly effective in triggering the "need" to travel

A number of authors, in fact, have demonstrated that the need to escape (related to the physiological need) is the strongest travel motivation. People see vacations as a way of escaping from everyday life rather than as a way of seeking pleasure. It has been suggested that two motivational factors simultaneously influence the leisure behavior of individuals. Leisure activities are sought because they allow individuals to escape from personal or interpersonal problems. At the same time people are seeking psychological rewards from participating in leisure activities. These rewards can be personal (sense of mastery, learning, exploration and relaxation) or interpersonal (involving social interaction). The model is illustrated in Figure 1.3. The unequal length of the lines indicates the fact that the desire to escape from personal or impersonal environments is greater than the desire to seek personal or impersonal rewards. This has practical implications for tourism businesses. It would suggest that promoting the need to escape and getaway vacations would be particularly effective in triggering the "need" to travel. It also suggests that the destination is less important than the need to escape. This makes it more difficult to sell the differentiating qualities of a particular destination.

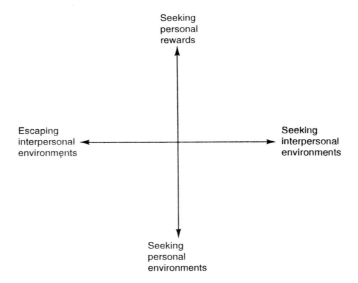

Figure 1.3   The escaping and seeking dimensions of leisure motivation. Adapted from: Seppo
E. Iso-Ahola, ''Social Psychological Foundations of Leisure and Resultant Implications for
Leisure Counseling,'' *Leisure Counseling: Concepts and Applications*, E.T. Dowd, ed.
(Springfield, IL: Charles C. Thomas, 1984), p. 111.

WHY TRAVEL?

We have said that an individual's needs—for safety, for belonging, and so on—can
be satisfied by setting different objectives or by taking certain actions. What determines how an individual will seek to satisfy a need? It is proposed that an individual
is motivated to satisfy a particular need in a particular way (by taking a vacation,
for example) based upon three factors. First, an objective will be set if the individual
perceives that the objective will satisfy her need: If she feels that taking a cruise will
result in her returning relaxed and refreshed and if it is important to her that she
do something to relax and refresh herself, then she is more likely to take that cruise.
(The process by which an individual perceives is covered in Chapter 2.) Second, a
particular action will be taken if the individual has learned that that action will satisfy
that need: If she has taken a cruise that has resulted in her returning home refreshed,
she will be more inclined to take it again. (The learning process is explored in the
remainder of this chapter.) Third, the decision as to what action to take in order
to satisfy a need must be taken within the limitations of the individual's external environment: She may perceive that a cruise will satisfy her need, she may have learned
that a cruise will satisfy her need, but if she does not have sufficient time or money
or if there are strong social or cultural factors that inhibit this option, she may not
be able to take the cruise. The effect of the external environment on the individual's
decision-making process is considered in Chapter 3.

Tourist's Learning Process

An individual will purchase a specific vacation package or trip if he has learned that the purchase will help satisfy an important need. This process is illustrated in Figure 1.4. The tourist weighs various alternatives against a list of criteria important to him to determine which alternatives are most likely to satisfy a particular motive. The inclination that results will have an effect upon the decision to purchase. This influence may be positive or negative, depending upon the "fit" between motives and alternatives—how well it is felt a chosen alternative will meet the motivation. Travelers have a low upper limit on the number of destinations that they perceive they may visit within a specified time period. Most travelers have identified seven or fewer destinations that they list as alternatives. The number of alternatives will vary relative to the characteristics of the travelers. Travelers who have previously visited foreign destinations have a larger number of alternatives to choose from than do those who haven't. It may be that travel broadens the number of destinations likely to be visited. Whether or not a destination will be included as an alternative depends in great part upon whether or not that destination has previously satisfied the individual. The level of satisfaction is a function of one's expectations of a situation and one's perception of the actual situation. If the level of expectation is higher than the actual experience, the individual will be dissatisfied. For an individual to be satisfied with a product, service, or situation, the level of actual experience must be equal to or greater than the level of expectation. Tourists can attempt to reduce the psychological risk involved in a purchase by expecting less from the vacation. This, however, is not a popular strategy, especially in travel.

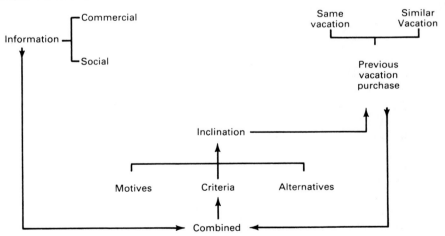

Figure 1.4 Tourist's learning process. *Adapted from:* John A Howard and Jagdish N. Sheth, *The Theory of Buyer Behavior* (New York, John Wiley & Sons, Inc. 1969).

We would expect that, as the amount of satisfaction increases, the number of alternatives considered next time decreases. The more an individual is pleased with a vacation choice, the higher that choice will be placed on the list of alternatives and the fewer will be the other alternatives considered. This places great importance on the level of service given the vacationer to assure a quality experience and a level of satisfaction that will bring the traveler back. The one exception to this might be the vacationer with a high need to know and understand. If this is very important, it may not matter how satisfied he or she is with, for example, a trip to Paris. Having visited that spot, the individual, making the most of limited resources of time and money, may never return to that city.

Serving as a bridge between the motives of an individual and the perceived alternatives are the criteria used for making a decision among those alternatives. A choice is made that the individual believes will produce maximum satisfaction of a need or needs. The criteria used to distinguish between alternatives are learned. These criteria are developed as a result of past experience and from information taken in from either the commercial (business) or social (friends and relatives) environment. The effect of information on learning will be considered in the following chapter when we look at the process of perception and image formation.

Learning, based on past experience, can come from having experienced the same thing that is being contemplated or from having experienced something similar. If you stayed in a particular town on vacation and were very satisfied, you learn that visiting that particular town is liable to satisfy you again. Those factors that accounted for your satisfaction—good weather, friendly service—are the criteria by which you determine where to take your next vacation.

People generalize their experiences at one chain hotel to all others in the chain

On the other hand, by staying at one property of a chain and having a poor experience, you may infer that you would have a similarly poor experience at all properties of that chain and behave accordingly when faced with a choice of places to stay. This process of generalization (which, by the way, may not be an accurate representation of what would have happened at another property in the chain) is known as the psychology of simplification. To make the decision-making process easier, the potential tourist generalizes from what he or she perceives to be similar situations. The more experiences you have, the more firmly established your decision criteria and the easier it is for you to generalize.

The individual moves from what is termed an extensive problem-solving process through a limited problem-solving process to a routine problem-solving process. In the process known as extensive problem solving, the tourist has little in the way of information or experiences from which to make a decision. The need and, consequently, the search for information is high, and a few decision criteria have been established. We may know what criteria are important to us, but we may be unaware of whether or not they can be satisfied by the various alternatives available. Additionally, as we experience certain destinations or vacations, we may find that the criteria that were important to us previously have become less significant.

Thus, our decision criteria are developed or modified (that is, learned) in great part by our actual experiences. As we become more confident in our decision criteria, decision making is easier for us. Our experiences, and the resultant generalization from them, are weighed more heavily than any information received. This is due, in part, to the fact that, as our decision criteria are strengthened, our need for information is weakened. Additionally, we have a tendency to filter incoming information so that it will support and reinforce our decisions. This is explored further in the next chapter. This progression leads to a routine problem-solving process whereby little or no information is sought and the decision is made rather quickly in reference to the decision criteria that have been established.

Consistency vs. Complexity

The movement described above—from extensive problem solving to routine problem solving—suggests that people seek to maintain consistency in their lives. Indeed, many psychologists adhere to this philosophy. Their theory is that inconsistency leads to psychological tension, which we constantly seek to avoid. Other psychologists argue the opposite. They feel that individuals find change and uncertainty extremely satisfying. This is referred to as the need for complexity.

The aforementioned two concepts are balanced by Edward J. Mayo and Lance Jarvis in *The Psychology of Leisure Travel*.[1] It is their feeling that individuals vary in the amount of psychological tension they can handle. Too much repetition or consistency can result in boredom for an individual creating a corresponding amount

---

[1]Edward J. Mayo and Lance P. Jarvis. *The Psychology of Leisure Travel* (Boston, C.B.I. Publishing Company, Inc. 1981), p. 172.

of psychological tension greater than the optimum for him. He will attempt to introduce some complexity in his life, thereby reducing the tension to an optimum level. Should this level be exceeded by an overly complex situation, the tension level will be greater than the optimum for him. This explains why someone, who for years has driven to a particular vacation spot, will change either the destination or the method of reaching that spot.

Similarly, too much complexity can result in more tension than an individual can handle. She will introduce consistency into the experience to reduce the tension level. An American tourist in Europe may find the different language and culture (complexity) need to be balanced by staying in a hotel chain with which she is familiar (consistency). This model may also help explain a person's choice of vacation. The individual who experiences a great deal of consistency in everyday life may compensate by seeking vacations which offer variety. People who have less stimulation in their lives than they desire prefer more novelty and stimulation on their ideal vacation.

SUMMARY

People are motivated to satisfy needs that may be innate or learned. Part of marketing's task is to make people aware of their needs and present them with an objective, the purchase or attainment of which will help satisfy that need. Vacations or trips are ways of satisfying various needs. There are, however, ways other than taking vacations to satisfy those same needs. An individual will purchase a vacation to satisfy a need or needs if he perceives that the vacation will satisfy those needs, or if he has learned that a vacation will satisfy those needs under the constraints of external factors such as time, money, and social pressure.

An individual learns of the alternative ways of satisfying her needs from personal experience, from the same or similar experiences, and from information gained from the commercial or social environment. The alternatives considered are linked to the person's motives by a set of decision criteria—guidelines used by the individual to select among alternatives. These guidelines are also learned from the sources described. If an individual has learned that a particular purchase results in satisfaction, strong decision criteria favoring that purchase will have been built up as the number of alternatives considered will have been reduced. There is a great likelihood that a specific motive under the conditions described above will result in a tendency to purchase a particular product, service, or experience.

REFERENCES

CROMPTON, JOHN, "A Systems Model of the Tourist's Destination Selection Process with Particular Reference to the Roles of Image and Perceived Constraints" (Ph. D. dissertation, Texas A&M University, 1977), pp. 34, 316, 345.

HARRELL, GILBERT D., *Consumer Behavior* (New York, Harcourt Brace Jovanovich, Publishers, 1986).

HOWARD, JOHN A. and J.N. SHETH, *The Theory of Buyer Behavior* (New York, John Wiley & Sons, Inc., 1969).

KRIPPENDORF, JOST, *The Holiday Makers: Understanding the Impact of Leisure and Travel* (London, Heinemann Ltd., 1987).

MANNELL, ROGER C. and SEPPO E. ISO-AHOLA, "Psychological Nature of Leisure and Tourism Experience," *Annals of Tourism Research*, vol. 14, no. 3, 1987, pp. 314–331.

MASLOW, A.H., "A Theory of Human Motivation," *Psychological Review*, vol. 50, 1943, pp. 370–396.

MAYO, EDWARD J., and LANCE P. JARVIS, *The Psychology of Leisure Travel* (Boston, C.B.I. Publishing Company, Inc., 1981), pp. 82, 156, 172.

"Vacations," *Psychology Today*, May 1980, pp. 62–76.

VAN RAAIJ, FRED W., "Consumer Research on Tourism: Mental and Behavioral Constructs," *Annals of Tourism Research,* vol. 13, no. 1, 1986, pp. 1–8.

WOODSIDE, ARCH and JEFFREY CARR, "Consumer Decision Making and Competitive Marketing Strategies: Application for Tourism Planning," *Journal of Travel Research*, vol. 26, no. 3, Winter 1988, pp. 2–7.

WOODSIDE, ARCH G., TEKKA RONKAINEN and DAVID M. REID, "Measurement and Utilization of the Evoked Set as a Travel Marketing Variable" (paper presented to The Travel Research Association, 1978).

MARKET SEGMENTS

	Deviation from overall statement mean
Segment 1	
Being daring and adventuresome	+ 0.7
Finding thrills and excitement	+ 0.4
Being physically active	+ 0.4
Participating in sports	+ 0.4
Roughing it	+ 0.3
Experiencing new and different lifestyles	+ 0.2
Learning new things, increasing knowledge	+ 0.2
Rediscovering self	+ 0.2
Trying new foods	+ 0.2
Reliving past good times	− 0.2
Indulging in luxury	− 0.2
Doing nothing at all	− 0.2
Meeting people with similar interests	− 0.3
Visiting places family came from	− 0.3
Visiting friends and relatives	− 0.5
Feeling at home away from home	− 0.5
Travel to places that feel safe and secure	− 0.6
Being together as a family	− 0.7
Segment 2	
Visiting friends and relatives	+ 0.8

Visiting places family came from	+ 0.6
Feeling at home away from home	+ 0.5
Being together as a family	+ 0.4
Meeting people with similar interests	+ 0.4
Travel to places that feel safe and secure	+ 0.4
Reliving past good times	+ 0.3
Talking about trip after return home	+ 0.3
Watching sports events	+ 0.3
Finding thrills and excitement	− 0.3
Trying new foods	− 0.3
Being daring and adventuresome	− 0.3
Getting a change from a busy job	− 0.5
Getting away from demands of home	− 0.5

Segment 3

Getting away from demands of home	+ 0.5
Doing nothing at all	+ 0.4
Getting a change from a busy job	+ 0.3
Indulging in luxury	+ 0.3
Travel to places that feel safe and secure	+ 0.3
Roughing it	− 0.3
Participating in sports	− 0.3
Going places friends haven't been	− 0.3
Watching sports events	− 0.3
Visiting friends and relatives	− 0.3
Visiting places family came from	− 0.3
Being daring and adventuresome	− 0.4
Being physically active	− 0.5

EXERCISE

A survey of people in Great Britain sought to identify what people interested in vacationing in the United States look for in choosing where and how to holiday.

Three segments were identified. A plus deviation from the overall statement mean indicates that people in that particular segment were more inclined to agree with the statement. The greater the plus number, the greater the agreement. For example, in segment one "Being daring and adventuresome" gets a "rating" of +0.7. People in this segment were much more inclined to agree with this statement than respondents on average. The reverse is also true. The greater the negative deviation from the statement mean, the greater the level of disagreement with the statement. For this segment there was much less importance given to "Being together as a family."

For each segment of the market:

1. What underlying need(s) are people seeking to satisfy?
2. Place an appropriate label or name on the segments that best describes the potential vacationers.

3. Knowing the underlying need(s) that people are seeking to satisfy, what are the implications for:
   a. the type of tourism product that will be most effective—i.e., what attractions will attract and what facilities should be offered?
   b. the price that should be charged?
   c. the type of promotion that would be effective?
   d. how it should be sold—directly or as a package.
4. Design an advertisement that would be appropriate.

2

SELECTING A TRAVEL DESTINATION:

Information Sources and Perceptual Biases

*"The people don't take baths and they don't speak
English. No golf courses, no room service. Who needs it?"
Jim McMahon, ex-Chicago Bear, on Europe. As quoted in
Newsweek.*

A travel destination is chosen in part based upon our perception of its ability to satisfy our felt needs.

This chapter examines the process by which we receive information about a destination and how our perception of that information influences the travel decision.

Information is received from both the commercial and social environments. The factors that influence where the information is sought from and how much is taken in are examined. The process by which the information taken is distorted by our perceptual biases is explored.

Implications for the marketer seeking to develop a specific image for a destination or to change an unsatisfactory image are pointed out.

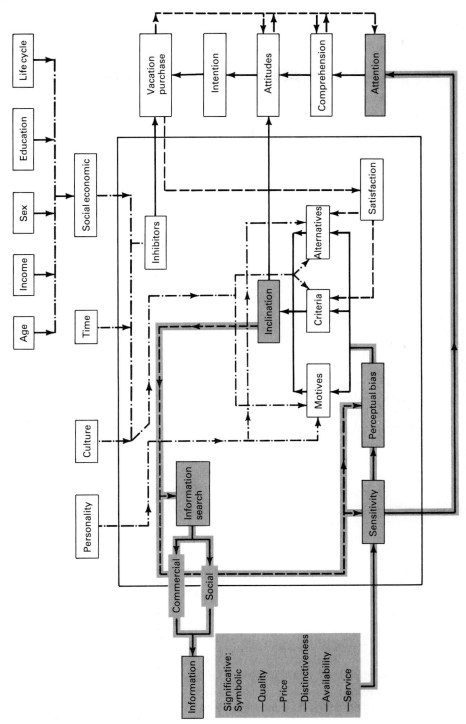

LEARNING OBJECTIVES

Having read this chapter, you should be able to:

1. Explain the importance of perception on travel decisions and the interpretation of travel information.
2. Define commercial and social information sources, indicating which is usually perceived to be the most objective of the two.
3. Describe how opinion leaders form a link between the social and commercial environments.
4. List and describe two factors that influence a person's sensitivity to receive travel information.
5. Explain the concept of *perceptual bias* and how this affects travel decisions.
6. Describe how a person's self-image influences his or her choices of travel destinations and services.
7. List seven technical factors that influence people's sensitivity to and perception of travel information and explain how they work.
8. Explain the process through which a person forms an image of a travel destination or service.

THE PROCESS OF PERCEPTION

In the previous chapter it was suggested that, in part, a travel purchase is made based on the extent that an individual perceives that the purchase will satisfy his or her needs. The key word is "perceive," for we buy based not so much upon what information is actually presented to us, but on how we perceive that information. This distinction will be explored in greater detail later.

It will be recalled that our inclination towards a particular product or destination is derived from the linking of our motives with the alternatives available to us through a series of learned decision criteria (see Figure 2.1). The strength of our preference has an effect on how new alternatives are perceived and even if any new alternatives are considered. For example, if an individual is well traveled and consequently knows which destinations please and which do not, a strong set of decision criteria will have been developed—"There must be a sunny climate"; "The culture must be significantly different from my own"; and so on. This, in turn, leads to a strong inclination towards certain destinations. The results are:

1. The tourist is less inclined to seek out information about new places.
2. The tourist is less sensitive to any information about vacation spots; the preferred destination is "protected" by a reluctance to allow in any information about other destinations.
3. Because a strong preference for a particular destination has been developed, any information about that destination is filtered to emphasize the positives while any negatives are rationalized or downplayed. The reverse is also true. In a study of perceptions regarding first-class and coach airline seating, those who preferred first class perceived a lesser difference in ticket price but a greater

difference in the positive aspects of choosing first class, such as more luggage allowance, better meal selection, and so on.[1]

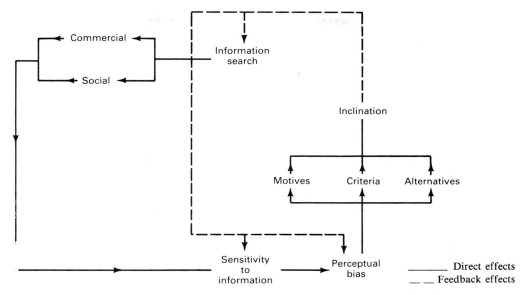

Figure 2.1 Information sources and perceptual biases. *ADAPTED FROM:* John A Howard and Jagdish N. Sheth, *The Theory of Buyer Behavior* (New York, John Wiley & Sons, Inc., 1969)

Sun and different culture as important decision criteria

[1]J.C. Makens and R.A. Marquardt, "Consumer Perceptions Regarding First Class and Coach Airline Seating," *Journal of Travel Research*, vol. 16, no. 1, 1977, pp. 19–22.

Information will come from two major sources—the commercial environment and the social environment. The commercial environment refers to information coming from companies, destinations, countries, or tourist businesses. These are businesses and organizations that have a vested interest in persuading the tourist to buy—those that would profit by such a purchase. The social environment, characterized by friends, relatives, and reference groups, presumably would have nothing materially to gain from the tourist's decision to buy. As such, it is presumed that their information or advice is more objective and worthy of trust. Although friends, relatives, and those in our reference groups may not benefit financially from the decision to buy a particular vacation, they may have their egos stroked if their advice is accepted and a decision is made based on their input.

It is likely that people will spend a longer time on an external search for a tourism purchase. There are several reasons for this. The greater the amount of risk in a purchase, the greater the search. Buying a vacation involves a great deal of risk involving both time and money. For many people the annual vacation is their only chance to get away. If they select a poor vacation, they may have to wait another year for the next opportunity. The vacation is also an expensive proposition—hence the risk. Second, because the purchase of a vacation involves buying an intangible that cannot be seen or touched ahead of time, there is heavy reliance on secondary and tertiary sources of information. It is, thus, likely that the search process will be longer than that for many other consumer products. Additionally, the greater the need for variety, the longer the external search effort. There is a tendency for many vacationers to select a different vacation destination each time they holiday. This would support the need for a greater information search.

INFORMATION SOURCES

What sources of information are sought when planning a vacation? Much evidence suggests that the social environment—the influence of friends and family—is instrumental in selecting a travel destination. It seems that the commercial environment performs an informing function—letting people know what is available. The social environment performs an evaluating function—being used by potential travelers as a means of evaluating the alternatives.

Knowing how people search for information can enable marketers to segment the market based on search behavior and develop specific strategies to appeal to and reach each segment. For this to happen there must be a sufficiently large number of people who engage in a certain form of search behavior to make the effort of marketing to them worthwhile. It would also be important to know whether different segments of the market use different types and numbers of information sources. The relative importance of these sources must be known in addition to the length of time taken in the planning process. This latter piece of information is necessary to ensure that information is available at the time when the potential travelers want it. If July vacationers plan their vacations six months in advance, the destinations should target their messages to reach that market in January. Advertising to them beforehand will have little impact because they are not thinking about the vacation. Advertising to them afterwards will be too late because they will already have decided where they will vacation.

In general, longer searches using a greater number of sources of information are undertaken by vacationers who want a well-planned trip, who seek excitement from their vacation, and who are planning longer trips over greater distances.

The role of the retail travel agent in this process has been documented in a series of reports by Louis Harris & Associates since 1971.[2] These reports indicate that, over the past twenty years, between 30 and 40 percent of those who visit travel agencies have only a general idea of where they want to go and thus rely, to some extent, on the agent's advice in selecting a destination. However, not everyone uses a retail travel agent. There is an increased tendency to use travel agents as the distance being traveled increases and as the tourist uses air transportation.

Thus, it appears that the social environment of friends, relatives, and reference groups is a prime source of information concerning vacations. Because the role of a retail travel agent increases in importance as the use of air transportation and the distance traveled increases, it might be better to view the important sources of information for the auto traveler separately from those used by the air traveler.

Travel to the United States

Many informative reports have been issued by the United States Travel and Tourism Administration. Table 2.1 summarizes information relative to sources used by travelers

TABLE 2.1   SOURCES USED TO PLAN TRIP TO U.S.

Sources	Japan	U.K.	Germany	France
Travel Agent	50%	59%	70%	48%
Brochures/Pamphlets	55%	44%	51%	37%
Friends/Family	26%	39%	44%	25%
Airline	5%	6%	13%	8%
Tour Operator	19%	12%	28%	7%
Read Articles	16%	19%	15%	15%
Books/Library	40%	19%	17%	12%

from four countries—Japan, United Kingdom, Germany, and France—in planning a trip to the United States. The primary sources used in planning the trip were travel agents, brochures and pamphlets, and friends and family. In three of the four countries, travel agents were the number-one source. In Japan brochures and pamplets were used slightly more often than were travel agents. In Japan, also, books and

---

[2]Louis Harris & Associates, "The Character and Volume of the U.S. Travel Agency Market," biennial since 1971.

library resources were used by more people than friends or relatives. It is also evident that travelers of different countries have different ways and priorities for obtaining information for travel purposes. The Japanese, as noted, make much more use of books and the library than do travelers in any of the European countries listed. West Germans, on the other hand, make much more use of tour operators. Thus, while the importance of retail travel agents and personal sources can be noted, the travel marketer must be aware of the fact that information to different travelers in different countries must be communicated through different channels to reach the intended audience.

Automobile Travel

A number of studies have been completed on the tourist's use of travel information sources when traveling by automobile. These studies indicate the importance of information from the social environment. Information from family or friends and from personal knowledge is regarded as more significant than that from commercial sources. The nonmedia preferred commercial sources are billboards and signs. It appears that as motorist travelers become more familiar with the location of establishments in

The importance of billboard advertising

a geographic area they rely more on previous experience than on physical appearance and on credit-card directories rather than on commercial billboards.

A link between the social and commercial environment is suggested by a consideration of the role of opinion leaders. There is evidence to indicate that the flow of communications is a two-step flow process. The tendency is for influence to flow from the mass media to opinion leaders who are receptive to the idea presented and from these opinion leaders to the general public. Opinion leaders act as channels of information. They tend to be demographically indistinguishable except for higher income or occupational levels, tend to read more media about related consumer issues, are more knowledgeable about new product developments, and participate more often in related consumer activities. Studies of travel opinion leaders found that they are active seekers of information but did not see either personal or media sources of information as being significantly important sources for them. It appears that travel opinion leaders may be better able to determine the credibility of various source materials and are not as easily swayed by the advice of friends and relatives as are the general population. Others, after all, look to them for advice—they do not look so much to others.

SENSITIVITY TO INFORMATION

Thus far we have considered the sources to which potential tourists turn to determine vacation patterns. The personal sources—those from the social environment—have been shown to exert considerable pressure compared with those from the commercial environment. All information from both the commercial and social environments reaches us if we are sensitive to the incoming information. Our sensitivity to receiving incoming information is first a function of how inclined we are to that information. If, for example, we feel strongly inclined towards taking a vacation, we will readily be open to information regarding vacations. If we have a strong preference for a Bahamas vacation, any information about the Bahamas—about travel packages, the weather, the political situation—is liable to receive attention. On the other hand, if we have definitely decided against a European vacation, our preference to go to Europe will be low, as will our sensitivity to information about Europe. Consequently, we will probably ignore any information that would affect those taking a European vacation. Our sensitivity to information is also a function of the ambiguity of the message. If the information received is familiar to us already, it may be too sinple and straightforward and thus be ignored. On the other hand, if the information presented—an advertisement, a travelogue, a personal opinion—is too complicated for us to absorb, the high level of ambiguity may lead us to put up a shield to "defend" ourselves, and the information will not get our attention. This process may be thought of as controlling the quantity of information received. In order to gain tourists' attention, the information presented should be aimed at their capacity to absorb it. Its chances of being taken in will be enhanced if the tourists have a preference for the destination or package being mentioned.

PERCEPTUAL BIAS

The information-receiving process, described above, controls the quantity of information taken in. The quantity of information received, however, is distorted by how that information is perceived. Two people presented with the same travel advertisement may perceive it differently. One person may view the advertisement positively, the other negatively. Feedback from our motives, the alternatives considered, and the decision criteria used will affect our image of information received. Various studies have shown, in fact, that visiting a destination or staying at a particular lodging chain causes a positive change in the image of that destination or chain. If we are strongly motivated to seek a historical, cultural vacation, one which could readily be satisfied by a trip to the province of Quebec, and if it is important (decision criteria) that we avoid crowds, then an advertisement showing throngs of people at an art festival in Quebec will be perceived negatively. Similarly, an advertisement that stresses the magnificent scenery of the province will not be perceived positively because that image runs counter to that which motivates us.

Although information from both the commercial and social environments is distorted, information received from personal sources is less subject to perceptual bias. This is because information from the social environment is regarded more favorably by the individual receiving the information. It should be remembered, however, that before a friend or relative gives us information, he or she has already distorted it to meet his or her value system. A recommendation of a "wonderful" place to visit, stay, or eat will only be given in those terms if it has met with what our friend determines is a wonderful place to visit, stay, or eat. This, of course, depends upon whether or not our friend perceives that his or her experience satisfied unmet needs. There is also liable to be less distortion when information is actively sought. When the tourist is unsure of which vacation will result in a more satisfying experience—when preference for any particular vacation is low—there will be less bias in the way information is perceived. In addition, there will be greater reliance upon the social environment for information if the tourist is unsure of the satisfactions from various alternatives and if the purchase is important. To the extent that we are influenced by the social group of which we are a part, our motives will be influenced by the (subjectively weighted) information from our social environment. Similarly, the social environment will affect the alternatives a buyer considers, particularly where experience is lacking. Also, information received will be fed into the buyer's decision criteria and will influence those criteria in the direction in which the information is perceived. A tourist, for example, may look for the lowest priced hotel. If information is received that suggests that paying a little more will actually be a better value, and if the tourist perceives this to be true, the decision criterion of "lowest cost" may change.

A link has been established between perception and behavior. We behave—buy, travel, stay at home, and so on—based in part upon our perception of information received. But how do we perceive products, for example, tourist destinations or services?

HOW WE PERCEIVE

It is generally felt that we perceive products and services as consisting of a bundle of benefits or attributes. A vacation package consists of a variety of parts—for example, in a ski vacation, excellent snow conditions, few lift lines, après-ski entertainment, saunas, continental cuisine, and so on. A significant association between overall preference for a particular brand and preference based on the attributes of that brand has been demonstrated in the choice of an airline, a destination, and a tourist attraction. Thus, we buy a bundle of benefits. The decision to purchase the overall brand or package will be based upon two factors. First, the skier, for example, must believe that the attributes of the package will help satisfy his or her felt needs. Second, the satisfaction of those felt needs must be important to the skier. The former contributes more to determining an individual's attitude towards a product or service. The implication is that, if we wish to sell a particular vacation, we should sell that vacation as consisting of a number of benefits that will contribute toward the satisfaction of the buyer's needs. As we saw earlier, an individual may be seeking to satisfy several needs at the same time. Our package, therefore, should contain many elements that will aim at satisfying different needs. The provision of American-type meals and English-speaking guides may satisfy primary physiological and safety needs during a trip to Europe, while the inclusion of side trips to certain "name" resorts may help in satisfying the need for status.

The provision of American-type meals may satisfy primary physiological and safety needs during a trip to Europe

Consumers have a tendency to buy things that have attributes consistent with their own perceived image. An individual's total image is made up of several parts. First, the *real self* is the objective person—what the individual is deep down. In reality, few of us know ourselves this well. Yet this true self governs our purchase and travel behavior, even if we are unaware of what it is that moves us in a particular way. Second, there is the ideal self. The *ideal self* is what we would like to be. This aspect of the individual is easier to discover for two reasons that are important to marketers: consumers are more willing to discuss what they aspire to than what they believe *really* motivates them and by simple observation of purchase behavior much can be learned about what a consumer is striving for. Last, the *self-image* is how consumers see themselves. It is a combination of the real and the ideal self. Consumers make purchases that will maintain or improve their self-image, as they perceive it. According to Walters, consumers attempt to preserve the self-image in several ways.[3] They

> Buy products consistent with self-image
> Avoid products inconsistent with the self-image
> Trade up to products that relate to an improved self-image
> Purchase products that relate favorably to group norms of behavior
> Avoid products that show a radical departure from accepted group norms

These three aspects of the self—the real, ideal, and self-image—are totally concerned with the individual. There are two other aspects of the self concerned with external facets. The apparent self—in essence a combination of the real self, ideal self, and self-image—represents how the consumer is seen by outsiders. The impressions that outsiders have of an individual will determine whether or not any commonality of interests or desires is perceived and whether or not any friendship will develop. This affects purchases because we tend to copy the purchases of those we admire. Thus, the picture of myself that I give to others—made up of my real and ideal selves and my self-image—will tell others if they and I seem to be the same "type" of people. If we are, buying patterns, for a vacation for example, may influence others to purchase that type of vacation. The *reference-group self* is how we believe others see us. What is believed, however, is more important than what is real, for behavior is predicted on what we *believe* others want us to do. The important influence of reference groups will be explored further in the following chapter. This self, then, is a combination of all of these aspects.

BENEFIT SEGMENTATION

So far the link between purchase of a product, attitudes towards that product, and perceptions of that product has been stressed. We have said that individuals perceive products and services in terms of bundles of benefits or attributes. Their likelihood of buying a product is determined by the extent to which they perceive the product to contain sufficient benefits to satisfy their felt needs and also the extent that the

---

[3]C. Glenn Walters, "Consumer Behavior: Theory and Practice" (Homewood, IL, Richard D. Irwin, Inc., 1978), pp. 182–86.

satisfaction of those felt needs is important to them. Also, consumers buy products that are consistent with their existing self-image or that they feel will allow them to improve their self-image. This is done within the boundaries of what kinds of purchases are sanctioned by their own reference groups. To make an effective marketing application of this process, it would be possible to divide up the tourist potential into segments and develop different vacation alternatives for the different segments based upon the various benefit bundles being sought by each segment. "Market segmentation is a technique used to divide a heterogeneous market into homogeneous sub-groups or market segments.[4] For example, in the skiing market people look for different things from the ski experience. To some, the quality of the slopes is of prime importance; to others, the *après*-ski entertainment is paramount. Each segment looks for different attributes. To the first segment a campaign stressing the quality of the slopes and the short lift lines would work. This campaign would not particularly interest the "entertainment" skiers. A brochure showing people sipping hot buttered rum round a blazing fire would be more effective.

It has been shown that the benefits sought from a specific destination vary by season and for different segments of the market. In the first study[5] visitors to Massachusetts were segmented by benefits sought and, further, by season of the year. Spring visitors were looking for a combination of such things as good road conditions, sporting activities, and historical and cultural attractions. The summer group were also interested in sporting activities and historical and cultural attractions. In addition, however, two new segments appeared—one group looking for a clean and scenic environment at a low cost, and the other, a clean environment with good climate and quality accommodations. The major benefit sought by fall tourists was a clean and inexpensive vacation with a large number of attractions that were cultural and historical. Winter travelers were concerned about climate and relaxation, the extent of commercialization, and the quality of shopping.

The second study[6] looked at the benefits sought by visitors to Hawaii. It was found that Canadians saw rest and relaxation as the main benefit from a vacation to Hawaii; mainland Americans sought cultural experiences; while Japanese visitors reported family togetherness as the major benefit from the trip.

These findings have implications for product and promotional strategy. Different travel products would be developed for different segments of the market and advertising messages would differ by market segment and by season.

There has been some question as to the individuality of specific destinations in providing unique benefit bundles. Does each destination contain those elements that will satisfy particular felt needs? It has been suggested that sociopsychological motives are unrelated to destination attributes. The emphasis may shift from the

[4]Bonnie D. Davis and Brenda Sternquist, "Appealing to the Elusive Tourist: An Attribute Cluster Strategy," *Journal of Travel Research*, vol. 25, no. 4. 1987, p. 26.

[5]Roger J. Calatone and Jotindar S. Johar, "Seasonal Segmentation of the Tourism Market Using a Benefit Segmentation Framework," *Journal of Travel Research*, vol. 23, no. 2, 1984, pp. 14–24.

[6]Arch G. Woodside and Laurence W. Jacobs, "Step Two in Benefit Segmentation: Learning the Benefits Realized by Major Travel Markets," *Journal of Travel Research*, vol. 24, no. 1, 1985, pp. 7–13.

destination itself to its function as a medium through which sociopsychological needs can be satisfied. If the "escaping from" motive is more important than the "seeking" motive (as suggested in Chapter 1), then destinations are, to a certain extent, interchangeable. Earlier we saw that a large percentage of tourists who use travel agents enter with only a general idea of where they wish to visit. This suggests the difficulty, from a marketing viewpoint, of establishing a destination as the unique place offering various unique benefits to satisfy particular needs.

Perception and Technical Factors

If the decision to travel to a particular destination is linked to our perception of that destination, then an examination of the perception process may help us understand if and how we can change an individual's perception of a destination in order to increase the likelihood of that individual's visiting the destination. Any information from either the social or commercial environment is molded into an image through our perceptual processes. The resultant image is less a function of the promotional message of a destination than of our individual perception of that message. There are many factors that affect consumer sensitivity and perception. Although these elements are working at the same time and although the effect of one often contradicts the effect of another, they are discussed individually. The first of these factors can be referred to as technical ones. Technical factors refer to the object, product, or service as it actually exists. The various elements of a particular product or service, such as price, quality, service, availability, and distinctiveness, can be communicated through the product or service itself. These inputs are termed significative stimuli. The elements may also be communicated in a symbolic way through the use of words and/or pictures. There are several factors that are termed technical. *Size* is an important consideration. To many, size is equated with quality. The larger the company, the airplane, or the hotel, the better the service is perceived to be. Generally speaking, larger advertisements will receive greater attention. A travel company might use a big advertisement or emphasize the largeness of its operation to gain more attention and give the impression of quality to the reader. *Color* also attracts more attention than black and white. Color advertisements are 50 percent more effective than are black and white ones. The *intensity* of a stimulus also affects the perception of it. The greater the intensity, the more the attention. Intensity can refer to the brightness of colors, the use of certain "strong" words, or the importance of a present or past purchase or experience. Stressing the importance of a decision to buy will increase the attention given a message. It can also refer to repeating the stimulus, thereby intensifying the message. The more a message is seen, the greater the chance that it will attract attention. *Moving objects* attract more attention than stationary objects. This accounts for much of the success of advertising on television. Point-of-purchase displays with moving parts—in a travel agency, for example—can also be used to good effect. The *position* of a piece of information can affect whether or not the information will attract attention. In a brochure rack, pamphlets at shoulder height will attract the most attention. When placing advertisements in a newspaper, it is important to consider that the upper part of the page attracts more attention. *Contrast* is another element that affects the attention given a stimulus. By varying the thought, color, size, pattern, or intensity of a stimulus, enough discontinuity may be created between what is expected and what is actually perceived to attract attention. If competing messages are bright, colorful, and somewhat gaudy, a very simple, dignified message may be noticed because of the contrast. The final technical factor is that of *isolation*. Advertisers are fond of putting a border, called "white space," around their messages to isolate them from other messages on a page. As noted earlier, these elements interact often in contradictory ways. The greatest impact comes when several factors combine to give a more significant effect. This is illustrated in Figure 2.2.

The task is to communicate these elements:	using these means:	to gain:
Quality	Size	Attention
Price	Color	
Distinctiveness	Intensity	
Availability	Movement	
Service	Position	
	Contrast	
	Isolation	

Figure 2.2   Getting attention

Size is an important consideration in advertising

Image-Shaping Forces

Technical factors are concerned with getting information through to the potential traveler. However, the information and impressions that do get through are distorted by a number of forces into an image. There is a tendency on our part to *stabilize our perception* even after the original basis for the perception has changed. A traveler may continue to stay at an old favorite hotel where the level of service has declined because the perception remains in the past. An image, whether positive or negative, may continue long after the factors causing that original image have been changed. This illustrates the difficulty involved in changing an image. Linked with this very closely is that, as a creature of habit, a traveler will perceive in a certain *habitual way* until forced to think differently. Stress here is placed on the need for marketers to break through the traveler's "habit barrier" by means of various stimuli mentioned above. A third shaping force relates to the extent to which individuals have a tendency to be *confident* or *cautious*. The confident individual takes in a complex situation more quickly, can more readily see positive elements in a situation, and can assimilate more detail. Decisions are made faster by confident persons, although those who are cautious make slower decisions and hence their perceptions tend to be more accurate. This factor points to the need to communicate different messages to different segments of an intended market. This, of course, will work only if marketers are able to determine that the more-confident traveler reads different newspapers or magazines or watches different television programs than the more-cautious traveler. The amount of information that can be perceived is limited by the fact that we have a *limited span of attention*. This refers to the number of stimuli that can be taken in at the same time. Experiments have shown this number to be approximately eight. This infers that messages should not consist of too many elements for fear that an important element may be missed or that the message may be disregarded because it is too confusing. The tendency to react to a given stimulus in a certain way is referred to as an *individual's mental set*. This suggests a learned response. It may be possible, for example, to suggest in a campaign, "Whenever you think of hotels, think of Hilton." If the campaign has the desired effect, an individual will think of Hilton (the response) whenever she or he thinks of hotels (the stimulus). Parts of this mental set are the *expectations* we bring to a situation. People tend to perceive what they expect to perceive. There is a tendency to round out a particular image in our minds by adding pieces that we do not have *based upon what we expect to be there*. For example, a highway traveler may see a sign for a motel that advertises an indoor pool. The traveler may expect that if a motel has an indoor pool, it will also have a certain high quality of service in other facilities. Because there is a pool, the expectation is that other high-quality facilities will be present. This is known as bringing "closure" to a situation. Another part of our state of readiness is the degree of *familiarity* we have with incoming stimuli. To the extent that we are familiar with the stimulus we will have some idea of how to respond to it. This effect of past experience manifests itself in several ways. First, if we have visited Germany, then information about Germany will be perceived by us, in part, based upon our experience there. If we experienced negatives, we will perceive new information about Germany negatively because it evokes memories of a negative experience. The reverse is also true. In addition, if we perceive new information to be *similar* to an experience with which we are familiar, we will tend to act upon that new information in a way similar to our behavior in our previous experience. For example, assume we perceive Austria and Germany to be similar as vacation destinations, yet we have visited only Germany and were pleased with the experience. Information received about Austria will be perceived positively in light of our German experience. This, of course, can work to encourage or discourage purchase behavior. If we know positive feelings exist for a product or service, we may wish to stress the connection when advertising a new product from the same company. A major selling point in a chain operation is the

If you stayed at one Holiday Inn and were pleased, you will be pleased when you stay at another Holiday Inn

uniformity of quality standards. The message is that if you stayed at one Holiday Inn and were pleased, you will be pleased when you stay at another Holiday Inn. This also can work in reverse. An unpleasant experience at one chain operation will be generalized into a perception about the entire chain. There are times when an advertiser will have to work hard against this tendency. Some tourists will have a tendency to perceive all "sun 'n fun" destinations as being similar. The task for any one such destination is to show that it is different from the others. A further complicating factor is that stimuli in close proximity to each other tend to be perceived as being similar. Despite the fact that islands in the Caribbean have unique identities because of different historical and cultural influences, the fact that they are relatively close together means they will be perceived as being similar. Again the marketing task is to differentiate one from another. Another related part of this perceptual process relates to *context*. A stimulus will be perceived relative to the context in which it is viewed. A resort will be judged, in part, by the perceptions of the media in which the resort is advertised. Advertising in a magazine viewed as exclusive will bring a certain perception of exclusivity to the resort.

How consumers perceive a situation is also affected by various *social and cultural factors*. A Mediterranean cruise, for example, will be perceived differently by individuals from different social classes. Males and females will perceive the same advertisement differently. It is also clear that the relative merits of attractions at a particular destination are perceived differently by those from different cultures. The difference in perception necessitates different marketing themes for those different market segments. Even within the same country a destination will be perceived in different terms by those in different social or cultural groups.

Perception of Distance

The subject of distance in general and perceptions of it in particular is very important in relation to the study of tourism. The reason for this is that much of tourist travel revolves around differences. People may travel to a different climate, from snow to sun; to see different scenery, from plains to mountains; or to experience a different culture, from modern to traditional. By its very nature, then, tourist travel to experience differences implies covering some distance. The distance to be traveled may act as a barrier, depending upon how it is perceived.

The perception of a particular distance is not a constant. Rather the perception of a particular distance seems to vary relative to various socioeconomic factors as well as to the activity to be undertaken. It appears that travelers in higher levels of occupation and income are inclined to travel farther. This may, of course, be partially explained by the fact that they can afford to travel farther. However, those who favored active vacations over inactive vacations are inclined to travel long distances. Some researchers feel that occupation is the key, while others link personality variables to the propensity to travel. Although all of the answers are not known, it does seem that distance can be viewed either positively or negatively in terms of its effect on travel. Certainly the greater the distance the greater the financial cost. As such, distance is a limiting factor. It may also be that great distances represent a psychological barrier because of the tediousness involved in traveling or the fear of being far from home. At the same time, a destination may increase in attractiveness because of the distance that must be traveled to get there. It has been demonstrated that, for some tourists, beyond a certain distance the friction of distance becomes reversed—the farther they go, the farther they want to go. Especially on unplanned trips there may be a tendency to view closer-to-home destinations and attractions as stepping stones to stopping points farther away rather than as competition for the farther destination.

Marketing Implications

It is important to consider the factors that influence image formation. According to Gunn[7] an image evolves at two levels. An organic image is formed as a result of general exposure to newspaper reports, magazine articles, television reports, and other specifically nontourist information. Thus, even the individual who has never visited a particular country nor even sought out information on that country will have some kind of image, perhaps incomplete, of that country. At this point, as mentioned earlier, other pieces of the image picture will be added that the individual perceives *should* be there to match the pieces already known in order to make a complete picture. The second level is that of an induced image. This refers to an image brought about by tourist-directed information, such as advertisements and travel posters. The organic image tends to develop first and, as such, may be regarded as a stronger influence than the induced one in overall image formation. There is little that can be done to influence the formation of an organic image. Filmmakers may be persuaded to shoot a movie such as *The Sound of Music* which, although not a travel film, influences people in their image of Austria. In general, however, little can be done. Marketers do seek, obviously, to induce an image through the production of films, posters, and advertisements. If the organic image is set in an individual's mind, an induced image may be disregarded in favor of the previously held organic image.

An image *can* change over time. Research has indicated that, although consumers have stable perceptions about frequently bought products, their image of an infrequently bought product changes over time. Although an image can change over time, can that image *be changed* over time? There is some literature that suggests that an image cannot be changed, but it appears that the task, though difficult, costly, and time consuming, is not impossible.

The topic of perception has very real marketing implications. Effective marketing strategies can be determined only after determining the extent to which potential visitors perceive that our destination contains those attributes that they consider important. This involves a three-step process:

1. What do you, the potential visitor, consider important?
2. Do you *perceive* that we have this?
3. Do we *actually* have this?

In a survey of potential tourists (see Table 2.2) individuals were asked what attributes they considered very important in planning a foreign trip and the extent to which they perceived that Britain did the best job of satisfying these same attributes. By comparing these responses, various strategies are suggested. The model for this process is contained in Figure 2.3.

The first consideration is "what does the market consider important or unim-

[7]Clare A. Gunn, "Vacationscape: Designing Tourist Regions." University of Texas 1972, pp. 110–13.

TABLE 2.2 COMPARISON OF IMPORTANT ATTRIBUTES
AND PERCEPTION OF BRITAIN*

		A Rank	B Rank
A.	Safety from physical harm	1	5
B.	Real scenic beauty	2	6
C.	Seeing things of historical interest	3	2
D.	Good weather and climate	4	18
E.	Having people make you feel welcome	5	7
F.	Getting really good food	6	16
G.	Cost of trip fits regular income without special saving	7	11
H.	Famous cities	8	3
I.	Visit more than one country easily	9	8
J.	Easy language communication	10	1
K.	Being sympathetic to people and their achievements	11	12
L.	Famous art museums	12	4
M.	Finding everything different from the United States	13	17
N.	Good beaches, swimming, water sports	14	21
O.	Shopping for things you'd like to buy	15	9
P.	Religious pilgrimage, seeing shrines	16	19
Q.	Being familiar with country and area	17	14
R.	American-style comfort, convenience	18	10
S.	Good nightlife	19	13
T.	Sympathy with political position of country's and area's government	20	15
U.	Being able to gamble at casinos	21	20

A: Attributes considered very important when planning a foreign trip

B: Attributes that travelers perceive Britain as doing the best job of satisfying
  Based on 1513 people interviewed at 200 locations throughout the U.S.

*Source: Michael Perry, "Comparison of Tourist Destination Image as Perceived by Travelers and
       Travel Agents," in New Perspectives and Policies Proceedings of the International Tourism
       Conference, Turkey, 1978.*

portant?" Potential visitors are particularly interested in physical safety, scenic beauty, historical attractions, climate, and hospitality. Because it is important to the market, it is important to us. The people in this segment of the market are not particularly interested in gambling, the country's political position, good nightlife, or American-style comforts. These latter elements should be ignored by us. To include them in any marketing effort would overload the consumer and may result in the potential visitors "protecting" themselves by ignoring the entire message.

We now know what is important to the visitors. Will they be satisfied with our destination if they visit it? The answer depends upon a comparison of their image of the destination compared to our knowledge of what actually exists relating to the attributes they consider important. Several outcomes are possible. First, the visitors' perception or image may be negative when we know that it should be positive. For example, climate is important (ranked 4), but Britain rates poorly (ranked 8). There are, however, times of the year when the British climate is good. In this case the image must be changed before visitors will feel positive. A campaign may stress the

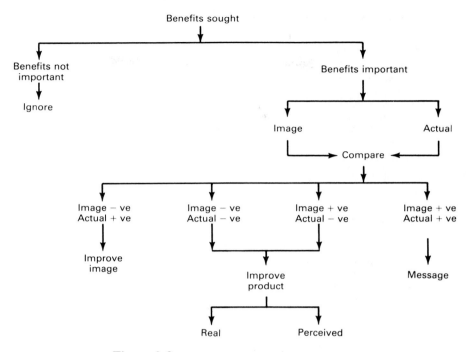

Figure 2.3 Perception—marketing implications

amount of sunshine or lack of rain in certain months. Some destinations in the Bahamas offer rain insurance. If you get more than a certain amount of rain during your vacation, your hotel room is free.

What if the image is negative and the actual condition is negative also? Britain's climate is rated poorly, and there certainly are some very wet months there. The solution is to change the product. If we score low on a factor important to the market, we have to get our own house in order before we can attract visitors. This may mean a real or perceived change. For example, to attract tourists during those wet months it may be necessary to develop more indoor facilities where activities can take place irrespective of the weather. The product change may, on the other hand, be perceptual. There is a segment of skiers who place high priority on short lift lines. If a ski area is perceived as having long lift lines, it will be necessary to change the product if, in fact, the lines are long. How can a lift line be shortened? A real change would be to open up more hill capacity. This, however, is expensive. A perceived change would be to make the wait *appear* shorter. Some Michigan ski areas provide entertainers or musicians to provide a diversion for those in line to make the time spent in line seem short.

The same strategy is appropriate if the image is positive but the actual situation negative. In such a situation we may attract visitors because they think they will be made to feel welcome. If we know that our employees do not have enough training to give this expected level of service, dissatisfaction will result unless the product (employee hospitality) is changed.

Last, what if the image is positive and the actual is positive? This becomes the thrust of our message. In this example, we would sell Britain on a combination of history and hospitality.

This process can be displayed visually in a perceptual map. A perceptual map shows the collective perceptions of a segment of the market for a particular destination on factors considered important to them. A perceptual map of Great Britain is shown in Figure 2.4. The importance of vacation attributes has been placed on the horizontal axis and the perception of Britain for these same attributes has been placed on the vertical axis.

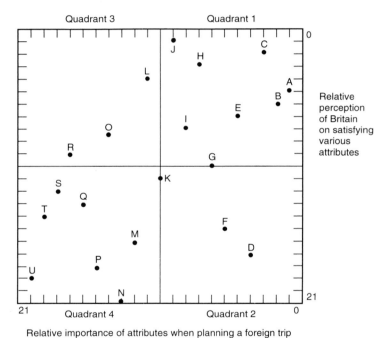

Relative importance of attributes when planning a foreign trip

Figure 2.4 A perceptual map and the marketing implications

Cross hairs dividing the map into four quadrants have been placed near the midpoint of the importance and perception scales. There are twenty one factors in all. Half of them are above the horizontal cross hair and half are below. Similarly, half are to the left of the vertical cross hair and half are to the right of it.

Items in Quadrant 1 consist of those attributes that are important to this segment of the market and on which Britain is perceived as doing a good job of providing. These items must survive a *reality check*. Do we *really* do a good job of providing these? Britain is perceived as a safe, scenic country with great historical

Visiting Great Britain allows the
opportunity to visit great cities

interest. The people are seen as being friendly; it is affordable; it allows the opportunity to see great cities and to visit more than one country easily; and there there
is no language barrier. To what extent is this really true? If this image is, in fact,
a true representation of the way it is, this would be the focus of the advertising
message. If any of these factors are less than the image, the product would have to
be improved. A positive image on items considered important to the market will bring
people in, but once they get to their destination and find that what exists is less than
what they imagined, they will be disappointed.

Quadrant 2 contains items that are important to the potential travelers but on
which Britain has a poor image. There are problems with the weather and the food.
These problems must be examined to determine the extent to which they are real or
imagined, and either the image or the product must be changed.

In Quadrant 3 there are items that are not important to the tourists, but items
on which Britain has a good image. Quadrant 4 contains items that are not important to the tourists and on which Britain has a poor image. Because Quadrants 3
and 4 contain items not important to the tourist, they should not be mentioned in
an advertising campaign for fear of overloading the viewer with information they
do not consider important to them.

Through the use of perceptual mapping, destinations can determine how or if they should change their tourism product and advertising.

REFERENCES

ABBEY, JAMES, "The Relevance of Life Style and Demographic Information to Designing Package Travel Tours" (Ph.D. dissertation, Utah State University, 1978).

BURNS, THOMAS, "Using Importance Performance Analysis to Measure the Opinions of National Park Concessioners," paper presented at the nineteenth annual conference of The Travel and Tourism Research Association, 1988.

CALATONE, ROGER, J., and JOTINDAR A. JOHAR, "Seasonal Segmentation of the Tourism Market Using a Benefit Segmentation Framework, "*Journal of Travel Research*, vol. 23, no. 2, 1984, pp. 14–24.

CROMPTON, JOHN, "A System's Model of the Tourist's Destination Selection Process with Particular Reference to the Roles of Image and Perceived Constraints" (Ph.D dissertation, Texas A&M University, 1977).

DYDKS, JERRY, "Overseas Travel to Canada: New Research on the Perceptions and Preferences of the Pleasure Market," *Journal of Travel Research*, vol. 26, no. 4, 1988, pp. 12–15.

GITELSON, RICHARD J. and JOHN L. CROMPTON, "The Planning Horizons and Sources of Information Used by Pleasure Vacationers," *Journal of Travel Research,* vol. 21, no. 1, 1983, pp. 2–8.

GARTNER, WILLIAM C., "Temporal Influences on Image Change," *Annals of Tourism Research*, vol. 13, no. 4, 1986, pp. 635–644.

GOODRICH, JONATHAN, "An Investigation of Consumer Perceptions of, and Preferences for, Selected Tourist Destinations: A Multidimensional Scaling Approach" (Ph.D. dissertation, State University of New York at Buffalo, 1977).

MAZANEC, JOSEF A., "How to Detect Travel Market Segments: A Clustering Approach," *Journal of Travel Research*, vol. 23, no. 1, 1984, pp. 17–21.

MAYO, EDWARD J., and LANCE P. JARVIS, *Psychology of Leisure Travel* (Boston, C.B.I. Publishing Company, Inc., 1981), pp. 43–48; 60–62.

MCQUEEN, JOSH, and KENNETH E. MILLER, "Target Market Selection of Tourists: A Comparison of Approaches," *Journal of Travel Research*, vol. 24, no. 1, 1985, pp. 2–6.

NICHOLS, CATHERINE M., and DAVID J. SNEPENGER, "Family Decision Making and Tourist Behavior and Attitudes," *Journal of Travel Research*, vol. 26, no. 4, 1988, pp. 2–6.

SCHUL, PATRICK and JOHN L. CROMPTON, "Search Behavior of International Vacationers: Travel-Specific Lifestyle and Sociodemographic Variables," *Journal of Travel Research*, vol. 22, no. 1, 1983, pp. 25–30.

TRAVEL WEEKLY, The 1988 Louis Harris Survey, 1988.

WOODSIDE, ARCH G., and LAURENCE W. JACOBS, "Step Two in Benefit Segmentation: Learning the Benefits Realized by Major Travel Markets," *Journal of Travel Research*, vol. 24, no. 1, 1985, pp. 7–13.

WOODSIDE, ARCH G., and ELLEN M. MOORE, "Word-of-Mouth Communications and Guest Retention by Competing Resort Hotels," paper presented at the seventeenth annual conference of The Travel and Tourism Research Association, 1986.

EXERCISE

A sample of Britons interested in visiting Colorado were given a list of vacation benefits and asked to rank them on a scale of 1 (not at all important to me) to 4 (very important to me). Their scores are reported in column A. They were then asked their perceptions of Colorado on these same benefits, also on a scale of 1 (very weak) to 4 (very strong). These scores are reported in column B.

Draw a perceptual map of Colorado and determine the marketing implications of this information to the state. Specifically:

1. What should their marketing message be?
2. What aspects of the product will they have to change? How?
3. What aspects of their image will they have to change? How?
4. What aspects of their image should they ignore in their advertising?

COMPARISON OF BRITONS' VACATION INTERESTS AND PERCEPTIONS OF COLORADO

Hygiene and Cleanliness	3.52	2.87
Warm, Sunny Weather	3.51	2.85
Reliable Weather	3.54	2.64
Personal Safety	3.49	2.9
Outstanding Scenery	3.55	3.5
Interesting and Friendly Local People	3.53	3.08
Warm Welcome for Tourists	3.27	3.04
Inexpensive Travel in Destination	3.14	2.21
Opportunities to Increase Knowledge	3.36	2.64
Public Transportation	3.25	2.53
Local Cuisine	3.17	2.5
Different Culture	3.01	2.9
Interesting Smaller Towns and Villages	3.18	2.72
Wide Open Spaces	3.15	2.84
National Parks and Forests	3.1	3.46
Good Beaches for Swimming and Sunning	2.9	1.6
Good Shopping	2.76	2.18
Sightseeing Excursions	2.83	3.09
High Quality Restaurants	2.74	2.69
Historic Old Cities	2.82	2.08
Wildlife or Birds	3	3.16
Wilderness and Nature	3.07	2.76
First Class Hotels	2.56	3.03
Lakes and Rivers	2.97	3.07
Manageable Size to See	2.63	2.73
Seaside	2.49	1.5
Local Crafts	2.74	2.57
Exotic Atmosphere	2.5	2.14

COMPARISON OF BRITONS' VACATION INTERESTS AND PERCEPTIONS OF COLORADO (cont'd)

Museums and Art Galleries	2.54	2.06
Resort Areas	2.37	3.24
Local Festivals	2.53	2.58
Budget Accommodation	2.69	2.57
Historical Sites	2.63	2.49
Unique Cultural Groups	2.66	2.42
Mountainous Areas	2.79	3.71
Live Theaters and Concerts	2.27	2.38
Nightlife and Entertainment	2.15	2.53
Amusement and Theme Parks	1.91	2.62
Big Modern Cities	1.87	2.82
Hiking and Climbing	2.17	3.38
Water Sports	1.78	2.37
Spectator Sporting Events	1.73	2.8
Golf or Tennis	1.59	2.63
Snow Skiing	1.57	3.7
Campgrounds and Trailer Parks	1.63	3.33
Casinos and Gambling	1.3	2.08
Good Fishing	1.29	3.09
Good Hunting	1.13	3.06

3

EXTERNALS:

The Environment
for Tourism

"Hurry Up, It's Leisure Time"

The MBA, April 1971.

The vacation decision is influenced, if not shaped, by various "forces" external to the individual. This chapter examines these forces.

The culture of which we are a part serves as a barometer of general trends within a country, and it exerts social pressure to conform to the broad cultural values represented by the majority of individuals making up that culture.

The amount and type of time available also helps determine if and where we can vacation.

Marketers have long segmented the travel market along the socioeconomic criteria of age, income, sex, and education. It is therefore appropriate to determine whether tourism demand differs on these criteria.

The characteristic patterns of demand at various stages in the family life cycle are examined, with particular reference to the effect of children on the family's demand, the demand pattern of the empty nester, and the various barriers to leisure enjoyment at different life-cycle stages.

Finally, the role of personality in shaping demand is explored. It has been felt that a link between personality and vacation behavior exists. Do certain types of people take certain kinds of vacations because of their personality characteristics? From a marketing viewpoint the segmentation of a target market by life-style provides a better picture of the characteristics, likes, and dislikes of the potential tourist.

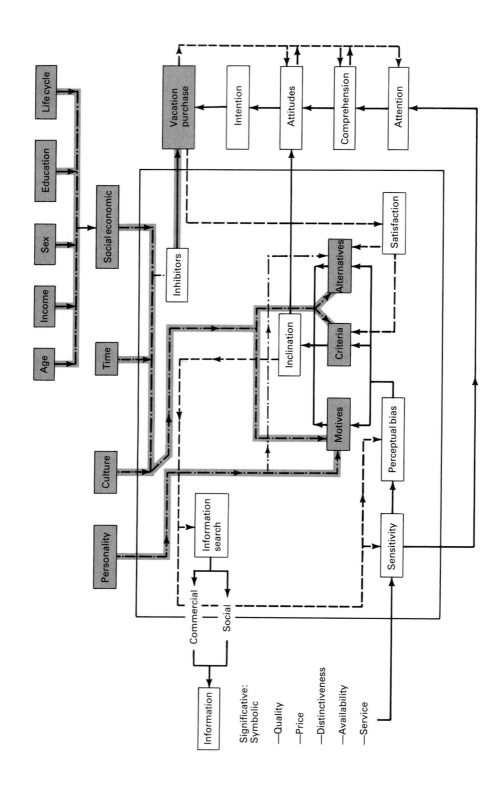

Significative:
Symbolic

—Quality
—Price
—Distinctiveness
—Availability
—Service

58

LEARNING OBJECTIVES

Having read this chapter, you should be able to:

1. Explain the effects of a culture and its component subcultures on travel decisions.
2. Describe a process for analyzing a culture.
3. Explain how the availability of time impacts on a person's travel and leisure decisions.
4. Explain the concept of resource value inversion.
5. Describe the effects of major socioeconomic variables on travel decision making.
6. Explain how family life cycle stages impact vacation and leisure decisions.
7. Describe how a person's personality influences travel decisions and choices of recreational activities.

Many factors external to the individual act as inhibiting factors on travel-purchase behavior. In this chapter the effect of these variables will be examined. Although these factors will be explored separately, it should be noted that their effect is often a compound one.

THE EFFECTS OF CULTURE ON TRAVEL

While an individual acts to satisfy certain internal needs and wants, the way in which these wants are satisfied is heavily influenced by forces external to the individual. As individuals, we are part of larger social groups by which we are influenced. These groups themselves are part of and influenced by the surrounding culture. *Culture* can be defined as a "set of beliefs, values, attitudes, habits and forms of behavior that are shared by a society and are transmitted from generation to generation."[1] A knowledge of the culture of a country or subunit within that country is important to an understanding of how individuals within that country or subunit will behave.

Culture and Society

Culture affects society in four ways. First, the overall values of the culture determine which goals and behavior will gain social approval or disapproval. To the extent that people are concerned about how others think of them, they will be influenced to seek gratification of their needs and wants in ways acceptable to society. This means that in order to induce those individuals to buy various products and services, it will be necessary to state the appeals and benefits of those products and services in terms acceptable to society. The many advertisements that feature the hedonistic vacation life-style can only work because society is increasingly condoning this value. Several decades ago, such an appeal would not have worked because it was not socially acceptable to be self-indulgent, even on vacation.

[1]Peter D. Bennett and Harold J. Kassarjian, *Consumer Behavior* (Englewood Cliffs, NJ, Prentice-Hall, Inc., 1972), p. 123.

Hedonistic life-style

The many social institutions of a society are also reflective of its culture. In the United States, for example, the ideas of individual initiative and equal opportunity for all (part of the culture) influence the way in which the educational system is organized to provide for mass education with a somewhat liberal child-rearing philosophy. Yet this expresses itself in different ways throughout society. Although lower-middle-class parents in the United States tend to be child-dominated and concerned with satisfying their children, upper-class parents are more interested in seeking ways to help their children seek status achievement. This suggests that upper-class parents can more readily be sold a travel vacation if that vacation is perceived by them as being something that will advance their child's progress in society.

The third way in which culture affects the social backdrop is in the established conventions and practices of society. Society adopts various practices relative to such things as which foods can be eaten, how to entertain, and which gifts are or are not appropriate. It is acceptable, for example, for horsemeat to be eaten in France but not in the United States; it is appropriate for a U.S. dinner guest to bring the host a bottle of wine, but in France this would be an insult. When attracting or servicing a market from a culture different from our own, it is necessary to know the established practices to avoid inadvertent behavior.

Last, culture's effect on society is felt in the language people use to communicate with one another. It is important to consider not only words, but also gestures, expressions, and other body movements. A smile in Western culture is a warm signal to further a relationship, but in Oriental culture it may be used to cover embarrassment and shame.

Culture and Social Groups

Social groups have roles or standards of behavior peculiar to each group. These group norms differ from one culture to another. Groups can be classified either as primary (family or friends) or secondary (unions, fraternities, church, and so on). An individual will belong to more than one group, and consequently, he or she will adopt a role for each social group. These roles may overlap. The surrounding culture will help define for each group the appropriate objects people use to show their membership in the group as well as the relevant status symbols.

Is there a distinct "vacation role"? One of the attractive features of taking a vacation is that it allows the freedom to be someone other than who we are in everyday life. Traveling to places where we are not known, meeting people who do not know us, allows us to choose how we will behave.

The social role that an individual takes is learned through socialization—*the process of social learning by which cultural role expectations are handed down from one generation to another.* The link between participation in recreational activities as a child and subsequent participation as an adult has been repeatedly demonstrated. If we also accept that travel is a learned experience, the importance of encouraging travel participation at an early age can be demonstrated. The norms of behavior for a group change by virtue of both internal and external sources. Within a group there are those people (innovators) who are more willing than others to try new things. Usually these group members are better educated, have high income, and are more achievement-oriented than others. The innovators also tend to be opinion leaders and, as such, highly sought-after by marketers. A common saying in explaining destination development is "mass follows class." This phrase suggests that a destination first attracts a relatively small number of high-status individuals whose actions are eventually copied by a larger number of less-innovative others.

Culture patterns also change by virtue of external forces. As a result of contact with other environments, previous attitudes and behaviors may change. A visit to a foreign country may result in a change in attitude towards the people of that country as well as a stimulation of a desire for cuisine from that country. Travel may also stimulate the sale of other products from the destination visited. A vacation in Germany might improve the chance of purchasing a German car upon one's return home.

Culture and the Individual

The effect of culture is felt by the individual in three ways. First, culture affects the daily life patterns of individuals in society. An afternoon siesta is common in certain countries in Southern Europe to cope with high midday temperatures. In the United States, the physical separation of work and residence leads to an uninterrupted workday and consequently a smaller lunch compared to those in Southern Europe. Concepts of time vary from culture to culture. In the United States, time is money; in other cultures time is of less consequence. Second, culture affects the way emotions are expressed. In the Latin culture there is much touching—people feel comfortable at distances from each other that would make an American or Briton uncomfortable—and emotions are expressed in a spontaneous and enthusiastic manner. Last, there is every indication that certain cultures have a predominance of certain personality types. The German national character exhibits a predominance of authoritative personality traits. In this culture, we would expect that a decision as important as an annual vacation would be made primarily by the male in a family.

It can readily be seen that in order to understand a consumer fully it is necessary to understand the surrounding culture of that consumer. A knowledge of how the culture affects the individual, the social groups to which that individual belongs, and society as a whole will better enable the marketer to sell a travel product. Insight will be gained as to what to say, to whom to say it, and how the message should be phrased. As hosts, we will be better able to understand why visitors act the way they do and be in a better position to anticipate and satisfy their needs and wants.

Analyzing a Culture

When marketing internationally, there are four possible strategies to overcome cultural barriers—adapt, do not adapt, pattern globalization, and changing the culture. In the first instance—adapt—the entire marketing mix is changed to fit the market better. In the second case a single message is given to all markets. Third, pattern globalization occurs when an overall image is adapted slightly at the local level while still following the overall plan. The message is the same but delivered differently. The final

TABLE 3.1   A COMPARISON OF CULTURAL DIFFERENCES

East Asian countries	United States of America
• Equity is more important than wealth. • Saving and conserving resources is highly valued. • Group is the most important part of society and is emphasized for motivation.	• Wealth is more important than equity. • Consumption is highly valued, awareness for conservation is growing. • Individual is the most important part of society, and the person is emphasized for motivation, although team emphasis is growing.
• Cohesive and strong families and ties often extend to distant relatives—even the nation and its leaders. Relationship society with strong network of social ties. • Highly disciplined and motivated work force/societies • Education is an investment in the prestige and economic wellbeing of the family. • Protocol, rank, and status is important. • Personal conflicts are to be avoided—e.g., few lawyers. • Public service is a moral responsibility.	• Nuclear and mobile family. Experimentation with new home/housing/commune living communities of nonrelatives. Fluid society that deemphasizes strong, social ties. • Decline in the "protestant work ethic" and hierarchy. • Education is an investment in personal development/success. • Informality and competence is important. • Conflict is energy, to be managed—many lawyers. • Distrust of big government and bureaucracy.

Source: Philip R. Harris and Robert T. Moran, *Managing Cultural Differences*, Second Edition (Houston, Texas, Gulf Publishing Company, 1987), p. 388.

option—expensive, time consuming, and ethically questionable—is to change the culture being marketed to. From a marketing viewpoint, the most desirable course of action is to adapt the marketing mix to the culture.

The cultures of different countries can vary greatly. In order to successfully attract people from a particular country, it is necessary to be aware of these cultural differences.

Table 3.1 illustrates some of the major differences between the culture of East Asian countries and that of the United States. A marketing effort aimed at people from these cultures would have to take these differences into account in order to be successful. For example, education is important to people from both cultures. However, East Asians look at education as an investment to help the family while, in the U.S., it is viewed as an investment in oneself. Thus, while the educational advantages of travel can be marketed to both groups, the approach taken would differ. Messages in East Asia would stress the educational impact on the family and the prestige involved for the family, while the individual benefits would be the focus to American audiences.

A marketing effort must take differences in culture into account in order to be effective

One model for doing this has been suggested by Hofstede.[2] He has analyzed certain work-related values of over 50 countries. He found that the value patterns dominant in these countries varied along four main dimensions:

1. Individualism vs. Collectivism
2. Masculinity vs. femininity
3. Large or small power distance
4. Strong or weak uncertainty avoidance

[2]Geert Hofstede, "The Cultural Perspective," *People and Organizations Interacting,* Edited by Aat Brakel (New York, John Wiley & Sons Inc., 1985).

On the first scale—individualism vs. collectivism—the issue is the closeness of the relationship between one person and other persons. At the individualistic end of the scale, individuals look after their own self-interests and those of their immediate families. At the other end of the scale, the ties between individuals are very tight. People are supposed to look after the interests of their in-group and have no other opinions and beliefs other than those of their in-group. Wealthy countries are on the individualistic side while poorer countries are on the collectivist side. We might speculate that people from countries that score high on individualism would have different motives and behaviors than those from countries with high-collectivist scores. High individualistics might be more inclined to travel independently than in groups and to be more motivated by the desire to improve themselves, for example.

The second dimension is masculinity vs. femininity—the division of roles between the sexes in society. The point is the extent to which societies try to minimize or maximize the social sex role division. Masculine societies make a sharp division between what men and women "should" do. In these cases, men always take more assertive and dominant roles, while women take more service-oriented and caring roles. In masculine societies more importance is given to such things as showing off, achieving something visible, and making money. In feminine societies more importance is placed on such things as people relationships over money, the quality of life, and preservation of the environment. Masculine countries are Japan, Germany, Austria and Switzerland, some Latin countries, and most Anglo countries. On the feminine side are the Nordic countries. Placement on this scale would have implications for appropriate marketing appeals. We would expect major decisions, such as for a vacation, to be made by the male in societies that score high on this scale, for example.

These two dimensions have been put together in Figure 3.1. The separation of the countries into distinct groupings suggests a similarity of culture within each segment. It also suggests that countries in separate segments have cultures sufficiently different to warrant different marketing approaches.

The third dimension is power distance—how society deals with the fact that people are unequal. Some societies let inequalities grow over time into inequalities in power and wealth, while others try to play down inequalities as much as possible. Asian, African, and Latin American countries have large power index scores (indicating inequalities), while France, Belgium, Spain, and Italy score rather high. The Nordic and Anglo countries score low on this scale. We might expect messages of a more humanitarian and egalitarian type to appeal to cultures low on this scale.

The last dimension is uncertainty avoidance—how society deals with the fact that the time runs only one way. We all have to live with the uncertainty of the future. Some societies teach their people to accept and live with this uncertainty. People will take personal risks rather lightly, will not work so hard, and will be relatively tolerant of behaviors and opinions different from their own. These are *weak uncertainty avoidance* societies. Others try to control the future through such things as formal and informal rules to protect themselves from the uncertainties of human behavior. In societies like this, the word of experts is relied upon much more heavily than in weak uncertainty avoidance societies. Latin countries score high, while Asian and

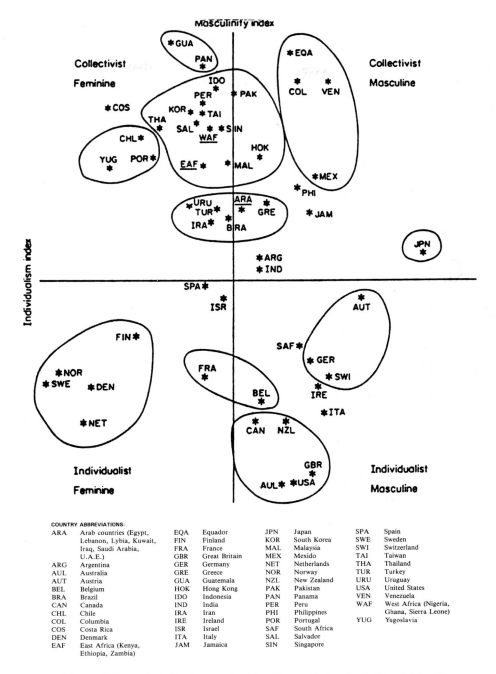

Figure 3.1 An individualism—collectivism X masculinity—femininity plot for 50 countries and three regions. SOURCE: Geert Hofstede, "The Cultural Perspective," in *People and Organizations Interacting*. (New York, John Wiley & Sons, 1985), p. 230.

COUNTRY ABBREVIATIONS:

ARA	Arab countries (Egypt, Lebanon, Lybia, Kuwait, Iraq, Saudi Arabia, U.A.E.)	EQA	Equador	JPN	Japan	SPA	Spain
		FIN	Finland	KOR	South Korea	SWE	Sweden
		FRA	France	MAL	Malaysia	SWI	Switzerland
		GBR	Great Britain	MEX	Mexido	TAI	Taiwan
ARG	Argentina	GER	Germany	NET	Netherlands	THA	Thailand
AUL	Australia	GRE	Greece	NOR	Norway	TUR	Turkey
AUT	Austria	GUA	Guatemala	NZL	New Zealand	URU	Uruguay
BEL	Belgium	HOK	Hong Kong	PAK	Pakistan	USA	United States
BRA	Brazil	IDO	Indonesia	PAN	Panama	VEN	Venezuela
CAN	Canada	IND	India	PER	Peru	WAF	West Africa (Nigeria, Ghana, Sierra Leone)
CHL	Chile	IRA	Iran	PHI	Philippines		
COL	Columbia	IRE	Ireland	POR	Portugal	YUG	Yugoslavia
COS	Costa Rica	ISR	Israel	SAF	South Africa		
DEN	Denmark	ITA	Italy	SAL	Salvador		
EAF	East Africa (Kenya, Ethiopia, Zambia)	JAM	Jamaica	SIN	Singapore		

African countries, with the exception of Japan and Korea, score medium to low. Germany, Austria and Switzerland score high, while the Nordic and Anglo countries score low. It might be expected that, in high scoring countries, the role of opinion leaders (as experts) would be stronger.

These last two dimensions have been put together in Figure 3.2. As before, it suggests that countries in separate segments have enough cultural differences to warrant different approaches in marketing to them.

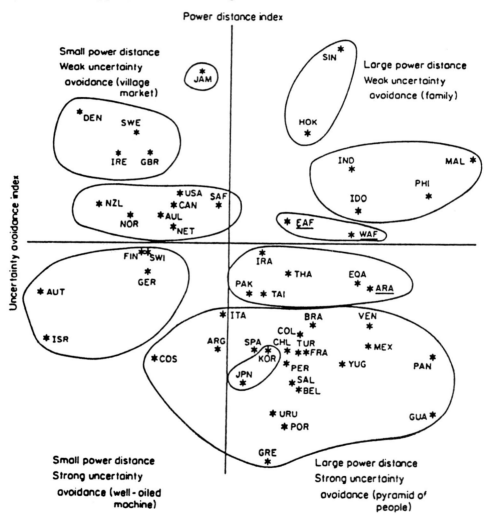

Figure 3.2   A power distance X uncertainty avoidance plot for 50 countries and three regions. SOURCE: Geert Hofstede, "The Cultural Perspective," *People and Organizations Interacting* (New York, John Wiley & Sons, 1985), p. 228.

Louden[3] has developed a checklist of factors to be considered in analyzing a culture. The analysis would be particularly appropriate before developing a marketing approach to people from different cultures.

1. Determine relevant motivations in the culture: Which needs do people seek to fulfill? In a comparison of travel motivations for vacations to the U.S., for example, Germans were particularly interested in status, while, to the Japanese, people were of prime importance.[4]

2. Determine characteristic behavior patterns: How often are vacations purchased. In Great Britain the annual vacation in the summer is paramount, while those who can afford it take an additional, off-season break. In the United States, on the other hand, there is a movement away from the long vacation once a year to several shorter breaks taken more often during the year.

3. Determine what broad cultural values are relevant to this product: Are vacations, leisure, and recreation thought of in positive terms? In Great Britain, the annual break is seen as very important, something to save for and look forward to all year.

4. Determine characteristic forms of decision making: Who makes the vacation purchase decision? When is it made? What information sources and criteria are used in making the decision? As noted above, we would expect the vacation decision to be male dominated in both Japan and Germany. The planning time varies by market segment. Japanese travelers interested in vacationing in Colorado begin planning their trip an average of 11 weeks ahead of time; the British begin 25 weeks ahead of time; and West Germans begin the process 31 weeks ahead of time.

5. Evaluate promotion methods appropriate to the culture: What kinds of promotional techniques, words, and pictures are acceptable or not acceptable to people of this culture? In Great Britain, for example, the humor is more subtle than in the United States. Advertisements use the double meaning to get the point across in a clever way. Such an approach would probably fail in the U.S. where the punch line has to be very direct to gain attention.

6. Determine appropriate institutions for this product in the minds of consumers: Do people tend to purchase vacations directly from suppliers, or are retail travel agents used? What alternatives, acceptable to the consumer, are available for distributing the product? Germans, for example, are more inclined to use retail travel agents than other Europeans when planning vacations to the U.S.

[3]David L. Louden and Albert J. Della Bitta, *Consumer Behavior: Concepts and Applications* (New York, McGraw-Hill Book Co., 1979), pp. 135–39.

[4]Harvey Shields, "Cross-Cultural Differences Among International Travelers: A Market Segment Probe," Paper presented at the seventeenth annual conference of The Travel and Tourism Research Association, 1986.

The U.S. Culture

Within the culture of a country various subcultures can be found. Nevertheless the following characteristics are those that are generally found in the dominant culture of the United States.

Evaluative and moralistic. The dominant culture in the United States is one that is evaluative and moralistic in its judgment of objects, people, and behavior. The judgments that people make are usually quite simple and concise, that is, something or someone is either right or wrong, good or bad, or moral or immoral.

Humanistic and egalitarian. Americans as a whole believe in equal rights for all and that people are created equal. If possible, these people are generous to charitable causes.

Human mastery over nature and human perfectability. This attribute is portrayed by corporations and individuals continuously devising new technology and ideas that will be of benefit to their economic goals and to the goals of people striving to become knowledgeable and well educated.

Materialism and progress. People place values on the number of possessions one has and the necessity to be progressive both materially and educationally.

Individualism and achievement. The U.S. dominant culture places a great deal of emphasis on a high level of achievement motivation, which distinguishes it tremendously from certain subcultures and cultures of other countries. We achieve goals and become individualistic through intense competition.

Time orientation. Time is important to many because it is equated with money. Many things are organized and run by the clock.

Youthfulness. Many people turn to youth activities and procedures for renewed inspiration. Advertising, promotion, and products are all geared toward youthfulness.

Activity. Americans value hard work and also hard play. This stems from the Puritan ethic that idleness is evil.

Efficiency and practicality. People in the United States are continually searching for better ways of doing things, whether it is with a new product, service, or procedure. A product or service that is quite "in" will be set aside and the new product or service will be implemented, even if the old product or service had not become obsolete.

Religious and moral orientation. A large percentage of Americans are religious. Many in the culture believe that the U.S. culture and way of life is the best and feel that it is their duty to bring others around to this country's way of thinking and acting.

Social interaction and conformity. Even though many in the United States value individualism, marketers promote products of all kinds that incorporate the theme of how beneficial these products are in achieving pleasurable social interaction.

Americans work hard and play hard

Subcultures

The point was made earlier that, not only do countries have unique cultures, but within a country subcultures exist. Within the United States there are, to name a few, Spanish, black, and Jewish subcultures. Each subculture is different in several ways from the national culture. In the Spanish subculture, family ties are very strong, with the husband having strong authority over buying decisions. The upper-class Spanish-American has been almost totally assimilated into American culture. Because Spanish-Americans are respected for this, they are regarded as opinion leaders and are a useful group to reach to penetrate the market.

In the black subculture, women have a great influence on the attitudes and behavior of black children and on purchase behavior in general. It is dangerous to generalize even when talking about the characteristics of a subculture. It appears, however, that blacks tend to spend their income on personal consumption items from which they feel they get value. Although some blacks base their purchase behavior on the whites they may seek to match, others go in the opposite direction.

The Jewish subculture is strongly family oriented, with joint decision making more common than in the subcultures of the previous examples. A strong emphasis is placed on education, and there is a willingness to buy new items, try new places.

Regional differences are also apparent. It has been suggested that North America is made up of nine distinct regional groupings.

1. *The Foundry.* Capital—Detroit. This industrialized, heavily urban region is heavily unionized and its people have a strong work orientation.
2. *Mexamerica.* Capital—Los Angeles. The region has a heavy Hispanic culture. The people are hardworking, entrepreneurial and growth-oriented.

3. *The Islands.* Capital—Miami. The diverse population of this area has a heavy Caribbean and Latin American influence and little in common with the rest of Florida.

4. *Quebec.* Capital—Quebec City. In the French-speaking part of Canada, the people have great history, tradition, and ethnic pride. Fiercely independent, the culture is extremely homogeneous.

5. *Dixie.* Capital—Atlanta. While this region is undergoing rapid social and economic change, it still exhibits a small-town way of life and an economy-minded population.

6. *New England.* Capital—Boston. This region is made up of politically diverse, cautious, and brand-loyal individuals.

7. *The Empty Quarter.* Capital—Denver. This region is characterized by hard-working, conservative, blue collar people who still have the frontier ethic.

8. *Ecotopia.* Capital—San Francisco. The young, educated, and affluent people of this region strongly believe in the importance of the quality of life.

9. *Breadbasket.* Capital—Kansas City. This is mainstream America with a stable, conservative population who are at peace with themselves.

From the thumbnail sketches given above, it can be seen that, even within one region, several cultures can exist. Diversified marketing approaches are necessary to appeal to people from specific geographic backgrounds.

THE EFFECT OF TIME ON TRAVEL

Time, or rather the availability of time, acts as a major inhibiting factor to tourist travel. The amount of available time and the form in which it is available is, in fact, a major shaper of the destinations that can be visited, the modes of travel that can be used, and the activities that can be engaged in at the destination or enroute. The desire to travel and the financial ability to travel are insufficient if one does not have the time to travel. All three factors must be present for travel and tourism to take place.

Our time can be spent in one of three ways (Figure 3.3).

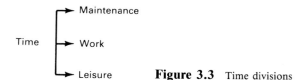

Figure 3.3 Time divisions

Spending Time

Time is spent in many maintenance activities. Maintenance activities can be thought of as activities that involve a certain degree of obligation and that are necessary to sustain and maintain life. Included in this definition are such activities as eating, sleeping, maintaining the house, and caring for the lawn. Time can also be spent at work. For many this involves a degree of obligation greater than that spent in maintenance activities. Leisure can be defined, although some people may feel it is a rather simplified definition, as the time remaining after work and maintenance activities have been completed. By its very definition leisure implies that the individual has a level of discretion over how to spend time that is not present in the other two categories. Leisure is often contrasted with the economic activity of work, and it is connected with pleasure and a feeling of freedom with a minimum of obligation. Leisure is also seen as inner directed rather than other directed. It is the time for one's self. Although leisure time offers opportunities for creativity and personal growth, the accent must be on freedom of choice. Traditionally, researchers have talked about leisure as time spent in productive pursuits. Yet this imposes a value system upon the individual's discretionary time. "Productive" is a term defined by the researcher. The crucial point is that leisure-time activities are those that are undertaken freely by individuals within their discretionary time.

Leisure time offers opportunities for creativity—Bungi jumping in New Zealand

By seeing time broken down into these three categories, it is easy to demonstrate a relationship between all three. Because time is absolute—there are twenty-four hours in a day, seven days in a week, fifty-two weeks in a year—any change in one of the three parts will automatically affect the others. As the workweek declines, more time is freed for maintenance and/or leisure activities. This is important because in the study of tourism, we are concerned with the use of leisure time, and a recognition that leisure time is bound to the other two concepts will help us to be concerned with changes in those concepts as they might affect leisure time.

How is time actually spent? In a "typical" week most time is spent on maintenance activities. This is true for both females and males. The significant differences between the sexes is that females spend more time on housework, necessary home maintenance, lawn care, and playing with or helping the children than do males. Leisure-time activities take up between 20 to 25 percent of the average workweek. This amounts to approximately thirty-nine hours per week. There are no major differences between the sexes as to how leisure time is spent. Most leisure time is spent watching television.

We might expect that the above distribution would change relative to changes in the family life cycle. This relationship is demonstrated in Figure 3.4. In the young and single phase, people are characterized by great physical capacity, disposable time, and few demands on their income. In the family phase, discretionary income and time decrease, and the physical capacity of the family is limited by that of its weakest member. The third phase is characterized by an excess of discretionary time and a decrease in physical capacity.

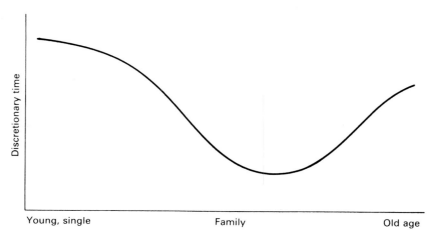

Figure 3.4 Time phases in the family life cycle

Historical Development of Leisure Time

The distribution of time between the three categories mentioned has changed over the years. In 1850 the average workweek was close to seventy hours; today it approximately forty hours. The reason for the long workweek in the nineteenth century have been traced to the industrial revolution. Prior to the industrial revolution in Britain, most people were connected with the farm. Hours of work and leisure were dictated by the farming seasons. People worked long hours when the harvest had to be brought in, but in winter, because of the lesser number of daylight hours, hours of work were less. The industrial revolution brought a movement of a rural population which had work hours conditioned by nature to an increasingly urban population, which had work hours determined by employers who sought to have output on a continuous basis year round. In addition, many of the leisure-time pursuits of the working class were rough and violent. In order to control their workers better, owners adopted various strategies. Wages were kept low so that saving money was difficult, and in order to live, people had to continue working rather than take time off. In addition, the Sabbath was strictly enforced. As a complement to this, the idea of work was made the most important part of life. The idea of spending time at work was praised almost to the point of sanctification, but the idea of spending time at leisure was derided. Religious movements developed this thought into an ethic—the Protestant ethic. Leisure time was first given to celebrate various religious festivals. These holy days were the forerunner of our holidays, as the idea of associating a break from work with religion has gradually diminished. The average number of weekdays enjoyed as paid vacation time varies greatly by country. In France and Sweden the workers have twenty five paid weekdays of vacation, not counting public holidays. Most European countries give their workers from eighteen to twenty five paid weekdays off. In contrast, Canadians get thirteen paid weekdays while Americans have a measly nine.

Although the workweek has undoubtedly decreased, other factors have prevented more people from seeing an increase in their leisure time. As affluence has increased the incidence of material possessions, much of the reduced work time has manifested itself in increased maintenance time to take care of the new possessions, such as the car and the house. In addition, as cities have grown as a result of the country's becoming more urbanized, commuting time to work has increased. A related factor is that, for many, the stress of big-city living means that more time is required before individuals are mentally ready for leisure pursuits. A third factor is that, as the economy moves from primary and manufacturing industries to a service economy, the distinction between work and nonwork becomes increasingly blurred. It is easier for the steel worker to punch out at the end of a shift and forget about work problems than it is for the manager of a business. In addition, the growing number of part-time workers has hidden the fact that over the past twenty-five years the average non-student workweek has remained steady at about forty-three hours.

Attempts have been made to show a relationship between the type of work and the type of leisure activities engaged in. Leisure has been seen as a compensation for work in that leisure activity is quite different from work activity. A passive job, for example, may result in active leisure-time activities. A second view is that the development of certain skills and life-styles learned at work will spill over into a demand for similar kinds of leisure-time activities. The problem, of course, is that any leisure-time behavior can be explained by reference to whichever theory is more appropriate to one's purpose. The link between type of work and leisure activities has not been demonstrated. In fact, several studies have demonstrated that there are no significant differences in leisure activity between workers who are doing what they consider boring jobs and those who are doing more interesting and enjoyable jobs. It does seem clear, however, that the place of leisure in a person's life is becoming more important relative to that of work.

More important than the absolute amount of leisure time available, however, is the way in which it is spent. An individual who finishes dinner at seven o'clock and plans to go to bed at midnight has five hours of leisure time. The amount of time available limits what activities can be done and where they can be pursued. Leisure time may be thought of as being divided into three categories (Figure 3.5).

Figure 3.5   Leisure time divisions

Leisure occurs on weekdays, weekends, and on vacations. The importance of this distinction can be illustrated by means of an example. If the workweek were to be reduced by 20 percent, the opportunities for tourism activities would be affected by the way in which the reduction was taken: the workday could be shortened to six-and-a-half hours from eight; the workweek could be shortened from five to four days; one week's paid vacation could be granted in each of three quarters of the year, with one month's vacation in the fourth quarter, and with six months' vacation every five years. All three alternatives represent a cut of 20 percent in the workweek, yet the form in which it is taken affects the opportunities to participate in various activities and to visit various destinations.

It is clear that, although the absolute amount of leisure time may have increased little over the past several decades, the form in which it is being taken is changing. Although most of the gains in leisure in the past century have been taken in the form of a shorter workweek, since 1950 added leisure time has increasingly been taken in blocks of extended periods away from work. Yet the vast majority of full-time U.S. workers still are engaged in a five-day workweek.

The concepts of work, leisure, and money are intertwined as far as tourism is concerned. Individuals need both leisure and money to travel. Usually this money is earned by working. Thus, it is necessary to work in order to earn money to engage in leisure-time pursuits. The more one works, the more money is earned (and, therefore, available for leisure activities), but the less time one has to spend and enjoy it. Consumers can thus be thought of as having both a time budget and a money budget, and some make rational decisions in allocating one over the other. The auto worker who takes Friday off to lengthen the weekend for a fishing trip chooses time over money; the college professor who chooses not to teach during the summer, but to travel cross-country chooses time over money. This idea has been expressed as the *principle of resource value inversion*. As consumers' incomes rise, time becomes increasingly precious to them compared to money. Money, after all, can be saved; time cannot. Combined with this is a perception on the part of many that "time is money." To what extent are people increasingly unwilling to put off gratification? Are people choosing more time over more money? Several generalizations can be made. First, although Americans desire both more income and free time, it appears that three units of income are preferred for every unit of free time worth one unit of income. Second, this preference gap seems to be closing as free time is gradually increasing in importance relative to more income. In times of economic slowdown, this statement does not hold true. Third, the income-free time choice is made within the context of other factors and values associated with an individual's perception of the quality of life. Fourth, the choice between income and free time may be affected by the way in which the free-time options are offered. Some options were demonstrated above with the example of the 20 percent workweek reduction. It appears that most workers prefer free time in the form of extended time away from work.

Much has been made of the effect of a four-day workweek on pleasure travel. People representing a nationwide sample were asked to indicate what activities would be undertaken if every week included a three-day weekend. The activities chosen by more than half of either male or female respondents are indicated in Table 3.2.

TABLE 3.2 ACTIVITIES RESPONDENTS WOULD ENGAGE IN WITH A THREE-DAY WEEKEND EVERY WEEK

Activity	Females (%)	Males (%)
Take weekend trips, visit places I've always wanted to see	70	63
Socialize, visit friends	56	45
Spend time with family, play with children	53	50
Drive around, go sightseeing	52	48
Spend time on outdoor hobbies	45	52

SOURCE: Douglas K. Hawes, "Time Budgets and Consumer-Time Behavior," in *Advances in Consumer Research,* Vol. 4, p. 228.

The major response given indicated that a significant proportion of both male and female respondents would take weekend trips. However, studies of workers engaged in a four-day, forty-hour workweek have indicated that, because of fatigue from the workweek, most people tended to be more favorably inclined to home-centered relaxaion. Another study compared the leisure participation of four-day-a-week and five-days-a-week workers. It found that both sets of workers devoted approximately equal amounts of time to participation in leisure activities. The only difference was that those who worked only four days a week pursued, on average, a greater number of different activities than the five-day-a-week worker. It may be that the extra day offers an opportunity to experiment with new activities, spending less time on each of more activities. This is rather interesting because, if this can be generalized, an extra day of nonwork actually places more time pressure on different leisure activities.

What will the effect of these time trends on travel products be? We can conclude the following:

1. A growing importance for goods and services that economize on the consumers' use of time.
2. A growing importance of goods and services that require spending leisure time in blocks.
3. A decline in the effectiveness of monetary incentives relative to leisure-time incentives.

These trends can already been seen in the development of shorter cruises, thus capitalizing on those who can afford the trip but not the traditional three weeks, which was a previously common cruise time. As these trends continue, we would expect an increasing demand for time-intensive activities such as golf, water skiing, and eating out, as well as for two- and three-day holiday weekends.

SOCIOECONOMIC VARIABLES AND THEIR EFFECT ON TOURISM DEMAND

Age

The relationship between tourism and age has two components—the amount of leisure time available relative to age and the type and extent of activities undertaken at various age levels. The amount of leisure time available changes curvilinearly, with the younger and older age groups having proportionately more leisure time.

Yet the amount of available time is, by itself, insufficient to explain age as a factor in tourism behavior. It is safe to conclude that the rates of participation in the overwhelming majority of leisure activities declines with age. The decline in participation varies relative to the type of activity. There is a greater decline for active recreational activities than for the more passive forms of recreation. Preferred activities among the elderly are the more passive ones such as visiting friends and relatives, sightseeing, fishing, and playing golf. Yet for many retirees, although the number of activities participated in may drop upon retirement, the amount of time spent on each remaining one in terms of participation often increases.

There appears to be several differences between patterns of travel based on age. Older people tend to represent a smaller share of tourists in proportion to their numbers than do younger people. This may also be influenced by other socioeconomic factors, such as income. Although younger people tend to select more adventurous destinations than do older people, older tourists tend to travel to farther destinations. The older tourists tend to dominate ship travel, spend less than middle-age tourists but more than younger tourists, and, while preferring to travel in the summer (in common with younger travelers), tend to travel more in the spring than do younger tourists.

In analyzing the impact of age on travel and tourism, the generational influence must be considered. The generational influence is the common set of values and attitudes shared by those who came of age during a particular decade. There are seven generational groups now living in American society. The groups and their implications for travel and tourism in the year 2000 are shown in Table 3.3. The key demographic trends facing the United States are these:[5]

TABLE 3.3   THE SEVEN GENERATIONAL GROUPS

Group	Born	Formative years	Dominant decade	Age in 1988	Age in 2000*	% of pop. 2000**
Baby Boomlet	1977–88	1989–2000	1990s	0–11	12–23	17%
Baby Bust	1965–76	1977–1988	1980s	12–23	24–35	17%
Late Baby Boom	1955–64	1967–1976	1970s	24–33	36–45	21%
Early Baby Boom	1946–54	1958–1966	1960s	34–42	46–54	18%
World War II Babies	1935–45	1947–1957	1950s	43–53	55–56	11%
Depression Babies	1924–34	1936–1946	1940s	54–64	66–76	8%
World War I Babies	1923 & earlier	1935 & earlier	1930s earlier	65+	77+	8%

*While actual ages are presented here, statistics have been compiled using traditional age groupings as follows: 15–24, 25–34, 35–44, 45–54, 55–64, 65–74, 75+

**Based on projected population 15 years of age and over in 2000.

Source: *Highlights of Discover America 2000,* (Washington, D.C., Travel Industry Association of America, 1988), pp. 2–3.

The U.S. population is getting older

[5]U.S. Travel Data Center, *Highlights of Discover America 2000* (Washington, D.C., Travel Industry Association of America, 1988) pp. 3–4.

- Between 1988 and the year 2000 the U.S. population will grow at its slowest rate since the 1930s, only 0.7 percent a year.
- The U.S. population is getting older overall as the Baby Boom advances into middle age. The greatest population growth between now and the year 2000 will be in the 35–54 age group.
- The marriage rate which has been declining for nearly 20 years may plateau or actually increase as a result of the AIDS threat and changing social values.
- Despite the Baby Boomlet, the total fertility rate in the U.S. is now and will continue to be at record lows, producing the same small families we see today.

The generational influence may impact future demand in the following ways:[6]

1. *Baby Busters,* who were raised in the less socially interactive environment of the 1980s, may prefer to travel independently in the future. However, the convenience of buying a package will appeal to their need for expediency in the arrangement of their leisure time.
2. *Late Baby Boomers* will be time-constrained working parents looking to create worthwhile family experiences. Their general familiarity and sophistication with travel will cause them to demand a high level of service.
3. *Early Baby Boomers* will be reaching the peak of their earning potential. Many will have sent their children to college and will have acquired long-term assets. One segment may be *early semi-retirees.* Because of the social environment in which they were raised, the less traditional vacation destinations could be very attractive to this group.
4. *Many World War II Babies* may find themselves encouraged to take early retirement to make way for the arrival of Early Baby Boomers into managerial ranks. Their upbringing could have them looking for opportunities for social interaction and learning as part of their travel experiences.
5. *Depression Babies* offer a challenge. They have life experiences very different from young Americans. They are intent upon hunting for bargains; they do not like to buy on credit; and they have strong family and community ties. Yet many will have time, money, and health to travel.
6. *World War I Babies* represent people for whom travel is not seen as an integral part of life.

In summary, leisure time decreases with age until children leave the nest; then the amount of leisure time increases. This increase continues with retirement. Though participation in physical activities declines with age (together with a corresponding rise in participation in the gentler forms of recreation) interest levels in activities previously participated in remains high. Opportunities may exist for tapping these interests by developing nonparticipatory means of expressing that interest. A skier,

[6]USTDC, pp. 5–6.

for example, may be unable to ski for reasons of age, but may be interested in other related activities such as watching skiers or sharing experiences.

Income

Income is obviously an important inhibiting factor in shaping the demand for travel. Not only does travel itself entail a certain cost, but the traveler must pay for services rendered at the destination as well as have money to engage in various activities during the trip. In addition, expenditures may be required in the form of specialized equipment to engage in various recreational activities while at the destination or enroute. It is difficult, however, to determine the relative importance of income per se, because this variable is interrelated with other socioeconomic variables. Generally speaking, higher income is associated with higher education, with certain jobs, and with certain age groups. Total family income has risen steadily as more wives have entered the labor force. The fact that family income has risen will have an effect upon tourism demand. Yet the fact that more families have two spouses in the labor force will also affect the shape of tourism demand. Different types of vacations and recreational activities may be demanded because of the time pressures involved in having two working spouses. The difficulty arises in determining the effect of these two interrelated variables on the demand for new tourism and recreation products.

It is important to see that the income spent on travel is spent at the expense of something else. (See Figure 3.6). Travel expenditures are in competition with other expenditures, some of which are discretionary.

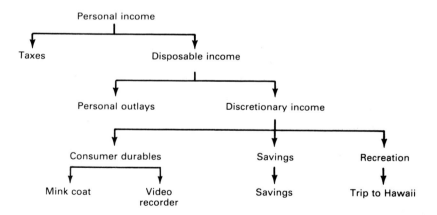

FIGURE 3.6 Personal income distribution

An individual's personal disposable income is the amount of income left after taxes have been paid. After various necessary personal outlays to maintain basic living needs have been spent, an individual has discretion to do with the reaminder whatever is desired. A mink coat may be purchased, money may be saved, or a trip taken to Hawaii. It is important to look at income in this way to realize that the trip to Hawaii is in competition not only with a trip to the Bahamas, but also with various other recreational activities and other uses of that discretionary income. As the level of personal income increases, so does the amount of discretionary income.

Many studies have attempted to determine the percentage of income spent on recreation as a whole. It appears that at the lower levels of income and education approximately 2 percent of income is spent on recreation. As income increases the proportion spent on recreation increases to between 5 and 6 percent for all education levels. The highest recreational expenditures, 7 percent, are reported by respondents who are heads of households, under forty years of age, and without children. Other studies have indicated a positive correlation between income and recreation expenditures. In fact, it appears that increases in income result in a proportionately greater increase in recreation expenditures. As might be expected, higher-income tourists stay longer and spend more per day than do those with lower incomes. The type of recreational activities participated in differs based upon income. Higher-income people tend to participate in activities such as reading, bridge, fencing, squash, and chess; and middle-income people tend to engage in bowling, golf, and dancing. Lower-income families are identified with television viewing, dominoes, and bingo. The implication of these activities is clear to companies who wish to put together travel packages with specific activities involved aimed at particular market segments. A package, for example, aimed at a high-income segment of the market might be built around a recreational activity in which that segment tends to participate.

In addition to the relationship between income and recreation expenditure, some work has been done on the amount of participation in recreation and income. It has been shown that participation in most recreational activities increases as income increases up to a certain point, but declines slightly at incomes higher than this.

The only significant demographic difference between U.S. domestic and foreign travelers is that of income. A greater percentage of foreign travelers had higher incomes.

Sex

There are more similarities than differences between the sexes in terms of leisure participation rates. Overall, participation rates in leisure activities do not differ between men and women, although many women engage in slightly fewer activities than do men. As might be expected, nonworking women have slightly higher participation rates than do employed women, except for such things as going out to dinner and either taking part in active sports or watching sports. There is a clear difference between the sexes in terms of preferred activities. Women are more involved in cultural activities, and men lead in outdoor recreation and playing and watching sports.

Education

The strong correlation between education as it relates to income has been well-established. Independent of income, however, the level of education that an individual has tends to influence the type of leisure and travel pursuits chosen. The amount of education obtained will most likely determine the nature of both work and leisure-time activities. By widening one's horizons of interest and enjoyment, education influences the type of activities undertaken. Education itself can serve as the primary reason for travel.

Researchers have found that participation in outdoor recreation tends to increase as the amount of education increases. There is also some evidence to suggest that the more educated prefer those activities that require the development of interpretive and expressive skills. Such activities include attending plays, concerts, and art museums, playing tennis and golf, skiing, reading books, attending adult education classes, and undergoing a wilderness experience.

In summary, it appears that the more education people have the broader their horizons and the more options they can consider. The more-educated travelers also tend to be more sophisticated in their tastes. They may not, however, be bigger spenders. A study of visitors to Hawaii found that visitors with less education spent more per day while on vacation in Hawaii. The authors suggested that the less-educated visitor may equate having fun with spending money.

LIFE-STYLE STAGES

Families evolve through a certain life cycle. The characteristics of the family at the various stages of its life cycle offer certain opportunities or exert various pressures that affect purchase behavior.

Single people take part in a much wider variety of activities outside the home than do married people. Married life brings about certain changes in leisure habits. Activities that were previously done alone or with friends are participated in less for reasons intrinsic to the activity itself.

Presence of Children

The narrowing of the types of activities participated in is intensified by the presence of children (see Table 3.4). When a married couple has children, there is a shift from activities engaged in primarily for intrinsic satisfaction to activities that are role-related, such as "family" activities. Before children came on the scene, the spouse was the chief leisure companion. This companionship is diluted by the presence of children. The presence of children seems to be crucial. Travel is curtailed; more leisure time is spent at home; and few new leisure interests are acquired. In at least one case, that of camping, the onset of parenthood has varied effects. Although the addition of young children in a camping family may produce a curtailment of camping activity, the shift to the empty-nest stage produces either an increase or a decrease in the activity. For those couples who enjoy camping, the situation of children leaving the

TABLE 3.4   A TRADITIONAL FAMILY LIFE CYCLE

Stage in Life Cycle	Buying or Behavior Pattern
1. Bachelor stage: Young, single people not living at home	Few financial burdens. Fashion opinion leaders. Recreation oriented. Buy basic kitchen equipment, basic furniture, cars, equipment for the mating game, vacations.
2. Newly married couples: Young, no children	Better off financially than they will be in near future. Highest purchase rate and highest average purchase of durables. Buy cars, refrigerators, stoves, sensible and durable furniture, vacations.
3. Full nest I: Youngest child under six	Home purchasing at peak. Liquid assets low. Dissatisfied with financial position and amount of money saved. Interested in new products. Buy washers, dryers, TV, baby food, chest rubs and cough medicines, vitamins, dolls, wagons, sleds, skates.
4. Full nest II: Youngest child six or over	Financial position better. Some wives work. Less influenced by advertising. Buy larger-sized packages, multiple-unit deals. Buy many foods, cleaning materials, bicycles, music lessons, pianos.
5. Full nest III: Older couples with dependent children	Financial position still better. More wives work. Some children get jobs. Hard to influence with advertising. High average purchase of durables. Buy new, more tasteful furniture, auto travel, nonnecessary appliances, boats, dental services, magazines.
6. Empty Nest I: Older couples, no children living with them, head in labor force	Home ownership at peak. Most satisfied with financial position and money saved. Interested in travel, recreation, self-education. Make gifts and contributions. Not interested in new products. Buy vacations, luxuries, home improvements.
7. Empty nest II: Older married couples, no children living at home, head retired	Drastic cut in income. Keep home. Buy medical-care products that improve health, sleep, and digestion.
8. Solitary survivor, in labor force	Income still good, but likely to sell home.
9. Solitary survivor, retired	Same medical and product needs as other retired group. Drastic cut in income. Special need for attention, affection, and security.

Source: William D. Wells and George Gubar, "Life Cycle Concept in Marketing Research," *Journal of Marketing Research,* November 1986, pp. 355–363, in J. Paul Peter and Jerry C. Olson, *Consumer Behavior: Marketing Strategy Perspectives* (Homewood, Illinois, Richard D. Irwin), p. 459.

nest may actually increase their participation. For others, who saw camping primarily as a family activity, the departure of children from the home may result in less camping.

Basic attitudes and behavior patterns of family life established in the early years of the family life cycle affect the future activities of both husbands and wives throughout the marriage. For the young child, leisure pursuits are restricted by the dictates of parents and the limitations of money. As children enter school, leisure activities outside the home increase. As children grow older, their leisure habits and attitudes are more heavily influenced by their peers. Because of the high rate of social interaction among young people, leisure fads are easily spread. There is also at this stage an attempt to duplicate the behavior and attitudes of older age groups. Particularly important in this respect are college students, who tend to be leaders, often being the first to try new products and services.

Empty Nesters

As children leave the home, more time and money tend to be available for leisure. The empty nesters left behind have been the subject of a focus group study conducted by Plog Research.[7] A focus group consists of a small group of people, usually ten to twelve, getting together for a two-hour discussion. The groups are made up of individuals who have already been screened through questionnaires and interviews to arrive at a group that has members similar to one another in background. The discussion is led by a psychologist who attempts to develop a picture of the needs, interests, and personal psychologies of the group. The findings of the study are quite revealing. The typical empty nester doesn't think of extended trips by air, especially to foreign destinations. Their thinking is geared to the kinds of trips taken with their children, trips which have typically involved travel by car and visits to friends and relatives. There appears to be a strong desire for travel experiences as a means of self-actualization. Several barriers present themselves. The surface barriers of lack of time and money are true up to a point. For couples who work, scheduling may be a problem, and there is a reluctance towards using all of one's vacation time at once. Financially, although more discretionary income may be available, many empty nesters feel uncomfortable in spending their money on an intangible, such as travel. In addition, they tend to believe that the cost of a trip is more expensive than it really is, estimating the cost at twice the actual one. More than anything, however, they express fear as a barrier to traveling. They are afraid of not knowing how to act in a new environment, of being taken advantage of. In a more subtle way, they feel that travel may be a way for them to learn how to be a couple again. Combined with this, however, is the fear that they may discover that they really do not like each other.

It is necessary to understand the particular inhibiting factors felt by each of these market segments at each stage of the family life cycle in order to be able to offer a product or service that will overcome the barriers and induce purchase behavior. For the empty nesters, for example, a tour would be very appropriate. A package tour relieves the participants of making decisions they may well feel inade-

---

[7]"Increasing Your Sales to New and Existing Markets," Plog Research, Inc., undated.

Empty nesters may increase their camping activity

quate to make. The regular tour may have a negative connotation for them, however. Empty nesters usually want to spend more time in fewer places than many tours offer. Popular kinds of destinations are those that help the empty nesters find their roots. This appeals to the need to find some meaning to their lives. The tour also helps alleviate some of the fears of being a couple again with no children around. The fact that there are other people around means that the empty nesters do not have to rely totally upon each other for companionship and support during the trip.

Barriers to Leisure Enjoyment

The barriers to leisure enjoyment have been the subject of a study by Witt and Goodale.[8] They identified the relationship between various barriers to the enjoyment of leisure and stages in the family life cycle. Understanding these barriers is a crucial step towards knowing what to say, do, and offer to lower those barriers. It was found that different patterns of change developed over the family life cycle relative to the barriers under discussion. Figure 3.7 illustrates the fact that various barriers (see Table 3.5) showed an approximately U-shaped pattern, with the barriers having the least effect when the youngest child was between six and eighteen years of age. These barriers refer to difficulties in knowing which activities to get involved with and with whom to share participation. This suggests that as children reach school age, parents have more knowledge of what is available and how to utilize those opportunities. It may also be, as mentioned earlier, that their leisure activities are more closely defined for them by the expectation of their role as parents of school-age

[8]Peter A. Witt and Thomas L. Goodale, "The Relationship Between Barriers to Leisure Enjoyment and Family Stages," *Leisure Sciences*, vol. 4, no. 1, 1981, pp. 29-49.

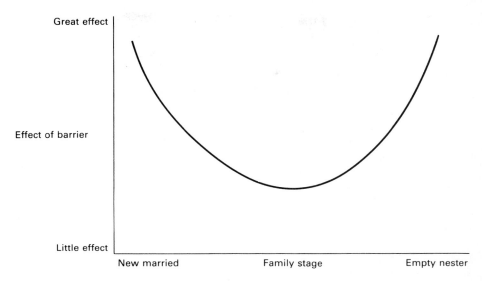

Figure 3.7 Barriers to leisure enjoyment at different family stages (U-shaped pattern)

TABLE 3.5 BARRIERS EXHIBITING A
U-SHAPED PATTERN

Not being sure what activities to be involved in
Not knowing what's going on or what's available
Not being sure how to use available resources
Difficulty in planning and making decisions
Not having anyone to do things with
Not being at ease in social situations
Difficulty in carrying out plans

children. The time when the youngest child leaves home appears to be a critical passage relative to these barriers, a point made in the earlier discussion of the empty nesters.

A second group of barriers exhibit an inverted U-shaped pattern when expressed over the life cycle of the family. (See Figure 3.8) During the child-rearing period, family obligations increase significantly for women and, to a similar but lesser degree, for men. This fact and the fact that neither parent feels there is enough free time represent the barriers felt; they increase until children leave the home, and then their effect drops off sharply.

The effect of various barriers has been found to increase as the family goes through various life-cycle stages. (See Figure 3.9) The expectations of family and friends increase for women, but for men they are more constant and less of a limitation over the family life cycle. The feelings of daily stress increase for both sexes as times goes on, while often the feeling of not doing anything stays somewhat constant during the child-rearing stage and increases dramatically when children leave

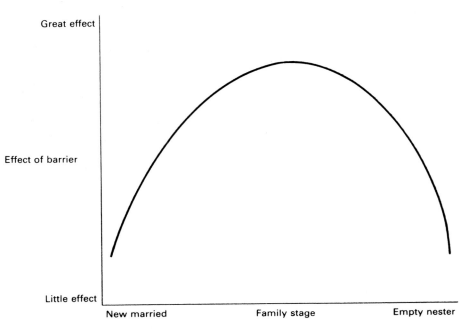

Figure 3.8 Barriers to leisure enjoyment at different family stages (Inverted U-Shaped Pattern)

Figure 3.9 Barriers to leisure enjoyment at different family stages (Direct effect pattern)

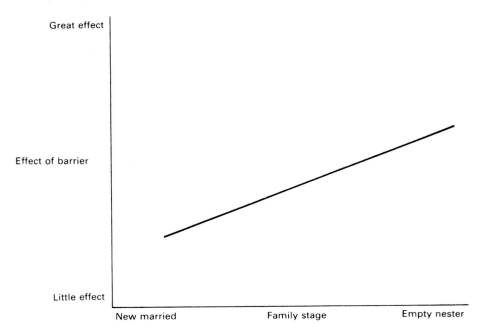

the home. Two other barriers have been analyzed for males only. It has been found that there is an increased effect by males who don't feel fit enough or don't have the physical skills for certain activities. This is reflected in the effect of a falling off in physical skills and fitness levels with age.

Certain points are worthy of note. First, it appears that stages in the family life cycle can help explain and help predict leisure-time behavior. Care must be taken, however, in the use of correlation or regression techniques for projecting or forecasting leisure activities because of the nonlinear pattern of many of these barriers. Second, it is noted that the family life-cycle stage can only explain leisure behavior very partially. Third, it is determined that noting which barriers are predominant at various lifecycle stages will enable product, packages, and messages to be targeted to reflect an undestanding of these barriers and potential objections of the many market segments.

PERSONALITY

An individual's personality has an effect on the purchase behavior described in Chapter 1. It has been suggested that most people view their vacation as an extension of their personality. Howard and Sheth have postulated that the effect of personality is felt on two areas—nonspecific motives and the alternatives considered for purchase. They have proposed that the more authoritarian a person is, for example, the fewer alternatives that will have to be considered in arriving at a purchase decision. The relationship between personality and nonspecific motives has been explored by various researchers in an attempt to understand existing behavior better and predict future behavior with greater accuracy.

The personality of an individual can be described as "the summation of the characteristics that make the person what he or she is and [that] distinguish each individual from every other individual."[10] It is logical that there is a link between the type of person one is and the type of purchases one makes. A "conservative" person will tend to make "conservative" purchases.

Personality Traits

Personality can be thought of as consisting of a variety of traits. Individuals who participate in recreational and tourist activities can be typed in terms of their personality traits in an attempt to determine whether such participants exhibit markedly different personality traits than do nonparticipants. The purpose of such analysis is to determine whether or not personality can be used as a variable for segmenting the market. If it is found that certain personality traits are dominant in winter vacations, marketers will know better the kind of tourist to appeal to and will gain valuable information as to what to say to appeal to this potential vacationer. To date, the research evidence is inconclusive as to whether or not personality is a significant

---

[10]C. Glenn Walters, *Consumer Behavior: Theory and Practice* (Homewood, IL, Richard D. Irwin, Inc., 1978). p. 296.

variable in explaining purchase behavior. Although several studies indicate a strong relationship between personality and consumer behavior and a few indicate no relationship, the great majority indicate that existing correlations are weak.

The relationship between personality and participation in recreational activities is also of interest. As we have seen, recreational activities can serve as a major reason or motivation for vacation travel. If a relationship between certain activities and certain personality traits can be established, an appropriate marketing strategy can be developed.

Personality Types

Often a person is described as having a certain type of personality. Personality types consist of characteristics that, when taken together, form a certain kind of person. One way of typing people is to the extent that they are perceived as being introverted or extroverted. Introverts look into themselves and tend to be shy and reserved. Extroverts are other-oriented, looking outside the self, and tending to be objective rather than subjective in outlook. Participants in vigorous physical activity in general tend to be extroverts. In fact, outdoor recreational activities in general are not participated in by introverted personality types.

Psychographics and Life-Style

The application of studies of personality to the business world has been hampered because the terminology of personality has come from clinical sources. Psychographics has developed as a way of describing consumer behavior in terms of a distinctive way of living in order to determine whether or not people with distinctive life-styles have distinctive travel behaviors. Psychographics is the development of psychological profiles of consumers and psychologically based measures of distinctive modes of living or life-styles. The most widely recognized use of this segmentation method is the VALS program. VALS stand for Values And Life Styles and is a copyrighted, syndicated lifestyle study conducted by SRI International (formerly the Stanford Research Institute). It divided Americans into nine lifestyles or types, which are grouped in four categories based on their self-images, their aspirations, their values and beliefs, and the products they use. It is possible for people to move from one category to another as they grow and mature.

The various categories and groups are depicted in Figure 3.10. Survivors and Sustainers make up the Need-Driven category. Survivors are struggling to survive. They seek to satisfy basic and immediate needs. Sustainers are struggling, but they are hopeful. They are the least satisfied with their financial status and the most anxious to get ahead economically.

The Outer-Directed Groups are middle America. They are very concerned about how they appeal to others, and their lives are influenced by others' perception of them. The largest group are the Belongers. They are uncomplicated, conservative, conventional, and lead comfortable lives. They are highly conforming and extremely patriotic. They are older, heavily female, little college education, and slightly below average income.

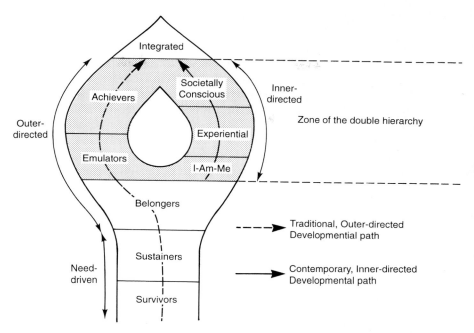

FIGURE 3.10 The Nine American Lifestyles. Reprinted with permission of Macmillan Publishing company from *The Nine American Lifestyles* by Arnold Mitchell. Copyright © 1983 by Arnold Mitchell.

While Belongers are satisfied, Emulators are trying to "make it" and become Achievers. They are competitive, macho, and very status conscious. Achievers are the second largest group. Its members are successful, happy, hard working, self-reliant, and wealthy. There are proportionately more men who are well educated with careers in managerial or professional occupations.

Approximately twenty percent of the population are what are called Inner-Directed. The basic rewards of life for them are internal and emotional rather than external and materialistic. The I-Am-Me's are young, typically single, and confused. They are fiercely independent. The Experientials are the most inner-directed of any group. They actively seek direct experience, personal involvement, and a sense of inner growth. They are young, well educated, artistic, and attracted to the exotic, the strange, and the natural. The Societally Conscious group are self-assured and well-off. They stress conservation, simplicity, and environmental concerns.

The Integrated group make up the Combined Outer- and Inner-Directed Category. This small group have it all together. They are self-assured, self-actualized, self-expressive, and have a global perspective on issues.

Earlier nine regional divisions of North America was suggested. Many of the regions have a greater than proportionate number of certain VALs types living in them. The Foundry, capital Detroit, has a large proportion of Emulators, Inner Directeds and I-Am-Me's. Emulators, Achievers, and the Societally Conscious predominate in Mexamerica, capital Los Angeles. Need-Driven and Belongers are found in Dixie, capital Atlanta; and New England, capital Boston, houses Inner Directed, Societally Conscious and Achievers. The Inner Directed are to be found in the Empty Quarter, Capital Denver; and Ecotopia, capital San Francisco, is home to the Inner Directed and Experientials. Last, the Breadbasket, capital Kansas City, is where there is a predominance of Belongers.

There is a similarity between the VALS typology and Maslow's hierarchy of needs outlined in Chapter 1. This is illustrated in Figure 3.11. The Survivors correspond to Maslow's survival needs, while security needs are most important for the Sustainers. Belongers are principally concerned with belonging or love, while the Achievers and Emulators focus on the need for esteem. Self-Actualization is the focus for those who are Integrated, in addition to being important to part of the Societally Conscious group.

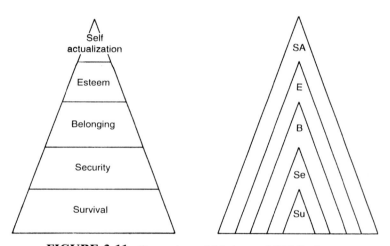

FIGURE 3.11   Comparison of Maslow and VALS schemes

Specific implications for travel and tourism are illustrated in Table 3.6. The most important segments for tourism are Achievers, Societally Conscious, and to a lesser extent, Experientials. Achievers travel frequently for both business and pleasure. They prefer luxury hotels and like to stay at resorts when on vacation. Of all the groups, Achievers are the group most likely to indulge themselves when on vacation. They tend to prefer independent travel, but they will take tours if it is the most convenient way to see the country. They enjoy traveling with their families and are most likely to travel with their spouses on a vacation trip. While on vacation they like to unwind and do not feel compelled to do anything.

Travel is very important for the Societally Conscious. They travel a great deal and look forward to it. They would rather spend their time and money on travel than on almost anything else. They take longer trips than any other group and get a great deal of pleasure from planning the trip. Having done extensive research and received personal recommendations from friends and ideas from travel articles, they are the best prepared upon arrival at the destination and may, therefore, be the most dif-

TABLE 3.6 TRAVEL HABITS BY LIFESTYLE

	Survivors	Sustainers	Belongers	Emulators	Achievers	I-Am-Me	Experientials	Societally conscious
Pleasure Travel								
Travel by air	−	−			+		+	+
Stay at hotels/motels	−	−			+			+
Use rental car	−				+			+
Use travel agent	−	−			+	+		+
Travel abroad					+	+	+	+
Business Travel								
Travel by air	−		−		+			+
Stay at hotels/motels	−			−	+		+	+
Use rental car					+			+
Use travel agent					+			+

Note: A plus (+) indicates that people in a given group participate in the activity more than ten percentage points above the average of all the VALS groups; a minus (−) indicates participation ten or more percentage points under average.

Source: Compiled by Shih based on Mitchell, *The Nine American Lifestyles.* Reprinted with permission of Macmillan Publishing Co.

ficult to please. They tend to distrust both advertising and travel agents. They prefer off-the-beaten-track vacation spots and, once there, are self-reliant, adventurous, and price conscious. The Societally Conscious are comfortable traveling alone. They explore, try new and unusual foods, like to experience the culture, and value the educational aspects of travel. They tend to avoid guided tours, chain hotels, and other tourists.

The socially conscious prefer off-the-beaten-track vacation spots

Differences can be expected when specific destinations are considered. The visitors to Pennsylvania, for example, consist largely of Achievers, Belongers, and Societally Conscious.

These three same types accounted for the bulk of travelers to Hong Kong. Each segment of the market, however, had travel patterns different enough to justify separate marketing action plans. The existing marketing program, based on the ''upscale traveler'' was on-target for the Achievers but needed adaptation for the Belongers and the Societally Conscious. This latter group was not as well represented as it should have been. The problem was that this group perceived Hong Kong as a tour destination where independent travel was not as readily available as they would prefer. This finding led to changes in the way the message was communicated to this group.

The Belongers who travel to Hong Kong are mainly the wives or widows of Achievers. Belongers prefer to travel domestically, most likely with their spouses or friends. On vacation, they are structured and cautious. They need to feel assured. They often select all-inclusive tours, staying in chain hotels. They are the least likely to indulge themselves when on vacation. To appeal to this group, the advertising message was changed to emphasize the fact that Hong Kong is more suited to their tastes than many European cities. English is spoken, it is easy to get around, and the water is drinkable. Savings on shopping would probably be a good idea also.

Segmenting the market in this way also has implications for where to advertise. Achievers, for example, are not big TV watchers but are interested in magazine and newspaper reading.

It has been shown that life-styles vary according to different socio-economic variables. Although it is beneficial to segment a market on the basis of life-style dimensions for marketing purposes, it is necessary to identify the socio-economic characteristics of these segments in order to reach the target markets effectively.

REFERENCES

AHMED, SADRUDIN A., "Understanding Residents' Reactions to Tourism Marketing Strategies," *Journal of Travel Research,* vol. 24, no. 2, pp. 13–18.

DUMAZEDIER, JOFFRE, *Sociology of Leisure* (Elsevier Scientific Publishing Company, 1974), ch. 3.

GROPP, MARVIN, M., "VALS—As a Media Evaluation Tool," *Magazine: Newsletter of Research,* no. 40, October 1982.

HARRIS, PHILIP R. and ROBERT T. MORAN, *Managing Cultural Differences,* second edition (Houston, Texas, Gulf Publishing Company, 1985).

HOFSTEDE, GEERT, "The Cultural Process," in *People and Organizations Interacting,* Aat Brakel (ed.) (New York, John Wiley & Sons, 1985).

MAYO, EDWARD J. and LANCE P. JARVIS, *The Psychology of Leisure Travel* (Boston, MA, C.B.I. Publishing Co., Inc., 1981), p. 234.

MITCHELL, ARNOLD, "Social Change: Implications of Trends in Values and Lifestyles," VALS Report no. 3, January 1979.

NEULINGER, JOHN, *The Psychology of Leisure* (Springfield, Ill., Charles C. Thomas, 1974).

OPPEDIJK van VEEN, WALLE M. and THEO W. M. VERHALLEN, "Vacation Market Segmentation: A Domain Specific Value Approach," *Annals of Tourism Research,* vol. 13, 1986, pp. 37–58.

PETER, J. PAUL and JERRY C. OLSON, *Consumer Behavior: Marketing Strategy Perspectives* (Homewood, Illinois, Irwin, 1987).

PITTS, ROBERT E. and ARCH G. WOODSIDE, "Personal Values and Travel Decisions," *Journal of Travel Research,* vol. 25, no. 1, pp. 20–25.

SHAMES, GERMAINE W. and W. GERALD GLOVER, *World Class Service* (Yarmouth, Maine, Intercultural Press, Inc., 1989).

SHIH, DAVID, "VALS as a Tool of Tourism Market Research; The Pennsylvania Experience," *Journal of Travel Research,* vol. 24, no. 4, pp. 2–11.

SKIDMORE, SARITA, "Lifestyle Segmentation of Vacation Visitors to Hong Kong," paper presented at the seventeenth annual conference of The Travel and Tourism Research Association, 1986.

UNITED STATES TRAVEL and TOURISM ADMINISTRATION, *International Travel to Colorado, 1988.*

US TRAVEL DATA CENTER, *Discover America 2000* (Washington, D.C., Travel Industry Association of America, 1988).

VOSS, JUSTIN, and ROGER BLACKWELL, "Markets for Leisure Time," paper presented at the Association for Consumer Research, 1974, pp. 7–8.

EXERCISE

In 1986 a five-year agreement was signed between Canada and the United States that allowed Tourism Canada and the U.S. Travel and Tourism Administration to undertake jointly funded research in overseas countries. The following data are a product of this work and were collected from people in Great Britain interested in visiting the United States.

The purpose of the exercise is to make suitable marketing recommendations in the areas of what tourism product should be offered, what price should be charged, what promotional theme should be used, and how the vacation should be sold or distributed to the specific market segments identified through the research.

1. Examine Table 3.7—Demographics of visitors to key destinations—and, on the basis of the information given, suggest what tourism destinations might be appropriate, what pricing strategy should be used, what advertising theme might be successful, and how the vacation should be sold.
2. Examine Table 3.8—Travel Philosophy Segments—and, for each segment, make similar recommendations. Note that each statement for the segments is given either a positive or a negative value that indicates its deviation from the overall statement mean. The greater the positive number, the more people in this segment agree with this statement; the greater the negative number, the more people disagree with this statement.
3. Repeat this process with the information in Table 3.9—Benefit Segments.
4. Repeat this process with the information in Table 3.10—Product Segments.
5. Which information is most helpful and which is least helpful in making specific marketing recommendations? Why do you say this?
6. Examine the information in Table 3.11—Product Segments vs. Travel Philosophy and Benefit Segments. Select one segment and make appropriate marketing recommendations along

the lines made previously. Compare your recommendations with those made earlier. Are they better? Why? How should a market be segmented in order to give the best data upon which to make marketing decisions?

TABLE 3.7   DEMOGRAPHICS OF VISITORS TO KEY DESTINATIONS

	U.S.		U.S.
Total respondents (100%)	447	Other	17
Sex		Not stated	2
Male	40	*Life cycle*	
Female	60	Living alone	4
Age		Living with one adult	28
18–24 years	12	Single with children	3
25–34 years	16	Couple with children	30
35–44 years	23	Other	35
45–54 years	18	*Mean no. of adults 18 years*	
55–64 years	17	*or over*	2.3
65 years or over	13	*Whether any children under 18*	
Marital status		*years in household*	
Single	20	Yes	35
Married	64	No	65
Divorced/separated/widowed	14	*1985 household income* (in pounds)	
Living together	2	3,000 and under	3
Occupation		3,001 to 8,000	19
Higher manager	5	8,001 to 15,000	25
Intermediate manager	21	15,001 to 30,000	23
Junior manager	42	30,001 or over	8
Skilled worker	11	Not stated	22
Semi/unskilled worker	14	*Region*	
Unemployed	5	London	27
Not stated	2	S. West	15
Education		Yorks/N.W.	26
No qualification	26	N.E./Scotland	10
High school	36	Midland	11
Undergraduate	14	Anglia	11
Post-graduate	4		

TABLE 3.8   TRAVEL PHILOSOPHY SEGMENTS

	Deviation from overall statement mean
Enthusiastic Independent Traveler (25%)	
Enjoy making own arrangements	+ 0.7
Like to make arrangements as go along	+ 0.5
Rather travel from place to place than stay put	+ 0.4
Don't have to spend a lot to enjoy vacation	+ 0.3
Usually use travel agent to help choose destination	− 0.4
Prefer guided tours	− 0.5
Like to stay put at destination	− 0.5
Worth paying for luxuries	− 0.5
Important that people speak my language	− 0.6
Prefer to leave organizing to co-traveler	− 0.7
Like to have arrangements made before leaving	− 0.7
Usually buy vacation packages	− 0.8
Affirmed Package Traveler (25%)	
Usually buy vacation packages	+ 0.9
Prefer guided tours	+ 0.9
Like to go to different places each trip	+ 0.4
Like to have arrangements made before leaving	+ 0.4
Usually use a travel agent to help choose destination	+ 0.3
Rather travel from place to place than stay put	+ 0.3
Worth paying for luxuries	+ 0.3
Take short pleasure trips whenever can	+ 0.3
Just as soon spend on things other than travel	− 0.3
Like to stay put at destination	− 0.3
Enjoy making own arrangements	− 0.3
Don't have to travel to enjoy vacation	− 0.3
Usually choose places been before	− 0.4
Like to make arrangements as go along	− 0.4
Guarded Package Traveler (19%)	
Prefer to leave organizing to co-traveler	+ 0.8
Usually use travel agent to help choose destination	+ 0.6
Like to stay put at destination	+ 0.5
Arrangements such a bother rather not travel	+ 0.4
Important that people speak my language	+ 0.4
Just as soon spend on things other than travel	+ 0.4
Don't have to travel to enjoy vacation	+ 0.4
Usually buy vacation packages	+ 0.3
Money on travel is well spent	− 0.3
Rather travel from place to place than stay put	− 0.4
Enjoy making own arrangements	− 0.8
Guarded Independent Traveler (21%)	
Enjoy making own arrangements	+ 0.5
Usually choose places been before	+ 0.5
Like to stay put at destination	+ 0.3
Worth paying for luxuries	+ 0.3
Rather travel from place to place than stay put	− 0.3

	Deviation from overall statement mean
Often choose places friends have been	− 0.3
Take short pleasure trips whenever can	− 0.3
Like to go to different places each trip	− 0.3
Prefer to leave organizing to co-traveler	− 0.3
Prefer guided tours	− 0.4
Usually buy vacation packages	− 0.5
Usually use travel agent to help choose destination	− 0.5

TABLE 3.9 BENEFIT SEGMENTS

A total of three benefit segments were identified in the analysis. The following descriptions indicate the ways in which each group is different from the average:

Adventure (35%)	This segment is looking for an active holiday and something different on their vacations, that is, thrills and excitement, feeling daring and adventuresome. They are open to new experiences and lifestyles, such as new foods, but mainly wish to be physically active as a way of releasing their energies, especially through sports.
Social Safety (34%)	This segment is more interested in being with people in a safe, secure environment than in seeing or experiencing new things on a vacation. They place more importance than average on feeling at home away from home, visiting friends and relatives, visiting where their family came from, and being together as a family. They also place more importance on reliving past good times and talking about their trip afterwards, likely because it is a means for them to be together with other family members with whom they want to share the experience.
Getaway 31%)	This group is looking for a temporary escape from the demands of home and a busy job. They are looking for rest and relaxation in a setting where they feel safe and secure. They do not wish to be tied to any activities or obligations but rather prefer to feel free to do nothing. For this reason, perhaps indulging in luxury is an appealing concept to them.

TABLE 3.10 PRODUCT SEGMENTS

The analysis yielded seven different product segments with the following comparative descriptions:

Developed Resort *(15%)*	While this group has some liking for beaches and seaside areas, these travelers are not looking for an area of wide open spaces away from it all. Rather they are interested in lots of facilities: first class hotels, high quality restaurants, nightlife and entertainment, sports facilities, and so on. In short they are looking for well developed resort areas with plenty of warm sun.
Beach (17%)	Although respondents in this segment seem to be mainly interested in the same beaches and seaside areas with good weather as Developed Resort travelers, they are much less interested in the facilities or leisure activities such as nightlife and water sports that one is likely to encounter at a resort. Instead the beach seems to provide a setting for a simpler retreat without all the extras of a resort vacation.
Culture and Comfort *(16%)*	This segment has above average interest in seeing historical sites and museums and art galleries, hence the culture aspect of their name. The comfort aspect comes partly from their liking of first class hotels and destinations that are a manageable size to see, and partly as a contrast with the Culture and Nature segment described below. Notwithstanding their greater interest in comfort, they exhibit some of the same interests in natural heritage as Culture and Nature travelers (for example, wildlife and national parks and forests).
Sports and Entertainment *(14%)*	This segment gave comparatively high ratings to a number of sports-related product items (skiing, fishing, hunting, spectator sporting events, water sports), as well as to a number of entertainment related items (casinos and gambling, nightlife and entertainment). This group appears to be looking to satisfy different product needs at different times, perhaps partly on a seasonal basis.
Culture and Nature *(12%)*	This group is similar in many ways to the Culture and Comfort group described earlier. They share an interest in historical sites, old cities, museums and art galleries, cultural groups and increasing their knowledge through travel. To some extent they also share an interest in such things as wildlife and national parks and forests.
	What strongly serves to differentiate the two segments, however, is the much lower importance attached by the Culture and Nature group to such items as first class hotels, high quality restaurants, and sightseeing excursions, as well as the relatively greater importance they attach to budget accommodation, campgrounds and trailer parks. In other words, with regard to culture, the two segments share highly similar importance values, with the main point of departure being the lower level of comfort required by Culture and Nature travelers.
Big City *(15%)*	Respondents in this group appear to be those who most desire the attractions of a large urban center: first class hotels, nightlife and entertainment, good shopping, amusement parks,

The analysis yielded seven different product segments with the following comparative descriptions:

	high quality restaurants, live theaters and concerts, and sightseeing around old cities. They least desire rugged outdoor physical activities such as hiking or climbing, wide open mountainous areas, and wilderness.
Outdoor Sports *(11%)*	This group is just the opposite of Big City. These travelers seek out strenuous things to do in the outdoors whether it be seaside water sports, hiking or climbing in the wilderness or skiing in the mountains. They also differ from Sports and Entertainment travelers with whom they share some interests because the latter rate spectator sports, theme parks, and other urban forms of entertainment equal in importance to the outdoor sports that this segment evidently values above other travel features.

TABLE 3.11   PRODUCT SEGMENTS VS. TRAVEL PHILOSOPHY AND BENEFITS SEGMENTS

Further insight into the product segments can be obtained by profiling them with respect to the travel philosophy and benefit segments. This reveals that the product segments are more likely than average to be represented as follows:

	Travel philosophy	*Benefit*
Developed Resort:	Guarded Package traveler	Getaway
Beach:	Guarded Independent traveler, Affirmed Package traveler	Getaway
Culture and Comfort:	Affirmed Package traveler	Social Safety
Sports and Entertainment	Guarded Package traveler, Guarded Independent traveler	Social Safety, Adventure
Culture and Nature:	Enthusiastic Independent traveler	Adventure
Big City:	Affirmed Package traveler	Social Safety, Getaway
Outdoor Sports:	Enthusiastic Independent traveler	Adventure

4

TRAVEL PURCHASE:

The Traveler's Buying Process

"What we do during our working hours determines what we have; what we do in our leisure hours determines what we are."

George Eastman, quoted in Reader's Digest.

When travelers are made aware of a vacation opportunity, they go through a series of stages before committing to a purchase decision.

The characteristics of each of these steps are examined.

The communications strategy of the marketer will vary depending upon where the target market is in the buying process. Appropriate strategies for each stage in the buying process are outlined.

The decision to take a vacation is, in fact, a series of subdecisions—where to go, when to go, how long to stay, how to travel, and so on. The order in which these decisions are made, as well as the influence of children on the various subdecisions, is examined.

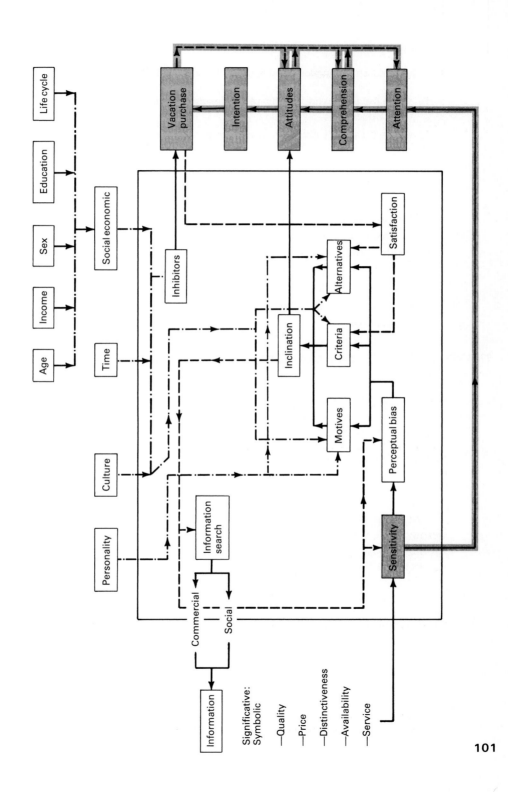

Significative:
Symbolic

—Quality
—Price
—Distinctiveness
—Availability
—Service

LEARNING OBJECTIVES

Having read this chapter, you should be able to:

1. Describe the seven buying-process stages that people go through when making travel decisions.
2. Explain the effectiveness of different communication strategies in each buying-process stage.
3. Identify which promotional techniques work best for each buying process stage.
4. Describe the appropriate communication objectives for each buying-process stage.
5. Discuss the principle of cognitive dissonance and what travel marketers can do to lessen its impact.
6. Explain the concept of buying-process feedback.
7. Describe how a vacation decision is actually composed of a series of subdecisions.
8. Explain the influence of family life-cycle stages on vacation subdecisions.
9. Discuss the role of husbands, wives, and children in making vacation subdecisions.

TRAVEL PURCHASE: THE TRAVELER'S BUYING PROCESS

It is easier, less time-consuming and less costly to sell London as a travel destination than it is to sell Tibet. Part of the reason is that more people know more about and have specific opinions or attitudes about London than about Tibet. To sell Tibet would require a rather lengthy educational process.

Attention and Awareness

When making a travel purchase, a consumer moves through several stages. The wise marketing manager realizes that different communication strategies are appropriate for different stages of the buying process. Fig. 4–1 illustrates the various stages as defined by several authors. When deciding whether or not to visit a previously unknown destination, for example, an individual may at first be unaware of the destination. The destination has, first of all, to be brought to the awareness or attention of the potential traveler. A prime function in communicating to the consumer is to gain attention. Advertising is very influential at this point.

Knowledge and Comprehension

The task in the next stage of the buying process is to make the customer goal directed. If the potential traveler's attention has been successfully stimulated, she or he will seek out more information on the destination. The attempt is to become more knowledgeable about what the destination has to offer, to comprehend what it is all about. The emphasis will be on information, and the task of the communicator will be to provide sufficient information to direct the potential traveler toward pur-

It is easier to sell London as a travel destination than it is to sell Tibet

Howard/Sheth	McDaniel/Crissy	McDaniel	AIDA	IUOTO
				Unawareness
Attention	Awareness	Awareness	Attention	Awareness
Compre-hension		Knowledge		Compre-hension
Attitudes	Interest	Liking	Interest	
	Evaluation	Preference	Desire	
		Conviction		
Intention				Conviction
Purchase	Trial	Purchase	Action	Action
	Adoption			

SOURCES: John Howard and Jagdish N. Sheth, *Theory of Buyer Behavior* (New York, John Wiley & Sons, Inc., 1969).
W. J. E. Crissy, Robert J. Boewadt, and Dante M. Laudadio, *Marketing of Hospitality Services: Food, Lodging, Travel* (East Lansing, MI, The Educational Institute of the American Hotel and Motel Association, 1975) pp. 94–95.
Carl McDaniel, Jr., *Marketing: An Integrated Approach* (New York, Harper & Row, 1979), pp. 170, 343-54.
IUOTO, *Study and Analysis of the Long-Term Effectiveness of Promotional Campaigns and Other Tourist Publicity and Advertising Activities*, undated.

Figure 4.1   The traveler's buying process

chase. Advertising is again important at this stage. The choice of media is crucial. Media should be chosen that can convey a great deal of information. Brochures or folders can do this, as can magazine and newspaper advertisements with a great deal of copy or words. Radio and television cannot provide the large amounts of information needed at this stage. It is important to talk about the destination in terms of the benefits offered. It will be remembered that destinations are perceived in terms of their benefits to the individual. To the extent that we understand a message, we will be more inclined to pay attention to it.

Attitudes, Interest, and Liking

The potential traveler next moves to developing a liking, interest, or attitude about the destination. The promotion objectives at this stage are to create or reinforce existing positive attitudes or images or to correct negative attitudes or images. A positive attitude is, in part, influenced by the individual's tendency or predisposition to visit that particular destination. (See Chapter 1.) It is also a function of how well we have gained the traveler's attention and provided sufficient information for him to determine whether or not the benefits of the destination match his needs and wants. Attitudes are difficult to change in part because, as a new attitude is developed, new incoming information is often screened to conform to an old attitude. (See Chapter 2.) It has been demonstrated that awareness or attention must exist before an attitude can change. The interest in a particular destination will influence how much effort is put into the comprehension of a particular message.

Evaluation, Preference, and Desire

After evaluating various alternatives, the consumer will develop a preference or desire for a destination.

In one study,[1] respondents were asked if, given the time, money, and opportunity, they would like to travel to other nations of the world. The figures in Table 4.1 indicate the percentage of respondents who answered in the affirmative. These figures give some indication of the overall place in the buying process of international tourism of these countries. It would appear that in countries such as Australia, France, and Scandinavia, a majority of the people are rather close to making a purchase decision, based on their strong desire to go. If one could determine the remaining barriers to travel in those countries, travel offers could be advertised, assuming that many of the earlier stages in the buying process had been reached. At the other end of the scale only 17 percent of the population of India (a sizable number in absolute terms) has reached the point of desiring foreign travel. Because the economic situation has to be considered even though the survey asked respondents not to use this as a barrier (people who do not have sufficient income to travel may be unable to envision a situation without that constraint), the people of India as a whole will need a much longer informative marketing campaign to get them to purchase foreign

---

[1]American Express V.P. Delineates Profile of the International Traveler," *Travel Weekly,* April 27, 1978, pp. 65–66.

TABLE 4.1   DESIRE TO TRAVEL TO OTHER NATIONS OF THE WORLD

Home Country	Percent desiring to Travel
Australia France Scandinavia	84%
Canada	79%
Mexico United Kingdom	74%
United States	68%
West Germany	67%
Brazil	60%
Africa (sub-Sahara)	57%
Japan	42%
India	17%

SOURCE: Travel Weekly, April 27, 1978, pp. 65–66.

travel. At this stage, there is heavy reliance on the opinions of other people and their experiences with what is being marketed. The importance of advertising is somewhat less at this stage. The most effective types of messages are testimonial ads and comparison ads. In a testimonial advertisement a person, usually a well-known public figure, praises what is being sold. The hope is that if the viewer or reader respects the person in the message their opinion on the product or service being sold will be respected. The same effect can be gained by "testimony" from someone who has already visited the destination being advertised. It is crucial that the spokesperson be believable. It is also important, for maximum impact, that the person chosen to be in the advertisement have some connection with what is being sold. A good example would be James Mitchener advertising Hawaii. Because he is the author of the best-seller entitled *Hawaii,* Mitchener is a well-respected personality with an obvious link to what is being advertised. A form of testimonial is the rating found in various guidebooks. To the extent that the rating system is respected, advertising the rating of a particular facility will gain the respect of the readers.

In a comparison advertisement one destination or facility is mentioned in a promotional message in comparison with another. The destinations are compared on particular attributes. For this kind of message to work, it is necessary to select for the basis of comparison attributes that the customer thinks are important. It is, obviously, crucial that the destination being advertised be stronger on those attributes than the competition.

Intention and Conviction

At this stage in the buying process, the potential travelers are convinced that the benefits of the destination will meet their needs and wants and are almost at the point of purchase. Studies have shown that the intention to purchase precedes the actual purchase. The international study mentioned earlier brought to light the fact that tourists differ in their travel intentions.

This research project sought to determine which countries the respondents would most like to visit. The United Kingdom, with 13 percent of the respondents, was the favorite choice of U.S. respondents, followed by Italy, which was chosen by 10 percent of the respondents. The United States was the first choice of Europeans, capturing 19 percent of the first-place votes. The United States was listed the top choice of all but those in the Benelux countries (Belgium, the Netherlands, and Luxembourg) who chose Spain ahead of the United States. People in the Latin American countries also chose the United States as the most popular destination. The only country in South America in which the respondents did not place the United States as a top choice was Brazil; citizens there slightly preferred France and Italy. Sub-Sahara Africans placed the United Kingdom in first position (22 percent of the responses) and the United States next (11 percent of the responses). In Japan the United States was ranked first, chosen by 13 percent of the respondents, followed by Switzerland with 7 percent. The Far East as a whole identified the United States the first choice by 13 percent of the respondents and Japan the second choice at 5 percent.

Studies such as the one described give an indication as to how many people in a potential market have, at the least, a postive attitude about foreign travel. By identifying the potential receiving country to which these people would like to travel, one can determine the size of the potential market and the appropriate communications strategy to use.

The United States is a favorite destination of Japanese tourists

Purchase, Trial, and Action

If the potential traveler has reached the conviction stage of the buying process, the barrier to travel is likely to be a physical one. It may be lack of time or money. It is clear, however, that the motivation is present. The marketing task is to identify the barrier and develop a product to breach it. If the problem is lack of money, a tour package may be successful. Lodging in smaller, cheaper hotels can be suggested. Research by Plog Research of several underdeveloped market segments indicated that people in all three segments estimated the true cost of a trip at twice the actual cost.[2] If the problem is one of time, it may be possible to offer a package that capitalizes on the time available. One of the reasons that fly-cruise packages have been developed is to respond to a market that has the money and the motivation, but not the time. Previously, when ships cruised out of New York much time was lost because two days of bad weather often had to be experienced before the ships reached sunny climates. The solution has been to fly travelers to Florida, sail out of a southern port, and give more sun for the time available.

Adoption

The final stage of the buying process is the adoption stage. At this point, the traveler has become a repeat purchaser. To achieve this end, it is necessary to provide a quality experience to the first-time traveler. However, advertising also has a role to play. The necessity for some form of communication to the purchaser arises because of cognitive dissonance. Cognitive dissonance arises after a choice between two or more alternatives has been made. It is a feeling of anxiety, a feeling that perhaps the choice made was not the best one. The amount of dissonance felt is influenced by the type of decision made. The anxiety is stronger if:

The rejected alternative is attractive.

The decision is important.

The purchaser becomes aware of negative characteristics in the alternative chosen.

The number of rejected alternatives increases.

The alternatives are perceived as being similar.

The decision made goes against a strongly held belief.

The decision is a recent one.

Because vacation travel represents an important decision, it has the potential for creating a great deal of anxiety after the purchase has been made. The potential is even greater if the traveler has chosen between a large number of attractive alternate destinations. The key is to indicate to the traveler as soon as possible after the decision has been made that the decision has been a good one. A note to the purchaser of a package tour or cruise may be sufficient to avoid second thoughts and cancelations. For advertisers, the key is to provide in their advertisements information that purchasers can use to justify to themselves the purchase made as well as the messages to convince people to buy.

[2]Plog Research, Inc., "Increasing Tour Sales to New and Existing Markets," undated report.

BUYING-COMMUNICATION PROCESSES INTERACTION

We have noted that there is an appropriate and different communications strategy for each stage in the traveler's buying process. This realization is particularly important because it helps in determining why a communications campaign failed. It is fairly easy to determine that a campaign did not work. For example, the promotion to induce travel to a particular destination can be assumed a failure if there has been no increase in visitors to the destination after the campaign. A more interesting question is not so much *did* the promotion fail, but *why* did it fail? Were enough people exposed to the message? Was the message memorable? Did it result in a change of attitudes? The only way that campaign managers can determine why the campaign failed is to break the process into its various stages and measure the results of each stage.

The information presented in Figure 4.2 refers to this process. At the first stage in the buying process, the objective is to expose the message to a certain number of people. The number of readers or viewers exposed to the message serve as a measure of whether or not the campaign reached this objective. At the next level, the objective is to transfer information to those exposed to the message. To determine the effectiveness, it is possible to measure the extent to which people exposed to the message have recalled the essential parts of it.

To measure a change in attitude it is necessary to survey attitudes both before and after a campaign. A similar strategy is necessary to measure whether preferences have been developed. The extent to which a message initiates action can be measured by the percentage of those who send in a response to a particular advertisement or the number who take an advertisement into a travel agent. Last, repeat purchases,

Buying Process	Communication Objective	Communication Measurement
Awareness/attention	Exposure	Number of readers/viewers exposed to message.
Knowledge/comprehension	Transmission of information	Percentage of readers/viewers who remembered essential parts of the message.
Attitudes/interest/liking	Attitude change	Attitude surveys before and after message to determine degree of change.
Evaluation/preference/desire	Creation of preferences	Preference surveys before and after message to determine preference.
Intention/conviction	Initiation of action	Number of actions taken (e.g., travel agent contact, tours booked, responses received) in response to a particular message.
Purchase/trial/action	Purchase	Number of bookings made, etc.
Adoption	Repeat purchase	Percentage of visitors who are repeat purchasers.

Figure 4.2   Interaction between the buying and communications processes

signifying the adoption of a product or service, can be measured by the percentage of visitors who are repeat purchasers.

By being aware of these different stages, communication objectives, and ways to measure their accomplishment, it is possible to determine where things went wrong. It may be, for example, that we reached a sufficiently large number of the right kind of people, a large percentage of whom remembered our message. It may be, however, that the message was not sufficiently strong to result in a change in attitude about the destination being promoted. The promotion manager knows that the media used were on target in terms of reaching the right numbers of prospects. The program has to be strengthened to result in an attitude change. A strategy offering cheap package tours, on the other hand, will be totally ineffective because the necessary prerequisite steps have not been taken in the minds of the readers.

Buying Process Feedback

Although each step in the buying process is a prerequisite for the next, there are also feedback effects. The adoption of a particular destination affects and reinforces the purchase of it. The purchase itself has an effect on future intentions, either a positive or a negative one. Each higher stage thus tends to reinforce the lower stages. Study abroad, for example, has been shown to result in a change in attitude about foreigners. It is, therefore, easier to induce a repeat purchase if a good job has been done of satisfying the traveler the first time than it is to get that first purchase.

VACATION SUBDECISIONS

Although the vacation buying process has been treated as a series of stages culminating in a buying decision, the vacation purchase is actually comprised of a series of subdecisions. From a marketer's viewpoint, it is important to know the order in which decisions are made and who makes the particular decisions. In this way, a marketing campaign can be developed that is aimed at the decision maker.

What the order of decisions is and who the decision maker is varies by which stage in the life cycle the family is in. At the stage in which the couple has been married for less than fourteen years and in which the couple is at most in their mid-thirties and may have young children at home, the decision to vacation tends to be a joint one. Although discretionary income is low, the first subdecision is "where to go," followed by "whether to go." This seems to reflect a more hedonistic attitude, which indicates an expectation to take a vacation despite income constraints. Decisions are next made concerning the amount to spend, the length of time to stay, and the accommodations to be used. In the next stage, in which the couple has been married for fourteen to twenty years, has a mid-forties age median, and has children eighteen years old or more, the husband tends to dominate the decision making slightly. This is due primarily to the vacation's being designed around the husband's work schedule. At this stage, the question of whether or not to go is most important, followed by decisions on destinations, amounts to spend, length of stay, and place to stay. When the spouses are in their mid-fifties and have been married twenty to thirty years, the process is largely wife dominated. This coincides with vacation purchases at a peak and disposable income close to a peak. The wife-dominated decision making continues until the husband is close to retirement; then he exerts a slight dominance, due perhaps to anxiety about financial matters. For couples married for over forty years, when the couple is retired, the wife once again takes over the decision making.

Other researchers have studied vacation decision making and have suggested that more joint decision making rather than individually dominated decision making occurs. Obviously more research is necessary to determine whether or not the decision focus changes with stages in the family life cycle.

The research to date on family vacation decision making indicates that the dominance of either spouse depends upon the particular subdecision to be made. External factors also come to bear on the decision. Vacation dates, for example, are probably determined by job and school dates, and hence decisions on these are husband dominated, with heavy influence by the children. There is some indication that the number of joint decisions is greater in middle-class families than in lower-class ones, but less than in the highest class ones.

A review of Table 4.2 will indicate that most vacation subdecisions are joint decisions. The husband tends to dominate in decisions regarding the length of stay, the dates of the vacation, the amount to spend, and the route to take. Although some studies indicate that husbands tend to dominate the vacation destination decision, most studies indicate this to be a joint decision.

TABLE 4.2   FAMILY VACATION DECISION MAKING

Subdecision	Standish[1]	Jenkins[2]	Myers[3]	Ritchie[4]	Omura[5]	3M6[6]	Kendall et al.[7]
Whether to go							
Whether to take the children		♀					
How long to stay		♂		♀			
How much to spend	♀	♂		♂			♂
Vacation dates		♂		♂			
Vacation destinations	♀	♀	♀	♀	♀	♂	♀
Mode of transportation	♀	♀					
Route		♂	♂				
Lodging	♀	♀	♀				♂
Activities							♀

Key: ♂   male dominated decision
           ♀   joint decision

SOURCES: [1]Theodore C. Standish, "How the Computer Views the Family Vacation Travel Market," in "Using Travel Research for Planning and Profits," *The Travel Research Association Ninth Annual Conference Proceedings,* Ottawa, Canada, 1978.
[2]Roger L. Jenkins, "Family Vacation Decision-Making," *Journal of Travel Research,* vol. 16, no. 4, 1978.
[3]Paul B. Myers and L. W. Moncrief, "Differential Leisure Travel Decision-Making Between Spouses," *Annals of Tourism Research,* vol. 5, no. 1, 1978.
[4]J. R. Brent Ritchie and P. Filiatrault, "Family Vacation Decision-Making—A Replication and Extension," *Journal of Travel Research,* vol. 18, no. 4, 1980.
[5]Glynn S. Omura, Mary Lou Roberts, and W. Wayne Talavzyk, "An Exploratory Study of Women's Travel Attitudes and Behavior: Directions for Research," *Advances in Consumer Research,* vol. 7, *(Proceedings of the Association for Consumer Research Tenth Annual Conference,* October 1979).
[6]3M National Advertising Company, "Psychographics of the Automobile Traveler," 1972.
[7]K.W. Kendall, D.J. Sandhu and Gordon Giles, "Family Decision Making in the Upscale Travel Market," Paper presented at the 14th Annual Conference of The Travel and Tourism Research Association, 1983.

Kendall et al.[3] found that decisions varied by time of year and by profession. In their study, husbands had greater influence on choosing vacations in the shoulder season, while in the prime season the decision was a joint one. In comparing trips taken by medical doctors and lawyers, they found that, on the decision to take a trip, the doctor husband has more influence while the wife of the lawyers had more influence on this subdecision.

Children influence some vacation subdecisions

[3]K.W. Kendall, D.J. Sandhu and Gordon Giles, "Family Decision Making in the Upscale Travel Market," Paper presented at the 14th Annual Conference of The Travel and Tourism Research Association, 1983.

Influence of Children

Studies by Jenkins and Ritchie (cited previously) indicate that children influence some vacation subdecisions. The children's effect is felt on the decision of whether to go on vacation, what dates and destinations to choose, what type of lodging is preferred, and which activities to undertake while on vacation.

A knowledge of who influences the various vacation subdecisions will aid marketing managers in selling their products and services. Facilities and messages can be more clearly geared to the decision maker in an attempt to increase the attention given the message, the comprehension of the message, and ultimately, the final purchase behavior.

REFERENCES

CRISSY, W.J.E., ROBERT J. BOEWADT, and DANTE LAUDADIO, *Marketing of Hospitality Services: Food, Lodging, Travel* (East Lansing, MI, The Educational Institute of the American Hotel and Motel Association, 1975), p. 95.

KENDALL, K.W. and D.J. SANDHU, "What Do You Do When You Get There: A Family Decision Making Analysis of Activity and Lodging Subdecisions of Vacationers," Paper presented at the 16th Annual Conference of The Travel and Tourism Research Association, 1985.

McDANIEL, CARL, JR., *Marketing: An Integrated Approach* (New York, Harper & Row, 1979), pp. 351, 354.

MICHE, DONALD, "Family Travel Behavior and Its Implications for Tourism Management," *Tourism Management,* vol. 7, no. 4, 1986, pp. 254–261.

NICHOLS, CATHERINE M. and DAVID J. SNEPENGER, "Family Decision Making and Tourism Behavior and Attitudes," *Journal of Travel Research,* vol. 26, no. 4, 1988, pp. 2–6.

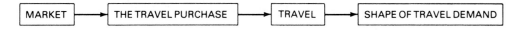

MARKET ⟶ THE TRAVEL PURCHASE ⟶ TRAVEL ⟶ SHAPE OF TRAVEL DEMAND

EXERCISE

The information in this exercise is taken from the study by Kendall, Sandhu and Giles referenced in Chapter 4.

A—% of WIVES who say wife has more influence than husband.

B—% of HUSBANDS who say wife has more influence than husband.

C—% of WIVES who say wife and husband have exactly the same influence.

D—% of HUSBANDS who say wife and husband have exactly the same influence.

E—% of WIVES who say husband has more influence than wife.

F—% of HUSBANDS who say husband has more influence than wife.

TABLE 4.E1 CRUISE VACATION—PERCEPTION OF INFLUENCE

Vacation Subdecision Area	A	B	C	D	E	F
Total Vacation Decision (To take a holiday)	29%	28%	46%	27%	25%	45%
To Take a Cruise	34%	32%	46%	27%	21%	42%
Particular Cruise Line	29%	25%	48%	31%	23%	44%
Cruise Area (Where to go)	28%	22%	43%	30%	29%	49%

Imagine you are marketing a cruise vacation. Given the preceding research data, what would be the implications for your marketing effort? To whom would you market—the wife, the husband or both? What differences, if any, should be made when appealing to the wife or the husband?

READINGS

This reading, though dated, is an excellent example of a tourism-related corporation putting into practice many of the concepts discussed in the first section of this book.

The paper was originally presented to members of the Travel and Tourism Research Association and was published in *The Impact of Tourism,* the Sixth Annual Proceedings of the Travel and Tourism Association. The authors wish to express their appreciation to the Association for permission to reprint this paper.

DESIGNING PRODUCTS FOR THE LEISURE TRAVEL MARKET FROM MARKET DEFINITION TO PRODUCT INFORMATION

Annabelle Bennetts, Manager, Marketing Research—Canada of Air Canada
Paul Burak, Vice President, Market Facts of Canada Ltd.

PART I—PAUL BURAK

Traditionally, airlines have marketed a product that was considered to be a seat from origin A to destination B and back again. Competitive products were differentiated by such things as departure and arrival times, destination points, and by such travel-related amenities as in-flight entertainment, meals, and friendly or attractive attendants.

This marketing approach is consistent with the definition of an airline as a transportation company, a means by which people get to their desired place at a desired time and in as comfortable a manner as possible. Although different kinds of advertisements may have been produced, the same basic product has been sold to the person who was travelling on business, or going to visit friends or relatives, or to the person who was trying to decide where to go or what to do on his vacation.

About four to five years ago, market planners at Air Canada decided that the time had come to market products that were fundamentally different for each type of traveller. For example, a major distinction was drawn between the traveller who had to travel to a particular destination, whether it be for business or personal reasons, and the potential traveller who might want to find a place to go.

For the nondiscretionary traveller who is committed to getting to a particular destination, the airline simply has to convince him that flying is the best way of getting there and back and, specifically, that their particular airline is the best way to do it.

As for the leisure traveller, the market task is much less clearly defined. This person is usually not committed to a particular destination place nor even necessarily to long distance travel. In fact, the choice of a particular destination place, if any, for his leisure time may be an integral part of his decision on how to spend his vacation. Certainly, the choice of an airline flight is only one element in the planning of a vacation.

116

From this emerged the concept that marketing to potential leisure travellers was not a matter of selling specific destinations but rather a matter of selling the right kinds of vacation experiences. Places such as London, Paris, Bermuda and other well-known vacation spots in the world today are clearly associated with the expectation of having special kinds of experiences. Moreover, it is the anticipation of having these kinds of experiences which people find appealing and which sell airline tickets.

As a result of this marketing concept, a large-scale market research program was launched in conjunction with Market Facts to analyze the leisure-time market for Canadians. The objectives of this research program were:

1. To analyze the demand structure in the leisure travel market
2. To identify possible new marketing opportunities
3. To develop a framework for the design of travel packages which would reflect the needs and desires of specific target groups among the population of potential leisure air travellers.

The first step in the market study consisted of in-depth group discussions. These were undertaken in order to develop an understanding of the range of attitudes toward leisure activities and vacation interests that might be found among different types of people and to develop hypotheses about what underlying factors contribute toward vacation needs, influence the kinds of experiences that different people look for in an ideal vacation, and which may constrain the realization of these vacations.

This approach to the market study allowed us to formulate a conceptual model on which to base the following market analysis. (See Exhibit A.)

Our first hypothesis was that a person's general attitudes, interests and outlook toward life are related to his or her attitudes toward different kinds of vacation experiences and to the kinds of things that he or she would want to do or encounter on a vacation. This hypothesis, if borne out, would influence the ways in which one should communicate to different kinds of potential customers.

The questionnaire that was designed included some 370 general lifestyle statements such as the following:

"I would rather live in a big city than in a small town."

"I have more stylish clothes than most of my friends."

"I don't like to take chances."

"My life is pretty dull."

"Spending money for an expensive vacation is a little like throwing money away."

"Memories make a vacation worth what it costs."

"I am interested in the cultures of other countries."

Exhibit A   Research model for the leisure travel market

I *agree* that—	I *agree* that—
I'd rather live in or near a big city than in or near a small town	I enjoy going through antique stores
I enjoy looking through fashion magazines	I'd rather save up and spend a longer time in a foreign country
I feel attractive to the opposite sex	I am interested in spices and seasonings
Dressing well is an important part of my life	I think the women's liberation movement is a good thing
Eye make-up is as important as lipstick	My greatest achievements are ahead of me
I would like to have a maid do the housework	I'd rather spend money on travel than on a new automobile
I *disagree* that—	I *disagree* that—
I am a girl watcher	I admire a successful business man more than a successful artist or writer
I enjoy watching sports on T.V.	In a foreign country I'd rather stay at a Holiday Inn than at a native hotel
I'd rather spend a quiet evening at home than go out to a party	Canada would be better off if there were no hippies

I *agree* that—	I *agree* that—
I will probably have more money to spend next year than I have now	I stay home most evenings
I am a girl watcher	I am in favour of very strict enforcement of all laws
I enjoy watching sports on T.V.	All men should be clean shaven every day
I like sports cars	I am a homebody
I like science fiction	I'd rather spend a quiet evening at home than go out to a party
I like to think I'm a bit of a swinger	Young people have too many privileges
I *disagree* that—	I *disagree* that—
I would rather write stories than run a business	I am active in sports
The kitchen is my favourite room	I am an impulsive buyer
I usually wear perfume	I like sports cars

I would *like* to—	I would *like* to—	I would *like* to—
See places I've always wanted to see	Visit relatives/friends	Be active
Absorb culture of a different place	Feel as comfortable as at home	Spend not too much money
Visit historic places	Spend not too much money	Meet young people
Go to an art gallery	Eat same kinds of food that I'm used to	Do something unique/ different
Go to a classical concert	Go somewhere that's familiar	Listen to rock music
Live with a foreign family	Watch T.V.	Ride a horse, a motorcycle, or a surfboard
I would *not like* to—	I would *not like* to—	I would *not like* to—
Do nothing	Absorb the culture of a different place	Do nothing
Lie on a beach	Do something unique and different	Stay in a fancy hotel
Have a frivolous vacation	Meet new kinds of people	Watch T.V.

I would *like* to—	I would *like* to—	I would *like* to—
Stay in a modern hotel with great entertainment, air conditioning, and good food	Have peace and quiet	Get away from snow and ice
Go to a night club	Cook over an open fire	Lie on a bench
Shop for new clothes	Get away from hustle and bustle	Be pampered
Get away from everyday routine	Drink from a mountain stream	Have breakfast in bed
Go to a luau	Spend summer at a cottage	Get into warm weather
Get a sun tan	Ignore the clock	Sit in the sun
I would *not like* to—	I would *not like* to—	I would *not like* to—
Be in a very quiet place	Go to a night club	Visit relatives/friends
Do it 'on the cheap'	Absorb culture of a different	Visit historic places
	Have an 'educational' vacation	Have an 'educational' vacation

In addition, the questionnaire included some 440 statements about different things that people might like to do when on a vacation. These included such statements as:

"Visit an historical place."

"Watch a sunset."

"Lie on a beach."

"Visit friends or relatives."

"Go shopping in out-of-the-way places."

"Paint the house."

Another set of statements described the kinds of things that people might encounter on a vacation:

"Pretty girls"

"Neon lights"

"Fine wine"

"Educational experiences"

"People who speak a foreign language"

Our second hypothesis was that the kinds of vacation experiences that people wanted are related to the kinds of vacation packages that would appeal to them. Moreover, it was hypothesized that the relationship between the desired kinds of vacation experiences and the vacation packages which people find appealing is influenced by their perceptions of different places, activities, accommodations, etc. Sociodemographic considerations, such as household income, age, number of dependents, etc., may be thought of as either opportunities or as constraints to people's ability to realize their preferred vacations.

In order to develop such vacation types, the survey respondents were asked to imagine that they had a specific amount of time and money available to them. Sixteen combinations of time and money were used, depending on each person's own demographic characteristics.

Two such scenarios involving different combinations of time and money were presented to each respondent. In each case, he or she was free to choose to go away somewhere or to stay at home and use the money in some way other than travel. If the respondent chose to use the time and money to go away somewhere, he or she was asked to describe the kind of place they would go to from a long list of descriptions. Some of these descriptions included the following phrases:

"A place where it is warm and sunny."

"A familiar place."

"A resort hotel."

"A foreign place with a different culture."

"A foreign place where nature is unspoiled."

Respondents were then asked to describe the kind of place where they would want to go, the activities they would like to take part in, and the kind of facilities or accommodations they would prefer to stay at using different sets of descriptive adjectives and statements. They were also asked to identify some specific places, activities, and types of accommodation that came closest to matching the description that they had selected as their ideal.

Other information collected included: the number and types of the people who would go along; whether they would prefer an all-inclusive package or not; the mode of transportation they would use to get to their vacation destination, as well as the type of transportation they would use while there; the time of year when they would probably go on this kind of trip; and their reasons for taking this kind of vacation. Those who thought it was unlikely that they would actually take such a vacation as they had described were asked for reasons why.

In order to determine the extent to which people's vacation desires are already being realized, respondents were asked about any vacations they had taken in the past two years. Additional information necessary to evaluate market opportunities for new vacation packages included at home leisure activities and interests plus ownership of recreational equipment.

The data base for the market analysis was a survey of about 3,000 people representing the adult population of Canada.

The major elements in the analysis of the market demand structure were two cluster analyses which were conducted on the same respondent base. One cluster analysis was conducted on the general lifestyle data and the attitudes toward different kinds of vacation experiences. Four different groups of people were found:

Lifestyle group	% of Total adult pop.
1. *Extravagant Consumers*—Are predominantly female, tend to have higher than medium household incomes, and include all age groups. An appealing vacation would emphasize luxury, service, pampering, and clothes in places like Europe, Hawaii and the Caribbean.	18
2. *Nature People*—Tend to be young, unmarried, and well-educated. They want to go to new and different places to avoid schedules and routines, and to experience the universe generally without the usual concern about the usual comforts.	20
3. *Playsters*—Are primarily young males involved in the active pursuit of sensual pleasure. A vacation for them would need to be relatively inexpensive, but swinging, modern, and active, featuring no social values other than fun.	23
4 *Cautious Homebodies*—Tend to be older, less affluent, less well-educated, and less concentrated in urban areas. They want safety, security, and a perfectly predictable environment on their vacation without any new experiences.	39

A second cluster analysis was carried out, using the same respondents, on the adjectives that people used to describe their ideal vacation. This analysis produced six distinct groupings of ideal vacation types:

Ideal Vacation Type	% of Total adult pop.
1 *Peace and Quiet*—Peaceful, quiet, and relaxing in a country setting; appeals to people in middle age and to those with less than average discretionary income.	20
2 *Aesthetic Appreciation*—A broadening, cultural, educational experience at historic places; appeals mostly to well-educated people and those in professional or managerial occupations.	22
3 *Hot Winter*—A vacation in a hot climate to get away from winters, lie on a beach and be pampered; appeals both to luxury and to fun seekers.	19
4 *Grand Hotel*—The luxury vacation providing entertainment, good food, and excitement; appeals both to luxury and fun seekers who have higher incomes.	19
5 *Inexpensively Active*—The low cost, active fun vacation good for meeting people; appeals most to males and young people.	9
6 *Relatives and Friends*—The family-centered vacation, full of familiar, friendly and inexpensive experiences; appeals most to older people who are not well-educated and have modest incomes.	12

Of course, not all of these people are equally likely to take vacations away from home, especially a vacation that involves travel by air. We therefore began to develop a set of probabilities for people that were based on:

1. Their responses to a short series of attitudinal statements about air travel;
2. Their reported likelihood of actually taking the kind of vacation that they described as being ideal;
3. Whether their ideal vacation involved air travel or not; and
4. Their actual vacation behavior over the past two years, taking into account any anticipated changes in their demographic circumstances.

When all of these factors were taken into account, the expected market potential for a vacation trip by air in any one year was found to be no higher than 35 percent of adult Canadians. Regionally across Canada we found some differences in this travel potential:

Maritimes	31 percent
Quebec English-speaking	35 percent
Quebec French-speaking	31 percent
Ontario	36 percent
Prairies	39 percent
British Columbia	37 percent

In the planning stages of this study, we had hypothesized that there is some relationship between the experiences that people want on a vacation and the type of vacation packages that they find appealing. If we cross-tabulate the lifestyle groups with the vacation types we get a 24-cell matrix. (See Exhibit B.)

The 35 percent potential air vacation travellers are distributed throughout all the cells of this matrix. However, if we compare the actual distribution with the distribution that would be expected to occur by pure chance, then we can find some significant relationships between lifestyle and ideal vacation types. (See Exhibit C.)

EXHIBIT B   TOTAL CANADA 24-CELL MARKET DEMAND MATRIX

	Total	Peace and quiet	Aesthetic appreciation	Hot winter	Grand hotel	Inexpensively active	Relatives and friends
Extravagant consumers	7.5	0.8	1.8	1.9	1.2	0.5	1.3
Nature people	7.7	1.3	3.0	1.2	0.8	0.8	0.6
Playsters	7.3	0.8	1.1	2.1	1.1	0.9	1.3
Cautious homebodies	12.3	1.3	3.3	2.3	2.3	0.5	2.6
Total	34.8	4.2	9.2	7.5	5.4	2.7	5.8

And where: Total Population is 100 percent (about 14,000,000)

Adjusted for: *Potential Leisure Travel by Air*
Likelihood of Taking Ideal Vacation
Propensity for Air Mode
Past Vacation Behaviour

EXHIBIT C   LIFESTYLE VS. VACATION CLUSTERS/ACTUAL VS. CHANCE INDEX

	Peace quiet	Aesthetic appreciation	Hot winter	Grand hotel	Inexpensively active	Relatives and friends
Extravant consumers	− 11.2		+ 12.3		− 13.3	
Nature people	+ 41.9	+ 47.8	− 28.1	− 33.0	+ 35.1	− 53.2
Playsters		− 42.9	+ 32.7		+ 60.1	
Cautious homebodies	− 11.3		− 12.5	+ 20.5	− 47.3	+ 26.9

And where: Total Population is 100 percent (about 14,000,000)

Adjusted for: *Potential Leisure Travel by air*
Likelihood of Taking Ideal Vacation
Propensity for Air Mode
Past Vacation Behaviour

From a marketer's point of view, however, the major interest in this distribution is the market size in each cell. Their relative size and potential provides some sort of rank order for market development opportunities.

Each cell in the matrix can be thought of as a distinct marketing opportunity, representing different target consumer groups. The six vacation types can be thought of as distinct groupings of vacation packages, while the four lifestyle groups indicate different kinds of experiences that can be offered to target groups of people and represent different communications approaches to be used in advertising.

At this stage of the market research program, we had been able to identify specific target groups within the leisure travel market for Air Canada and to provide sufficient analytical information for the development of new vacation packages and communication strategies.

PART II—ANNABELLE BENNETTS

When we first began to research, as was mentioned earlier, it was intended to carry it right through to the testing of holidays designed from it. The identification of the consumer segments had involved such a large scale survey, however, that by the time it was completed, we had almost lost sight of the fact that it was only the beginning.

The communication and interpretation of this first phase of the work took some months to complete. All of Air Canada's product development and communications people were involved, and each, because of his route responsibilities, was interested in a different mix of lifestyle and vacation-type segments.

While the communication of the research was being done, plans were underway for the next two stages, those of vacation testing and forecasting.

It was planned that the study be useable over a period of at least five years. We wanted it to be the basis of both product design and of product testing. But having completed the first phase, we still had to develop a methodology for testing the travel concepts we were yet to design. We felt we knew how many groups of people and vacation types there were and what the make-up of each was. The next problems then were how to design vacations to suit these types, how to find out whether the designs were all accepted by people, and most difficult, how to predict how many people would buy each one.

The job of designing the vacations to suit the various segments was done by Air Canada's product development group, having ascertained which lifestyle groups and which vacation types went together. What went toward the makeup of each holiday type (e.g., accommodations, destination, activities), was used to design new holidays around specific Air Canada destinations. The desire among extravagant consumers for a holiday in the sun with the luxuries of high class hotels and good service became one of Air Canada's "Sun Living" vacations. It included a one or two-week stay in Montego Bay, Ocho Rios, and Kingston, accommodations in first class hotels, entertainment, sightseeing, beach parties, etc. The desire of the cautious homebodies to be led around and made to feel secure, as opposed to being on a wild solo fling, was recognized and turned into a guided coach tour of England. In total, 20 vacation concepts were designed based on profile and need information from the study.

As the vacation packages were being designed, a methodology for testing them was worked out. It was planned to type a large body of people according to their lifestyles and preferred vacation types and to keep this group of people in reserve for testing purposes. Economics of time and money prevented us from trying to recontact the original sample of people to whom the first questionnaire had been administered. Instead, a methodology was worked out whereby an individual could easily and reliably type himself. A number of approaches were tried, and the one which was found to be the most successful was, as is often the case, the simplest.

It was found that each of the four lifestyles and the six vacation types could be described with about nine statements. The nine statements for each of the four lifestyles were listed vertically and boxed off separately so that the four descriptions were side by side on a single page. The same was done for the six vacation types. The respondent had merely to check off one of the four lifestyles and one of the six vacation summaries which he felt to be most like him. The statements used were those that best discriminated each group from all of the others. Thus, while a statement such as "I would like to absorb the culture of a different place," might have received a positive reaction from a cross-section of people, it was believed in much more strongly by the "Aesthetic Appreciation" group than by any other. The boxes of statements were not, of course, labelled by the terms we now use to identify the requirements. It is unlikely that anyone would have recognized himself too readily with a title such as Cautious Homebody or Extravagant Consumer.

A test was done to check people's ability to classify themselves as one of the types described. The check involved having a sample of people answer a scaled questionnaire similar to the one used in the original study. At a later date, after we had categorized them, they were sent a self classification questionnaire. The results compared favourably and it was decided that the simplified test would be used to categorize a large body of people to be used as future respondents for the concept testing.

The descriptions were sent to Market Facts mail panel members, and the yield was about 6,500 people classified by lifestyle and vacation type. Information was also obtained on the sample's past and present vacation habits and demography. Having set up the data bank of people, we were then ready for the first series of concept testing. About half of the already classified panel was sent a questionnaire for this phase of the study. The rest of the panel was used later for further testing.

While the mail panel was being divided into lifestyle/vacation groups, the Market Development department was designing vacation packages based on the data from the first phase of the study. Air Canada is divided into four route areas (Canada, U.S.A., South America, Europe) and five concepts were formed for each of them. Each of the 20 concepts was laid out in the pattern as shown here. Each concept was presented on a single page containing seven columns of information (see below). The destination, what was included in the trip and paid for, the time of year the vacation was offered, special features such as golf, watersports, sightseeing tours, the length of stay, and the cost were each dealt with separately.

Included in the list of 20 concepts was one which had already been on the market for a few years. It was called Skifari, and it had been attracting steadily increasing numbers of travellers from one year to the next. Accurate counts of the number of people who had bought Skifari and some estimates of the number who were likely to buy it in the next couple of years were available from industry sources. It was also felt that Skifari would appeal to only a small and well defined group of people and that this group was, in all probability, not found in more than one or two lifestyle/vacation groups of people. This concept was tested with the sole purposes in mind of checking how well it was targeted and how accurate our market forecasts for the other 19 concepts might be. It was felt that if the forecast model, yet to be developed, could accurately predict roles for Skifari, we could be fairly confident that the forecasts for the other concepts were not too far off the beam.

The model was designed from values assigned to respondents for their answers to various questions on both the self-classification and the concept testing questionnaires. Approximately 35 percent of adult Canadians had been judged to be potential travellers and this group became the base for concept projections. Included in the concept test itself had been a question on the likelihood of the respondent actually taking his chosen vacation. The answers to this question and others were included in the model for market projections. One interesting part of the formula was a factor derived from questioning the respondent as to whether his or her chosen vacation or that of the spouse would be most likely to be taken first. Thus, the impact of the influence of each household member on the decision to take a certain type of vacation was taken into account.

The forecast model which was developed was experimented with somewhat before a final format was established and the results of the ensuing forecasts were quite fascinating. We were able to predict sales for Skifari which were so close to what are actually expected for the coming season that they almost seemed a little suspicious. It remains to be seen whether the other concepts will be bought by Canadians in approximately the same numbers as we have forecast. The terms of the sale of some for these vacations are not as strictly "package" as are those for Skifari. Thus, someone may buy a touring trip of Europe very similar to one of the test concepts but not actually be purchasing the exact holiday called "City Roamer" being sold by Air Canada. The job of counting all the "City Roamer"-type tours will be more difficult than that of counting well defined Skifari-takers. It may be found that checking our forecast model's accuracy will be just as difficult a task as developing it was in the first place.

A number of reports were written on the concept test at various stages of its completion. It was, however, the generation of the actual forecasts for the concepts that elicited the most interest from the users. Since it was really our first attempt at cranking out these numbers from research data, the test will be closely monitored for its success or failure over the next couple of years. Undoubtedly, refinements will have to be made before we come up with something in which we are totally confident, but the first try shows signs of being a pretty reasonable start.

We were able to direct and design the communication of a concept to specific audiences based on the information we collected much more accurately than had been the case previously. We were able to check the rightness or wrongness of offering a specific vacation to a certain group of people and to make changes to the holidays based on their suggestions. Information gathered included which vacations were the most preferred, additions or deletions the respondents would like made to the vacations, perceived monetary value of the vacations, reasons for choosing a particular

VACATION PACKAGE DESIGN

Destination	Includes	When	Special Features	Length of stay	Cost (For each of two people sharing a room)
Jamaica	Return air fare Toronto to Jamaica	All year	Sightseeing in each place	Summer	
Montego Bay	4-5 day stay in each of the places		Entertainment and tours in	9 days	$470
and	Accommodations in first class hotels		each of three places	14 days	$650
Ochos Rios	Transportation from airport to hotel		Tours to places of interest	Winter	
and	Motor coach transfers from hotel to hotel		Rafting	9 days	$549
Kingston	Night entertainment		Visits to waterfalls	14 days	$799
	Sightseeing		Beach parties		
			Picnics		

concept, and the likelihood of actually going on the vacation chosen. The final task was one of having the respondent create his or her own ideal vacation within certain parameters of time, money and mode of travel.

When the concepts were designed, it was the intent to structure them for specific target audiences such as Extravagant Consumers on Hot Winter holidays. Ideally, we should have been testing only among the groups for whom the vacations had been intended. However, it was felt that the buyers of some of the holidays might overlap among a few groups, and with this in mind, the research was structured to identify the groups for whom each vacation was ideally suited as well as to refine the structure of each of the holidays. Thus, while it had been the original intent to send only Cautious Homebody concepts to Cautious Homebodies, for example, all concepts were sent to a mix of everyone, regardless of lifestyle or vacation type.

The methodology proved to be the right one on the whole. Some of the concepts, most notably Skifari, were found to be perfectly targeted at only one or two groups of people. Others, however, unexpectedly found followers in a number of groups. Of all those who chose and were likely to go on Skifari, 84 percent were either Playsters or Nature People, and 74 percent preferred a Grand Hotel or Peace and Quiet Vacation. One of the Southern concepts, on the other side of the coin, appealed to all groups in almost the same proportions as are actually found in the general population. Hopefully, by the next round of product testing, our ability to understand the needs of the various groups will be somewhat more advanced, and we will come closer to being able to target a vacation as precisely as was the case for Skifari. It is clear that only by contacting people over and over will we be able to fully appreciate the differences among the segments originally defined in the study.

Some of the concepts which were tested in the first place are now on the market, a full three years after the fieldwork for the Leisure Market study was begun and at least four years after the work was authorized.

In any study of this magnitude, there are bound to be mistakes made and areas found in which changes could improve the work, and this study was no exception to the rule. We were given the opportunity recently to try our hand again in the European markets and were successful in anticipating most of the major problems which surfaced in the Canadian study. It remains to be seen how well we teach ourselves. Our success in correctly targeting well designed and accepted concepts in the next series of tests will be the test of our expertise.

EXERCISE

The following letter was received by your company, an organization specializing in market research.

Dear Sir/Madam:

> We understand that your organization specializes in consumer research and has previous experience with research in tourism promotion.

Our marketing aim is to increase significantly the number of tourists from your country who visit ours. Tourists from your country represent a surprisingly small number in our overall tourist visits. What puzzles us is that the number and share of tourists from your country to our immediate neighbors and closest competitors have increased considerably during the last few years. The statistics also indicate that the majority of our tourists come from countries neighboring yours.

In our view the first step will be to have a research project whose aim would be to obtain answers to these questions:

1. *Awareness and Knowledge.* What is known about our country as a place to visit, its attractions and climate, its people, the political and economic situation, its hotels and restaurants, how one can get there, and how much it will cost to stay there? What is the image of our country in general? (We would not be surprised if the existing knowledge is found to be limited and to some degree erroneous).

2. *Motivation and Behavior.* In this part of the inquiry an attempt should be made to find out why so few tourists from your country visit ours. Is it mainly lack of information or are there other real or imaginary factors.

3. *Information Gathering and Decision Making.* Where do potential tourists in your country gather information about places to go? What is the role of travel agents? How important are noncommercial sources?

It seems to us that the research project will have to be designed in such a way as to find out any differences of awareness, motivation, and information-gathering and decision-making behavior that might exist between the various groups of the population.

We would like you to make a proposal to us on the research work described above. In particular, we would like to know how you would plan to carry out the investigation, what sample would be used, which interviewing techniques you would recommend, and how you would present the results in a final report. We would like to receive a questionnaire outline, a preliminary cost estimate, and a time plan.
Yours Sincerely,

Director of Tourism

Question: How would you respond to this request?

SUMMARY

The first section of *The Tourism System*—Chapters 1 through 4—has explained the factors that influence the decision of an individual, any individual, to purchase travel. Individuals decide to purchase travel because they have *learned* that it satisfies various needs and wants they consider important (Chapter 1), and because they *perceive* that it will satisfy various needs and wants that they consider important (Chapter 2), yet within various external constraints (Chapter 3). In actually making the purchase, travelers go through a series of steps in their own minds (Chapter 4). The "end product'' of this process will be, hopefully, a decision to "buy travel." Individuals decide in this way that they will "move round the tourism system" to their chosen destination.

It is impossible to describe the travel characteristics of each and every individual. Travel movements of the major *segments* can, however, be described. This is the task of the second part of the text—to describe *who* is traveling, *where* they are traveling to, and *how* this is being done.

Travel is done for either business or pleasure and personal reasons (Chapter 5). People in these market segments choose destinations that are international, regional, or domestic (Chapter 6) and travel by a variety of means to reach their destinations (Chapter 7). The shape of travel demand at the destination is a result of the interaction between who is traveling, when they are traveling, where they are going, and how they are going to go.

5

PURPOSES OF TRAVEL:

The Characteristics of Traveler Segments

". . . the explorer seeks the undiscovered, the traveler that which has been discovered by the mind working in history, the tourist that which has been discovered by entrepreneurship and prepared for him by the arts of publicity."

Paul Fussell, "The Stationary Tourist" Harper's, April 1979.

The two major classifications of travel purpose are business travel and pleasure/personal travel. The patterns and needs of people in both segments are the topic of this chapter.

Business travel is the "bread and butter" market for many tourism-related businesses. Business travel is broken down into regular travel, business travel related to meetings, conventions, and congresses, and incentive travel, which is somewhat of a hybrid as the people on the trip are traveling for pleasure although the purchasers of the trip are businesses. The characteristics of those in these market segments are explored in detail.

The pleasure/personal travel market is examined from the viewpoint of traditional segments, such as resort travelers and family pleasure travelers, and other major growth segments, such as the elderly, singles, and black travelers.

THE TOURISM SYSTEM

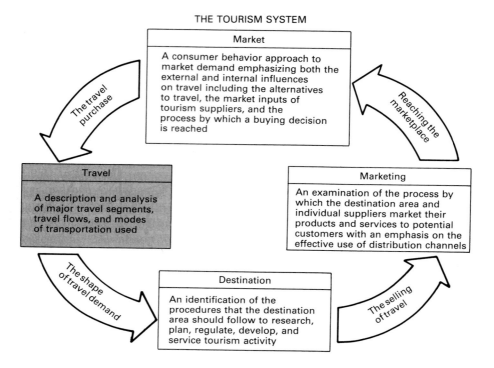

LEARNING OBJECTIVES

Having read this chapter, you should be able to:

1. Describe the various segments of the travel market.
2. Explain the various components of the business travel market.
3. Describe the marketing programs airlines, hotels, and other travel suppliers have been introducing to attract executive and frequent business travelers.
4. Describe the recent growth that has occurred in the women business traveler, incentive travel, and "hybrid" travel trip markets.
5. Explain the significance of the VFR (visiting friends and relatives) portion of the pleasure-personal market.
6. Describe the trip classification system developed by Tourism Canada to segment the U.S. pleasure travel market into eight distinct groups.
7. Explain how changes in the age composition of the population have affected pleasure travel in North America.
8. Describe the four travel philosophy segments developed by Tourism Canada.
9. Explain the approaches and travel "products" that have been used recently to appeal to the elderly, singles and couples, and the handicapped.

Chapters 1 to 4 have examined how an individual—any individual—makes a travel decision. In order to describe the larger picture of travel flows, it is necessary to describe not individuals but segments of the total travel market. Those travelers relevent to tourism are either tourists, if they are in a destination for more than a day but less than a year, or excursionists, if they arrive and depart the same day. In either case their travel may be for reasons of business or pleasure (Fig. 5.1).

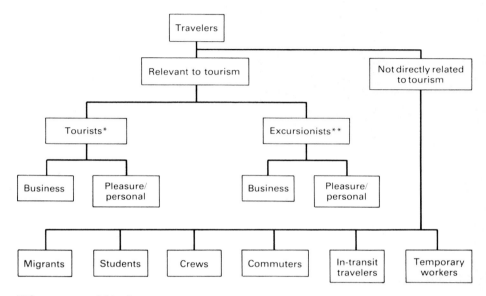

Figure 5.1 Segments of the travel market

THE BUSINESS TRAVEL MARKET

In most developed countries, business travel is the "bread and butter" market for the tourism industry for much of the year. This is certainly the case in the United States, Canada, and the United Kingdom. Just as it is inadequate to use the "jumbo jet" approach to analyzing pleasure/personal travel markets, it is equally wrong to view the business travel market as an amorphous mass that cannot be further segmented. In fact, this first major travel market has many component segments, and the number of segments appears to grow from year to year. The business-related travel market segments can be broadly categorized as follows:

1. Regular business travel
2. Business travel related to meetings, conventions, and congresses
3. Incentive travel

Service quality is particularly important to the business traveler

The third category of incentive travel is really a ''hybrid'' segment since it is a type of pleasure travel that has been financed for business reasons. Thus, the persons on the incentive trips are pleasure travelers and the purchasers are businesses.

Over 40 percent of the business trips taken in the United States are to attend a conference, convention or trade show. Just under 30 percent are for company business or sales meetings, while about one in four is to see present or potential clients or to attend a training meeting or seminar.

Regular Business Travel

Approximately 30 percent of all trips in Canada and the United States are taken for business reasons. (Note: A trip in the United States is defined as one of over 100 miles from home; in Canada it is defined as one of over eighty kilometers or fifty miles from home.) The growth in business travel has outpaced that of pleasure travel in both countries. In addition to these levels of domestic business travel by United States and Canadian residents, there is also significant cross-border travel and travel from the two countries to other foreign nations.

Business travelers are more important to travel suppliers than their total numbers would indicate. They use airlines, rental cars, hotels, and travel agents to a greater extent than pleasure travelers. Business travelers, for example, account for over 40 percent of all airline trips and hotel stays and account for almost two thirds of rental car revenues. In selecting an airline business travelers are primarily concerned with the convenience of the airline schedule. To a lesser extent, low or discount fares and the on-time departure record of the airline influence their choice. Reasonable rates, on the other hand, are the most important factor when choosing a car rental company. This is followed in importance by the convenience of the location and the condition of the cars. Location is the number one factor in selecting a hotel, followed by clean, comfortable rooms and room rates.

Compared to the pleasure traveler, the business traveler is more time sensitive; service quality is more important than price; and she or he is more experienced and demanding.

Approximately 12 percent of business travelers belong to frequent flyer programs, many to several. To a majority of travelers, this is a major factor in their choice of an airline. Belonging to a frequent flyer program means that credit is collected for mileage flown on that particular airline. After a specified number of miles have been flown, the traveler can qualify for upgrades to first class and free trips. In recent years airlines have reduced the attractiveness of their awards, making it necessary to fly greater distances in order to obtain a particular reward. It seems likely that these programs will be phased out for several reasons. First, passengers of many airlines have accumulated significant amounts of travel that, if and when these amounts show up on the company's balance sheet as a liability, will have a significant impact on the airline. Second, it is only a matter of time before the Internal Revenue Service looks at these awards and begins to tax them. As part of the effort to reduce corporate travel costs, some companies are seeking to have the award given to the company rather than to the individual.

Business travel is a nondiscretionary expenditure. The business traveler must travel to specific places to do business. For the pleasure tourist, taking a vacation is a discretionary purchase—one that he or she does not need to make. As a result, business travel is more stable and less price resistant than vacation travel. Business trips are taken consistently throughout the year, while pleasure trips tend to be concentrated in the summer months.

Business travelers are likely to be more upscale than pleasure travelers. They are more likely to be men (although there is a trend towards more and more female business travelers), to be between the ages of 25 to 44, and to have better educations, professional or managerial occupations, and higher incomes than pleasure travelers.

People traveling on business tend to get frustrated with the many demands of travel which are beyond their control. Principal among these are the time required to travel, the long waits, and the delays of arrivals and departures. They also have more personal frustrations—being away from home and families, being alone, and living out of suitcases.

More and more companies are concerned about the high cost of travel and are putting more time and effort into controlling their corporate travel costs.

The business executive travel market is proving to be more "segmentable" today, with many airlines and hotels making specific efforts to cater to these higher echelon persons. Airlines have been offering first-class seat service and first-class passenger lounges in airport terminals to these travelers for many years. More recent innovations include special check-in arrangements, bigger seats, and sleeper seats. Many hotel chains have begun to allocate whole floors or wings of their buildings for those business travelers seeking greater luxury in their accommodations. The rooms or suites are more spacious, contain more personal "giveaways," and they provide their guests with complimentary drinks and express check-in, check-out service. Normally the airline and hotel companies add a surcharge to their regular prices for the extra comforts and convenience provided to executive travelers; they have achieved considerable marketing successes in so doing.

While we have been talking about the business traveler, there are actually several segments to this market, each with distinct characteristics. Business travelers can be divided into segments as follows:

1. frequent business traveler
2. women business traveler
3. luxury business traveler
4. international business traveler
5. occupational designation

Frequent business travelers are those who take a minimum of ten trips a year. While they are just over 10 percent of all business travelers, they account for slightly less than one-half of all the business trips taken. They average 22 trips and 70 nights away from home each year. The average number of nights per trip is less than for other business travelers. They tend to be upscale professionals between the ages of 35 and 44, college graduates with high incomes. They are much less interested in rates and much more interested in frequent travel programs.

In 1970 women accounted for 1 percent of all business travelers; today they account for approximately 40 percent of all business travelers. This figure is estimated to increase to 50 percent by the year 2000. They tend to have less formal education and have lower incomes than men business travelers. They are also more likely to have another household member with them on the trip and to add on vacation days to the business part of the trip. As hotels sought to attract this segment of the market, several mistakes were made. Early attempts to provide "women's floors" and pink wallpaper were viewed by many women as patronizing. They were concerned about such things as security, however. This has resulted in such things as a "club floor"— open to both sexes—and accessed by a special key. More hotels are building suites so that women can hold meetings in their rooms without having a bed in view. Room service hours have been expanded as many women dislike eating alone. Lighting in hallways and parking lots is getting brighter.

The luxury business traveler comprises one in every six business travelers. They are defined as business travelers who fly business or first class on airlines and who stay in more expensive hotels.

Almost one in five business travelers travel abroad on business trips each year. Business travelers account for one third of all air trips abroad by U.S. citizens. They have higher incomes than business travelers in general and are concentrated in the Mid-Atlantic and South Atlantic states. They are more likely to be including vacation time and to be accompanied by others, either family members or business associates.

Business travelers can also be segmented based on their occupations. Twenty-eight percent of business travelers are managers (president to self-employed consultants); twenty-seven percent are salespeople; twenty-two percent are professionals (doctors to lab technicians); twenty-three percent are administrators (operational workers, office workers and skilled workers, who produce the products that the salespeople sell and who carry out the decisions of the managers).

Managers, the largest segment, travel primarily for sales and consulting, take the most but the shortest trips, visit the same destinations most often, use their own cars most often, and use hotels frequently. *Salespeople* travel frequently for sales and consulting, include more vacations with business trips, fly frequently, and use hotels most often. *Professionals* include many women, take fewer but longer trips, travel primarily to attend meetings, often travel to new destinations, and often use their own cars. *Administrators* tend to be younger, travel infrequently and stay longer. They are the most likely of all business travelers to use airlines, rental cars, and travel agents for their trips.

There are four factors which influence the future of business travel. These factors are economic, regulatory, communications, and automation. As a general rule, the rate of growth of the economy determines the level of business travel and the extent to which that level changes. Business travel activity tends to match the growth of the economy when overall economic performance is weak, but business travel moves ahead of the rate of growth of the economy during times of economic stability and expansion. The market in the U.S. follows this pattern more strongly than does the European market. The strong signs for business travel are strong trade, investment, and output growth, while the weak signs are high interest rates and unemployment levels.

Exchange rates are economic factors. The rate of exchange refers to the relative value of one's own currency to other currencies. Changes in exchange rates are not felt as much in business travel as in pleasure travel. There is, however, an impact. When a substantial change in exchange rate occurs, the trade balance moves in favor of the weaker economy. When the dollar loses value against the pound, for example, U.S. goods are less expensive for the British than they were previously. The reverse is true of the cost for the traveler on either business or pleasure. It is more expensive to travel to and stay in Britain to sell the cheaper U.S. goods. This represents a psychological barrier which business travelers, however, seem to overcome.

The second factor affecting the future of business travel is regulatory. Its impact is felt in two areas—deregulation of travel and government policy regarding the treatment of business travel expenses for tax purposes. In 1978, deregulation came to the U.S. air industry. Airlines were free to set rates based on market demand without their being subject to government approval beforehand. As a result many new airlines came into being and many went out of business. Increased competition kept fares between major cities low. Airline deregulation in Europe will evolve in a much slower way. It remains to be seen how the Economic Community's decision to eliminate trade barriers in 1992 will effect the cost of air travel.

Business travel is treated as a business expense. Recent moves in the United

States to limit the tax deductibility of business meals to 80 percent of the cost of the meal has not seemed to limit travel but has changed the way clients are entertained. For example, by bringing a speaker into a luncheon, the entire cost of the meal can be deducted. Various attempts have been made to limit the tax deductibility of meetings abroad. Any attempt to do this would have an impact on the amount and type of travel undertaken.

As the potential for international communications continues to increase, the opportunities for globalization also increases. The economies of countries are increasingly interdependent. With the interdependency comes a greater demand for international business travel.

Automation can work both to increase travel and to limit it. The development of sophisticated computer systems makes it easier to make, confirm, and change travel reservations and control the costs of travel. On the other hand, innovations, such as picture phones and teleconferencing, eliminate the need for much travel.

Meetings, Conventions, Congresses

A major segment of the business travel market is concerned with travel for the purpose of attending meetings, conventions, congresses, trade shows and expositions. The major division that can be made in these types of public and private gatherings is into the institutional and the corporate/government markets. Here the word "institutional" refers to associations and other groups that share a broad affinity; "corporate/government segments" refer to organizations that deal with specific corporate or government business matters and that are private in nature. Several subdivisions can usefully be made within the institutional group. Normally the terms *conventions, conferences, congresses,* and *assemblies* are used for institutional gatherings. Lawson[1] has put forward the following definitions for these types of gatherings:

> A *congress, convention,* or *conference* is a regular formalized meeting of an association or body, or a meeting sponsored by an association or body on a regular or ad hoc basis. Depending on the objectives of a particular survey, this may be qualified by a minimum size (e.g., 12 or 25 attendees), by the use of premises, by a minimum time or/and by having a fixed agenda or program.
>
> *Congresses* are usually general sessions, mostly information giving, and the commonly accepted traditional form of full-membership meeting. Meetings are usually large and formal and the word *congress* carries a connotation of a serious working purpose. Congress halls are designed to accommodate large numbers of delegates, usually in close-seated auditorium or theater-style arrangements.
>
> *Assemblies* are mainly policy-making or legislatory meetings attended by large numbers of representatives or representative groups who may formally speak and vote on the subjects of the agenda. Assembly layouts may require double banks of seats and tables for the principles and their advisors.

[1]Fred R. Lawson, "Congresses, Conventions and Conferences: Facility Supply and Demand," *International Journal of Tourism Management,* September, 1980, p. 188.

Convention is a term widely used in North America and the Pacific region to describe major or total-membership meetings. Over 80% of American associations hold a major annual convention for their total membership, and many companies provide similar opportunities for their staff to meet, formally as well as socially, in attractive surroundings.

Conferences are usually general sessions and face-to-face groups with a high participation, primarily concerned with planning, obtaining facts and information, or solving organizational and operational problems. Conferences are mainly confined to members of the same company, association, or profession. Meetings are less formally organized but encourage collective participation in reaching stated objectives or goals. Numbers of delegates attending a conference may range up to 150 or more but 30-50 is more typical.

Although Lawson uses the term *conferences* to include corporate groups, the most common North American interpretation of the word is that it refers to institutional and not corporate gatherings.

CONVENTION MARKET

1. International associations
2. Continental associations
3. National associations
4. Regional associations

The institutional or association convention market can be segmented geographically into four parts, namely international, continental, national, and regional conventions. International conventions usually involve members and non-members from more than two foreign countries, and they take place in different countries each year. They are nongovernmental events, and it has been forecast that the numbers of delegates attending these will double in the twenty-year span from 1973 to 1993. The groups or associations are generally of the nonprofit variety and attract persons with common fields of interest.

Continental conventions have attendees drawn primarily from a continent, such as North America. The annual Travel and Tourism Research Association (TTRA) Conference is an appropriate example of a continential convention, being held in either the United States or Canada. It has members and draws conference delegates primarily from these two countries.

National conventions are limited by their by-laws or traditions to holding their gatherings within the countries in which they are located. Generally, their attendees are residents of that country. The Tourism Industry Association of Canada (TIAC) is an example of such a body which rotates its annual convention between Canadian cities.

Regional conventions are those meetings organized by associations at the state, provincial, or another regional level. Normally these organizations hold their conventions within their own regions.

The most comprehensive survey of this segment of the business travel market in North America is carried out once every two years by *Meetings & Conventions* magazine. The 1987 survey estimated that just over 1 million conventions and meetings were held that year by the magazine's subscribers.[2] (These subscribers are based primarily in the United States). Approximately 81 percent, or 807,200 of these events were corporate meetings. There were 12,700 major association conventions, and the balance, or 181,700 meetings, were also staged by associations. It should be noted that all 1,001,600 conventions and meetings were "off-premises," meaning that they were held outside of the plants and offices of the corporations and associations. Quite obviously there are a large number of other "on-premises" meetings that generate business travel between corporate and association offices.

Approximately one half of all corporate meetings are evenly split between training seminars and management seminars. An additional 16 percent are regional sales seminars. These seminars averaged 56 attendees and lasted an average of 2.6 days.

Many corporate meetings are management seminars

[2]"The Meetings Market Report," *Meetings and Conventions,* April 1988, pp. 83–85.

Average delegate attendance at major association conventions is about 1,100. A major segment of this market is the medical field. There are at least 35,000 medical or health-care professional meetings and conventions each year. Educational meetings are also important; the typical educational seminar has 250 people attending. The insurance industry spends more than $2 billion a year on meetings. On average, insurance companies (there are at least 5,000 of them) hold meetings 20 times a year with attendance ranging from 20-200.

There are more than 8,000 trade shows a year. It is projected that by 1991 delegate attendance will average 30,000.

The International Association of Convention & Visitors Bureaus determined that in 1985 out-of town convention delegates spent an average of $419 per trip. When amounts paid by associations, trade show exhibitors and exposition service contractors were added in, the average figure rose to $660 per delgate over a four-day period. Slightly less than half of a delegate's expenses go to paying for lodging. Food takes up an additional quarter of the budget. Over 10 percent of the expenditures are in retail stores, while the remainder (18 percent) is spent on such things as hospitality suites, entertainment, and local transportation.

Conventions and meetings contribute significantly to the economies of host cities. An individual convention/trade show attendee generates over $800 to the host community during the average four-night stay. Half of this money is spent on hotel accommodations, almost one quarter on food, slightly less than one fifth on entertainment and local transportation, while the remainder is spent in retail stores.

The 188 members of the International Association of Convention and Visitors Bureaus spent over $330 million in 1987 to attract business to their cities. The major source of funds for U.S. convention and visitors bureaus is a tax on hotel room sales. In 1987 hotel guests paid an average room tax of 5.15 percent.

The factors that motivate the destination choice for conventions are different from that for meetings. Attendance at conventions is voluntary and many delegates must pay their own way. Consequently, a destination must be chosen that is attractive to delegates. Because so many attendees combine a business trip with a vacation, the destination should have recreational facilities and access to sightseeing and entertainment facilities. Spouse attendance can be increased if they can do something interesting while their wives or husbands are in meetings. The most popular states for major conventions are California and Florida (11 percent); Illinois (6 percent); New York, Ohio, Louisiana and Arizona (4 percent); and Nevada, Pennsylvania and Georgia (3 percent). Canada was cited as the prime destination for an international convention or association meeting. Europe, Mexico, the Caribbean, Asia, Hawaii, and Bermuda were also mentioned.

Almost two thirds of all international conferences are held in Europe, while one in five is held in North and South America. The region of the world that is the fastest growing for international conferences is Asia, which presently accounts for just over 10 percent of the annual total. The most important cities for international meetings are, in order, Paris, London, Brussels, Geneva and Vienna. New York, the highest ranking U.S. city, is eighth in the listings; Washington, Chicago, and San

Francisco follow at positions 16, 34 and 35, respectively. The highest ranking Asian city is Singapore, number 10, while Montreal is the number one ranked Canadian city at 20.

Convention locations usually change from year to year as attendees do not want to return to the same spot each year. Many associations have a policy of rotating the meeting destination on a geographic basis—east one year, west the next.

The number one factor in choosing a particular meeting site for association convention planners is the availability of suitable meeting rooms. Conventions may require a large auditorium for general meetings and several smaller rooms for break out sessions.

Attendance at corporate meetings is required. As a result the choice of destination has no effect on the number of people attending. Many corporate meetings are held at the same place year after year if the host hotel can show it can deliver quality service. The site chosen is usually close to the corporate facility. The dollar and time cost of traveling to and from the meeting is thereby minimized. Since the accent at a corporate meeting is on work, privacy and a lack of distractions is appreciated more than recreational facilities and sightseeing opportunities.

Prior to leaving the subject of conventions and meetings, we should note one barrier to this travel in recent times in North America that was imposed by the U.S. government in 1976. Section 620 of the Tax Reform Act of 1976 permitted U.S. corporations to hold only two tax-deductible meetings a year outside of the United States and required detailed record-keeping on the part of convention and meeting organizers and attendees. Individuals attending conventions were allowed to deduct their expenses from only two foreign conventions per year. This was the law in the United States for a four-year period between January 1, 1977, and December 31, 1980. It proved extremely unpopular with meeting/convention organizers, delegates, and with host cities outside of the United States, particularly those in Canada and Mexico. A new law is now in effect that allows U.S. residents and corporations to deduct all qualifying expenses incurred from every convention and meeting taking place in the "North American zone," which includes the United States, Canada, and Mexico.

Incentive Travel

> Travel is the answer to a dream—a dream of luxury, prestige, in exotic places. It is the ultimate escape from daily routine[,]. . .and travel which is earned through effort salves not only the ego, but the conscience as well.

The above statement is indicative of the lure of travel trips as work incentives for employees and the reason why the incentive travel market segment has been booming in popularity.

Incentive travel uses travel as a motivational award for the accomplishment of a business objective. In the United States it generates over $2 billion dollars a year, while in the United Kingdom the annual value of incentive travel is over 150 million pounds. Incentive travel is used by half of the corporations in the U.S., although twelve major industries account for two thirds of the market. The top users of incentive travel are the insurance, electronics, automotive parts, cars and trucks and farm equipment industries. Over three quarters of these companies use incentive travel to increase sales. Other important aims are to boost morale and goodwill and to introduce new products. Some companies report an increase in sales of over 20 percent as a result of a promotion. This increase in sales more than offsets the cost of the program.

If the award is given to a salesperson who has met a prescribed goal and the predominant purpose of the trip is pleasure, the company can deduct the cost of the award from its taxable income. The award recipient must, however, include the value of the trip in his or her income for income tax purposes.

Increasingly incentive travel programs are being introduced to other than salespeople as a means of cutting costs or reducing turnover. It is expected that programs to accomplish these types of things will increase significantly in the years ahead.

On average, approximately 30 percent of those participating in incentive travel contests qualify for the awards. The two main types of trips involved in incentive travel are dealer trips and sales-force trips. Each accounts for about half of the total cost of incentive trips, although more money is spent per capita on dealer trips, with some estimates that there are twice as many sales-force trips as dealer trips. Dealer trips are rewards for having met a required performance objective. The destination is the major factor that will motivate employees to strive for the sales target. Dealer trips tend to be longer and are more likely to use foreign destinations. They focus on pleasure and relaxation, and usually there is little or no business content.

Sales-force trips are briefer, favor domestic destinations, and have some business content, such as a conference or the introduction of new products.

The most popular length of stay for incentive trips is one week. Planners, however, are developing more weekend trips, not to replace the one-week incentive trip but to expand to other users. Most trips invite the spouse at company expense. As a result the average group size is just under 150 people, although the median is about half that. The greatest increase in recent years has been in the small-group market, with an average of 10 people per trip.

The mushrooming popularity of incentive travel has given rise to the creation of a number of companies specializing in the organization of these trips. Many of these companies belong to an association known as SITE (Society of Incentive Travel Executives). In the United Kingdom the Incentive Travel Association of the United Kingdom (ITA:UK) has recently been formed by the leading incentive travel specialists.

The costs of incentive travel trips depend on the rates the incentive travel companies can negotiate with suppliers such as hotels, airlines, and so on. In this way they act as a specialized type of tour wholesaler. To their prices they add a markup for their own services and costs in packaging the incentive travel trip, typically in the 15 percent to 20 percent range.

Incentive travel programs in the U.S. strongly favor domestic destinations. There are two major reasons for this. First, with most trips lasting one week, travel to and from domestic destinations is less time consuming. Second, if there is any business component to the trip, it is restricted to the North American area to maintain its tax deductibility. The most popular domestic destinations are Florida, Hawaii, California, Nevada and Arizona. Mexico and the Bahamas—areas for which U.S. citizens do not need passports—top the list of favored international incentive destinations, followed by the United Kingdom, the Caribbean, Bermuda, and Canada. In the United Kingdom the most popular destinations are France, Spain, and the United States.

Incentive travel is also growing in other European countries. In Holland, for example, the most popular destinations are those associated with the manufacturing companies' main head offices. Car dealers with Japanese franchises will journey to Japan, with a stopover in Singapore or Bangkok. In France, price and budget are the major concerns in choosing a destination. The top destination is the United States, with the Far East becoming increasingly popular. For shorter trips the North African coast is popular, particularly Morocco. Sixty percent of all West German incentive trips are to European destinations. Paris, London, Athens, and Budapest are favored for short haul weekend trips. Interestingly, 90 percent of incentive trip participants travel without partners.

The people who "buy" destinations for incentive trips are influenced by:

a. *Budget.* However, incentive trip planners look for high quality rather than low prices.

b. *Time of year.* Employee participation on incentive trips tends to take place in that particular industry's slow season. The most popular months for incentive travel are February and April. Planners would look at destinations that are attractive during these months.

c. *Participant background.* The level of sophistication and previous travel experiences of the likely participants.

d. *Incentive history* of the users and the competition. There must be a distinction between the last use of the destination and its use again if the competition is to be successful.

e. *Accessibility.*

f. *Facilities,* including hotel rooms, meeting rooms, restaurants, local transport.

g. *Activities,* recreation and sports facilities

Europe has lagged behind the United States in the development of specialist incentive travel services. However, in the last few years, a number of small, specialist, agency-type companies have come into existence to organize incentive trips. A major reason for the lack of development in Europe is confusion regarding the objectives of incentive travel and a certain amount of suspicion of its ability to generate sales increases greater than the cost of the program.

Prior to beginning the discussion of the pleasure and personal travel market, the "hybrid" travel trip must be clearly identified. The hybrid trip is one in which the traveler mixes business and pleasure, be it on a regular business travel junket or in conjunction with a convention or a corporate meeting. Travel promoters at every travel destination should realize that having a business traveler really provides a three-part opportunity. First, the business traveler visits to carry out his or her work-related activities. Second, he or she, and perhaps his or her spouse, may be convinced to spend pleasure travel time before or after the meeting, convention, or other business activity. Third, he or she may be attracted to return to the destination in the future on a pleasure or a business travel trip.

With the rise of two-income households in the North American work force, there is a higher incidence of situations in which both spouses travel. In situations in which their business travel plans match, or come close to coinciding, as to destinations and dates, this provides another incentive for hybrid travel trips by both partners.

In summation, the business travel market is a major component of tourism. It has several segments within it, and as with pleasure travel, more new, viable segments appear to emerge as time progresses. Businesswomen, executives, attenders of corporate meetings and conventions, incentive travelers, and hybrid travelers are some of the most readily identifiable of these segments.

THE PLEASURE AND PERSONAL TRAVEL MARKET

We can begin by trying to pinpoint the approximate total scale of the pleasure/personal market.

U.S.A.   In 1988 Americans took 1,030,000,000 person trips for personal vacation reasons, spending an average of 4.3 nights away from home. (A trip is defined as travel of at least 100 miles away from home).

Canada.   In 1986 Canadians took 64,202,000 person trips for personal pleasure reasons in Canada, spending an average of 3.5 days away from home. (A trip is defined as travel of at least 50 miles away from home).

A study of The Longwoods Research Group Ltd. for Tourism Canada broke the U.S. pleasure travel market into eight types, based on trip purpose.[3] The study noted, however, that most travelers are in the market for more than one type of vacation trip and suggested segmenting the market on types of trips rather than types of markets.

Segments of the Market

Visiting friends and relatives accounts for 44% of total trip nights (one trip night is one trip that lasts one night; two trips that last four nights each would be eight trip nights). These trips tend to be relatively unplanned, involve little use of travel agents or the media, and are of short duration.

Close-to-home leisure trips account for 13% of all trip nights and are also relatively unplanned and of short duration. Additionally, little use is made of the media for information on where to go. The average length of stay is between two and three days. Eighty-five percent of the travelers use their own cars. The most widely used form of accommodation is a motel. Others stay in hotels or with friends and relatives. Over 10% camp or take a trailer.

[3]Travel & Leisure's *World Travel Overview 1986/1987,* American Express Publishing Company, 1986, pp. 116–119.

Those taking outdoor trips are interested in beautiful scenery

Touring vacations make up 14% of all trip nights. These trips have no single focus. They last an average of eight days, are planned one to two months in advance, and while friends are the most-used source of information, travel agents and the media are also important. One out of five trips involves a package deal. This type of tourist is interested in beautiful scenery with lots to see and do. They want to visit a well-known, popular area that offers well-known landmarks and is definitely not dull. In over one quarter of the trips, at least part of it is booked through a travel agent. These tourists tend to travel by car, although in one quarter of the cases, a plane is used. One out of eight travel by bus. Friends and relatives provide the accommodation 20% of the time; the remainder of the stays are split between motels and hotels.

Those taking outdoor trips represent 10% of all trip nights. These people tend to plan their trips less than one month in advance and rely most on the advice of friends for places to go. The average length of each trip is between three and four days. They are interested in beautiful scenery with lots to see and do. They want real adventure, but not too wild, want to travel moderate distances, and want, in most cases, some fishing and hunting. This tourist travels exclusively by car, truck, or van, and in two thirds of the cases, stays in a campground or trailer park.

Eight percent of the trip nights are spent on resort vacations. Travel by plane accounts for almost 30% of the travel. Tourists stay either in a hotel (31%), motel (26%), lodge (14%) or condominium (13%). The average length of stay is five days, and in one out of five cases, the trip is part of a package deal. This segment accounts for the greatest use of a rental car (15%). Tourists want to visit a place that is popular in a well-known area and that has beautiful scenery with lots to see and do. They want a place that is exciting yet can offer the opportunity for walking and strolling. Over one third of these trips are planned more than three months in advance, while another third are planned between one and two months ahead of time. Travel agents are used both for information and for booking the trip in one fourth of the trips. The resort traveler is interested in relaxing, getting away, and being entertained. Less than 20% are interested in golf or tennis.

City trips make up 7% of all trip nights. Half of these trips are booked less than one month in advance. They tend to be a short, impulsive getaways. The family car is the predominant (70%) mode of transportation while, at the destination, three quarters of the travelers stay in a hotel or motel. Staying with friends and relatives makes up the remainder. For this tourist it is important that the city be famous, with first class hotels and elegant restaurants. It should be popular, definitely not dull, and should have well-known monuments. People are less interested in nightclubs and bars.

Visits to theme parks or special events make up only 3% of all trip nights. Over 40% are planned less than one month ahead, while just over one quarter are planned between one to two or over three months in advance. This traveler is interested in a well-known, even world-class attraction—something that offers activities for all ages, lots to see and do, that is exciting, and that the children would enjoy. The average trip lasts just under four days. Three quarters of the trips involve the use of a car; in one out of ten situations, it is a rental car. Just less than 20% of the trips involve staying with friends or relatives; the remainder of the stays are split between hotels and motels.

Last, there is the cruise. Accounting for one percent of total trip nights, people who take cruises want to see beautiful scenery and want to experience something different with lots to see and do. They want real adventure, do not want the trip to be dull, and are interested in all the comforts. Trips average over six days, and in almost two thirds of the cases, they are packages. Most cruises are planned more than three months in advance. This segment of the market is the only one where the advice of a travel agent (67%) is sought more than a friend's (51%).

Travel Philosophy Segments. A study of Canada's pleasure market revealed four travel philosophy segments.[4] The *planned adventurer* comprises 30 percent of the Canadian population. These people like to make all their travel arrangements before setting out on a trip. They tend to travel to a different place each trip and prefer places they have heard of. This group includes slightly more females than the average, is better educated, more affluent, and is more likely to live in the smaller metropolitan area of Canada. They are also more inclined to visit the U.S., particularly the southern states, in addition to other foreign destinations.

[4]Gordon Taylor, "Multi-Dimensional Segmentation of the Canadian Pleasure Travel Market," *Tourism Management*, vol. 7, no. 3, 1986, pp. 146-153.

The *casual traveler* makes up 27 percent of the population. These people arrange their travel as they go. They go to different places on each trip and tend to take shorter trips. They are younger, better educated, and more affluent than average. They also prefer traveling in Canada, and when they do venture out of the country, prefer the northern U.S. states.

Twenty-four percent of the population are classified as *low risk travelers*. They tend to return to places they have visited before. Almost one third have a second home, mobile home, or camp they use on a regular basis. They are older, less likely to live in a metropolitan area, and less likely than the previous groups to travel outside Canada.

The *stay-at-home traveler* comprises 18 percent of the population and is made up of those who do not view travel as an important part of their life style. They would prefer to spend their money on other things. They do not need to travel to enjoy a vacation and find the making of travel arrangements a nuisance. They are older, less educated, less affluent, and tend to live in smaller towns and rural areas. Over a third have not taken a vacation in the past three years.

Benefits and Interests and Activities Segments.   Each group identified above is capable of further segmentation by benefits sought and activities or interests. One example of the process is shown in Figure 5.2. The "planned adventurer-getaway-outdoors" segment differs from the "planned adventurer-experiences-resort" segment.

Table 5.1 shows the distribution of planned adventurers, casual travelers, low-risk travelers, and stay-at-homes across the four benefits sought. Those seeking *family getaways* comprise 32 percent of the total. This tends to involve visiting friends and relatives as well as being together as a family. They tend to be young families, college educated with above average household income due, in great part, to slightly more two-income earners than the average. Over represented in Ontario and the three Prairie Provinces, they travel mostly in Canada and are average in their travel out of the country. They are represented more by the stay-at-home philosophy than any other.

The *going home* benefit is sought by 28 percent of the population. This group is very cost and security conscious. They are drawn to places their family came from, historical places and prestige destinations. This segment has proportionately more older females and has the lowest education level, lowest incomes, and the fewest multiple earner households of any benefit group. They also travel the least of any of the four benefit groups. Interestingly, while they are less likely to travel to the United States, they are above average on travel to overseas destinations. They are more likely to be found with a low-risk traveler or stay-at-home travel philosophy.

The *experience* group, 24 percent of the total, is looking for a change from job and family, excitement and a desire to see as much as possible. Family-oriented benefits rate low for this group. They tend to be young and are often single or young couples without children. They are well educated, have good incomes, travel to the U.S., and venture overseas more than any other group. They are most likely to be planned travelers.

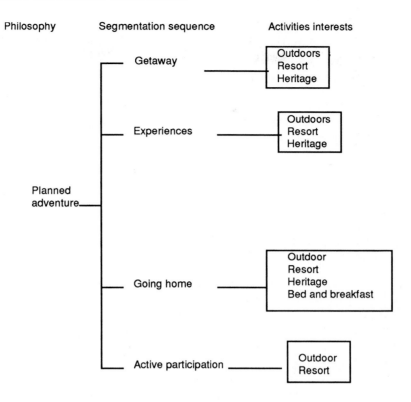

Figure 5.2 Segmentation Sequence. Source: Gordon Taylor, "Multi-Dimensional Segmentation of the Canadian Pleasure Travel Market," *Tourism Management*, vol. 7, no. 3, 1986, p. 148.

TABLE 5.1 TRAVEL PHILOSOPHIES AND BENEFITS

| | Benefits | | | |
Travel philosophy	Family getaway	Going home	Experiences	Active participation
Planned				
Adventurer	23%	27%	36%	13%
Casual Traveler	33%	21%	28%	18%
Low-Risk Traveler	37%	36%	13%	14%
Stay-at-Home	51%	34%	0	15%

Source: Gordon Taylor, "Multi-Dimensional Segmentation of the Canadian Pleasure Travel Market," *Tourism Management*, vol. 7, no. 3, 1986, p. 149.

Those seeking *active participation* make up 15 percent of the population. They are strongly oriented towards physical activity, sports and excitement. They are mostly male, single, and between the ages of 17 and 34. They are better educated than most and earn a good income. They also travel in Canada more than any other group, taking more short trips and traveling less overseas than others. They are fairly evenly distributed over the four travel philosophies.

The third segmentation is by activities and interests deemed important in achieving the benefits sought. *Outdoors* is the largest of the group, accounting for 30 percent of Canadian travelers. This group enjoys wilderness, mountains, parks, lakes, and rural areas ripe with outdoor recreation opportunities.

Twenty-two percent fell into the *resort* segment. They prefer beaches for swimming, a warm climate with predictable weather, quality restaurants, nightlife, and first class hotels. This segment tends to travel to the southern U.S. states.

The *bed and breakfast* group is made up of 10 percent of the population. They are attracted to small towns and villages and rural areas. They are interested in budget accommodation and inexpensive meals.

The *city culture* segment (8 percent) is interested in museums and art galleries, live theater, cultural activities, historic sites, and local crafts. They are attracted to big cities and the first class hotels and quality restaurants provided there.

The *heritage* group, also with 8 percent, is similar to the city culture segment except that the big-city atmosphere is not as important, and they are less likely to travel outside Canada. For the purposes of marketing these two groups are combined as one—heritage.

The last group—*city spree* (3 percent)—was later dropped as a segment. The small number of people who make up this group are young, single, well educated, reasonably affluent. They live outside major metropolitan areas and look to the city for short trips to enjoy shopping and nightlife.

Family Pleasure Travel

The family pleasure-travel market can be segmented into three groups, namely mature families, mid-range families, and junior families. These are defined according to the husband and wife's ages and the educational stages of their children as follows:

The junior family. Families with parents aged 20-34, having preschool and/or grade-school children only.

Mid-range families. Families with parents aged 35-44, with grade-school and/or high-school children only.

Mature families. Families with parents aged 45 or over, with children who are of high school age and older.

What motivates family pleasure-travel trips? For all three family groups the first priority is to use travel as an educational experience for their children. The second priority is to do something different, and this factor is especially highly rated by mid-range families. The third priority is to use travel to bring the family closer together. Another important motivator is to visit friends and relatives, and this is particularly prevalent with the junior families. The major deterrents to family pleasure-travel are the costs of travel—particularly the cost of transportation, accommodation, and food—the ability of the parents to have privacy from their children, and the problems of organizing and coordinating family pleasure travel plans. Marketers in destinations appealing to families would therefore be well-advised to promote the experiences that families are seeking and to take steps to lessen the impact or perceptions of the deterrents.

While 85 percent of all Americans live in families, the traditional "nuclear family" is no more. Only 7 percent of the families in the United States consist of a working father, a mother at home, and children under the age of 18 living at home. Sixty percent of all married women work, two thirds of them full time.

Because of decreasing birth rates and the baby boomers' putting off marriage, the size of U.S. households has dropped from an average of 3.37 persons in 1950 to a projected 2.32 persons in the year 2000. Meanwhile, the total number of households has more than doubled since 1950. Although married-couple households still comprise the largest percentage of households in the United States, female-headed households with no adult male and male-headed households with no adult female are of growing importance. It is predicted by the Census Bureau that by the year 2000 the total number of households will have increased 13 percent; married-couple households, 10 percent; male-headed households, 43 percent; and female-headed households, 22 percent.

The Elderly

An examination of population trends in North America and Europe clearly indicated that the population is aging. There are many more people today of fifty years of age and over, including greater numbers of retirement-age persons in the sixty-five-plus category. These population shifts have made the "elderly" persons pleasure-travel market and its component segments an increasingly lucrative target for tourism destination areas. The strong growth that has occurred in the bus tour and recreational-vehicle market is indicative of the increasing relative importance of the "fifty-plus" market.

Figures 5.3 and 5.4 visually demonstrate the aging population trend in various countries of the world. They also depict the phenomenon of the "baby boom" market, a significant segment of today's North American population that has members who were born approximately within twenty years of the conclusion of World War II. This group, which in 1981 consisted primarily of people in the fifteen to thirty-four year age categories, represents the major concentration of the United States and Canadian populations. As the baby boomers age further, the "bulge" in the U.S. and Canadian population age distributions will also move towards the older age categories. For example, by 1991 the major concentrations will be in the twenty-five to forty-four age groups.

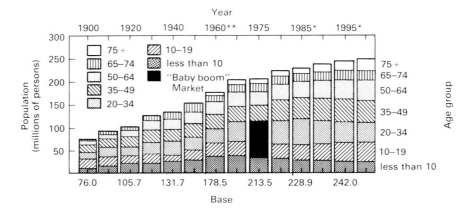

Base: Total U.S. population
*Series III Projections
**65–74 and 75 + age breaks were not
available prior to 1960 date Base

SOURCE: U.S. Bureau of the Census. Adapted from Yvonne Crissey, "Over Forty-Nine: The
Active Affluent," in *Research and the Changing World of Travel in the 1980's* (Travel
Research Association, Eleventh Annual Conference Proceedings, 1980), p. 130.

Figure 5.3   The 65 + Age Group as Percent of Population

One of the important elements of the over 50s market are the "empty nesters" who were profiled earlier in Chapter 3. Another group which Crissey[5] isolates are the "active affluents," most of whom are at the same time empty nesters. She stated that the active affluents search for unique experiences, cultural enrichment, learning and high degrees of participation in their pleasure travel trips. Other researchers have also found that the older people are the more emphasis they place on learning experiences, socialization, and activities which lead to self-fulfillment.

Older travelers differ from others in that they tend to take longer vacations. The reasons are that they have more leisure time and also that they tend more to vacation in the off-peak seasons when the costs are lower. They also, as a group, tend to be more concerned about health, including the fear of being taken ill when away from home.

One of the most important patterns of travel for the older traveler, both in Europe and North America, is the winter vacation, especially the long-stay winter vacation. Many people who take these holidays do so to escape the weather at home. In Europe this means vacationing in Spain and other Mediterranean countries, while Florida remains a favorite spot in the United States. The low costs involved in vacationing in the off-season can mean that it is as cheap to live in Spain, for example, as to pay the fuel bills at home.

[5]Yvonne Crissey, "Over Forty-Nine: The Active Affluent," in *Research and the Changing World of Travel in the 1980's* (The Travel Research Association Eleventh Annual Conference Proceedings, 1980), pp. 127–33.

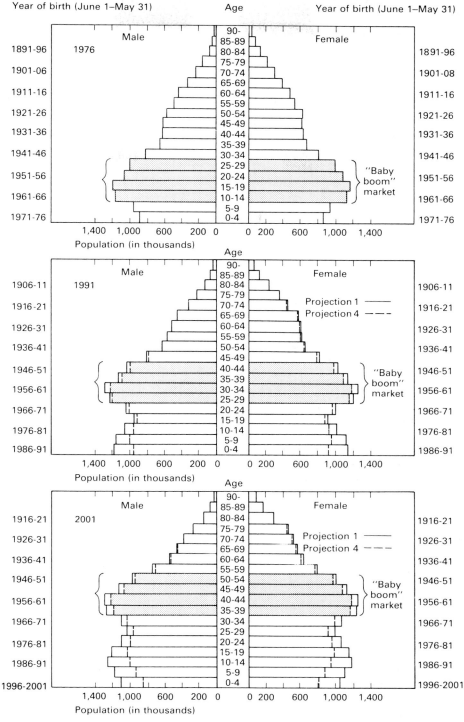

Year of birth (June 1–May 31)   Age   Year of birth (June 1–May 31)

Population (in thousands)

SOURCE: Statistics Canada, *Population Projections for Canada and the Provinces 1976–2001* (Ottawa, Ontario, Statistics Canada, 1979), p. 42.

Figure 5.4 Age Pyramids of the Population of Canada, 1961 and 1986

153

There are, in fact, several segments to the older traveler market. In the 55 to 64 age group, 30 percent are retired. For travelers 65 to 74 and 75 plus, the number of retirees increases to three quarters. Different tourism products and approaches would be appropriate for each group. A change in travel behavior seems to occur when a significant watershed event happens—retirement or the loss of a spouse, for example. Hawes[6] identified three segments of older women—the traveler, laid back, and the dreamer—each with her own set of travel behaviors. Foster,[7] on the other hand, broke the senior market into eight segments:

Marketing lifestyle	Travel lifestyle
Senior Urban Professionals	Independent Traveler
Retired Affluent Professionals	Group Tour Taker
Suburban Seniors	The I-95 Traveler (Coach Tours)
Culture Vultures	Backpacker
Independent Singles	Adventurous Traveler
Newly Widowed	Companion Seeker
Homebodies	Educational Traveler
Sunbelters	Snowbirds

A common mistake of marketers is to aim their marketing at the chronological age of their target markets rather than the cognitive age—the age people feel. There is a tendency on the part of older people to see themselves anywhere from eight to fifteen years younger than they really are. The stereotype of the old, physically inactive retiree no longer holds.

Singles and Couples

Another growing segment of the travel market that one resort chain has targeted most successfully has members wanting their vacations to fulfill their "psychological, intellectual, and physical needs" by giving them the opportunity "to rest, relax, escape the routine of pressures of daily living, to indulge their fantasies, enjoy the naturalness of life, and to express total freedom.[8] The chain is Club Mediterranee, and the market segment consists of singles and couples. The hedonistic appeal of the Club Med-resort formula, in fact, ties in directly with many of demographic/socioeconomic, and life-style/social changes highlighted earlier. Approximately 60 percent of Club Med vacationers are couples or pairs, and 40 percent are singles vacationing

[6]Douglass K. Hawes, "Travel-Related Profiles of Older Women," *Journal of Travel Research,* vol. 27, no. 2, pp. 22-32.

[7]Jerry Foster, "1988 Outlook for the Senior Travel Market," proceedings of the Thirteenth Annual Travel Outlook forum, 1987.

[8]Roz Gibbons, "Singles and couples," in *Research and the Changing World of Travel in the 1980's* (The Travel Research Association, Eleventh Annual Conference Proceedings, 1980), pp. 113-16.

on their own. This is certainly not the family travel market. Growth in the numbers of persons visiting Club Med resorts has been spectacular. Also of note is that North Americans account for a growing proportion of Club Med's visitors each year. Club Med is not the only organization to have tapped into the singles and couples pleasure-travel segment. Other resorts and destinations, particularly in the Carribbean region, have initiated the successful Club Med formula or at least learned about this market segment. Club Med's success can be attributed to the fact that there are many more singles and childless married and unmarried couples in the North American market today who have the means and the desire to travel for these hedonistic experiences.

Handicapped Travelers

Handicapped travelers make up another segment of the travel market that is growing and is deservedly receiving greater consideration in the physical design of tourism facilities. Many destination areas have published booklets and guides for handicapped travelers, including the British Tourist Authority that has produced a pamphlet entitled ''Britain for the Disabled.'' The positions of tour operators and wholesalers specializing in arrangements for handicapped people have been created, and organizations such as the March of Dimes are also actively assisting these persons in their travel. The International Year of the Disabled did a great deal to build more public awareness of the needs of those in this particular market segment, and many government agencies have introduced more stringent standards for making buildings more accessible to the handicapped.

Handicapped travelers make up a segment of the travel market that is growing

REFERENCES

BEATTIE, CINDY and THOMAS J. BEGGS, "Needs of the Female Business Traveler," unpublished study, 1984.

BRUDEMEIER, JUDY, "Incentive Travel in the USA," *Travel & Tourism Analyst,* September 1986, pp. 25–36.

CLEVERDON, ROBERT, *International Business Travel: A New Megamarket,* Special Report No. 189, (London, The Economist Intelligence Unit, 1985).

CUFF, MAX, "Incentive Travel in Europe: Survey of a Rapidly Growing Market," *Travel & Tourism Analyst,* May 1986, pp. 37–45.

DE ROOIJ, NIKO, "Mature Market in Europe: Forecasts For Holiday Taking by the Over 55s to 2000," *Travel & Tourism Analyst,* May 1986, pp. 17–27.

DYBKA, JERRY M. "A Look at the American Traveler: The U.S. Pleasure Travel Market Study," *Journal of Travel Research,* vol. 25, no. 3, 1986, pp. 2–4.

FORBES, ROBERT, "Research on the Mature Traveler," *Annals of Tourism Research,* vol. 14, no. 4, 1987, pp. 586–588.

GATRELL, RICHARD D., "Destination Marketing for Convention and Visitors Bureaus" (Dubuque, Iowa, Kendall/Hunt Publishing Company, 1988).

HASTINGS, COLIN, "Conference Industry in Asia," *Travel & Tourism Analyst,* September 1986, pp. 37–48.

HAWES, DOUGLASS K., "Travel-Related Lifestyle Profiles of Older Women," *Journal of Travel Research,* vol. 27, no. 2, 1988, pp. 22–32.

"The Meetings Market Report 1987," *Meetings and Conventions,* April 1988, pp. 83–85.

SHOEMAKER, STOWE, "Segmentation of the Senior Pleasure Travel Market," *Journal of Travel Research,* vol. 27, no. 3, 1989, pp. 14–21.

STEVENS, BLAIR, "The U.S. Pleasure Market Study," proceedings of the seventeenth annual conference of The Travel and Tourism Research Association, 1986, pp. 177–180.

STATISTICS CANADA, *Touriscope: 1988 Tourism in Canada.*

TAYLOR, GORDON, "Foreign Pleasure Travel by Americans," *Journal of Travel Research,* vol. 25, no. 3, 1986, pp 5–7.

THE TRAVEL WEEKLY/U.S. TRAVEL DATA CENTER, *1985/86 Survey of Business Travelers.*

U.S. TRAVEL DATA CENTER, *1988 Outlook for Travel and Tourism.*

U.S. TRAVEL DATA CENTER, *1989 Travel Outlook Forum.*

EXERCISE

Tourism Canada, the national organization responsible for tourism development and marketing in Canada, recently conducted a major study of their most important market—the United States. This exercise is based on their findings. Given the information provided, develop a regional effort to attract the "touring trip" tourist from the United States to Canada.

FINDINGS:

1. Canada's share of American travel is:

Touring trip	6.8%
Outdoors trip	5.4%
City trip	2.8%
Trip to theme park, exhibition, special event	1.5%
Visit to friends and relatives	1.4%
Close-to-home leisure trip	1.2%
Resort trip	0.8%

2. A touring trip is defined as one by bus, car or train through areas of scenic beauty or of cultural or general interest. In regional terms, the most preferred areas for touring are the Pacific coast (38%), followed by Quebec (21%), Ontario (20%), the Rockies (15%), and the Maritimes (9%).

3. Touring travelers have no focus on a single product; their tour involves a mix of experiences and products. The average duration of their trip is eight days; one in five trips is a package deal; 60 percent travel by car; 71 percent of the visitors are over 40 years old; 64 percent stay in hotels; half of the market seeks out first class accommodations and food; they are more concentrated in the Mid- and South Atlantic census divisions.

4. The top ten benefits sought by Americans from a touring trip are:

   1. Being together as a family
   2. Having lots of things to see and do
   3. Spending time with someone special
   4. Getting away from pressures
   5. Resting and relaxing
   6. Having fun, being entertained
   7. Being safe and secure
   8. Fulfilling a dream
   9. Visiting friends and relatives
   10. Experiencing different cultures and ways of life

5. The top ten benefits sought by Americans *when planning a touring trip in Canada* are:

   1. Having lots of things to see and do
   2. Spending time with someone special
   3. Fulfilling a dream
   4. Being together as a family
   5. Getting away from pressures
   6. Experiencing different cultures and ways of life
   7. Being safe and secure

      8. Resting and relaxing

      9. Visiting friends and relatives

    10. Visiting places important in history

6. For Americans seeking a touring trip the most important activities on the trip are:

      1. Walking and strolling

      2. Visiting small towns and villages

      3. Dining in a variety of restaurants

      4. Sampling local cuisine

      5. Visiting national parks

      6. Seeing wildlife

      7. Being close to mountains

      8. Being by the ocean

      9. Being by a lake

    10. Taking guided tours

7. In terms of image, Canada's individual products are not seen as being superior to those in the United States; the U.S. has a 16 percent edge in "lots of things to see and do." Americans do not think that prices in Canada are out of line. Canada's primary strength is that Americans see Canada as a foreign destination.

6

GEOGRAPHY OF TRAVEL:

The Characteristics of Traveler Flows

"It seems Nepal is the really fashionable place to go at present."
"Not at all, that's passe. Ladakh is the place to go."
"I don't even know where Ladakh is!"
"Of course, that's why it's now the place *to go."*

Elery Hamilton-Smith, "Four Kinds of Tourism" Annals of Tourism Research, *vol. 14, no. 3, 1987, p. 334.*

Tourist flows, both domestic and international, are not random. The movement of travelers, when measured and explained, can be used as a basis for forecasting future tourist movements. The characteristics of traveler flows is the subject of this chapter.

International tourist movements are described and recent trends noted. One of the most significant trends for North America has been an increase in the number of overseas travelers to Canada and the United States. The origins of these visitors and reasons behind this trend are explored.

The unsteady growth pattern of outbound overseas travel from North America is examined and reasons for this discussed.

Regional flows of tourists (between Canada, the United States, and Mexico) far outweigh flows of overseas visitors to North America. The size and characteristics of travel flow between the countries in North America are covered in detail.

Domestic travel within North American countries is the next topic of this chapter. The major characteristics of domestic travel are examined; we draw heavily from the findings of the U.S. National Travel Survey and the Canadian Travel Survey.

A profile is given of the major European tourism countries, as well as a country growing in importance as far as outbound tourism is concerned—Japan.

LEARNING OBJECTIVES

Having read this chapter, you should be able to:

1. Describe a number of theoretical models of travel flows.
2. Explain the impact of demand/origin and demand/resource factors on travel flows.
3. Indicate the magnitude of worldwide travel flows and identify the major originators and recipients of these flows.
4. Identify and explain the relative orders of magnitude of various types of travel flows within the U.S. and Canada, and to and from the U.S. and Canada.
5. Describe the growth in the numbers of foreign travelers visiting the U.S. and Canada during the past two decades.
6. Identify the countries which generate the most visitors for the U.S. and Canada.
7. Identify the most popular international travel destinations for U.S. and Canadian residents.
8. Explain the magnitude and flows of travelers to and from other major tourism countries.

The study of tourist movements is important for several reasons. For those at a destination it is vital to know the origins of the visitors. By knowing *where* the market comes from, marketing plans can be drawn up to reach potential travelers. Also, by studying the geographic characteristics of existing tourists, it may be possible to identify additional untapped market areas. For example, we may note that visitors to a particular "sun and fun" destination tend to come from cold weather cities within a 600-mile radius of the destination. Further analysis might show several large cold-weather centers of population within 600 miles where there is no marketing effort at present. These would be potential market areas for expansion of the marketing effort.

From a theoretical viewpoint the study of tourist flows is also imporatnt. By *analyzing* existing tourist flows, general principles can be developed to *explain* the movements of tourists. By *applying* these principles to other destinations, we can *forecast* potential future tourist movements. This kind of information is important, not only to those who market destinations, but it is also vital information to people who plan airline routes and develop attractions for the tourist areas of the future.

THEORETICAL MODELS OF TRAVELER FLOWS

The study of traveler flows has been called by many of the geography of travel/tourism or simply *tourist geography*. As Matley notes, there is quite obviously an "uneven spatial distribution of international tourist activities."[1] He attributed this to the following factors:

[1] Ian M. Mately, *The Geography of International Tourism* (Washington, DC, Association of American Geographers, Resource Paper no. 76-1, 1976), p. 11.

The uneven distribution of tourism resources between destinations
The wide variety of activities in which travelers participate
Changes in season
Weather
International and domestic political situations
Economic changes in countries of origin and destination
Fluctuations in monetary exchange rates
Increases or decreases in the prices of tourist services
The staging of special, short duration attractions and events

A number of authors and researchers have attempted to explain past travel-flow patterns and their unevenness by developing and using theoretical models.

The hypothesis put forward by Williams and Zelinsky is that travel flows are not random but have distinctive patterns that can be explained by several identifiable factors.[2] They suggest that these factors include:

1. *Spatial distance*
   The travel time and costs involved when going between origin and destination points.
2. *Presence or absence of past or present international connectivity*
   The existence of economic, military, cultural, and other ties or linkages between countries. The flow of travelers between Canada and the United States and between Canada and the United Kingdom are good examples of strong international connectivity.
3. *Reciprocity of travel flows*
   The belief that a flow in one direction creates a counterflow in the opposite direction. Williams and Zelinsky have found that this is a poor predictor of travel flows between two countries.
4. *Attractiveness of one country for another*
   The attractive features of one country that can induce travel; these include such items as a favorable climate; cultural, historical, and sporting attractions; and so on. The attractiveness of Florida, Hawaii, and the Caribbean to North Americans is a good example of this, as is the climatic attractiveness of Spain and other mediterranean countries to northern Europeans.
5. *Known or presumed cost of a visit within the destination country*
6. *Influence of intervening opportunities*
   The influence of attractions and facilities between the origin and destination points that cause travelers to make intermediate stops and even to forego the journey to their original destination.

[2]Anthony V. Williams and Wilbur Zelinsky, "On Some Patterns in International Tourist Flows," *Economic Geography,* vol. 46, no. 4, 1970, pp. 549–67.

7. *Impact of specific, nonrecurring events*
   The influence of major international events such as the Olympic Games, the World's Fair, and the World Cup of Soccer that can cause temporary increases in travel between a destination and various points of origin.
8. *The national character of the citizens of originating countries*
9. *The mental image of the destination country in the minds of the citizens of originating countries*

Williams and Zelinsky developed and tested their hypothesis by examining the flows of travelers between fourteen destinations, including the United States, Japan, the United Kingdom, France, and Netherlands, Benelux, West Germany, Scandinavia, Austria, Switzerland, Italy, Iberia, Greece, and South Africa. These authors illustrated the relationships of the flows between these fourteen destinations through the use of cartograms. They developed a model with which they calculated the actual and expected travel flows between individual pairs of origins and destinations. They then computed a "relative acceptance index" (an "RA") by dividing the difference between the actual and expected flows by the expected flows. Williams and Zelinsky found strong interactions between several origin and destination pairs, including the United States and Japan, the United Kingdom and South Africa, and France and Iberia. It is probable, however, that the authors have created an artificial situation by limiting their analysis to only fourteen countries.

The simplest model of a travel flow consists of an origin point, a destination, and a transportation link. This basic system has been adapted by introducing the two factors of the *resistance of the link* (a function of distance and cost) and the propensity to participate at the origin. The basic equation[3] is that the flow for a link is equal to *P* (propensity to participate) × 1/resistance of the link.

This gravity model is an adaptation of Newton's law of universal gravity, which states that two bodies attract each other in proportion to the product of their masses and inversely by the square of their distance apart. The propensity to travel may, for example, be a measure of the population at the origin—the more people who live in the country of origin, the greater number of potential tourists to travel from that country of origin to a particular destination. The number of travelers is tempered by the time and money it takes to travel from origin to destination. This model assumes that tourist flows decrease as distance from the origin increases. This tends to be true; however, for many people, after a certain point, distance becomes an attraction rather than a deterrent. The farther a destination is, the more status might be given by traveling there. It is speculated that this might be the case where the travel is for a "generic" reason. For example, take the case of people traveling from Britain to Spain for beaches and sun. The fact that "everybody goes to Spain" may induce people seeking the sun to travel farther. There is more status in traveling to

---

[3]Michael Chubb, "RECSYS-SYMAP-Michigan's Computerized Simulation Approach to Demand Distribution Prediction," in *Predicting Recreation Demand* (Technical Report No. 7, Michigan State University, 1969), pp. 23–33.

Greece or Yugoslavia for a suntan than to Spain. (Cost factors also come into play in understanding the reasons behind such movements.)

The model also assumes two-way flow. We have seen, however, that tourism flows tend to be one way from generating areas to destination areas. A last proviso is that the model predicts relative flows rather than absolutes. The model might, for example, predict that the flow of tourists between countries A and B would be twice that between countries A and C. It would not predict the actual number of tourists who would travel between these countries.

A model of tourist flows is shown in Figure 6.1. To understand tourist flows, it is necessary to examine factors at the origin, the destination, and in-transit routes that influence these flows.

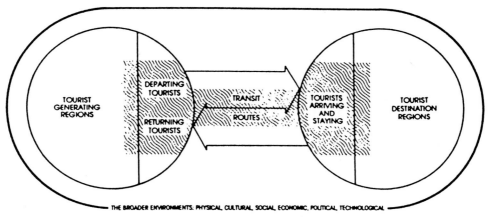

Figure 6.1 The tourism system. *Source:* Leiper, N., "The Framework of Tourism," *Annals of Tourism Research*, vol. 6, no. 1., 1979, p. 400.

Demand and Origin Factors

The demand for tourism occurs at the origin. Demand is either *effective* or *actual*— the number of people who actually travel. Suppressed demand comes from the number of people at the origin who, for one reason or another do not travel. If, however, the factors that prevented them from traveling (lack of income or time, for example) were removed, they would be inclined to travel. This is referred to as *potential* demand. *Deferred* demand, on the other hand, refers to demand that is put off because of a scarcity of supply. There may, for example, be a lack of package tours to where the tourist wants to travel. Both potential and deferred demand can be converted into effective demand by, for example, an increase in income or the development of package tours to specific destinations. Lastly, these people who have, and will continue to have, no desire to travel exhibit a category of *no demand*.

Travel propensity is used as a measure of actual demand. The travel propensity of a population is the percentage of the population who actually take a trip or are tourists. The net travel propensity refers to "the percentage of the population who take at least one tourism trip in a given period of time, while gross travel propensity gives the total number of tourism trips taken as a percentage of the population."[4] As more people take second and even third vacation trips each year, the gross travel propensity becomes more important. Dividing the gross travel propensity by the net gives the travel frequency—the average number of trips taken by the population.

Because of suppressed demand and no demand, the maximum net travel propensity is likely to be 70 to 80 percent. In the United States, for example, about two thirds of the population travel away from home each year while four out of five Swedish residents take a holiday of four nights or more every year. On the other hand, only one in three Italians take a holiday each year. Gross travel propensity, however, can exceed 100 percent if many in the population take more than one trip a year. In 1989, for example, the U.S. Travel Data Center reported that Americans took 1,261,000,000 person-trips (a person trip is one U.S. resident on a trip to a place 100 miles or more away from home). Of this total, 882.7 million person-trips were for vacations, 233 million were on business or to attend a convention, and the remainder, 145.3 million, were for personal travel. The gross travel propensity would be the number of person-trips (882.7 million) divided by the population of the United States (246 million), expressed as a percentage, or 359 percent.

The travel propensity for a given population is determined by a number of factors.[5] The demand for tourism is, first, a function of the country of origin's level of economic development. As a country moves towards a developed economy, more people move from being employed in the primary sector (fishing, agriculture, etc.) to getting jobs in the secondary or manufacturing sector and, eventually, in the tertiary or service sector. The percentage of the population who are economically active increases from 30 percent or less in developing countries to 50 percent or more in developed countries. More people have more money to spend as they wish and have the time for such things as recreation and tourism. Paid vacations, a healthier population, and greater educational opportunities all combine to produce a greater demand for travel and tourism.

Second, the demand for tourism is affected by the growth, development, distribution, and density of the population. Population growth is important in terms of the numbers of people and the relationship between births and deaths. As a society progresses, it tends to move from a stage characterized by high birth and death rates to continued high birth rates while death rates decline due to improved health care. The country still cannot afford to care for its growing population, and tourism is a luxury. As countries continue to develop, birth rates decline, and both birth and death rates stabilize at a low level. The population increasingly can afford to travel.

The distribution of the population between urban and rural areas has a significant impact upon the demand for travel and the travel patterns. Densely populated rural areas tend to indicate a population dependent upon agriculture with neither

[4]Brian G. Boniface and Christopher P. Cooper, *The Geography of Travel and Tourism* (London, England, Heinemann Professional Publishing, 1987), p. 9.

[5]Ibid, pp. 9–14.

the time nor the money to travel. In contrast, densely populated urban areas suggest an industrialized society with the time, the money, and the motivation (the "escape from the urban jungle" mentality) to travel. The distribution of a population also affects travel patterns. In the United States two thirds of the population is concentrated in the eastern one third of the country. A major travel flow in the U.S. is from the populated east to the open spaces of the west.

Densely populated urban areas suggest an industrialized society with the time, the money, and the motivation to travel

The politics of the country of origin also affects travel patterns. Countries can, and do, act to control such things as the amount of currency that can be taken out of the country as a deterrent to people's traveling abroad. In 1966, for example, the British government imposed a 50 pound travel allowance in an attempt to curtail travel abroad. (Interestingly enough, this policy encouraged package tour operators to put together creative packages to maximize value within the travel allowance. In 1967, 18 percent more British tourists traveled to the U.S. than in the previous year). Outbound travel can also be controlled by the need for an exit visa.

Patterns of international travel are affected by patterns of domestic tourism. On a world-wide basis, domestic tourism far exceeds international tourism. Some divisions between domestic and abroad tourism for various countries are displayed in Figure 6.2. The Netherlands and Belgium have low domestic travel volumes due to the small size of the countries and the ease of travel to other countries that offer excellent attractions. The sheer size of the United States and the variety of high quality tourism resources assures a high volume of domestic tourism compared to international departures.

Finally, tourism demand is a function of the demographics and life styles of the population. This was explored in great detail in Chapter 3. It is, in part, a measure

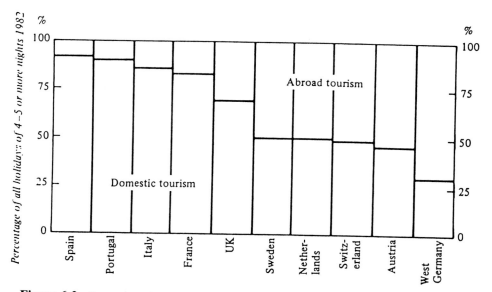

Figure 6.2 Domestic and abroad tourism in selected Western European countries. *Source:* Brian G. Boniface and Christopher P. Cooper *The Georgraphy of Travel and Tourism* (London, England, Heinemann Professional Publishing, 1987), p. 205.

of the amount of discretionary income enjoyed by the population. Discretionary income is the amount of money left over when taxes have been paid and the basics of life have been provided for. The number of employed and the types of jobs they have is an important demographic consideration also. This factor is closely related to income. Education is also important. Education broadens the mind and leaves the individual more aware of travel opportunities, while stimulating the desire to travel. The number of paid holidays will affect travel demand. Greater numbers of paid holidays or entitlements will encourage travel. However, the high cost of travel may mean that more of this entitlement will be spent at home. We are seeing, in industrialized nations, more demands for blocks of time that could be used for short vacations. The stage in the family life cycle will influence the type of vacation chosen. The young adult has the need for independence and a fair amount of free time tempered by a lack of money. There is great demand for budget vacations using surface transportation and self-catering accommodations. Patterns change with the arrival of marriage and, even more dramatically, with the appearance of children. Marriage may bring high income, especially with more and more dual-income families. Travel abroad may increase. As children arrive on the scene, families are constrained by more responsibility and less discretionary time and money. Vacations are role-related, with an emphasis on domestic holidays, self-catering, and visiting friends and relatives. With the advent of the empty nest and retirement, people again have the time and, importantly, the money to travel.

Finally, travel demand is a function of the values and life styles of the population. How important is travel to them? What do they like to do on vacation? An examination of the culture of the country (see Chapter 3) can reveal different values regarding travel, both domestically and internationally.

Destination and Resource Factors

While factors at the origin "push" people to travel, destination characteristics "pull" them to vacation. Basically tourists seek what they cannot get at home. A number of factors help pull tourists.

Climate is a key factor. Everything from sunbathing to skiing is dependent on climatic factors. Climate is the major determinant of the length of the season for many destinations. When the snow is gone, so is the ski season. The long-term weather conditions at a location are influenced by latitude, continental or maritime influences, and relief.

Latitude is the distance from the Equator. The zone between the Tropic of Cancer (23.5 degrees north of the Equator) and the Tropic of Capricorn (23.5 degrees south of the Equator) experiences a warm climate all year long. The farther from the Equator, the shorter is the summer and the greater the difference between day length between summer and winter.

Because land surfaces heat and cool faster than large bodies of water, the oceans act as a source of heat. Both coastal areas and islands enjoy temperate conditions compared to the extremes experienced by large land masses. The Gulf Stream, which brings warmth from the ocean, brings relatively mild winters to much of western Europe.

Mountain areas experience great extremes in temperature because the thinner atmosphere at high altitudes means that more solar radiation reaches the ground during the day while heat is lost faster at night. Mountains also affect the weather conditions in that moist air from the seas is forced to rise above them, and it becomes drier and warmer as it descends. This is the situation faced by Denver in its position relative to the Rocky Mountains.

From a climatic viewpoint, visitors are concerned about the temperature, humidity, amount of sunshine, precipitation, and wind. The climates of the world are displayed in Figure 6.3. The significance for tourism for each of the 10 regions is shown in Table 6.1.

The combination of climate and land surface produces conditions that affect the type of tourism appropriate to the location. The land surface of the earth is either mountains, plateaus, hill lands, or plains. Approximately three quarters of the earth is mountain or hill land. These are suitable for recreation all year long. In winter, skiing and other snow-based recreation is possible, while the clear, crisp air at other seasons allows opportunities for such things as walking, sightseeing, and photography. As noted above, they can provide relief from the summer heat for those in the lowlands. The lack of population adds to the attractiveness of these areas. Most of the world's population lives on the plateaus and plains. Coastal plains are ideal for tourism development providing, as they do, access to beach and sea. Inland waters are also attractive to tourists, allowing a variety of recreational pursuits in addition to their attractiveness as a scenic resource.

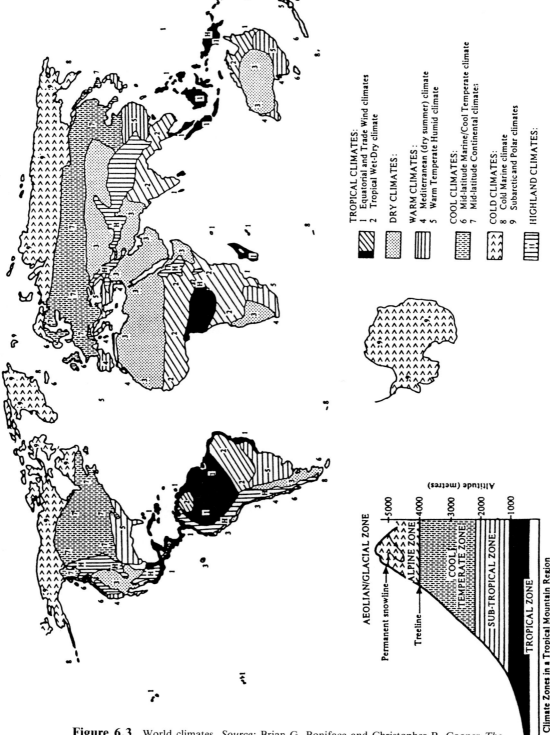

Figure 6.3 World climates. *Source:* Brian G. Boniface and Christopher P. Cooper *The Geography of Travel and Tourism* (London, England, Heinemann Professional Publishing, 1987), p. 23.

TABLE 6.1 WORLD CLIMATIC REGIONS AND THE IMPLICATIONS FOR TOURISM

Climatic Region	Significance for tourism
1. Tropical trade wind and equatorial climates	High temperatures discourage high activity. Warm year-round water temperatures encourage beach tourism.
2. Tropical wet-dry climates	Dry season suitable for sightseeing, safaris, and beach tourism. High rainy season temperatures and storms discourage tourists.
3. Dry climates	Plentiful sunshine encourages outdoor recreation most of the year. Problems with water supply, dust storms, and high summer heat.
4. Mediterranean climate	Beach tourism most of the year.
5. Warm temperate humid climate	High summer temperatures may deter active recreation. Water sports most of the year
6. Cool temperature climate	Beach activities only in the summer. Favors strenuous outdoor recreation. All-weather indoor facilities desirable.
7. Mid-latitude continental climates	Outdoor recreation in the summer. Skiing and snow-based activities in the winter.
8. Cold marine climate	Unfavorable for recreation. Rich bird and marine animal life.
9. Subarctic and polar climates	Adventure holidays requiring much advance preparation. Canoeing and fishing in some areas in the summer.
10. Highland climates	Recreation including trekking, climbing, and naturalists. The thin air may restrict strenuous activities. Mountains in tropical countries offer relief from summer heat, while in middle latitude countries snow cover encourages winter sports.

Source: Adapted from Brian G. Boniface and Christopher P. Cooper, *The Geography of Travel and Tourism* (London, England, Heinemann Professional Publishing, 1987), pp. 24–25.

While climate and natural resources are major factors in drawing tourists to a destination, tourists are also attracted by culture, history, ethnicity, and accessibility of a destination. These factors are explored in Chapter 8.

Transit Routes

While tourists may have the means and the motivation to travel and while destinations may have features likely to attract visitors, they must be able to reach the places where they want to go. That is the *function* of the transit route which links origin to destination.

The vast majority of travel between origin and destination is by road. For tourists, the advantage of traveling by car is that they have the flexibility of stopping where they wish, when they wish, for as long as they wish. It also allows for the transport of sizable (depending upon the size of the car) amounts of luggage. Travel by coach is more restrictive; however, the number of destinations served by coach is significantly greater than are served by other means of transportation.

In the mid-nineteenth century rail travel opened up areas that were previously inaccessible. Some lines added special carriages, raised to allow viewing of the scenery. It offers a relaxing way to travel with the opportunity to get up and walk around.

Air travel ushered in the era of mass tourism. The speed and the range of the jet aircraft has opened up large areas of the world to millions of people. The individual with two weeks' annual holiday can get to the destination within a few hours instead of the several days that it might have taken by road or rail.

Travel by sea is now essentially limited to cruising and ferry crossings. The major selling point for the cruise is relaxation, luxury, and comfort.

The travel route and mode of transportation are decided upon by the tourist after evaluating the options in terms of availability, frequency, price, speed, and comfort. The various modes of transportation are covered more fully in the following chapter.

TRAVEL FLOWS

Global Travel Flows

By some estimates tourism will be the world's largest economic sector by the year 2000. The World Tourism Organization (WTO) estimated 1989 expenditures for worldwide domestic and international tourism at more than $2 trillion. Over 90 percent of all trips were domestic. However, international arrivals have been growing at a faster rate than domestic arrivals. Worldwide International tourism arrivals were estimated at 400 million with receipts of more than $200 billion (excluding expenditures on transportation).

Since only a limited number of industrialized countries provide reliable data, regional figures must be considered rough estimates. However, in 1987, 51 percent of all domestic trips occurred in Europe, 38 percent in the Americas (North America, Central and South America, and the Caribbean) and slightly less than 10 percent in East Asia and the Pacific. South Asia, Africa, and the Middle East together accounted for less than 2 percent of worldwide domestic traffic. These percentages have remained relatively constant for the past decade.

The regional market share for international tourism has also changed very little in recent years. Europe receives over two-thirds of all international arrivals and approximately 60 percent of all receipts (Figures 6.4, 6.5, 6.6). The Americas recorded about 18 percent of the worldwide total of international arrivals and over 20 percent of all receipts (Figure 6.7). Other regional shares of international arrivals were relatively small —East Asia and the Pacific, 9.3 percent; Africa, 2.8 percent; Middle East, 2.1 percent; South Asia, less than 1 percent.

The showing by Europe is due to the propensity of Europeans to travel and the fact that countries in Europe are smaller than in other regions of the world. A

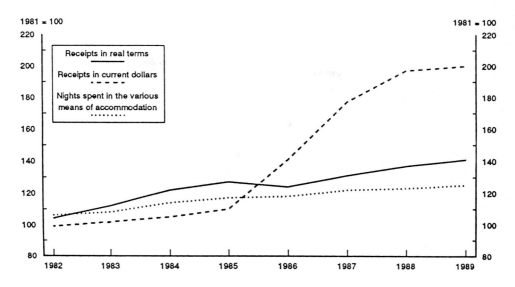

Figure 6.4 Trends of international tourism in Europe. *Source:* Organization for Economic Co-operation and Development.

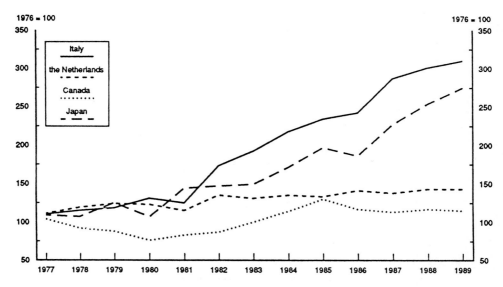

Figure 6.5 Trends of international tourism in Europe, from: *Source:* Organization for Economic Co-operation and Development.

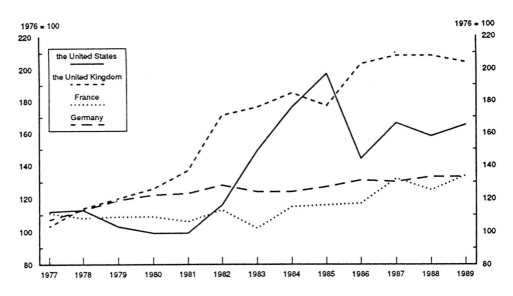

Figure 6.6 Trends of International tourism in Europe, from: *Source:* Organization for Economic Co-operation and Development.

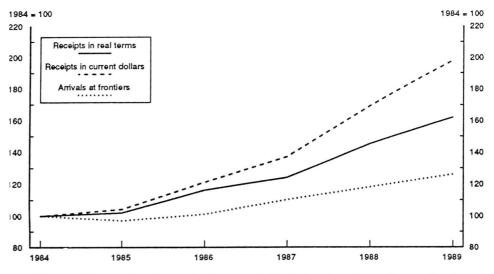

Figure 6.7 Trends of International tourism in North America. *Source:* Organization for Economic Co-operation and Development.

trip of 100 miles in the United States, for example, might get an individual into another state. This would be recorded as a domestic arrival. In Europe if that 100-mile trip meant traveling to another country, it would be classified as an international arrival.

Working with a small base, regions that presently have a small market share have the greatest potential for higher percentage growth. The East Asia/Pacific region has seen the largest percentage growth in recent years (Figures 6.8, 6.9, 6.10) while South Asia and Africa have also experienced percentage growth rates higher than the worldwide average.

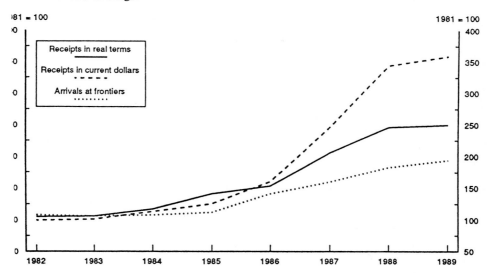

Figure 6.8 Trends of International tourism in Australasia-Japan. *Source:* Organization for Economic Co-operation and Development.

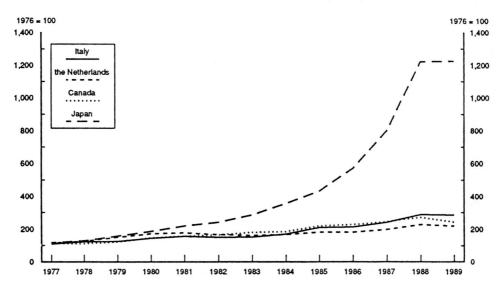

Figure 6.9 Trends of International tourism in Australasia-Japan. *Source:* Organization for Economic Co-operation and Development.

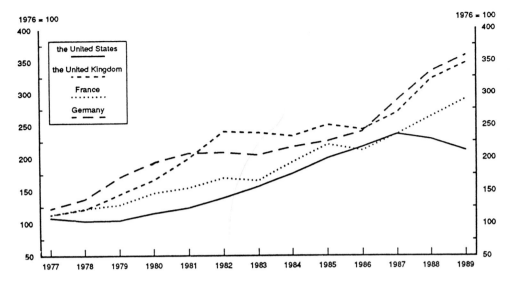

Figure 6.10 Trends of International tourism in Australasia-Japan, from: *Source:* Organization for Economic Co-operation and Development.

The pattern of international arrivals and receipts is shown in Table 6.2. Which is the number one tourism country? It depends upon the definition being used. The top generators of tourism expenditures are the United States, West Germany, and Japan. They are followed, at some distance, by the United Kingdom, France, and Canada.

The United States is the major beneficiary of tourism receipts. It is followed by France, Spain, Italy, the United Kingdom and West Germany. In terms of arrivals, however, the order is different. Italy receives the most international tourists followed by Spain, France, the United Kingdom, and Canada. The figures and order for 1989 are shown in Table 6.3.

TABLE 6.2 PATTERN OF INTERNATIONAL ARRIVALS AND RECEIPTS

Region	International tourist arrivals (percent world total)	International tourism receipts (percent world total)
Europe	67%	60%
Americas	18%	21%
East Asia Pacific	9%	12%
Middle East	2%	3%
Africa	3%	2%
South Asia	0.8%	1%

Source: Travel & Leisure's *World Travel Review* 1988/1989 (New York), pp. 9, 11.

TABLE 6.3 WORLD'S TOP TOURISM EARNERS AND SPENDERS (1989)

	A	B	C
United States	34,430	35,249 (TR)	34,977
Spain	16,252	54,058 (NV)	3,080
Italy	11,987	55,000 (NT)	6,773
France	16,500	43,000 (RT)	10,292
United Kingdom	11,248	17,204 (RV)	15,195
West Germany	8,658	NA	24,129
Canada	5,013	15,122 (RT)	7,376
Japan	3,156	2,835 (NV)	21,130

Key:
A - International Tourism Receipts (Million US $)
B - International Tourist Arrivals (Thousands)
C - International Tourism Expenditures (Million US $)
T - Tourists
V - Visitors
R - Tourist count by country of residence
N - Tourist count by country of nationality
Note: West Germany does not provide figures of arrivals of visitors or
tourists at frontiers to OECD. They did report 14,653,201 arrivals of
foreign tourists at all means of accommodation in 1989.
*Source: Tourism Policy and International Tourism in OECD Member
Countries* (Paris 1990, Organization for Economic Cooperation and
Development), pp. 39, 53, 99.

International tourist flows of 1 million or more from the main generating countries for the year 1989 are shown in Table 6.4. In interpreting these figures the reader should bear in mind that not all countries report figures. Additionally, comparisons are difficult because of inconsistencies in definitions. In some cases the figures represent tourists only, tourists and excursionists, or arrivals at hotels.

TABLE 6.4 INTERNATIONAL TOURIST FLOWS OF ONE MILLION OR MORE
FROM MAIN GENERATING COUNTRIES (1989)

Destination	Country of origin	Number of arrivals
Austria (AH)	West Germany	6,362,138
Canada (T)	USA	12,195,400
France (T)	West Germany	9,113,000
	United Kingdom	6,645,000
	Netherlands	4,047,000
	Italy	3,441,000
	Switzerland	3,378,000
	Belgium/Luxembourg	3,146,000
	United States	1,950,000
	Spain	1,310,000
Greece (T)	West Germany	1,655,000
	United Kingdom	1,632,000

TABLE 6.4 *(cont.)*

Destination	Country of origin	Number of arrivals
Ireland (T)	United Kingdom	1,668,000
Italy (TE) (1)	Switzerland	10,190,559
	West Germany	10,134,213
	France	9,390,152
	Austria	6,083,370
	Yugoslavia	5,909,741
	United Kingdom	1,906,236
	Netherlands	1,840,884
	United States	1,356,662
	Belgium	1,048,930
Mexico (T) (3)	USA	14,800,000
Portugal (T)	Spain	3,246,826
	United Kingdom	1,207,281
Spain (TE) (2)	France	11,994,421
	Portugal	10,044,244
	United Kingdom	7,345,831
	West Germany	6,783,753
	Netherlands	2,034,717
	Italy	1,511,618
	Belgium	1,374,776
	Switzerland	1,138,923
Switzerland (AH)	West Germany	2,130,168
	USA	1,032,600
United Kingdom (T)	United States	2,814,100
	France	2,254,300
	West Germany	2,011,700
	Ireland	1,301,800
United States (T)	Canada	15,365,937
	Mexico	7,200,000 (3)
	Japan	3,080,396
	United Kingdom	2,221,871
	West Germany	1,076,385
West Germany (AH)	USA	1,963,587
	Netherlands	1,606,800
	United Kingdom	1,276,221
Yugoslavia (AH)	West Germany	1,309,745

Key: 1 - Includes about 53 percent of excursionists
        2 - Includes about 34 percent of excursionists
        3 - Source: United States Travel and Tourism Administration
        T - Arrivals of foreign visitors at frontiers
   AH - Arrivals at hotels
   TE - Tourists and excursionists

Source: Tourism Policy and International Tourism in OECD Member Countries
(Paris 1990, Organization for Economic Cooperation and Development)

The vast majority of international travel occurs between neighboring countries. For Italy, the largest numbers of arrivals come from Switzerland, West Germany and France. For Spain, the major generating countries are France, Portugal, and the United Kingdom. In the Americas, people of the United States, Canada, and Mexico all visit each other. The prominence of Japan as a market for the United States can also be explained in part by geography. Nearly 60 percent of Japanese travelers to the United States visit Hawaii, while an additional 20 percent travel to Guam.

Nearly 60 percent of Japanese travelers to the United States visit Hawaii

For Eastern Europe, other Eastern block countries and the Soviet Union produce the most international travel volume.

Japan is a major generator of tourism for Hong Kong, as is neighboring China. In East Asia, Singapore and Malaysia are the most important markets for each other.

Forecasts for international tourism to the year 1999 are shown in Table 6.5. The rank of the United States is expected to slip significantly while that of the United Kingdom is forecast to grow. These projections assume that the U.S. dollar will continue to be soft and real private consumption expenditure will slow. They also assume that the oil exporting countries will experience economic standstill, accompanied by sharply declining currency values in real terms.

It is projected that, between 1986 and 1999, the number of international trips will more than double for West Germany, Denmark, and Norway; almost triple for the United Kingdom, Spain, and Japan; and more than quadruple for Sweden. The number of U.S. international trips taken by U.S. residents is forecast to decline by 17 percent.

TABLE 6.5 INTERNATIONAL TOURISM FORECASTS TO 1999

	Trips (millions)				Nights Abroad (millions)				Expenditures ($US billions)[1]			
	1986	1991	1995	1999	1986	1991	1995	1999	1986	1991	1995	1999
West Germany	120.1	187.9	229.8	268.3	551	782	900	1,018	16.6	23.1	26.1	28.9
United States	61.6	54.2	51.5	51.2	273	233	216	234	17.3	15.2	14.4	15.8
Netherlands	26.2	27.4	28.6	27.8	100	108	116	116	3.6	3.9	4.2	4.3
Switzerland	25.6	35.2	39.5	40.3	89	128	148	155	2.8	4.3	5.2	5.6
United Kingdom	25.2	47.3	60.3	77.9	312	577	698	863	7.3	13.9	17.1	21.6
Austria	23.0	29.5	31.5	33.9	72	89	90	91	2.6	3.3	3.4	3.5
Belgium-Luxembourg	15.9	19.8	21.5	24.8	66	80	87	98	2.4	2.9	3.2	3.7
France	14.7	17.2	20.0	23.2	192	215	241	271	4.9	5.8	6.8	8.0
Canada	13.0	16.7	18.5	21.3	131	161	172	194	4.1	5.4	6.1	7.3
Italy	9.4	14.3	17.3	19.4	78	118	142	160	2.5	3.8	4.6	5.2
Spain	7.5	12.0	17.3	21.1	50	74	101	116	1.3	2.0	2.8	3.3
Denmark	7.3	9.2	12.1	14.9	48	59	77	96	1.8	2.2	3.0	3.8
Japan	7.1	11.4	15.0	19.6	62	107	149	206	6.8	10.2	12.5	15.5
Sweden	5.4	9.7	15.6	22.9	45	83	136	210	2.4	4.2	6.8	10.3
Norway	4.8	5.5	7.8	11.8	39	45	64	96	2.1	2.4	3.5	5.4
Malaysia	4.7	3.7	6.5	9.2	31	25	43	61	1.0	0.9	1.7	2.6
Mexico	3.8	3.5	7.5	9.5	22	19	37	44	2.0	1.8	3.7	4.5
Saudi Arabia	2.3	1.3	1.2	2.1	24	14	13	21	2.5	1.4	1.2	1.9
Kuwait	1.5	0.9	1.0	1.1	19	12	14	16	1.4	0.9	0.9	1.0
Australia	1.4	1.3	1.4	1.5	42	44	50	58	1.7	1.7	1.8	2.0
Total—20 Main Countries	380.8	508.0	603.9	702.2	2,247	2,975	3,496	4,125	87.1	109.3	129.0	154.2
WORLD TOTAL	497.8	655.3	799.5	909.7	2,808	3,720	4,414	5,251	108.9	136.7	162.9	196.2

[1]Excluding fares, at constant relative prices, expressed in 1985 dollars and exchange rates.

Surce: "International Tourism Forecasts to 1999" by Anthony Edwards, The Economist Intelligence Unit, July 1988, and *Travel & Leisure's World Travel Overview* 1988/1989, p. 17

Travel to neighboring countries is expected to grow at a rate less than the overall average, while other trips of short to medium distance are projected to increase at a faster than average rate. Long-haul travel (over 1,500 miles or 2,400 kilometers) would decline initially then rise.

International Travel to the United States

The United States accounts for approximately 9 percent of world tourist arrivals and just over 16 percent of world tourism receipts (Figures 6.11, 6.12). The U.S. Travel and Tourism Administration projected 44 million foreign visitors in 1991.

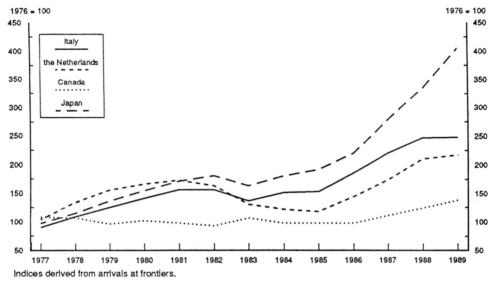

Figure 6.11 Trends of International tourism in North America, from: *Source:* Organization for Economic Co-operation and Development.

Canada accounts for just over 40 percent of the foreign arrivals in the United States. While the number of Canadian arrivals has increased by over 70 percent between 1985 and 1991, their share of the market has dropped from 1970 when nearly three quarters of all international visitors to the U.S. were Canadian residents. Their travel patterns have changed also. Over the past decade there has been a substantial increase in the number of Canadian visitors who fly to the U.S. and a slight decline in the number who drive. This change in transportation has resulted in a lessening of the seasonality of Canadian tourism demand. In the 1970's Canadians visited the U.S. mainly during the summer months. By the 1980's, while summer was still the dominant season, long-haul winter travel to warm weather states had picked up considerably. There has also been a shift towards more vacations in U.S. cities and resorts and away from rural sightseeing/outdoor activities vacations.

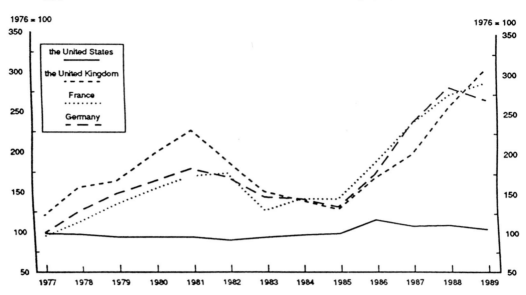

Figure 6.12 Trends of International tourism in North America, from: *Source:* Organization for Economic Co-operation and Development.

In 1970 Mexico accounted for 9 percent of the total number of international visitors to the U.S. By 1991 Mexico was accounting for 37 percent of all arrivals, Europe, 16 percent; Asia/Middle East, 12 percent; and South/Central America, 4 percent. The total number of overseas visitors continued to grow in the latter part of the 1980's and the early 1990's due, in great part, to the weak U.S. dollar. The largest growth during this time came from overseas tourists. The largest generators of foreign visitors to the U.S., after Canada and Mexico, are Japan (8 percent), the United Kingdom (6 percent), and West Germany (3 percent). Almost half of all visitors (business and pleasure) confined their visit to the U.S. to a single state. Almost one third visited three or more states.

The British and the West Germans tend to prefer the outdoor and beach holiday as well as wishing to experience the "American way of life." French travelers, on the other hand, are more interested in visiting historical places, museums, and art galleries. Japanese visitors are attracted by the cultural and historical aspects of the U.S. in addition to the night life, shopping, and the opportunity to meet the U.S. people. There is also a great deal of interest in participative sports like golf and tennis.

The distribution of foreign visitors to regions of the United States is shown in Figure 6.13. Thirty percent of all foreign visitors to the United States visit the Pacific Census Region. (See Figure 6.14 for the states included in each census division). Approximately one quarter of the regional total come from Canada while an additional 17 percent are from Mexico. The East South Central and South Atlantic Census Divisions together attract 22 percent of the U.S. total. Over 40 percent of them come from Canada while only 2 percent are from Mexico. The Middle Atlantic Census Division receives 21 percent of the U.S. total of international visitors, with 44 per-

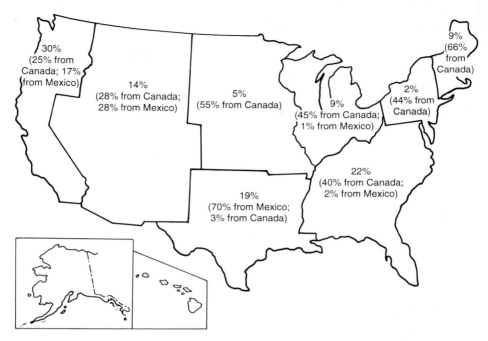

Figure 6.13 Distribution of foreign visitors to U.S. regions. *Source:* U.S. Travel and Tourism Administration.

Figure 6.14 Bureau of Census regions used by the National Travel Survey. **181**

cent coming from Canada and less than 1 percent from Mexico. Nineteen percent of international visitors travel to the West South Central Census Division. Over 70 percent come from Mexico and just 3 percent visit from Canada. The Mountain Census Division attracts 14 percent of the total, with 28 percent each coming from both Canada and Mexico. New England and the East North Central Census Divisions each receive 9 percent of the total number of international visitors. Almost two thirds of the international visitors to New England are from Canada, a negligible number from Mexico. Forty five percent of the East North Central's international visitors come from Canada, while only 1 percent come from Mexico. The West North Central Census Division receives 5 percent of the U.S. total, with 55 percent coming from Canada and a very small amount from Mexico.

Table 6.6 gives a profile of overseas visitors to the United States. The highlights of the 1987 profile are:

- Almost half of all trips were for vacation or holiday; over one third were for business reasons; one in five was to visit relatives, and an additional 16 percent were for the purpose of visiting friends.
- Over three quarters had already visited the U.S.
- Travel agents were used by over 70 percent of the visitors to book air reservations, by over 60 percent as a source of travel information, and by over half to book lodging.
- The average trip was planned 49 days in advance (median 32 days).
- On average, visitors spent an average of 26 nights away from home, 22 nights being spent in the U.S. Medians were 14 and 11 nights respectively.
- The leading ports of entry were New York City, Los Angeles, Miami, and Honolulu.
- Within the U.S. almost half of the visitors traveled by domestic airlines, almost 40 percent rented a car, while over a third used a private automobile.
- Nearly half visited one state; about a quarter saw two states, while 30 percent visited three or more states.
- The most popular destinations were California, New York, Florida, Hawaii, and Washington, D.C.

A gradual trend is for more European visitors to move beyond the traditional city destinations in the east to attractions in the west, for Asian visitors to expand beyond Hawaii and the west coast to destinations further east, and for visitors from South America to travel beyond Florida to major cities throughout the continental United States.

Beginning December 15, 1988, Americans and Japanese were able to visit each other's countries without a visa for as long as 90 days if they held transit or return-trip tickets. In addition to relieving U.S. consular offices of a massive burden, this lowering of travel barriers should help increase the flow of travel between residents of the countries. Prior to this time Japanese have had to wait up to two days to obtain a visa at a travel agency or up to two hours at the U.S. consulate. Japan has agreements with 50 other countries allowing reciprocal visa-free travel.

International Travel from the United States

Throughout the 1980's and early 1990's the numbers of Americans traveling abroad also rose. The outbound U.S. travel market has been called a *mini mass-market* in that, while substantial in size, it represents only a fraction of the U.S. population. About 10 percent of vacation trips taken by U.S. residents are outside the contiguous U.S.

In 1948 only 200,000 U.S. nationals traveled to Europe and 70 percent of them went by ship. In 1991 over seven and a half million Americans traveled to Europe, all but a few thousand traveling by plane.

Two thirds of U.S. departures to foreign countries are split between Mexico (36 percent) and Canada (29 percent). Europe accounts for an additional 16 percent of the total. The major destinations in Europe are the United Kingdom, Germany, France, Switzerland, and Italy. Over 70 percent of U.S. travelers overseas visit only one country; one in eight visit three or more countries.

California sends twice as many visitors as the next leading contender, Texas. Pennsylvania is the third leading state of origin. The median length of stay is seven nights, with Cancun, Mexico City, and Puerto Vallerta the major destinations.

Table 6.7 gives a profile of U.S. residents traveling to overseas destinations. The highlights of the 1987 profile are:

- Most travelers are from California, New York and Florida.
- Over 60 percent of the trips are for vacation purposes; about one third are for business or attending a convention; about one third are to visit friends and relatives.
- Most use a travel agent to book air reservations and as an information source. About three quarters travel independently.
- Less than three quarters stayed at a hotel or motel during their trips; one third stayed in a private home.
- Over 70 percent visited just one country.
- Western Europe remains the most frequent destination, but its lead over other areas is declining.
- The average number of nights spent outside the U.S. is up slightly from previous years, while the median is slightly less.

The U.S. outbound market continues to show a seasonal effect with the majority of travel being during the months of June, July and August. The market has

TABLE 6.6 PROFILE OF OVERSEAS VISITORS TO THE UNITED STATES

	1987 Percent		1987 Percent		1987 Percent
Residence		**Type of Airline Ticket** (Continued)		**Port of Entry** (Continued)	
Western Europe	44	Economy, tourist	72	Seattle	3
France	6	Other	3	Other ports	NA
Germany—West	9	**Advance Trip Decision Time**		**Types of Accommodations**[1]	
Italy	3	Mean (days)	48.7	Hotel, motel	77
Scandinavia	3	Median (days)	32.0	Private home	42
United Kingdom	13	**Type and Size of Traveling Party**		Campsite	3
Eastern Europe	1	Traveling alone	48	Other	5
Caribbean	9	Family group	34	**Transportation in the U.S.**[1]	
South America	8	Busines group	8	Domestic airline	50
Central America	3	Mixed business, family, other	11	Intercity train	7
Africa	2	Average party size (persons)	1.4	Intercity bus	18
Oceania	4	Median party size (persons)	1.0	City bus or subway	22
Far East	27	**Sex and Age of Visitors**		Rented auto	38
Japan	19	Children under 18	5	Private auto	36
Middle East	4	Male adults	62	Other	38
Purpose of Trip[1]		Female adults	33	**Number of States Visited**	
Business	37	Average age of male adults (years)	40.7	One state	47
Attend convention	8	Average ag of female adults (years)	37.0	Two states	24
Vacation, holiday	48	**Occupation of Visitors:**		Three or more states	30
Visit friends	16	Manager, executive	30	Average (states)	2.1
Visit relatives	20	Professional, technical	27	Median (states)	2.0
Study	5	Clerical, sales	10	**Main U.S. Destinations Visited**[1]	
U.S. Trip Experience		Craftsman, mechanic	3	California	37
First-time visitors	22	Government, military	7	Los Angeles	22
Repeat visitors	78	Homemaker	9	San Francisco	20

184

Means of Booking Air Trip[1]

Travel agent	71
Self	14
Company travel department	10
Other	3

Means of Booking Lodging[1]

Travel agent	51
Self	15
Company travel department	20
Friends and Relatives	12
Other	9

Information Sources[1]

Airline	17
Travel agency	62
Government sources	3
Friends, relatives	20
Newspapers, magazines	6
Published sources	11
Company travel dept.	12
Other	3

Type of Airline Ticket

First class	6
Executive business	19

Student	8
Retired	4
Airline employee	3

Annual Family Income

Average	$46,820
Median	$43,113

Nights Away From Home

Average (nights)	25.6
Median (nights)	14.0

Nights Spent in the U.S.

Average (nights)	21.9
Median (nights)	11.0

U.S. Port of Entry

New York City	29
Miami	11
Honolulu	9
Los Angeles	13
Chicago	8
Atlanta	6
Dallas/Ft. Worth	4
San Francisco	7
Boston	4

New York	28
New York City	26
Florida	20
Miami	9
Orlando	9
Hawaii	14
Washington, D.C.	10
Texas	8
Illinois	7
Chicago	7
Massachusetts	8
Nevada	7
Arizona	8
Pennsylvania	4
Washington	4
New Jersey	4

Expenditures in the U.S.A.

Per visitor	$1,384
Per visitor/day	$ 63

NA = Not Available.

[1] Multiple responses tabulated.

Source: *In-Flight Survey of International Air Travelers*, January–December 1987, U.S. Travel and Tourism Administration and *Travel & Leisure's World Travel Overview*, 1988, 1989, pp. 48–49.

TABLE 6.7 PROFILE OF U.S. RESIDENTS TRAVELING TO OVERSEAS DESTINATIONS

	1987 Percent		1987 Percent		1987 Percent
Residence		**Type of Airline Ticket**		**Type of Accommodations**[1]	
New York	12	First class	7	Hotel, motel	74
New York City	8	Executive, business	15	Private home	35
California	16	Economy, tourist	75	Other	7
Los Angeles	5	Other	3	**Number of Countries Visited**	
San Francisco	4	**Use of Pre-Paid Package Inclusive Tour**		One country	71
Texas	8	Yes	24	Two countries	18
New Jersey	6	No (Independent)	76	Three or more countries	12
Illinois	4	**Type and Size of Travel Party**		Average (countries)	1.5
Florida	11	Traveling alone	35	Median (countries)	1.0
Pennsylvania	3	Family group	47	**Main Overseas Destinations Visited**[1]	
Massachusetts	4	Business group	8	Western Europe	44
Washington	3	Mixed business, family, other	13	France	8
Purpose of Trip[1]		Average party size (persons)	1.6	Germany	12
Business	28	Median party size (persons)	1.0	Italy	7
Attention Convention	4	**Sex and Age of Visitors**		Switzerland	4
Vacation, holiday	61	Children under 18	5	United Kingdom	19
Visit friends	11	Male adults	55	Eastern Europe	2

Visit relatives	21	Female adults	41	Caribbean	24
Study	3	Average age of male adults (years)	43.7	South America	6
Foreign Trip Experience		Average age of female adults (years)	41.7	Central America	2
First-time visitors	10	**Occupation of Visitors**		Oceania	7
Repeat visitors	90	Manager, executive	25	Australia	5
Means of Booking Air Trip[1]		Professional, technical	34	Far East	18
Travel Agent	71	Clerical, sales	7	Hong Kong	6
Self	14	Craftsman, mechanic	3	Japan	7
Company travel department	8	Government, military	4	Middle East	3
Other	5	Homemaker	9	Africa	2
Information Sources[1]		Student	7	**Nights Outside the U.S.**	
Airline	20	Retired	8	Average	20.9
Travel agency	63	Airline employee	NA	Median	11.0
Government sources	6	**Annual Family Income**		**Average Non-U.S. Expenditures**	
Company travel dept.	10	Average	$54,204	Per traveler	$971
Friends, relatives	27	Median	$55,138	Per traveler per day	$ 46
Newspapers, magazines	11				
Published Sources	14				

[1]Multiple responses tabulated.

Source: *In-Flight Survey of International Air Travelers*, January-December 1987, U.S. Travel and Tourism Administration, and *Travel & Leisure's World Travel Overview*, 1988, 1989, pp. 45–46.

also been opting for shorter vacations. From 1973 to 1985 the average stay in Europe declined from 27 days to 18. The trend and financial effect of international travel to and from the U.S. is shown in Figures 6.15 and 6.16. In 1989 the U.S. tourism account produced a surplus for the first time ever.

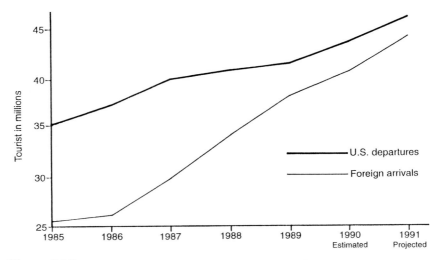

Figure 6.15 The Traveler Gap is rapidly closing as U.S. outbound wains, inbound gains. *Source:* United States Travel and Tourism Administration.

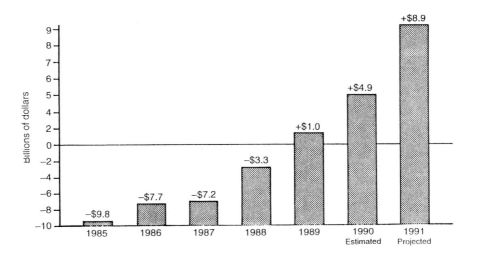

Figure 6.16 U.S. Tourism account in surplus for the first time ever in 1989. *Source:* United States Travel and Tourism Administration.

Domestic Travel Within the United States

In 1989 over two thirds of all U.S. residents took 1.26 billion person-trips. Approximately 70 percent of them were vacation trips. About 90 percent of all vacation trips are taken within the contiguous United States. About half are less than four nights in duration, concentrated on weekends and within 310 miles of home. Another one third of those trips are four to nine nights long to places 550 miles away from home on average.

Long vacation trips—those of ten or more nights away from home—account for 14 percent of domestic vacation trips. However, they account for 40 percent of all vacation nights, averaging 15 nights away from home. Destinations for long vacation trips are an average of 960 miles away from home. They are more popular in the winter months than are shorter trips.

People on longer trips are considerably older than for other types of vacation

People on longer vacation trips are considerably older than for other types of vacations. Well over one quarter of such trips are taken by people 55 years or older. Long vacation trips are less likely to include children—long vacationers being twice as likely to be retired. The regions which produce the most long vacation travelers are the Mid-Atlantic, South Atlantic and East North Central areas. New England residents produce a disproportionate share of long vacation trips compared with either shorter trips or the size of their resident population. Residents of the Mountain region are also more active than their population size would indicate.

The characteristics of long vacation trips reflect the older age of the travelers and the requirements and restrictions of traveling away from home for more than a week. The trip is more apt to consist of only one or two people and is more likely to include a visit with friends and relatives. Indeed, more than half of such trips include staying with friends or relatives. Long vacationers are also more likely to rent a cabin or condominium or stay in their own second home. About one quarter of long vacation trips—higher than the average for all trips—are primarily for outdoor recreation. This is tied in to the preference for winter travel and the demand for skiing. Only about 5 percent of these trips involve a package tour, the same as for all trips. This is probably due to the lack of supply of good-quality domestic tours for long trips (compared to Europe, for example).

The South Atlantic region is overwhelmingly the most popular destination for the long vacationer. It receives over one third of all such tourists, with Florida being a prime beneficiary. The Pacific region is the second most popular destination region, mostly to California. The Mountain region attracts the third largest number of travelers based on its ski resorts and summer opportunities for recreation. New England also attracts big numbers to its winter sports activities and its summer coastal attractions.

Forty percent of all vacation trips are taken during the summer. The seasonal effect, however, is not as great as for the U.K. or West Germany, for example. The average summer trip lasts 6 nights. Over 80 percent of all summer vacation travel is taken by auto, truck, or recreational vehicle. About one in eight vacationers travel by air. Summer trips average shorter travel distances than those taken in other seasons. Just over half involve distances of less than 500 round-trip miles. Forty percent of all summer vacationers each stay in hotels and motels or with friends and relatives. The third most popular way to spend overnights is camping, which accounts for 11 percent of the total.

Americans prefer to vacation in cities, on ocean beaches and in small towns and rural areas. Cities are preferred by people in the Midwest, while ocean beaches are the most popular destinations for those in the East. Those in the Great Lakes favor small towns and rural areas while residents of the West are fond of mountain areas.

International Travel to Canada

Three quarters of the trips in Canada are taken by Canadian residents, slightly less than one quarter by U.S. residents, and only 1.5 percent of the total by visitors from other countries. Canadian residents accounted for approximately two thirds of total expenditures on these trips, U.S. residents accounting for one quarter of the total, with the remainder coming from residents of other countries.

Of the trips of one or more nights, an even greater percentage, 83 percent, is taken by Canadian residents, compared to 15 percent by U.S. residents.

The last ten years have seen significant structural changes in Canada's international tourism markets. While the United States remains Canada's most important international market by far, its share of the total tourism market has declined. Within the non-U.S. market there were also changes. The United Kingdom's share of the market has dropped while Japan's, the third largest international market, has increased dramatically. West Germany's share remained constant while France and Australia have very slightly increased their market share in recent years. Figure 6.17 shows the distribution of visitors to Canada for 1990.

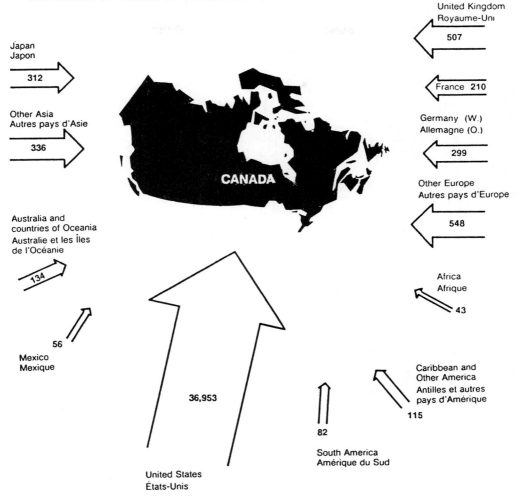

Source: **Travel Between Canada and Other Countries** Catalogue No. 66-001.
Source: **Voyages entre le Canada et les autres pays,** no 66-001 au catalogue.

Figure 6.17 Canada's visitors, 1990, (number of trips in thousands). *Source:* Statistics Canada

Both the Middle Atlantic and the East North Central regions within the U.S. account for 25 percent of U.S. trips of one night or more to Canada. Both these regions have seen their share of the market increase in the 1980's, while the Pacific region saw its share of the market decline. These flows are depicted in Figure 6.18.

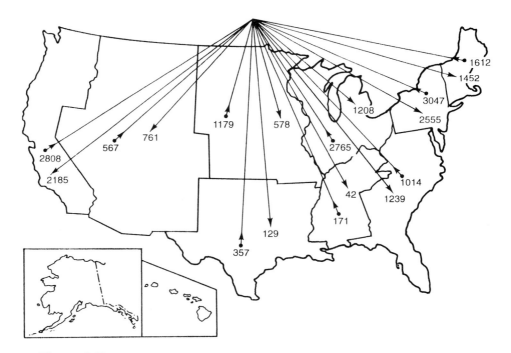

Figure 6.18 Person trips of one night or more between Canada and the U.S. travel regions—1986 in thousands. *Source:* Statistics Canada, *Touriscope: Tourism in Canada 1988* (Ottawa, Ontario, 1988, pp. 53, 73).

International Travel by Canadians.

The vast amount of all international visits by Canadians—88 percent in 1987—are to the United States. Of the remainder 14 percent are to the Caribbean countries, 11 percent to the United Kingdom and 7 percent to France. Both Asian countries and Mexico received 6 percent of all visits, while trips to Germany accounted for 5 percent of the total. South America and Asia have increased in popularity for Canadians. Canadian travel to South America tripled in the mid 1980's, while travel to Asia doubled between 1980 and 1986. The distribution of outbound international visits is shown in Figure 6.19.

Most Canadian trips in the U.S. are to the Middle Atlantic states, which attract 24 percent of the total. The Pacific region attracts 17 percent of the total, followed by New England with 13 percent, and the South Atlantic and East North Central with 11 percent each. These percentages have remained fairly constant throughout the 1980's. These flows are shown in Figure 6.18.

Forty percent of the person trips of one or more nights in Canada are connected with business, attending a convention or otherwise employment related. Slightly less are for pleasure, recreation, or holiday, while 15 percent are to visit friends and relatives. On the other hand, most person trips to the United States and to other

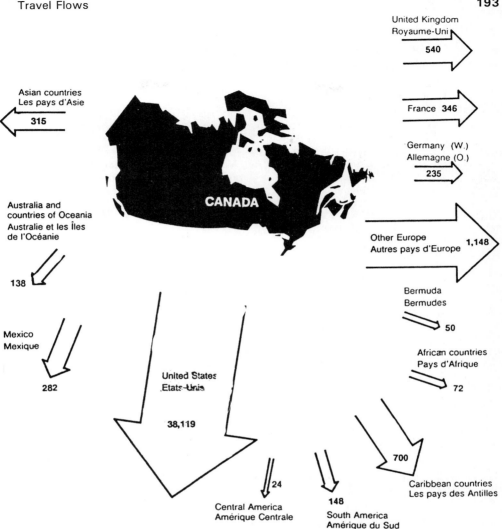

Source: **International Travel**, Catalogue No. 66-201.
Source: **Voyages internationaux**, no 66-201 au catalogue.

Figure 6.19 International visits by Canadians, 1986, Les visites internationales des Canadiens, 1986, (thousands of visits - milliers de visites). *Source:* **International Travel,** Catalogue No. 66-201. *Source:* **Voyages internationaux,** no. 66-201 au catalogue.

countries—54 percent—were pleasure trips. One in four were to visit friends and relatives, while one in eight were for some aspect of business or to attend a convention.

The flows of international travelers to and from Canada and the resulting balance of payments on the Canadian travel account indicate that Canadians traveling abroad continue to spend more than the rest of the world spends in Canada.

The distribution of travelers between Canada and the United States by month for 1987 is shown in Table 6.8. It clearly illustrates the seasonal effect of travel, with travel peaking in July and August. For Canadian travelers to the U.S. there is a "mini peak" in March and April. This is most likely due to travel to warmer climates over Easter breaks.

TABLE 6.8   U.S./CANADIAN AND CANADIAN/U.S. TRAVELERS BY MONTH (1987).

Month	U.S. travelers to Canada	Canadian travelers to U.S.
January	395,828	734,760
February	470,996	671,275
March	512,184	1,127,230
April	655,899	1,055,612
May	1,196,515	978,732
June	1,649,395	888,031
July	2,533,518	1,673,314
August	2,512,096	1,850,510
September	1,434,100	1,074,942
October	878,546	950,370
November	520,930	759,522
December	520,930	653,910

Source: *Travel & Leisure's World Travel Review 1988/1989* (New York, 1988), p. 50.

Domestic Tourism in Canada

Canadians' favorite city destinations are Toronto, Montreal, Vancouver, and Ottawa. Most Canadians—over 30 percent—are described as planned adventurers while just over a quarter are casual travelers who typically make no formal pre-trip planning. A trip is most importantly seen as a getaway, followed by going home to visit family, and third, the desire for a new experience. The most important activities and interests on a trip relate to the outdoors, followed by a stay at a resort.

The patterns of domestic travel can be seen in Table 6.9. Of the 88 million trips of one or more nights by Canadians in 1986, 82 percent are spent in Canada. Over two thirds are taken within the same province, while one in eight are spent in the United States. Trips to other countries constitute 3 percent of the total.

In examining the travel patterns of the residents of the provinces, residents of Ontario take 37 percent of all trips. They are slightly more inclined to stay within their own province, to travel to the U.S. and other countries, and slightly less inclined than the average to travel to other provinces. The people of Quebec take 23 percent of total trips. They are more inclined to stay in Canada and within their own province, while being slightly less inclined than the average to visit other provinces.

TABLE 6.9 PATTERNS OF DOMESTIC TRAVEL IN CANADA—1986: IN THOUSANDS

Province	Trips	Canada	Interprovincial	Interprovincial	U.S.	Other Countries
Total	88,353	82%	69%	16%	12%	3%
Ontario	32,758	82%	71%	12%	14%	4%
Quebec	20,514	86%	73%	13%	12%	3%
Alberta	10,902	92%	68%	24%	7%	1%
British Columbia¹	8,879	77%	65%	12%	20%	3%
Newfoundland						
Prince Edward Island	6,086	92%	65%	27%	7%	1%
Nova Scotia						
New Brunswick						
Saskatchewan	4,761	94%	69%	25%	5%	1%
Manitoba	4,472	88%	64%	24%	11%	1%

¹Includes Yukon and the Northwest Territories

Source: Statistics Canada, Touriscope: Tourism in Canada 1988 (Ottawa, Ontario, 1988), p. 48. Author's calculations.

Twelve percent of total trips are taken by residents of Alberta. They are more inclined to vacation in Canada and to visit other provinces but less likely to visit the U.S. and other countries.

Residents of British Columbia take 10 percent of all trips taken by Canadian residents. They are less likely to take a trip in Canada, but are more likely to travel to the United States. Residents of the four north-eastern provinces—Newfoundland, Prince Edward Island, Nova Scotia, and New Brunswick—take 7 percent of all trips. They are more likely than the average to vacation in Canada, but travel outside of their own region. They are less inclined to visit the U.S. or other countries. Residents of Saskatchewan, who take 5 percent of all trips, are the most inclined to vacation in Canada. Ninety-four percent of their trips are within Canada. They travel to other provinces as well as their own and are less likely to vacation in the U.S. and in other countries. Residents of Manitoba also account for five percent of all trips taken by Canadian residents. They are more likely to vacation within Canada and to visit other provinces, but less inclined to visit countries other than Canada and the United States.

One in four interprovincial trips of one or more nights in Canada is to Ontario. An additional one in five are to British Columbia, while 18 percent are to Quebec and one in eight are to Alberta. (See Figures 6.11–6.19.)

Tourist Flows To and From Major Tourism Countries

Changes in destination trends for mass market holidays are shown in Figure 6.20. While travelers have ventured further from home in the past 50 years, two items are constant—the north-south movement and the importance of Europe.

Because of the importance of Europe as a region of origination and as a destination, it is appropriate to examine certain intraregional flows. One way of doing this

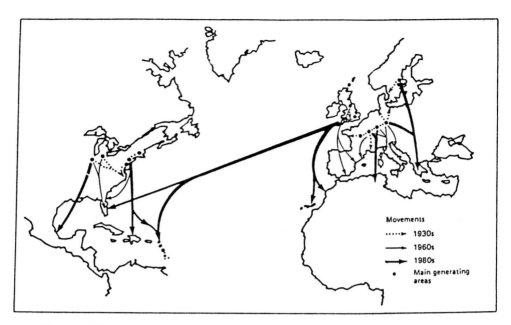

Figure 6.20 Changes in destination trends for mass market holidays, 1930s to 1980s. *Source:* J. Christopher Holloway, *The Business of Tourism*, (London, Pitman Publishing, 1985), p. 44.

is through the data of the European Civil Aviation Conference (ECAC) of inclusive tour charter flights. One of the most significant factors in the development of tourism in Europe since the 1960s has been the increasing number of package tours by air. The ECAC defines an inclusive tour as one which ''consists of a round-trip or circle tour performed in whole or in part by air, organized by a tour organizer and offered to the public at a comprehensive price including, besides air transport, accommodation for the duration of the trip, surface transport and, where appropriate, other amenities. An inclusive tour is normally paid for before departure, is for a predetermined period, and is to an announced destination or destinations.'' An inclusive tour flight ''is a flight operated with an aircraft chartered, for example, by a tour organizer or travel agent, to carry inclusive tour passenters. The flight may constitute a round or circle trip and be one of a regular series of flights.''[6] These flights are also called Inclusive Tours by Charter or ITCs.

In Figures 6.21 and 6.22 the major Intra-ECAC flows are shown for 1970 and 1980. In 1970 the main direction of flight movements was north-south, with traffic being centered in Spain and, to a lesser extent, Italy. Spain was linked to the eight major European markets, the most important being the United Kingdom. In fact, the U.K.–Spain route was the most important route in terms of volume, accounting for over one quarter of total traffic within Europe between countries which had at least one percent of the market.

[6]Douglas Pearce, ''Spatial Patterns of Package Tours,'' *Annals of Tourism Research*, vol. 14, no. 2, 1987, p. 185.

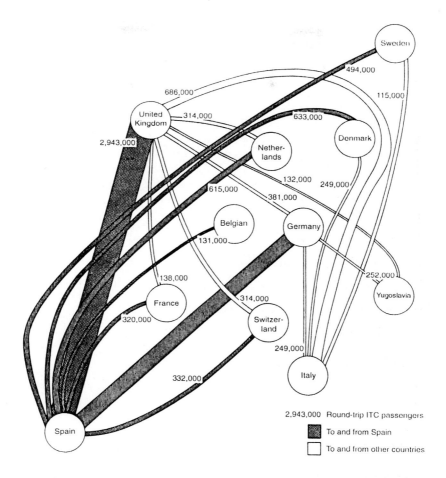

Figure 6.21 Major Intra-ECAC ITC flows (for 1970). *Source:* Douglas Pearce, "Spatial Patterns of Package Tours," *Annals of Tourism Research,* vol. 14, no. 2, 1987, p. 190.

Movements became more complex in the 1970s as new destinations opened up. The U.K.–Spain route, while still important, reduced its market share to 20 percent. Links between the U.K. and France and the U.K. and the Netherlands fell below 1 percent, as did those between Scandanavia and Italy. Greece not only emerged as a new destination, but as the second most important after Spain. Of its four markets— U.K., France, West Germany, and Sweden—the U.K. was the most important. During this time major flows also developed between the U.K. and two new destinations— Malta and Portugal.

The north-south movement intensified as new southern destinations were developed, and Norway emerged as a growing originating country. The reasons for these changing flows can be explained by developments in the countries of origin, in the destinations, and in the linkage itself. Population growth in the countries of

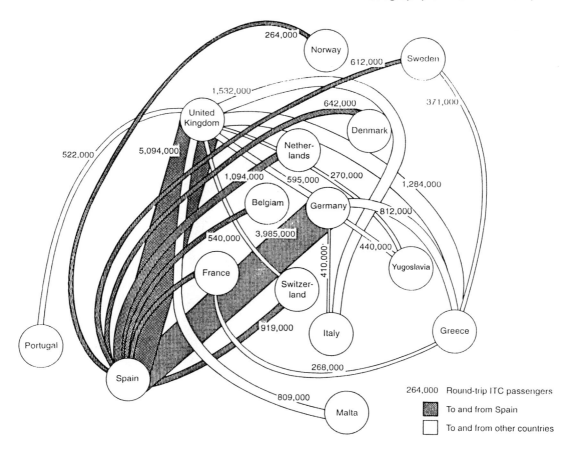

Figure 6.22   Major Intra-ECAC ITC flows (for 1980). *Source:* Douglas Pearce, "Spatial Patterns of Package Tours," *Annals of Tourism Research,* vol. 14, no. 2, 1987, p. 191.

origin is one reason for the growth. More people with sufficient discretionary income produced a larger "pie." Complementarity is another reason. The north-south traffic is strong because of the movement from colder, northern countries to warmer, southern areas around the Mediterranean coast. The distances involved and the fact that certain markets, in particular the U.K. and some destinations: are insular explains the rise in importance of ITCs. The long coastline of Spain and the short distances involved between airport and hotel, together with the close proximity of other tourism features, lead to an ease of packaging. The availability of surplus military aircraft also helped spur the development of package tours. The Berlin airlift of 1947 and 1948 showed the advantage of having a pool of operators able to move large quantities of items on short notice. The movement of large numbers of people was seen as an appropriate use of their skills in peace time.

Yet why did the U.K. develop a strong ITC movement when France, for example, did not? To answer this question, it is necessary to examine the characteristics of the countries more closely. First, France has an attractive coastline of its own. Second, it is relatively close to and has overland links with other Mediterranean countries. Third, the French as a nation are very individualistic. Fourth, there have been a number of industry practices which induced the potential for ITCs. These included such things as high commissions by travel agents and restrictive practices by the authorities and parent airlines. The net result was that, in 1980, the proportion of French tourists taking an organized tour was 5 percent, while 50 percent of all British holidays abroad involved inclusive tours.

This kind of analysis shows many of the factors that must be considered in explaining and understanding the reasons for tourist flows. Only with such an understanding can future flows be predicted.

The major tourism countries outside of North America are Spain, Italy, France, the United Kingdom, West Germany, and Japan. The tourist characteristics of each will be summarized.

Spain.   Spanish receipts from international tourism are surpassed only by those of the United States. The value of tourist comsumption is approximately 10 percent of the gross domestic product.

Tourism has grown steadily since the 1950s, with annual growth rates during this time of 15 percent. The devaluation of the peseta and the Stabilization Act, which opened up the economy to foreign investment, provided additional momentum for increased tourist visits. An increasingly affluent population in northwest Europe were offered guaranteed sun, a low cost of living, a stable society, and government-controlled prices.

Foreign tour operators also played a significant role in the growth of Spanish tourism by marketing the country and organizing the flow of foreign tourists.

Foreign tourists take up more than half of all bed nights in all tourist accommodations and more than 80 percent of all bed nights in hotels. About 40 percent of all visitors to Spain are excursionists (visits lasting less than 24 hours), with heavy representation from Portugal and France. In terms of bed nights, the most important markets are the British, the West Germans, and the French. The first two account for over one third of all bed nights in hotels and graded pensions. The West German market has been steadily increasing and accounts for one in every 8 visitors.

Over 60 percent of visitors to Spain arrive by land. The French and the Portuguese predominate in the land route, but large numbers of Germans arrive by auto also. Over 30 percent arrive by air, with the British dominating this market, followed by the Germans. These two nationalities account for about 60 percent of air arrivals. Significant numbers of French and Portuguese visitors arrive by rail, while sea arrivals account for only 3 percent of foreign visitors.

Italy.   The Italian outbound market has been the fastest growing in Europe, averaging 20 percent annual growth in recent years. In 1985 28 million Italian vacationers—half the population—took 30 million trips. Of these, about 10 percent were to international destinations, up from 6 percent in 1981.

Almost two thirds of Italians travel within Europe, but North America and North Africa also sell well and represent just under 10 percent each of outbound travel. The most popular destination countries are France, Spain, Yugoslavia, Greece, and the United Kingdom.

The four major tourist markets, which account for over 70 percent of total visitors, are Switzerland, bringing in just under one in every four visitors, closely followed by West Germany (22 percent), with France and Austria accounting for 16 and 10 percent respectively. There has been a continued growth of visitors from Yugoslavia and the United States, while the number of British tourists has declined in recent years.

France.   Just under 60 percent of French adults take an annual holiday of four or more days. Over 80 percent of the 60 million trips taken in 1985 were within France. The average trip taken was 29 days. From 1975 to 1987 domestic travel grew 41 percent, while international has increased 51 percent. However, the proportions of domestic to international trips have remained relatively constant.

Seasonally, nearly two thirds of holiday trips are taken in summer, one third in winter. The most popular summer destination is Spain followed, at some distance, by Italy, Greece, and Portugal. Favored winter destinations are Spain, Morocco, the United Kingdom, West Germany, and Switzerland.

It is projected that by the year 2000 the French will take 77.5 million trips. They will be slightly less dependent on the automobile and more likely to travel by plane.

Seven generating countries account for over 80 percent of France's tourists. West Germany heads the list, bringing in one quarter of the France's visitors. The United Kingdom accounts for 16 percent of the total, while the Netherlands and Switzerland both account for 10 percent. Belgium, the United States, and Italy bring in 9, 8, and 7 percent respectively. In recent years growth rates have been experienced from the United States, Germany, Italy, and Switzerland.

United Kingdom.   In 1986 U.K. residents took 24 million trips and spent 300 million nights abroad, an average length of stay of 12.5 nights. Approximately two thirds of all trips are for pleasure.

The most important element of the U.K. outbound market is the inclusive tour (IT). Sales of the IT have doubled in volume between 1979 and 1986 and now account for over 60 percent of all U.K. travel to destinations abroad. In an inclusive tour the price of the travel and accommodations cannot be separated out. Other parts of the holiday may be included also, such as entertainment, excursions, and car rental.

The most popular destinations are those on the "sun routes" to southern Europe. Spain attracts over 20 percent of British tourists, over two thirds of them in inclusive tours. France is a close second as a destination favorite, followed, at some distance, by Greece with less than 8 percent of the market, and Italy with less than 5 percent. U.K. traffic to France is essentially non-IT independent travelers traveling by car and trailer via a Channel ferry crossing. North America captures about 2 percent of the total outbound market.

The market is very sensitive to prices and, correspondingly, exchange rates have a great deal of influence on travel patterns. Since 1979 the proportion of outbound visits by air and sea has remained fairly constant at 60:40.

Recent years have seen an increase in the popularity of self-catering villas and apartments. It is equivalent to one third of the hotel sector. This has given rise to a demand for "seat-only" sales which, by some estimates, account for 10 to 20 percent of all air ITs. The outbound market is very seasonal, with most holidays being taken during July, August and September.

Four countries account for half of the visitors to the United Kingdom. In order, they are the United States, Ireland, France, and West Germany. The next five most important countries—Belgium, Canada, Italy, Austria, and the Netherlands—account for an additional 20 percent of all tourist arrivals.

It is likely that growth in the volume of travel abroad will come from short breaks of two to five nights and in additional holidays rather than for annual summer vacations.

West Germany.   Because of their geographical position, the strength of their economy, and the ease of cross-border travel, West Germans travel more internationally than any other people. They generate greater than one-and-one-half times more overnights abroad than their closest contender, the U.S.A., and 40 percent more than the U.K., France and Italy combined.

Just under 60 percent of West Germans 14 years and older take vacation trips each year. The travel intensity rate (number of travelers as a percentage of the population) increased enormously during the sixties and seventies, going from 28 percent in 1960 to 57 percent in 1985. At the same time the proportion of domestic travelers to all travelers fell from two thirds in 1960 to one third in 1985. The vast majority of the vacation market consists of visits to other European countries. Less than 10 percent of the holidays of five or more nights taken abroad are spent outside Europe.

The most favored vacation destinations for West Germany are Italy, Spain, and Austria. Italy owes much of its popularity to the ease of access by car. Nearly 60 percent of all holiday trips and at least half of all trips abroad are by auto. There has been, however, a steady increase in coach and rail travel over the past 15 years. The importance of Austria can be traced to its location as a transit country on the way to Italy, Yugoslavia, Hungary, and Greece. France is the fourth most popular destination, while the fastest growing vacation destination is Yugoslavia. The value of this country for the money is a major factor in its growth in popularity.

The most popular long-haul destinations are North America, followed by the Far East.

Approximately two thirds of all West German travelers make their own travel arrangements independent of any travel agent or tour operator. The high number of independent trips can, in great part, be explained by the amount of trips taken by auto vacationers who are more likely to plan things themselves. This percentage, however, has been declining in recent years as people realize that it may be more expensive to organize their own vacations.

There have been several recent trends in West German tourism:[7]

1. Increase in foreign travel, in particular to the Mediterranean countries for the sun and the high country in the Alps in winter.
2. Increase in second and third trips, primarily to domestic destinations.
3. Increase in visiting different areas.
4. Increase in level of activity on vacation, particularly hiking and walking.
5. Increase in popularity of vacation homes. Vacation homes and apartments have risen in popularity, since they allow the opportunity to be independent and self-sufficient.

Between 1983 and 1995 the long-haul vacation market is expected to triple in size, largely at the expense of the more traditional short-haul charter destinations. By 1995, however, the long-haul vacation market will still represent only 20 percent of nights spent abroad. While Sweden and Switzerland have a travel intensity approaching 70 percent, it seems that the West German outbound market is near maturity and that the majority of any increase in its size will come from an increase in additional holidays as opposed to an increase in the base number of vacations taken.

Japan.   The Japanese represent the fastest-growing, consistently growing outbound market in the world. This growth began in 1964 when restrictions on outbound travel were first relaxed. The growth can be attributed to such things as the post-war development of Japan as an industrial power, which led to an increase in expendable income that was available to most Japanese. In addition, outbound travel has increasingly become recognized in Japan as an important part of life's experiences. Developments in the industry also helped. In 1973 there was an increase in Japanese traveling abroad of 64 percent despite the shock of rising oil prices and problems with supply. During that year the number of packaged tours being offered increased dramatically, while bulk air fares to Hawaii, a major market, increased only slightly and fares to the west coast of the U.S. actually declined.

The total number of Japanese traveling abroad remains a small percentage of the total population. The numbers are increasing quite dramatically, however, to the point where Japan is regarded as a "mature" market with much growth ahead. The importance of the Japanese market is seen, not only from the numbers traveling abroad, but also from the fact that those who do travel spend a great deal of money on a per-capita basis.

The top five destinations for the outbound market are Hawaii, South Korea, Hong Kong, Taiwan, and Singapore. Nearly 20 percent of all outbound travel is to Hawaii. Well over half of all Japanese travelers to the United States visit Hawaii.

[7]Becker, Christopher, "Domestic Tourism in FRG: Trends and Problems, *Annals of Tourism Research*, vol. 14, no. 4, 1987, pp. 520–523.

When the figures to Hawaii and Guam are subtracted, the actual visitors to the U.S. are low, less than to many European countries. However, the United States is growing in popularity as a destination, in great part because it is the major foreign culture with most impact in Japan. More and more Japanese are visiting the mainland and moving across the country from the west to the east coast.

Destinations in Asia are next in importance after Hawaii. In Europe the major destinations are France, Italy, Switzerland, and the United Kingdom. The attraction of mountain scenery and the activity of Swiss tour operators account for the numbers to Switzerland.

Although the numbers visiting Australia and New Zealand are low, both countries have experienced recent growth rates.

The Japanese travel for many of the same reasons as other markets. "Curiosity," "sightseeing," "shopping," and "seeing beautiful natural landscapes" are reasons commonly given for traveling. The importance of exploring different cultures is a major motivation for visiting the west. They are extremely security conscious and, also, do not travel to countries where they perceive they are not liked.

After years of growth the honeymoon travel market has stabilized as fewer couples are now getting married. The peak number of marriages occurred in 1975 and was related to the post-war baby boom. There has, however, been an increase in the "office ladies" market. As women get married later and have access to their own income for longer and become more important in travel decision making, this market is likely to grow. However, older travelers still make up the majority of outbound travelers.

The Japanese continue to work longer hours and, consequently, have less time off for travel than workers in any other industrialized country. Larger companies have only recently begun giving employees a week off in the summer. On the other hand, 70 percent of Japanese companies give holidays of four or more days during the "Golden Week" in March. August and March, the period of the "Golden Week" holidays, account for 20 percent of all outbound travel.

It is forecast that in 1995 the Japanese will take 14 million trips abroad, of which over 60 percent will be long-haul. These long-haul trips will account for 87 percent of trip-nights spent abroad.

REFERENCES

BAILEY, MURRAY, "Japan Outbound: A Study of the Japanese Travelling Abroad," *Travel & Tourism Analyst*, April 1986, pp. 13–23.

BECKER, CHRISTOPHER, "Domestic Tourism in FRG: Trends and Problems, Annals of Tourism Research, vol. 14, no. 4, 1987, pp. 516–530.

BERROL, ED, "USA Outbound," *Travel & Tourism Analyst,* August 1986, pp. 3–18.

BONIFACE, BRIAN G. and CHRISTOPHER P. COOPER, *The Geography of Travel and Tourism* (London, England, Heinemann Professional Publishing, 1987).

COOK, NANCY, "West German Outbound: A Study of the West Germans Travelling Abroad," *Travel & Tourism Analyst,* June 1986, pp. 27–38.

Cook, Suzanne, "1988 Summer Travel Forecast," paper presented at the nineteenth annual conference of The Travel and Tourism Research Association, 1988.

Frechtling, Douglas, "US Domestic Holiday Travel," *Travel & Tourism Analyst,* November 1986, pp. 3–18.

Middleton, Victor, "U.K. Outbound," *Travel & Tourism Analyst,* December 1986, pp. 17–27.

1991 Outlook for Travel & Tourism (Washington, D.C., U.S. Travel Data Center, 1990).

National Travel Survey, Full Year Report (Washington, D.C., U.S. Travel Data Center, various years).

Pearce, Douglas, "Spatial Patterns of Package Tours," *Annals of Tourism Research,* vol. 14, no. 2, 1987, pp. 183–197.

Salmon, Keith, "Spain: National Report No. 103," *International Tourism Quarterly,* No. 3, 1985, pp. 20–41.

Touriscope: Tourism in Canada—1988 (Ottawa, Ontario, Statistics Canada, 1988).

Tourism Policy and International Tourism in OECD Countries (Paris, Organization for Economic Cooperation and Development, 1990).

Travel Industry World Yearbook: The Big Picture—1988 (New York, Child & Waters Inc., 1988).

Travel & Leisure's World Travel Overview 1988–1989 (New York, Travel & Leisure, 1988).

Travel Trends in 1988 (Washington, D.C., U.S. Travel Data Center, 1989).

United States Travel and Tourism Administration, "In-Flight Survey: U.S. Travelers to Mexico and Overseas Countries, 1987" (Washington, D.C., 1988).

United Stated Travel and Tourism Administration, "In-Flight Survey: Overseas and Mexican Visitors to the United States, 1987" (Washington, D.C., 1988).

Wynegar, Don, "Forecasts for Inbound Travel to the USA in 1986 and 1987," *Travel & Tourism Analyst,* March 1986, pp. 5–18.

EXERCISE

The leading international destinations and patterns of arrivals from the main tourist generating countries are shown in Table 6.4 for 1989. Plot these flows on a map of the world (Figure 6.E1). What factors explain these flows? Can you determine specific principles to explain these flows? Use the principles which explain these tourist movements to identify other potential geographic markets for each major destination.

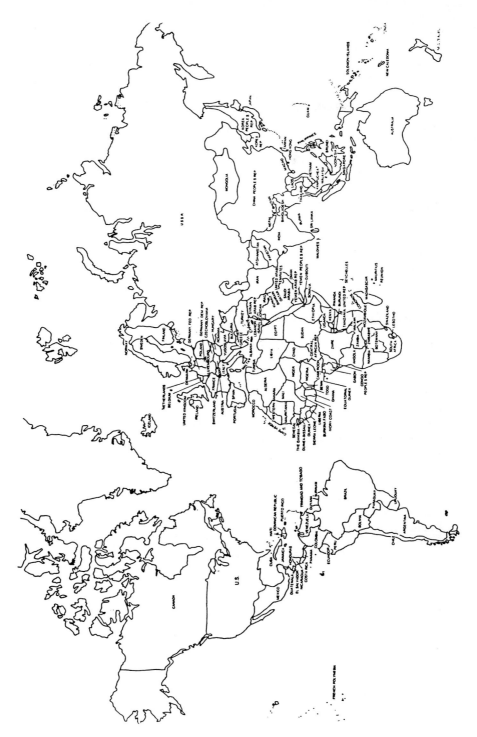

Figure 6.E1 Map of the World

205

7

MODES OF TRAVEL:

Travel Alternatives

"Far away is far away only if you don't go there,"

O Povo, *Brazil, quoted in* Reader's Digest.

The means travelers use to reach their destinations is the subject of this chapter.

A model is presented to explain the reasons people select one transportation mode over another. Marketing implications for the various modes are suggested.

An in-depth treatment of each of the travel modes is provided. The rise and fall of travel by rail is chronicled and its competitive edge today defined. The major change through which ocean liners have gone is the shift from scheduled to cruise trips. The reasons and ramifications are explained. Automobile travel is the single most predominant mode in North America. The extent and advantages of automobile travel to the tourist are covered in a section that includes material on recreational vehicles and rental cars. The airplane has had a revolutionary impact on tourism. The history, scope, and significance of travel by air is an important part of this chapter. The importance of bus travel is indiciated by the fact that the industry annually carries more passengers and provides service to more destinations than any other common carrier mode.

This subject would not be complete without a consideration of the effects of energy problems on travel modes. A summary of responses to energy problems is given.

A final segment suggests that travel may face competition from a rather unusual source—the telecommunications industry. As people are able to "travel electronically," will the same technological advances that aided travel's growth contribute to its demise?

LEARNING OBJECTIVES

Having read this chapter, you should be able to:

1. Describe the criteria people use to select their preferred modes of transportation.
2. Describe the major growth in air and automobile travel since World War II.
3. Explain the recent trends in the popularity of cruises.
4. Describe the increasing importance of the bus charter and tour market, and the typical reasons why people select this mode of transportation.
5. Explain the characteristics of demand and supply that affect the marketing of passenger transportation.
6. Explain the reasons for the demise of passenger travel by train and scheduled ocean liners.

There can be no doubt that the development of new transportation modes, routes, and alternatives has opened up the world to tourism. People travel either in their own private mode of transportation or alternatively use a group travel mode offered by a common carrier. The following diagram (Figure 7.1) defines today's major travel alternatives:

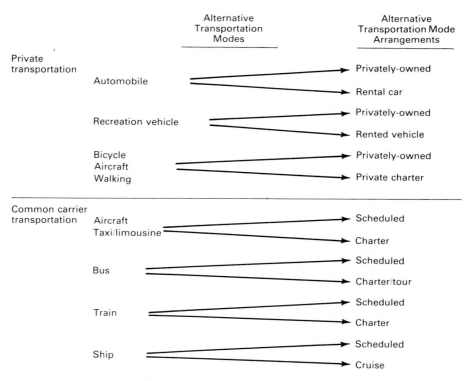

Figure 7.1 Travel alternatives

TRANSPORTATION MODE SELECTION DECISIONS

Model

Why do people select one transportation mode over another for business and pleasure/personal trips? Many theories have been put forward on mode selection decision processes. Most theorists, however, consistently identify availability, frequency, cost/price, speed/time, and comfort/luxury as the mode decision variables. Other factors that have been suggested are safety, convenience, ground services, terminal facilities and locations, status and prestige, and departure and arrival times. People in different segments of the travel market place varying degrees of value or utility on these criteria. For example, a business traveler is unlikely to have the same value perceptions as a pleasure traveler. Speed/time and departure/arrival times may be all-important to the business traveler, while cost/price may be the pleasure traveler's first criterion. One useful classification of selection variables and values has been put forward by Sheth.[1] He suggests that travelers choose a travel mode based upon the actual compared to the desired performance on five dimensions, namely the functional, aesthetic/emotional, social/organizational, situational, and curiosity utilities of the alternative modes. The functional utility of a mode is simply its likely performance for a specific purpose. Departure and arrival times, safety records, the directness of routes, and the absence of stops or transfers are examples of functional considerations. The functional utility is the *net* outcome of the positive and negative evaluations the user makes of a particular mode.

Aesthetic or emotional reasons relate to such things as fear and social concerns that affect fundamental values of the individual. Often users associate strong emotional feelings derived from early experiences with a mode of travel. Associations are also developed by early childhood socialization processes. These values often manifest themselves in terms of such things as style, interior/exterior decoration, comfort, luxury, and safety.

Social or organizational utilities refer to the stereotypes that various transportation modes have. For example, bus tours and cruises have been stereotyped as being a mode of transportation and vacation type for persons of retirement age. This may dissuade younger people from taking bus tours and cruises.

Situational utilities refer to the locational convenience of the mode and its terminal facilities to the traveler—the *total* set of activities associated with a trip. This might relate to the time in getting to and from the airport as a disincentive to fly. It is similar to the functional utilities except that the stress is on the activities that are antecedent and subsequent to the actual travel itself.

Curiosity utility concerns the traveler's tendency to try something because it is new and different. For example, flying transatlantic on the Concorde when it first came into service may have had a high curiosity value for many travelers. This feeling is usually short-lived.

---

[1] Jagdish N. Sheth, "A Psychological Model of Travel Mode Selection," in *Advance in Consumer Research, vol. 3* (Proceedings of the Association for Consumer Research, Sixth Annual Conference, 1975), p. 426.

Bus tours have been stereotyped as being a mode of transportation for persons of retirement age

The model presumes that the individual has desired expectations on these five utilities and that the discrepancy between the image or perception of the utility and the actual experience determines the extent to which that mode of travel is acceptable or not.

Certain supply-oriented and trip-purpose/traveler-profile factors influence the traveler's utility assessments. The availability of the mode—the number and convenience of flights, for example—influences the perception of functional and situational utilities. Mode design, including the variety of products or services offered to customers, affects the image of functional, curiosity, and aesthetic/emotional utilities. The way the mode is operated—on-time departures, quality of service, careful handling of the traveler's luggage—influence perceptions of functional and situational utilities. The way the mode is marketed wiill have an impact on functional, situational and social/organizational utilities. For example, advertisements for cruises that show young people onboard having a great time may dispel perceptions that cruises are just for older people. These supply-oriented factors combine to generate differential psychological utilities for different travel modes. These factors often create mass acceptance or rejection of a mode in the marketplace.

In a similar fashion, various demand-oriented factors produce differential psychological utilities for the same mode among a cross section of users, leading to acceptance by some and rejection by others. Differences can be expected on the basis of personal demographics, personal life-style, familiarity and satisfaction of the traveler with a particular mode, and the purpose of the trip. For example, income level will influence the mode of transportation chosen. A person who values status will select a way of traveling that reflects that self-image. A person traveling from

New York to London on business may choose to fly but, when traveling the same route on vacation, may choose to sail on the QEII.

Last, there is the impact of unexpected events. A death in the family requiring attendance at a funeral will influence a person to fly to the destination, even if the cost is perceived as too high or if the individual is afraid of flying.

Sheth's explanation of the transportation mode selection decision-making process is illustrated in Figure 7.2.

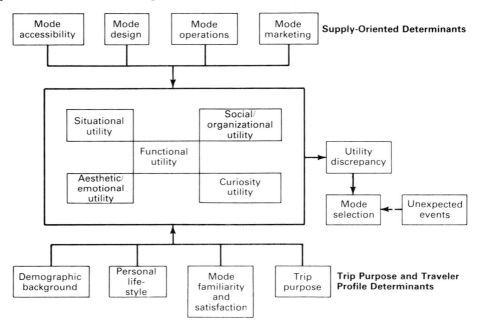

*Needed to account for occasional deviations from regular mode usage.

ADAPTED FROM: Jagdish N. Sheth, "A Psychological Model of Travel Mode Selection," in *Advances in Consumer Research, vol. 3* (Proceedings of the Association for Consumer Research, Sixth Annual Conference, 1975), p. 426.

Figure 7.2   Travel mode selection model

Travel by Train

It seems fitting to begin our review of individual transportation modes by talking about trains. They opened up the North American continent from its Atlantic to Pacific coasts, and they were the major stimulant in the nineteenth and early twentieth centuries to vacations within the United States, Canada, and Europe. The first transcontinental route in the United States was completed in 1869. Britain had its first organized tour on the train in 1841 when Thomas Cook put together an excursion between Leicester and Loughborough. In 1851, three million English took the train to the Great Exhibition that was being staged in London. The train was also instrumental in Britain for spurring the development of many of its seaside resorts.

In the United States in 1929, the first year for which comprehensive statistics are available, approximately 780.5 million paying passengers took the train. This number had fallen to about 268.9 million by 1975. In fact, the heydays of the train in most of the major developed countries lasted approximately one-hundred years from the 1830's to the 1930's. In the 1920's and 1930's the automobile began to gain more popularity as a passenger transportation mode, mainly drawing away traffic from the train. Rail passenger traffic in the United States began to decline in the 1920's during what some persons have called the "age of abundant energy." It was not until the mid-1970's to the early 1980's, which could be referred to as the "age of uncertain energy," that the slide in the popularity of the train as a passenger transportation mode seemed to be halted. Although the U.S. railroads had accounted for approximately 77 percent of the nation's common carrier passenger miles in 1929, this market share had slid to about 7 percent by 1970.

The demise of the railway as a passenger travel mode was so alarming that in 1958 the U.S. Interstate Commerce Commission (ICC) ordered a detailed study of the situation. The results of this study became known as the Hosmer Report, and it predicted the eventual disappearance of the train as a passenger travel mode in the United States. The recommendations of the Hosmer Report were never officially accepted, and it was not until 1970 that the federal government took some concrete action to improve the failing rail-passenger travel business. In October 1970, the Rail Passenger Service Act became law. The act created the National Railroad Passenger Corporation, now commonly known as Amtrak. Amtrak began its operations in May 1971, and it was intended to be a profit-making corporation. Canada's equivalent of Amtrak, Via Rail Canada, was created in 1977 in the form of a crown corporation.

Both Amtrak and Via Rail have the sole national responsibility for marketing and providing intercity passenger rail transportation. Since their inception both organizations have been successful in increasing passenger volumes that had been falling continuously beforehand. They have done so primarily by improving the equipment and services they offer, and by more effectively promoting the benefits of traveling by train.

Several attempts have been made to determine why travelers select the train as a transportation mode. Four factors seem to emerge consistently; these are cost/price, comfort, safety, and the ability to see the area through which the train is passing. Via Rail's on-board surveys of business travelers have identified user cost, convenience, travel time, and comfort as being of prime importance. A survey of Amtrak users has indicated that travelers favored the train for the following reasons:

Safety
Ability to look out of trains and see interesting things enroute
Ability to get up and walk around
Arriving at the destination rested and relaxed
Personal comfort

Negative factors often associated or perceived with rail travel are slowness in reaching the destination, relatively inflexible departure times, and a lack of quality in food service. Trains are certainly perceivied as being a very safe mode of transportation and are thought to attract a significant "fear of flying" market. Recent promotions by Via Rail and Amtrak have emphasized the rest and relaxation benefits of taking the train. They have also begun to point out that the downtown-to-downtown routing of trains actually saves passengers time.

In West Germany, France, and Japan, high-speed trains have been developed and are in operation. These trains travel faster than the automobile, and they actually cut down on the time that passengers would take to drive between major cities. For example, the Train Grande Vitesse in France travels at over two-hundred kilometers per hour between Paris and Lyons, reducing this trip to about two hours. (A comparable trip by car takes a minimum of five hours.) Via Rail introduced some of these LRC (light, rapid, comfortable) trains to Canada in 1984.

In the 1970s and 1980s British Rail became more marketing-oriented in an attempt to increase its share of the tourist market. Their policies were helped by shortages of gas and the subsequent increase in prices which had a dampening effect on travel by private automobile. Package holidays were developed with hotel companies, while other programs were aimed at the rail enthusiasts who were mainly interested in the trip itself. Originally organized as charters, these excursions were later provided on scheduled services. Longer packages, which offered travelers a short break away from home, were introduced. The high speed 125 train—capable of speeds of 125 miles per hour—now offers a service competitive in time from city center to city center with that of the airlines.

Of the 12,720,000 person trips of one or more nights by international visitors to Canada in 1987, only 58,000 were generated by rail travel. Travel by train accounted for only 0.7 percent of all person trips in 1986. This compared to 3.7 percent for bus travel and 7.7 percent for travel by air. In the early 1980s, intercity train travel was beginning to show significant increases. In the period 1980–81, business travelers using first-class service grew tremendously. The upward effect of energy-cost increases on airline ticket prices was a main contributor to this trend. However, demand has fallen off in the latter part of the 1980s. While the number of person trips of one or more nights away from home has risen slightly, the number attributed to train travel has declined.

In the United States AMTRAK generated over $760 million in passenger revenue in 1988. However, they still operated at a loss. Their revenue to cost ratio in that year was 69 percent. They have had success in developing travel on their short-distance corridors. These include the Northeast Corridor between New York and Washington, the Empire Corridor between New York City and Niagara Falls, and the Los Angeles to San Diego Corridor. Approximately 70 percent of all intercity rail and air travelers in the Northeast Corridor travel on AMTRAK. The long distance market has been approached through the All Aboard America Fare, which divides the country into three zones with the fare varying by the number of zones crossed. These fares involve few restrictions and allow for up to three free stopovers.

Before leaving the subject of rail travel, the role of railways as tourist attractions should be highlighted. Short-duration train excursions through scenic surroundings have proven to be major attractions to pleasure travelers in recent years. For example, two major excursions of this type in Canada are the Algoma Central Railway in Ontario and the Royal Hudson Steam Train in British Columbia. The Strasburg Railroad in Pennsylvania is a U.S. example of a popular train excursion of this type. The experience of riding aboard the Orient Express, made famous by Agatha Christie, was reintroduced in 1983 after a complete restoration of the train had been completed.

Travel by Ship

Travel by ship did in fact precede travel by train, but it was not until the mid-nineteenth century that travel by ocean liner began to show its greatest prominence. Although ocean liners used to provide an important link for passengers between continents, water transport today plays two main roles in travel and tourism—ferrying and cruising.

The steamship era had its beginnings in the 1840s. Sir Samuel Cunard pioneered the first transatlantic scheduled liner trips at that time. Just as the automobile led to the demise of the train, the introduction of intercontinental commercial airline service precipitated the rapid decline in the use of ships as a scheduled passenger transportation mode. In 1957, transatlantic ship traffic reached a new post-World War II high as some 1,036,000 passengers were transported on ocean liners. Although travel by ship remained strong for several years thereafter, the aircraft had by 1958 eclipsed it in terms of volumes of transatlantic passengers.

Transatlantic scheduled passenger ship traffic declined rapidly. Passenger departures from New York fell from approximately 500,000 in 1960 to 50,000 in 1975. So great has been the decline in scheduled liner passenger transport volumes that it has almost completely disappeared in ths modern-day era.

Cruising has taken the place of scheduled liner services.

Ships built for ocean crossings do not make the best cruise ships. Ocean liners were large and heavy—built to withstand the rigors of the Atlantic ocean. As a result the fuel costs were great. As cruising took off, the lines built ships specifically for cruising. These ships were smaller—800 to 850 passengers and 20,000 tons—lighter, with smaller cabins, larger deck space and public areas, and a smaller ratio of staff to passengers. Fuel costs were also reduced by spending time in more ports, a move that satisfied passengers. Recent building has resulted in overcapacity in the industry. As a result, between 1983 and 1989 there were 16 major mergers and consolidations.

About two thirds of the passengers who cruise each year are from the United States. The number of cruise passengers in the United States has increased by 600 percent since 1970—from 500,000 to 3 million in 1987. However it is estimated that only 5 percent of the U.S. population have taken a cruise in the past 15 years, while there are an additional 28 million potential customers—8.6 percent of the population—who have both the time and the money to buy a cruise.

The size of the market is limited by a number of negative perceptions about cruising. First, there is the association that ships have with isolation, storms, and seasickness. Second, many perceive that ships are slow, cramped, and boring, with regimented activities. However, cruises offer high levels of satisfaction, with the industry reporting an 85 percent repeat business ratio.

The dominance of Americans in the cruise market has meant that strict standards have been imposed on all foreign flag carriers which operate out of U.S. ports. There are strict standards expected in the areas of hygiene, safety, and financial protection for passengers in case of the collapse of the carrier.

The most important areas for cruises from the U.S. are the Caribbean, the Mexican Riviera, and Alaska. Seventy percent of all passengers leaving the United States cruise in this area. The popularity of the Caribbean has been built on warm winter weather, good sailing conditions, the ability to visit a number of varied ports in a relatively short time, and the capacity of Miami International Airport to bring in passengers. The Port of Miami projects that 4 million passengers will embark from there by 1995.

Approximately 15 percent of the total number of cruises sail out of San Diego and Los Angeles, largely to the Mexican Riviera. Cruises to Alaska originate in San Francisco, Seattle, and Vancouver, Canada. Because of the Passenger Service Act of 1886, foreign vessels may sail from Seattle, but those passengers may not disembark in Alaska, another U.S. port. Passengers must return to Seattle via a foreign port. Since most vessels operating out of the U.S. are foreign, this poses a problem for Seattle. A popular package to Alaska is the seven-day fly and cruise package which involves a one-way trip by ship and a fly or land return. This type of tourism must originate in neighboring Vancouver, Canada. Restrictions on the number of cruise ships into Glacier Bay have placed limits on the growth of this market.

The smallest segment of the U.S. cruise market-about 5 percent—is around the Hawaiian islands.

About 90 percent of passengers in the North American market are U.S. citizens, with the largest proportion of the remainder being Canadians. Small but growing numbers come from Mexico, Brazil, and Venezuela, with a very small number from Europe.

In the United States about 60 percent of the cruises are for seven days, while approximately 30 percent are in the three- to four-day market. These latter appeal to segments of the market who have traditionally avoided cruising because of high prices or perceived boredom. They tend to originate in Miami and include two to three ports of call. The market is drawn on a regional basis from Florida and other nearby states. There has also been an increase in the popularity of one-day "cruises to nowhere." Here the passengers do not know their itineraries prior to the departure of the ship.

One study of U.S. cruise passengers[2] identified three segments of the market. The *cruise enthusiast* represents one-third of the market of nationally representative cruisers. They prefer a blend of features on each cruise, but place little emphasis on

[2]William K. Tripp, "A Market Segmentation Strategy for Cruise Package Design," paper presented at the Nineteenth Annual Conference of The Travel and Tourism Association, 1988.

About 5 percent of the U.S. cruise market is around the Hawaiian Islands

the actual cruise line. As cruise enthusiasts, they are willing to pay the higher price for the experience. Forty percent of the market is identified as *cruise line* or *brand* oriented. Two of the leading cruise lines were the dominant choice for these cruisers. While they do not prefer the luxury-priced cruise, neither were they strictly price-sensitive. The third segment is the *price-sensitive* cruiser. Comprising about one quarter of the existing cruise market, this group is looking to get the longest cruise possible visiting the greatest number of ports for their money.

The next largest cruise markets are West Germany, the United Kingdom, and Australia, although this latter consists almost entirely of domestic round-the-coast cruises. Vacationers from West Germany and the United Kingdom cruise mainly in the Mediterranean, which, in the mid-1980s, was the second most popular cruising destination in the world. The U.S. market comprised only 20 percent of the total Meditteranean market in the mid-1980s.

One of the reasons for the growth of the U.S. market to the Caribbean was the deregulation of the airlines in 1978 which allowed cruise operators to offer cheap fly-cruise packages. Flights from northern cities were heavily subsidized. By flying to Florida, the time spent in warm weather was maximized. In theory deregulation in Europe could offer the same boost to Meditteranean cruising. However, deregulation in Europe has continued to proceed at a very slow pace. In addition, marketing campaigns in Europe must take into account the diversity of national markets and cannot benefit from economies of scale enjoyed in the U.S. The Mediterranean cruise industry took off in the late 1960s and early 1970s as lines expanded their fleets. The extra capacity generated additional interest from tour operators in West Germany and the United Kingdom. This interest coincided with significant growth in the overseas inclusive vacation market.

While West Germany and the United Kingdom make up the largest market segments for Mediterranean cruises, the development of the market differs greatly in both countries. In the United Kingdom tour operators set up their own cruise divisions, negotiating charter deal with cruise lines. The initial effect was to increase the size of the market. However, lack of expertise and experience in operating a cruise ship meant that the narrow profit margins that were a result of concentrating on volume and market share put companies at risk. Tour operators now have no operating responsibility for the cruise and tend to feature cruises in their vacation brochures on an open-sale basis with no charter commitments. A major problem for cruise operators in the United Kingdom is the difficulty of selling a rather sophisticated travel product through retail travel agents. By some estimates less than one in ten travel agents are productive in terms of cruise sales, lacking the expertise or experience to sell cruises.

In West Germany tour operators dominate the cruise booking market. In part this is because a flight must be packaged in to get the vacationer from West Germany to the Mediterranean. About 75 percent of the Mediterranean cruise market travels on tour-operated chartered ships.

In the United States travel agents sell about 95 percent of all sea vacations.

One of the fastest growing areas worldwide is the Far East. The major cruise routes of the world are illustrated in Figure 7.3.

Incentive travel accounts for 15 percent of all cruise berths, perhaps more in the United States. Yet, because cruise lines tend to be registered in foreign countries, they have been unable to penetrate the business or convention markets to a larger extent. Legal restrictions prevent the tax deductability of convention-oriented expenses if they are incurred with a cruise on a non-U.S. flag vessel.

Most cruise-line marketing has been oriented to capturing market share from other lines rather than to increasing the size of the total market. Some lines have successfully found themselves a market niche. Premier Cruise Lines has developed a unique package by combining three days in Disney World with four days of cruising. In addition to appealing to families who want a balanced vacation, the competition will find the product truly difficult to duplicate. Another niche has been developed by Windstar Sail Cruises. Aimed at the affluent active vacationers who would normally not cruise, Windstar markets cruises on a sail-cruising ship, which offers a wide variety of water sports activities and visits to remote, small islands that traditional ships do not visit.

Ships are becoming both bigger and smaller. In the 1970's the optimum size for a cruise was seen as being 20,000 tons and 750–850 passengers. Excess capacity in the industry has meant that operators are looking to larger ships to spread overheads and to capitalize on economies of scale. The cruise ships being built now tend to be in the 40,000 tons range. The commercial life of a cruise ship is about 20 years, but there is increased pressure on them to make a profit by the third year of operation. This has resulted in a selling orientation on the part of the operators to fill their berths through heavy price discounting. The corresponding battle for market share has done little to expand the size of the market for cruises.

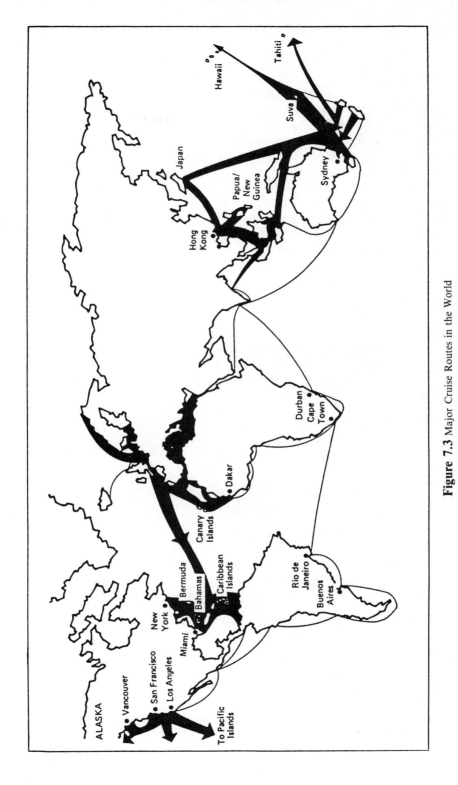

Figure 7.3 Major Cruise Routes in the World

Source: J. Christopher, *The Businees of Tourism*, 2d ed Pittman Publishers, London,

217

Ships are also becoming smaller with the development of a number of ships with a capacity of 150 passengers or less to cruise the more remote waters of the world.

Cruises share a kinship with other unique transportation offerings, such as traveling on the Orient Express train, in that they are more of a vacation experience than a transportation mode. The romance of cruising has been heavily promoted, and this has been helped along by a popular television program known as *Love Boat*. Today cruise ships are like portable resort hotels that ply the waters of the Caribbean, Mediterranean, and other regions.

Special interest or hobby-type cruises have grown, packaging such things as the theater, gourmet dining, bridge, flower arranging, aquasports, jazz, country and western music, and many other themes and activities. This ties in closely with the trend toward more vacation travel for the purpose of learning or improving upon a leisure time or recreation activity.

The ship remains an important passenger transportation mode in its role as a ferry service. The "floating bridge" is an essential complement to the automobile, recreational vehicle, and bus in many parts of the world, including the English Channel, the Irish Sea, the Hebridean Islands of Scotland, the North Sea, the Maritime provinces and British Columbian coast in Canada, and on the Great Lakes.

The ship remains an important transportation mode in its role as a ferry service

As with its "partner" in history, the train, the ship also has considerable importance in tourism as an attraction. Examples of short-duration sightseeing cruise-ship attractions are abundant in North America and elsewhere. Characteristically, these cruises are for a day or for an even shorter period of length. Viewing scenic surroundings is the major focus of many of these operations, including those featuring the Thousand Islands (New York-Ontario), the Mississippi River, Muskoka Lakes (Ontario), Niagara Falls (New York-Ontario) and many others. Other cruises combine nostalgia with scenic viewing. Steamer and riverboat cruises are examples of these. One study of a restored steamer sightseeing cruise operation indicated that its appeals were in learning about the history of steamships and the history of the surrounding area, seeing the scenic beauty of the area, watching the visible operations of steam engines, and using its dining/bar service.

Travel by Automobile

The introduction of the automobile precipitated the demise of the train in most developed countries. As mentioned earlier, the automobile as a passenger travel mode gained its momentum as far back as the 1920s. Lundgren refers to the period after this as the automobile-based travel-system era characterized by "individual travel diffusion." He explained this point as follows:

> The private motor car siphoned off a larger portion of the potential travel market from the established mechanisms and routes toward a new tour destination concept with quite different distance dimensions. Thus, the (international) tourist dollar became diffused over wider territories.[3]

The advent of the automobile, therefore, spread the benefits of tourism more widely and provided more and more people with the means to travel individually or in private, smaller groups. Nonprivate group travel had been a characteristic of the railway and steamship era that preceded the automobile. Due to the nature of the railroad's infrastructure and the limited routing possibilities by water, travel patterns were very predictable. People could only get to the destinations to which the trains and steamships would take them. Many famous resort areas, resort hotels, and city center hotels flourished at important destination and staging points for the trains and steamships. With the increased popularity of the automobile, the attractiveness of these areas and facilities began to decline, and many of them suffered significantly.

The automobile brought about a more random pattern of travel movements, opened up new destinations, and spurred the development of elaborate networks of new automobile-oriented facilities and services along highways and roads. The tourist court, motel, and the motor hotel were three of the new facility types that developed in the United States and Canada after World War II. In fact, the whole development pattern in North America was fashioned directly and indirectly to accommodate the private automobile.

Traveling by automobile is now the single most predominant travel mode in North America. Most travel surveys have shown that automobile trips account for over 85 percent of the pleasure and personal and business trips taken by Canadians and 75 percent of intercity passenger miles in the U.S. The nuclear family unit traveling by private automobile has been the major source of pleasure and personal travel demand and the marketing target for a majority of tourist-oriented businesses in the

---

[3]Jan O. J. Lundgren, "The Development of the Tourist Travel Systems," *The Tourist Review,* January 1973, p. 10.

United States and Canada. It is not difficult to see why, considering the statistics that have been discussed earlier.

Just as they have done with the train, many experts have tried to explain why the automobile is selected over other modes of transportation. One such report[4] found the major attractive attributes of the automobile to be as follows:

Control of the route and the stops enroute

Control of departure times

Ability to carry baggage and equipment easily

Low out-of-pocket expense of traveling with three or more persons

Freedom to use the automobile once the destination is reached

Other surveys have shown that many persons perceive the automobile to be a relatively safe mode of transportation, and others indicate that people like driving as a recreational experience.

Two other important aspects of automobile travel that remain to be discussed are recreation vehicles and car rentals, or as they are called in Britain "car hires." These two areas have developed so extensively in North America and elsewhere that they are now both significant elements of tourism.

The recreation vehicle, or RV for short, was a further extension of North Americans' love affair with the automobile. The President's Commission on Americans Outdoors found that 43 percent of American adults consider driving for pleasure a main recreational pastime. RVs offer the opportunity to combine driving and camping. RVs have grown tremendously in popularity in recent years. New RV sales in the United States in 1987 topped 200,000. There has been an increased interest in touring the country in rented recreational vehicles.

The trends in production and ownership of RVs in the 1970s were closely tied to the "energy crisis" pattern, as the graphs shown in Figure 7.4 indicates. This figure indicates that the major drops in RV production in the United States occurred in 1974 and 1979 following the main "crisis" periods in 1973 and early 1979. Ownership has now increased since 1979.

Since World War II, camping has grown rapidly in popularity in North America and elsewhere. The United States has more than 14,000 public and private parks and commercial campgrounds containing about a million campsites. Canada has been said to have 250,000 campsites and Mexico 10,000 campsites. The increasing popularity of the RV led directly to a number of new camping phenomena during the 1980's, including the franchised, condominium, and time-sharing condominium campgrounds. In a condominium campground the RV owner buys the site and pays a monthly fee for the maintenance of the common areas. In a time-share operation the use of the site for one or more weeks each year is purchased.

Yet another phenomenon to which the RV has led is that of many European

[4]Marcia Stockton and Harriet Thiele, *Group Transportation to Public Recreation Areas: Literature Review* (Madison, WI, University of Wisconsin Extension, May 1980).

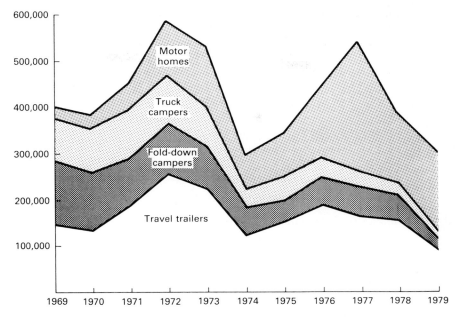

NOTE: 1976-79 shipments of motor homes includes B-2 chassis estimates.

SOURCES: Automotive News 1979 Data Book Issue (from Recreation Vehicle Industry Association).
Canadian Government Office of Tourism, *Planning for the 80's: A Perspective of Canada's Private Campground Industry* (Ottawa, Ontario, Canadian Government Office of Tourism, 1980).

Figure 7.4   Trends in shipments of recreational vehicles in the United States, 1969–1979. NOTE: 1976–79 shipments of motor homes include B-2 chassis estimates.

visitors to Canada and the United States renting these vehicles for cross-continent trips. Many companies have been formed to provide this service to overseas pleasure travelers.

The rental of automobiles was another sector of tourism that demonstrated rapid growth in the 1970's and 1980's. The highest utilization of rental cars takes place on Mondays to Fridays by business travelers (about 75 percent of the total business). Weekend demand comes primarily from pleasure/personal travelers. A high proportion of car rentals takes place at airport terminals in North America and, therefore, it is understandable that the fortunes of this business are closely tied to that of the airline industry. The top four car rental companies account for 95 percent of airport market share. Hertz has 32 percent of the market; Avis has 25 percent, while National and Budget each have 19 percent.

Recent changes in the rental car business have included significant shifts in car fleets towards smaller and more fuel-efficient models. Fly-drive packages offering rental cars together with flights have made significant gains in popularity as more travelers have begun to substitute air travel for travel by the private automobile.

Travel by Air

Continuing our chronology of transportation modes, the airplane had a revolutionary impact on tourism from World War II onward. This point was already highlighted in Chapter 6 where the plane's refashioning of the global travel market was mentioned.

The history of air transportation can be divided into at least three parts, pre-World War II, World War II, and post-World War II. The first period, from 1918 to 1938, was a period of infancy for the scheduled airlines of North America, while the modern era can be termed the mass air-travel era. The present era has been marked by steadily improving aircraft technology and the advent of air charters and of the packaged vacation, or as it has sometimes been called, the "inclusive" or "all-inclusive vacation."

A few dates in history allow us to put the facts discussed later in perspective:

The first scheduled domestic air service in the United States was in 1918 on the New York-Philadelphia-Washington route.

In 1939 Pan American operated the first transatlantic passenger flight using a "clipper" flying boat.

BOAC (now British Airways) offered its first transatlantic passenger service in 1946.

BEA (now also a part of British Airways) offered its first passenger service to Europe in 1946.

The first of the wide-bodied jets was introduced into service in 1970.

As was just pointed out, the modern era of air travel really began at the end of World War II. Between 1945 and 1960 we have seen that travelers increasingly switched from trains and ships to automobiles and airplanes. In the 1960s this trend continued, and airfare reductions further stimulated air travel. The 1970s was the decade of the wide-bodied jets, and it was then that the "mass tourism" phrase was coined.

In 1975 the airlines of the world carried 534 million passengers and achieved a passenger load factor—number of passengers carried divided by number of seats available—of 59 percent. In 1987 over 1 billion passengers were carried, and the airlines achieved a passenger load factor of 67 percent.

The North Atlantic route is the world's largest international route, accounting for approximately 20 percent of the world's internationally scheduled passenger-kilometers and 10 percent of the world's internationally scheduled passengers. The proportion of trans-Atlantic passengers carried on charters has declined in recent years, as a result of more attractive fares with fewer restrictions provided by the scheduled airlines.

Of the world's total domestic scheduled air traffic, 79 percent is carried by the United States—57 percent of the total—and the U.S.S.R., with 22 percent. Rapid growth in domestic air traffic is presently being felt in the United States, Brazil, and Australia, although many feel that air traffic in the United States is in the mature stage of the life-cycle. At this stage of the life-cycle, sales continue to grow but at a decreasing rate. The Boeing Company estimated that revenue passenger miles grew worldwide at an annual rate of 5.9 percent between 1986 and 1990, while the Federal Aviation Administration estimates that U.S. air traffic will grow at an annual rate of 5 percent between 1986 and the year 2000.

The United States carries 17 percent of all international air traffic, while the United Kingdom carries 10 percent. Trans-Pacific routes are the fastest growing international routes in the world. It is difficult to operate non-stop trans-Pacific routes between Asian countries and the U.S. The 1990's will see the introduction of advanced-technology long-range aircraft capable of flying nonstop on these routes. This will undoubtedly make trans-Pacific travel more enticing to the pleasure traveler. For the airlines nonstop service offers greater economic performance as more fuel is used on takeoffs and landings than when the plane achieves cruising altitude.

Almost 40 percent of the world's air travelers who are carried on scheduled airlines travel on U.S. air carriers. Eight major U.S. airlines control 95 percent of the market. Air travel accounts for about 90 percent of common-carrier passenger miles in the United States. In 1971 only 49 percent of the U.S. population had ever flown. In 1987 that percentage was 79 percent. This represents 126 million out of 175 million adults. In that one year alone 30 percent of the U.S. population reported that they had taken a flight.

In Canada travel by air accounted for 14 percent of all person trips of one or more nights made to, from, and within Canada in 1986. Air carriers recorded 86 percent of intercity passenger revenue in Canada in that same year.

In 1978 the U.S. airline industry was deregulated. The National Transportation Act of 1988 accomplished the same thing in Canada. The impact of deregulation will be explored in more detail in Chapter 11.

Air transportation can be broken down into scheduled and nonscheduled or charter operations. Scheduled services fly on defined routes and times on the basis of published timetables irrespective of passenger-load factors. Scheduled airlines may be publicly or privately owned. The amount of private vs. public ownership will vary with the political philosophy of the host country. In most countries the public airline will be the national flag carrier and is usually the only airline designated for international flights. In the U.S. the airlines are privately owned. U.S. carriers are designated as either major carriers, national carriers, or regional carriers. Carriers are classified as major carriers if they have annual gross revenues of over $1 billion. They include United, American, and Continental airlines. National carriers have annual gross revenues of $75 million to $1 billion. Companies that run commuter airlines are now classified as regional air carriers. A large regional airline is one whose annual gross revenue falls between $10 and $75 million, while a small regional is one with annual gross revenue of less than $10 million.

In Canada airlines are designated as Level I, II, III, or IV carriers, depending upon their size. There are three Level I carriers in Canada—Air Canada, Canadian Airlines, and Wardair. These three airlines account for over 80 percent of passenger revenue. For many years Wardair flew only charter services, primarily to Europe, the U.S., and the Caribbean. In 1985, however, it introduced scheduled service on some of its most popular international routes, and in 1986 it began scheduled domestic operations. Its routes are restricted to major cities because, unlike Air Canada and Canadian Airlines, it does not have any working agreements with feeder airlines to provide scheduled service from smaller airports to and from the major centers with smaller airplanes.

Charter airlines fly only on routes where they can generate high passenger-load factors—typically 85 to 90 percent. Because they are not obligated to fly regardless of load factor, their revenues per flight are much higher than those of scheduled airlines. Additionally, they keep costs low by saving on marketing, offering less in the way of service both in the air and on the ground, and having lower overhead costs. In this way they can offer, in many cases, substantial fare savings over scheduled airlines. As a result, charters tend to operate to high-volume destinations. A recent trend has been the tendency for tour operators to form or take over their own charter airlines in order to ensure seat availability for their passengers. Prior to the 1960s, charters could operate only through closed groups made up of members of a club or organization whose main purpose was something other than low-cost travel. Many bogus clubs were formed, and policing became increasingly difficult. The 1970s saw a liberalization of charter restrictions. The scheduled airlines had a difficult dilemma. They did not wish to discount prices for passengers who were willing to pay the higher fares, but they wished to capture a share of the market. One answer was the advanced purchase excursion fare (APEX), which required passengers to book and pay for their trip in advance.

Increased capacity brought about by deregulation has meant that scheduled airlines were forced to reduce prices to attract the traveler. The result was that charter flights lost their price competitive edge in many cases.

Charter airlines accounted for 20 percent of passenger revenue in Canada in 1986. The largest charter airlines in Canada are Nationair, based on Montreal, and Worldways, which is headquartered in Toronto. Both operate large jets to Europe, the Caribbean, and Mexico.

Charters remain popular in Europe, where deregulation is moving slowly. The success of charter airlines in Europe will depend upon their ability to move with the changing demands of the market. This might mean selling seats only (instead of an air-land package), offering scheduled flights, and new, less crowded destinations. There will also be a demand for more activity holidays, winter vacations, and more flexible packages, such as multi-center and fly-drive options. Increased demands for higher-quality service will also challenge charter operators.

A major problem for airlines—particularly in North America—is the safety of air travel. The average age of the U.S. fleet is nearly 13 years. This compares to 8 years for German and Japanese fleets and 10 years for British Airways planes. The hub and spoke system of airline routes puts increased pressure on the planes. Instead of flying from one airport to the destination, passengers gather at outlying airports and fly to hub airports where they catch connecting flights to their destinations. This means more takeoffs, which cause the body of a jetliner to expand and elongate by an inch to accommodate changes in air pressure. The supersonic Concorde jet grows by 11 inches. While aircraft design takes expansion into account, the more takeoffs and landings, the faster metal fatigue begins to set in.

New aircraft are being developed, however, that are safer as well as being more fuel efficient. The newest 747-400 jet airliner can fly from New York to Tokyo entirely by computer and, if necessary, even land automatically. It offers more range, better fuel economy, and lower operating costs. Its 8,400-mile range almost doubles that of the original 747, while it consumes one third less fuel. One factor that makes it particularly safe is the triple and quadruple redundancy of its systems. Complete failure of any one system is a million-to-one possibility.

In addition, concern has been expressed over security at airports. The General Accounting Office reported the existence of security deficiencies at U.S. high-security airports. Chief among these were ineffective passenger screening and inadequate controls over personnel identification systems and over access to those parts of the airport where aircraft operate. Concern for safety has been felt in the response of travelers to terrorist threats. Concern about terrorist attacks on Americans in the mid-1980's led to dramatic reductions in travel from the U.S. to Europe, for example.

In summary, the airplane has in the post-World War II era taken over as the major international and intercontinental transportation mode. It also predominates among the common carriers in domestic transportation in the United States and Canada. It is a particularly important mode for the business travelers who have the time factor as a major consideration. Additionally, charter flights, since their introduction, have become increasingly important as vacation travel modes, particularly in Europe.

Travel by Bus and Motor Coach

The third principal common-carrier mode is the bus. The term *bus* is used to describe intercity travel while *Coach* or *motor coach* describes charter or tour travel.

Only 15 percent of person trips on Greyhound were for pleasure travel, excluding visits to friends and relatives. This compares to 43 percent of total person trips in the U.S. for this purpose. As can be seen, most travel by bus is of the intercity type.

In 1983 the bus industry in the United States was deregulated. Prior to that time an Interstate Commerce Commission-licensed bus company or tour broker had to prove need before receiving authority to operate. At that time few motor coach operators employed marketing representatives. Many had a small individual tour program, and most had a larger group tour program. The majority were still charter operators, while many operated regular group service as well. Tour brokers were generally smaller operations, many tied to a retail travel agency. The impact of deregulation can be seen in the growth of motor coach companies. In 1983 there were 1500 motor coach companies licensed by the ICC. In 1989 that figure had jumped to 3600. Tour brokers were deregulated out of existence. Many became tour operators or tour organizers.

In 1987 the second largest motor coach company in the U.S., Trailways, Inc., was purchased by the nation's largest, Greyhound Lines, Inc. A recent study of Greyhound riders revealed five distinct market segments:[5]

Roost-to-Roost Travelers represent 27 percent of total Greyhound passengers. Extremely traditional and family and home oriented, they like the experience of traveling and like the whole family to participate. They do not, however, like to travel far from home and family.

Spontaneous/Impetuous Mixers make up 21 percent of riders. They travel for the social experience, preferring to start out alone and meet new people. They are more likely to be on vacation; however, plans for the trip were probably made less than two weeks in advance.

Independent Explorers make up 10 percent of total passengers. They are dedicated travelers who like to explore new and unusual places. They perceive travel as too much fun to hurry through. They tend to choose destinations that are tourist-oriented and travel to see new places rather than friends and relatives. Enjoying the social experience of meeting strangers, they have a good time when traveling alone.

Apprehensive Travelers are 17 percent of total ridership. Worried and anxious about traveling, they are negative to the whole idea of travel.

Nervous Travelers represent 16 percent of passengers. They are compulsive about keeping to a schedule. Lacking curiosity, they do not find travel enjoyable and cannot enjoy a trip without a familiar companion.

For the purposes of tourism, the potential lies with the use of coaches for touring vacations. In 1986 the National Tour Foundation explored in depth the market's response to domestic group travel.[6] People go on tours for reasons that are practical and emotional. The practical benefits are convenience, expertise, safety, and price.

Tours are convenient in that the vacation can be spent concentrating on the experience rather than on making the arrangements. Having someone else doing the driving is important in terms of dealing with city traffic, driving in unfamiliar areas, and spending time reading maps rather than enjoying the scenery. Tours offer the convenience of being picked up and delivered to hotels, sights, and entertainment. Accommodations and event tickets are guaranteed. This is particularly important for high-season events or times. Last, the idea of the baggage being taken care of is appreciated. This is particularly true for single women and older people.

People who take tours feel that they can see and do more than if they were traveling alone. There is the feeling that the operator has the expertise to select the best places to see. Because of this, participants can actually see more because they do not have to spend time evaluating all of the options. Also, there is safety in numbers. This is particularly true for older or female travelers and for urban or "strange" destinations.

The fixed price of a tour is an important feature. The most important part,

[5]Gary Graley, *1989 Outlook For Bus Travel,* paper presented at the U.S. Travel Data Center's 1989 Travel Outlook Forum, 1988.

[6]*T.R.I.P. Report and NTA Group Travel Summit Procoeedings 1986,* Lexington, Kentucky, National Tour Foundation, 1986.

however, is not the absolute price but the fact that the costs are known beforehand. There is little or no danger of being halfway through one's vacation and running out of money because of poor budgeting. The tour is prepaid. The only other costs are some meals, sightseeing, and shopping.

People also take tours for emotional reasons—companionship, an opportunity to learn, shared activities, and security. Tours offer the opportunity to meet new people and make new friends. Many see it as an opportunity to get an overview of a destination—to discover and learn. Adventure touring is important to younger travelers, while historical touring is mentioned by older tourists.

Group travel is seen as a way of participating in activities with others who have the same interests. This can include physical activity tours such as skiing or water sports, as well as theater, garden, or historic homes tours. In all of this, there is the opportunity to be further educated in a particular area.

Group travel can include historic tours

The security angle comes from the feeling of being an insider even in a strange place. This is an emotional appeal compared to the physical feeling of safety, explored previously.

The negative images that people have about tours fall into four categories—perceptions of the bus, the tour experience, the group concept, and the types of people who take tours. For a number of people, tours are associated rather negatively with buses. The term *motor coach* is used by the industry to designate touring buses. Particularly in Europe most coaches are extremely comfortable with videos, hostesses who serve drinks, and reclining seats. However, despite the fact that such equipment is available in the United States (albeit on a lesser scale), the image brought to mind is too often the school or commuter bus. The bus is seen as too slow, too confining, and too uncomfortable. It is viewed as a cheap and old-fashioned way to travel. Travelers also have a negative image of bus terminals and view this as an undesirable place to start a vacation. Additionally, some people—particularly men—dislike the idea of giving up control to the coach driver. They complain about not being able to control the lights, the fans, or where and when to stop.

For people who do not take tours, the tour experience itself is perceived negatively. Touring, to many, is equated with regimentation, inflexibility, and passivity. The tour is seen as a shallow, boring, and impersonal experience. There are those who think that, rather than receiving the advantages of group power, being part of a group involves getting second-class treatment from hotels and restaurants. Yet another barrier to be overcome in selling tours is the group aspect of the tour. There is a fear of not relating well to other members of the group. To many people, a vacation involves having personal space and freedom. Being part of a group limits both. Last, many have a negative perception of the kinds of people who take tours. People who travel as part of a group are seen by many, stereotypically, as infirm, older, inexperienced travelers. This translates into a personality profile of tourgoers as passive and lacking in self-confidence.

To rid itself of these negatives, those who package tours need to be more innovative in upgrading the image and the content of tours. Perhaps even the word *tour* needs to be changed into "adventure holiday, expedition, discovery trip or excursion." Different modes of transportation can be used in conjunction with each other—air to get the traveler there and coach to see the destination. Hub-and-spoke concepts can be used to bring people to a destination where they can relax on their own. Shorter mini-trips can be packaged with more free time, and tours themed around recreational activities can be developed to appeal to the younger, more active crowd.

MARKETING OF PASSENGER TRANSPORTATION

Transportation marketing seeks to satisfy the needs and wants of the traveler by providing the right mix of services. To appreciate the difficulties involved, it is necessary to consider the characteristics of supply and demand for passenger transportation.

Characteristics of Demand

The demand for passenger transportation has a number of characteristics, all of which affect the way a company markets. First, demand is instantaneous. For carriers there is great uncertainty as to what the demand will be on a particular day at a particular time between two points. While past trends are useful, they cannot be totally reliable. When demand is greater than supply, travelers are unhappy. By the time adjustments are made to supply more capacity, customers may have changed carriers or found an alternate means of transportation. The tendency, then, would be to provide more capacity than is needed. Overcapacity shows up in the load factor. In a perfect match of supply and demand, load factor would be 100 percent. Anything less indicates the measure of overcapacity. The challenge in marketing is to create programs to fill each plane, train, ship, or bus on each trip.

Overcapacity is the result, not only of instantaneous demand, but also of the variability of demand. Demand for transportation is not the same each hour of each day of each month. It shows what is known as *peaks and valleys.* At certain times of the day or week or month, there is great demand; at other times the demand is light. Yet sufficient planes, boats, trains, buses, and terminal facilities have to be provided to cover peak demand. The result is that excess capital has to be invested. As a result, the costs of operation are increased. How should demand be priced? Should the peak traveler pay more than the off-peak traveler? Peak-load pricing states that those traveling at peak times should pay more for the extra capacity provided to meet peak demand. Some off-peak pricing is found in the airline industry and with passenger trains. Reduced mid-week and night fares are an attempt at peak pricing.

The third characteristic of demand is that there is, in fact, more than one type or segment of demand for transportation. In its simplest terms, demand is either business demand or pleasure demand. The motivations, frequencies, and responses to price are different. The motivation for the business traveler is *derived*—that is, the demand for travel exists because of the desire to do business in a particular territory. Demand for the pleasure travel is *primary*—the motivation is to travel to a vacation spot. The distinction is important because derived demand tends to be affected more by factors external to the transportation industry. No matter how good the services between New York and Detroit, if business is bad in Detroit, travel demand may go down. A reduction in fares, for example, may affect primary demand but may not affect derived demand.

The business traveler travels more frequently than does the pleasure traveler. This makes this person very valuable to the airline. Frequent Flyer programs, which offer rewards based on miles traveled, have been targeted toward the business traveler in an attempt to capture customer loyalty. As mentioned above, derived demand may not be affected by changes in price. The company may absorb a fare increase as a cost of doing business. The business traveler may choose a more convenient, but more expensive, flight, since the company and not the individual is paying for it.

In some situations people can substitute one mode of transportation for another—train for plane, bus for train, and so on. This affects the way transportation is marketed. *Elasticity* is the economic term for the sensitivity of travelers to changes in price and service. An elastic demand is sensitive to substitution; an inelastic demand is not. The extent of elasticity is dependent upon the price of the other mode of transportation and the type of demand. Pleasure travel is more price elastic than is business travel; primary demand is more price elastic than derived demand. When people choose how to travel, the decision is made on the basis of price, prestige, comfort, speed, and convenience. AMTRAK could successfully compete with the plane on certain distances on the basis of several of these factors.

Competition also exists within one mode between carriers. Generally prices and the speed of the journey are the same or similar among competing carriers. Carriers must then market on the basis of the factors mentioned above—prestige, comfort and convenience. Often a small change in departure time can capture a significant number of passengers. This explains much of the congestion at airports at certain times—everyone wants to offer flights at what are felt to be the most convenient times for the traveler.

A sixth aspect of demand is that some transportation modes offer more than one type of service. Passengers can fly economy, business class, or first class; trains also offer various classes of service. The different types of service are in competition with each other. Airlines, for example, have to decide the proportions of first class, business class, and economy or tourist class seats to offer on a plane. They then decide what additional services are necessary to justify the price differential—more leg room, better meals, free drinks, and the like.

Demand for transportation is also affected by the relationship between the price charged and the income level of the traveler. Pleasure travel is income elastic; that is, the demand for travel is affected by changes in the traveler's income. Economists say that demand is elastic when a reduction in price results in more demand that will result in more revenue. (Revenue equals price times number demanded.) The company gains revenue because the increased demand brought about by a drop in price makes up for the reduced price. Similarly, an inelastic demand is one where a reduction in price results in less revenue generated. More passengers may be attracted but not in sufficient numbers to offset the loss of revenue brought about by the reduction in price. Pleasure travel is discretionary—the traveler has a choice of whether or not to travel. An increase in price may mean the traveler will postpone the vacation.

Business travel is also influenced by the income of the company. Much business travel is essential; some is discretionary. Businesses may turn to teleconferencing as a way of reducing the travel bill if costs increase too much. Last, the demand for travel makes itself felt in a demand for nonprice items. The frequency of departures, the condition of the equipment, the service of the employees, on-time performance—the whole package—is often more important than the price. Companies have to find out what is important to the different segments of the market they are going after (the list will be different for each) and seek to provide it.

Characteristics of Supply

Just as the marketing of transportation is affected by the characteristics of demand, so is it influenced by the supply characteristics. The supply of transportation is unique in eight distinct ways. First, the transportation industry is a capital-intensive industry. Terminals and equipment cost a great deal of money. The costs are also *indivisible*—airlines cannot put "half a plane" in the air if the plane is only half full. Because the industry is capital-intensive and much of the capital is borrowed, many of the costs of running a transportation company are fixed—interest on the debt must be paid in full, irrespective of the number of passengers and revenue. This puts a great deal of pressure on management to fill seats that would otherwise be empty. This may affect both the promotional and pricing decisions.

Related to this previous point is the fact that transportation costs are "sunk" with few alternatives. The cost of a plane is "sunk" in that the company has incurred the cost of it. It is up to the company to generate revenue to pay for the plane. It is not like a light that can be turned off, thereby saving money. The plane also has few alternative uses. It can fly; it might be possible to sell it as a unique type of restaurant, but essentially all the company can do with it is fly it. This puts additional pressure on the company to use the resource rather than have it lie idle. The large amounts of sunk costs also mean that there is a tendency to use old equipment rather than invest in more modern (and more expensive) equipment.

A third characteristic of supply is that, although demand is instantaneous, supply is not. There is a long time between planning for a piece of equipment and placing the order for it, between placing the order and getting it, and between putting it into service and scrapping it. Thus, while demand can shift very quickly, it takes a great deal of time to adjust supply. A company must live with its mistakes for a very long time.

Because of the high level of fixed costs, the incremental costs of operation are small. The incremental cost is the cost of adding one more unit. The running costs of adding another passenger car to a train, another bus to a route, or even a plane between two points is small compared to the costs of the actual piece of equipment. If a plane is scheduled to fly anyway, the cost of an additional passenger is incredibly small—an extra meal and some services. This means that, above a certain point, it makes economic sense to reduce the price charged in order to get some revenue coming in. This is the rationale behind discount fares. Airlines can predict, based on past records, how many seats on a particular flight will sell within a week before a flight. The people who book within a week before a flight are usually business people. Assume, for example, that on a particular flight 80% of the seats will be bought at the regular fare in the last week before the flight. This means that the airline can sell up to 20% of the seats at a discount for people who will book and pay for tickets more than seven days before the flight.

A fifth characteristic is that supply cannot be stored for future use. A grocery store can sell a can of dog food today or tomorrow or the next day. Every seat on a plane or train or bus must be sold only for that trip. The sale that is lost today is lost forever. This puts additional pressure on management to sell, sell, sell.

Transportation services must be available on a continuous basis. The traveler expects the same level of service whether it is day or night, summer or winter, if the plane is full or almost empty. Because transportation is expected to be reliable on a continuous basis, there is little opportunity to cut costs for inferior service at odd hours. This adds to the cost of providing the service.

Last, there is the problem of labor. In transporting people, the company takes on a great responsibility. Often the service—whether in operations or in maintenance—is offered 24 hours a day. Employees must be equally alert, no matter what the time. There are strict rules about the amount of time that pilots, drivers, or operators can be on duty at any one stretch. F.A.A. limits pilots to 30 hours of flying in any seven-day period. Although the operating costs are small compared to the sunk costs, they can still be considerable. Airline pilots are paid well for their skills. A further complication is that there is little opportunity for the substitution of capital for labor. This is, after all, a service business.

Marketing has the task of ensuring that there is sufficient demand to utilize the supply of equipment and facilities fully. It must also ensure that there is enough of the right kind of supply to meet the demands of the passengers. Just as demand influences supply, so supply influences demand. The demand for vacations to Jamaica will influence a decision to operate flights to Jamaica; however, the existence of flights to Jamaica at times and prices appropriate to the market will stimulate demand. Marketing brings supply and demand together.

Marketing Strategies

In marketing, the offerings of the firm are known as the 4 p's—product, promotion, place, and price. In tourism it is appropriate to change the "product" to include *service* and to replace "place" with *distribution*.

Service refers to getting the ideal mix of services to satisfy existing or potential customers. This means offering transportation at the right times, in the right kinds of equipment, while giving a level of service before, during, and after the journey that will meet the needs of the customer—all while making a profit.

Most carriers use a linear route structure—the equipment travels from one point to another, turns round, and travels back. In the airline industry most fuel is used at takeoff and landing. Also, the speed of travel by plane is only appreciated on longer flights. Thus, for reasons of cost and customer benefit, jet aircraft operate in the most efficient manner when they fly on long hauls. A piece of equipment may, however, make an intermediate stop. While this increases the time and fuel costs, it can add significant additional revenue.

The airlines also operate what is known as a hub-spoke concept. Airlines have identified several major cities which serve as hubs (as in hub of a wheel) for them. Smaller towns serve as the spokes of a wheel connected to these hubs. Airlines attempt to have passengers fly into their hub city on a smaller or commuter plane for connection to a larger plane for travel to their ultimate destination. Colorado Springs is a spoke city for the Denver hub (on Continental), which is itself a spoke city for Chicago, which is a spoke (on United) for London. Increasing hub development will result in more convenient service for passengers. There will be more nonstops as smaller cities become hubs and displace larger cities as connecting points.

Major air carriers have made increasing use of code-sharing agreements with regional airlines. Code-sharing involves the joint use by a regional carrier of a major airline's two letter designation on its air routes and usually involves a commuter traffic fleet at the major's hub. In this way, the regionals serve as feeder lines to the majors. Service is improved through more convenient ticketing and baggage checking.

The first frequent-flyer program was introduced by American Airlines in 1981. The idea was successful in building brand loyalty to a single airline. According to some sources, however, airlines owe participants more than three million round-trip domestic tickets, enough for travelers to fly 5.4 billion miles at no cost. In an attempt to minimize this cost, airlines have placed restrictions on the use of this free travel.

Service must be provided on the right kind of equipment. Equipment has two facets that must be matched—identifying the operating costs of one piece of equip-

Denver is a hub for Continental Airlines and a spoke for St. Louis on T.W.A.

ment over another while offering equipment that will attract the traveler. One example is Concorde. While this supersonic aircraft could draw passengers because of its speed and unique shape, the operating costs are so high that the potential market is relatively small.

Scheduling is a major marketing weapon for carriers. Traveling from point A to point B leaves little opportunity for differentiating one firm from another. Offering departures at times most convenient for the passenger is one way to do this. Unfortunately, everyone wants to do this. The result, certainly in the airline industry, is severe congestion at the most popular times. Generally speaking, the demand for business travel peaks on Monday mornings and Friday afternoons. It is also heavy during the morning and early evening hours during the week—Monday through Thursday. The demand for pleasure travel peaks on Friday evenings, Sunday afternoons, and early evenings.

Service can also be altered by such things as upgrading the quality of the interior of the vehicle. Research has shown that, for flights of less than two hours, the most influential factor in a choice of flight is the schedule (70 percent), followed by the airline or airplane (18 percent), and the fare (11 percent). However, for flights longer than five hours, the passengers' priorities change. Sixty-three percent rate the airline or airplane as being most important, compared to 19 percent who listed schedule, and 17 percent who listed fare as most influential. SAS used results like this to change the interior of their intercontinental planes. They had found, additionally, that on 767s people are less comfortable in the middle seats. Given the importance of the airplane in making a trip of five hours or more, they removed the middle seats from their business class cabin. Service could also be altered by providing tie-ins with other modes, such as fly-cruise or rail/drive.

The subject of promotion will be dealt with in greater detail towards the end of the book. However, several points can be made. Promotion can be seen as the communications link between carrier and passenger. It is the responsibility of the carrier to communicate its message effectively. If the passenger has not understood, it is the fault of the carrier. To this end, it is important that clear promotional objectives be defined. These objectives should identify which target markets are to be reached, what tasks have to be done to reach the markets, who is to perform the tasks, and when they have to be completed. It is vital that the promotional theme be in synch with the marketing plan, which, in turn, must be consistent with the overall objectives of the carrier. A carrier may, for example, feel that, in order to meet its financial targets, it must emphasize "quality" and "service." The way then, to reach the target is to stress quality and service. These concepts become the essence of the marketing campaign. As part of that plan, communicating the ideas of service and quality to the public becomes the promotional objective.

Distribution involves the mechanisms by which passengers can obtain the information they need to make a trip choice and, having made that choice, make the necessary reservations. Direct distribution occurs when passengers get in touch with the carriers directly. Indirect distribution is when the sale is made through an intermediary.

This latter has taken four forms. First is the emergence of independent companies to handle all aspects of travel. It might involve a wholesaler who arranges the specifics of a tour, for example; it might be a retail travel agent who serves as an independent distributor for a wholesaler or carrier; it may be one of the wholesaler-retailers who package their own tours or who buy packages from other wholesalers for distribution.

A second movement has been the marketing of tourism, either regionally or nationally. Countries, provinces, and states promote travel to their particular destinations. This effort supplements the marketing plans of the carriers. In some cases the marketing effort of the carrier can dovetail with that of the destination.

A third trend has been the coordination of marketing plans by various private-sector companies. Tie-ins between airlines and hotels or bus lines and various attractions are becoming more prevalent.

Last, there is the movement toward vertical integration. Airlines have moved in to take control of hotels and car-rental agencies. This has been an attempt to develop a "one-stop travel shop" experience for the traveler. The strategy recently backfired for United Airlines, which formed Allegis—an amalgamation of airline, hotel, and car-rental companies. Under stockholder pressure they were forced to divest themselves of the nonairline parts of the company.

When the majority of airline passengers consisted of people traveling on business and rather wealthy tourists, the airlines felt that the demand for travel was inelastic. That is, if prices were reduced, any increase in number of passengers would not produce more revenue. Because of this and a fear that open pricing would lead to price wars that might result in bankruptcy for smaller airlines, airline pricing was closely controlled. Pricing was a reflection of operating costs. The average costs of carriers serving particular markets were calculated, and a reasonable return on investment

A third trend has been the coordination of marketing plans by various private-sector companies

was added to come up with the price that could be charged. With deregulation a new era has come to pricing in transportation in general and in the airline industry in particular.

Three economic concepts are important when looking at pricing alternatives. They are the ideas of *differential pricing,* the *contribution theory,* and the *incremental concept.* Underlying differential pricing is the idea that there is not one demand curve but many. A separate demand exists for coach than exists for first-class; separate demand exists for travel from Denver to New York than from New York to Denver. As such, carriers can calculate how price-sensitive demand is in one particular class or on one particular route and price accordingly. The demand for business travel, for example, is probably less sensitive to price changes than the demand for pleasure travel on that same route at that same time. A higher price can be charged where demand is inelastic.

The idea of contribution theory is that prices should be set at the level that contributes most to paying off fixed costs while still allowing traffic to move. The fare charged might be low on a route where the demand is elastic and higher where demand is inelastic. In effect, segments of the market that are price inelastic are subsidizing others that are price elastic. How low should the price be? Low enough to ensure the passenger travels while contributing as much as possible to paying off fixed costs.

Tied to the ideas above is the incremental concept. Incremental costs are those incurred by running an additional service. The operating costs of a particular plane or train are its incremental costs. Each fare should cover its incremental costs while contributing as much as possible to fixed costs and ensuring that the traffic moves. It is up to management to analyze each route and each segment of the market to price accordingly.

REFERENCES

BREDEMEIER, JUDI, "U.S. Car Rental Industry—Surviving the 1980s," *Travel & Tourism Analyst,* March 1986, pp. 47–55.

FARRIS, MARTIN T., and FORREST E. HARDING, *Passenger Transportation* (Englewood Cliffs, NJ, Prentice-Hall, Inc., 1976).

HOFTON, ANDY, "Trans-Atlantic Air Travel," *Travel & Tourism Analyst,* January 1987, pp. 3–18.

HOLLOWAY, J. CHRISTOPHER, *The Business of Tourism* (London, Pitman Publishing, 1985).

HUUTINEN, HEINI, "Charter Airlines in Europe," *Travel & Tourism Analyst,* November, 1986, pp. 19–36.

JAMES, GEORGE, "Air Travel in North America—Forecasts for the Market and its Carriers," *Travel & Tourism Analyst,* April 1986, pp. 3–12.

JENKS, CRAIG, "U.S. Airlines Hubs and Spokes," *Travel & Tourism Analyst,* August 1986, pp. 29–42.

KENDALL, K.W., BERNARD H. BOOMS and JAMES P. NEEDHAM, "The Passenger Service Act and the Transfer of Economic Impacts in the Alaska Cruise Market," paper presented at the nineteenth annual conference of The Travel and Tourism Research Association, 1988.

LEWIS, JAY and DAN SAREL, "Cruise Industry in the USA: Matching Supply and Demand by 1990," *Travel & Tourism Analyst,* August 1986, pp. 43–55.

LOVIN, CLAXTON E., "Regional/Major Airlines Partnership," paper presented at the seventeenth annual conference of The Travel and Tourism Research Association, 1986.

MATHESIN, HEIDI, "Adjusting the Aircraft Product to Emerging Customer Needs," paper presented at the nineteenth annual conference of The Travel and Tourism Research Association, 1988.

MEAD, KENNETH M., "Security at Nation's Highest Risk Airports," Statement before the Subcommittee on Government Activities and Transportation, Committee on Government Operations, House of Representatives, December 17, 1987.

MORRELL, PETER, "European Air Travel," *Travel & Tourism Analyst,* March 1986, pp. 33–46.

"Motorcoach Deregulation and Traveling Marketing—5 Years Later," Special Report distributed by the National Motorcoach Marketing Network, Inc., 1988.

PIESLEY, TONY, "Cruise Industry in the Mediterranean—Prospects for 1986 and Beyond," *Travel & Tourism Analyst,* April 1986, pp. 24–37.

REICHEL, GERNOT P., "Pleasure Cruises in the 1990s," paper presented at the seventeenth annual conference of The Travel and Tourism Research Association, 1986.

Touriscope 1988: Tourism in Canada, A Statistical Digest (Ottawa, Canada, Statistics Canada, 1988).

TRIPP, WILLIAM K., "A Market Segmentation Strategy for Cruise Package Design," paper presented at the nineteenth annual conference of The Travel and Tourism Association, 1988.

World Travel Overview 1988/1989 (New York, Travel & Leisure, 1988).

U.S. TRAVEL DATA CENTER, *1988 Outlook For Travel and Tourism* (Washington, DC, 1987).

U.S. TRAVEL DATA CENTER, *1989 Outlook For Travel and Tourism* (Washington, DC, 1988).

WATERS, SOMERSET R., *Travel Industry World Yearbook: The Big Picture 1988* (New York, Child & Waters, Inc., 1988).

WELLS, ALEXANDER T., *Air Transportation* (Belmont, CA, Wadsworth Publishing Company, 1989).

EXERCISE

The National Tour Association recently sponsored research on the image of group travel and touring in the North American marketplace. Based upon the information given below and in this chapter, develop a marketing program to:

- reposition the image of group travel;
- identify market segments with tour potential;
- develop different products to overcome customer resistance;
- develop strategies and tactics to market the products developed effectively.

Group Travel and Touring Described

Consumers tend to describe group travel and touring as a type of experience, not just a method of travel. It is an experience that is shared, organized, passive, carefree.

REPEAT USERS	NON-USERS
"A relaxing way to travel"	"Too slow a way to travel."
"It's all planned for you"	"It's too regimented."
"You get special attention"	"The herd treatment"
"It's more fun"	"It's boring"
"Well paced"	"Hurry up and wait"
"You see the best things"	"You see things too quickly"
"People like me"	"Not my kind of people"

The Appeals of Groups and Touring

Practical benefits.   Someone else does all the work

Convenience: someone else does the driving, door-to-door service with group travel, entrance to events or entertainment is prearranged, baggage handling included.

Expertise: more organized and complete, see and do more on a tour, better accommodations, tour escorts handle problems.

Safety: safety in numbers.

Emotional benefits.

Companionship: meet new people and make new friendships, share experiences.

Opportunity to learn.

Shared activities: participate in hobbies and interests with like-minded people, intellectual element, gain expertise in field of interest.
Security: feeling like an insider in a strange place.

Price/value.

Value enhanced by operator's expertise and presence of tour escort.

Barriers to Group Travel.

The bus: uncomfortable or confining, cheap, old fashioned, not high tech, little glamour, relinquish control (men particularly dislike).

The tour experience: regimentation and inflexibility, shallow experience, boring experience, too passive, impersonal, less than special treatment, tourist traps.

The group concept: being constantly attached to a large number of people, fear of not relating well to group members, being cooped up on a bus, not having enough personal space and freedom, more aggravating than relaxing, hurry up and wait.

People who like to travel in groups: infirm, older, inexperienced, passive, lacking in self-confidence, all the time in the world, shallow interests.

The second part of *The Tourism System* ends with the arrival of tourists at the destination. The third part of the system looks in detail at a destination.

The aspects that define a destination are identified, and standards for the attractions and services necessary for tourism are given (Chapter 8). Chapter 9 explores the reasons that people at destinations seek tourism and considers the economic and social effects of tourism on those at a destination. Guidelines are given to ensure the "best" type of development from the destination's viewpoint.

In order to get the most benefits from tourism while minimizing the negatives, people at a destination must establish a policy (Chapter 10) within the confines of the regulatory framework (Chapter 11). Having done this, those people at the destination are free to plan (Chapter 12) and develop (Chapter 13) tourism resources for the long term benefit of the destination.

Although planning and development must take into account the characteristics of the potential tourists, the major emphasis on tourists occurs when people at the destination seek to move tourists round *The Tourism System* from origin to destination. To sell travel requires the implementation of a marketing plan. That plan can only be formulated and implemented once those at the destination have developed a policy, a plan, and a development strategy for tourism.

READINGS

This reading analyzes tourist flows from the viewpoint of a geographer. It is an all-inclusive study of the characteristics of people and places from a tourism outlook.

This reading is a chapter in a Resource Paper (No. 76–1, 1976) written by Ian M. Matley, Professor of Geography at Michigan State University, and titled *The Geography of International Tourism*. The authors wish to thank the Association of American Geographers for permission to reprint this reading.

Physical and Cultural Factors Influencing the Location of Tourism

The study and analysis of tourist flows and their patterns on the surface of the earth form the core of the geography of international tourism. We have seen the various forms of transportation which permit the rapid and widespread movement of tourists around the world. We have also looked at the methodology for the study of these flows and at the impact of tourism on the economies of places and regions. However, people do not travel considerable distances and are not willing to expend money and experience discomfort to get to a specific destination unless that place offers certain attractions which their own place of residence does not possess. In other words, flows and patterns of tourism result because of a variety of physical and cultural attractions possessed by different places which appeal to people with different backgrounds, tastes, and needs. The uneven distribution of tourism on the surface of the earth is explained to a great extent by the complex interrelationships between attractions of various types and the interests and desires of tourists.

In order to be able to explain these interrelationships and in turn the tourist movements which develop from them, the geographer needs to know the various characteristics of the people and places involved. Therefore, it is necessary to look at the various factors which make a place attractive for tourism and also at the way in which people perceive a place as attractive or not.

SUN, SEA, AND THE RESORT

Of all the factors influencing the location of tourist activities, the most important are the physical. The mass development of tourism in Europe derives from the existence, on one hand, of urbanized regions with a cool, cloudy climate and, on the other, of relatively underpopulated regions with a warm, sunny climate. It has been said that the large migration of Germans to Spain and Italy is not a reflection of an interest in Latin culture, but of the shortness and coldness of Germany's coastline (Simpson: 1968, p. 233). A large number of resorts[1] ring the Mediterranean coast for housing and feeding the worshipers of sun and sea from Northern Europe. Other amusements and entertainments may be provided, but they are sidelines to the major attractions of the sun and the beach. To many tourists, the country matters little. Spain may have bullfights and flamenco dancers and Italy may have Latin lovers and the Leaning Tower of Pisa, but what matters to most is the promise of reliable

[1]Place visited by people for the purpose of recreation, health, etc.

sunshine, warm temperatures, a beach to lie on, warm water to swim in, and clean but cheap hotels and restaurants. In fact the relative popularity of Spain in the last couple of decades over Italy and the south of France has been attributed to its relatively low prices. Yugoslavia, Romania, and Bulgaria have been the latest countries to develop their coasts for tourism and to offer low-cost vacations to sun-hungry northerners. The complex of new hotels stretching along the Black Sea coasts of Romania and Bulgaria is a good example of development designed primarily to exploit warm summer temperatures and broad sandy beaches which slope gently into a sea free from dangerous currents and jellyfish. Foreigners are housed in hotels according to nationality and language and, although trips can be made to various inland natural and cultural attractions, contact between the guest and the local people is limited.

PROBLEMS OF COASTAL RESORTS

This isolation of resort visitors from the surrounding native people is also a phenomenon of modern tourist development in areas other than Eastern Europe. In many countries new resorts and hotels are being built from scratch on empty coastlines, with tourists, waiters, cooks, and maids all coming from outside the area. This can produce an "ocean liner" atmosphere, insulated from the outside world (Simpson: 1968, pp. 233–34). It is probably true that many people like it this way, as it limits the need to communicate with foreigners and reduces contacts with possibly unpleasant or perhaps puzzling aspects of local life.

This tendency towards isolating tourists from local life runs counter to the view of tourism often propagated by writers in the communist countries. A Romanian view is that "tourism in general, including tourist geography, serves a high humanistic ideal of education, of progress and peace between peoples" (Iancu: 1976, p. 374). To a Soviet writer tourism is "a form of cultural contact between peoples of different countries" and "tourism between socialist countries plays an important role in developing social connections between them and helps to develop the world system of socialism" (Anan'yev: 1968, pp. 11–12). This somewhat idealistic view of tourism, difficult to associate with present trends in mass tourism, is tempered by the warning that "the Soviet people constantly remember that tourist exchange between socialist and capitalist countries takes place at the same time in the arena of a political and ideological struggle with its own specific features" (Anan'yev: 1968, p. 13). This last remark would suggest the advisability of isolating tourists from capitalist lands as much as possible from contacts with the local population. In fact, the attraction of the tourist mark or dollar for the governments of many of the communist countries is offset by the dangers of excessive contact between their peoples and Western tourists.

Although the Mediterranean beaches of Southern Europe and North Africa, along with those of the Black, North, and Baltic Seas, have virtually monopolized the seaside tourist trade of the Old World (Exhibit A,[2]), other continents are begin-

[2]Readers may find Exhibit A useful in locating the various place names of European and Mediterranean resort areas.

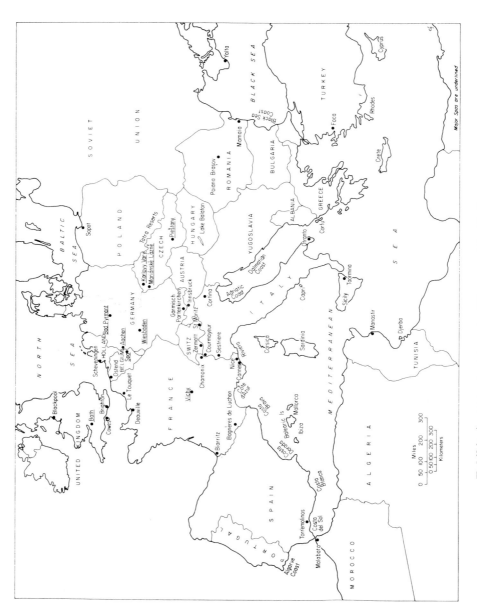

Exhibit A Major tourist resorts of Europe and the Mediterranean.

ning to develop their resources. The United States has seen the development of the Florida beaches along with those of the Carolinas, and California. Mexico has its Acapulco, and the Caribbean Islands have developed their resorts at a rapid rate during the last two decades. Uruguay attracts other Latin Americans with its excellent beaches and casinos. In West Africa, the Ivory Coast is developing a major coastal resort for foreign tourists.

This development of seaside resorts in sunnier climates has had considerable repercussions on resorts in northern Europe. With an increase in the number of persons able to afford vacations which occurred during the Victorian period in Great Britain, a number of major seaside resorts had developed. They were located mainly near large urban concentrations, the most notable being Brighton, serving the London area, and Blackpool, serving the industrial North. Their growth was speeded by the development of rapid railroad transportation (Robinson: 1972, p. 384). On the continent similar types of resorts arose, such as Scheveningen serving the Hague, Ostend serving Brussels, Deauville serving Paris, and Le Touquet serving Paris and Brussels, whereas in the United States, Atlantic City served the New York-Philadelphia region. Apart from offering the visitor a beach and the sea, and, with luck, some sunshine, these resorts developed various other attractions, such as promenades, piers, amusement galleries, dance halls, casinos, and theaters, and accommodations ranged from cheap bed-and-breakfast establishments to giant luxury hotels. The development of resorts in the Mediterranean and other sunnier and warmer regions, along with the ability of more people to afford longer vacation journeys, has led to the demise of many of the seaside resorts of northern Europe. Luxury hotels have been closed or converted to other uses and many resorts rely now for their income on the day tripper, whose range of activity has been increased greatly by the automobile, or on a more stable population of retired persons. Because of the great increase in day tourism by car and the resultant traffic congestion in resort towns, many tourists are seeking small, unspoiled villages and towns, which, in their turn, will become overcrowded.

It should be noted that the transition from northern to southern European resorts involves factors other than purely climatic ones. The earliest resort development in the Mediterranean region took place on the French Côte d'Azur. The period from 1865 until World War I saw the rise of Nice and Cannes as winter resorts for the moneyed classes from northern Europe and England, in particular. These luxury resorts have undergone considerable changes since World War II, as a new class of tourist has arisen with different tastes and more limited finances than the prewar group. The new group consists mainly of working people, who have their vacations in the summer months, a fact which has changed Nice into a predominantly summer resort (Latouche: 1963, pp. 369–70). The rich have in turn joined the "jet set," who now seek the more exotic and distant shores of Acapulco or Tahiti. Nice and Cannes have lost their old glory and must now compete in the field of the new mass tourism not only with newer resorts on the French Mediterranean coast, especially in the Languedoc-Roussillon region, but with a host of others in neighboring countries. Between the war and 1955 the French Riviera had some competition from the Spanish

Costa Brava and the Biarritz-San Sebastian area on the Bay of Biscay. During the period 1955–1965, however, new resorts began to appear in Corsica, on the Costa del Sol and the Costa Blanca in Spain, along the Italian Riviera di Ponente and di Levante, on the Adriatic coast north of Rimini, in the Naples-Capri area and in Sardinia, and on the Dalmatian coast of Yugoslavia. Since 1965 new developments have taken place on the Costa Dorada of Spain and on the Balearic Islands, especially Majorca, in Portugal on the Algarve coast and in the north, in Calabria and Sicily in Italy, and on the Greek islands, including Corfu and Rhodes. A large number of new hotels have been built on the Yugoslav coast, while Morocco, Tunisia, and Turkey have been investing in the development of several major new resorts. The rapid growth of the Black Sea resorts of Bulgaria and Romania also began during this period. During the last few years the European tourist agencies have added Madeira and the Canary Islands to their lists, especially for the wealthier winter tourists.

This move away from the traditional vacation of the past is a reflection not only of a search for exotic sunny shores, but also of the development of cheap air transportation, mainly organized on a charter basis. The lower costs of accommodations and food in many of the economically less developed regions on the fringes of the Mediterranean also make it possible for tourist agencies to offer attractive package vacations within the financial ability of many working-class families in northern Europe. Tourist organizations and agencies in many north European countries have organized hotels and other facilities in southern resorts for the exclusive use of their own nationals. For example, the Dutch have developed hotels in the Spanish resorts of Torremolinos and Benalmadena on the Costa del Sol, and Dutch tourists arrive in large numbers by charter plane during the summer. Some have bought houses, apartments, or land in the area for vacation use or for retirement, and a small but growing Dutch colony is developing. These people are bringing a steady stream of foreign currency in exchange for services into a region which offers few alternatives for employment.

Most resorts owe their development to government activity and investment, and the tourist industry is to a great extent nationalized. For example, the French government is involved in the development of six resorts in Languedoc to house two million tourists (Lavery: 1974, p. 193). Only a few individuals, such as Baron Edmond de Rothschild, who is aiding the development of a resort at Caesarea in Israel, and the Aga Khan, who is backing a resort in Sardinia, can afford the necessary investments (Simpson: 1968, p. 240, footnote 18). In the developing countries, in particular, investment in the tourist industry by the government is essential if any development is to take place at all, and in some countries the development of tourist facilities stands very high on the list of investment priorities. As Christaller pointed out, it is precisely in the peripheral regions of Europe and in the underdeveloped countries that tourism has most to offer in terms of economic development (1964, pp. 95–103). It is in these regions that the greatest expansion of the "sun and fun" variety of mass tourism should be expected in the future.

A recent development of significance for the future of tourism in the Mediterranean and beyond is the development of organizations such as the "Club Méditerranée." The concept of this club is based somewhat on the holiday camp as devised by Butlin in Great Britain. The Butlin holiday camps, first started at Skegness in 1936, consist of villages of chalets, with communal restaurants and amusements, located near the sea. The keynote of the holiday camp, however, is organized entertainment and activities, whereas the Club Méditerranée, although using the village format, does not attempt to organize the vacations of its members to the same degree. The aim of its founder, the Belgian Gerard Blitz, is to create an atmosphere directly opposed to that of life in a large urban center. Life in the villages is informal and democracy is stressed, and sports form the major occupation of the guests.

The first village was started in 1949 on Majorca, and at the moment there are over 75, stretching from Tahiti to Senegal, including villages in such diverse places as Egypt, Israel, Cuba, Spain, Morocco, Turkey, Hawaii, and Mexico. There are several winter sports resorts. The Club is trying to attract American tourists by developing bilingual villages where English is spoken along with French. About nine percent of the Club's one million members are North Americans. The Club Méditerranée is now a public company, with Baron Edmond de Rothschild and a company owned by Giovanni Agnelli of the Fiat corporation as major stockholders.

The village resorts of the Club Méditerranée are open to the same criticism as most other modern resorts which have appeared along the coasts of the developing countries; they are self-contained, isolated islands of middle-class European or American urbanites who have little contact with the local people. The Club does not encourage members to leave the premises of the resort except on conducted tours (Francke: 1976, p. 47).

Although long hours of sunshine and warmth are the basic ingredients for a successful seaside resort, another aspect of the physical environment, although independent of the climate, cannot be neglected. This is the quality of the beach. Such resorts as Copacabana, Palm Beach, Mamaia in Romania, Muizenberg in South Africa, and Montego Bay in Jamaica offer the combination of sunshine and fine sandy beaches. The sandy, dune-backed beaches of the Dutch and the Belgian coasts are good enough to offset the disadvantages of climate for the thousands of Germans from the Ruhr industrial region who invade them during the summer. In the British Isles the quality of the beaches varies from one resort to another and can be an important factor in attracting families with children, who are looking for a sandy beach where the children can dig and build sand castles and which has a gentle slope into a sea without dangerous currents.

The character and slope of the beach creates the necessary conditions for surfing, which has increased greatly in popularity in recent years. Although suitable conditions for the sport exist at locations in California, Hawaii, South Africa, and other regions, the major area of development is in Australia. For example, a twenty-five mile stretch of coast south of Brisbane has been developed as a surfing and water sports area, known as the Gold Coast. This region, with Surfers Paradise as its center, now contains over 2,600 hotels and has begun to attract foreign tourists, including Japanese.

The nature of the coastline may be important in the development of resorts, apart from the presence or absence of good beaches. Boating and sailing have played a major role in the development of some coastal resorts, and the existence of a sheltered bay or channel, the lack of reefs or rocks, and the presence of a good harbor, natural or otherwise, are favorable for the sport of sailing. The resort of Cowes on the Isle of Wight in southern England has the above features and has become a major center for international yachting. Marinas, which provide mooring, provisions, repairs, and in some cases overnight accommodations and other services for yachtsmen, are beginning to appear in increasing numbers along the coasts of many countries. Although sunshine and warmth make sailing more pleasant, warm temperatures are not as important for sailing as for swimming, and many of the northern countries offer good conditions for the sport.

Pollution

A major problem which may have a limiting effect on the development of seaside resorts in the future is that of pollution, both of beaches and of the adjacent waters. Beach users are major polluters. Their litter is not only unsightly but creates hazards, such as broken glass and tin cans which can cause injury to the feet of bathers. More serious, because it is less easy to control and to remove, is the pollution caused by oil spills from passing ships, either in the form of deliberate release of oil or because of an accident. Several serious oil spills along the coasts of the United States and the British Isles have received considerable publicity in recent years. Although the damage to sea birds and other fauna has been stressed, the threat to a resort beach from even a small spill can be serious.

The dumping of industrial waste, sewage, and garbage into the sea close to resort beaches can make swimming not only unpleasant but also dangerous to health by increasing the possibility of infectious diseases. It also limits the possibility of safe recreational fishing in many coastal areas because of the danger of eating the polluted fish.

Some tourist countries are already seriously affected by pollution. Almost two-thirds of the beaches of Italy have been polluted to some degree by sewage and garbage. Some Eastern Mediterranean countries, such as Israel and Lebanon, also report that pollution is becoming a major problem facing the future development of their tourist industry. So far Greek, Yugoslav, and Turkish resorts have not yet encountered serious pollution, but they will have to exercise extreme caution to prevent the present situation from deteriorating. Pollution is also affecting inland waters. For example, in Switzerland no swimming is permitted on Lake Lugano, and some beaches have been closed on the shores of Lake Geneva.

Apart from environmental pollution, the seaside resort may suffer from what is often referred to as *visual pollution*. Many of the nineteenth century resorts were built with taste and style, and some modern resorts, such as the villages of the Club Méditerranée, make an attempt to blend with the local architectural styles and physical environment. However, many resorts are characterized by poorly designed and shoddily built hotels, restaurants, other recreational buildings, garish advertisements and signs, and a general lack of control of architectural style. Some Mediterranean coastal resorts consist of rows of apartments constructed en masse with cheap and rapid construction techniques. In some cases overcrowding has resulted in a second row of apartment blocks from which it is impossible to obtain a view of the sea. There is a sameness to many of these resorts which makes it difficult at times to know in which country one might be.

WINTER RESORTS

Although warm summer temperatures may be the major component of climate affecting the location of tourist development, cold winter temperatures are also important. Although the majority of people employed in a modern industrial society take their vacations during the summer there are more and more who find it possible to take some time off from their work in the winter. Some summer resorts keep hotels and facilities open for a clientele seeking relief from northern winters and who benefit from cheaper off-season rates, both in accommodations and transportation. This is especially true of the more southerly resorts in North Africa, Madeira, and the Canary Islands. It was, in fact, the warm winters of the French Riviera which led to its early development as a tourist region. However, cold winter temperatures are more significant than warm ones in the development and location of modern winter tourism, and the growth in popularity of winter sports is one of the most noteworthy developments of the tourist industry of the last few decades.

Of all the modern winter sports activities, skiing is by far the most popular. Skiing as a form of winter transportation has an ancient history, but as a sport it is of relatively recent vintage. Skating is an older sport, being popular in northern Europe, especially in Holland, in the seventeenth century. The lack of long periods of freezing temperatures results in a rather limited skating season in England or Holland, but no major skating resorts were ever developed in countries with a more suitable climate. This was partly because of the relative unpopularity of skating as a modern sport and partly because of the development of the artificial indoor ice rink, which made skating a sport independent of climate. Skiing requires quite different physical conditions from skating. First of all, it is an outdoor sport, and second, it requires a good snow cover and a mountainous or, at least, hilly terrain. The last item is not so necessary for crosscountry skiing as practiced in the Nordic countries, a type of skiing which is becoming rapidly more popular in the Alpine countries and North America. However, few skiing resorts have been developed in areas which do not have a hill in the vicinity. Modern skiing as a mass sport developed in the Alps, and Alpine-type downhill skiing still forms the model for the sport in most parts of the world.

The use of mountain regions as areas for recreation and tourism is of relatively recent origin. It was only in the eighteenth century that Europeans began to perceive mountains as anything but regions of danger and horror. Mountain climbing in the Alps began in the late eighteenth century, and skiing was introduced from Norway by the English to the Swiss Alps in the 1890's. The development of the ski lift in the 1930's led not only to the rapid development of skiing for sport, but opened up the Alps to all forms of tourism. By giving access to higher slopes and glaciers, it has enabled resorts such as Chamonix and Zermatt to develop a summer skiing season.

Because of differences in climate and terrain between the different mountain regions of Europe, conditions for developing winter sports vary considerably from region to region. The lack of sufficient snow for long periods makes much of the southern Alps unsuitable for skiing, although a few resorts have recently been developed in this region. Even in the northern Alps weather and snow conditions can be quite variable, depending on the time of the year and the altitude. For this reason some resorts can offer guaranteed good conditions for skiing from Christmas until Easter, whereas others have a more restricted season. In the Norwegian mountains, on the other hand, snow conditions are more uniform from place to place throughout the winter, but the short daylight hours of the winter months, along with the cold temperatures, reduce the popularity of Norwegian resorts with the foreign tourist until the spring (Heller: 1969, pp. 60–61). Scotland has seen more commercial development of its winter sports facilities in recent years, but suffers from the variable weather associated with a west-coast marine climate, with a resultant uncertainty about snow and weather conditions at any given time in the winter (Perry: 1971, pp. 197–201). In fact, commercially organized skiing in Scotland is only really practical in the snow-filled corries and gullies of the major mountain ranges, such as the Grampians. Scottish skiing, however, attracts few tourists from outside Britain. Other mountain regions of Europe have varied conditions for winter sport development. The Pyrenees have some centers, such as Bagnères de Luchon and Barèges on the French side, but in general the Pyrenees are not easily accessible from the main urbanized regions of Europe; and in the western Pyrenees the snow cover is uncertain (Ritter: 1966, pp. 227–28). In Eastern Europe the best conditions for skiing are found in the Carpathians, in particular in the Tatra mountains between Poland and Czechoslovakia. Some resorts in Romania and Yugoslavia attract some foreign visitors, but very few from the West.

North American skiing has so far attracted few foreigners, although the Laurentian region of Quebec and some other Canadian resorts attract U.S. tourists from the East and Midwest. The other continents have seen some development of their winter sports potential in recent years, but this is mainly of regional or national rather than international importance. In South America the ski resorts of the Andean region of Chile and Argentina have some potential to attract tourists from other Latin American countries.

Development of Winter Sports Resorts and Centers

It should be noted that suitable conditions of climate, snow, and terrain are not enough to guarantee the success of a particular location as a winter sports resort. Much capital must be invested in the form of hotels with central heating, ski lifts, snow plows to keep access roads clear, and special care for the ski slopes (Blanchard: 1958, p. 202). At some resorts snow-making machines are used to reinforce inadequate snow cover on the slopes or snow may even be brought in from areas where it is abundant. Besides, the prospect of good skiing is not enough to attract many people to a winter sports resort, and night clubs, restaurants, and bars are important features of most of the larger resorts. There are, however, two main types of winter sports bases: the village, with a self-contained life and transportation system, which can best be thought of as a "resort" and the much larger area, with ski lift stations far apart and linked by public transportation, which has more of the nature of a "center." A variant of the latter is the "created center," built from scratch on an empty mountain side (Heller: 1969, p.49). The "created center" is found in its most extreme form in France and Italy, where small urban-type settlements with skyscrapers have been developed virtually in the wilderness. One of the most spectacular of these is La Plagne in the Tarantaise Valley of Savoie, with skyscraper apartment buildings, a shopping center with covered arcades, including boutiques with the latest fashions, and a central plaza where all the ski runs end. In Italy, Sestriere has been developed along the same lines. These "created centers" are more compact than some of the other large centers such as Davos and St. Moritz, but they are typical Latin developments in the sense that they are an attempt to reproduce an urban way of life in the wilds. In Austria and Switzerland the architecture of resorts and centers is more traditional and in keeping with the rest of the human landscape. Austria in particular encourages the natural growth of existing villages rather than the construction of new centers. In general the large centers appeals to the tourist who wishes a sophisticiated after-ski night life, and the smaller resort may appeal to the person who desires only good skiing.

Some winter sports resorts have been moving from the development of hotels as the main form of lodging for tourists to the construction of apartments and condominiums. In the United States complexes of condominiums have been built near major ski resorts in mountain states such as Colorado, but have not proved as popular as hoped. In some European ski resorts the richer clientele from the big cities own their own apartments which they use themselves or rent to others.

Safety is one of the problems inherent in the development of new centers. Apart from the question of preventing accidents on the slopes, there is the much more serious problem of avalanches. Recent major tragedies, in the French Alps in particular, where avalanches overwhelmed ski resorts causing destruction of buildings and loss of life, have drawn attention to the lack of safety planning in locating new ski resorts and centers.

Earlier we mentioned cross-country skiing, which has recently become very popular in North America. Although ski touring and crosscountry ski racing has been extremely popular for many years in Scandinavia, it was virtually unknown in North America and Alpine Europe until the early 1970's. Its main attractions are that equipment is considerably cheaper than for downhill skiing; it is good exercise in the fresh air in pleasant surroundings; it is not dangerous; and as long as there is some snow, it can be carried out on almost any type of terrain, including flat country. It is this last feature that makes cross-country skiing independent of resorts. It does not require ski lifts and prepared runs and as long as some accessible country can be found, the skier may not have to travel far from home. Cross-country skiing, thus, is much more important as a local form of recreation than as an attractor of foreign tourists.

Downhill skiing still remains much more significant as a generator of international tourist traffic.

Some mention should be made of snowmobiling, a winter sport which has shown such rapid growth in North America recently. So far this sport has been confined mainly to the flat or slightly hilly regions of the northern United States and Canada. Apart from North America the only region where snowmobiling has seen some growth, principally as a means of transportation, is northern Scandinavia. It is not a sport which can be carried on effectively in mountainous areas, and being mechanized, requires considerable service facilities. It has become necessary to control the use of these potentially dangerous machines, and special terrain and trails are being developed for their use. Damage to the environment and excessive noise are also problems which are difficult to control. Snowmobiling has not yet developed into a sport attracting foreign tourists in any number, and it is doubtful if it will ever challenge skiing as a major international sport. It offers little as a form of exercise and requires little skill in return for a large financial expenditure on equipment.

Mountain regions do not always rely exclusively on their winter climate to attract visitors. Local people in regions adjacent to mountainous areas use the mountains to escape the summer heat. Darjeeling and Simla in the Himalayas were developed as summer resorts for the British seeking relief from the summers of the plains, and the Blue Mountains of Australia and the Adirondacks and Catskill Mountains of New York State contain resorts serving the populations of the Sydney and New York metropolitan areas, respectively. Although these resorts were developed mainly to serve a regional population, in some cases they attract foreign tourists as well.

The importance of climatic factors in the location of tourism has much to do with the seasonal nature of tourism. The summer still remains the peak period of tourist activity, and in industrial Europe and North America, June, July, and August are the main vacation period. This is, of course, not only because the summer is the warmest period of the year, but because most persons are given their vacations from work at that time. In some countries, such as France, the Scandianvian countries, and New Zealand, almost the entire nation takes its vacation during a one-month period in the summer, with a resultant strain on tourist and transportation facilities. As noted above, the tourist facilities which cater to summer tourism are often not the ones which serve the winter tourist. Thus, many tourist resorts have a short but intensive season. Winter tourism appeals mainly to the young and to the sportsman, and even with the great rise of interest in winter sports, it may never have the popularity of the more varied activities that can be carried on in summer. The winter season does not compete in intensity of tourist activity with the summer.

That the southern hemisphere experiences its seasons at the opposite time to those of the northern hemisphere might suggest the possibility of refugees from the northern winter seeking the sun south of the equator, but this difference in seasons has little influence on the pattern of world tourism at the moment (Zachinyayev and Fal'kovich: 1972, pp. 44–45).

THE ATTRACTIONS OF THE LANDSCAPE

Apart from climate and terrain, there are other aspects of the physical environment which are important in the development of tourism. In particular, the landscape or scenery of a region has much to do with its attraction for the tourist. The word "landscape" is used here in the sense of a tract of country considered as scenery. A seaside resort or a winter sports center adds to its attractions if the countryside around it creates a pleasant impression. The beauty of the Alps not only adds to the popularity of its winter sports resorts, but attracts many visitors to these same resorts during the summer months, when the excitement of skiing is replaced by the quieter pleasures of walking amid spectacular scenery. The growth of the popularity of the Dalmatian coast of Yugoslavia is due not only to the sun and the beaches but also to the rugged beauty of the coastal mountains. Many regions which offer little in the way of good climate or exciting sports have built up a tourist industry virtually on scenery alone. Such regions are the Scottish Highlands, the English lake District, the Norwegian fjords, Iceland, and, to a lesser extent, the Rocky Mountains. Resorts have arisen in some of these regions which offer little else than scenery, such as Pitlochry in Scotland, Interlaken in Switzerland, and Keswick in the Lake District.

Water plays an important role in forming an attractive landscape. The sea, lakes, and rivers not only add to the visual beauty of a region but also offer the possibilities of swimming, sailing, canoeing, and fishing. Hence, the popularity not only of the sea coast and other large bodies of water, such as the Great Lakes, the Lake of Geneva, or Lake Balaton, but also of such regions as the Finnish lakes, the Scottish lochs, the Italian lakes, and the Andean lake district of Bariloche. Forest areas also have considerable attractions for relaxation and sport. In North America the development of state parks and wilderness areas has taken place largely in response to demand for forest scenery. In the case of wilderness areas there is the added attraction, at least for some people, of isolation and solitude combined with an element of "roughing it." For more information on the use and misuse of wilderness areas, see *Wilderness as Sacred Space,* by Linda H. Graber (1976).

Apart from the pleasures of viewing the scenery of a region in general, there are certain specific natural phenomena which may draw tourists, such as volcanoes, waterfalls, caves, and canyons. Examples are the Grand Canyon in the U.S., Vesuvius in Italy, Niagara Falls in the U.S. and Canada, Mammoth Caves in Kentucky, the geysers of Iceland and New Zealand, the Great Barrier Reef of Australia, or the Plitvice Lakes of northern Yugoslavia. Some of these phenomena, such as Niagara Falls or the Grand Canyon, are impressive enough to be a major attraction on their own, but in most cases they are visited in the course of a general tour. This is especially true if they are located in a region which also offers other features of interest to the tourist.

The particular fauna or flora of a region sometimes draws tourists. In Kenya and other countries of southern Africa wildlife safaris are rapidly increasing in popularity, the camera being substituted in most cases for the gun. Game reserves often provide accommodations and services for tourists. The Arctic and Antarctic regions attract a small but significant number of tourists to view the icy wastes, the polar bears, or the penguins. The Amazon, with its exotic rain forest vegetation and its wildlife, is also seeing an increase in its tourist trade. On a less exotic level, the tulip fields of Holland or cherry blossom time in Japan or Washington, D.C. are added attractions to the other sights.

HUNTING AND FISHING

Apart from the pleasure of viewing animals in their natural habitat, there is the added attraction for some people of hunting them. Although hunting remains basically a local sport, there are persons who are willing to pay for the privilege of shooting big game in Africa, bear, boar, and chamois in the Caucasus, or grouse in Scotland. In particular the Soviet Union and other East European countries, such as Poland and Hungary, offer hunting vacations to Western tourists who are willing to pay the high prices. The attraction is the possibility of shooting species of animals which have vanished or are in short supply in Western countries. For example, the Polish government permits a limited hunting of the European bison, which at one time was almost extinct and is now increasing in numbers in a forest preserve in eastern Poland.

Fishing attracts tourists to both the sea and to inland waters. Again, fishing is primarily a local pastime, but several countries have developed it as a significant branch of tourism. European countries such as Ireland, Scotland, and Norway attract foreigners to fish their salmon and trout rivers and streams, and many Americans travel to Canada for the pleasure of fishing in unspoiled waters and wild natural surroundings. River and lake fishing is limited primarily to the northern countries where physical conditions are conducive to the breeding of sport fish such as trout and salmon.

Sea fishing as a sport of international significance is located mainly in the tropics or sub-tropics. The deep-sea game fish, such as swordfish or tuna, are found in southern waters. Attempts to popularize shark fishing in northern waters have not proved very successful. Spearfishing by divers equipped with snorkels or breathing apparatus is also a predominantly southern sport, but is confined to onshore waters and does not involve game fish.

Although hunting and fishing may constitute very important branches of a country's internal tourism, they have less significance as attractors of foreign tourists.

The physical attractions of a particular region may appeal to some persons and not to others. Attitudes may vary from individual to individual within a particular culture, depending on perception of an attractive place or environment in which to spend a vacation. Although the sea, and lakes or rivers are usually perceived as desirable features for vacation resorts, there are people who are not interested in the presence of water and who may even find it distasteful. The author has heard the view expressed that a seaside resort is only "half a place" because its hinterland is only half that of an inland resort. Some persons find a mountain landscape too confining and may even experience a type of claustrophobia in mountain valleys.

The perception of the attractiveness of places from the point of view of tourism has been little studied as a phenomenon. The work of Gould and White (1974) on the subject of mental maps suggests the possibility of constructing mental maps of a country, region, or continent which would indicate the most desirable places for a vacation as perceived by the population of selected places or regions. In many cases these mental maps would not differ greatly from those which indicate preferences for areas for living and working. However, mental maps have generally been constructed on the basis of a single country, whereas mental maps for the purposes of international tourism would involve the perception of foreign areas and places. Gould and White touch on the theme of perception of residential desirability in Europe from the point of view of Swedes, West Germans, and Italians (1974, pp. 181–86).

Although attitudes may vary from individual to individual within a particular culture, there are still clearly identifiable attitudes towards the natural environment which differ from culture to culture (Lowenthal: 1962–63, pp. 19–23). The seaside has a particular attraction for the British, partly because of their long association with the sea and partly because of its relative accessibility. The forests are particularly popular with the Swedes and Finns, who value the isolation of a forest cottage during the summer months. The love of northern nature among the Scandinavians is, however, balanced by a love of the southern sun, which sends them in large numbers to the south of Europe, if possible during the long, dark northern winter. The Italians and some other peoples of Latin culture have neither a particular admiration for untamed nature nor a desire for isolation and prefer more sophisticated pleasures. Hence, the urbanized nature of most Italian winter sports centers and the necessity of good restaurants and cafes in resorts catering to Italian tourists. Tourists from Moslem countries also have a perception of recreational attractions which are characteristically different from those of the inhabitants of other cultural regions (Ritter, 1974). In spite of these differences in national attitudes, the modern tourist industry has by advertising created a mass demand for sun or snow which embraces the nationals of most countries of the industrialized West.

SPAS AND HEALTH RESORTS

One component of the physical environment which was once a major attractor of tourists, but which has a more limited significance, is mineralized water found in springs or tapped by wells. By the seventeenth century people developed a widespread conviction of the medicinal value of various varieties of mineral waters, either for drinking or for bathing, and began to visit such spas, the general name given to places where these waters occurred. As the name suggests, Spa in Belgium was one of the earliest of these medicinal watering places, but the spa saw much early development in England. Bath and Tunbridge Wells became the most fashionable. The clientele of the spas can be numbered among the earliest tourists in Europe (Robinson: 1972, p. 383). On the continent certain spas became world-famous and attracted a rich and fashionable clientele from abroad, especially during the latter half of the nineteenth century. In general, spas also offered their clientele parks and gardens, concerts, theatrical performances, and other recreation, the quality of which helped to determine a spa's popularity. English and American spas in particular were more social than therapeutic (Lowenthal: 1962, p. 127).

With the development of modern methods of medical treatment and a lack of faith in the curative powers of mineral waters, the spas have ceased to attract the clientele of the past. This is particularly true in Great Britain and the United States, whereas in Central and Eastern Europe some spas still retain considerable popularity. For example, the Czech spa of Karlovy Vary (Karlsbad) still attracts a large number of tourists, not only from the Soviet bloc countries, but also from West Germany. The Germans in particular retain a strong belief in the curative powers of mineral springs and Karlovy Vary offers a cheaper vacation than does a German spa. Piešťany in Slovakia treats rheumatic complaints with mudbaths and, strangely enough, has a large clientele from the Arab countries. The necessity of visiting spas to drink the water is offset to a great extent by the practice of bottling the waters and selling them cheaply to a wide public.

Along with the spa can be classed the sanatorium, which, although scarcely a tourist attraction, nevertheless uses a "healthy" climate to attract persons suffering from certain diseases, especially those of the lungs. The Alpine region, and Switzerland in particular, contains a large number of sanatoria specializing in the treatment of tuberculosis. These sanatoria achieved their greatest popularity among foreigners during the inter-war period, before the development of antibiotics. In recent years the necessity of sanatorium treatment has greatly diminished, although some sanatoria are used as convalescent homes or as health resorts for children. The sanatorium has ceased to be a major attractor of foreign visitors.

URBAN CULTURAL AND HISTORICAL ATTRACTIONS

It is impossible to estimate with any accuracy the number of tourists who move from one country to another in response to the attractions of the physical environment alone. There are few countries which do not have some man-made attractions to offer the visitor, and in any decision to visit another country, cultural factors have a certain influence. This influence may be the major one, as in the case of a person who visits a city to attend the theater or visit the art galleries, or marginal, as in the case of the visitor to a Spanish beach resort who attends a bullfight. In the case of a large number of tourists who simply want a couple of weeks on the beach in the sun, the choice of country is probably dictated by the cheapest package deal which they can get from a tourist agency. As already noted, the isolation of many resorts from the surrounding region and its population makes it immaterial to many tourists which country they are visiting. However, even the most isolated and self-contained resort usually arranges some cultural attractions for the tourist. For example, the resort of Mamaia on the Black Sea coast of Romania provides special plane and bus trips for its visitors to such places as Bucharest, the Danube Delta, and the monasteries of northern Moldavia.

Urban Tourism

Apart from the large numbers of tourists who travel abroad to find a natural environment which they do not have at home, there are many who visit other countries primarily because of their cultural attractions. Many of these tourists find what they are seeking in urban centers rather than in the countryside. These people form the basis of the important urban tourist industry.

It is difficult to itemize all the factors which attract people to certain cities. Apart from the buildings, churches, art galleries, museums, theaters, restaurants, and shops which individually or collectively interest and attract tourists, many cities have an individual character and atmosphere which transcend the mere sum of their buildings and other physical attractions. An obvious example is Paris. It is doubtful if the average tourist visits the city with the specific intention of seeing the Eiffel Tower or visiting the Louvre or the Folies Bergère. He does so because he wishes to experience the atmosphere and spirit of the legendary city about which he has heard so much in song and story. The same is true to a certain degree of other world cities, such as London, Rome, Venice, New York, or Amsterdam. This atmosphere is difficult to define, being a combination of visual impressions based on pleasant or characteristic architecture, attractively laid-out streets or picturesque canals, along with restaurants and cafés serving good food and drink and also the life-style of the inhabitants. The organizations and agencies responsible for propagating urban tourism known the characteristics of these places well and their advertising stresses the atmosphere and the character of the city they wish to sell to the tourist.

From the viewpoint of tourism, cities can be divided into two major groups: old and modern. Old cities, such as Rome, Athens, Venice, or Jerusalem attract the tourist mainly with their ancient ruins, castles, classical architecture palaces, museums, and art galleries, whereas modern cities, such as New York, Chicago, West Berlin, or Düsseldorf, offer modern architecture, theaters, department stores, boutiques, luxury hotels, restaurants, and night clubs. Of course, many old cities combine the attractions of old and new, such as Paris, Rome, London, or Amsterdam. These cities are the main centers of mass urban tourism. Many tourists not only visit these cities while on tour, but may regard a stay in one of them as their main tourist goal. Many visitors to France or Great Britain see little of these countries outside Paris or London, although the increased mobility of the modern tourist has resulted in shorter stays in more places in a given country.

Apart from the world cities of major interest to tourists, there are many smaller cities of historical or cultural interest which are generally visited as part of a wider tour of a country or region. Such are York, Stratford-on-Avon, and Oxford in England, Edinburgh in Scotland, Bruges and Ghent in Belgium, Florence and Pisa in Italy, Granada in Spain, and Heidelberg in Germany, to name only a few. In some cases these towns are known for a particular feature of attraction, such as the Leaning Tower of Pisa, the Alhambra in Granada, or the Castle and Holyrood Palace in Edinburgh.

Youth Tourism

An aspect of western urban tourism of recent origin is the so-called "youth" tourism. Although numbers of young people with packs, bundles, or suitcases can be found hitchhiking along most of the main highways of Europe, their goal is generally the city. Cities such as Paris, London, Copenhagen, and, above all, Amsterdam became the rallying-points for young people from many countries, including the United States, during the 1960's. They formed the clientele for cheap hotels and hostels and in the summer slept in the parks and streets, local police permitting. In Amsterdam the Vondelpark was virtually turned into a dormitory for the young tourists in the summer months. Some countries attempted to restrict this youth tourism as it brought in little money and created problems, such as drug use and theft. In the case of Amsterdam, however, many conventional tourists came considerable distances to be shocked by the "hippies," who in themselves had become a tourist attraction.

This type of youth tourism changed considerably in the 1970's. The hippies have been replaced largely by a more conventional type of young traveller who is less willing to sleep under a tree in a park, but who nevertheless is looking for cheap lodgings and restaurants and is willing to hitchhike. The travel agencies and transportation companies are aware of this market and have offered cheap air fares, special prices for passes on the European railroads, and other attractions. Special guidebooks on several countries have been written for young tourists with information on inexpensive eating-places, night-life, how to meet the opposite sex, and other useful hints.

A subcategory of cities with tourist attractions are the cities of the non-Western world, with their exotic architecture, food and customs. These are the Moslem cities of the Middle East and Africa, such as Tangier, Marrakesh, Tunis, or Istanbul, cities of the Far East, such as Tokyo, Hong Kong, or Bangkok, and cities of Latin America, such as Rio de Janeiro, Bogotá, or Mexico City. These cities may combine aspects of ancient and modern, but it is the exotic elements of these places that attract most Western tourists.

Some urban areas offer what are best described as "economic" attractions. These include such features as ports and harbors, airports and trade fairs, as well as interesting industries, such as automobile factories, salt mines, and breweries (Christaller: 1955, p. 3). In many port cities groups can take organized tours of the harbor by boat, and visits to large airports to watch the planes take off and land are a popular form of family recreation with many city people. These economic attractions are of little significance in international tourism, except for the trade fairs, such as the Leipziger Messe, which provides about the only reason for foreigners to visit that city. A few foreign tourists visit such places as Wieliczka salt mines near Cracow in Poland or the Chartreuse distilleries in France, but most of these visits are only incidents on a tour with other major objectives.

Religious Pilgrimages

Some urban centers have an ancient history as sites of objects of religious veneration and thus have become the object of pilgrimages. Classic examples for the Christian world are the tombs of the Apostles at Rome, the relics of the Three Kings at Cologne, Germany, the tomb of St. James at Santiago de Compostela in Spain, the tomb of St. Thomas in Canterbury, England, the house of the Virgin at Loreto in Italy, and the highest goal of all medieval Christians, the Holy Sepulchre in Jerusalem. Of these, only Rome and the Holy Land still attract pilgrims from abroad in any numbers. Of much greater significance in terms of modern religious tourism are the shrines of more recent origin, such as Fatima in Portugal and Lourdes in France. The latter shrine is the supreme example of an object of religious veneration forming the basis of a major tourist industry. Special trains bring the sick and the faithful from all over Europe, and their needs are catered to by many hotels, boarding houses, hospitals, and nursing homes, restaurants, and shops selling religious souvenirs. Numerous Americans visit Lourdes and Fatima on organized trips.

The Moslem world has several places of religious pilgrimage, such as the mosque in Kairouan in Tunisia and the Dome of the Rock in Jerusalem, but these are overshadowed by the great pilgrimage of *hajj* to Mecca. Large numbers of pilgrims still visit Mecca annually, coming not only from the Middle East and North Africa but from Pakistan, Bangladesh, Malaysia and Indonesia. The pilgrims travel in ships, often highly overcrowded, to the Red Sea port of Jidda, which is connected by rail with Mecca, or by charter plane directly to Mecca. For the average pilgrim, accommodations in Mecca are primitive, consisting usually of a tent in a large camp, although in recent years the Saudi Arabian government has improved accommodations and services in the city. The places of pilgrimage of other religions, such as Banaras for the Hindus, or Buddha's footprint in Ceylon for the Buddhists, have little significance as centers for international tourism.

RURAL HISTORICAL AND CULTURAL ATTRACTIONS

Apart from buildings of historical interest in urban areas, either because of their architecture or their connection with historial characters or events, there are many places in the country with historial associations. Chief among these are castles, palaces, abbeys, monasteries, and country houses, either of architectural interest or associated with a particular person, family, or period. Examples are the French chateaux of the Loire Valley, Malmaison near Paris, with its relics of Napoleon, the castle of Chillon in Switzerland, immortalized by Byron, and the many palaces and country houses open to the public in the British Isles. In order to add to the attractions of country houses with no particular historical significance and to pay for the expenses of their upkeep, many of their owners have devised added entertainments for the visitors. The Marquis of Beaulieu has opened a zoo and a museum of old cars on his estate in Hampshire, U. K., while other country houses offer medieval style dinners or tea with the duke.

Apart from buildings and estates there are other places of historical importance in the countryside. Battlefields, such as Waterloo (Belgium), Verdun and the Somme (France), and Gettysburg (U.S.), and the military cemeteries associated with them are of interest to many tourists, especially those with family connections in the case of more recent battles. The sites of concentration camps from World War II still receive many visitors. Oswiecim (Auschwitz) near Cracow is still of major interest to tourists visiting Poland.

In the developing countries the major historical tourist attractions are mainly the ruins of ancient civilizations, such as the Pyramids and Sphinx of Egypt. Angkor Wat in Cambodia, Borobodur in Java, Machu Picchu in Peru, or Palmyra in Syria. A lack of knowledge of the more recent histories of the countries of Asia and Africa limits the interest of the American or European tourist in more modern monuments and relics.

Just as a beautiful natural landscape may please the tourist, so may a cultural one. Part of the attraction of the Alps lies in the contrast between wild nature and the cozy, comfortable villages of the inhabitants. The highly artificial, well-organized landscapes of the polderlands of the Netherlands or the rice-lands of the Far East have a charm of their own, while many picturesque villages in the British Isles, such as those of the Cotswolds or Devon, are in themselves objects of tourism.

"Ethnic" Tourism

Some rural areas offer what might be described as "ethnic" attractions, such as a colorful folk-life, native costumes, house-types, customs, regional foods and drink, fiestas, and wine festivals. In Europe many folk costumes and customs are maintained specially for the tourist, and folkloric events, such as dance or song festivals, are purposely organized to attract visitors, although in some cases the local people are genuinely interested in their own folklore. Much of this rural culture has been transferred to the city, and many East European countries in particular maintain dance groups, choirs, and folk orchestras in the major cities to entertain the foreign tourists. In Asia, Africa, and Latin America, where an active folklife still exists in the rural areas of many countries, this artificial stimulus is not so necessary. In North America about the only areas with genuine ethnic attractions are the Southwest, with its Indian and Mexican population, and French Canada. Other ethnic attractions, such as offered by German, Dutch, or Swiss communities in the Northeast and Midwest may be artificial and some are not even authentic.

Another type of "ethnic" tourism consists of the return of people to the country of their origin. Much of the flow of American tourists to Ireland is made up of immigrants and other persons of Irish origin paying a nostalgic visit to the old country. Immigrant societies organize charter flights for their members to a number of countries, including the countries of Eastern Europe. In recent years even the Soviet Union has organized tours of the Ukraine and the Baltic States designed to attract persons originally from these regions or with family connections there.

SPORTING EVENTS

Major sporting events such as the Olympic Games or, to a lesser degree, the Wimbledon tennis championships or international soccer matches, attract visitors who may also spend some extra time in the country for sightseeing. However, the proximity of the site of the event to major regions of tourist origin will influence the number of visitors. For example, the Winter Olympics at Sapporo in northern Japan were too distant to attract a large number of European tourists.

ARTIFICIALLY CREATED ATTRACTIONS

Some mention should be made of the artificially created attractions of such institutions as Disneyland in California and Disney World in Florida. These amusement centers, which have proved to be prime attractions for foreign visitors to the United States, including heads of state, are an elaboration on the traditional urban amusement park, such as the old Vauxhall Gardens in London or Tivoli in Copenhagen, with a suggestion of the open-air museum, such as Skansen in Stockholm or Greenfield Village in Detroit. The Disney creations are, however, highly artificial in that all their indoor and outdoor exhibits and amusements rely little on the physical and cultural features of the areas where they have been developed, except that the sites have been located in areas with a good climate all the year round. Disneyland and its counterparts, including some of the ''Western'' towns inhabited by ''cowboys'' which one finds scattered throughout the Midwest and West of the United States, are a new development in the tourist field in that they can create a major tourist attraction in an area which has virtually no physical or cultural features of note.

A less desirable, but nevertheless important aspect of tourism must not be overlooked. This is the number of establishments often found in frontier areas devoted to gambling, drinking, prostitution, or the sale of goods or services unobtainable or more expensive in the neighboring country. In North America this situation not only exists between the United States on one hand and Canada and Mexico on the other, but between the states themselves. Examples are the gambling casinos of Reno and Las Vegas, Nevada, the bars along the state lines which attract minors from one state who are of legal drinking age in the next state, and the supermarkets of northern Illinois which sell margarine to Wisconsin housewives who cannot buy it legally in their own state.

On the international level the red-light districts of such towns as Tijuana, Ciudad Juarez, Nuevo Laredo, and others just over the Mexican borders are said to bring in an annual revenue of $900 million, or 60 percent of Mexico's tourist revenue, and attract some 90 million Americans (Young: 1973, p. 122). These figures are probably exaggerated as it must be difficult to distinguish this type of tourist from the many other Americans who cross the border for more innocent pleasures. Besides, statistics for visitors to Mexico by car are not accurate. The phenomenon of ''frontier prostitution'' exists also along the Belgian side of Belgian-Dutch border, where a number of red-light cafés cater to the Dutch from the towns of the southern Netherlands. A strange twist to this situation is the existence of the large number of sex-shops and pornographic bookstores which have been opened in towns on the Dutch side of the border to cater to Belgian tourists. This type of tourist traffic is generally the result of differences in national or local laws or sometimes in national attitudes and customs.

Crossing a national frontier to get cheaper drink or food or to be free of legal restrictions on drinking hours is an important factor in a limited number of cases. One example in North America is the small detached fragment of the state of Washington known as Point Roberts, which is located at the end of a small peninsula south of Vancouver in British Columbia. This two-mile long, three-mile wide strip of U.S. territory has some 200 inhabitants, but over one and a half million Canadians a year visit it. The reason is that dancing is not permitted in bars in British Columbia, and they are closed on Sundays. A couple of the largest bars in the United States are located in Point Roberts, offering dancing every night to well-known bands. On a larger scale, this type of tourism exists between England and some of the French and Belgian channel ports, such as Calais, Boulogne, and Ostend, where tourists from Dover and other southern English towns on cheap day or other short-period trips can drink inexpensive drinks all day and night, generally starting on the boat, where drinks are free of the high British taxes on liquor, wine, and beer. This type of "alcoholic tourism" has very questionable value. It generally attracts the worst type of tourist and often results in drunkenness, disturbance of the peace, and even violence or vandalism, and alienates the local inhabitants, whose opinion of a particular nation may be formed from the tourists which they encounter.

A more innocuous form of border tourist is the shopper who wishes to take advantage of cheaper prices in a foreign country. An example is Calexico, California, which attracts shoppers from Mexicali in Mexico. In 1974 the stores of the town, which has a population of 13,000, had total receipts of $54 million. Every day some 50,000 Mexicans cross the border to buy eggs, meat, and groceries because of their better quality and lower price. Mexican peddlers from the rural areas come by train and bus to Mexicali and cross the border to shop for goods which they later sell back in their local villages. On a broader front, the same phenomenon can be seen in border areas in Europe. For example, Trieste in Italy attracts shoppers from Yugoslavia. New tariff agreements between West European countries have limited this type of tourism in recent years.

OTHER FACTORS OF ATTRACTION OR REPULSION

Apart from the major physical and cultural factors which attract tourists to a particular country or region, there are a few minor, but nevertheless important, ones which should be mentioned. One of these is the economic level of development of the country to be visited. Low prices compared with those of the country of origin or with those of competing tourist countries may be a strong attraction for tourists. For example, the very low level of the Argentinian peso compared with the U.S. dollar during 1975 and 1976 has attracted a large number of tourists from surrounding Latin American countries who enjoy a cheap vacation and return laden with goods bought in Argentina. In Europe, many people choose Austria for a winter vacation because of the relatively low level of prices compared with West Germany and Switzerland. The lower prices of the East European countries also partially account for their increasing popularity with West European and American tourists. The drop in the value of the British pound has made Britain an attractive country for foreign visitors.

However, a low level of prices may reflect a low standard of living, and this in turn may be associated in many people's minds with poor food, unsafe drinking water, a lack of hygiene in restaurants, or dirty bed linen. It must be admitted that in some cases this association is true, and many a person's vacation has been ruined by intestinal disorders or even serious illness. The fact that many of the developing countries which are trying to attract tourists are located in the tropics means that disease can be a serious hazard, and many tourists are not keen to visit a country for which innoculations against various diseases are necessary. This problem has been partially overcome in some areas by the developing self-contained resorts, where the developer can exercise some control over hygiene, food preparation, and laundry.

The general standard of tourist services is also important. If hotels are badly built, faucets do not work, hot water is not available, roads are bad, and gasoline stations few, the news spreads by word of mouth or through travel articles in newspapers. Potential visitors may decide that the physical attractions of the place may not be sufficient to outweigh these other factors. In other words, factors of repulsion may be as important in some cases as factors of attraction in explaining tourist flows.

REFERENCES

ANAN'YEV, M. A., 1968, *Mezhdunarodnyy Turizm* (International Tourism), Moscow: Izdatel'stovo "Mezhdunarodnyye otnosheniya."

BLANCHARD RAOUL, 1958, *Les Alpes et Leur Destin* (The Alps and their Destiny), Paris: Librairie Arthème Fayrad.

CHRISTALLER, WALTER, 1955, "Beitrage zu einer Geographic des Fremdenverkehrs" (Contributions to a Geography of Tourism), *Erdkunde,* vol. 9, no. 1, pp. 1–19.

FRANCKE, LINDA, 1976, "Sun Spots," *Newsweek,* January 5, pp. 44–50.

GOULD, PETER, and RODNEY WHITE, 1974, *Mental Maps,* Harmondsworth: Penguin Books.

GRABER, LINDA H., 1976, *Wilderness as Sacred Space,* Monograph No. 8. Washington, DC: Association of American Geographers.

HELLER, MARK, 1969, *Ski,* London: Faber and Faber.

IANCU, MIHAI and SILVIA, 1967, "Citeva consideratii asupra geografiei turismului" (Several considerations about the geography of tourism), *Studia Universitatis Babes-Bolayi,* series geologia-geographia, no. 2, pp. 371–75.

LATOUCHE, ROBERT, 1963, "Un colloque scientifique sur le tourisme à Nice" (A scientific colloquy on tourism in Nice), *Revue de Geographie Alpine,* vol. 51, no. 2, pp. 369–70.

LAVERY, PATRICK, 1974, "Resorts and Recreation," in P. Lavery (ed.), *Recreational Geography,* New York: John Wiley and Sons, pp. 167–96.

LOWENTHAL, DAVID, 1962, "Tourists and Thermalists," *Geographical Review,* vol. LII, no. 1, pp. 124–27.

PERRY, ALLEN H., 1971, "Climatic Influences on the Scottish Ski-ing Industry," *Scottish Geographical Magazine,* vol. 87, no. 3, pp. 197–201.

RITTER, WIGAND, 1966, *Fremdenverkehr in Europa* (Tourism in Europe), Leiden: A. W. Sijthoff.

ROBINSON, H., 1972, *Geography for Business Studies,* London: Macdonald and Evans.

SIMPSON, ANTHONY, 1968, *The New Europeans,* London: Hodder and Stoughton.

YOUNG, GEORGE, 1973, *Tourism: Blessing or Blight?* Harmondsworth: Penguin Books.

ZACHINYAYEV, P.N., and N. S. FAL'KOVICH, 1972, *Geografiya Mezhdunarodnogo Turizma* (Geography of International Tourism), Moscow: Izdatel'stvo "Mysl'."

8

THE DESTINATION MIX:

Attractions and Services for the Traveler

"A voyage to a destination, wherever it may be, is also a voyage within oneself; even as a cyclone carries along with it the center in which it must ultimately rest."

Lauren van der Post

At a destination there is a mix of interdependent elements. The elements are interdependent because in order to produce a satisfying vacation experience, all elements must be present.

The destination is composed of:

Attractions
Facilities
Infrastructure
Transportation
Hospitality

Attractions draw visitors to an area. Facilities serve the needs of the visitors while away from home. Infrastructure and transportation are necessary to help ensure accessibility of the destination to the visitor. Hospitality is concerned with the way in which tourist services are delivered to the visitor.

LEARNING OBJECTIVES

Having read this chapter, you should be able to:

1. Describe the destination mix concept listing its five elements.
2. Explain the interdependencies between the five destination mix elements.
3. Identify the differences between primary and secondary attractions.
4. Explain the differences between site and event attractions.
5. List six of the major types of attraction characteristics.
6. Explain the concept of clustering related to the development and design of attractions.
7. Describe the three principal categories of facilities.
8. Describe the eight major components of a destination area's infrastructure/transportation system.
9. Explain how employees in the tourism industry can be trained to have more hospitable attitudes.
10. Describe the techniques that can be used in a community to increase public awareness of the benefits of tourism.

THE TOURISM SYSTEM

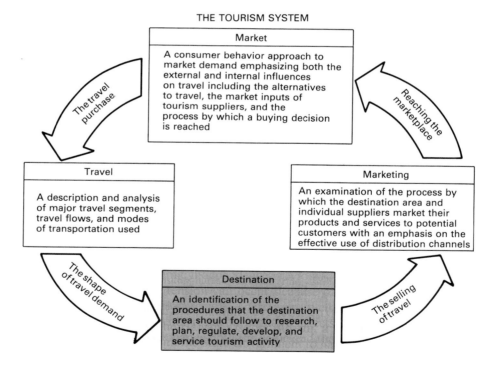

ATTRACTIONS

The central aspects of tourism are attractions. Attractions, by definition, have the ability to draw people to them. Although attractions for the tourist concern the satisfactions perceived from various experiences, the task for the developer and designer is to create an environment made up in part of "attractions" that will provide an opportunity for the tourist to enjoy a visit. The addition at a site of factors other than attractions (services, transportation, hospitality) will help ensure that enjoyment.

Attractions have many characteristics. As mentioned above, they tend to draw visitors to them—they aim to serve the recreational needs of visitors. They can to a large extent be developed anywhere and act as a growth inducer, tending to be developed first in a tourist region.

Scope

The way in which attractions are characterized has implications for development and marketing. Attractions can be characterized in terms of their scope, ownership, permanency, and drawing power. A typology is suggested in Figure 8.1. Destinations may be primary or secondary (sometimes called stopover or touring destinations). A primary destination is one that is attractive enough to be the primary motivation for tourism visits and one that is aimed at satisfying tourists for several days or longer. A secondary or stopover destination is either an interesting or a necessary place to visit on the way to a primary destination, and it aims at satisfying tourists for one to two days. It may be interesting enough to attract tourists on their way somewhere else, or it may, in fact, be a required stop on the way to a final destination. Certain areas can be primary destinations for one segment of the market or stopover destinations for other segments.

Attractions at a primary destination have to have sufficient breadth of appeal to entice tourists to stay for many days. There have to be sufficient things to do and see to keep all members of the party occupied. At a stopover destination, the length of stay will be shorter and the need for a diversity of attractions is less. From a marketing viewpoint, the primary destination or attraction seeks fewer tourists staying longer periods of time, compared to the secondary destination that relies on attracting larger numbers for shorter periods of time. In terms of location, primary destinations tend to be oriented towards the location of the market (Disney World) or to the site of the resource (Aspen). Secondary destinations, although located between tourists and resources, are more reliant on their accessibility to transportation networks.

Ownership

The form of ownership of the attraction has great implications for tourism. Approximately 85 percent of all outdoor recreation lands in the U.S. are owned by the federal government. The agencies that manage this land often do not have tourism as a primary use of the land. Their outlook will determine the degree to which tourism and recreation are encouraged.

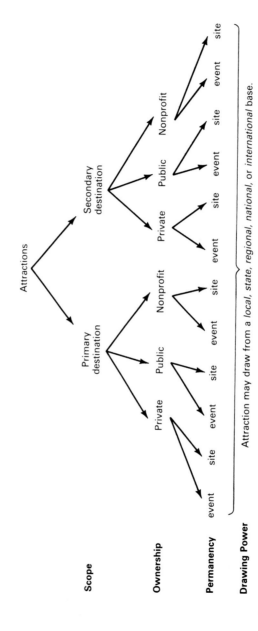

Scope

Ownership

Permanency

Drawing Power

Attraction may draw from a *local*, *state*, *regional*, *national*, or *international* base.

Figure 8.1 Typology of attractions

Hawaii is a primary destination for most people and a stopover destination for U.S.
travelers on their way to Australia

The nonprofit sector is usually oriented to some aspect of the social good. Yet
when nonprofit organizations get involved in work for the social good, such as
historical preservation, their efforts can have great implications for tourism. Limited
tourism may be a vehicle for getting sufficient revenue to continue the historical work.
Care must be taken to ensure that the means does not become the end. The nonprofit organization involved may back out of the project and the resource may become
overcommercialized and lose its original appeal.

The private sector's motivation is that of profit making. The wise manager will
realize that short-run profit maximization may be detrimental to the long-run success of the attraction and the destination.

Permanency

Site attractions concern attractions of a physical nature. They are largely permanent,
with their locations being fixed. Event attractions are rather short in duration, and
their location can be changed. Site attractions are more dependent upon the resource
base. Event attractions can be developed at places more convenient to the market.
Because site attractions cost more to develop in terms of both time and money than
do event attractions, new tourist regions can conceivably develop event attractions
as a way of publicizing the area and bringing in cash to help finance more permanent
site attractions.

Drawing Power

Attractions may also be defined in terms of the distance from which they are able to draw people. Attractions may be locally, state-wide, regionally, nationally, or internationally significant. The rating is inclusive in that a national attraction will draw from the state and local level also. If proposed and existing attractions can be objectively viewed in terms of their drawing power, appropriate strategies for the marketing of existing attractions and the development mix of future attractions can be developed. Attractions do not become attractions for the purpose of tourism until a certain amount of development has occurred to make the natural resource accessible to and attractive for tourists.

Although tourists are motivated to visit a destination to satisfy various needs and wants, they are also motivated to visit a destination because of certain characteristics. The characteristics that attract tourists are:

Natural resources
Climate
Culture
History
Ethnicity
Accessibility

Natural resources.   The natural resources of a destination provide an excellent asset to sell to tourists. When studying the landscape or scenery of an area, it is important to note not only the natural resources but also the human imprints on the area, for this is also part of the scenery. In this respect it is important to point out that any change in one aspect of the scenery changes the whole landscape.

For many markets, an outstanding natural resource has been, and still is, sandy beaches. In urban areas, where children do not have the opportunity to run free in safety or the chance to see the sea, an exodus occurs on weekends and holidays to spots offering such attractions. So it is that Jones Beach becomes a weekend mecca for Manhattan residents, while Manitoba advertises 100,000 lakes, together with soft warm sands and sparkling blue waters.

Two important points should be stressed when considering scenery. First, from the visitor's viewpoint, there is no cost for it. A beautiful sunset, Niagara Falls, the Grand Canyon—these cost the tourist nothing. The second point is concerned with the variety of scenery. Variety in an area can be an important selling point. In this way, Britain with a variety of views and types of countryside every few hundred yards can compete—successfully so—with such dwarfing structures as the Canadian Rockies and the Swiss Alps.

Climate.   Climate is perhaps the most common marketing theme used as the basis for selling a tourism area once it has suitable tourist attractions. Although a region in some cases can be sold largely on the basis of climate, for maximum effect the area must be readily accessible to large concentrations of population. One reason for the popularity of California's coastline resorts is their proximity via automobile to millions of people. Florida, meanwhile, to attract vacationers from the northeastern and the north central states must advertise that its sun is only an hour or so away by plane.

In addition to ready accessibility, the destination area should promise something that tourists cannot get at home. In a populous center, where most people live with enough disposable income to travel, one market segment may be attracted by warm sunshine at a time when it is cold and gloomy at home, while another segment may seek accentuated winter conditions of a ski resort. Conversely, when the population centers are sweltering with summer heat, one market segment may head for the seashore—Maine, Oregon, Florida, or even the Caribbean—for cooling breezes, while another segment wants a mountain area, whether it's New Hampshire, the Canadian Rockies, Scotland, or Switzerland.

When considering summer weather, the most comfortable living is in the populous temperate zones of the Mediterranean, which have warm, sunny, and dry climates. Tropical conditions are too hot and too wet to sell solely on this basis, so that selling of tropical climates must be amplified with a number of other attractions, which is the case of the Caribbean.

An interesting corollary of climate advertising is that those who have left home want to be kept informed about the bad conditions they have fled. In Florida and Puerto Rico, hotels post weather conditions in northern cities during the winter. In summer, it may also be cooler in Florida and Puerto Rico than it is back home because of ocean breezes.

Recreational activities are undertaken considering the combination of natural resources and climate on hand. Over the past several years we have seen a remarkable growth in recreational pursuits in general and participative recreational pursuits in particular. This has resulted in a decline in the business of many sedentary holiday areas and the upsurge of resorts offering sporting facilities. The type of recreation facilities offered is usually determined by the nature of the surrounding countryside—skiing requires mountains, water sports need water, and so on. However, we are seeing the introduction of artificial ski slopes, "dry" ski slopes, artificial lakes for boating and fishing, and artificially stocked waters and bird and hunting grounds.

The important point to remember in selling an area on its recreational facilities is to sell a variety of pursuits, not just one. This way one does not rely solely on one sport, one market, or one season for one's business.

Culture.   Each country has its own unique culture—a state of manners, taste, and intellectual development. Some countries are found to be more interesting culturally and better developed than others. Culture is, for practical tourism purposes, interwoven with history. Today's way of life is tomorrow's culture.

Thus, although one can "sell" the way of life of the people of a foreign land, that way of life must be radically different from the visitor's own to induce excitement and the desire to view it.

America and the Americans have always exhibited, perhaps because of their relatively young existence, an almost insatiable appetite for historical culture. With a fusing in this country of so many races from so many different lands, these groups have jealously clung to preserving their own ethnic culture. Today, however, these cultures are not guarded quite so tightly, but are sold to the rest of the country. Williamsburg, the Pennsylvania Dutch, and western ranch country demonstrate this feature remarkably well.

Historical resources.   Historical resources may be defined by function into the following subdivisions: (1) war, (2) religion, (3) habitation, and (4) government. Past wars hold a fascination for many people. Depending on the chronological distance from the event, the emotions aroused range from morbid curiosity and excitement to sorrow and remembrance. Thus, people throng to the Tower of London and Edinburgh Castle to see the chamber of horrors and the bottleneck dungeons, excited by the thought of such distant gory deeds. The most popular World War II sites in Europe are Margraten in the Netherlands, Omaha Beach Ceremony in France on the site of the D-day landings in Normandy in 1944, and the Luxembourg City cemetary, where General George S. Patton, Jr. lies buried. In America, the popularity of Arlington Cemetery in Washington, D.C., attests to the national feeling of remembrance for those who died for their country.

Since the times of the earliest pilgrimages and the travelers in Chaucer's *Canterbury Tales,* pilgrims have made journeys to shrines, monuments, and cathedrals in the name of their Lord. Although religion can be a tremendous selling force, it can act negatively for the country. The obvious present example is in Northern Ireland, where past demonstrations against parades commemorating William of Oranges's defeat of the militant Catholics have erupted into long, and sometimes bloody, battles that have served to disrupt trade, industry, and tourism from progressing into the area.

Religion forms the basis for the Outdoor Biblical Museum at Nymegen, Holland, which is a beautiful and moving attempt to bring all faiths to a point where they can worship together. Visitors walk along narrow paths cut through a forest to arrive at a scene from the Bible. A minimum of figures and a natural landscape leave the visitor awestruck by the simplicity of it all.

From the simple house tour to the elaborate view of Buckingham Palace, man's natural curiosity to see the trappings of others' homes is a marketable item. Thousands will flock to the homes of Anne Hathaway and William Shakespeare, or to the houses of George Washington and Abe Lincoln, in an attempt to achieve some sense of rapport with the memory of these famous people. However, one need not be numbered amongst the dead to enjoy this admiration and visitation. The White House and Buckingham Palace are favorite tourist stops while, in Britain, many stately homes are being opened to the public, and the promise of dining with a duke and thereafter spending the night in one of the state rooms is an appealing attraction to many. After the success of the movie *Mary, Queen of Scots,* the Scottish Tourist Board ran a promotion centered around "Mary, Queen of Scots country."

Religious shrines are major attractions
for many

Visitors can also be encouraged to visit places where ficticious people lived. World Travel Tours advertise special *Song of Norway* tours and *Sound of Music* trips to Norway and Austria, respectively. Pan Am has run tours to Dracula's Transylvania (now a part of Romania).

A nation's capital will always hold a fascination for those who desire to see where the decisions are made. The Houses of Parliament are as well known as the House of Representatives and the Kremlin. The chance to see the country's leaders in session is an experience few visitors would miss. Even on the state and local levels, council sessions can become the focal point of an educational tour, while the City Hall "you can't fight" may also be visited.

Ethnicity. The United States is a cosmopolitan mixture of first-, second-, and third-generation Scots, Irish, Dutch, German, Russian, and so on. As such, it is easy to appeal to people's basic sentimentality to coax them "back to the homeland." The ethnic groups may be classified as first and later generations. For the first generation, no development is needed at all, for these people wish to see the area they left just as they left it.

However, first-generation travelers will generally stay with friends, and one finds that it is the later generations that will spend more money in a particular spot. This latter group of travelers, experiencing a different environment, will require some of the creature comforts afforded them at home. It should not be thought, however, that the only viable market for this kind of promotion consists of present-day U.S. citizens, though many examples of such marketing exist. One of the definite movement channels that can be readily traced is that from Ireland to New York and Boston.

In North America itself, Michigan's Tulip Festival, the Highland Games at Alma, the Beer Festival at Frankenmuth, and the weekly summer ethnic concerts in downtown Detroit show the success of a campaign on this asset.

It is possible also to spotlight movements within a country. In the United States, it is estimated that one out of every five Americans moves each year. Nor are these movements random. States like Florida, Nevada, Arizona, and California have attracted decennial population increases in the order of 50 to 80 percent, and states like Arkansas and West Virginia have suffered population decreases in the order of 6 to 10 percent. There may well be a significant market to be reached through the sentimental pull of old friends and places.

Accessibility.   The last item to consider in this section is accessibility. Though germane to every asset listed above, certain areas owe their popularity—and some their very being—to the fact that they are readily accessible to large urban areas. The development of Brighton, England, as a weekend and holiday resort despite its completely stony beach is due to its proximity to London with a potential market of 8 million people.

The accessibility of an area to a particular market should be measured in terms of time, cost, frequency, and comfort. Although attention should be paid to each factor, an area can sell on its comparative advantage in providing exceptional services in one or a combination of several of the above factors at the expense of another.

Traveling to Europe by plane, for instance, may cost more and be less comfortable than land or sea travel, but Europe is more accessible in terms of time and frequency of service. An advertisement for a sea ferry declares, "All that divides Scotland and Ireland is two-and-a-half hours." The motorist immediately knows how long it will take him to get to Ireland, and a seemingly large and time-consuming obstacle—the Irish Sea—becomes a mere two-and-a-half hour expressway.

Part of Mexico's appeal to the American market is its accessibility in terms of cost—not necessarily in terms of cost to reach the country, but in terms of what can be bought there. A two-week vacation in Mexico may be more accessible in terms of cost than fourteen days in the United States.

Other areas have become attractions because of the difficulty in reaching them. In those few cases in which lack of accessibility increases the attractiveness, the end result (the destination) should be somewhat spectacular—a magnificent view, great food, or a wonderful culture.

Development and Design

Gunn has suggested several design principles to guide the development of attractions.[1] It is important to remember that the dependencies of the attraction vary. Certain types of attractions, such as ski areas and battlefields, are extremely dependent upon the resource base, but others, such as theme parks, are much less so. All attractions are, to some extent, dependent upon their relationship to the tourist's origin, upon their accessibility, and upon the number of facilities and services available. In terms of the tourist origin, the time relationship may be more important than the distance relationship. Zones of tourist origin will differ, depending upon the mode of transportation considered. A two-hour zone, for example, may include tourists 100 miles away by car and 500 miles away by plane.

As noted earlier, accessibility, although important, is more crucial to the touring destination because the time available is a major constraint.

Services and facilities tend to grow up to support the developed attraction. However, if a service center is already developed, its location may effect the development of a new attraction.

Attractions tend to be clustered for several reasons. First, there is an increased desire on the part of tourists to do more in one place. Second, clustering allows a destination a better opportunity to satisfy more people. To explore a major theme fully, a variety of different attractions may be required. A group of museums, each exploring part of an overall theme, is more effective than one. A cluster of different but related historic buildings may be necessary to explore and explain a particular time in history fully. Different rides, clustered into a theme park, are necessary to appeal to all of the senses.

The extent of clustering depends upon the type of destination involved. For the primary destination, clustering is obviously more important. This is particularly true if accessibility is dependent upon modes of transportation oriented towards mass tourism. Destinations that rely on tourists arriving by plane, boat, or train will be apt to develop more clusters of attractions than those appealing to the motorist.

Events

Events can be developed for several reasons. Events may be staged to make money, to celebrate particular holidays, seasons, or historical events, to provide cultural or educational experiences, or to unite and give a feeling of pride to a particular community. An event may seek to combine these reasons. It is important that objectives be developed, agreed upon, and ranked in order that subsequent conflicts over strategy can be solved by referring to the action that will help to achieve the most important objective.

An examination of special events in Illinois revealed that most events included from eight to sixteen different activities. The most common activities were parades,

[1]Gunn, *Tourism Planning,* and Clare A. Gunn, *Vacationscape: Designing Tourist Regions* (Austin, Texas, The University of Texas, 1972).

queen and beauty contests, carnivals with featured entertainers, lunches and dinners, musical entertainments, dancing, and children's activities.

In approximately one-third of the cases, a nonprofit corporation takes major planning responsibility. The planning of the event can take anywhere from a month to over a year. Most groups used from five to eleven committees to organize the event that involved a total of 12 to 350 people, almost all of them volunteers.

FACILITIES

While attractions draw visitors from their homes, facilities are necessary to serve these visitors away from home. Facilities tend to be oriented to attractions in their location because of the need to locate close to where the market will be. They tend to support rather than induce growth and, hence, they tend to be developed at the same time as or after the attractions are developed.

It is possible for an attraction to be a facility. A case in point would be a well-known resort hotel that not only serves to draw people to an area but satisfies their needs as well.

Lodging.   While away from home, the tourist needs to eat and sleep. Sleeping accommodations can range from hotels of an international standard and condominiums, to campgrounds, and the homes of friends and relatives. Lodging accounts for between one-fifth and one-fourth of total tourist expenditures, despite the fact that almost half of U.S. tourists stay in the homes of friends and relatives when taking a trip. It is vital to the success of a tourist region that a sufficient quantity of accommodations of the right quality be provided for tourist needs.

The type of accommodation provided will be determined primarily by the characteristics of the market segment being sought. Some prefer the full-amenity type of property. In destination areas these properties will tend to have greater demands placed on them in terms of room size and services offered because guests will be staying a long time. Tourists whose prime motivation is to visit friends and relatives will likely stay with them.

The type of accommodation provided is also partly determined by what the competitors are providing. A key concept to remember in marketing is that the facilities provided should be at least equal those provided by the competition for the same market. The type of lodging is also determined by the transportation used by visitors to the destination. In Roman times, resting places were determined when the horse, not the rider, was tired. In the United States in the early seventeenth century, taverns were located about fifteen miles or one day's carriage ride apart. The development of rail travel led to accommodation clusters near the stations. An increase in auto travel encouraged the roadside motel, but the growth of air travel has led to clusters of hotels and motels around airports.

Food and Beverage.   More of the tourist dollar is spent on food and beverage than on any other service. It is probably no coincidence that those states highest in per capita eating place sales are also top tourist states.

The type of food service provided will be related to tourist needs. Many areas have successfully developed menus indigenous to the area to promote local economy foods, while they also use the local items as a unique selling point.

Support Industries.   Support industries refer to the facilities provided for tourists in addition to lodging, food, and beverage. These may include souvenir or duty-free shops (for goods), laundries and guides (for services), and festival areas and recreational facilities (for activities).

Support industries can either be subsistence-related by providing staple needs or requirements or pleasure-related by providing impulse or entertainment purchase opportunities.

For tourism, support industries tend to be small businesses. This fact can be both positive and negative for the destination area. It can be positive in that the encouragement of small businesses will allow for the wide distribution and sharing of the financial benefits of tourism with those in the community. On the other hand, small businesses may lack the capital and expertise required to provide a quality part of the vacation experience. Several considerations can assist in maximizing the potential of support industries. It is important that the support industries be located in places accessible to tourists. It will be necessary to observe or predict tourist movement patterns to locate facilities to serve them optimally. The number and types of facilities offered will also have to be determined relative to tourist needs. Facilities should be provided that match the quality and price level of lodging, food, and beverage operations that should themselves be provided in light of visitor expenditure levels.

Shopping is an important support industry

If a sufficient number and mix of services is provided, the supply may actually stimulate demand or increase the length of stay of visitors by offering such a number of attractive alternatives that they will have enough things to buy and do to encourage them to stay longer. At the same time, too many facilities at one place may mean that there is insufficient sales volume to assure a reasonable rate of return for the businesses involved.

The two primary techniques for helping assure the effective development of support industries are:

Zoning and operating regulations enforced by law

Ownership or control exercised through leasing of facilities to individual entrepreneurs.

The methods can, in fact, be combined with good results. People at destination areas may designate certain areas as being appropriate for tourist-support industries, and within those areas they may lay down restrictions as to theme, design, building height, and density; and they may place restrictions on signs in order to ensure the development of a destination that has attractions and facilities that meet expectations of the tourist market sought. The problem can also be effectively managed if a developer or public agency can own a large tract and establish control through requirements in the lease agreement.

INFRASTRUCTURE: TRANSPORTATION

Attractions and facilities are not accessible to tourists' use until basic infrastructural needs of the destination have been met. Infrastructure consists of all the underground and surface developmental construction of a region and comprises:

Water systems
Communication networks
Health care facilities
Transportation terminals
Power sources
Sewage/drainage areas
Streets/highways
Security systems

There has been some criticism of tourism's overreliance on a fully developed infrastructure. In certain parts of the world newly discovered tourist destinations may be able to satisfy tourist needs without developing a full infrastructural system. The lack of modern highways may, in fact, be an added attraction for some kinds of tourists. As a destination attracts more tourists, the increase in numbers may actually stimulate the development of the infrastructure. In most cases, the reverse is true. Infrastructural development is necessary to stimulate the development of tourism.

The infrastructure of an area is shared by both tourists and residents. An upgrading of the elements of the infrastructure primarily for the purpose of attracting tourists will benefit the host population.

The development of infrastructure is almost always a public-sector responsibility. It is one way that the public sector has created a climate suitable for tourism development.

The development of a proper infrastructure requires engineering input, but it is wise to consider the reports of engineers in light of the effects on tourism. The best placement of a coast road from an engineering perspective may not be the best route for tourist viewing.

It is necessary also that visitors receive enough communication so that their questions about travel within the state are answered. Because of federal pressure in the United States to restrict billboards on the highway, various alternatives have been explored. Vermont has developed a successful travel information system comprised of the following parts:

1. Local chambers of commerce are located in many Vermont communities, with manned offices or booths.
2. Vermont visitors handbooks, containing details on the facilities offered by over 600 Vermont traveler-oriented businesses, can be obtained from local chambers of commerce.
3. Official state maps, containing historic sites, museums, golf courses, campgrounds, and ski areas are offered. These maps, highway route numbers, and town destination signs will guide the visitor between towns. Once the desired town is reached. . .
4. Official business directional signs replace billboards for services available in that town and may indicate the number of miles to a hostelry or other service. These signs are located just before road junctions that require the visitor to change direction from one numbered highway to another, except at congested intersections and other important locations, and on interstate highways at rest areas, where these signs are replaced by listings on. . .
5. Travel information plazas, from which are dispensed the area. . .
6. Travelers services guide pertaining to the section of Vermont in which the dispensing plaza is located. These guides provide directions to businesses that are listed on each plaza where the guide's dispenser is located.

The important parts of a tourist infrastructure are the following:

- *Water*—Sufficient quantities of pure water are essential. A typical resort requires 350 to 400 gallons of water per room per day. An eighteen-hole golf course will require 600,000 to 1 million gallons of water per day, depending on the region in which it is located.
- *Power*—The important considerations are that adequate supplies of power be available to meet peak-load requirements, that continuity of service be assured,

and that, if possible, the type of power supplied be compatible with that used by the target markets of the destination.

- *Communication*—Despite the fact that many tourists may wish to get away from it all, it is necessary for most that telephone and/or telegraph service be available. The lack of telephones in hotel rooms will often deter visitors from staying at a particular property because of the security aspect.
- *Sewage/drainage*—Sewer demand is often placed at 90 percent of domestic water demand. Although water-storage reservoirs and sewage treatment plants can be designed on the basis of maximum average demand, transmission lines must be designed on a basis of maximum peak demand.
- *Health care*—The type of health-care facilities provided will depend on the number of visitors expected, their ages, the type of activities in which they will engage, and local geographic factors. Ski areas will tend to specialize in broken bones, for example.
- *Streets/highways*—The availability of first-class roads adds greatly to the accessibility of a region. Some areas have, in fact, refused to upgrade their road systems in order to slow down tourism development. The effect of a highway system was noted by the U.S. Department of Transportation when it estimated that the development of the U.S. interstate system meant that the distance that could be safely driven in one day increased from 350 to 500 miles. There are certain ways to make use of the highway more interesting for tourists.
  1. Privide close-range view of local scenes
  2. Change the elevation
  3. Develop viewpoints and overlooks
  4. Independently align dual-lane highways to fit into the land contour
  5. Selectively thin trees to reveal views. It is crucial to consider to what extent resident (or local) traffic is to be integrated with tourist (or regional) traffic. It may be desirable to design a dual system of higher-speed lanes flanked by roads for low-speed local traffic. Roads should be engineered for safety, taking appropriate measures designed to safeguard the highway user.
- *Transportation terminals*—There should be a degree of coordination between the three modes of air, rail, and bus to facilitate passenger transfer between modes. Directional and informational signs should be easy to see and of a uniform design throughout the mode. A security system should be in place to prevent theft of luggage and/or misclaiming of checked baggage at terminals. Personnel should be available to assist passengers, particularly the aged, the handicapped, and non-English speaking passengers. Complete information should be provided on the location, fares, schedules, and routes of local transportation services.
- *Security*—While on vacation tourists are in an unfamiliar environment. Because of this, the need for assurances regarding their safety is important. Especially when traveling long distances and to foreign countries, the image gained of the destination may be distorted. Europeans, for example, are fed television programs that sensationalize the American crime scene. This creates an image of

Clean streets are an important part of a destination's infrastructure

the United States as a place filled with violence. In addition, the costs of medical care are so expensive that concerns about health in foreign countries may generate additional fears. Insecurities about food, water, or police protection may dissuade visitors from visiting. It is necessary that the basic needs for security and safety be considered and assured to make the potential tourist feel secure prior to and during the vacation.

HOSPITALITY RESOURCES

Hospitality resources refer to the general feeling of welcome that visitors receive while visiting a destination area. It is the way that tourist services are delivered by service providers, as well as the general feeling of warmth from the general resident population. It is a combination of a certain amount of knowledge and a positive attitude that results in specific hospitable behaviors. The way in which services are delivered is particularly important because tourism is consumed on the spot. Sales and service occur at the same time. Although excellent service cannot totally make up for a hard bed, tough steak, bumpy bus ride, or rainy weather, poor service can certainly spoil an otherwise excellent vacation experience. In the broader sense, tourists will have a much more rewarding vacation if they feel welcomed by the host population and will certainly feel awkward and unhappy if they feel resented.

Hospitality resources can be improved by, in effect, training tourism personnel to be hospitable and encouraging positive feelings toward tourism and tourists on the part of the general public. These two aspects will be dealt with separately.

Hospitality Training

A program of hospitality training is generally aimed at motivating service providers to be hospitable in their dealings with tourists. The assumption is that providing more hospitable service will result in a more satisfied tourist who will be inclined to return and/or spread positive reactions through word-of-mouth advertising to other potential tourists. To achieve hospitable service on the part of service providers, it may be necessary to change their present behavior. Many believe that a change in behavior is brought about by a change in attitude and an increase in the level of knowledge. The three aspects of attitude are toward self, toward others, and toward the subject matter.

Attitude toward self.   If an individual's self-esteem, or attitude toward self, is low, that individual will tend to behave in such a way that the feedback from others will confirm this low opinion of himself or herself. Traditionally the tourism industries have lacked prestige. Those who work in the tourism industries have, by association, lacked prestige. Behavior is thus precipitated that will reinforce this feeling. The key then is to change the individual's perception of self in order to improve behaviors. If service providers can be made to believe that their work and they themselves are important, the hope is that their work and specifically their actions toward tourists will reflect this new feeling. This aspect can be put into practice by highlighting the vital part that service providers play in ensuring a positive vacation experience. If service providers can be viewed as hosts and hostesses rather than "just" employees, their self-image may be raised. Stress should be placed on the fact that dealing with and serving people is, indeed, a most difficult task. Visitors often bring demands with them that are difficult to satisfy. Although it is relatively easy to deal with a satisfied guest, it is very challenging to deal with visitors who are dissatisfied or extra demanding. The ability to create a satisfied guest is a very demanding task. Those people who can do this have skills that should be highly regarded by themselves as well as by others.

Attitude toward others.   The second aspect of attitude relates to attitude toward others. An individual's feelings toward people that she or he comes into contact with will affect, positively or negatively, behavior toward them. The task is to assist the service provider in developing positive feelings toward fellow employees and tourists that will result in positive behavior toward the tourists. This can be achieved by training the individual in the importance of teamwork and interdependence in getting the job done. Oftentimes employees are not aware of all the people and actions that are necessary to ensure a satisfied guest. It is important that employees see where they fit into the big picture of a satisfied tourist, not only to see how important their role is, but also to be aware of the interfacing roles of others.

It is obviously important to consider the employee's attitude toward visitors. The key to the development of positive attitudes toward visitors is being able to develop the ability to put oneself in the visitor's place. Role-playing can be successfully used for this purpose. If a service provider can emphathize with the tourist, accept tourists as they are, understand that for them this vacation is something that they have saved for all year, and appreciate how tired they may be after a long trip, then the attitude is likely to be more positive.

Attitude toward subject matter. The third aspect of attitude concerns attitude toward subject matter. The individual who does not believe in the work being done will display a negative attitude that will be reflected in poor service toward the guest. A positive attitude on the part of service providers toward tourists can come about only when employees are made aware of how important tourism is to their state, country, city, and property. By being aware of the amount of revenue, jobs, and taxes generated and the dispersion of the tourist dollar throughout the community, employees may become convinced of the economic and social significance of the industry of which they are a part.

The hope is that more hospitable behavior will come, in part, from a better self-image, more empathy with others, and a positive attitude about tourism's role in the community.

To precipitate a change in attitude, it is necessary to raise the knowledge level of the individual. This may be done in group sessions or through a variety of audiovisual means.

Teaching Specific Behaviors

A second theory of behavior change is that a change in behavior affects attitudes. If people can be trained in specific desired behaviors and act them out, the positive feedback they receive will result in a positive attitude. The task is to develop specific behaviors that will be termed *hospitable* and instruct employees in these behaviors. If the employees act out these hospitable behaviors, the positive reactions (tips, recognition, advancement, and so on) will result in positive attitudes toward hospitality. To this end, employees can familiarize themselves with the surrounding attractions and services (to be able to give advice or direction). Some attractions will have an open house for those involved in tourism to acquaint them by means of a mini-familiarization tour. Sessions can cover both verbal and nonverbal behavior. Employees are often unaware of the negative messages their facial expressions or posture give.

By means of this joint approach—attempting to change attitudes about the self, others, and tourism through increasing the level of knowledge and teaching specific hospitable behaviors—an attempt is made to raise the hospitality behavior level of service providers.

Community Awareness Programs

Although the tourist is most directly affected by the degree of hospitality shown by service providers, the overall feeling of welcome within a community will also enhance or detract from the vacation experience. Residents of a destination area cannot be trained to act in a hospitable way toward tourists, but a community awareness program can help develop a more positive attitude toward the tourist. The objectives of such a program are twofold—to build acceptance of tourism and to build an understanding of the tourist.

An acceptance of tourism cannot be built unless the benefits of tourism are made relevant to members of the community. The benefits of tourism are many, yet many people do not realize that they are positively affected by it. To some it may mean a summer job, while to others tourism may ensure that a playhouse can survive year-round for the cultural benefit of the community. It is necessary to communicate to each part of the community messages that are important and relevant to them.

An understanding of who the tourist is can assist in a greater acceptance of the visitor. Knowing why people visit the area might result in a renewed civic pride.

There are different ways to communicate with the local community. Public meetings can be held to discuss particular problems. Some areas have successfully organized a speaker's bureau consisting of tourism community leaders who talk to community groups. Information sheets and newsletters, though infrequently used, can be distributed to the general public. Some communities have shown the effect of tourism by giving two-dollar bills in change to tourists to distribute throughout the area. In the off-season in Niagara Falls, Ontario community groups can tour many of the tourist attractions free of charge. Whatever methods are used, the objective remains to create a feeling of welcome for the tourist within the community.

Hospitality—the aloha spirit

REFERENCES

Destination U.S.A., Vol. III, Implementation: Visitor Services (The University of Missouri, 1978), pp. 14–20, 89.

GUNN, CLARE A., *Tourism Planning* (New York, Crane Russak & Company, Inc., 1979), pp. 54–61, 76, 83–86.

"It's All Up to You," Facilitator's Training Manual, Gulf Coast Community College, Florida, undated.

KAISER JR., CHARLES, and LARRY E. HELBER, *Tourism Planning and Development.* (Boston, CBI Publishing Company, Inc., 1978), pp. 28–29, 61, 169, 191, 193–94.

KASTARLAK, BULENT, "Planning Tourism Growth," *Cornell Hotel and Restaurant Administration Quarterly,* February 1971, pp. 27–29.

MCINTOSH, ROBERT W., *Tourism: Principles, Practices, Philosophies,* 2nd ed. (Columbus, OH, Grid Inc., 1977), p. 127.

Planning Community-Wide Special Events (University of Illinois at Urbana-Champaign, Cooperative Extension Service, undated).

EXERCISE

A 1972 report by the Department of Transportation in the U.S. identified the following problems in terminal facilities and ground transportation. Use this list to evaluate a terminal facility in your town—either an airport, train station, or bus terminal. To what extent have things improved? What problems remain?

General—There is an almost complete lack of coordination between the three modes of air, rail, and bus. In addition, there is a noticeable lack of consistency in standards and procedures within each mode.

Directional and informational signs are often difficult to see; signs are not uniform throughout the system; public-address announcements are often unintelligible.

Air—Long walks are required in many terminals.

Rail—Parking is inconvenient and inadequate near larger terminals; use of facilities by local transients and inadequate cleaning procedures lead to crowded, unsanitary waiting rooms and restrooms; security to prevent thefts is lacking; information and directional maps are not provided in most rail terminals; special transportation to and from rail terminals is not provided; and the urban transit and taxi service is often inadequate.

Bus—Terminals are dirty and crowded due to use by unauthorized people and to inadequate cleaning procedures; boarding gates lack a system of orderly procedures resulting in crowding when passengers are boarding; inadequate protection is afforded to passengers against traffic.

The following suggestions regarding terminals and ground facilities have been made and serve as a guide to the provision of adequate services:

1. Full information about facilities, terminal location, and local transportation at destination should be made available to all originating passengers.

2. A security system should be provided to prevent theft and misclaiming of checked baggage at terminals.

3. The information system should provide data on connecting or alternative rail and bus service, including information on fares and schedules.

4. A system of standard signs and symbols should be developed and installed in all air terminals.

5. Rapid updated arrival and departure information should be available on posted information boards, through public address announcements, and to telephone callers.

6. Personnel should always be available to assist passengers, particularly the aged, the handicapped, and non-English speaking.

7. Complete information should be provided on the location, fares, schedules, and routes of local transportation services.

8. City maps should be made available to passengers.

9

TOURISM
AND ECONOMIC
AND SOCIAL PLANNING

The Contributions
of the Travel Industry

*"The tourist brochure refers to Saint Maarten as unspoiled.
Unspoiled, in the vernacular of tourism, means that the
place is hardly worth a visit."*

Kenneth R. Morgan, "Speaking You English?
A Lighthearted Guide to World Travel."

Tourism can have a significant impact upon a destination country. This chapter explores the potential economic and sociocultural effects of tourism upon a destination and suggests appropriate strategies to maximize tourism's economic effects. It is recognized that tourism may be one of several development options open to a location. The characteristics of tourism compared to other development possibilities are therefore examined. The full effect of tourism on the economy in terms of foreign exchange, income, and employment is detailed. Although tourism can bring economic advantages to a destination country, it can also bring social changes. The possibilities are outlined.

The effect of tourism on the U.S. and Canadian economies is detailed, and suggestions are given to help those at a destination develop policies to maximize tourism's economic effect.

LEARNING OBJECTIVES

Having read this chapter, you should be able to:

1. List and explain three potential categories of economic impacts of tourism on a destination country.
2. Discuss the possible sociocultural impacts of tourism on a host country, including the potential tensions between the hosts and the visitors.
3. Explain the input-output and cost-benefit analysis techniques.
4. Describe the major impacts of tourism on the U.S. and Canadian economies.
5. Identify and describe the strategies to maximize the economic impact of tourism.

"Currently second only to oil and almost certain to become the biggest sector in international trade by the year 2000, tourism is increasingly providing a large number of developing countries an avenue of escape from the quagmire of the international commodity markets. Once frowned upon and described by many as neocolonialistic and dangerous to the social and moral fabrics of the Third World, the growth of tourism is all the more remarkable for its consistency . . . If tourism has weathered the storms of the world economic recession and the political upheavals and conflicts that characterized many parts of the globe in the 1970s and '80s, it is clear that the urge in man to travel either for business or for leisure is very strong indeed."[1]

This quotation provides an excellent opening for the discussion of tourism and its impacts on a host destination. It clearly indicates that tourism as an economic endeavor has both positive and negative effects, some of which are very real and others of which have a tendency to be overexaggerated by tourism's proponents, on the one hand, and its critics, on the other. The statement not only reflects that tourism is not all bad and not all good, but shows a new maturity about our understanding of tourism. Tourism has, by and large, demonstrated that it is relatively "recession-proof," and its consistent performance can help alleviate the cyclical patterns of other sectors of the host community's economy.

TOURISM'S ROLE IN ECONOMIC DEVELOPMENT

Tourism development has been advanced as a policy alternative, particularly for developing countries, to aid economic growth. There are several arguments for this. First, the demand for international travel continues to grow in developed countries. Second, as incomes in the developed countries increase, the income elasticity of demand for international travel will mean that it will increase at a faster rate. Third, developing nations need foreign exchange earnings to aid their own economic development to satisfy the rising expectations of their growing populations.

Developing countries have tended to rely upon agriculture and other primary industries for economic growth. Indeed, the World Bank, indicating that between

---

[1]General Secretariat of the ACP Group of States, Tourism, (The ACP-EEC Courier, July–August 1990, p. 50).

fifty percent and seventy percent of the population of middle- and low-income developing countries is directly dependent on agriculture, supports the necessity for full agricultural growth as a key to industrialization and further economic and employment growth. Noting that almost all developing countries have followed import-substitution (the substitution of locally produced products for those presently imported), they stress the need to reward exports with incentives. A basic problem, however, with the reliance on agricultural development is that the developing country can easily be overly dependent on a few primary products. The price of primary products is unpredictable and dependent on such things as weather, disease, and outside manipulation by large buyers from the developed countries.

The development of the manufacturing sector is not always a viable option. Problems include the fact that:

1. The processing of raw materials is related directly to the base amount available in the area, and possible projects are likely to be few for all but the most richly endowed nations.
2. For industries aimed at import substitution, the relatively small size of many domestic markets restricts growth.
3. Developing countries are characterized by a chronic shortage of skilled labor.
4. For export-oriented industries, their products will have to face full international competition in terms of price and quality, as well as in terms of marketing techniques used.

This is not to say the development of tourism does not face similar problems for a developing country. Yet each country has the "raw material" for tourism within its borders. In most cases, there are fewer restrictions on international travel than on international trade. The distance of the destination from the market is becoming less of a problem and may in itself be an attraction. Also, prices charged are more under the control of the seller than of the buyer in comparing tourist-related industries with primary industries. The Organization for Economic Cooperation and Development (OECD) has concluded, in fact, that tourism provides a major opportunity for growth for countries that find themselves at the intermediate stage of economic development and that are experiencing rather fast economic growth and increasingly require more foreign-exchange earnings. They also caution that "there are few if any developing countries which could or perhaps even should rely principally on tourism for their economic salvation."[2]

Tourism is an invisible export that differs from international trade in several ways:

1. The "consumer" collects the product from the exporting country, thereby eliminating any freight costs for the exporter, except in cases in which the airlines used are those of the tourist receiving country.

[2]Robert Erbes, International Tourism and the Economy of Developing Countries, OECD, June 1973, p. 4.

2. The demand for the pleasure segment of tourism is highly influenced by noneconomic factors, such as local disturbances, political troubles, and changes in the fashionability of resorts or countries created mostly by media coverage. At the same time, international tourism is usually both price elastic and income elastic. Changes in either of these two variables normally result in a more-than-proportional change in pleasure travel.

3. By using specific fiscal measures, the exporting (tourist receiving) country can manipulate exchange rates so that those for tourists are higher or lower (normally the latter in order to attract a greater number of tourists) than those at other foreign trade markets. Also, tourists are permitted to buy in domestic markets at the prices prevailing for the local residents (the exceptions being the duty-free tourist shops operated in many Caribbean islands and elsewhere).

4. Tourism is a multifaceted industry that directly affects several sectors in the economy (such as hotels and other forms of accommodations, shops, restaurants, local transport firms, entertainment establishments, and handicraft producers) and indirectly affects many others (such as equipment manufacturers and utilities).

5. Tourism brings many more nonpecuniary benefits and costs (that is, social and cultural) than other export industries.

ECONOMIC IMPACTS OF TOURISM

Increasing Foreign Exchange Earnings

Because of the findings stated above, many countries have embraced tourism as a way to increase foreign exchange earnings to produce the investment necessary to finance economic growth. This certainly can and does occur. Some countries even require tourists to bring in a certain amount of foreign currency for each day of their stay and do not allow them to take it out of the country at the end of their vacation.

However, the foreign exchange earnings generated by tourism can be overstated unless the import factor is known. The value of goods and services that must be imported to service the needs of tourism is referred to as *leakage*. The money spent leaks from the host economy and must be subtracted from foreign exchange earnings to determine the true impact.

Leakage. Leakage occurs from a variety of sources. The extent to which a destination can minimize these effects will determine the size of the foreign exchange earnings. Leakage occurs first from the cost of goods and services that must be purchased to satisfy the needs of tourists. If a tourist wishes a steak and if that steak is imported, the cost of the steak is an import cost set against earnings. Local industries may also import part of their raw materials to produce goods for tourists. This also is a cost. A second cost may occur when importing goods and materials for infrastructure and buildings required for tourism development. The use of materials indigenous to the area will not only reduce import cost but will also add a distinctive look to the facilities. Payments to foreign factors of production represent another import cost. Commissions might have to be paid to overseas tour operators. If foreign capital is invested in the country's tourism, plant interest payments, rent, or profit may have to be paid to those outside the country. The amount of local ownership and control is crucial in this regard. Foreign-owned chain hotels will often be staffed, stocked, and furnished by people, food, furnishings, fixtures, and equipment from a central foreign source. A fourth area of cost is in direct expenditure for promotion, publicity, and similar services abroad. The cost, for example, of setting up a national tourist office (NTO) is a large expense to be set against earnings. There are several ways that transfer pricing can reduce foreign exchange earnings. If tourists make purchases in the country of origin for services to be delivered at the destination, the transfer payments need not be made for the services provided. If a tourism company is multinational, payments may be recorded in the country of tourist origin rather than in the destination country, thereby reducing profits and taxes in the destination country. In a similar situation, purchases by a foreign-owned hotel at the destination country may be made from a foreign-owned subsidiary at inflated rates to reduce the taxable income in the destination country. The use of credit cards and traveler's checks can mean that local banks will not be able to participate in the exchange. Last, foreign exchange earnings can be reduced when host governments exempt duties or taxes on foreign-owned companies or offer financial inducements to them to attract investment.

Leakage occurs when a destination must import goods and services to satisfy the tourist

A critical issue for destination areas is to determine the net foreign exchange earnings from different types of tourists. High-income tourists may be few in number and may spend large amounts of money, but they may require a substantial infrastructure and facilities resulting in a high import cost. Is this better for the destination country than the mass market that comes in greater numbers and spends less per person, but requires fewer imported goods and services? The answer comes from a rather complex economic analysis. It breaks down tourism earnings into component economic sectors and then determines to what extent each of the sectors depends on imports. Countries can be characterized as follows on the basis of the proportion of net foreign exchange earnings (subtracting the import content) from tourism:

- *Less than 10 percent:* Totally import reliant (such as Mauritius)
- *10–50 percent:* Heavily import reliant (such as the less-developed Caribbean and South Pacific islands)
- *50–70 percent:* Import luxuries and a few necessities (such as the better developed Caribbean islands)
- *70–90 percent:* Import principally luxuries; have advanced manfacturing sectors with good resources (such as Kenya, Tunisia, Greece, and Yugoslavia)[3]

There are relatively few studies in this area, and the works that exist do not use the same methodology. However, a certain pattern seems to be true regarding foreign exchange earnings. The foreign exchange cost will be high initially as a country begins to develop its tourism potential. Materials will probably have to be imported and incentives given to attract investment. After this heavy initial cost period, the foreign exchange cost will gradually diminish for a period and then will tend to increase again. This is due in great part to what is known as the demonstration effect. The demonstration effect describes the process by which local residents, exposed to goods imported for tourist use, begin to demand those goods for themselves. This automatically increases the demand for imports. This is illustrated in Figure 9.1. To

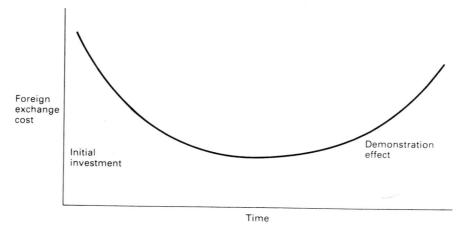

Figure 9.1 Foreign exchange cost over time

[3]Robert Cleverdon, The Economic and Social Impact of International Tourism on Developing Countries (E.I.U. Special Report No. 60, The Economist Intelligence Unit Ltd., May 1979), p. 32.

what extent this cost should be ''charged'' to tourism is debatable. As incomes rise and as communications relay messages to residents, they increasingly have the means for and are exposed to many new products. Tourism may be said to hasten the process by exposing at first-hand such goods and services to the local residents.

Increasing Income

The multiplier effect.   The tourism industry obviously generates income within a destination country. The amount of income generated, however, is difficult to determine. The difficulty arises from the fact that tourism is comprised of many different sectors of the economy. Additionally, many small businesses are involved, which leads to great difficulty in getting precise data.

Probably the most common method for estimating the income generated from tourism is by determining the multiplier for a destination. The multiplier effect is illustrated in Figure 9.2. A tourist makes an initial expenditure into the community.

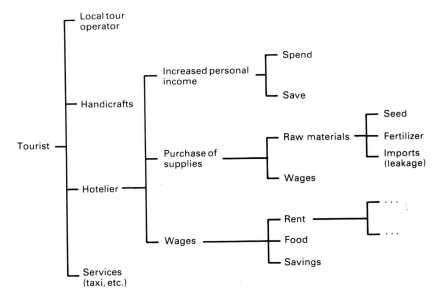

Figure 9.2   The multiplier effect

This expenditure is received as income by local tour operators, handicrafts store owners, hoteliers, and taxicab drivers. In the first round of transactions, a hotelier may use some money received to buy some supplies, pay some wages, and retain some profits. The income in the second round may be spent or saved, while the employee who has received payment for services rendered may spend some of that on rent and some on food and may put some into savings. The money spent on supplies in the third round of spending, goes for things such as seed, fertilizer, and imported raw materials. Any income spent on imports has leaked out of the local economy. This process continues until the additional income generated by a new round of spending essentially becomes zero. The multiplier is given by:

$$K = \frac{Y}{E}$$

where

      K = the multiplier
      Y = the change in income generated by E
      E = the change in expenditure (the initial sum spent by the tourist)

(Because of the difficulties in generating the data for an additional unit of expenditure, the analysis is generally conducted relative to an average unit of spending.)

The size of the multiplier depends upon the extent to which the various sectors of the economy are linked to one another. This is largely a function of the diversity of activities within the destination. When the tourism sectors buy heavily from other local economic sectors for goods and services, there will be a correspondingly smaller propensity to import, and the multiplier will be greater than if the reverse were true.

A simplified formula for the multiplier is:

$$K = \frac{1 - L}{1 - (c - cj - tic)\,(1 - td - b) + m}$$

where

K = the multiplier
L = the direct first-round leakages
c = the propensity to consume
cj = the proportion of that propensity spent abroad
tic = the indirect tax
td = the value of direct deductions (income tax, national insurance, and so on)
b = the level of government benefits
m = the value of imports[4]

Most island economies have an income multiplier range between 0.6 and 1.2, while developed economies have a range between 1.7 and 2.0.[5]

The *simple multiplier*, which we have been discussing, has come under criticism for several reasons. For two reasons, it is suitable for use in only small countries with relatively small economies. First, the model does not take into account the fact that the destination country may increase export sales to other countries from which it presently imports. Although it may be necessary to import certain items to cater

[4]Robert Cleverdon, pp. 234–35.

[5]Brian Archer, "Input-Output Analysis: Its Strengths, Limitations and Weaknesses, in The 80's: Its Impact on Travel and Tourism Marketing" (The Travel Research Association, Eighth Annual Conference Proceedings, June 1977), p. 98, and Cleverdon, p. 33.

to visitors, once these former tourists return to their home country, they may desire foods or other items from the country visited. Second, the model fails to take into account the fact that the additional income generated may produce investment in the destination country.

Input-Output Analysis

A more serious criticism of the simple multiplier formula, has to do with the assumption that each type of income injected into the economy has the same general effect. To remedy this, it is necessary to break the increase in expenditure into its component elements in order to analyze the effect of each element separately. This is done through *input-output analysis*. An input-output table shows how transactions flow through an economy in a given time period. A matrix is developed, the rows of which show the total value of all the sales made by each sector of the economy to all the other sectors. The columns of the matrix show the purchases made by each sector from each of the other sectors. Input-output analysis is a method of looking at these interactions and determining the effects of any possible changes. Here again, problems exist. It is extremely difficult and expensive to get sufficient data for a detailed model, largely because tourist spending affects so many sectors of the economy. Analysis is suitable for only the short and medium term. Last, it is argued, input-output analysis makes too many unrealistic assumptions. It assumes that supply is elastic. Any increases in demand will require more output that can be met by purchases from the economic sectors that provided the previous supply. It is unlikely that this will happen in the short run because of production hindrances. It also assumes that production functions are linear in form and that trade patterns are stable. It assumes that when production increases, purchases of imports will be made in the same proportions and from the same sources as before, negating any thought of economies of scale. Additionally, it is assumed that increases in income will be spent on the same items and in the same proportions as previously. In reality, none of these assumptions are likely.

Certainly, input-output analysis can show the economic impacts of different kinds of visitors, which will assist in target market selection. It can also show short-term economic effects compared with the effects of other sectors of the economy. Other tools, however, are needed to demonstrate the best long-term policy option for investment in the various available economic sectors.

Cost-Benefit Analysis

Cost-benefit analysis is a technique used to determine which economic sector will produce the most benefit in terms of foreign exchange, employment, taxes, or income generated relative to the costs of development. The factors of production are valued at their *opportunity cost*—the marginal value of their next best use. It is then possible to compare several investment options. The social cost-benefit analysis of a project determines the average annual rate at which benefits accrue to society. Such an analysis also draws critics who argue that the results are too dependent upon the appropriateness of the assumptions made. It is not possible to check actual performance against prediction. Certainly, it does appear possible to make value judgments that will produce the appropriate results.

Structural Analysis

As growth takes place, long-term changes in the economy can be determined through structural analysis. It is necessary to determine and study three different processes:

1. Accumulation processes (investment, government revenue, education)
2. Resource allocation processes (structure of domestic demand, production and trade)
3. Demographic and distributional processes (labor allocation, urbanization, demographic transition, income distribution)

In recent years, countries have tended to become primary or industrial specialists, have balanced production and trade, or have moved through the process of import substitution. Insufficient work has been done to determine the development pattern of a country's economy as it builds its tourism sector. Early work suggests that there is a danger of developing the tourism sector at the expense of other exports, such as agriculture. For maximum economic impact, care must be taken to achieve as much integration of tourism with the internal economy as possible.

INCREASING EMPLOYMENT

A principal argument made for encouraging the development of tourism is that it produces many jobs. Tourism creates primary or direct employment in such areas as lodging, restaurants, and sightseeing operations. Indirect employment can also be created in the construction, agriculture, and manufacturing industries. The amount of indirect or secondary employment generated depends upon the extent to which the tourism sector is integrated with the rest of the local economy. The more integration and diversification that occurs, the more indirect employment that is generated.

It is often argued that tourism is more labor-intensive than other industries, and for this reason it deserves developmental support. The degree of labor intensity can be measured in terms of the cost per job created or the employment-output ratio. The employment-output ratio is the number of workers employed divided by the contribution of tourism to the national income. Although research conclusions are not unanimous, for the most part they agree that the cost per job created in tourism is no less than in other sectors of the economy. A major reason for this is the fact that tourism is also capital intensive. The heavy costs of providing necessary infrastructure drastically increase the cost of creating jobs.

In the early stages of tourism development, the cost per job created is likely to be rather high due to the costs described previously. Similarly, the capital-output ratio will also be high because of the low volume of tourists in the initial stages of tourism development. As the destination country develops and as more tourists are attracted, the capital-output ratio declines. The cost per job created will also be reduced due to the experience and organization of those at the destination. In addition, as tourism increases, physical development takes place in facilities that are less costly than the construction of hotels. Jobs can thus be created at a lower average cost. In the third stage of tourism development, the average cost per job created may increase due to higher land prices and increased engineering costs because of the necessity of using sites that are more difficult to develop. Also, as tourism increases in importance, a greater infrastructure may be necessary, because the tourism plant will be geographically spread out. Also, greater infrastructural demands may be made by larger numbers of tourists.

The cost per job created obviously depends upon the type of facility constructed. The cost will be greater for a luxury hotel than for a smaller, more modest property. Also, the luxury hotel will offer more job opportunities per room and higher employment-output ratios than will the smaller properties. The larger properties are more inclined to use imported labor, at least for managerial positions. The key to maximizing the economic and job returns for the destination is to use materials and personnel indigenous to the region while maintaining a quality standard acceptable to the target market.

Can tourism development be an aid to regional development by producing income and jobs in areas previously lacking in economic development opportunities? Many people feel that this is a key role for the tourism industries. The fact, however, that tourism requires a heavy infrastructure means that the cost of developing tourism in a rural, outlying area may be as great as for developing its agricultural or industrial market potential.

Several additional criticisms of tourism as an employer have been made. In many areas, tourism is a seasonal business. To ensure a balance between market demand and staff requirements, a business tends to adopt one of two strategies. Either employees are laid off during the low season, or additional employees are imported from other regions during the high season. In the former situation, tourism cannot provide a meaningful job to a resident. In the latter situation, there is an increased need for housing for employees who will spend most of their wages outside of the destination region. Thus jobs and income are lost to the local area.

Because the tourism industries rely so heavily upon people for delivering a service, productivity gains are difficult to come by. The national output may be difficult to improve if tourism becomes a dominant part of the economy, particularly if the destination lacks a strong industrial sector where productivity gains are easier to obtain.

MODIFYING THE DESTINATION'S SOCIOECONOMIC STRUCTURE

Tourism development does indeed change the economic structure of the host country. Although such changes can easily be integrated into the developed economy, the

Tourism can create jobs in the building trades

effects in a lesser-developed country (LDC) are more profound. Stresses can occur when the old and the new exist side by side. Traditional methods of farming and primitive industries contrast with modern hotels and polished tourist entertainment. This, in fact, causes a movement away from traditional forms of employment. The fisherman turned tour-boat entrepreneur and farm girl turned waitress undergo not only a change in income but a change in status. The fisherman's catch is lost to the local people, but his own income may improve. The waitress may view her task of serving as a throwback to earlier colonial times or may look at the new-found job as a cleaner and less arduous way to earn a living. The satisfaction for locals may well depend upon the range and type of jobs available, together with the opportunity for advancement. The problem of seasonality is a major concern.

As with any other development industry, tourism encourages work-force migration, with the corresponding possibility of breaking down the traditional family unit. It does appear, however, that, even though migration occurs, family ties and responsibilities are maintained.

Because of tourism, profound changes can occur within society in terms of economic power. To the extent that tourism businesses attract women and young people, they gain an economic independence previously unheard of. Particularly in traditional societies, great tension can occur because of this shift in the economic resources within a destination region. There is inconclusive evidence to show that such changes may or may not result in negative effects upon the family.

Finally, tourism does change both the value and the ownership pattern of land. As tourism is developed, the value of potential sites increases. Land sold to outsiders results in a short-term profit to the local landowner. However, the land may be lost to agricultural production or local recreational use, and control of the land goes out of the community. Some destination regions take steps to prevent unhealthy (from the viewpoint of the destination) land speculation.

Tourism obviously has certain impacts upon the host region. Many of these impacts are direct (such as the raising of land values) while others are indirect (such as the increase in imports brought about by local exposure to goods imported for tourist consumption). Many of these changes would occur no matter what type of economic development took place. Whether these changes are good or bad is often a value judgment. The important point is to realize that these impacts are likely to occur, to decide whether or not they are desirable for the destination in question, and to plan accordingly.

Affecting Societal and Cultural Values

Tourism is concerned with the movement of, and contact between, people in different geographical locations. In sociological terms this involves[6]

1. Social relations between people who would not normally meet
2. The confrontation of different cultures, ethnic groups, life-styles, (possibly) languages, levels of prosperity, and so on
3. The behavior of people released from many of the social and economic constraints of everyday life
4. The behavior of the host population, which has to reconcile economic gain and benefits with the costs of living with strangers

The degree to which conflict will occur between host and guest depends upon the similarity in their standards of living, the number of tourists at any one time, and the extent to which tourists adapt to local norms.

The sociocultural impact of tourism can be both positive and negative. If host regions recognize that their indigenous cultures will attract tourists and serve as a unique factor in distinguishing one destination from another, attempts may be made to keep the culture alive. In some cases, traditional ways and goods may be restored because willing buyers (tourists) can be found. The Aaraya women of Cuna, Panama, had to be taught to sew the traditional dress of their culture. The skill had been lost. In London, England, many theaters can survive only because of the influx of tourists. In other areas, festivals are produced for tourists by the community which helps to keep its culture alive. Thus, entertaining the tourist may be the impetus for the performing of cultural activities or the production of goods, but the effect on the local community is that of preserving part of the old culture.

There are two negative sides to this. First, a process of cultural involution can take place. The modernization of an area and a people can be halted because of tourist demand for the old ways. Tourism, in essence, can encourage the host people to remain artisans at the expense of their industrial modernization. Second, the authen-

---

[6]Tourism Supply in the Caribbean: A Study for the World Bank by the Shankland Cox Partnership, November 1974, p. 84.

ticity of culture packaged for the tourist may be questionable. Many people feel that when a cultural event is prepared for tourist consumption its original, often spiritual, meaning is lost. In the United States, the moving of certain historic celebrations (Columbus Day, Washington's Birthday, and so on) to Mondays to give more three-day weekends throughout the year delighted many people in tourism. The purpose of the celebrations, however, was lost. In a smaller destination such changes in festivals, foods, and traditional ways of life have a greater impact.

Tourism's effect on architecture has largely been to the detriment of local styles. Part of this pressure comes from tourist demands, part from the multinational companies who seek economies of scale in construction, and part from the host countries themselves who see the building of Western-type hotels as a step toward modernity. A decision to build in the local style using materials indigenous to the area gives the region a different selling point while reducing economic leakage.

Tourism appears to act as a medium for social change (because of the contact between host and guest) rather than as the cause itself. The host-guest interaction offers the opportunity for each to learn more of the other, and as such, it can contribute to a greater understanding between peoples. Each destination region must weigh the cultural gains to be had—revived arts, theater, exposure to new ideas—against the losses to be had—overcrowding, a cheapening of the culture, possible social change.

TOURISM IN THE U.S. ECONOMY

Attempts to develop economic impact data for the United States have been hampered by the cost involved. Because tourism cuts across so many industries, the expense of obtaining accurate and detailed figures is considerable.

The U.S. Travel Data Center has developed the travel economic impact model designed to estimate the economic effects of tourism at the national, regional, and local levels. Their work indicates that approximately 26 percent and 21 percent respectively of the U.S. resident and foreign visitor spending is initially for food, and about 38 percent and 13 percent is spent on a combination of private and public transportation. Expenditures on lodging are about 17 percent of total resident spending and 27 percent foreign-visitor spending. The proportions spent on incidentals, entertainment, and recreation account for approximately 19 percent resident and 39 percent foreign-spending. During the 1980's, domestic expenditures varied between sixteen and twenty times greater than that of foreign visitor totals. In the same time period, approximately 40 percent of the states accounted for 75 percent of the resident and foreign visitor expenditures. The leading states in terms of income and jobs generated from tourism are California, Florida, New York, Hawaii, and Texas.

The food-service industry is by far the major recipient of jobs created by tourism. Approximately 45 percent of all travel-related employment in the United States is in the food-service industry. Lodging accounts for about 20 percent of all of the jobs. Public transportation accounts for 12 percent of the jobs, while entertainment and recreation account for about 11 percent. The remaining jobs are in the general retail trades, auto transportation, and in travel arrangement.

The food-service industry is by far the major recipient of jobs created by tourism

The greatest impact of tourism jobs is felt in states such as Nevada and Vermont and least in the larger, more industrialized states that have more diversified economies. In about 80 percent of the states, tourism is among the top three private-industry employers and is the first private-industry employer in 26 percent of the states.

TOURISM IN THE CANADIAN ECONOMY

Tourism Canada estimates that 60,000 Canadian businesses are involved in tourism and that these businesses employ around 632,000 Canadian residents or 5% of Canada's labor force.[7] Of the $24 billion (Canadian) spent by all visitors in Canada in 1988—equivalent to 4% of Canada's Gross Domestic Product—the amounts allocated to the various economic sectors were: transportation (45%), food and beverage (21%), lodging (16%), recreation and entertainment (7%), and miscellaneous (11%).

Tourism is Canada's third largest export industry, with foreign visitors spending $7.1 billion (Canadian) in Canada in 1989. The ratio of resident to foreign tourist spending—at about 4 to 1—is much lower than that previously mentioned for the United States (at around 16-20 to 1).

As in the U.S., the economic importance of tourism varies according to the region of the country. From an income standpoint, the Atlantic Provinces and British Columbia are the most dependent on tourism. Some 7.4% of Prince Edward Island's Gross Provincial Product (GPP) results from tourism, while the percentages for the three other Atlantic Provinces were 5.6%, 4.7%, and 4.4% respectively in 1988 for Nova Scotia, New Brunswick, and Newfoundland. Approximately 5.5% of British

[7]Industry, Science and Technology Canada, Tourism on the Threshold, 1990, pp. 4-10.

Columbia's GPP was contributed by the tourism industry. Among the ten Canadian provinces, the lowest percentage contributions by tourism to GPP—at 3.6% for Ontario and 2.9% for Quebec—were not surprisingly in the most developed and economically diversified provinces.

Tourism Canada contends that tourism plays a strategic role in the Canadian economy, and the agency's summary of the benefits of tourism to Canada provides an excellent synopsis of what has been discussed to date in this chapter. According to Tourism Canada, tourism:

1. Creates jobs at all skill and experience levels.
2. Can drive development and growth in any region of the country.
3. Is a significant contributor to GDP.
4. Is a major earner of foreign exchange.
5. Enhances Canada's global trading relations: the international tourism marketing campaign promotes an appealing image of Canada abroad, and the personal contacts and experiences developed during tours and visits to Canada can later turn to fruitful business dealings.
6. Has a direct effect on other economic sectors including transportation, hospitality, entertainment, and the cultural industries.
7. Has a potential for growth that exceeds that of many other industries.

MAXIMIZING TOURISM'S ECONOMIC EFFECT

Growth Philosophy

Traditional economic growth theories have suggested one of two strategies to maximize economic impact within a region. Supporters of *balanced growth* suggest that tourism be viewed as an essential part of a broad-based economy. This philosophy stresses that tourism supply (the goods and services delivered as tourism) needs the support of other interrelated industries. To obtain the maximum economic benefit, these inputs should be locally produced. This necessitates a significant economic effort. The objective is thus to integrate tourism with the other economic activities.

Proponents of *unbalanced growth,* on the other hand, see tourism as the spark to economic growth. Although balanced growth supporters emphasize the development of supply, unbalanced growth proponents stress the need to expand demand. As demand is established through the vigorous development of tourism, other industries will see the need for their products and services and will move to provide them locally, thus expanding the economic base of the region. The dangers of relying upon tourism have been mentioned earlier. Certainly, it is preferable to develop tourism along with industrial activity.

A compromise strategy is that of *coordinate growth.* Economic efforts are concentrated into areas that "either provide a promising or existing base (i.e., the balanced growth concept) or. . .exhibit valid, yet incomplete, recreational opportunities and/or substantial market flow (utilizing tourism as the linchpin industry in an unbalanced situation, but limiting implementation to those cases where the proposed project can have considerable spillover effects upon the other, existing tourism elements in the area''[8] (for example, the development of a convention center to alleviate problems of seasonality).

Strategies for Minimizing Leakage

The key to maximizing the economic effect of tourism is to maximize the amount of revenue and jobs developed within a region. This entails developing and marketing to bring tourist money in and organizing the tourism sector to minimize leakage of both money and jobs. Developing and marketing will be dealt with in remaining chapters of the text. Strategies for minimizing leakage will form the basis for the remainder of this chapter.

Import substitution. A major economic problem, especially for lesser-developed countries, is the lack of linkages from the tourism industry to other industries within the economy. Foreign exchange earnings can be increased if ties can be developed between the tourism industry and primary, industrial, and other service industries. The economic feasibility of local development can be investigated in industries ranging from handicrafts to furniture. The industries showing most promise can be supported through specific subsidies, grants, or loans. Also, quotas or tariffs can be placed on the importation of goods that can be developed locally. This latter strategy may invite retaliation from other countries or regions, however. Last, it may be possible to encourage the use of local architecture, design, and materials by means of incentives.

Incentive programs. The wise use of incentives can encourage the influx of capital, both local and foreign, necessary to develop tourism supply. The common forms of incentives are[9]:

1. Tax exemptions-reductions on imported equipment, machinery, materials, and so on
2. Reduction in company taxation by means of favorable depreciation allowances on investment, or special treatment in relation to excise taxes, sales taxes, income taxes, turnover taxes, profits taxes, or property taxes
3. Tax holidays (limited period)
4. Guarantee of stabilization of tax conditions (for up to twenty yeras)
5. Grants (for up to 30 percent of total capital costs)
6. Subsidies (guaranteeing minimum level of profit, occupancy, and so on)
7. Loans at low rates of interest
8. Provision of land freehold at nominal or little cost or at low rents

[8]Tennessee Tourism Investment Study, Leisure Systems Inc., February 1975, p. 12.

[9]Robert Cleverdon, Economic Impact, p. 47.

9. Free and unrestricted repatriation of all or part of invested capital, profits, dividends, and interest, subject to tax provisions

10. Guarantees against nationalization or appropriation

Incentives are often offered on the basis of what the competition is offering rather than on what is best for the destination region. As a result, capital-intensive activities may be encouraged when, for many destinations, the problem is a surplus of labor. Several other difficulties can arise. The easy importation of materials may make it more difficult for local industries to develop. Destination regions have also found that it is difficult to phase out tax concessions. Managers may lose interest in the project or let the quality standards run down as the tax holiday comes to a close. Care must be taken to ensure that the burden of risk is borne not only by the local government, but by local or outside investors as well. Overall, the specific effect of incentives in encouraging development has not been demonstrated. Before implmenting an incentive strategy a destination should:

1. Examine the performance of other countries' schemes in the light of their resources and development objectives

2. Research the actual needs of investors

3. Design codes of investment concessions related to specific development objectives, with precise requirements of the investors (such as in terms of job creation)

4. Establish targets of achievement and periodically monitor and assess the level of realization of such targets

Multinational control. As tourism has developed among nations, the opportunity has arisen for international expansion of businesses in four areas—hotels, airlines, restaurants, and tour operations. Much criticism has been leveled at the multinational businesses (multinationals), charging that they operate to benefit their own operations at the expense of the destination region.

Overwhelmingly, multinationals have their home offices in developed countries. Approximately 80 percent of the hotels abroad are accounted for by companies headquartered in the United States, France, and the United Kingdom, and there is a trend toward more ownership by Japanese and Hong Kong interests. Most problems for the destination countries have resulted when the multinational corporations have had no financial investment in the hotels. Most overseas properties are operated without any foreign equity involvement, which is a trend that is increasing. Control is exercised through management contracts, or to a far lesser extent, through franchise agreements.

Although it is true that a foreign-owned hotel may engage in policies that run counter to the national tourism plan, it is impossible to identify this activity as a trend. The chances of this happening are lessened by a direct financial involvement of the overseas company. Likewise, criticisms stating that a type of internatinal property is out of context with the host country must be viewed in the larger scope of the target market. If a country has correctly identified the type of tourists it is seeking, it may seek a larger ''international-type'' facility. In general, however, multinational corporation hotels usually generate lower foreign exchange receipts than do local hotels, especially the smaller locally-owned and managed properties. The charge that foreign-owned properties import too much seems to be ill-founded. The import content of constructing, equipping, and operating a hotel in a lesser-developed country has been analyzed as follows[10]:

	Cost Component Analysis (percent)	Import Content (percent
Construction and capital equipment	87.5 to 92.5	50 to 80
Furniture and furnishings	4 to 6	10 to 50
Hotel operating equipment	4 to 6	20 to 70
Overall	100	45 to 80 (average 60)

There has been no clear evidence, however, that the import content would have been less if the hotel had been developed by a local developer. Hotels seem to be willing to purchase food locally if prices are competitive and supplies are assured.

Another concern among host countries has been that a foreign-owned hotel allows limited opportunity for local employees to reach positions of responsibility. International hotel chains usually have a core expatriate management team of three in a 100-room hotel, five in a 250-room hotel, and eight in a 350-room hotel. The wage bill, however, is proportionally higher than the number of employees. Some management contracts will stipulate that within, say, three to five years the management team must be made up of locals.

It appears that foreign ownership of hotels is of greatest benefit to the host country in the early stages of tourism development. At this point, the destination can really benefit from the foreign know-how. Maximization of benefits comes from direct financial involvement of the transnational business in the development of local managerial and supervisory talent.

Most countries have a national airline, although the airline may be owned and operated by a foreign company. Tourists will generally prefer to travel by the airline of their country of origin rather than by the airline of the destination country. This is particularly true, because of the perception of quality and safety in the event of travel to a lesser-developed country.

To protect their investment, destination countries have attempted to develop pooling agreements whereby technical services may be reciprocated or revenue earned and costs incurred on a route shared by the airlines serving that route. Lately, attempts have been made by the United States to dismantle this procedure on the grounds of antitrust violations. Virtually every charter airline is owned and operated

[10]Robert Cleverdon, p. 59.

by companies in developed countries. If an airline is a charter operation of another country, the host country receives less than 10 percent of the airline's revenue in the form of landing fees, fuel costs, and passenger handling. This figure may be as low as 2 to 3 percent if fuel is excluded. Although some countries have successfully banned charter aircraft from their airports, the development of mass tourism usually, though not always, requires the development of charter traffic.

Tour operators can wield a great deal of influence over destinations. Operators have the ability to direct large numbers of tourists to particular destinations. If a country has made a decision to develop tourism to the masses, and if it has consequently built the infrastructure and facilities to service these tourists, it must attract sufficient numbers of visitors to utilize and pay for the facilities. This type of country can become dependent on large tour operators who have the ability to sharply influence where the masses will vacation. In both Europe and the United States a large percentage of the charter tour market is increasingly controlled by a small number of companies. The larger foreign operator dealing with the mass market is much more likely to bypass local tour operators and deal directly with the local hotels. If hotel owners are in a situation in which supply is greater than demand, they can be forced to promise rooms at uneconomic rates or else face a total loss of business. If destinations are dependent on foreign-based tour operators, they have lost control of their own development. Also, the foreign exchange revenues may suffer. Destination regions benefit more from short-haul tourism than from long-haul. In addition, by dealing with smaller operators who specialize in a smaller but more discriminating market, there is more chance that local operators will be used.

Foreign exchange.   To maximize foreign exchange earnings, many countries have placed restrictions on spending. Countries have limited the amount of their own currency that tourists can both bring in and take out of the destination in order to ensure that foreign currency is used to pay bills in the host region. Tourists may be required to pay hotel bills in foreign currency. Before being allowed into the country, visitors may have to show that they have enough money for their stay, or they may even be required to enter with a specified amount of foreign currency for each day of their visit. Foreign tour operators will often barter with operators of local facilities to avoid an exchange of cash. Destination countries may require that tour operators pay in foreign currencies for services in the host country. In other cases, tour operators may issue vouchers in the country of origin for services to be provided at the destination. Some destination countries will require that these vouchers be cashed by the service provider inside the host country. Although there has been some talk of a number of destination countries issuing, on a regional basis, their own credit card or travelers's check program, the idea has not yet been implemented.

SUMMARY

Tourism can have a significant, positive economic impact on a destination area. The three major categories of these economic impacts are through increasing foreign ex-

To maximize foreign exchange earnings, many countries have placed restrictions on spending

change earnings, increasing income, and increasing employment. A variety of techniques can be used to measure such impacts, including multiplier calculations, input-output analysis, and cost-benefit analysis. In the past, tourism development has also modified the socioeconomic structures of destination countries and affected their societal and cultural values. These societal and cultural impacts have in some cases been negative, and tourism has been widely criticized for permanently altering the societies and cultures of some destinations.

This situation highlights an area of conflict that may exist in the tourism system between economic development and societal-cultural values. Therefore, it is vitally important for those involved in tourism policy setting and planning to recognize and give equal consideration to both the potential positive and negative effects of tourism.

REFERENCES

ARCHER, BRIAN, "Input-Output Analysis," pp. 93–95.

CLEVERDON, ROBERT, "Economic and Social Impact of International Tourism on Developing Countries," *International Tourism Quarterly,* May 1979, pp. 10–11, 13, 32, 38–39, 59, 64, 66, 70, 74, 115.

"Development in Perspective: World Bank Assessment," Tourism International Air-Letter, August 1979, p. 2.

GRAY, H. PETER, International Tourism: International Trade (Lexington, MA, D. C. Heath & Co., 1971), p. 131.

OECD, Tourism Development and Economic Growth, May 1966.

SMITH, VALENE L., ed., Hosts and Guests: The Anthropology of Tourism (Philadelphia, The University of Pennsylvania Press, Inc., 1976), pp. 8–12.

The Impact of Travel on State Economies, 1977–78 (U.S. Travel Data Center, Washington, DC, 1978).

"The Role of Tourism in Economic Development," Special Article No. 8, International Tourism Quarterly, no. 2, 1973, p. 57.

"Transnationals in Developing Country Tourism," Special Report No. 39, International Tourism Quarterly, no. 1, 1981, p. 43.

United States Travel Service, Tourism State Structure, Organization and Support—A Technical Study, 1978, p. 25.

10

TOURISM POLICY FORMULATION:

The Political Framework for Tourism Development

"Cities put their libraries, museums, zoos off limits to non-residents, except for a fee, though the city fathers argued, while funding these projects, that they were to be tourist attractions as might bring in money from the outside."

Editorial, Niagara Gazette, *April 1, 1973.*

To guide the development of tourism at a destination area, it is necessary to establish a tourism policy. Because of the potential importance of tourism to the destination area, public-sector involvement is often desirable for setting and carrying out that policy.

This chapter examines the political framework within which tourism policy is established and implemented. The various roles played by members of the public sector in tourism are reviewed and a model for establishing tourism policy is given.

Tourism policy is implemented through the efforts of tourism organizations. The functions of international, multinational, national, state or provincial, and community tourism organizations are examined in regard to their role in carrying out tourism policy.

The efforts of the U.S. public sector to establish tourism policy are traced from 1940 to the present, and problems with and primary functions of organizations at the national, state, and local levels are outlined.

LEARNING OBJECTIVES

Having read this chapter, you should be able to:

1. Identify the reasons why the public sector (government) should be involved in tourism development.
2. Describe the roles and functions of the public sector in tourism.
3. Explain the elements of a tourism policy model and how models are used to form a tourism policy for a destination.
4. Compare and contrast the external and internal constraints that must be considered in formulating a tourism policy.
5. Describe the roles and functions of the World Tourism Organization (WTO).
6. Describe the roles and functions of National Tourism Organizations (NTOs).
7. Explain the functions of the United States Travel and Tourism Administration (USTTA) and Tourism Canada.
8. Explain the functions of state and provincial government tourism agencies in the United States and Canada.

REASONS FOR PUBLIC SECTOR INVOLVEMENT IN TOURISM

There are several reasons why the public sector should be involved in tourism. First, there are *political reasons*. Tourism by its nature involves travel across national boundaries. Government must get involved in terms of policies relating to the procedures regarding the entry and exit of travelers and nationals. The encouragement of tourism can also be used for political purposes as a means of furthering international relations between two countries or as a means of enhancing the national and international image of a particular destination. Japan, for example, embarrassed by its huge international trade surplus during the 1980s, initiated the "Japan Ten Million Programme" to encourage Japanese people to take trips to foreign countries. This move was in stark contrast to other countries, including Canada and the United States, who remained concerned about their international "travel gaps" (the differences between what their residents spent abroad and what foreigners spent in their countries on travel).

Second, there are *environmental reasons* for public-sector involvement. Tourism "sells" such things as the scenery, history, and cultural heritage of a region. One of the dangers of tourism is that in attempting to make the national environment more acceptable to a foreign market, the true nature of that environment, physical or cultural, maybe permanently damaged, altered, or lost.

Finally, as discussed in Chapter 9, there are *economic reasons* for public-sector involvement in tourism. Tourism generates income, creates jobs, helps in economic diversification, complements certain other local industries, is an export industry, and provides foreign exchange earnings. In order to enhance these economic advantages to the host destination, the government, to some extent, must get involved.

The type and amount of government involvement varies from country to country. The greater the importance that the government attaches to tourism, the greater will be the involvement. We might expect, for example, government involvement in tourism to be greater in the Bahamas—where visitor spending represents about 50% of Gross Domestic Product (GDP)—than in the United States, which has a much more diverse economy. The conditions existing in the country also affect the type and amount of government involvement. The political-economic-constitutional system is an important factor. We would expect the level of involvement of a socialist government to be greater than in a country that has a predominantly free-enterprise philosophy.

The level of socioeconomic development is another important factor determining the level of a government's involvement. The greater the economic development of a region, the less the need for government involvement. In connection with this, the maturity and financial capabilities of the private sector are important factors. The greater the capabilities of the private sector, the less the need for public-sector involvement. In the United States, the argument has been made with some success that its tourism private sector is so highly developed, sophisticated, and resourceful that there is little need for the Federal Government to be concerned with its development or marketing. This philosophy is clearly reflected by the fact that the United States Travel and Tourism Administration (USTTA) does not have a development function and has no official role in the promotion and development of domestic (resident) tourism within the U.S.

PUBLIC-SECTOR ROLES AND FUNCTIONS IN TOURISM

Coordination of public-and private-sector groups. The public sector often plays a coordinating function. Coordination is necessary among the many governmental bodies concerned with different aspects of tourism. Immigration may, for example, wish to relax the frontier formalities in order to expedite the entry of tourists into a country. This obviously helps tourism. The appropriate agency for drug enforcement may be against this proposal of relaxation, though, for fear that it will increase the flow of drugs as well as tourists into the host country. Some kind of coordination is obviously necessary. Coordination is also necessary among governments at the national, state or provincial, and local levels. To be truly effective, tourism within a country must be coordinated so that all regions are moving toward the same goals. For the same reason, coordination is necessary between the public sector and the private sector, as well as between the public sector and nonprofit organizations. Many educational and cultural organizations, although they do not have tourism as their major focus, do much to provide resources that attract tourists. The private sector is obviously very involved in tourism. To avoid duplication of effort, it is vital that goals and strategies be coordinated. This responsibility needs to be assigned to one specific agency responsible for tourism.

Tourism policy-setting and tourism planning.   In lesser-developed countries (LDCs) as well as in some developed countries, government is involved in the planning for tourism development. National tourism policies and development plans are drawn up in which the government decides which sectors of tourism will be developed, what the appropriate rate of growth will be, and who will provide the needed capital for expansion. The key is to balance the development of supply (attractions, facilities, transportation, infrastructure, and human resources) and the promotion of demand (the number of tourist arrivals). In its Federal Tourism Policy, Canada has established as two of its priorities to "improve the supply of qualified human resources to meet demand" and to "improve the productivity of human resources and the quality of employment in the tourism industry."[1]

Legislation and regulation of tourism.   An important role of government is that of a legislator and regulator. Government legislation can affect the number of paid vacation days during the year and hence the amount of discretionary paid time available for vacations. Policies on passports and visas also directly affect tourism. Visas are required by many tourists entering the United States (the exceptions being for residents of Canada, UK, France, Germany, Italy, Japan, The Netherlands, Sweden, and Switzerland); the reverse is not true for U.S. residents visiting many other countries. The appropriate policy is determined by the government. Government influence may also be felt in the regulations necessary to run a tourism business. In some countries, guides must be licensed. Businesses may have safety and health regulations to abide by; they may also have to meet zoning, building, and licensing requirements. The need to protect the environment and other resources that attract tourists may result in restrictions regarding entry to and use of fragile natural resources. Tourists are no longer allowed to enter certain European monuments, and U.S. and Canadian National and State or Provincial Parks have certain areas set aside as wilderness, the uses within which are severely limited.

Tourism development and operations.   The public sector is generally expected to provide the infrastructure (roads, airport facilities, sewerage, electricity, water, and other essential services) for tourism development in various parts of the destination. In addition, however, many governments are involved through the ownership and operation of certain attractions, facilities, and services. In the U.S. and Canada, this involvement is limited to National, State, and Provincial Parks, and historic and government sites, monuments, and buildings. Many countries operate state-owned airlines, including Jamaica (Air Jamaica) and Trinidad & Tobago (BWIA), while in India, Greece, Spain, and Portugal the government owns and operates hotels. Government ownership and operation of hotels and resorts is not very prevalent in the U.S. and Canada, the exception being within certain National and State or Provincial Parks including those in Kentucky, Ohio, and Indiana.

[1]Industry, Science and Technology Canada, Tourism on the Threshold, 1990, p. 33.

Stimulation of investment, development, and marketing. A government can stimulate tourism within a country, state, or locality in one of three ways. First, financial and fiscal incentives, such as low-interest loans or nonpayment of taxes for a specified period of time, may be offered to induce private-sector investment. Second, the public sector may sponsor research that will benefit an industry in general rather than one company in particular. For instance, research may be conducted on the characteristics of a particular foreign market. The results then can be made available to those in the private sector who can develop their own plans to attract this market to use each particular facility. Last, government can stimulate tourism by spending money on promotion. The effort should be aimed at promoting the entire county or state, and it usually consists of travel promotion aimed at generating tourist demand. In some cases, it may also involve investment promotion aimed at inducing capital investment for tourism attractions and facilities.

Education and training of tourism personnel. Another important role played by many of the world's government agencies is in the provision of education and training programs for those involved in the tourism industry. Some programs focus on training at the skills levels, including the many national governments which operate their own hotel and restaurant training schools. Other agencies, including Tourism Canada, assist with the development of training programs (courses, seminars, workshops) and materials (books, manuals, guides, audio and videotapes) for management. Some governments are concerned with the establishment of minimum standards or competencies that tourism employees must be able to meet. In Canada, for example, the Province of Alberta assisted in the establishment of the Alberta Tourism Education Council, which has since developed certification standards for many key job positions in hospitality and tourism.

ESTABLISHING A TOURISM POLICY

It should be clear by now that whether those in the public sector like it or not, they are or need to become, involved in tourism. To guide the government's own programs and the actions of private and nonprofit organizations, it is essential to give top priority to the establishment of a tourism policy. A statement of tourism policy must provide a set of guidelines for all those directly and indirectly involved in tourism by specifying the broad goals and objectives, priorities, and actions that will provide the basis for the future development of tourism in the destination area. Despite the clear need to establish a tourism policy as a precursor for future tourism planning and development, many government agencies have yet to develop statements of their tourism policies.

Tourism Policy Model

The model presented in Figure 10.1 illustrates the process by which a tourism policy can be formulated. The many needs of a region, such as the creation of employment,

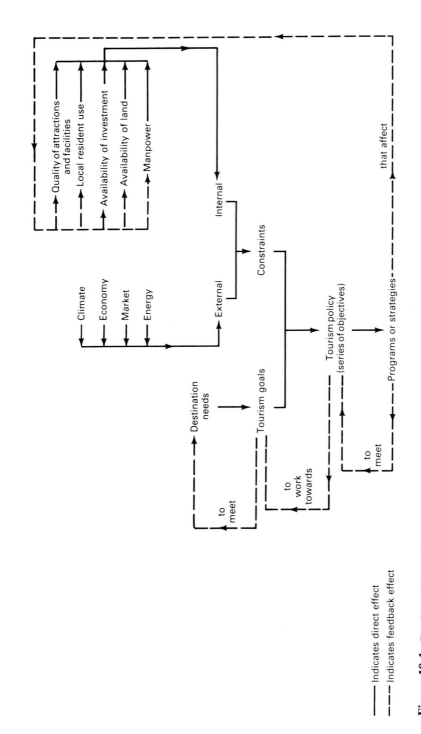

Figure 10.1 Tourism policy model

ADAPTED FROM: Harry G. Matthews, *International Tourism: A Political and Social Analysis* (Cambridge, MA, Schenkman Publishing Company, 1978). Scottish Tourist Board, *Planning for Tourism in Scotland: Preliminary National Strategy*, 1975. U.S. Senate, "National Tourism Policy Study: Ascertainment Phase," *Committee on Commerce, Science and Transportation*, 1978.

economic diversification, or resource protection-conservation, are identified by using appropriate research techniques. Tourism goals must reflect these overall needs, but they are constrained by the existing market and resource factors. A series of strategies and programs should flow from the overall policy that is aimed at achieving the tourism goals and satisfying previously identified needs. Also, the constraints of market and resources are affected as a result of feedback resulting from the generated policy. The individual elements of the tourism policy model will now be explored in greater depth.

Tourism goals.   Goals for tourism have to be set before policy statements can be developed. In so doing, it is crucial that these tourism goals not be set in isolation. For example, there is a very close link between tourism and recreation. It can be argued that tourism is a form of recreation involving overnight travel or a certain distance away from home. In addition, both tourists and residents often share some of the same recreational facilities.

It is also essential that tourism goals are set in concert with the broader economic, social, cultural, and environmental objectives of the destination. They must support broad national or regional interests. A U.S. study identified the following principles of national public policy by which the federal government achieves a consensus for guiding federal legislation.[2] They can be used as an expression of the U.S. national interest:

Energy conservation

Full employment

Economic growth with minimum inflation

Improved operation of the federal government

Environmental protection

Judicious use of natural resources

Urban revitalization

Preservation of national heritage resources

Consumer protection

Equal opportunities for people in disadvantaged segments of the population

Improved physical and mental health

Reduced international trade deficits

Equitable taxation

Economic viability of small businesses

Minimum regulation of private industry

Improved international goodwill

Balanced national transportation system

[2]U.S. Senate, "National Tourism Policy Study: Ascertainment Phase," Committee on Commerce, Science and Transportation, 1977, p. 30.

In the preamble to its Federal Tourism Policy, the Canadian government stated that its overall policy was to:[3]

> Build a strong economy fully competitive among the world's trading nations.
>
> Reduce the deficit as a vital component in securing Canada's future.
>
> Preserve Canada's environment and encourage increased public interest and involvement.
>
> Foster a confident sense of Canada's cultural and national uniqueness.
>
> Mobilize entrepreneurship for the economic, social, and cultural development of all parts of the country.
>
> Foster a comprehensive human resource strategy to meet the challenges of increasing competition, diminishing reliance on traditional industries, growth in the service sector, and increasing sophistication and application of technology.

Against the backdrop of these national interests, tourism goals can be developed into at least six categories—economic, sociocultural, market (demand) development, resource protection and conservation, human resources development, and government operations. These tourism goals must also be tempered by the external and internal constraints discussed below. Typical tourism goals are:[4]

ECONOMIC GOALS

To optimize the contribution of tourism and recreation to economic prosperity, full employment, regional economic development, and improved international balance of payments.

SOCIOCULTURAL GOALS

To contribute to the personal growth and education of the population and encourage their appreciation of the geography, history, and ethnic diversity.

To avoid the encouragement of activities that have the potential of undermining or denigrating the social and cultural values and resources of the area and its traditions and lifestyles.

To make the opportunity for and the benefits of travel and recreation universally accessible to residents and visitors.

MARKET DEVELOPMENT GOALS

To encourage the free and welcome entry of foreigners, while balancing this goal with the need to monitor persons and goods entering the country with laws protecting public health.

---

[3]Industry, Science and Technology Canada, Tourism on the Threshold, 1990, p. 30.

[4]Adapted from "National Tourism Policy Study," p. 31.

RESOURCE PROTECTION AND CONSERVATION GOALS

To protect and preserve the historical and cultural foundations as a living part of community life and development and to ensure future generations an opportunity to enjoy the rich heritage of the area.

To ensure the compatibility of tourism, recreational, and activity policies with other broader interests in energy development and conservation, environmental protection, and judicious use of natural resources.

The judicious use of natural resources is a guiding principle for federal legislation

HUMAN RESOURCE DEVELOPMENT GOALS

To ensure that tourism has an adequate supply of professionally-trained skilled and managerial staff to meet its future needs.

To ensure that the education and training programs and materials are available to meet the needs of tourism.

GOVERNMENT OPERATIONS GOALS

To harmonize to the maximum extent possible all government activities supporting tourism and recreation; to support the needs of the general public and the public and private sectors of industries involved with tourism and recreation; to take a leadership role with all those concerned with tourism, recreation, and heritage conservation.

Constraints.   Before more specific objectives can be developed in the five above-mentioned categories, it is necessary to recognize and consider certain constraining factors. These constraints are both external and internal to the host destination. External constraints are those outside the direct control of the host destination, while internal constraints can be influenced by the tourism policy and other direct means.

External Constraints.   Because the volume of demand for travel is closely related to levels of disposable income, policy is constrained by general economic conditions in the tourist-generating countries. A stagnant economic situation suggests that a destination should plan for, at best, limited growth and a policy of improved quality rather than quantity of resources.

Policy is also constrained by the world energy situation. The price and supply of oil particularly affects destination regions that rely upon auto tourists. The overall effect of an increase in the price of gas or uncertainty over gasoline supplies may mean a reduction in the number of auto-based tourists, a redistribution of tourists to more accessible areas, and a more center-based vacation than a touring one. Such a situation will have important policy implications for the development of facilities and the encouragement of public transportation. Airlines also are sensitive to the price of gasoline, as it is a major element in their cost structure, and they buy it on a week-to-week basis. Increases in costs tend to be passed on to the traveler. Since the demand for pleasure travel is particularly sensitive to price, gas price increases can have a significant impact on demand.

The travel potential of various segments of the market will also influence policy. For example, the best potential for increased travel to certain parts of the Caribbean is from Europe because of its increased affluence and shorter-duration air trips. This suggests that Caribbean nations develop policies encouraging more European flights to their countries.

Climatic factors constrain the types of tourism that can be developed. For example, the climate of Scotland is regarded unfavorably by many people in Britain. To a certain extent, the image is not totally justified and may be remedied by promoting the seasons when the climate is conducive to holiday-making. If poor weather limits vacation activities, the obvious implication for policy makers is to develop more wet-weather facilities.

Internal Constraints.   On the one hand, internal constraints influence tourism policy but, on the other hand, can themselves be modified as a result of the tourism policy that is created.

The quality of attractions and available facilities limits, for example, the type of vacationers that can reasonably be attracted. U.S. and Candian visitors are very accustomed to private bathrooms in hotels. If these are lacking, a policy implication may be to allow financial incentives to modernize existing facilities by building more rooms with private bathrooms. Facilities that have been built without private bathrooms may not be eligible for such aid.

It was mentioned earlier that tourism policy cannot be separated from recreation and leisure policy. The use of attractions and facilities by the local population has to be considered as a possible constraint to tourism policy. In and around urban areas it may be that only a small portion of the recreational capacity will be available for tourists, particularly on weekends. On the other hand, certain cultural and recreational facilities may be viable and available to the local community only because of the support from tourist demand. The extensive theater facilities in London are a prime example. Many of these theaters rely upon tourist traffic to make them commercially viable. If this demand were not present, many theaters would be forced to close, and this resource would be lost to the local population.

The availability of land and investment capital is also of concern to destination areas. Particularly in smaller countries and regions, such as Singapore and the island of Tobago, difficult decisions must be made regarding appropriate land uses. In both Canada and the U.S., considerable controversy has arisen over the proposed uses of public land for parks and other wilderness or recreational uses. The scarcity of investment capital raises particular problems for many destination countries, especially the lesser-developed nations. The lack of money for investment can hold back tourism development, but the attraction of foreign capital may result in a loss of local control and leakages from the economy. This problem is felt not only by countries but also by local areas within a country that seek financing from domestic sources of capital. Decisions to expand, contract, build, or close facilities—decisions that vitally affect the local community—are made by executives outside the community.

The availability of manpower also acts as a constraint to tourism policy. Tourism is a people industry. The characteristics of the tourism industries create particular employment problems. Tourism jobs are often seasonal, part-time, or low-paying. In order to deal with the public from another social class and culture, it may be necessary to learn different behaviors or different ways of serving food than those used in the home. In some cases, U.S. hotel companies, prior to the opening of an overseas property, have had to support the development of a school for training local employees in methods of serving the American market.

Tourism Objectives.   Having stated the broad tourism goals after due consideration of external and internal constraints, more specific tourism objectives should be articulated. At this point, it is not unusual to find that conflicts arise between goals or within goals. For example, should casino gambling be encouraged? To do so may be consistent with tourism's economic goals, but may conflict with the country's sociocultural goals. In setting its tourism policy in 1988, the government of Trinidad and Tobago stated that it "will not permit the establishment of gambling casinos and/or any similar activities that are likely to have undesirable consequences for the society.''[5] Although they recognize the earning potential of casinos, it is felt that the potential social costs are too great. Similar fears for their citizens have stopped several U.S. states and Canadian provinces from allowing casino gambling.

Conflicts can also arise within goals. For example, encouraging more foreigners to visit tourist ports of entry may help to improve the international balance of payments, thus helping achieve part of an economic goal, but this may not be compatible with another economic goal of maximizing regional economic development. Only when local interests weigh what is best for their community, what meets the community needs, can such conflicts be solved in the best intersts of the community.

In 1990, Industry, Science and Technology Canada stated the following objectives as the basis for Canada's tourism policy:

1. Increase international tourism revenues to Canada
2. Ensure that Canada has the products demanded by the customer
3. Provide long-term growth and prosperity for Canadian tourism through a balance between tourism development and maintenance of Canada's physical and cultural environment
4. Ensure that visitors from Canada's primary international markets can reach Canadian destinations
5. Harness technology to the task of improved competitiveness
6. Improve service to visitors through improved training of human resources
7. Improve the flow of financing to the right demand-driven tourism products
8. Facilitate the (tourism) industry's ability to undertake more information-based advocacy and decision-making[6]

Tourism Policy.   The agreed-upon tourism objectives, carefully formulated to complement the tourism goals, constitute the main element of the tourism policy for a destination area. The many alternative ways to meet tourism's goals have been resolved by Trinidad and Tobago in the form of its "tourism development philosophy":[7]

The development and promotion of the Tourism Industry in Trinidad and Tobago will place emphasis on the country's cultural heritage, natural resources and history, and not merely perpetuate the image of sea, sun, and sand for marketing the tourism product.

The Government is committed to the development of the industry in a manner that will preserve the national pride and the dignity of the peoples of Trinidad & Tobago, while simultaneously encouraging foreigners to visit and experience our way of life.

In developing tourism plant, the Government will take into account the need

[5]Trinidad and Tobago Tourism Development Authority, Tourism Policy 1988, p. 3.

[6]Industry, Science and Technology Canada, Tourism on the Threshold, 1990, pp. 31–34.

[7]Trinidad and Tobago Tourism Development Authority, Tourism Policy 1988, p. 3.

to stimulate the expansion of domestic tourism in harmony with the drive to increase international tourism.

In marketing the tourism product, the Government will not encourage the creation of enclaves that exclude nationals on the grounds of race, colour, religion and sex.

The Government will not permit the establishment of gambling casinos and/or similar activities that are likely to have undesirable consequences for society.

The Government will pursue a policy of exploiting the tourism market selectively, stressing to the various target groups the uniqueness of the tourism product within the Twin Island destination.

Tourism Strategies and Programs.   Having established the tourism policy, government officials and others involved in the industry can begin the task of developing tourism strategies, plans, programs, and perhaps also the required legislation and regulations, to achieve the policy's stated objectives. Chapter 11 considers the legislation and regulations required to support tourism and other policy areas. Chapter 12 examines how—through the process of tourism planning—specific programs and actions are selected to support policy goals and objectives. Examples of such programs include establishing specific investment incentives, setting immigration rules, organizing the tax structure, and marketing efforts aimed at specific target markets.

TOURISM ORGANIZATIONS

World Tourism Organization (WTO).   Many types of organizations have been created at the international, national, state or provincial, and local levels to develop and implement tourism policy. The only organization that represents governmental interests on a worldwide basis is the World Tourism Organization (WTO). The forerunner to WTO was the International Union of Official Travel Organizations (IUOTO) set up at The Hague (Netherlands) in 1923 to promote tourism for the economic, social and cultural advancement of all nations. WTO, an intergovernmental technical body, came into existence in January 1975. Based in Madrid (Spain), WTO is the official tourism voice to the United Nations and represents its main instrument for the promotion of tourism. The major aim of WTO is as follows:

> The fundamental aim of the Organization shall be the promotion and development of
> · tourism with a view to contributing to economic development, international understanding, peace, prosperity, and universal respect for, and observance of, human rights and fundamental freedoms for all without distinction as to race, sex, language or religion. The Organization shall take all appropriate action to attain this objective. In pursuing this aim, the Organization shall pay particular attention to the interests of the developing countries in the field of tourism.[8]

[8]World Tourism Organization, WTO: What is it; What it does; How it functions.

As this statement shows—although its members include many developed countries including Canada, the United States, Australia, Germany, and France—WTO generally aims to promote and develop tourism with particular emphasis on the interests of the developing countries. WTO has three membership categories—full, associate, and affiliate members. Its 109 Full Members in 1989 were the national governments of countries, and there were an additional 4 Associate Member territorial governments (including Puerto Rico). WTO's affiliate members are international and regional tourism bodies—such as the Pacific Asia Travel Association (PATA), European Travel Commission (ETC), and Caribbean Tourism Organization (CTO)—and private sector companies, associations, and educational institutions.

Three main groups are responsible for the policies and programs of WTO. The WTO Secretariat consists of the Secretary General of WTO and the full-time WTO staff located in Madrid. The General Assembly, held every two years, brings together all members to consider WTO's policies and programs. The General Assembly has created six Regional Commissions representing Africa, the Americas, Europe, Middle East, the Pacific and East Asia, and South Asia, who oversee the implementation of WTO programs in their respective regions. The third WTO body is its Executive Council, consisting of one member for every five Full Members. This Council meets at least twice a year to take whatever measures are necessary to implement the decisions and recommendations of the previous General Assembly.

Some of the main functions of WTO include the collection of information and issuing of publications on travel statistics and trends. It represents a "World clearing house" for all available information, including statistical data on international and domestic tourism, legislation and regulation, facilities and special events. Some of its regular publications include *World Travel, Tourism Compendium, International Travel Statistics, Economic Review of World Tourism,* and *Travel Abroad—Frontier Formalities.* WTO also publishes several special studies and manuals on such subjects as the marketing of tourism products, physical planning, and the protection of environmental and cultural resources.

WTO helps to encourage the adoption of measures that make travel between countries easier through the reduction and simplification of frontier formalities (for example, passport and visa requirements) and the removal of other barriers to the free movement of travelers. WTO also plays a major role in tourism education and training, including offering correspondence courses and short-term training programs throughout the world. Other types of assistance are provided to the National Tourism Offices (NTOs) of Full-Member states, including technical cooperation and the organization of international conferences, seminars, round-tables, and technical meetings on various aspects of tourism. Finally, WTO works toward the preparation of draft international agreements on tourism and their eventual implementation. Three important past agreements include the "Tourism Bill of Rights and Tourist Code" (Sofia, Bulgaria, September 1985), the "Manila Declaration on World Tourism" (Manila, Philippines, September 1980), and the "Acapulco Document" (Acapulco, Mexico, August 1982).

International Civil Aviation Organization (ICAO).   Established in 1944, the International Civil Aviation Organization (ICAO) is made up of representatives from the governments of 157 contracting states. The principal task of the ICAO is to promote worldwide civil aviation. To achieve this, international standards and practices regarding air navigation have been adopted. Proposals have been developed for the construction of facilities and the reduction of frontier formalities to help ensure the growth of international civil aviation in a safe and orderly way.

Multinational Tourism Organizations.   Several multinational organizations have been established to assist in the development of tourism in different regions of the world. Some, such as the Organization for Economic Cooperation and Development (OECD), were created for reasons of general economic growth and stability. Founded in 1960, the member states of OECD include the United States, Canada, the United Kingdom, Australia, New Zealand, Japan, Turkey, and other developed countries in Europe and Scandinavia. Within OECD, a tourism committee was established to deal specifically with tourism, including the assessment of the effect of member country policies on tourism.

In other cases, organizations have been created to implement policies to develop, promote, and facilitate travel to specific regions of the world. PATA, the Pacific Asia Travel Association, was organized in 1951 to promote travel in the Pacific-Asia area. Similarly, the Caribbean Tourism Organization (CTO) and the European Travel Commission (ETC) have been created to assist Caribbean nations and Europe, respectively.

National Tourism Organizations (NTOs).   The tourism policy of a country is typically developed and implemented by its national tourism organization (NTO). An NTO is the official body responsible for the development and marketing of tourism. The functions of NTOs vary acording to the governmental status they are given in specific countries. First, it may be governmental—part of the civil service system as either an independent ministry, such as the Bahamas Ministry of Tourism, or part of another related ministry. In France, the State Secretariat for Tourism is part of the Ministry of Cultural Affairs and the Environment, but in Spain the Ministry of Commerce and Tourism contains the NTO. Approximately 30 percent of WTO's members have an independent ministry for tourism.

Second, the NTO may be a governmental agency or bureau responsible for tourism set within a larger department. Tourism Canada, formerly the Canadian Government Office of Tourism (CGOT), is located within the Department of Industry, Science and Technology Canada (ISTC) under the leadership of the Minister of State (Small Businesses and Tourism). In the United States, the U.S. Travel and Tourism Administration (USTTA) is an agency within the Department of Commerce. Government agencies have, in general, less influence and status than the ministry form described above. Mexico, for example, has an independent government agency called the National Tourism Council that is responsible for international promotion, but it reports to and receives policy guidance from the State Tourism Secretariat. Tourism bodies that have governmental status have the broadest range of functions of NTOs.

Third, the official tourism organization may be a quasi-public government-funded corporation, board, or authority, such as the Hong Kong Tourist Association, the Irish Tourist Board, or the British Tourist Authority. A key advantage of the government-funded board is that it has greater management flexibility in dealing with the commercial aspects of tourism development and promotion. A closer liaison with the private sector and the consuming public is possible. In fact, members of the private sector are often asked to serve as board directors.

Last, the official tourism organization may be a private industry association indirectly supported by government funding, such as the Japan Tourist Association. Less than ten percent of WTO members have a national tourism organization that has nongovernmental status. A primary advantage of having a government agency as an NTO is that it has the authority within government to represent tourism and develop and interpret tourism policy.

The typical functions of NTOs can be categorized into the six main roles and functions discussed earlier in this chapter: (1) coordination of public- and private-sector groups; (2) tourism policy-setting and planning; (3) legislation and regulation of tourism; (4) tourism development and operations; (5) stimulation of investment, development, and marketing; and (6) education and training of tourism personnel. These roles and functions of NTOs affect both the supply of and demand for tourism destinations, facilities, and attractions.

Supply-Side Functions.   NTOs' functions vary depending upon the governmental status given to them. On the supply side, these programs may include conducting inventories of tourism resources prior to the formulation of a tourism plan. In fewer cases, NTOs are involved with maintaining the quality of the tourism product. This may include protecting the environment that tourists come to view or setting minimum standards for hotels or tour guides. NTOs in free-enterprise countries tend to have less of a quality control role. The input of the NTO in free-enterprise economies is usually limited to providing advice on the effects of certain industry practices on tourism. When another agency sets policy that affects tourism, the NTO may have some advisory input into that policy.

Although the state's role in economic activities in free-market economies is generally confined to legislation and regulation, the role of the state in socialist countries has historically been quite different, although the differences are now becoming less obvious. In socialist countries, governments have traditionally been involved in owning and operating tourist facilities, as well as in controlling domestic travel agencies and in-country tour operations. Developing countries that lack private industry capital and expertise have often found it necessary for the state to develop, own, and manage facilities and attractions. To ensure the proper supply, it has been necessary for some governments to provide financial incentives for the development of facilities and attractions and for human resources development to produce sufficient numbers of qualified personnel.

Some national tourism organizations regulate tour guides

Demand-Side Functions. On the demand side, NTOs tend to be involved in matters of facilitation, marketing research, marketing (including promotion), and representation in foreign countries. The role of the NTO in facilitation tends to be an advisory one, commenting on the effect of government policies regarding visas, passports, and customs formalities on tourist demand. NTOs are primarily known for their roles in marketing, especially in attracting foreign visitors to their respective countries, and in sponsoring or generating tourism marketing research data. Some agencies, including the USTTA, have no direct supply-side functions and are also not involved in the marketing of tourism to their own residents (domestic tourism). Others such as Tourism Canada have traditionally had both supply- and demand-side functions.

UNITED STATES GOVERNMENT INVOLVEMENT IN TOURISM

Historical Review[9]

Prior to World War II, the federal government of the United States had done little to involve itself with either domestic or international tourism. In 1940, however, the Domestic Travel Act was passed. This act authorized the National Park Service (NPS), a part of the Department of the Interior, to promote and administer tourism functions of the department. World War II halted any plans the NPS might have had.

[9]This section is abstracted from Destination U.S.A., final report of the National Tourism Resources Review Commission, Vol. 4, "Federal Role," June 1973.

After the war, NPS was faced with restrictions of budget and a need to expand park facilities to meet the increasing numbers of park visitors. Thus, travel activities were given no attention.

At the same time, two developments led to a tourism balance of payments deficit for the United States. First, Americans were encouraged to visit Europe to help the devastated European economies. This was partly justified by the argument that the inflow of U.S. dollars would better enable Europe to purchase American goods. Second, many foreign countries, because of their need to acquire American dollars, restricted foreign travel by their own citizens in the immediate postwar years.

In 1960, President Eisenhower proclaimed a "Visit U.S.A. Year" but felt that, although government involvement in tourism could be justified on economic grounds, it was not a proper function of government to advertise and promote travel. Pushed initially by the Senate Commerce Committee, the International Travel Act, passed by Congress in 1961, established the United States Travel Service (USTS) within the Department of Commerce. The USTS represented the first real attempt to promote the United States to foreigners. The office was authorized to set up overseas offices and to promote and advertise U.S. travel destinations to people in foreign countries. The goals of the USTS were to:

- Contribute to the maximum extent possible to the balance of payments position of the United States
- Contribute to the maximum extent possible to the health and well-being of the American people
- Contribute to the maximum extent possible to international goodwill and understanding

Emphasis was placed on the economic goal of achieving as favorable a balance of payments position as possible.

By the mid-1960s the travel deficit had increased to $1.6 billion. In an attempt to reduce this, President Johnson proposed in 1968 the imposition of a tax on international tickets and a reduction in the duty-free allowance upon return to the United States. The proposal was not enacted because of the widespread opposition generated. Recognizing that a travel deficit could be reduced not only by discouraging American travel abroad but also by encouraging foreign travel to the United States, Congress in 1970 amended the 1961 International Travel Act to authorize matching funds to states or nonprofit organizations for projects aimed at promoting foreign travel to the United States. At the same time, the position of director of the USTS was elevated to that of assistant secretary of commerce for tourism.

In 1975, the authority for domestic tourism that the Secretary of the Interior had agreed to transfer to the Secretary of Commerce was given to USTS, which was later renamed the U.S. Travel and Tourism Administration (USTTA). Passage of the National Tourism Policy Act in 1981 ended an eight-year industry lobbying effort. The Act, which survived strong objections from the Executive Branch including a Presidential veto, resulted in the USTTA being headed by an Under Secretary of Commerce for Travel and Tourism, which was an elevation in status from an assistant secretary. Funding, however, has been kept at a level so low, having declined from $30 million in 1977 to approximately $11 million in 1988–89, that meaningful activities at the federal level have been curtailed. In fact, despite increasing competitiveness in international travel marketing and inflation, USTTA's budget remained in the range of $11 to $12 million between 1984–85 and 1988–89. Notwithstanding the nation's position as a world leader, the USTTA's total budget in 1988–89 ranked 22nd among NTOs, being about one-third of Tourism Canada and British Tourist Authority's budgets. It is also interesting to note that much smaller countries—including Singapore, Switzerland, and Ireland—allocate budgets two to three times greater than USTTA's to their NTOs.

Present Role

Policy and other coordination problems.   The tourism system is comprised of natural resources, attractions, facilities, services, transportation, facilitation, and marketing. The blend of these factors determines the effectiveness of the system. A major difficulty in the United States is that the role of the federal government in tourism is so fragmented that integration of the various tourism elements is exceedingly difficult.

There are over one-hundred different programs in approximately fifty different departments or agencies that directly affect tourism, travel, or recreation. The difficulties caused by this fragmentation are obviously felt in problems of communication. A study by Arthur D. Little found a "widespread lack of understanding among Federal officials of the degree of their agencies' current involvement in and/or impacts on tourism and travel."[10] The study team also found that the federal interagency coordination on travel and tourism was poor to nonexistent. Little or no coordination existed between those agencies viewed as influencing tourism and the USTTA. There was general agreement that there were too many federal programs involved in an aspect of tourism and no effective means of coordinating existing efforts, resulting in an ineffective federal involvement.

To overcome some of these and other coordination problems, USTTA has created an Office of Policy & Planning. This Office implements USTTA's tourism policy program and also chairs the Tourism Policy Council. The Tourism Policy Council has four roles: (1) coordinating the policies and programs of Federal agencies that have a significant impact on tourism, recreation, environmental quality, economic development, transportation, and national heritage preservation; (2) identifying areas of cooperation between Federal agencies and programs they administer; (3) assisting in resolving interagency policy and program conflicts; and (4) seeking out and reviewing concerns of the U.S. travel industry and state and local governments relative to Federal policies and programs deemed to conflict with the orderly growth and development of tourism.[11]

[10]U.S. Senate, "National Tourism Policy Study: Ascertainment Phase," Committee on Commerce, Science and Transportation, 1977, p. 15.

[11]United States Travel and Tourism Administration, Budget Estimates, Fiscal Year 1990 Congressional Submission.

Another part of USTTA's policy program is aimed at identifying foreign government-imposed impediments to international travel and the development and implementation of policy initiatives designed to eliminate these barriers.

Tourism marketing.   The marketing of U.S. tourism is the responsibility of the USTTA. The agency is primarily involved in international tourism marketing, but also does a variety of marketing research projects and has an Office of Policy & Planning. Programs range from promotional campaigns aimed at atracting conventions and sponsorship of international trade shows to the development of gateway reception areas to provide language assistance to the international visitor. The organization chart for USTTA is shown in Figure 10.2.

Natural resources.   The natural resources of the United States are the responsibility of the Department of the Interior, the Department of Agriculture, the Department of Defense, and additional independent government offices. The primary research, development, and planning function is undertaken by the former Bureau of Outdoor Recreation, now the Heritage Conservation and Recreation Service (HCRS). HCRS has the primary responsibility of maintaining a comprehensive nationwide outdoor recreation plan. The agency can only make recommendations on recreation policy, planning, and research, and it has no authority to manage land, water, and recreation areas.

The link between tourism and recreation is again shown by the fact that of the 771 million acres of land owned by the federal government, around 450 million acres have been set aside for recreation use by tourists. Federal lands represent approximately 85 percent of the recreation space in the United States. The principal agencies that manage federal lands for recreation and tourism are the Corps of Engineers, the U.S. Forest Service, and the National Park Service. The Corps of Engineers is responsible for navigation, beach erosion control, hurricane flood protection, major drainage, flood control, and water resources on both federal land waterways and improved inland and intercoastal waterways. The corps takes recreation into account in their cost-benefit analysis to determine whether or not a project should be undertaken. Although recreation sites at project sites are operated by the corps, the agency prefers to turn over operation to nonfederal units.

The U.S. Forest Service controls both national forest areas and national grasslands areas. Recreation is a major activity on forest land, as is timber harvesting, mining, livestock grazing, and protecting wildlife. Approximately half of the nation's ski areas operate under permit from the U.S. Forest Service.

The original purpose of the National Park Service (NPS) was to preserve the unique natural wonders of the country for the use and pleasure of all people. Later legislation added historic preservation, intensive outdoor attractions, and cultural activities to that mandate. NPS areas serve as attractions for nearly 300 million visitors every year.

A major problem as far as tourism is concerned is the question of preservation versus development. The agencies mentioned above are very concerned about the resources they manage. Critics argue that a certain level of development is necessary

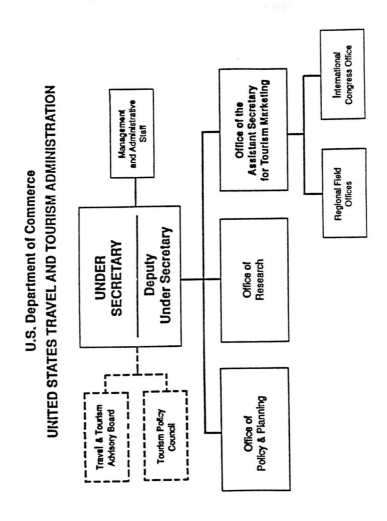

Figure 10.2 Organization chart for USTTA

to service the visitors that travel to the natural resource attractions. This is answered by those who are concerned that too much development will ruin the attraction of the natural resources. Although tourism is heavily dependent on the proper management of the natural resources of land and water, it also relies upon physical improvement of the base. The controversy arises over this balance.

Facilitation. The Departments of State, Transportation, Treasury, and Justice are concerned with the movement of tourists. The USTTA is authorized to encourage the simplification, reduction, or elimination of travel barriers. In reality, apart from transportation, the influence of arguments for encouraging tourism is very low.

ROLE OF STATE AND PROVINCIAL GOVERNMENTS

Structure

The role of tourism and government involvement in tourism varies by state and province. In the U.S. and Canada, two types of organizational structures are most commonly found: (1) a public or quasi-public tourism department, commission or bureau; and (2) an independent or semi-independent tourism ministry, department or division.

The Hawaii visitors bureau works to bring visitors to the state

Hawaii and Michigan are examples of the first type of structure. In Hawaii, leadership is provided by the Hawaii Visitors Bureau, a private, nonprofit corporation which has a contract with the State Government to handle all of Hawaii's tourism marketing and research. It also has a State Government tourism office known as the Hawaii Tourism Office. In contrast in Michigan's case, leadership comes from the public sector. The Michigan Travel Commission acts as the board of directors and is made up of representatives of convention bureaus, representatives of the State Government's Michigan Travel Bureau (located within the Department of Commerce) and consumer representatives appointed by the Governor.

There are several examples of the second organizational type in Canada. For example, both British Columbia and the Yukon have a Ministry of Tourism with their own Ministers of Tourism. In the U.S., the State of Tennessee represents another example of the second type of organizational structure. It has a Department of Tourist Development with an independent cabinet-level status. This allows for a simplification of the decision-making process because of the access that the Commissioner of Tourist Development has to the Governor due to the incumbent's position as a member of the Governor's Cabinet. Another important plus is the advantage the Commissioner has, especially at the time of the budget, in dealing with the State Legislature as a full Department.

Those states with the most active travel and tourism programs have certain characteristics:

1. They have the personal interest and active support of either the Governor or Lieutenant Governor and the Legislature.
2. A committee of the Legislature deals specifically with travel and tourism.
3. A program of research and evaluation is carried out to indicate the effectiveness of the marketing effort and the impact of tourism on the state.
4. The economic development aspects of tourism are emphasized.
5. Active advisory councils or commissions are present, and the liaison between the private and the public sectors is strong.
6. State travel-tourism plans are part of the planning and budgeting process.
7. Spending of promotional dollars has shifted from promoting the natural resources to promoting urban, convention, and man-made attractions.

Roles

The roles of state and provincial tourism agencies tend to parallel those of their respective NTOs but, in this case, at the state or provincial levels. All fifty states and ten Canadian provinces have some kind of official government agency responsible for tourism marketing. The marketing programs of the 50 state tourism offices are discussed in detail in Chapter 15. The primary role of state and provincial tourism agencies is domestic travel promotion, that is, promoting their respective states and provinces to their own residents and the residents of nearby states or provinces. In recent times, these agencies have become more involved in international travel promotion, devoting more funds to attracting foreign visitors. In this respect, they are playing an increasingly important role as a cooperative partner for their respective NTOs. A large portion of this promotional money is allocated to generating and fulfilling enquiries.

These agencies also play an important role in disseminating various types of travel information at state or provincial welcome centers. Some maintain information offices in other parts of the country and overseas. They participate in a variety of travel, trade, and consumer travel-recreation shows. They host travel writers, retail travel agents, and tour wholesalers visiting their states and provinces on familiarization trips.

State and provincial tourism offices make significant investments in gathering statistics on ongoing visitor volumes and on other special tourism research studies. The level of research effort has been increasing as these agencies attempt to target their marketing programs better and to measure the effectiveness and impacts of their marketing efforts.

Many state and provincial tourism offices play a role in tourism development and in the education and training of tourism industry personnel. This is especially true of the Canadian provinces and territories where significant investments, some in cooperation with the Canadian Government, have been made in tourism planning and stimulating the development of new attractions and facilities and in the improvement and expansion of existing ones. The Canadian provinces and territories have also had a well-established role in educational-training programs to upgrade management and other staff skills. Although these programs seem to be on the increase among the 50 states, these agencies have traditionally been involved solely in tourism promotion and not in tourism planning and development.

Almost all states, provinces, and territories play some role in encouraging the development and promotion of package tours. In some cases, particularly in Canada, this has involved financial and/or technical assistance with tour development. Again, the vast majority of these agencies in the U.S. and Canada have cost-sharing programs which provide grants to local groups to promote their locales.

Overall, the role played by state, provincial, and territorial tourism offices in Canada and the U.S. seems to be increasing in importance. Certainly, in the U.S. where several state tourism offices outspend the USTTA, these agencies play the key role in domestic travel promotion and tourism development.

REGIONAL TOURISM ORGANIZATIONS WITHIN DESTINATIONS

Within a country, state, or province, it is desirable for local communities, under the umbrella of the national and state or provincial efforts, to prepare their own policies and strategies for tourism development. This may involve the creation of regional tourism organizations, as in Michigan and Ontario. Funded in part by a state or provincial grants and in part by contributions from private businesses, these regional tourism organizations supplement the state and provincial programs while encouraging a joint public-private sector involvement.

COMMUNITY TOURISM ORGANIZATIONS

At the local community level a tourism organization typically evolves in the following way:

1. A small, informal group of people (most likely a special-interest group) interested in increasing tourism in the community gets together to seek additional support and help by visiting governmental or community agencies such as the county or city council.

2. Once the agencies are made aware of the many things involved in the community affecting and affected by tourism, there develops the realization that a proper community involvement is necessary; a subcommittee on tourism is formed as part of the chamber of commerce or county or city council.

3. When it is realized that certain jobs can best be accomplished by people who share the same priorities, an association forms, either as a part of the chamber of commerce, as a part of the local government under the city council, or as an independent entity (for example, a convention and visitors bureau). As the quantity of work increases, a regular office and secretary may be established to complement the volunteer leadership.

4. At the final stage, a full-time executive director is hired to direct the organization's work.

The way a community tourism organization forms depends in great part upon the tradition within the community, the resources that are available, the organizational structure in the community, the strength of the local chamber of commerce, and the amount of confidence in the local elected officials. At the state or provincial level, assistance may be given to local communities in one of two ways:

1. States or provinces can assist local efforts by passing legislation enabling communities to collect taxes to support local promotional activities. In the U.S. and Canada, this is usually in the form of a room or innkeeper's tax, but some cities derive support from a tax on mixed drinks, entertainment, tickets, or from an earmarked sales tax.

2. States or provinces can provide matching (50-50 cost sharing) grant funds, either for general purposes or for activities specified by the state or provincial government. The types of activities receiving such funding are usually such things as promotion and public relations, familiarization tours for tour wholesalers and travel writers, brochure preparation, tourism planning studies, and marketing research projects.

A model organizational structure for a regional or community tourism organization is shown in Figure 10.3. Referred to as a Tourism Council in this case, the organization establishes the tourism philosophy for the community and sets the overall goals for the tourism master plan. With input from related organizations, the Council develops policies that are carried out by a full-time staff. Eight planning Committees and two full-time Departments (Research and Information; Marketing and Promotion) are established.

The Committee on Community Involvement and Leadership is responsible for maximizing the involvement of community leaders in the work of the Council. The

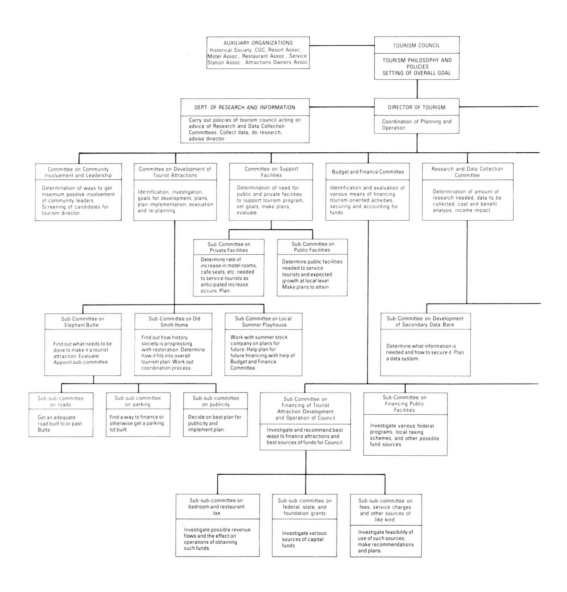

Figure 10.3 Destination area tourism council organizational structure

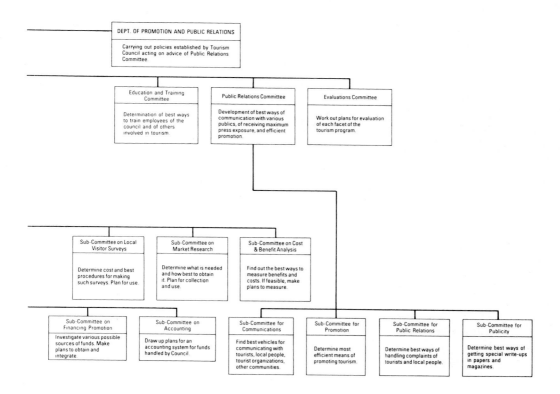

DEPT. OF PROMOTION AND PUBLIC RELATIONS

Carrying out policies established by Tourism Council acting on advice of Public Relations Committee.

Education and Training Committee

Determination of best ways to train employees of the council and of others involved in tourism.

Public Relations Committee

Development of best ways of communication with various publics, of receiving maximum press exposure, and efficient promotion.

Evaluations Committee

Work out plans for evaluation of each facet of the tourism program.

Sub-Committee on Local Visitor Surveys

Determine cost and best procedures for making such surveys. Plan for use.

Sub-Committee on Market Research

Determine what is needed and how best to obtain it. Plan for collection and use.

Sub-Committee on Cost & Benefit Analysis

Find out the best ways to measure benefits and costs. If feasible, make plans to measure.

Sub-Committee on Financing Promotion

Investigate various possible sources of funds. Make plans to obtain and integrate.

Sub-Committee on Accounting

Draw up plans for an accounting system for funds handled by Council.

Sub-Committee for Communications

Find best vehicles for communicating with tourists, local people, tourist organizations, other communities.

Sub-Committee for Promotion

Determine most efficient means of promoting tourism.

Sub-Committee for Public Relations

Determine best ways of handling complaints of tourists and local people.

Sub-Committee for Publicity

Determine best ways of getting special write-ups in papers and magazines.

A bed or transient tax is a common way of obtaining funding for a a destination-area tourism council

Committee on Development of Tourist Attractions seeks to identify new attraction opportunities and develop them. Similar tasks are undertaken by the Committee on Support Facilities in regard to the need for both private and public facilities to support the goals of tourism development.

The role of the Budget and Finance Committee is to identify and evaluate the various ways of financing the operations of the council. As mentioned above, a room tax is a common method of obtaining funding. This requires passage of a county or city ordinance after state or provincial enabling legislation has authorized counties or cities to establish such a tax. Room tax proposals are usually resisted by local lodging groups as an unfair tax on only one segment of the industry. On the other hand, local residents are normally inclined to support it, since these are taxes paid by the visitor, not the resident, that is, they represent a "user-pay" approach. Counties and cities in some cases also receive allocation from the general funds of the city, county, or state or province. However, cities are often reluctant to allocate general revenue funds to agencies over which they have little or no control and, in some cases, such allocations may not even be legal. Many U.S. states and Canadian provinces provide matching grants to help regional tourism organizations, counties, and cities attract tourists. Restrictions are usually placed on the use of these grant funds to ensure that they are used for advertising or other promotions rather than for staff salaries and that they are used to achieve specific objectives, for example, attracting out-of-state or out-of-province business that the state wants to target.

Another common method of financing local tourism marketing and development is through membership dues. Dues are often set on a sliding scale, based upon the member's volume of business or the number of employees. A major responsibility of the council's Executive Director or President is to convince local businesses that it is worth their time and money to belong. Some communities obtain money through a variety of fund raisers, including special dinners or events, such as races and auctions. These events require a great deal of effort by the council's staff, as well as the support of many local people and businesses. However, they do provide a focal point for galvanizing community support. Although not often done, it is possible to have property owners agree to have an additional mill levy on their property or building taxes that is specifically used for tourism development. The major problem with this funding alternative is that monies so collected do not keep pace with inflation unless new properties are constructed.

The Research and Data Collection Committee determines the amount of research needed and what data should be collected. An important, though often overlooked function, is that of ensuring that the level of service given visitors at the destination is of sufficiently high quality. The Education and Training Committee is concerned with determining the best ways that employees in various tourism businesses can be trained. This is usually done by the individual operation, but in some cases, it may be more effective and efficient to have a group training session on, for instance, fire safety or the importance of customer service.

The Public Relations Committee tries to develop the best ways of communicating with the community's different publics. This typically involves getting press releases and articles in newspapers and magazines, preparing a newsletter, handling tourist complaints, and determining how best to market the destination. The last committee, the Evaluation Committee, is responsible for determining how to evaluate each part of the tourism program.

SUMMARY

Because of the economic, sociocultural, and environmental importance of tourism, government agencies have found it necessary to take a role in organizing tourism. The amount of involvement depends upon such factors as the political philosophy of the government and the degree of maturity of the destination area. A clear tourism policy must be established to guide the tourism destiny of the country, region, state, or province. Without a policy and a mechanism for implementing it, tourism will increase or decline at the destination in a haphazard and potentially negative manner.

To bring a tourism policy into effect, it is necessary to have an organization responsible for its implementation. There are various levels of tourism policy and, therefore, a variety of policy-implementing agencies spread throughout the world. For example, the World Tourism Organization has a global responsibility for tourism, while there are several multinational and regional tourism organizations. Within an individual country, there is usually a National Tourism Organization (NTO), state or provincial tourism agencies, and regional and community tourism organizations.

REFERENCES

"America's Best Kept Secret: The Tourism Industry" (Address before the National Conference of Lieutenant Governors), Vital Speeches, 42(24), pp. 756–57.

Destination U.S.A., vol. 4, "Federal Role," June 1973, p. 9.

MCINTOSH, ROBERT W., and GOELDNER, CHARLES R., *Tourism: Principles, Practices and Philosophies,* Sixth ed. (New York, John Wiley & Sons, 1990).

UNITED STATES DEPARTMENT OF COMMERCE, Tourism USA: Guidelines for Tourism Development, 1986, pp. 28–34.

U.S. SENATE, "National Tourism Policy Study: Ascertainment Phase," Committee on Commerce, Science and Transportation, 1977, p. 28.

UNITED STATES TRAVEL SERVICE, Planning for Tourism, vol. 2, "Development," 1978, pp. 2–3.

UNITED STATES TRAVEL SERVICE, Tourism: State Structure, Organization and Support, A Technical Study, 1978, pp. 56, 89–90.

WAHAB, SALAH ABDEL, "Aspects of Organization for Tourism at the Destination End," Tourist Review, no. 2, April/June 1975, pp. 49–57.

CANADIAN FEDERAL TOURISM POLICY

INTRODUCTION

It is the policy of the Government of Canada to:

- build a strong economy fully competitive among the world's trading nations;

- reduce the deficit as a vital component in securing Canada's future;

- preserve Canada's environment and encourage increased public interest and involvement;

- foster a confident sense of Canada's cultural and national uniqueness;

- mobilize entrepreneurship for the economic, social, and cultural development of all parts of the country; and

- foster a comprehensive human resource strategy to meet the challenges of increasing competition, diminishing reliance on traditional industries, growth in the service sector, and increasing sophistication and application of technology.

Considering that:

- Canada's tourism industry contributes significantly to economic growth across the country;

- tourism is a major source of foreign exchange to Canada;

- Canada's goals for sustainable development find much resonance within the tourism industry inasmuch as Canada's environmental assets are of long-term mutual interest;

- tourism attractions and events integrate and sustain Canada's historical, cultural, and national identity;

- the tourism industry in Canada is comprised largely of small and medium-sized businesses, which are vital to Canada's goals for entrepreneurial development and job creation;

- in a time of fundamental shifts in labour requirements and structural unemployment the tourism industry acknowledges the need for increased investment in human resource development;

the Government of Canada seeks to strengthen its commitment to tourism and to work with the provinces, territories, and the Canadian tourism industry to meet the challenges and secure the opportunity.

To this end, it is the intention of the government that the following policy will provide a framework within which government and private sector initiatives can be co-ordinated to achieve greatest effectiveness.

STATEMENT OF POLICY

The Government of Canada recognizes the tourism industry as a strategic sector of the Canadian economy inasmuch as it makes an essential contribution to the economic well-being of Canadians and to the economic objectives of government. Equally, the Canadian tourism industry is vital to the social and cultural identity and integrity of Canada.

In the interest of maximizing the net benefit to the tourism industry and the country, the Government of Canada confirms its international focus with respect to its activities in support of tourism.

The Government of Canada is committed to the growth and international competitiveness of the Canadian tourism industry and recognizes that, in order to realize this commitment, a co-ordinated approach is required by those federal departments and agencies whose policies and programs have an impact upon the tourism industry.

In recognition of the need to integrate efforts on the part of all partners committed to the international competitiveness of the Canadian tourism industry, the Government of Canada reaffirms its policy of co-operation and co-ordination with provincial and territorial governments and with the industry itself.

THE FEDERAL ROLE

The federal government has an impact upon the tourism industry through the spending, planning, policy, and regulatory decisions of many departments and agencies with diverse economic, social, or horizontal responsibilities. The tourism industry benefits from such decisions in many ways. The management of Crown lands by the Canadian Parks Service within Environment Canada, Public Works Canada, and the St. Lawrence Seaway Commission results in attractions of considerable interest to tourists. Cultural assets, multiculturalism, cultural development, and national identity are federally vested with, for example, National Museums of Canada, Communications Canada, and the Department of Multiculturalism and Citizenship. Rail service, international air service, airports, ferry service, and other federal transportation responsibilities reside with Transport Canada, External Affairs and International Trade Canada (EAITC), and the National Transportation Agency. Competitive human resource development is supported by Employment and Immigration Canada.

(Reprinted with permission. *Tourism on the Threshold*, copyright Minister of Supply and Services Canada 1990, pp. 30–33.)

Environmental awareness and protection and issues of sustainable development are governed by Environment Canada. Regional economic development and diversification are the mandate of the Atlantic Canada Opportunities Agency and the Western Economic Diversification Office.

ISTC has been mandated by the Government of Canada to support and promote the international competitiveness and excellence of Canadian industry. ISTC's activities in support of the tourism industry fall within three areas: *advocacy, business services,* and *international marketing.* The latter is a shared responsibility with EAITC, which has the mandate for the delivery of the tourism program abroad through its tourism officers stationed at posts in the United States and overseas.

The objective of *advocacy* activities is to position tourism industry considerations in the planning and policies of other federal departments and agencies having an impact upon tourism.

Business services include those activities aimed at contributing to the strategic planning and decision making of both the private sector and government. Information gathering, analysis, and dissemination are central activities. ISTC collects data, research, intelligence, and other types of information relating to tourism markets, products, and issues.

For several years, the focus has been on improving and streamlining the type of information gathered. Significant progress has been made in performing this "info-in" function. The new focus will be on "info-out," i.e., on getting the information to partners in a timely manner and useable format with the objective of facilitating their decision making.

International marketing by ISTC and EAITC is that set of activities aimed at increasing the awareness of Canada in its primary markets, at developing new opportunities in selected markets with growth potential for the Canadian tourism industry, and at co-ordinating the marketing efforts of other partners.

While the domestic market comprises more than 70% of all tourism receipts for Canada, federal trend research indicates stagnant growth in the domestic market, continued growth in certain segments of the U.S. market, and the greatest overall growth potential in Canada's overseas markets. This international demand will drive federal activity in tourism.

The governing premise for federal tourism policy is net economic benefit to Canada. In the interests of securing such net benefit, new revenue to Canada is the objective and maximizing that revenue is the basis of the high-yield strategy that will govern federal international marketing plans. On the product side, it is clear that the development of products of international calibre also serves the Canadian domestic market, since high-quality products will appeal to Canadian travellers as much as to international ones.

FEDERAL TOURISM AGENDA FOR THE 1990s

ISTC will focus on the following priorities selected to contribute directly to the international competitiveness of the Canadian tourism industry.

Market Development

Objective
increase international tourism revenues to Canada.

Priorities

- maximize the yield on marketing dollars invested by targeting market segments offering the greatest return in terms of international receipts; and

- increase the dollars available to the national marketing program from private and public sector partners.

Activities

- allocate a larger portion of marketing resources to packaging strategic marketing information for dissemination to industry in order that they can spend "smarter" in the markets of greatest potential;

- secure additional partners to sell particular product lines to high-yield markets;

- explore new ways to do business under the federal marketing program to more effectively integrate the efforts and expenditures of the federal and provincial/territorial governments and private sector in the international market place; and

- work more closely with EAITC to deliver a more strategically targeted tourism program by the posts abroad.

The Right Products

Objective
ensure that Canada has the products demanded by the customer.

- work closely with Transport Canada, EAITC, the National Transportation Agency, and Canada's international air carriers to ensure that the interests of the tourism industry regarding routes and capacity are represented in the air bilateral negotiation process; and

- collaborate with Transport Canada to develop a comprehensive study of air capacity and passenger processing requirements incorporating ISTC visitor volume projections by primary market.

Technology

Objective

harness technology to the task of improved competitiveness.

Priorities

- increase productivity by technological innovation and application to tourism operations; and

- increase the use of technology in the distribution of Canadian tourism products globally.

Activities

- expand federal programming for technology diffusion to include the tourism industry as an eligible sector;

- monitor and inform industry partners on the implications of technology applications for human resource planning;

- work closely with industry owner/operators of international travel information networks to ensure that Canadian products are "on-line" with these sales and distribution systems; and

- promote the development of consortia of firms to achieve economies in technology investment.

Human Resource Development

Objective

improve service to visitors through improved training of human resources.

Priorities

- improve the match between the service requirements of the customer and delivery by staff;

- improve supply of qualified human resources to meet demand; and

- improve productivity of human resources and the quality of employment in the tourism industry.

Activities

- provide to industry "best case" scenarios that demonstrate the value of and link between training and productivity, reduced labour costs, and increased profitability;

- diffuse to a broader industry audience the results of research, standards and certification, and career awareness work;

- improve the integration and co-ordination of federal and provincial/territorial policies, programs, and agendas with respect to human resource development;

- work with Statistics Canada and EIC to analyse and evaluate supply/demand data to permit better human resource planning by industry and other levels of government;

- develop a Memorandum of Understanding between the federal government (ISTC and EIC) and the tourism industry to develop and implement the measures required to promote human resource planning and to overcome human resource problems;

- work with EIC to determine the priority to be placed on the tourism industry in the Labour Force Development Strategy; and

- collaborate with the Department of Multiculturalism and Citizenship to assist the Canadian tourism industry with the provision of culturally sensitive services to a diverse clientele and the management of a multicultural labour force.

Financing

Objective

improve the flow of financing to the right demand-driven tourism products.

Priorities

- improve the awareness and understanding of the business of tourism among financial institutions; and

- increase the profile of tourism as a priority sector for targeted foreign investment.

Activities

- implement an information program designed to improve business planning in the industry and an understanding of tourism among financial institutions such as Canadian chartered banks, foreign banks, trust companies, mutual funds, venture capitalists, etc.;

- develop and implement with EAITC an investment prospecting plan for the tourism industry; and

Priorities

- the creation of packages that effectively integrate products and services into the tourism experiences that will compete in the marketplace; i.e., packages highlighting Canadian diversity and cultural assets;

- maximization of tourism development opportunities existing in selected properties owned by the Government of Canada;

- identification of opportunities for new product development or major upgrading/expansions to meet international market demands and circumstances; and

- focus on
  - attractions and service development complementary to principal touring routes,
  - increasing the four-season capacity of the resort product,
  - development of the surrounding areas of selected national parks, and
  - adventure product development in wilderness or remote areas.

Activities

- bring together product suppliers, tour operators, wholesalers, and retailers both in Canada and abroad into consortia for developing new packaged products;

- increase the range of business services offered by ISTC such as: extension of the Business Opportunities Sourcing System (BOSS) to include a data base on international-calibre tourism products and suppliers, seminars on new products and technologies, and improved packaging and dissemination of commercial intelligence to better inform industry decision makers;

- pursue joint planning with Environment Canada, Public Works Canada and other custodians of federal Crown lands to identify opportunities for development such as: provision of further service facilities within certain national parks, extension of the operating season of selected parks, further animation of historic sites, leasing arrangements of undeveloped Crown lands;

- work in joint consultation with industry, regional development agencies and other federal departments as well as with the provinces and territories to identify new development opportunities and to perform a brokerage function in identifying financing for those opportunities; and

- work closely with the Aboriginal Economic Program and the Department of Indian and Northern Affairs, within the context of the Aboriginal Economic Development Strategy, to facilitate the participation of aboriginal peoples in the planning and implementation of tourism initiatives.

Sustainable Development

Objective

long-term growth and prosperity for Canadian tourism through a balance between tourism development and maintenance of Canada's physical and cultural environment.

Priorities

- foster awareness within the industry of the importance of a balanced approach to tourism development, i.e., that it must self-regulate or be regulated; and

- increase the level of community-based tourism planning and development.

Activities

- disseminate the Action Plan for Tourism and Sustainable Development emanating from the Globe '90 Conference to provide guidance on retaining the integrity of environmental and cultural resources;

- support the Tourism Industry Association of Canada in its efforts to develop an "environmental code" for the industry; and

- provide an assessment of the industry's current level of sustainable development activity and disseminate "best case" scenarios to encourage further progress.

Transportation

Objective

ensure that visitors from Canada's primary international markets can reach Canadian destinations.

Priorities

focus on air transportation to:

- seek to ensure establishment of route rights that provide adequate capacity and reasonable tariffs in order to bring visitors from our markets of greatest potential to Canadian destinations; and

- influence airport management and infrastructure development to enable international passengers to move quickly and easily to their ground destination.

11

TOURISM REGULATION

Controlling
the Tourism Industries

"From March to October tube queues (translation: subway line) should be organized like passenger entry into Heathrow. One queue for UK passport holders and another for the rest of the world. This would mean that foreigners would have to queue for at least an hour in order to buy a ticket to go two stops."

Hugh Thompson, Midweek, *July 16, 1987.*

The role of the public sector in regulating tourism is regarded by many as essential and by most as controversial. This chapter explores the many ways in which tourism is regulated by the public sector. Tourism legislation and regulation in the United States is examined in depth. The role of regulatory agencies is discussed, and arguments for and against regulation from the viewpoints of consumers, government, and industry are given. Legislation and regulation in Canada is described in full, and the situation is compared with that in the United States.

Beyond the national level, there are a number of international regulations that affect tourism. The most significant of these involve air travel between countries. The specifics of how such agreements are reached are discussed.

The chapter concludes that governments act primarily to protect the resources of the destination area as well as the visiting tourist. Thus, their role in tourism is a positive one. However, the lack of cooperation and coordination between the government agencies that directly or indirectly affect tourism means that the public sector is too often unable to react with the speed desired by the private sector.

LEARNING OBJECTIVES

Having read this chapter, you should be able to:

1. Discuss the notion that government's role in establishing tourism-related legislation and regulations is both essential and controversial.
2. Explain the two common methods that governments use to enforce regulations.
3. Discuss the evolution and apparent advantages and disadvantages of airline deregulation in the U.S.
4. Identify and explain the major multinational and bilateral regulations that affect travel and tourism.
5. Discuss the need for government regulations in tourism destination areas.

CONTROLLING THE TOURISM INDUSTRY

In Chapter 10 it was pointed out that one of the public sector's roles in tourism was that of setting and enforcing various forms of legislation and regulations. This role is at the same time essential and controversial in most free-enterprise-system destination areas. It is thought to be essential because governments cannot totally rely upon the private sector to control and regulate its activities effectively; it is often controversial because the private sector feels that the public sector goes too far in enforcing its regulations. For example, in Canada a major private-sector task force reached the following conclusions on government regulations:

> The tourism industry. . .could optimise its contribution to the Canadian economy if there were less intervention from all levels of government. Regulations have largely impeded the growth of tourism, rather than hastened its growth. There is a requirement to modernize these regulatory processes and have them respond to needs of the industry and the market rather than as a policing function.[1]

In the United States as well as in Canada a multitude of government agencies have programs and regulations that directly or indirectly affect tourism. Other countries, especially those with socialist or communist governments, regulate tourism even more comprehensively. The complexity of the tourism regulatory framework in most destination areas is a direct reflection of tourism itself; tourists cross international borders, are exposed to all of the cultural, historic, man-made, and natural resources of the destination area, and must be catered to in a safe, secure, and hygienic fashion. It follows, therefore, that a variety of government agencies have tourism-related programs and regulations.

As Chapter 10 has pointed out, those in the public sector generally get involved in tourism for political, environmental, and economic reasons. The specific func-

[1]Tourism Sector Consultative Task Force, A Report By the Sector Task Force on the Canadian Tourism Industry (Ottawa, Ontario, Department of Industry, Trade and Commerce, 1978), p. 126.

tions of governments normally encompass coordination, policy-setting and planning, legislation and regulation, development and operations, stimulation of investment, development and marketing, and education and training of tourism personnel. The degree of emphasis given to each of these six principal roles varies from destination to destination, but it is usually directly related to the importance attached to tourism as an economic activity. It is important to realize that the actions of those in the public sector have to be supported by various bodies of law (legislation) and specific regulations to have legitimacy in democratic societies. It is with the actual enforcement of the laws and with the structuring of regulations that the most controversy and conflict occurs between the private and public sectors of the tourism system.

Taxonomy of Tourism Legislation and Regulations

Before the specific types of legislation and regulations that have been introduced in the United States, Canada, and elsewhere are described, it will be useful to classify them as they are commonly found in most destination areas. One method of classification is to group the tourism legislation and regulations into functional areas, such as those related to the protection of the environment, those related to economic development, those related to frontier controls, and so on. The material on the U.S. is organized in this way. Another means of classification is to group on an industry

Building and zoning codes for accommodation establishments are common forms of regulations found in tourism destinations

sector basis by identifying the legislation and regulations that relate to airlines, hotels, travel agents, and so on. In this respect, *horizontal* legislation or regulations are those items that affect every industrial sector, whether it be a tourism or nontourism one, such as income tax and labor legislation. *Specific* legislation or regulations are those items that relate directly to an industrial sector. An example of this is a grading system for hotels. The following chart illustrates commonly found legislation and regulations classified on a sector-by-sector basis in tourism:

ACCOMMODATION ESTABLISHMENTS

Classification and grading or rating of hotels and other establishment types

Fire safety regulations and codes

Health safety regulations and codes

Building and zoning codes

Issuance of operating and liquor licenses and other regulations of the terms and conditions of operation

Liability laws with respect to guests and their belongings

Labor and taxation legislation

TRAVEL AGENTS, TOUR WHOLESALERS, AND OPERATORS

Regulations and licensing of travel agents, tour wholesalers, and operators

Definition of responsibilities and limitations

Regulations of promotions

Labor and taxation legislation

AIRLINES, RAILWAYS, BUSES, SHIPS, AND OTHER CARRIERS

Control of fares and tariffs

Licensing of carriers

Regulation of safety procedures

Control of route entry and exit

Limitation of weights and capacities

Negotiations of services

Subsidization of routes

Labor and taxation legislation

Other sectors of tourism, including retailers, car rental agencies, commercial attractions operators, and other businesses, have their own specific legislation and regulations in addition to the horizontal laws and regulations that apply to all.

The Legislation and Regulation of Tourism in the United States

The role taken by the U.S. Federal Government in preparing legislation and regulations relative to tourism reflects the country's national interests in tourism and tourism's interrelationship with other aspects of U.S. society and business. The U.S. Senate Committee on Commerce has identified these national interests related to tourism as follows:[2]

1. Health and other aspects of the quality of life:
    a. The national interest in public health
    b. Other aspects of the quality of life
    c. Protection of the quality of the tourism experience
    d. Ensuring opportunities for participation in tourism
2. Tourism as an economic activity:
    a. The efficient satisfaction of consumer demand
    b. Increasing employment, income, and regional development
3. Meeting business travel demand
4. Facilitation of international tourism
5. Tourism's impact on publicly-owned lands

In addition to recognizing tourism's direct impact and interrelationship with these five factors, the committee has also recognized that tourism interacts with the national economy, the functioning of the transportation system, the system of social and economic statistics, the forms of environmental protection, the clearance of international visitors, the public revenues, and the forms of consumer protection.

It is obvious from these expressed national interests and interactions that tourism is perceived as having a broad-scale and pervasive impact on U.S. society, as in most destination areas that have embraced it as an important economic activity. The broad scope of these impacts is mirrored by a diverse range of legislation and regulations that directly and indirectly affect tourism within the United States.

The most comprehensive analysis of federal legislation in the United States was completed in 1976 as part of the National Tourism Policy Study. One of the major conclusions emerging from this analysis was that "Federal legislation has seldom been addressed explicitly to national interests in travel or tourism. . ."[3] The Senate Commerce Committee separated the existing tourism legislation in the United States into two main categories, namely federal tourism legislation and federal tourism-related legislation. The Committee also identified the following nine subcategories of federal legislation:

FEDERAL TOURISM LEGISLATION
1. Tourism promotion and development legislation
2. Tourism resources legislation

FEDERAL TOURISM-RELATED LEGISLATION
3. Interstate transport investment and regulation

[2]U.S. Senate, A Conceptual Basis for the National Tourism Policy: Appendix B (Washington, DC, U.S. Government Printing Office, 1976), pp. 23–27.

[3]Conceptual Basis for the National Tourism Policy Study, pp. 5–70.

4. Nonimmigrant visa and customs legislation
5. Economic development legislation
6. Environmental quality control legislation
7. Energy legislation
8. Land-use legislation
9. Tax legislation

Within these subcategories, there were forty-five existing or proposed acts that had some impact on tourism within the United States. It is quite obvious, and the U.S. Senate Commerce Committee has confirmed it, that the major direct pieces of tourism legislation in the United States, that is, the Domestic and International Travel Acts, have been structured without sufficient regard to other legislation and the programs of affected federal agencies. The reverse is also true, since the programs and legislated mandates of other agencies have not given sufficient attention to tourism. This situation is not uncommon among destination areas, as few of them have systematically developed legislation in an effectively coordinated fashion. As is discussed later in this chapter, Canada for example, moved to ease its regulatory and legislative overlaps and conflicts by forming an Interdepartmental Committee on Tourism.

We turn our attention now to regulation as opposed to legislation. Governments have two common methods of enforcing regulations, namely by establishing regulatory agencies and by utilizing regulatory techniques. In the United States, the regulatory agencies include the Federal Aviation Administration (FAA), the Interstate Commerce Commission (ICC), the Federal Highway Administration (FHWA), the National Highway Traffic Safety Administration (NHTSA), the Federal Maritime Commission (FMC), the United States Coast Guard (USCG), and the Federal Trade Commission (FTC). The former Civil Aeronautics Board (CAB) was phased out in 1984 and represented the Federal Government's first attempt to deregulate drastically a once closely regulated business sector. The regulatory techniques used by governments include, among others, establishing land-use controls, setting admission policies, and withholding government funds.

Many of the regulatory agencies in existence in the United States have been created as a result of the passage of federal tourism-related legislation. For example, the CAB was established in 1938 through the Civil Aeronautics Act. Its mandate was to protect the safety of the public and to maintain the viability of the U.S. airline industry. The CAB was given the authority to determine which airlines could operate in the United States, which routes they could operate on, and what fares they could charge. It was given powers over airline schedules, airline profit margins, and the types of working relationships permissible. From the time of its inception, the CAB was probably the most influential regulatory agency in the United States with respect to its impact on tourism within the nation. The successful passage of the Airline

Deregulation act in October 1978 was, therefore, a most significant event in terms of U.S. tourism. This act was historically unique, since it was the first time ever that the Federal Government virtually abolished its role in the economic regulation of an industry. The decision to wind up the powerful CAB came after much public criticism of the agency and of its perceived overregulation of the airline industry. The general concern was that the CAB had gone too far in trying to maintain the viability of the airline industry and was beginning to engage in activities that were not beneficial to the traveling public. The following statement succinctly expressed the paradox that the CAB represented:

> The CAB in recent months has been accused of sheltering the airline industry, stifling competition, fueling inflation, discriminating against the charter of the marketplace. It has also been praised for presiding over the development of one of the finest and most efficient air transportation networks anywhere in the world.[4]

Another major problem with the CAB was its tardiness in responding to proposals presented by individual airline companies. During the long lag time, airlines often changed their minds about their proposals, or they lost the benefit of the marketing opportunity they were seeking. Because of the apparent inability of government regulatory agencies to react with the speed which the private sector requires, a great deal of friction has existed within the tourism system. Thus, as has been the case with the CAB, it is often not the question of regulations being good or bad for the industry, but of their being good and bad. In other words, the private sector sometimes may agree wholeheartedly with the underlying principles behind the regulations, but often they will be opposed to the manner and to the degree with which the regulations are enforced.

The Airline Deregulation Act of 1978 envisaged that the CAB would be completely phased out by January 1985. The CAB "sunset" timetable included the loss of its authority over route entry in 1982 and its jurisdiction over tariffs and pricing in 1983.

The air travel experiment in the United States, which was motivated by the desire to let the marketplace operate more freely to the ultimate benefit of travelers, has had its advantages and disadvantages. George James of the Air Transport Association has identified these advantages and disadvantages in the context of the three parties affected, namely consumers, government, and airline companies.[5]

As a result of the deregulation of the airline industry, several new airline companies emerged and were certified by the CAB. More discounted fares became available and the existing airline companies were better able to rationalize their route

---

[4]Bill Poling, "Behind the Scenes at the CAB" (New York, Travel Weekly, Ziff-Davis Publishing Co., Inc., 1975), p. 15.

[5]Karen Rubin, "How's Business?" The Travel Agent, November 1980, p. 82.

systems. Overcrowded planes and airports and the overbooking of flights were the most frequent criticisms of the results of deregulation.

The roles of existing U.S. regulatory agencies are as follows:

FEDERAL AVIATION ADMINISTRATION (FAA)

- Regulates air commerce in ways that best promote its development and safety and fulfill the requirements of national defense.
- Controls the use of navigable airspace of the United States, regulating both civil and military operations in such airspace in the interest of safety and efficiency.
- Promotes, encourages, and develops civil aeronautics.
- Consolidates research and development with respect to air navigation facilities.
- Installs and operates air navigation facilities.
- Develops and operates a common system of air traffic control and navigation for both civil and military aircraft.
- Develops and implements programs and regulations to control aircraft noise, sonic boom, and other environmental effects of civil aviation.

INTERSTATE COMMERCE COMMISSION (ICC)

- Regulates various types of interstate surface transportation that takes place within the United States, including trains, trucks, buses, water carriers, freight forwarders, transportation brokers, and a coal slurry pipeline in interstate and foreign commerce.
- The Bus Regulatory Reform Act of 1982 sharply reduced the Federal role in regulating the bus industry. Various other acts enacted in 1980 reduced the ICC's role in regulating the trucking and railroad industries.

FEDERAL HIGHWAY ADMINISTRATION (FHWA)

- Provides funding to States for highway construction and improvement.
- Provides funding to States for construction programs to increase highway safety.
- Develops highway safety standards and guidelines.
- Regulates the safety performance of all commercial motor carriers engaged in interstate and foreign commerce.
- Inspects common carrier terminals and vehicles for safety.
- Identifies and monitors locations where serious accidents have occurred.
- Involves itself in highway planning and design, construction, maintenance, and beautification.
- Assists in obtaining uniformity among the States in the area of commercial motor carrier registration and taxation reporting.
- Establishes requirements for a single national commercial vehicle driver license for State issuance.
- Runs various training programs related to highway safety and other aspects of highway administration.

The National Highway Traffic Safety Administration regulates vehicle safety standards

NATIONAL HIGHWAY TRAFFIC SAFETY ADMINISTRATION (NHTSA)

- Regulates vehicle safety performance standards through the Federal Motor Vehicle Safety Standards program.

FEDERAL MARITIME COMMISSION (FMC)

- Regulates waterborne foreign and domestic offshore commerce of the United States.
- Assures that the United States international trade is open to all nations on fair and equitable terms.
- Protects against unauthorized, concerted activity in the waterborne commerce of the United States.

UNITED STATES COAST GUARD (USCG)

- Polices coastal and inland waters and navigable rivers of the United States for water pollution by ships and boats.
- Formulates, administers, and enforces various safety standards for the design, construction, equipment, and maintenance of commercial vessels of the United States and offshore structures on the Outer Continental Shelf.
- Develops and directs a national boating safety program aimed at making the operation of small craft in U.S. waters both pleasurable and safe.
- Controls traffic on waterways and establishes and maintains the U.S. aids to navigation system.

FEDERAL TRADE COMMISSION (FTC)

- Has authority to prevent "unfair methods of competition" and "unfair or deceptive acts or practices" (including deceptive advertising).

The other method that the public sector used to enforce its regulations is through regulatory techniques. Normally these techniques are concerned with the use of land. They include setting access or user quotas based upon a resource's carrying capacity, establishing reservation systems, making restrictive convenants on property ownership transfers, and in the United States using *eminent domain* that enables the Federal Government to take over endangered lands and historic sites. In the United States these techniques are exercised mainly in lands owned by the Federal Government.

State, regional or county, and municipal governments in the United States also have legislation and regulations that affect tourism, either directly or indirectly. Although the U.S. Constitution provides the federal government with specific powers, state governments automatically have the responsibility for all areas left unspecified. These responsibilities include the authority to regulate land uses and to acquire land within the state. Historically, these powers have been passed on to local governments at the city, town, and county levels. Cities, towns, and counties within the United States exercise these powers through zoning and the structuring of municipal plans.

Like the Federal Government, State Governments have legislation and regulations specifically dealing with state-owned lands, including state parks. Certain states have also enacted legislation that deals specifically with sectors of the tourism industry. A common characteristic of this sectoral legislation is that it has been motivated by a desire to protect the interests of consumers. Rhode Island, for example, passed a Travel Agency Act in 1977 giving the state the power to license retail travel agencies. The law was passed as a result of serious complaints from consumers about their experiences with certain agencies. Rhode Island was the first state in the United States to introduce such legislation, while Puerto Rico had done so earlier in 1974. Several Canadian provinces did likewise during the 1970's. Another part of the tourism industries that has received considerable attention has been the condominium real estate developments within resort areas, particularly time-sharing projects. Nebraska was the first state to introduce a time-sharing act to protect its citizens against any misleading claims of time-sharing resort developers in Nebraska and elsewhere.

The Legislation and Regulation of Tourism in Canada

Like its larger neighbor to the south, Canada has a myriad of legislation and regulations at both the federal, provincial, and municipal levels that directly or indirectly impinges upon tourism. As mentioned at the beginning of this chapter, the Sector Task Force on the Canadian Tourism Industry concluded in 1978 that the industry would be more effective economically if some of these laws and regulations were dismantled or updated. In response to this suggestion, the Canadian government established the Interdepartmental Committee on Tourism (IDCT). In addition, Canada's national tourism office, Tourism Canada, has accepted as one of its basic goals the improvement in levels of cooperation and coordination between government agencies and the private sector. It established its own coordination secretariat to establish liaison and consult with other federal agencies through the IDCT. It should also be noted that the Conference of Canadian Tourism Officials (CCTO) and the Federal/Provincial Conference of Tourism Ministers have been formed to improve

Federal and Provincial government coordination and cooperation relative to tourism.

Tourism Canada has recognized that due to the diversity of the tourism system within Canada many federal agencies have established regulations, policies, and programs that affect tourism. In their tourism sector strategy of 1981, Tourism Canada stated that the activities of these agencies:

> In some cases,. . .address the particular needs of the tourism industry. In others, the pursuit of goals different from those of the tourism industry exacerbate current industry problems or constrain the industry's ability to respond to opportunities. Tourism industry concerns have focused on several government horizontal policy measures. . .namely labor legislation, manpower policy, taxation policy, transportation regulations, environmental control, and the myriad of regulations at the federal, provincial, and municipal levels affecting facilities development.[6]

In its 1990 statement of Federal Tourism Policy, the Federal Government stated that "a co-ordinated approach is required by those federal departments and agencies whose policies and programs have an impact on the tourism industry."[7]

As in the United States, Canada's tourism legislation and regulations have their roots in the late nineteenth century. The Rocky Mountain Parks Act of 1887 established the first National Park surrounding Banff, Alberta. This was the parallel in history to the Yellowstone National Park Act of 1872 in the United States. The National Parks Act followed in Canada in 1930, and in 1953 the Historic Sites and Monuments Act was passed. The 1930 act stated that only such uses would be permitted within national parks that would "leave them unimpaired for the enjoyment of future generations."[8] This clause has been quite controversial, since certain of Canada's national parks, such as Banff and Jasper, are clearly among the nation's major tourist attractions and most favored destinations, particularly with respect to the desires of foreign visitors. The private sector of the Canadian tourism industry via the Sector Task Force on the Canadian Tourism Industry stated that these visitor needs and potentials were not being satisfied due to unnecessarily stringent development controls on the part of Parks Canada (now the Canadian Parks Service). This is a classic case of conservation versus development in tourism and of the unavoidable, inherent conflicts between the private sector and certain parts of the public sector of the tourism system.

In addition to the Canadian Parks Service, located within Environment Canada, at least sixteen other federal departments have tourism-related legislation and regulations. These include among others Industry, Science and Technology Canada (that includes Tourism Canada), Transport Canada, the National Transportation Agency, Public Works Canada, National Museums of Canada, External Affairs and International Trade Canada, Finance, and Employment and Immigration Canada.

[6]Canadian Government Office of Tourism, Tourism Sector Strategy (Ottawa, Canadian Government Office of Tourism, April 1981), pp. 59–68.

[7]Industry, Science and Technology Canada, Tourism on the Threshold, 1990, p. 30.

[8]Parks Canada, Parks Canada Policy (Ottawa, Parks Canada, 1979), p. 7.

There are several regulatory agencies within Canada whose mandates impact upon tourism. Principal among these is the Canadian Transport Commission (CTC), which historically was Canada's parallel organization to the now defunct CAB. The Air Transport Committee (ATC) was the specific group within CTC that makes airline regulatory decisions. The history of airline regulations within Canada has been quite different from that of the United States, primarily due to the existence of a nationally owned airline, Air Canada. The Canadian government established Air Canada through an act of Parliament, which gave the authority for its operation to a Crown Corporation. Although regulations were eased over the years to allow private airline companies to provide scheduled services within Canada, Air Canada (originally established as Trans Canada Airlines) was always preeminent, and the scheduled air service market up to the mid to late 1980s could therefore be described as being one of "regulated competition." This is in sharp contrast to the open market situation that developed in the United States from 1978 onwards as a result of airline deregulation. This situation changed in the last half of the 1980s as the Canadian Federal Government began to privatize Air Canada by selling off part of the ownership of the national airline. This was also the time that the Federal Government initiated the process of deregulating the domestic airline business in Canada.

The CTC is responsible for the regulation of railways and merchant shipping in Canada. The Canadian Coast Guard, located within Transport Canada, regulates nonmerchant boats and ships traveling in Canadian waters, including recreational crafts and cruise or sightseeing vessels.

As in the United States, the ten Canadian provinces and two territories have legislation and regulations that affect tourism directly and indirectly. Several of the provinces have specific tourism acts that give them the authority to license and, in some cases, to inspect tourism businesses. The Province of Quebec, for example, has the power through its tourism act to inspect and grade commercial accommodation facilities. Additionally, certain provinces, including Ontario and Quebec, have legislation that permits them to license and regulate retail travel agencies. All of the provinces and territories have considerable legislation governing the use of their parks and other natural resource areas.

Multinational Regulations Affecting the Travel Industry

In addition to the layers of national, state and provincial, regional and county, and city and town legislation and regulations affecting tourism, there are certain agreements that have been reached between foreign countries which have a direct impact upon travel.

Perhaps the most significant of these agreements are those which relate to air travel between countries. The embryonic period for these air travel agreements was during World War II. The five freedoms of international air travel were first discussed at an international civil aviation conference in Chicago in 1944. These five freedoms were:

1. Right of transit. The freedom to fly over another country without stopping.
2. Right of technical stop. The right to stop at another country's airport for fuel and servicing.
3. Right to discharge passengers at another country's airport.
4. Right to pick up passengers from another country's airport and return them to their homes.
5. Right to discharge passengers at another country's airport and to then load passengers for countries farther on.

Although these freedoms had considerable support, especially from the United States, they were never agreed to universally. This meant that there was a need to establish bilateral agreements between countries. The Bermuda Agreement of 1946 was the first of these, and it dealt with air travel between the United States and Britain. The formation of the International Civil Aviation Organization (ICAO) in 1944 and the International Air Transport Association (IATA) in 1945 paved the way for these types of agreements. ICAO is an organization of national governments; IATA represents the airlines. Approximately one hundred and sixty countries, including the United States, Canada, and the United Kingdom, belong to ICAO. Its objectives are:

1. To adopt international standards and recommended practices for regulating air navigation.
2. To recommend installation of navigation facilities by member countries.
3. To set forth proposals for the reduction of customs and immigration formalities.
4. To plan for the safe and orderly growth of international civil aviation throughout the world.
5. To encourage the improvement of the art of aircraft design and operation for peaceful purposes.
6. To seek the development of airways, airports, and air navigation facilities for international civil aviation.
7. To provide for safe, regular, efficient, and economical air transportation.
8. To discourage unreasonable competition.
9. To ensure that the rights of contracting countries are fully respected and that every member country has a fair opportunity to operate international airlines.
10. To discourage discrimination between contracting countries.
11. To promote the development of all aspects of international civil aeronautics.

Approximately 140 scheduled airline companies belong to IATA, some of which are nationally owned airlines. Any company offering a scheduled international air service may belong to IATA. The association's purpose is basically to resolve problems that the airline companies would not be able to resolve if they acted individually.

Its objectives are to encourage safe, regular, and economical international air services, to encourage international air commerce, and to research problems and issues affecting the industry.

One of IATA's key roles is that of setting rates on international routes to which all member airlines agree. It also acts as a clearing house for air-ticket coupons that allow passengers to fly internationally on several airlines while requiring only one flight coupon. It acts in an advisory capacity on mutual problems, such as fuel shortages, hijacking, navigation, and safety. Also, IATA is an important source of statistics on international air travel. Unlike the national regulatory agencies, IATA does not certify airlines, award routes, or act on market exit decisions. These powers remain with the national governments and their regulatory authorities. The International Airlines Travel Agents Network (IATAN), a nonprofit subsidiary of IATA, endorses retail travel agencies to sell tickets on IATA-member airlines.

Bilateral air agreements are struck between governments addressing these matters; the United Kingdom-United States-Bermuda agreement of 1946 is the forerunner of these. These bilateral agreements are frequently somewhat loose and often mask ongoing disputes between two countries over transborder air services. The 1973 bilateral agreement between the United States and Canada is a good example of this latter point. It is indicative of the inherent problems of a tourism system in which the market or political philosophies of nations are quite different. Since 1978 the United States has deregulated its airline industry and has been a strong proponent of an "open skies" airline policy internationally. In contrast until more recently, Canada maintained a highly protectionist stance with respect to its airline companies. Canada's refusal to open up the international air border between itself and the United States completely led in 1983 to a serious dispute over a proposed package of heavily discounted fares to be offered by Air Canada to several cities in the southern United States. The CAB's obstinacy in not allowing these fare schedules caused many Canadians prebooked on these flights to cancel their trips. Quite obviously the destination areas within the southern United States suffered because of the loss of potential income from the Canadian travelers. It is hoped that the final implementation of the Free Trade Agreement (FTA) between Canada and the United States may help to liberalize cross-border air travel.

Before leaving the subject of international air travel regulations and agreements, mention must be made of the many pacts that have been made between countries with respect to airlines' liabilities for passenger injuries and damage or loss of baggage. Historically, there have been three such major agreements—the Warsaw Convention, the Hague Protocol, and the Montreal Agreement. The Warsaw Convention dates back to 1929 and constitutes the main body of international rules in this respect. The United States accepted the Warsaw Convention regulations in 1934; Canada and the United Kingdom are other adherents to it. Several Central American and South American countries are not members of the treaty. The Hague Protocol and the Montreal Agreement represent international agreements that have raised the dollar limit on an airline's liability to an individual passenger.

Hotel classification on an international level also represents a tacit attempt by several nations to regulate standards within another important component of the

The world tourism organization supports an international organization system for
hotels—hotels in New Delhi

tourism system. The World Tourism Organization (WTO) has taken the lead role
in this regard. It was given this authority in 1963 when the United Nations Conference
on International Travel and Tourism asked it to draft these standards. The main rationale for setting these standards was as follows.

> Traveling problems can be eased to a considerable extent if hotels of a par-
> ticular category in all countries were to present more or less the same
> characteristics of comfort and service.[9]

Although many countries appear to agree in principle with the classification
method and criteria that the WTO has developed, many have chosen to create their
own classification and grading or rating systems, since they have found the WTO
guidelines to be too broad for their purposes.

In addition to these specific agreements, there are a plethora of treaties and
agreements governing trade and travel or customer procedures between nations and
groups of nations. Although they are too numerous to mention, they also play a key
role in the tourism regulatory framework of destination areas.

The Need for Government Regulation of Tourism in Destination Areas

A close analysis of the legislation and regulations described above would clearly show
that governments are acting in the general interests of their citizens. They do so

[9]World Tourism Organization, International Hotel Classification (Madrid, Spain, World Tourism
Organization, 1969), p. 2.

primarily to protect and conserve their destination area's natural, historical, and cultural resources, to ensure the health and safety of visitors, and to protect the visitors from unscrupulous business practices. In these respects, the value of a government's role cannot be questioned.

From time to time, however, governments are accused of being overly bureaucratic, of developing unnecessary red tape, and of going too far in their policing efforts. This is especially true when the political pendulum and public sentiment swing more toward the free-enterprise approach, as they have in the U.S. airline industry. It is also true of Canada where those in the tourism industries have sharply criticized governments for hindering the development of tourism destination areas because of their lengthy and complex project approval processes. Certainly, government agencies seldom appear to act or react with the speed with which the private sector requires.

The lack of coordination and cooperation between government agencies in their policies and programs is often quite prevalent in tourism. This is a reflection of the diversity of the tourism system itself and of the inherent and unavoidable conflicts between the goals of some agencies, such as natural resource conservation versus tourism promotion and development agencies. Any destination area with a vital interest in tourism should undertake steps to bring about the highest amount of coordination and cooperation among its government agencies. It seems logical that the national and state or provincial offices should take the lead role in this respect.

SUMMARY

Experience has shown that tourism development can have both positive and negative impacts on a host destination. Tourism also affects and is influenced by various national interests of a country, including its natural and cultural resources and its immigration laws and policies. For these and other reasons, it is essential that governments play a role in developing legislation and in regulating specific aspects of the tourism industries. While most agree that this is a valid role for governments to play, many in tourism often feel that government goes too far in implementing various laws and regulations. This appears to be a perennial source of public-private sector friction in most developed countries.

In recent years, there has been a definite trend in certain developed countries toward deregulating parts of the tourism industries. The United States has been a leader in this regard, having removed its regulation of the airline and bus industries. Canada and certain European nations are also now considering airline deregulation.

REFERENCES

Destination U.S.A., Report of the National Tourism Resources Review Commission, vol. 4, Federal Role, June 1973, p. 12.

HUDMAN, LLOYD E., Tourism: A Shrinking World (Columbus, OH, Grid Inc., 1980), p. 74.

JOHNSTON, EVERETT, E., and J. R. BRENT RITCHIE, "Regulation of Air Travel: A Canadian Perspective," Journal of Travel Research, vol. 20, no. 2, Fall 1981, p. 9.

SOLBERG, CARL, Conquest of the Skies: A History of Commercial Aviation in America (Boston, Little, Brown & Co., 1979), p. 286.

TOURISM SECTOR CONSULTATIVE TASK FORCE, A Report By the Sector Task Force On the Canadian Tourism Industry (Ottawa, Ontario, Department of Industry, Trade, and Commerce, 1978), p. 125.

U.S. SENATE, A Conceptual Basis for the National Tourism Policy Study: Appendix C (Washington, DC, U.S. Government Printing Office, 1976), pp. 82, 92.

12

TOURISM PLANNING

Selecting among Alternatives for the Tourism Industries

"See the sunset—only 3 dollars a car."

Cartoon caption, *Niagara Gazette*, April 1, 1973.

Because of the wide-ranging effects of tourism on a destination area, it is vital that development be undertaken within the context of a plan. This chapter deals with the planning process as a method for selecting among alternatives for the destination. A comparison is made between planned and the unplanned destination areas, and reasons are given why planning should take place. The consequences of unplanned development are noted.

The purposes of planning are laid out and barriers to planning examined in an attempt to understand why the planning stage is often avoided. A process for planning tourism is detailed, and an examination of each step in the process is undertaken to provide a road map for the destination planner.

LEARNING OBJECTIVES

Having read this chapter, you should be able to:

1. Identify the reasons for tourism planning in destination areas.
2. Describe the consequences of unplanned development of tourism.
3. Explain the five basic purposes of tourism planning.
4. Describe the relationship of tourism planning to tourism policy formulation.
5. List the four common barriers to tourism planning in free-enterprise systems.
6. Describe the five essential phases in the tourism planning process.
7. Explain the concept of the hierarchy of tourism goals and objectives.
8. List the seven major components of a destination area's market potential.
9. Describe the research techniques that can be used to assess a destination area's and business' market potential.

THE DESTINATION AREA
WITH AND WITHOUT TOURISM PLANNING

Tourism planning is an essential activity for every destination area, especially in today's fast-changing business environments. Although it is true that some destinations have flourished without any conscious planning, many have eventually suffered serious consequences for not carefully considering future events and their impacts.

Planning refers to the selection between alternative courses of action. All planning involves an analysis of the future. It also involves setting the basic goals and objectives for the destination area, which is the point at which other supportive actions follow.

Reasons for Tourism Planning

There are many valid reasons for tourism planning. One of these relates to the destination life-cycle concept as defined by Plog.[1] Plog's hypothesis is that destination areas tend to rise and fall in popularity according to the whims of those in the predominate *psychographic* groups to which they appeal at different stages in their development histories. This concept is somewhat similar to the product life-cycle and product adoption-curve ideas discussed in most basic marketing texts (see Figure 12.1), except that it relates certain personality profiles to the destination area's stages of growth. Thus, a new and/or exotic destination tends to appeal first to Plog's *allocentric* group—the innovators in the travel market that seek out uncrowded and unique destinations. As the destination area becomes more widely publicized and better known, it loses its appeal to the allocentrics and they are replaced by the *midcentrics,* who greatly outnumber the allocentrics in the population in general. Plog relates the midcentric appeal stage in the destination area's history to the maturity phase of the

[1]Stanley C. Plog, "Why Destination Areas Rise and Fall in Popularity," Cornell Hotel and Restaurant Administration Quarterly, Ithaca, New York, 1973, pp. 13–16.

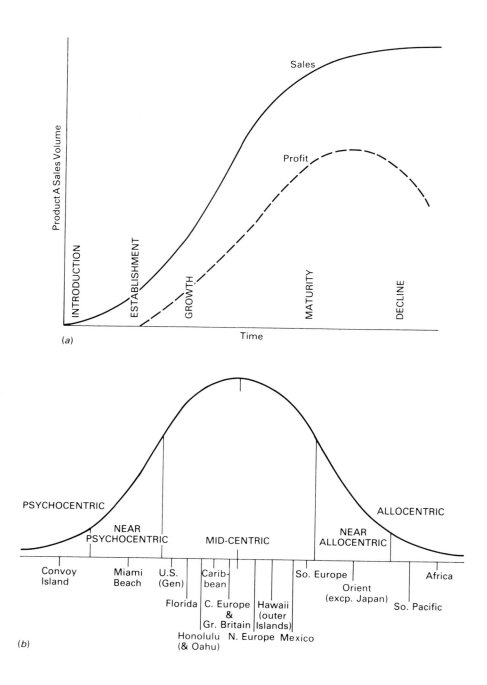

Figure 12.1 (a) Lazer's Product Life Cycle; (b) Plog's Destination Life Cycle; (c) Rogers' Product Adoption Curve.

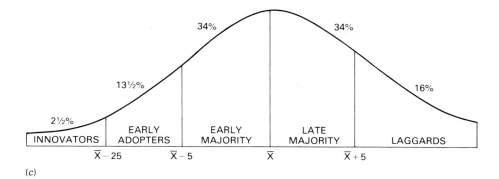

(c)

Adapted from: Stanley G. Plog, "Why Destination Areas Rise and Fall in Popularity," *Cornell Hotel and Restaurant Administration Quarterly*, November 1973, pp. 13-16.
Everett M. Rogers, *Diffusion of Innovation* (New York, Free Press of Glencoe, 1962), p. 162.
William Lazer, *Marketing Management: A Systems Perspective* (New York, John Wiley & Sons, 1971), p. 272.

product life cycle where sales volumes are at their peak. Basically, the destination area can be said to have mass-market appeal at this point. Eventually as time progresses, this destination area also loses its appeal to the midcentrics, and they are replaced by the *psychocentrics* who, like the allocentrics, represent a much smaller proportion of the population. According to Plog, the psychocentric stage is the final point in the destination area's life cycle; it has lost its appeal to both the market innovators and the mass market. One of the most important messages of the Plog hypothesis is that destination areas can "carry with them the potential seeds of their own destruction" if they allow themselves to become over-commercialized and to forsake the unique appeals which made them popular in the first place.

Although Plog's concept appears to suggest that all destination areas eventually face the same fate, the years of experience which have been gained since it was first publicized have shown that there have been several exceptions to this rule. This experience indicates that destination life cycles can be extended if change is anticipated, and if steps are taken to adapt to the change. One of the core functions of tourism planning is to provide the basic framework to allow the destination area to cope with change.

The point is that both the external and internal variables mentioned in a previous chapter are constantly changing. The destination has two choices: (1) react to changes after they occur; or (2) develop a method or plan to assess the present situation, forecast the future situation, and select an appropriate course of action to make the most of available opportunities.

Consequences of Unplanned Development

What can happen if a destination area does not involve itself in tourism planning? The examples are numerous and often well-documented, especially as they relate to tourism's impact on the physical environment. Some of the symptoms of a lack of tourism planning may include the following:

PHYSICAL IMPACTS

Damage or permanent alternation of the physical environment

Damage or permanent alteration of historical/cultural landmarks and resources

Overcrowding and congestion

Pollution

Traffic problems

HUMAN IMPACTS

Less accessibility to services and tourist attractions for local residents resulting in local resentment

Dislike of tourists on the part of local residents

Loss of cultural identities

Lack of education of tourism employees in skills and hospitality

Lack of awareness of the benefits of tourism to the destination area

MARKETING IMPACTS

Failure to capitalize on new marketing opportunities

Erosion of market shares due to the actions of competitive destination areas

Lack of sufficient awareness in prime markets

Lack of a clear image of destination area in potential markets

Lack of cooperative advertising among individual operators

Inadequate capitalization on packaging opportunities

ORGANIZATIONAL IMPACTS

Fragmented approach to the marketing and development of tourism, often involving "competitive" splinter groups

Lack of cooperation among individual operators

Inadequate representation of the tourism industries' interests

Lack of support from local public authorities

Failure to act upon important issues, problems, and opportunities of common interest to the industry

OTHER IMPACTS

Inadequate signage programs

Lack of sufficient attractions and events

High seasonality and short lengths of stay

Poor or deteriorating quality of facilities and services

Poor or inadequate travel information services

Although the critics of tourism as an economic activity have made much of these negatives, particularly as they relate to environmental conservation and negative cultural or social effects, the blame can more properly be attached to the lack of tourism planning than to the inherent nature of tourism itself.

A lack of tourism planning can result in pollution and traffic problems

THE PLANNING CONTEXT

Tourism activity in a destination area is generated through the existence of unique attractions. These can include beaches, natural scenery, parks, historical buildings and landmarks, unique cultural characteristics, unique local events and activities, outdoor sports areas, and so on. It follows that if the destination area wishes to maintain tourism as a long-term economic activity, it must show its concern through planning to preserve and enhance these special factors that make it different from all other destinations. Planning in this context has five basic purposes:

1. Identify alternative approaches to
   Marketing
   Development
   Industry organization
   Tourism awareness
   Support services and activities
2. Adapting to the unexpected in
   General economic conditions
   Energy supply and demand situation
   Values and life-styles

Fortunes of individual industries
Other factors in the external environment

3. Maintaining uniqueness in
Natural features and resources
Local cultural and social fabric
Local architecture
Historical monuments and landmarks
Local events and activities
Parks and outdoor sports areas
Other features of the destination area

4. Creating the desirable, such as in
High level of awareness of benefits of tourism
Clear and positive image of area as a tourism destination
Effective industry organization
High level of cooperation among individual operators
Effective marketing, signage, and travel information programs
Other objectives

5. Avoiding the undesirable, such as in
Friction and unnecessary competition among individual tourism operators
Hostile and unfriendly attitudes of local residents toward tourists
Damage or undesirable, permanent alteration of natural features and
  historical resources
Loss of cultural identities
Loss of market share
Stoppage of unique local events and activities
Overcrowding, congestion, and traffic problems
Pollution
High seasonality
Other factors

As the reader will quickly realize, the purposes of tourism planning are basically to avoid the negative physical, human, marketing, organizational, and other impacts that can occur when planning is not practiced. Although the authors do not advocate that tourism is necessarily the answer to every destination area's economic and social problems, or indeed that every community should pursue it, tourism is much more likely to be a successful activity if planning is pursued.

Roles and Responsibilities for Tourism Planning

In communist countries all planning is done by the national government. As such clear centralization of power and responsibility is not found in noncommunist countries, the roles of the public sector (government) and the private sector (tourism industries) are much less easily demarcated. Clearly in a democratic nation, there is a valid role to be played in tourism planning by both the public and private sectors.

Experience has shown that the process of joint participation and close industry and government cooperation produces the best results and that plans are more likely to be successfully implemented if the private sector is actively involved in the planning process.

Historically, tourism planning appears to have originated in Europe, quickly being adopted thereafter in several developing nations in Africa and Asia. France, Eire, and the United Kingdom were among the pioneers of the technology of tourism planning, with all three nations being involved in some form of planning for tourism in the early 1960's. Canada has also been in the forefront of tourism planning, its efforts originating in the late 1960's and early 1970's. The United States has seen little organized tourism planning to date and certainly lags badly behind its northern neighbor in this respect.

Tourism planning should take place at many levels within a country. The starting point for the tourism planning process in any country should be development of a national tourism policy. In Chapter 10 a tourism policy model was described (see Figure 10.1), and it was suggested that a national tourism policy represented an amalgam of the principles upon which a nationwide course of action for tourism is based. As such, the tourism policy represents the basic foundation from which more specific goals, strategies, objectives, and plans are developed. It follows that all planning efforts should be complementary to the national tourism policy. A national tourism policy, as well as all tourism plans, should be given finite time spans and be reviewed and modified at the expiration of these time periods. Because change is inevitable and continuous, it follows that tourism policy making and planning have to be dynamic processes. Because policies tend to be more broad scale than tourism plans, they usually are valid for a greater number of years. The life span of a tourism plan is normally not more than five years.

Barrier to Planning

There are often many barriers to tourism planning and numerous problems associated with it. First, many people are against planning in principle, particularly within the free-enterprise system. This is especially true in North America, where tourism has developed and existed for many years without tourism planning. Many business people view tourism planning as an encroachment into their domain of activity, and they are quite skeptical of this ultimate value. Cost is a second barrier to tourism planning. Because effective tourism planning must be based upon detailed resource analysis and market research, it inevitably means that is has to be funded by one or more groups. The public sector generally funds the planning efforts on behalf of itself and the private sector. A third barrier is the complexity and diversity of the industry and the large number of government departments that have activities that impinge upon tourism. Unlike, say, the automobile manufacturing business, the tourism business is not a readily identifiable industry. Although the front-line recipients of tourists' expenditures—such as hotels, motels, resorts, airlines, car rental agencies, campgrounds, commercial attractions, and restaurants—are quite obvious, others, including retail stores, banks, and municipal governments, are not normally seen as being part of the "industry." Another complication is that many tourism businesses receive their income from both visitors and from local residents. In the public sector, the complexity is no less great, as was noted earlier.

The situation in Canada is the same, as the programs of a multiplicity of departments and agencies have some effect on tourism. Tourism planning is often made more difficult because the policies of these departments are not coordinated and, indeed, are sometimes in direct conflict with one another.

A fourth barrier to planning is the fact that tourism usually is characterized by a few large businesses and a multitude of smaller enterprises. There is also a tendency for individual operators to categorize themselves as being in the campground industry or the hotel industry or the restaurant industry rather than accepting their broader role in tourism. Other problems encountered in planning tourism include the seasonality of business activity and the relatively high ownership turnover in the industry.

Despite these barriers to tourism planning, an increasing number of plans are produced each year around the world. Indications are that tourism planning will be given a higher priority in the future and that more destinations will become involved in this important process. As they become involved, they will have at their disposal the previous planning experience of many other areas and thus a more refined "technology" of tourism planning. The remainder of this chapter is devoted to the steps in the tourism planning process itself.

STEPS IN THE TOURISM PLANNING PROCESS

As was pointed out earlier, tourism planning in a destination country should take place at a variety of levels. The approaches utilized in producing the plans, however, should follow a similar step-by-step pattern. Figure 12.2 provides an illustration of a conceptual model for the tourism planning process incorporating these steps. Actual experience has shown that some of the elements of the conceptual model have been overlooked in some past planning efforts and that varying degrees of emphasis have been attached to the individual phases of the planning process.

There are five essential phases in the tourism planning process, and these are as follows:

1. Background analysis phase
2. Detailed research and analysis phase
3. Synthesis phase
4. Goal-setting, strategy selection, and objective-setting phase
5. Plan development phase

Each of the five phases involves a variety of activities, participants, and outcomes, and these are illustrated in Figure 12.2.

Background Analysis Phase

The first phase in the tourism planning process could be classified as situational analysis that produces the basic direction for the succeeding phases. Because most destination areas, be they countries, states, provinces, regions, or local communities, have some level of existing tourism activity and regulatory or policy framework for the industry, this is a logical launching point for most tourism plans.

In establishing a national tourism plan, the national tourism policy must be first considered and interpreted. Also if a state or province has a tourism policy, then it should be carefully reviewed at the outset of the plan. In Chapter 10, it was stated that tourism policy goals normally fall into four categories: economic, consumer-social, resource-environmental, and government operations. In the province of Ontario, the Ministry of Tourism and Recreation identified the *economic* policy goal as being its prime mandate. It defined this goal as follows: "To stimulate employment, income and economic development through the systematic improvement, development and marketing of Ontario's tourism industry."[2]

In tourism policy making and planning, there is a hierarchy of goals and objectives. The tourism policy goal or goals, like those of Ontario, are the long-term targets in the destination area that provide the framework and rationale for supporting goals and objectives (see Figure 12.3). At each level in the hierarchy, the goals and objectives become more specific and more action oriented. Using the Ontario example again, the Ministry of Tourism and Recreation defined two policy objectives and six subobjectives on the basis of the policy goals as follows:

Policy Objective 1. To increase the volume and diversity of tourism opportunities throughout Ontario.

SUBOBJECTIVES

1.1 To develop a system of attractions and events of provincial and regional significance

1.2 To provide traveler support services (accommodation, food, transportation, information) in response to existing and projected consumption patterns

1.3 To ensure the existence of an effective and efficient infrastructure to complement provincial tourism resources

Policy Objective 2. To increase the quality of the tourism experience in Ontario.

SUBOBJECTIVES

2.1 To encourage orderly growth and increased efficiency within the tourism industry

2.2 To assist in upgrading the tourism plant

2.3 To encourage integration of supply components to better satisfy tourism requirements

[2]Balmer, Crapo & Associates, Inc., Tourism Development in Ontario: A Framework for Opportunity (Waterloo, Ontario, Ontario Ministry of Tourism and Recreation, 1977).

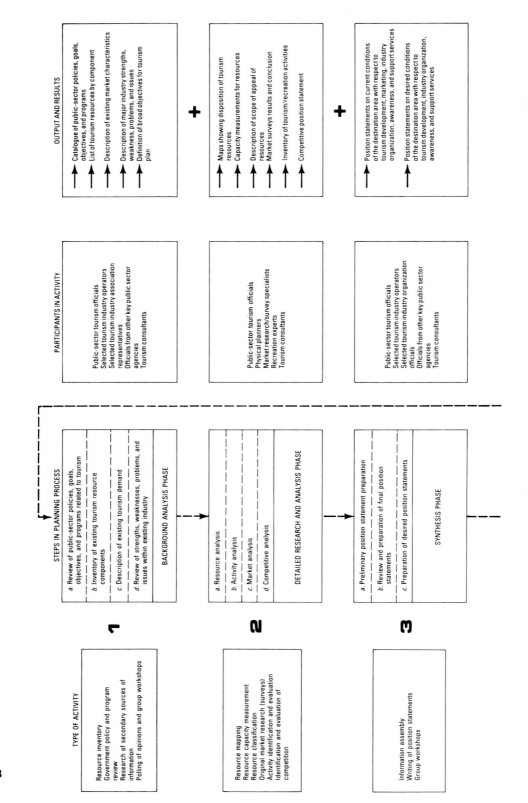

STEPS IN PLANNING PROCESS

a. Review of public-sector policies, goals, objectives, and programs related to tourism

b. Inventory of existing tourism resource components

c. Description of existing tourism demand

d. Review of strengths, weaknesses, problems, and issues within existing industry

BACKGROUND ANALYSIS PHASE

a. Resource analysis

b. Activity analysis

c. Market analysis

d. Competitive analysis

DETAILED RESEARCH AND ANALYSIS PHASE

a. Preliminary position statement preparation

b. Review and preparation of final position statements

c. Preparation of desired position statements

SYNTHESIS PHASE

TYPE OF ACTIVITY

Resource inventory
Government policy and program review
Research of secondary sources of information
Polling of opinions and group workshops

Resource mapping
Resource capacity measurement
Resource classification
Original market research (surveys)
Activity identification and evaluation
Identification and evaluation of competition

Information assembly
Writing of position statements
Group workshops

PARTICIPANTS IN ACTIVITY

Public-sector tourism officials
Selected tourism industry operators
Selected tourism industry association representatives
Officials from other key public sector agencies
Tourism consultants

Public-sector tourism officials
Physical planners
Market research/survey specialists
Recreation experts
Tourism consultants

Public-sector tourism officials
Selected tourism industry operators
Selected tourism industry organization officials
Officials from other key public sector agencies
Tourism consultants

OUTPUT AND RESULTS

➤ Catalogue of public-sector policies, goals, objectives, and programs
➤ List of tourism resources by component
➤ Description of existing market characteristics
➤ Description of major industry strengths, weakness, problems, and issues
➤ Definition of broad objectives for tourism plan

+

➤ Maps showing disposition of tourism resources
➤ Capacity measurements for resources
➤ Description of scope of appeal of resources
➤ Market surveys results and conclusion
➤ Inventory of tourism/recreation activities
➤ Competitive position statement

+

➤ Position statements on current conditions of the destination area with respect to tourism development, marketing, industry organization, awareness, and support services
➤ Position statements on desired conditions of the destination area with respect to tourism development, industry organization, awareness, and support services

1

2

3

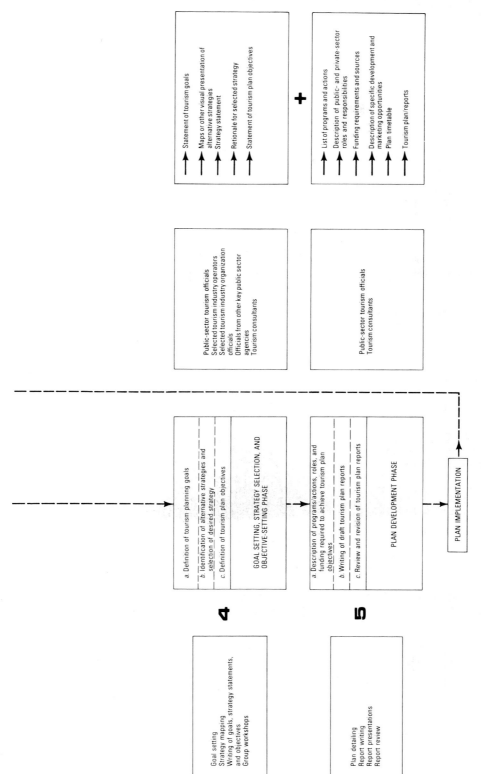

Figure 12.2 Tourism planning model

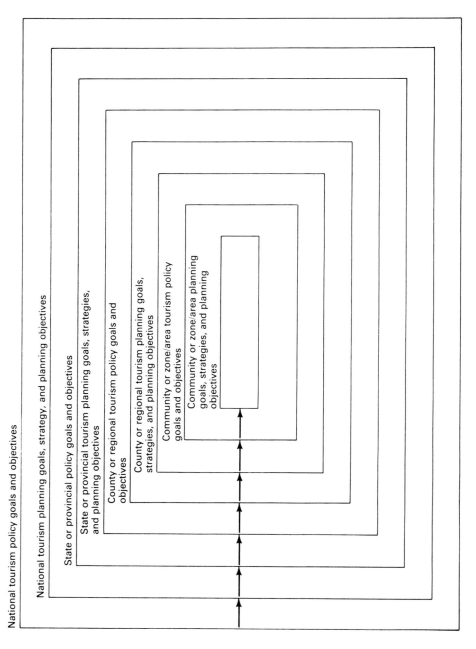

Figure 12.3 A hierarchy of tourism policy and planning goals and objectives.

Because other public sector agencies normally have policies, goals, and objectives that impact upon tourism, these must be considered in the background analysis stage. Existing tourism-related programs or activities of public and private sector organizations should also be identified.

The background analysis should produce an inventory or listing of the destination area's tourism resource components. Figure 12.4 provides a basic categorization of these tourism resource components and their subcomponents. These resource components and subcomponents constitute the existing tourism "product" of the destination area.

The third step in the background analysis normally involves a description of existing tourism demand in the destination area, utilizing readily available secondary (published) sources of information. Ideally this information will give a profile of demand along the following lines:

Component	Subcomponent
Natural Features	Landscapes Scenery Unique features Flora and fauna
Historical and Cultural Features	Buildings Sites Themes Communities/subcommunities
Tourist Operations and Facilities	Attractions Accommodation Food service Events
Hospitality Services	Information centers Reservation systems Commercial stores and services (banks, retail stores)

Infrastructure	Transportation systems:
	  road
	  rail
	  airport
	  boat
	Underground services

Human Resources	Population and work force Ethnic community Attitude toward tourism
General Socioeconomic	Employment/unemployment Industries Economic conditions Social problems
Present Land Uses	Land ownership Planning and zoning regulations Future growth and development

SOURCE: The Economic Planning Group of Canada.

Figure 12.4 Categorization of tourism resource components

- Modes of travel to and within the destination area and past usage volumes (aircraft, bus, train, ship, private automobile, etc.)
- Visitation volumes and patterns by month or season
- Geographical origins of tourists
- Geographical destinations of tourists
- Tourist demographics (such as age, sex, income, education, occupations, and travel party composition)
- Trip purposes
- Activity participation
- Market segments (families with children, singles, tour groups, business groups, etc.)
- Lengths of stay in area
- Tourist expenditures within area
- Usage of facilities (such as accommodation, attractions, events, and recreation facilities)

The quantity and quality of this information will be determined by the priority that the destination area has attached to tourism market research in the past. If gaps are found in the available information, these are usually identified in this first phase and an attempt is made to fill them in the detailed research phase.

The final step in the background analysis phase should be a review of the major strengths, weaknesses, problems, and issues within the destination area's existing tourism industries. This is an important scene-setting step for the remainder of the tourism planning process, and it should be both introspective, critical, and objective. It should involve a variety of individuals, including public sector tourism officials, officials from other key public sector agencies, selected tourism industries operators, and selected industry organization representatives. This exercise is likely to be most objective and productive if a broad variety of opinions and interests are sought. In North America, private consulting organizations specializing in tourism are often utilized in the planning process. These organizations inject a degree of objectivity and broad industry experience that may not be readily available in the area itself.

Another step that is taken in some tourism plans at this point is that of staging a series of public meetings with citizen groups in the destination area. These sessions can be useful in determining community attitudes and awareness levels of tourism and the type of future direction citizens wish for tourism in their locales.

Detailed Research and Analysis Phase

A valid tourism plan cannot be formulated without research. Tourism plans developed without research tend to reflect the subjective opinions of their authors and to perpetuate existing situations. As the Scottish Tourist Board has noted[3], these types

---

[3]P.A. Taylor and M. R. Carter, "Using Tourism in Regional Development: Planning for Tourism in Scotland," in Tourism Planning and Development Issues (George Washington University, 1980), p. 309.

of plans normally "provide what seems to be most in demand at the time" but they do not necessarily lead to the achievement of tourism policy goals and objectives.

Research should be concentrated in four distinct areas—resources, markets, activities, and competition. The very basic level of research carried out during the background analysis phase should have helped to pinpoint where the more detailed research should be focused.

Using the inventory of tourism resource components as a base, the first step in the resource analysis involves the preparation of maps identifying the location of key resources. With the mapping completed, the capacities of the various tourism resources are then measured. Although the capacities of some of the tourism resource components are easily measured (such as in guest rooms, restaurant seats, camp sites, and golf courses), the capacities of others (such as boating on lakes and rivers, beaches, and historical landmarks) are not.

The final stage of the resource analysis could be referred to as resource classification. Basically, this represents a ranking or grading of the scope of appeal of the tourism resources of the destination area. Thus, individual resources or zones within

St. Paul's Cathedral in London is a tourism resource with international appeal

the destination are normally defined as being of international, national, regional, or local significance, or as having international, national, regional, or local market appeal. Two examples can be used to illustrate this process. In the Auvergne region of central France, the classification was done on an area-by-area basis. Three classifications were developed: Class A areas having tourist attractions of national and international importance, Class B areas having regionally important attractions capable of attracting people from the rest of France, and Class C areas having attractions of only regional or interregional importance. Another example is illustrated in Figure 12.5, which is taken from a tourism development plan prepared for the Collingwood-Midland-Orillia Zone in Ontario. This plan has classified the various resource components as having local, regional, provincial, Canadian and U.S., or international appeal with respect to both the existing, desired, and potential markets.

The second component of the detailed research phase is the activity analysis. Activities include all of the things that the tourist can do while visiting the destination area, ranging from outdoor recreational pursuits, such as alpine skiing, to more passive pursuits, such as shopping and viewing scenery. Every destination area has a variety of existing activities and potential activities not yet being capitalized upon. As the activity or activities available at the destination are often a prime motivating factor to travel, this exercise can be most useful in highlighting new demand generation opportunities. Again, it is necessary to classify the activities in terms of their range of appeal (see Figure 12.5). It is also essential to identify the months of the year in which the activities can be pursued (see Figure 12.6). Because many destination areas suffer from a seasonality of demand problem, this part of the analysis helps to pinpoint those activities that will generate demand outside of peak periods.

A good tourism plan will incorporate some original research on the existing and potential markets for the destination area. As will be recalled, the market-related research carried out in the first phase was based upon already available information. The original research is done by carrying out one or more surveys of existing tourists and potential tourists. Surveys of existing tourists are normally carried on while they are traveling within the destination area, and they are useful in producing information of the following types:

Overall degrees of satisfaction with trips
Evaluations and ratings of attractions, facilities, services, and other resource components
Likelihood of return visits
Awareness levels of area attractions and other resource components
Motivations for travel to area
Identification of items that would increase likelihood of return visits
Sources of information utilized in planning trips
Major constraints or barriers to return visits
Images of the destination area

Tiny Shoreline Region

TOURISM RECREATION OPPORTUNITY			RESOURCE OPPORT	EXISTING MARKET					DESIRED MARKET					POTENT MARKET				
				Local	Regional	Provincial	National/U.S.	International	Local	Regional	Provincial	National/U.S.	International	Local	Regional	Provincial	National	International
Water-based Recreation Opportunities	Boating	Sailing	●	●	●	○			●	●	○			●	●	○		
		Power Boating/Touring	●	●	●	○	○		●	●	○			●	●	○	○	
		Ice Boating	○	○	○				○	○				●	●			
		Canoeing	●	●	●				●	●				●	●			
		Windsurfing	●	●	●				●	●				●	●			
	Fishing	Sportfishing	◐	●	●				●	●				●	●			
		Icefishing	○	○	○				○	○				○	○			
	Swimming/Bathing		◐	●	●				●	●	○			●	●	○		
	Water Skiing		◐	●	●				●	●				●	●			
	Scuba Diving/Snorkeling		◐	●	●	○			●	●	○			●	●	○	○	
Land-Based Recreation Opportunities	Skiing	Alpine																
		Cross-Country	●	●	●	○			●	●	○			●	○	○		
	Hunting	Big Game	◐	●	●				●	●				●	○			
		Small Game	◐	●	○				●	○				●	○			
		Water Fowl	◐	●	○				●	○				●	○			
	Camping	Auto Touring	○	○	○				○	○				●	●	○		
		Wilderness	●	○	○				○	○				○	●	○	○	
	Hiking/Backpacking	Day	○	○	○				○	○				○	●			
		Overnight	●	○	○				○	○				○	●			
		Snowshoeing	◐	○	○				○	○				○	●			
	Rock Climbing														○			
	Cave Exploring																	
	Picnicking		●	●	○				●	●				●				
	Cottaging/Chalet		●	○	◐		○		○	●				○	●	●	○	
	Snowmobiling		●	●	●				●	●				○	●	●		
	Cycling		○	○	○				○	○				○	●			
	Equestrian Trails		○	○	○				○	○				○	○			
Land and Water-Based Recreation Opportunities	Viewing Natural Attractions		●	●	●	○	○		●	●	○	○		●	●	○	○	○
	Gathering/Collecting		●	○	○				○	○				○	○			
	Photography/Painting		●	●	●	○	○		●	●	○	○		●	●	○	○	○
Air-Based Recreation Opportunities	Hang Gliding																	
	Hot Air Ballooning																	
	Gliding		○	○	○				○	○				○				
Natural Resource Opportunities	Natural Parks and Sites	National	●	○	●	○			●	●	○	○		●	●	○	○	
		Provincial	◐	●	○				●	●				●	●	○	○	
		Crown Land	●	●	○				●	●				●	●	○		
	Game Sanctuaries/Reserves		●	●	●				●	●				●	●	○		
	Game Farms																	
Historical Resource Opportunities	Historic Parks and Sites	National	◐	○	●	○	○		●	●	○	○		●				
		Provincial	○	●	○				●	●				●				
		Local	○	●	○				●	○				●				
	Archaeological Attractions	Existing	○	○	○				○	○				○	○			
		Potential	○	○	○				○	○				○	○			
Cultural Resource Opportunities	Population Centres	Cities/Towns	○	●	●	○			●	●	○	○		●	●	○	○	
		Ethnic Settlements	○	○	○				○	○				○	○			
	Cultural Attractions	Fairs/Celebrations	○	●	○				●	●				●	○			
		Crafts/Events	○	●	○				●	●				●	○			
		Museums/Galleries																	
Recreation Leisure Developments	Accommodation Recreation Resorts	Hotel Motel Cottage	◐	○	●	○	○		○	●	●	●		○	●	●	●	
		Vacation Farm																	
		Ski Developments													●	○	○		
		Marina Developments	◐											●	○	○		
		Convention Centres	○											○	○			
	Travel Touring Corridors	Air	○	○	○				○	○				○	○	○	○	
		Rail	○	○	○				○	○				○				
		Boat	●	●	●	○	○		●	●	○	○		●	●	○	○	
		Car	◐	●	○	○			○	●				●	●	●	○	
	Recreation Leisure Developments	Ski Developments - Alpine	◐	●	○				●	●				●	○			
		Ski Developments - Cross Country	●	●	○				●	●				●	○			
		Marina Boating Developments	●	●	●	○	○		●	●	○	○		●	●	○	○	
		Golf Courses	○	●	○				●	○				●	●			
		Campgrounds Trailer Parks	●	●	●	○	○		●	○				○	●	○		
		Beaches	○	○	○				○	○				○	○			
Attractions			◐	○	○				○	○				○	○			

NATURAL RESOURCES (Water-based through Air-Based Recreation Opportunities)

MAN-DEVELOPED MAN-CONTROLLED RESOURCES (Natural Resource through Recreation Leisure Developments)

a. RESOURCE OPPORTUNITIES
- ● Abundant resource opportunities; existing and/or potential.
- ◐ Moderate resource opportunities; existing and/or potential.
- ○ Limited resource opportunities; existing and/or potential.
- ☐ No resource opportunities.

b. EXISTING MARKET
- ● Heavy use/demand
- ○ Limited use/demand
- ☐ No use/demand

c. DESIRED MARKET
- ● Strong desire to attract as a primary market.
- ○ Limited desire to attract as a primary market.
- ☐ No desire to attract as a primary market.

d. POTENTIAL MARKET
- ● Strong market attraction for this activity.
- ○ Weak market attraction for this activity.
- ☐ No market attraction for this activity.

Figure 12.5 Recreational opportunities and market associations.

Honey Harbour Region

TOURISM RECREATION OPPORTUNITY

Column groups: RESOURCE OPPORT. | EXISTING MARKET (Local, Regional, Provincial, National/U.S., International) | DESIRED MARKET (Local, Regional, Provincial, National/U.S., International) | POTENT MARKET (Local, Regional, National, International)

NATURAL RESOURCES

Water-based Recreation Opportunities
- Boating
  - Sailing
  - Power Boating/Touring
  - Ice Boating
  - Canoeing
  - Windsurfing

Land-Based Recreation Opportunities
- Fishing
  - Sportfishing
  - Icefishing
- Swimming/Bathing
- Water Skiing
- Scuba Diving/Snorkeling
- Skiing
  - Alpine
  - Cross-Country
- Hunting
  - Big Game
  - Small Game
  - Water Fowl
- Camping
  - Auto Touring
  - Wilderness
- Hiking/Backpacking
  - Day
  - Overnight
  - Snowshoeing
- Rock Climbing
- Cave Exploring
- Picnicking
- Cottaging/Chalet
- Snowmobiling
- Cycling
- Equestrian Trails

Land and Water-Based Recreation Opportunities
- Viewing Natural Attractions
- Gathering/Collecting
- Photography/Painting

Air-Based Recreation Opportunities
- Hang Gliding
- Hot Air Ballooning
- Gliding

MAN-DEVELOPED MAN-CONTROLLED RESOURCES

Natural Resource Opportunities
- Natural Parks and Sites
  - National
  - Provincial
  - Crown Land
- Game Sanctuaries Reserves
- Game Farms

Historical Resource Opportunities
- Historic Parks and Sites
  - National
  - Provincial
  - Local
- Archaeological Attractions
  - Existing
  - Potential

Cultural Resource Opportunities
- Population Centres
  - Cities/Towns
  - Ethnic Settlements
- Cultural Attractions
  - Fairs Celebrations
  - Crafts Events
  - Museums Galleries

Recreation Leisure Developments
- Accommodation Recreation Resorts
  - Hotel Motel Cottage
  - Vacation Farm
  - Ski Developments
  - Marina Developments
  - Convention Centres
- Travel Touring Corridors
  - Air
  - Rail
  - Boat
  - Car
- Recreation Leisure Developments
  - Ski Developments - Alpine
  - Ski Developments - Cross Country
  - Marina Boating Developments
  - Golf Courses
  - Campgrounds Trailer Parks
  - Beaches

Attractions

---

a. RESOURCE OPPORTUNITIES
- ● Abundant resource opportunities; existing and/or potential.
- ◐ Moderate resource opportunities; existing and/or potential.
- ○ Limited resource opportunities; existing and/or potential.
- ☐ No resource opportunities.

b. EXISTING MARKET
- ◉ Heavy use/demand
- ○ Limited use/demand
- ☐ No use/demand

c. DESIRED MARKET
- ● Strong desire to attract as a primary market.
- ○ Limited desire to attract as a primary market.
- ☐ No desire to attract as a primary market.

d. POTENTIAL MARKET
- ● Strong market attraction for this activity
- ○ Weak market attraction for this activity.
- ☐ No market attraction for this activity.

Figure 12.5 Continued.

Midland/Penetanguishene Region

TOURISM RECREATION OPPORTUNITY

Category	Sub-category	Activity
NATURAL RESOURCES		
Water-based Recreation Opportunities	Boating	Sailing
		Power Boating/Touring
		Ice Boating
		Canoeing
		Windsurfing
Land-Based Recreation Opportunities	Fishing	Sportfishing
		Icefishing
		Swimming/Bathing
		Water Skiing
		Scuba Diving/Snorkeling
	Skiing	Alpine
		Cross-Country
	Hunting	Big Game
		Small Game
		Water Fowl
	Camping	Auto Touring
		Wilderness
	Hiking/Backpacking	Day
		Overnight
		Snowshoeing
		Rock Climbing
		Cave Exploring
		Picnicking
		Cottaging/Chalet
		Snowmobiling
		Cycling
		Equestrian Trails
Land and Water-Based Recreation Opportunities		Viewing Natural Attractions
		Gathering/Collecting
		Photography/Painting
Air-Based Recreation Opportunities		Hang Gliding
		Hot Air Ballooning
		Gliding
MAN-DEVELOPED MAN-CONTROLLED RESOURCES		
Natural Resource Opportunities	Natural Parks and Sites	National
		Provincial
		Crown Land
	Game Sanctuaries Reserves	
	Game Farms	
Historical Resource Opportunities	Historic Parks and Sites	National
		Provincial
		Local
	Archaeological Attractions	Existing
		Potential
Cultural Resource Opportunities	Population Centres	Cities Towns
		Ethnic Settlements
	Cultural Attractions	Fairs Celebrations
		Crafts Events
		Museums Galleries
Recreation Leisure Developments	Accommodation Recreation Resorts	Hotel Motel Cottage
		Vacation Farm
		Ski Developments
		Marina Developments
		Convention Centres
	Travel Touring Corridors	Air
		Rail
		Boat
		Car
	Recreation Leisure Developments	Ski Developments - Alpine
		Ski Developments - Cross Country
		Marina Boating Developments
		Golf Courses
		Campgrounds Trailer Parks
		Beaches
Attractions		

Column groups: RESOURCE OPPORT | EXISTING MARKET (Local, Regional, Provincial, National/U.S., International) | DESIRED MARKET (Local, Regional, Provincial, National/U.S., International) | POTENT MARKET (Local, Regional, Provincial, National, International)

a. RESOURCE OPPORTUNITIES
- ● Abundant resource opportunities; existing and/or potential.
- ◐ Moderate resource opportunities; existing and/or potential.
- ○ Limited resource opportunities; existing and/or potential.
- ☐ No resource opportunities.

b. EXISTING MARKET
- ● Heavy use/demand
- ○ Limited use/demand
- ☐ No use/demand

c. DESIRED MARKET
- ● Strong desire to attract as a primary market.
- ○ Limited desire to attract as a primary market.
- ☐ No desire to attract as a primary market.

d. POTENTIAL MARKET
- ● Strong market attraction for this activity
- ○ Weak market attraction for this activity.
- ☐ No market attraction for this activity.

Figure 12.5 Continued.

Activity	April	May	June	July	Aug.	Sept.	Oct.	Nov.	Dec.	Jan.	Feb.	Mar.	Present Availability
Boating													
General													*
Sailing													*
Canoeing													*
Ice sailing													Z
Cruise boat trips													Z
House boat rentals													Z
Fishing													
General													*
Ice fishing													*
Hunting													
Grouse and duck													*
Bear													*
Moose													*
Deer													*
Camping													*

Figure 12.6 List of potential travel-recreation activities by season.

Outdoor Recreation
Swimming
Scuba diving
Water skiing
Windsurfing
Hiking
Snowmobiling
Cross-country skiing
Downhill skiing
Orienteering
Wilderness survival
Snowshoeing
Golf
Tennis
Horseback riding

Key: ——— Prime months for the activity

- - - Activity possible in these months, but not as popular as in prime time

** Activity/facilities available in quantity in the area

* Limited availability of activity/facilities in the area—some room for expansion

N Activity/facilities not available presently in the area

SOURCE: A Strategy and Action Plan for Tourism in Atikokan Area (Waterloo, Ontario, Balmer, Crapo & Associates, Inc., 1979), p. 66.

Normally the personal interview technique is utilized in these surveys of existing visitors, either at exit and entry points or at key tourism facilities.

The background analysis phase and the detailed resource-activity analysis should have provided some clues as to the sources of potential new market demand for the destination area. If the tourist market in an area is first divided into its business- and pleasure-travel components, then its market potential will have the following seven major components:

> The attraction of pleasure travelers from other geographical markets than those which are currently being drawn from
>
> The attraction of pleasure travelers from other segments of the pleasure-travel markets than those which are currently being drawn from
>
> The increased penetration of those geographical markets from which pleasure travelers are currently being drawn from
>
> The increased penetration of those segments of the pleasure- travel market which are currently being drawn from
>
> The increased penetration of those segments of the business-travel market which are currently being drawn from
>
> The attraction of current business travelers as future pleasure travelers
>
> The attraction of current pleasure travelers as future pleasure travelers (that is, repeat patronage)

A variety of survey techniques are available and can be utilized to research these potential markets. These include personal interviews, focus group sessions, telephone interviews, and mail-out mail-back questionnaires. They can be directed towards the individual pleasure travelers in a specific geographic market (household surveys) and/or be aimed at the channels of distribution (tour wholesalers-operators and travel agents) and other travel influencers (convention planners, club-affinity group executives, corporate travel departments, and so on). This research helps to determine attitudes toward future travel to the subject destination area, levels of awareness of the area's tourism resource components, images of the area, the major competitive destinations, and the steps needed to be taken to attract patronage from these potential visitors. It can also provide an opportunity to *market test* new tourism attraction-packaging-activity ideas that those in the destination area have identified earlier in the planning process.

Another important aspect of the detailed market analysis should be an evaluation of the likely impact of future travel trends on the destination area. The information on these trends comes from a variety of available *futures* research studies and ongoing *tracking* research programs on travel trends. It is a fairly common practice at this point in the tourism planning process to forecast tourism demand volumes for the period covering the term of the tourism. A number of techniques can be utilized in such forecasting, and these are described later in Chapter 13. When the forecasts have been completed, a supply (capacities of resource components), demand (forecast demand volumes), matching exercise is normally carried out. This step helps those in the destination area determine where there are likely to be shortfalls in different tourism resources and where there could be problems in preserving tourism resources due to excessive demand levels.

No destination area is without competition, and thus a tourism plan must consider the competitive advantages and future plans of other areas as well as its own. Normally, it is most useful to define competitive markets in terms of their relative distance from prime geographic markets. Those destination areas closer to a prime market are often referred to as being *intervening opportunities*—the tourist must pass them to reach the subject destination area. The detailed market research described earlier can assist in identifying the most competitive destinations, their individual strengths and weaknesses, and the steps that can be taken to make the subject destination area unique among its competitors.

Certain other avenues of research and analysis may also be incorporated in the second phase of tourism planning. These may include an evaluation of the tourism industries organization, tourism awareness levels, and the tourism marketing programs of the destination area. The background analysis phase will indicate the degree of emphasis to be given to these factors. For example, in some areas, organizational problems or conflicts may be so acute that they require detailed research and evaluation.

Synthesis Phase

The third phase of the tourism planning process represents the point in which the major conclusions regarding all of the previous work are formulated. Some tourism planning experts consider it to be one of the most important and creative stages in the process. A comprehensive tourism plan will produce conclusions on five distinct subjects:

1. Tourism development
2. Tourism marketing
3. Tourism industries organization
4. Tourism awareness
5. Other tourism support services and activities

The first step in the synthesis phase should be the preparation of position statements on each of these five subjects. The position statement indicates *where we are now* with respect to development, marketing, industry organization, awareness, and other support services. One of the participating groups is given the responsibility for preparing preliminary position statements, usually either the tourism consultants or the public sector tourism officials. These are then reviewed and discussed by all participants, and a consensus is reached on the final wording of the statements. Position statements may be simply expressed in one sentence or be documented in several pages of text. A simple position statement on development could be "our destination area has historically been developed to appeal to a summer, warm-weather market; facilities to attract tourism at other times of the year have not been constructed."

The second step is that of determining "where we would like to be" or the desired future situation. Again, it is useful for the destination area to verbalize these desired states in terms of tourism development, marketing, industry organization, awareness, and support services. In our simple example this could be "it is our desire to have year-round tourism facilities in our destination area." Tourism strategies and plans provide the *bridge* between the present situation and desired future situations in a destination area. They provide the means to the end.

Before we move on to the fourth phase of the planning process, some classification of tourism planning terminology is necessary. First, it should be realized that the terms *tourism plan* and *tourism strategy* are often used to refer to the same thing. In this text, we refer to the entire task described in this chapter as being tourism planning, irrespective of whether the eventual outcome is called a tourism strategy or a tourism plan. Under our definition, all tourism planning exercises produce alternative tourism strategies and a tourism plan. The tourism plan itself is a very specific course of action, and the tourism strategies are the alternative approaches available to achieve the tourism planning goals. The strategies therefore precede the plan in chronological order.

Goal Setting, Strategy Selection, and Objective Setting

Now that the destination area has decided upon the fundamental future directions for tourism, tourism planning goals, alternative strategies, plan objectives can be defined. The planning goals, strategies, and plan objectives must be complementary to policy goals and objectives.

A destination sets goals as to the intensity of development desired

In the Ontario example cited earlier, the major policy goal for tourism was "to stimulate employment, income and economic development through the systematic improvement, development and marketing of Ontario's tourism industry." This can be classified as an economy-oriented approach to tourism. Another destination area suffering from overcrowding or an already too rapid pace of development might have chosen a more conservation-oriented approach. Remember that a tourism plan has a relatively short life span, usually five years, and its planning goals should be achievable within that time period. A destination area with an economy-oriented policy approach may wish to obtain the maximum economic impact from tourism within the term of the plan. This area will therefore probably adopt a planning goal that emphasizes the development and marketing of those subareas or specific resource components likely to produce the greatest economic return within the planning period; it will concentrate on its major strengths. Yet another destination may have an economy-oriented approach but be more concerned with spreading the economic benefits of tourism more evenly throughout its subareas. Its planning goals might therefore be to concentrate upon the development and marketing of those subareas with the lowest levels of existing tourism activity.

Once the planning goals have been set, there are usually a variety of approaches or strategies that can be employed to achieve them. Within a specific destination area, it should also be realized that different approaches or strategies may be utilized for the subareas within it—some subareas may have economy-oriented strategies and some may have conservation-oriented strategies.

A commonly found tourism development strategy in North America involves dividing the destination into destination zones, touring corridors, and other areas (see Figure 12.7). This type of strategy was utilized in Ontario and was later adopted by other Canadian provinces and certain states of the United States. It can be applied to many geographic areas, including countries, states or provinces, counties, and regions within counties. As well as being visually displayed in this fashion, a strategy is usually verbalized in a series of strategy statements. A comprehensive strategy will incorporate in these statements the five elements of development, marketing, industry organization, awareness, and support services. Once more it should be mentioned that a strategy is an approach to translating the current conditions in these five fields into the desired situations. For example, a destination area highly dependent on one specific geographic market for its demand may wish to adopt a strategy of diversifying its geographic markets, thereby reducing its dependence on one market. Those in a destination area with the planning goal of increasing the economic benefits of tourism to a specific subarea may select a strategy to increase visitation to that subarea.

The tourism plan objectives flow logically from the selected strategy. Figure 12.8 provides an example of this for a region within Ontario showing the linkage among planning goals, strategy, and plan objectives.

Plan Development Phase

The final phase of the tourism planning process is the development of the plan itself. The plan details the actions needed to achieve the objectives, implement the strategy,

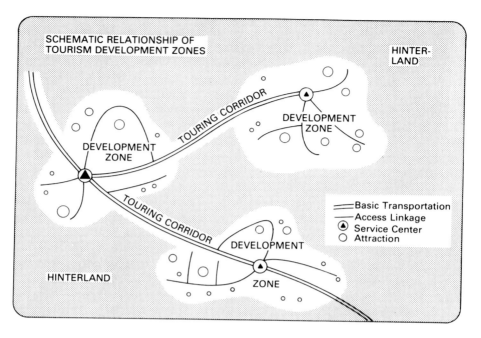

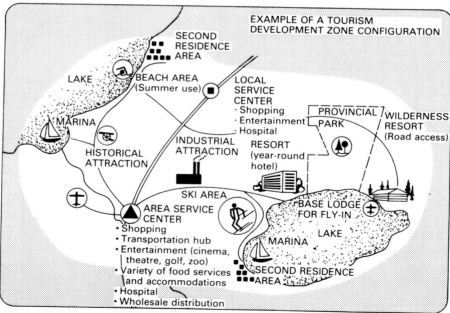

SOURCE: *Tourism Development in Ontario: A Framework for Opportunity* (Waterloo, Ontario, Balmer, Crapo & Associates, Inc., 1977).

Figure 12.7

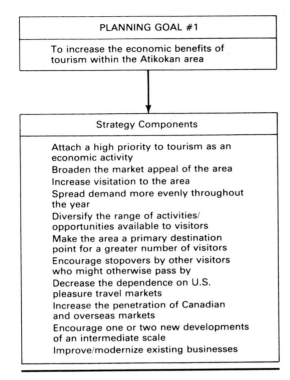

| PLANNING GOAL #1 |
| To increase the economic benefits of tourism within the Atikokan area |

| Strategy Components |
| Attach a high priority to tourism as an economic activity |
| Broaden the market appeal of the area |
| Increase visitation to the area |
| Spread demand more evenly throughout the year |
| Diversify the range of activities/ opportunities available to visitors |
| Make the area a primary destination point for a greater number of visitors |
| Encourage stopovers by other visitors who might otherwise pass by |
| Decrease the dependence on U.S. pleasure travel markets |
| Increase the penetration of Canadian and overseas markets |
| Encourage one or two new developments of an intermediate scale |
| Improve/modernize existing businesses |

Figure 12.8

and satisfy the planning goals. A comprehensive plan deals with the five subjects of development, marketing, industry organization, awareness, and support services. It takes each of the plan objectives and specifies the following for each of them:

The program and actions required to achieve each plan objective

The roles and responsibilities of the public and private sector in carrying on these programs and actions

The specific development and marketing concepts and opportunities that will help achieve certain objectives

The funds required to carry out specific programs and actions

The sources of these funds

The timetable for carrying out specific programs and actions within the plan

The method for monitoring the success of the plan on a periodic basis during its term

Once it has been laid out in this detail, the tourism plan is then written up in formal reports, either by a private tourism consulting firm or by public-sector tourism officials. The tourism plan reports are often presented in two parts—the first being a summary report containing the plan itself, the second being a larger and more detailed technical report providing all of the research, findings, and conclusions produced during the planning process. The reports are usually prepared in draft and are reviewed and revised by public and private sector representatives prior to being finalized for publication.

SUMMARY

Every destination area interested in tourism should be involved in the tourism planning process. Although tourism planning can be arduous, time consuming, costly, and hard to sell, it is an essential activity in today's rapidly changing business environments. The absence of tourism planning in a destination can eventually lead to irreversible economic, social-cultural, and environmental damage and to loss of market share. There are many barriers to tourism planning in every destination area, but the rewards resulting from an effective tourism planning process far outweigh the efforts needed to surmount these. Empirical evidence throughout the world clearly shows that the "model" destinations for successful tourism are those that have embraced the tourism planning concept.

REFERENCES

BALMER, CRAPO & ASSOCIATES, INC., A Strategy and Action Plan for Tourism in the Atikokan Area (Waterloo, Ontario, Township of Atikokan, 1979), p. 66.

BALMER, CRAPO & ASSOCIATES, INC., Tourism Development in Ontario: A Framework for Opportunity (Waterloo, Ontario, Ontario Ministry of Tourism and Recreation, 1977).

BOSSELMAN, FRED P., In the Wake of the Tourist: Managing Special Places in Eight Countries (Washington, DC, The Conservation Foundation, 1978).

GUNN, CLARE A., Tourism Planning, (New York, Crane Russak, 1979), p. 23.

MARSHALL MACKLIN, MONOGHAN, Tourism Development Strategy: Collingwood-Midland-Orillia Zone (Toronto, Ontario, Ontario Ministry of Tourism and Recreation, 1980).

MORRISON, ALASTAIR M., The Planning and Development of Tourism in a Large Rural Area: Regional Tourism Planning in Auvergne-Limousin (East Lansing, MI, 1973), pp. 32–33.

POLLOCK, ANN M./B.C. RESEARCH, A Framework for Tourism Development Planning (Victoria, British Columbia, Tourism British Columbia, 1977), p. 22.

THE ECONOMIC PLANNING GROUP OF CANADA, Tourism Development Strategy and Action Plan for the County of Bruce, Owen Sound and North Grey (Toronto, Ontario, County of Bruce, 1983).

TURNER, LOUIS, and JOHN ASH, The Golden Hordes: International Tourism and the Pleasure Periphery (London, England, Constable, 1975).

WOLMAN, FRANK and ASSOCIATES, Yukon Tourism Development Strategy (Toronto, Ontario, Yukon Department of Tourism and Information, 1978), pp. xi-xiii.

YOUNG, GEORGE, Tourism: Blessing or Blight (Middlesex, England, Penguin Books, 1973).

13

TOURISM DEVELOPMENT:

Building a Future for the Tourism Industries

"The chief feature of every monumental structure is the swarm of beggars and curio vendors at the entrance. Since, like the monuments, they look the same everywhere you go, rumor has it that they follow the tourist buses by taxi."

Kenneth R. Morgan, Speaking You English? A Lighthearted Guide to World Travel.

Within the context of a tourism plan, development can take place. The specifics of tourism development is the topic of this chapter.

The necessity for defining the tourism product in its widest sense is stressed. The respective roles of the private and the public sectors in tourism development are outlined.

A process for analyzing individual tourism development projects is suggested, and each step is detailed. Particular attention is paid to the analysis of the project from an economic viewpoint. Sources of financing from both the private and the public sectors are examined.

LEARNING OBJECTIVES

Having read this chapter, you should be able to:

1. Explain the linkage between tourism planning and tourism development.
2. Discuss public- and private-sector roles in tourism development.
3. List and explain nine criteria that government agencies tend to use when evaluating applications for financial, technical, and other assistance.
4. Describe the objectives of a prefeasibility study.
5. Explain the objectives of an economic feasibility study.
6. Identify the two principal groups concerned with the results of economic feasibility studies and discuss the questions that they typically want answered.
7. Discuss the steps that are followed in completing a site analysis for a tourism development project.
8. Explain the steps and research techniques used in conducting a market study.
9. Explain the steps and techniques used in forecasting.
10. List and describe the seven steps that are followed when preparing an economic feasibility analysis.
11. Define and explain the purpose of cost-benefit analysis.
12. Explain the role of government financial incentives in tourism development and discuss the two major categories of incentives provided.

BUILDING A FUTURE FOR THE TOURISM INDUSTRIES

The Linkage between Tourism Planning and Tourism Development

The tourism planning process described in Chapter 11 should be designed to produce goals, strategies, and objectives for the destination area related to tourism development, marketing, industry organization, and awareness, and to other support services and activities. The tourism development plan normally provides overall guidelines for development, outlines broad development concepts, and identifies individual development opportunities worthy of in-depth analysis (through feasibility studies and/or cost-benefit analyses).

When proceeding with tourism development, those in the destination area will first find it necessary to establish overall development guidelines to ensure that when development occurs it complies with the area's economic, environmental, social and cultural policies and goals. It may also be prudent for those in the destination to draft more specific guidelines describing the basic characteristics of the scale, quality, and types of development that it wishes to encourage.

The final outcome of a tourism development plan is often that a series of individual development opportunities are identified for further investigation. For the purposes of this text, the term *tourism product* is used to describe all categories of development opportunities, both commercial and noncommercial. The economic feasibility of commercial (profit making) development opportunities is usually established at a later date, using techniques similar to those outlined in this chapter. The noncommercial development opportunities can include such support facilities as travel information centers, infrastructure, and nonprofit-making attractions, such as museums and other historic landmarks. The advisability of proceeding with these facilities or services cannot be measured through an economic feasibility study, since they may produce little or no revenue. These opportunities are thus often the subject of a technique known as cost-benefit analysis, or else they are considered in the context of their importance to the achievement of the tourism plan's goals and objectives.

Public and Private Sector Roles in Tourism Development

Both the public and private sectors have important roles to play in tourism development in a free-enterprise system. The role of the private sector in tourism development is more limited and certainly more clearcut. Its principal role is to provide tourism facilities and services to the traveling public while maximizing financial returns in the process. In more enlightened societies, the private sector has come to accept that it has certain social and environmental responsibilities that it must respect in achieving its profit goals.

Not all tourism development projects are identified through the tourism planning process. Many project ideas emerge from the private sector itself through sponsored research studies and assessments of supply-demand relationships. Idea generation is, therefore, a key role of the private sector.

The entrepreneurial role is at the heart of the private sector's involvement in tourism development. This role embraces idea generation, development project implementation, financial risk taking and investment, and the management of operations. The private sector also provides the specialized technical skills required in the development process through tourism consultants, market research firms, economists, architects, engineers, designers, lawyers, project managers, and builders.

The private sector, through its financial institutions, other corporate lenders, and individual citizens, provides a large proportion of the capital funds for the investment in tourism projects.

Nonprofit private organizations also play an important role in tourism development in most destinations. These organizations include chambers of commerce, travel associations, foundations, historical and cultural societies, recreation and sports associations or clubs, service clubs, community associations, religious groups, and so on. The roles played by these groups vary from destination to destination, but typically the groups are involved in operating attractions (such as pioneer villages, historic buildings, museums, and art galleries), creating and running events and special meals, providing travel information services, and financing the development of community-oriented facilities (such as recreation and community halls, historical and cultural centers, and trail systems).

In North America and the majority of Western Europe, the most widely accepted function of government in tourism development is to act as a catalyst and to complement the efforts of the private sector, including nonprofit organizations. The World Tourism Organization points out that as a general principle, a government should not seek to do itself what the private sector is able and willing to do. Although this can be said to be a generally accepted principle in North America, there are still numerous instances of overlapping activities and conflicts between the public and private sectors. In both the United States and Canada, the federal, state or provincial, and local governments are heavily involved in the operation of parks, most of which include camping facilities. Many private campground operators feel that the government-operated facilities offer unfair competition and that the government should not be in the campground business. Another area of contention often found is in the provision of boat-docking facilities where both the private sector and government agencies sometimes operate competitive facilities. A further area of direct competition is that of state-owned airlines versus private air carriers.

There can be several valid reasons behind the reversal in the public and private sector roles in tourism development. The most important of these is that it is not always reasonable to expect tourism to develop along the lines and at the speed desired by the government in its tourism program if left entirely to the operations of the private sector. Government agencies often find themselves with a more direct role in tourism development for the following reasons:

In India the government operated its own tourist buses

The private sector is unwilling to finance the development of a project because of its limited profit potential; the government may, however, have given this project a high priority due to its regional economic contributions or its pivotal role in stimulating tourism activity.

An existing tourism facility is bankrupt and cannot be sold on the market; for reasons similar to those mentioned in the first point, the government feels obliged to acquire the facility.

The government may wish to provide low-cost vacation opportunities for disadvantaged groups within its population, such as the poor, the sick, and the aged; this is often called *social tourism.*

The government may wish to encourage private-sector development by pioneering new types of developments through *demonstration* or *pilot* projects.

Due to one or both the first two reasons just listed, several provinces within Canada and several states in the United States are directly involved in the resort business. These include Kentucky, Indiana, Ontario, Manitoba, Quebec, New Brunswick, Prince Edward Island, and Nova Scotia. In these areas, the resorts are owned by the respective governments and are either operated directly by the government or by the private sector through a management contract. The social tourism function is not yet prevalent in North America, but is a widely accepted phenomenon in many countries in Western Europe. For example, France has established a network of *village de vacances* (family-oriented resorts) and *gites familiaux* (family homes in resort settings) for its disadvantaged citizens. As an example of the last point listed above, Tourism Canada sponsored the design of four styles of low-cost accommodation units for use in areas with particularly short operating seasons. It subsequently provided assistance to a private developer in constructing some of these units.

THE ANALYSIS OF INDIVIDUAL TOURISM DEVELOPMENT PROJECTS

Individual development opportunities in tourism are either generated through the tourism planning process or by the private sector (entrepreneurial role) independent of this process. In destinations without tourism plans, those in the public sector may also be involved in identifying development opportunities for private-sector investment.

Although these development opportunities can have the potential of satisfying tourism planning goals and can have considerable initial appeal to those in the private sector, they may be undesirable due to financial, environmental, social, or other reasons. All individual tourism development opportunities must, therefore, be carefully researched and analyzed prior to the reaching of a decision to proceed with their construction.

Before this process of research and analysis is described, it is important to realize some fundamental differences in the range of potential tourism development projects. The first difference between projects is their capability to generate financial profits. Some projects, such as hotels and commercial attractions, are inherent profit generators, while others, such as travel information centers and infrastructure facilities, are usually not. Although the latter facilities may not generate any direct revenues or may only break even in a financial sense, they are nevertheless often essential components of the destination area's tourism product. Profit-generating projects are generally investigated by means of economic feasibility studies, and the remaining projects are the subject of cost-benefit analyses or other types of *contribution analysis* exercises.

Tourism development encompasses many elements. Some of these include projects that involve building construction (such as a superstructure); others require only human resources and equipment (such as guided canoe trips, under the category of programming and events). Despite these major differences in the tourism project ingredients of the eight product elements, individual projects can be analyzed by using similar techniques.

A government agency involved in providing financial incentives and technical or other assistance to individual tourism projects should as a first step establish a set of project selection criteria. These criteria will assist the agency in identifying those projects that merit its assistance and in screening out others that are not as desirable. Typically, criteria fall into the following nine categories:

1. *ECONOMIC CONTRIBUTIONS:* That the project creates a significant level of income and employment benefits.
2. *ENVIRONMENTAL IMPACT:* That the project is developed in compliance with existing legislation and regulations governing the conservation and protection of the environment.
3. *SOCIAL-CULTURAL IMPACT:* That the project does not jeopardize the social well-being of citizens.
4. *COMPETITIVE IMPACT:* That the project complements, rather than competes with, existing tourism businesses, and that it does not seriously jeopardize the financial viability of any individual enterprise.
5. *TOURISM IMPACT:* That the project adds to the destination's tourism potential by creating an attraction, by improving the area's capacity to receive and cater to visitors, or by being beneficial to tourism in some other fashion.
6. *DEVELOPER AND OPERATOR CAPABILITIES:* That the developer and operators of the project must be capable of developing and operating the business successfully.
7. *COMPLIANCE WITH POLICIES, PLANS, AND PROGRAMS:* That the project complies with the destination's tourism policies, plans, and programs.
8. *EQUITY CONTRIBUTIONS:* Where the project is profit-generating, that the investors have sufficient equity to inject into the venture.
9. *FEASIBILITY:* Where the project is profit-generating, that it be economically feasible.

Figure 13.1 visually displays a tourism project evaluation and analysis system. It shows that there are at least seven important decision points in project analysis in which further consideration of the project may be terminated. These are as follows:

- A prefeasibility study produces negative results
- The site for the project is not found to be suitable, and no alternative site is available
- The market analysis indicates that the potential market is not large enough to support the project as envisioned
- The project is not found to be economically feasible
- The results of a cost-benefit analysis are negative
- The government decides that the project does not warrant financial incentives and is not feasible without these incentives
- Sufficient financing from private sources cannot be obtained

The remainder of this chapter is devoted to a description of the key steps in the tourism project evaluation and analysis system.

Prefeasibility Study

A prefeasibility study is an analysis that determines whether a more detailed economic feasibility study of a project is justified and which subjects the detailed study should address. Because detailed economic feasibility studies are costly and time-consuming, this type of preliminary project assessment can be extremely valuable to the developer. The four principal objectives of a prefeasibility study are to determine whether:

1. The available information is adequately detailed to indicate that the project will not be viable or will not be attractive to investors or lenders
2. The available information indicates that the project is so promising that an investment decision can be made on the basis of the prefeasibility study itself; that is, a detailed study is not needed.
3. Certain aspects of the project are so critical to its viability that they must be analyzed as part of the detailed economic feasibility study.
4. The availability of certain factors critical to the viability of the project (such as the availability of a specific site location) must be confirmed prior to a detailed economic feasibility study being initiated.

Prefeasibility studies can be completed by the private developers themselves, by a government agency considering financing projects, or by private consulting organizations on behalf of the developers and/or a government agency. In some cases, the tourism development plan component of the tourism planning process produces prefeasibility analyses of key tourism project opportunities.

Detailed Economic Feasibility Study

If a project survives the prefeasibility screening process, then it normally becomes the subject of a detailed economic feasibility study. In North America, the majority of tourism-project economic feasibility studies are carried out by private consulting

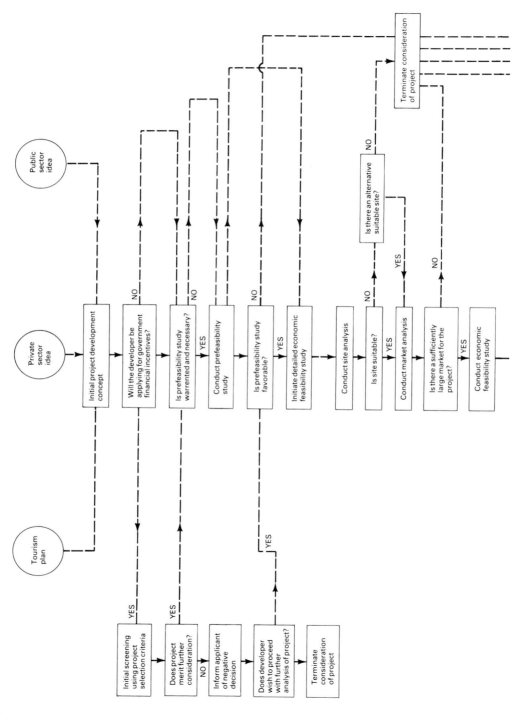

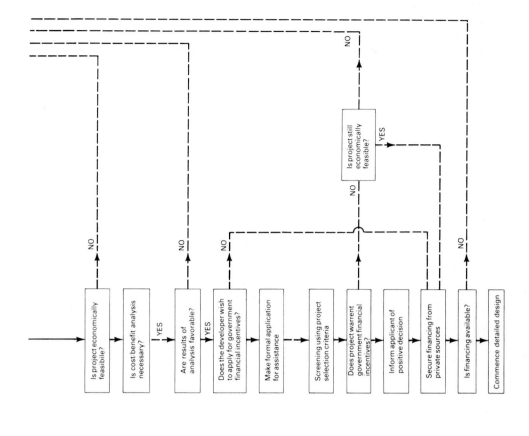

Figure 13.1 Conceptual model of a tourism project evaluation and analysis system

organizations on behalf of private developers-investors, government agencies, or a combination of the two.

Although many successful tourism projects have been developed without detailed economic feasibility studies, as have many that have not proven successful, these analyses are vitally important to a variety of participants involved in the development process. Such participants include developers, investors (if they are different from the developers), and potential lenders. Other players involved in the process can include management companies interested in operating the projects on behalf of the developers-investors. Also, the potential lenders may often fall into two groups—those providing the construction (interim) financing and those providing the long-term (permanent) financing.

An economic feasibility study is a study that determines the economic feasibility of a tourism project. A project is economically feasible if it provides a rate of return that is acceptable to the investors in the project. A market study is one component of an economic feasibility study dealing with the project's market potential. Sometimes the term *economic feasibility study* is abbreviated to just *feasibility study*. Because of the need to acquire an unbiased opinion on a project's viability, economic feasibility studies are usually prepared by an independent third party and not by the developers-investors or the potential lenders. Many lenders, including both private financial institutions and government agencies providing financial incentive programs, require that these independent studies be completed before they will seriously consider projects.

An economic feasibility study is designed to answer the following questions that are of concern to the various participants in the development process:

DEVELOPERS AND INVESTORS

Which of several alternative site locations is the most appropriate for the project?

Is a specific project site appropriate for the development?

If not, is there another site available that would be suitable?

Is there a market of sufficient size available to support the project?

What are the optimum scale and components of the project?

What style of operation and quality levels should be provided?

What revenues and expenses will the project earn and incur?

What will the capital costs of the project be?

Will the project produce a satisfactory return on investment?

Should the developers-investors proceed with further analysis of the project?

LENDERS

All of the questions pertinent to developers and investors should also be of concern to the lenders.

How much money will have to be loaned to the developers-investors?

Do the developers-investors have a sufficient amount of equity to invest in the project, given the financing required?

Will the project produce sufficient operating profits and cash flow to cover the interest and principal payments when they become due?

The economic feasibility study has another important use for the developers. It produces recommendations on the scale, sizes, facility types, and quality levels of operation. These recommendations are based upon the size and expectations of the market as dictated by the findings of the market study. At a later date in the development process, these will be used as the basis for the architect's preliminary drawings.

Site analysis. Although not all tourism-related projects require physical site locations, a very large proportion do. An economic feasibility study can either specify a site (site specific), if a specific site location has been chosen for the project, or determine if an appropriate site exists within a given geographic area.

A tourism project site normally requires certain specific characteristics for it to be successful. This is not true of all industry sectors in an economy, as there are many "footloose" enterprises that are not location dependent. In tourism, location has an extremely important bearing upon financial viability.

The characteristics or criteria for site selection and evaluation vary according to the type of tourism project under consideration. For example, a proposed new alpine ski area is highly dependent on the snow conditions and slope characteristics in a given location, while an urban hotel requires proximity to a concentration of industry and commerce. Similarly, a motor hotel requires ease of access and proximity to highways, while the placement of tennis courts is dictated by the wind and sun conditions at the site. The first step in the site analysis must, therefore, be to identify the critieria that are crucial to the project being considered.

Alpine Ski Areas are highly dependent on snow conditions

Tourism project site critieria or characteristics can be divided into three categories:

1. Market-related site criteria
2. Criteria related to the physical characteristics of sites
3. Other criteria

Typically, the market-related site criteria encompass the site's proximity to potential markets, transportation facilities and routes, essential support facilities (such as accommodations, restaurants, and shopping centers), and competitive facilities. Figure 13.2 provides a master list of individual criteria within each of the categories. The selection from this of characteristics most crucial to a given project requires both a knowledge of the particular business type, experience with it, and a broad knowledge of construction and site engineering. Ideally, therefore, a multidisciplined team consisting of a specialized tourism consultant, engineer, landscape architect, and architect should be utilized for this purpose.

When the site analysis is not site specific, it is a common practice to first identify a "long list" of potentially suitable sites and then to rank these sites on the basis of their compatibility with the project. This is often accomplished by attaching a weighting factor to each site selection criterion-characteristic and by then giving each site under consideration a numerical score for that criterion-characteristic. The weighting factor reflects the relative importance of each individual criterion-characteristic, and the numerical score (say on a 0 to 10 basis) indicates the quality and/or quantity of that criterion-characteristic at one of the alternative sites. The multiplication of the weighting factor and the numerical score provides a final score for each criterion-characteristic at each given site. The final scores for all criteria are added to give a total score for each alternative site. The most appropriate site for the project is usually the one earning the highest total score.

A modification of this type of site ranking system is demonstrated in Figure 13.3. This recreation facility site evaluation system, developed in Wisconsin, is designed to produce numerical scores for alternative sites relative to a variety of recreation and tourism land uses. The main factors that it considers are surface water conditions, ground water conditions, land characteristics, vegetation, climate and regional market characteristics. Figure 13.3 shows one page from among the several contained in this site evaluation matrix. Each criterion is divided into four measurable units; for instance, the distance from a metropolitan area is divided into (a) over four hours, (b) one and a half to four hours, (c) one half to one and one half hours, and (d) under one half hour. Each unit is given a score of between 1 and 4. Each site under consideration is assigned scores on the basis of this matrix, and the site with the highest total score for a particular project type is the most appropriate for that use.

It should be realized that the evaluation of sites for some forms of recreational and tourism projects requires a high degree of specific technical expertise. Generally, these cases occur when the project is highly dependent for its ultimate success on the characteristics of the natural resource base and also when the construction

1. MARKET-RELATED SITE CRITERIA

Proximity of site to potential markets
Proximity and ease of accessibility to
  transportation facilities and modes:
  Highways and roads
  Airports
  Railroad services
  Marina and harbor facilities
  Trail systems (hiking, cross-country/
  Alpine skiing, snowmobiling, bicycling,
    etc.)
  Bus services
  Ferry services

Proximity of site to essential support
  services (such as accommodation,
  restaurants, and shopping centers)
Proximity of site to other major tourism
  demand generators
Visibility of site to passing vehicular
  traffic
Proximity to major competitive facilities

2. CRITERIA RELATED TO THE PHYSICAL CHARACTERISTICS OF SITES

Aesthetics of adjoining lands and land uses
Natural conditions
  Climate and microclimate
    Temperature
    Precipitation
    Sunshine and clouds
    Humidity
    Winds
    Seasons
    Purity of air
  Water supply
    Natural springs
    Waterfalls and cascades
    Rivers and streams
    Lakes and seas
    Drainage patterns
    Flooding problems
  Geology and geomorphology
    Bedrock type
    Water-table level, well depths,
      quality
    Geologic history
  Soils and topography
    Soil types
    Slopes
    Depths

Site aesthetics
  Scale
  Views
  Focal points
  Variety (feature, form, color)
  Noise
  Smells
Vegetation
  Tree types
  Ground cover type
  Visual and physical condition
  Clearing problems
Wildlife and fish
  Species and type
  Effects of development on these
Available infrastructure
  Sources of energy
  Water supply
  Sewer system and waste disposal
    services
  Transportation facilities
  Other needed services
Other site characteristics
  Dimensions and shape
  Existing rights of way and easements
  Length of shoreline available
  Height above sea level
  Geographical orientation
Ability of land to support various types
  of recreation activities

3. OTHER CRITERIA

Manpower availability
Availability of staff accommodation
Availability of suitable quality of land
  for project
Cost of land
Zoning laws and other legal regulations

Social and economic characteristics of
  host area
Sources and types of financial assistance
  in host area
Labor laws and labor relations history

SOURCES: *Checklist of Factors Determining the Selection of Sites for Tourism Development*
(Madrid, Spain, World Tourism Organization, undated), pp. 1-16.

Manual for the Preparation of Industrial Feasibility Studies (New York, United
Nations, 1978), pp. 94-97.

Project Investigation/Recreation Facility Site Evaluation (Wisconsin Department
of Local Affairs and Development: Bureau of Recreation, undated), pp. 4.2-4.9).

Figure 13.2   Master list of tourism site selection criteria

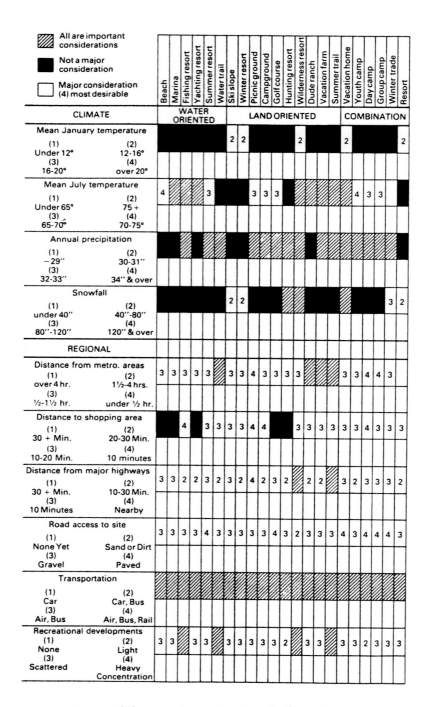

Figure 13.3 Recreation facility site evaluation system

costs are high. Examples of such projects include alpine skiing areas and large full-service marina projects. Private organizations specializing in site evaluations for these types of projects have been formed and are normally engaged to perform these analyses.

An economic feasibility study may be terminated during or after the site analysis if an essential site characteristic is missing or if some insurmountable legal or zoning restriction or other barrier to development is uncovered. The study will move on to an analysis of potential market demand if this is not the case.

Market analysis. The market analysis phase of an economic feasibility study is often the most costly and time-consuming element of the entire study process. The costs and time required are directly dependent on the mix of primary (original) and secondary research utilized. Secondary research involves an analysis of readily available, published sources of information and is far less expensive than original research. Market surveys aimed at producing new information and conclusions specific to the subject project are classified as being original or primary research. Although prefeasibility studies can be based solely on secondary research, detailed economic feasibility studies must contain a mixture of both secondary and original research.

The market analysis usually commences with the collection and review of secondary sources of information, since this provides a clearer focus upon the type and scope of original market research needed. With the growing attention being given to tourism on a worldwide basis, the amount of tourism-related research that has been carried out to date is enormous, and it grows rapidly from year to year. An analysis of secondary sources in tourism can, therefore, be both time consuming and exhausting, unless the researcher is familiar with the major tourism-related bibliographies and the institutions at which the major tourism library sources are located.

Once the review of secondary sources of information is completed, a plan of original research is drawn up and implemented. This generally involves carrying out a variety of surveys, and it requires that the researchers have a thorough understanding of marketing research techniques. Although it is not appropriate to provide an exhaustive description of these techniques in an introductory tourism text, a brief overview of the most commonly used methods can be given. These methods include the following:

1. Questionnaire method
   Personal interview
   Telephone
   Mail
2. Focus group or delphi methods

The questionnaire method in its various forms of communications is certainly the most frequently used technique in tourism project feasibility studies. Researchers direct their questions to potential users of the project and/or to the owners and

Observing tourist behavior can uncover
what is of interest to them

managers of competitive or similar enterprises. In the latter case, the questions are
normally aimed at gathering information on the facilities and services offered and
on the existing market volumes and characteristics through such competitive-
performance statistics as room occupancy rates, attendance figures, and so on. The
common factor in all forms of the questionnaire is that they require verbal responses
(written or oral) to questions (written or oral). The three major advantages of the
questionnaire method are its versatility, its speed, and its cost. Questionnaires are
said to be versatile because almost every research problem can be addressed by using
this method, including the respondent's knowledge, opinions, motivations, and intentions. The use of questionnaires is usually faster and cheaper than an observational method of research. An observational method is a process of observing and
studying the behavior of people, objects, and occurrences rather than of questioning
for the same information.

The questionnaire method also has recognized disadvantages. The first is that
respondents may be unwilling to provide information. They may either refuse to be

interviewed or may refuse to answer specific questions. Mail questionnaire surveys typically have low response rates, with sometimes as many as 90 percent of the questionnaires not being returned. Skilled and experienced researchers can usually bring the response rate up to 50 percent. Personal and telephone questionnaire surveys generally have higher response rates. A second disadvantage of the questionnaire method is that a respondent may be willing to cooperate but at the same time may be unable to provide accurate answers to some of the questions. For example, the respondents may not have thought through their basic motivations for particular purchases or activities. A third limitation of the questionnaire method is that the respondent may intentionaly supply incorrect or inaccurate information. Some respondents may give the types of answers that they think the researchers are looking for, or they may deliberately give misleading information. Others may answer in a particular way so as not to be embarrassed or to have their egos damaged. Respondents may also wrongly interpret the semantic meanings of particular questions and may give less-than-satisfactory answers because of this.

Broad-scale questionnaire surveys, although relatively inexpensive when compared to other market research techniques, can be very expensive to mount if they ae carried out at the individual householder level. This is particularly true if the potential users reside in countries or regions far distant from the destination area. Unlike consumer product research, market research using broad-scale questionnaires may often encounter difficulties in determining the exact geographical origins of potential users of a tourism project and their relative proportions. Because there are these problems in defining the statistical universe, it is also extremely difficult to state accurately what the size and structure of a respective sample should be.

Due to these rather unique difficulties in carrying out market surveys of individual potential users of proposed tourism projects, it is also a common practice to survey persons active in the channels of distribution (such as travel agents, tour wholesalers, and tour operators) and other group or individual travel decision makers (such as convention-meeting planners, corporate travel departments, and club executives) or to utilize the focus group and/or delphi methods as a supplement to questionnaire surveys.

The focus-group method involves bringing together a small group of persons (ideally eight to twelve) in one place and causing these persons to focus upon the particular research subject. The research team supplies an experienced focus group leader. The objectives of these sessions are to get the group to reach consensus on qustions or statements posed by the leader. The focus group can be drawn from householders in general, or each participant may have some common affinity, such as being convention-meeting planners, travel agents, tour operators, tour wholesalers, or club executives. Because focus group participants tend to interact with one another and because there is a greater opportunity to explore individual preferences and attitudes, this method overcomes some of the principal drawbacks of the questionnaire approach. It is a common practice to prescreen focus-group participants prior to their being invited to the sessions.

The delphi method is another research technique that has broad application. It is most often associated with forecasting and futures exercises in tourism, but it can also be applied to an individual tourism project. It could also be called the *knowledgeable panel* method, since it involves assembling a team of experts in a particular field and using this team as a sounding board on alternative approaches, ideas, or concepts. The delphi group need never physically meet, but individual participants are required to give their responses to a variety of written propositions prepared by the researchers, such as: What probability do you attach to this resort's succeeding at this location? (Provide a probability percentage between 0 percent and 100 percent.)

Another type of research that has been used for some tourism projects can be termed *analogy research*. This does not involve any surveying of potential users; rather it is composed of detailed research into the performance of comparable (or analogous) businesses. By studying how comparable projects have fared, conclusions are drawn on the likely performance levels of the proposed project. Because there are a multitude of variables that contribute to a business's success, this particular research method must be utilized with great caution.

In economic feasibility studies and evaluations of noncommercial projects, it is often necessary to forecast demand for either the project itself or for the destination in general, or for both. There are many forecasting techniques available to the researcher. These include:

1. Extrapolation
    Linear
    Exponential
    Cyclical
2. Covariation
3. Correlation
4. Summation
5. Tests
6. Calculation Methods
    Calculation by indices
    Calculation by sales potential
    Calculation by unit sales
    Calculation by elasticity coefficient
    Calculation by models
7. Guesstimate
    Individual
    Group
       Committee
       Delphi process

Forecasts are generally divided into time spans that are considered to be accurate. There is general agreement that there are four basic forecasting horizons: (a) short-term (one day or two years), (b) medium-term (between two and five years), (c) long-term (between five and fifteen years), and futurism (over fifteen years). Figure 13.4 provides basic definitions of the forecasting methods listed earlier and indicates

Forecasting Method	Suggested Forecasting Horizon for Use			Potential Users of Methods*			Definition of Methods	Types	Caveats
	Short-term	Medium-term	Long-term	National Tourist Offices		Commercial Tourist Enterprises			
				National Tourism	International Tourism				
1. Extrapolation	✓	–	–	X	X	–	Process whereby a statistical series is extended by adding new terms to the known terms, following the same law as the series; or by graphically determining the ordinate point situated on the extension of the curve, proving its equation.	Linear (uniform series) Exponential (accelerating series) Cyclical Time series analysis	It should be used for short-term forecasts only and only when more accurate methods are not available.
2. Covariation	✓	✓	–	XX	XX	X	A relation between the variations in time of two or more magnitudes or statistical series, any increase or decrease in the one being accompanied by an increase or decrease in the other or others.	–	There are no "stock" models of covariation. Every destination should establish its own.
3. Correlation	✓	✓	✓	XXX	XXX	XX	Coefficients of correlations are calculated to measure the relationship between variables. There is a correlation between two factors when they are related in such a way that their values always vary in the same or contrary sense.	Simple correlation Multiple correlation Partial correlation Linear regression models	It should be used only where experience and reasoning suggest that there is some basis for correlation.

Continued

Figure 13.4 A sample of techniques available for preparing tourism forecasts

FIGURE 13.4 (*cont.*)

Forecasting Method	Suggested Forecasting Horizon for Use			Potential Users of Methods*			Definition of Methods	Types	Caveats
	Short-term	Medium-term	Long-term	National Tourist Offices		Com-mercial Tourist Enter-prises			
				National Tourism	Inter-national Tourism				
4. Summation	✓	✓	–	XXX	XXX	XXX	Adding together and, where necessary, incorporating weighting factors into a number of separately es-tablished forecasts.	–	It is only as good as the individual forecasts upon which it is based.
5. Tests	–	✓	✓	XXX	XXX	XX	An experimental process in which the objective is to look for a section of the market that reacts in advance of the others.	–	It is a method that is not entirely math-ematical and therefore is difficult to translate into figures.
6.1 Calculation by Indices	–	✓	–	X	X	X	An index can be defined as a unit of measurement defining a ratio between one tourist movement and others or be-tween a tourist movement and the general situation.	–	It is a rather simple exercise since the rela-tionships be-tween variables are often very complex.

						Description	Examples	Disadvantages
6.2 Calculation by Sales Potential	✓	✓	–	–	XXX	A method in which sales are calculated by multiplying the number of points of sale (such as hotels and travel agencies) by the average sales volume per point of sale.	–	It requires experienced judgment and specific research.
6.3 Calculation by Unit Sales	✓	✓	–	–	XXX	A method in which sales are calculated by multiplying average expenditures per tourist.	–	It requires experienced judgment and specific research.
6.4 Calculation by Elasticity Coefficient	✓	✓	XXX	XX	X	A method in which travel volumes are related to elasticity coefficients that display the relationships of price levels to demand levels.	–	It is extremely difficult to find and develop reliable elasticity coefficients.
6.5 Calculation by Models	–	✓	X	–	–	A variety of mathematical and statistical models that attempt to simulate the relationships of various factors affecting travel.	Econometric models Gravitational models Computer systems simulation models	It does not eliminate the need for value judgments and is often very expensive to develop and use.
Economic and Planning Factors	✓	✓	XXX	XX	XX	Means using general economic forecasts and plans for places of visitor origin in preparing travel forecasts for the destination.	–	They are only as good as the individual forecasts on which they are based.

NOTE: * The number of X's shown indicates the author's opinion of the degree of desirability of applying the methods in various circumstances. (–) meant not to be used while XXX is a most desirable application.

SOURCE: Adapted from *Guidelines on Methodology Applicable for Making Annual and Medium-Term Forecasts (Relating to Tourism Development and Promotional Plans) for Members*, World Tourism Organization, p. 73.

the time spans for which they are considered to be most accurate. For example, the extrapolation method is thought to be useful only for short-term forecasts, while correlation techniques are considered to be good for short-, medium-, and long-term forecasting.

Returning again to the individual tourism project and the evaluation of its economic feasibility, the forecasting of potential market demand usually covers the medium-term to long-term forecasts, that is, the initial five to fifteen years of operation. This seems quite appropriate since the critical financial years of a purely commercial project are its first one to ten years. Most commercial tourism projects are expected to reach their full financial and operating potential within their first five years of operation and to pay back their investor's equity within ten years. Also, as will be seen later, the present value concept dictates that the earlier the financial returns are received from a project the greater will be their contribution to economic feasibility.

The actual forecasting of potential demand levels for an individual project can be approached in several different ways, including the following:

1. *The Market Share or Market Penetration Approach.* Using information obtained from competitive facilities, historic demand growth rates, and anticipated future occurrences, or other forecasting techniques, total market demand is calculated and the subject project's share of total demand is estimated.

2. *The Calculation Methods.* As shown in Figure 13.4, these methods use known "rules-of-thumb" (industry averages) or consumer expenditure and behavior patterns to project potential demand.

3. *The Survey and Potential Demand Quantification Approach.* Using the results from questionnaires and other survey methods, total potential demand is quantified by "grossing up" from the sample size taken.

4. *The Alternate Scenario Approach.* Uses either or both of the above approaches and produces optimistic, realistic, and pessimistic scenarios of potential demand levels.

5. *The Analogy Approach.* Assumes that the subject property will achieve certain demand levels based upon the known performances and penetration levels of similar facilities elsewhere.

As a general rule, it is advisable to use two or more of these approaches independently and then to cross-check and rationalize the results of each. Once a technically acceptable potential market demand forecast has been developed, an initial judgment can be made as to whether the market is of sufficient size with the appropriate characteristics to support the project. To make such a judgment at this stage requires considerable experience with the business type under consideration. It has to be very clear that the potential demand levels will obviously not render the project viable if a hotel requires an annual occupancy percentage of 70 percent to be viable and the potential demand will generate an occupancy of only 30 percent in the project's fifth year of operation. In many instances this judgment will not be as clear-cut, and the analysis will have to proceed further to determine if the demand levels justify the investment.

Economic feasibility analysis.   The economic feasibility analysis determines whether the project is capable of producing a satisfactory financial return for its investors. Using the forecast demand levels and other pertinent market analysis data as a base, this step is composed of the following seven distinct steps:

1. Description of components, scale and sizes, and quality levels required to capture the potential market demand
2. Specification of unit prices and rates
3. Estimation of revenues (market demand levels times unit prices and rates)
4. Estimation of operating expenses and profits
5. Preparation of a capital budget
6. Estimation of capital expenses, net income, and cash flow
7. Calculation of rate of return on investment

The forecasts of potential market demand and the expressed desires and expectations of persons interviewed provide the key inputs in describing a detailed project concept. This project concept will describe the components, scale, sizes, and quality levels of facilities and services needed to satisfy the potential demand discovered. Again, based upon expressed market expectations, together with a review of competitive price levels and proposed market positioning, unit prices and rates are then prepared.

The next two steps are commonly referred to as the production of pro forma (or forecast) income statements that indicate the estimated revenues, operating expenses, and operating profits for the project. When estimating revenues, the total potential demand must be broken down into segments, and the applicable unit prices and rates must be multiplied against the resulting volumes in each segment. The operating expenses include those costs incurred directly in operating the project, such as the cost of food and other merchandise for resale, the cost of labor, the cost of marketing, the cost of energy, and the cost of repairs and maintenance. Publications containing industry average performance statistics can be helpful in estimating these operating costs. In North America such publications are readily available for hotels and motels, resorts, and alpine ski areas. Greater individual accuracy occurs when the forecaster is familiar wth the type of business under consideration and when detailed staffing schedules and other operating standards are developed for the project at this stage.

There are other ongoing expenses that the project will encounter, and these are all related to the capital investment in the development. To estimate the expenses requires that a capital budget be prepared first. A capital budget is a detailed, itemized forecast of the capital investment required by the project. For a tourism project, these items will normally include building construction costs; professional fees; infrastructure costs; recreational facility costs; furniture, fixtures, and equipment costs; interim financing costs; contingencies; and miscellaneous other costs. The most realistic capital budgets are usually produced by a multidisciplined team consisting of specialized tourism consultants, civil engineers, quantity surveyors, interior designers, architects, and landscape architects. The capital budget is prepared by first identifying all of the capital costs that will be encountered and then pricing out each item. A contingency factor, normally between 10 and 20 percent, is added to the other items to cover unforeseen cost overruns or items overlooked. Once the capital budget has been completed, the capital-related expenses for the project can be calculated. These expenses include financing charges on long-term debt, depreciation, municipal taxes, and insurance premiums on fixed assets. When these expenses have in turn been estimated, they are deducted from the forecast operating profit levels to give net income figures (after tax profit) and cash flow forecasts. The net income and cash flow projections generally cover the useful life of the project, which for most tourism enterprises, does not usually exceed fifteen to twenty years of operation.

As the final step in this process, one or more financial analysis techniques are used to measure the rate of return produced by these net income and cash flow levels which were forecast. Most experts in the field favor the time-value yardsticks, especially the net-present-value and internal-rate-of-return techniques. These two methods are based on the present value concept that implies that money has a time value. Thus, a dollar received today is worth more than a dollar received a year from now, since the dollar received today can be reinvested to produce a higher overall return. It follows that under the present value methods the dollars received in profits in the earlier years are more valuable than those earned in later years. Both the net-present-value and internal-rate-of-return techniques use cash flow figures as a basis for their projections and discount the value of future cash flows at certain assumed rates of return.

Based upon the rates of return predicted through the use of one or more of these financial analysis techniques, a decision is made as to whether the project under consideration is economically feasible. If the rate is less than that which investors require, the project is normally considered not to be economically feasible; the reverse is also true.

It should be realized that to date the positive impact of government financial incentives upon a project's economic feasibility has not been discussed. Later in this chapter the role of these incentives in tourism development is reviewed in detail. At this point, it should be realized that many projects that would not have been economically feasible with private sector financing alone have been developed because of an injection of financial assistance from those in the public sector. By reducing the interest burden on projects or by reducing financing costs in some other way, these incentives have the effect of increasing the rates of return that the investors earn. In many instances, the increases are great enough to change an infeasible project into a feasible one. However, if a project has been found to be infeasible and if there is no possibility of receiving government financial assistance, it will probably be terminated at this point.

Cost-benefit Analysis

Commercially-oriented projects that have been found to be economically feasible may or may not have to be further analyzed using cost-benefit analysis techniques. Cost-benefit analyses are also useful for evaluating noncommercial tourism projects that either generate no direct revenues or that have, at best, operating revenues equaling operating expenses. Cost-benefit analyses are generally carried out by or on behalf of government agencies. They help these agencies measure and weigh all of the costs and benefits of alternative projects. In so doing, the agencies are able to determine which project will produce the largest net benefit for their economies and for their society as a whole.

Economic feasibility analyses are just one aspect of cost-benefit analysis. There ae several financial analyses or capital budgeting techniques available that will permit comparisons between alternative projects. In purely financial terms, the project that creates the highest rate of return for its investors is usually the best alternative for them. However, from a government agency's viewpoint, the size of the return on private investors' capital cannot be the sole criterion for support. A government agency has broad-scale economic, environmental, and social-cultural responsibilities that have to be considered prior to giving financial incentives or other support or approvals to a project. For example, a proposed casino may generate spectacular returns for the investors, but a government agency may feel that such a project will undermine the social well-being of its destination area. If a government agency makes financial incentives available for tourism development projects, it usually can satisfy only a small proportion of those who apply because of budgetary limitations. The agency must, therefore, have some means and criteria available to it to rank projects against each other and to support those that earn the highest rankings. Earlier in this chapter, the following criteria were suggested for government project screening purposes:

1. Economic contributions
2. Environmental impact
3. Social-cultural impact
4. Competitive impact
5. Tourism impact
6. Developer and operator capabilities
7. Compliance with policies, plans, and programs
8. Equity contributions
9. Feasibility

Some of the factors related to certain of the above criteria can be measured quantitatively; others cannot. For example, as should be clear from the material presented in Chapter 9, the economic contributions of a project can be forecast in a numerical way; the social-cultural impacts, however, cannot be reduced to numbers.

A cost-benefit analysis, therefore, should attempt to weigh the quantifiable and unquantifiable costs and benefits of a tourism project against each other. Some subjectivity and judgment has to enter into this because there can be no single measurement or set of measurements of a project's overall worth to a destination area. Assuming that the cost-benefit analysis results have proven positive, the project can progress to the next level of evaluation. Some project developers may wish to apply for government financial incentives, while others may go ahead without such assistance.

Role of Government Financial Incentives in Tourism Development

One of the major hurdles that all tourism projects face before they are realized is that of securing the financing needed for their development. Many tourism projects have been proven to be economically feasible but have not been developed because their promoters have been unable to attract the right amount or types of financing. The number of government agencies providing specific financial incentives for tourism projects has increased rapidly in recent years on a worldwide basis. In this respect, these agencies are playing their dual roles as "stimulators" and "entrepreneurs."

In Canada, for example, almost all of the provincial and territorial governments have financial assistance programs specifically tailored for tourism development projects. The federal government has played an active role in this process by sharing the costs of some of these programs with individual provinces.

Government financial incentives for tourism projects can be classified into two broad categories. Fiscal incentives are special allowances for income tax or other tax purposes. Direct and indirect incentives constitute the second main category, and include a wide variety of programs aimed at easing the financial requirements of projects. The basic objective of most of these incentive programs is to help businesses carry out tourism development projects that, without assistance, might have been completely abandoned or seriously delayed. On a global basis, all levels of governments get involved in providing these types of incentive programs. The following is a list of some of the types of financial incentive programs provided by government agencies to tourism projects:

DIRECT AND INDIRECT INCENTIVES

Nonrefundable grants—reduce a project's capital budget

Low-interest loans—reduce the amount of interest that the project must pay during its operating life

Interest rebates—the government agency rebates a portion of the project's interest costs during its operating life

Forgiveable loans—the government agency loans funds to the project and then

Government agencies often assume the cost of building and maintaining roads as part of the tourism infrastructure

"forgives" all or part of these over an agreed-upon time period; this acts like a phased nonrefundable grant

Loans guarantees—the government agency guarantees a loan or loans given to a project by a private financial institution

Working capital loans—the government agency loans funds to meet the working capital needs of a project

Equity participation—the government agency purchases some of the available shares in the project, and it therefore becomes an equity investor

Training grants—the government agency provides a nonrefundable grant to the project for staff training purposes

Infrastructure assistance—the government agency assumes the costs of some or all of the infrastructure required for the project

Leasebacks—the government agency purchases land, buildings, or equipment and then leases them to the project

Land donations—the government agency donates land free of charge to the project

FISCAL INCENTIVES

Tax holidays or deferrals—the government agency defers the payment of income taxes or other taxes for a predetermined time period

Remission of tariffs—the government agency relaxes or removes import duties on goods and services required by the project

Tax reductions—the government agency lowers the normal tax rates that would be paid by the project

Because most government departments providing these financial incentives generally receive more applications for assistance than their budgets can handle, it is inevitable that not all projects that request monetary help receive it. In certain cases, this results in these projects not proceeding any further.

Private Sector Financing for Tourism Development

Although governments continue to play a greater role in providing financing to tourism projects, it is the private sector that generally supplies the majority of the financing. These private sources range from individual citizens to major institutional lenders such as banks, trust companies, credit unions, insurance companies, and other commercial finance companies. Typically, a private financing source requires that the following five points be satisfied before lending money to a tourism project:

1. Previous management experience in tourism and an established credit record within the management team
2. Proof of economic feasibility via an independent economic feasibility study
3. Adequate collateral or security for the funds to be borrowed
4. Adequate equity capital to be invested by the owners of the project
5. Proof of stability in the tourism industry in which the project will function

Tourism projects require equity as well as borrowed capital from owners and investors. These individuals are the true *risk takers* in the development, and they are rewarded with profits from a return on their investments.

Not all projects are able to secure the types and amounts of private financing that they require, although they may have successfully survived all of the earlier screening mechanisms.

Detailed Design and Construction

In the final stages of realizing a tourism development project, various levels of architectural designs and drawings are prepared. Normally this procedure includes the following:

1. Preparation of preliminary architectural concepts
2. Preparation of preliminary architectural design
3. Preparation of final architectural design
4. Construction

At each of the first three stages, the drawings become increasingly more detailed and exact. When the final drawings have been approved, the project moves into construction.

SUMMARY

The tourism development strategy or plan for a destination area provides overall guidelines for development, outlines broad development concepts, and identifies individual development opportunities thought to be worthy of more in-depth analysis through economic feasibility studies and/or cost-benefit analyses. Obviously the public sector has a key role to play in ensuring that developers abide by the overall guidelines and that broad development concepts are realized. The public sector is also playing an ever-increasing role in stimulating the development of individual project opportunities through many types of financial incentive schemes.

Probably only a small proportion of tourism project ideas actually reach the construction stage, as most are unable to meet certain criteria or to secure the necessary financing. Many are screened out by tourism project evaluation and analysis systems similar to the one described in this chapter.

REFERENCES

BALMER, CRAPO & ASSOCIATES, INC., Tourism Development and Marketing Strategies for the Northwest Territories (Calgary, Alberta, Northwest Territories Department of Economic Development and Tourism, 1979), p. 30.

BAR—ON RAPHAEL RAYMOND V., "Forecasting Tourism—Theory and Practice," in a Decade for Achievement (The Tenth Annual Conference Proceedings of the Travel Research Association, Salt Lake City, Utah, 1979), p. 27.

BERGERON, PIERRE G., Capital Expenditure Planning for Growth and Profit (The Canadian Institute of Chartered Accountants, Toronto, Ontario, 1977), p. 60.

BOYD, HARPER W., and RALPH WESTFALL, *Marketing Research: Text and Cases* (Homewood, IL, Richard D. Irwin, Inc., 1972), pp. 131–36.

CCH CANADA LIMITED, Industrial Assistance Programs in Canada, 1979, (Don Mills, Ontario, 1979), p. 1.

GUNN, CLARE A., *Tourism Planning* (New York, Crane Russak, 1979), p. 318.

MORRISON, ALASTAIR M., The Planning and Development of Tourism in a Large Rural Area: Regional Tourism Planning in Auvergne-Limousin (East Lansing, MI, 1973), pp. 35, 76.

NAIR A., The Role of the State in the Field of Tourism (Madrid, Spain, World Tourism Organization/CIEST, 1970), p. 20.

ONTARIO MINISTRY OF TOURISM and RECREATION, Framework for Opportunity: A guide for Tourism Development in Ontario/Canada (Toronto, Ontario, undated), p. 10.

ORGANIZATION FOR ECONOMIC CO-OPERATION and DEVELOPMENT, Tourism Development and Economic Growth (Paris, France, 1966), p. 23.

SCHUMACHER, E. F., *Small is Beautiful: A Study of Economics As If People Mattered* (New York, Harper & Row, 1973), p. 38.

UNITED NATIONS, Manual for the Preparation of Industrial Feasibility Studies (New York, 1978), p. 11.

WORLD TOURISM ORGANIZATION, Guidelines on the Methodology Applicable for Making Annual and Medium-Term Forecasts (Relating to Tourism Development and Promotional Plans) For Members (Madrid, Spain, undated), pp. 57–72.

14

TOURISM MARKETING:

Bringing It All Together

"If this is your first visit to the U.S.S.R., you are welcome to it."

Sign on the door of a Moscow hotel room.
Quoted in English Well Speeched Here by Nino Lo Bello.

This chapter is concerned with the marketing of tourism services. The factors that make tourism marketing different from the marketing of other products and services are highlighted, and a definition of tourism marketing is provided. This definition stresses the need for a marketing orientation and market segmentation and describes the product life-cycle concept.

A procedural model for marketing planning is described. The model suggests that forces external to the destination, overall development objectives, and the analysis of the market, product, and competitors be taken into account in producing marketing objectives. Target markets are selected, and an appropriate marketing mix for each target market is determined. The elements of the marketing mix are examined.

LEARNING OBJECTIVES

Having read this chapter, you should be able to:

1. Describe the differences between marketing tourism services and traditional product marketing.
2. Compare and contrast the different approaches to marketing associated with production, selling, marketing, and societal marketing orientations.
3. Explain the concept of market segmentation and how it is used in tourism.
4. List and describe six criteria used to determine the viability of market segments.
5. List and explain seven general categories of segmentation criteria.
6. Differentiate between *a priori* and *factor-clustering* segmentation methods.
7. Explain how a tourism destination or organization should select target markets.
8. Define positioning and explain how it is used.
9. Explain the product life-cycle concept.
10. Describe each of the steps of the marketing planning process in tourism.
11. List and describe the elements of the marketing mix.

TOURISM MARKETING IS UNIQUE

The problems of marketing in tourism are somewhat different from those of traditional product marketing. The differences are the result of the characteristics of tourism supply and demand. An intangible experience is being sold, not a physical good that can be inspected prior to purchase. Because it is a service, production and consumption take place at the same time. In manufacturing, goods are produced, stored, and sold. The inventory process serves as a way of linking these stages of production and consumption. Tourism supply cannot be stored. Unlike a can of food which, if it is not sold one day can be sold the next, airline seats, hotel rooms, or restaurant seats not sold today lose that particular sale forever. Although the inventory cannot be stored and adjusted to changes in demand, the capacity to produce these tourism services must be developed ahead of time. This puts a great deal of pressure on producers to plan the proper amounts of facilities effectively and, having developed these facilities, to keep them used as fully as possible. This in itself creates another kind of problem, for tourism supply is relatively fixed. The resources and infrastructure of a destination cannot change as quickly as can tourist demand.

A second important factor that makes tourism different from other industries is that the service provided—a vacation—is in fact an amalgam of several services and some products. Most vacations have information, transportation, lodging, food and beverage, attraction, and activity components. These components are usually offered by different organizations and may be marketed directly to the tourist by the individual organizations or combined into a package where the services are supplied by a set of the organizations. This lack of one single organization's control over the entire vacation experience means that a great deal of interdependence exists among tourism organizations. For the visitor to leave having had a satisfactory experience, each individual tourism organization must have performed to the same standard. One bad service experience can spoil an otherwise perfect vacation or business trip. The marketing success of each organization in the *tourism service chain* is thus dependent on the efforts of the other organizations providing the other trip service components.

The guest's satisfaction is also a function of the staff providing the service. Tourism is a people business, people providing personal services to other people. Because of the vagaries of the human personality, a consistent quality of service is difficult to provide on an ongoing basis. As one writer has said, although we may want to, "we can't paint a smile on a human being's face." Those destinations and organizations that invest most heavily in hospitality and other types of service training are the ones most likely to enjoy the greatest success.

A third factor that makes tourism different from other industries is the role of travel intermediaries. Because tourist services are located at a distance from potential customers, specialized intermediaries—organizations that operate between the producer and the tourist—are often necessary to bridge the gap. Also, the fact that many tourism producers are relatively small means that they cannot afford to set up their own retail outlets. Thus, while in most industries the producer exerts much control over every stage in the development and delivery of the product, in tourism the travel intermediaries can influence, if not determine, which services should be offered, to whom, when, and at what price.

The last factor that makes tourism different from other industries relates to demand. Tourism demand is highly elastic, seasonal in nature, and influenced by subjective factors such as taste and fashion as well as the more objective factors such as price. In many cases, the services and experiences sought can be provided by any number of destinations or organizations, with particular emphasis on no one in particular.

DEFINITION OF MARKETING

There are numerous definitions of marketing, although few specifically address the unique characteristics of marketing tourism services. One of the definitions designed to fit tourism states "marketing is a management philosophy which, in light of tourist demand, makes it possible through research, forecasting, and selection to place tourism products on the market most in line with the organization's purpose for the greatest benefit."[1] This definition suggests several things. First, it indicates that marketing is a way of thinking about a situation that balances the needs of the tourist (as indicated through tourist demand) with the needs of the organization or destination. This can be explained by an examination of the development of an appropriate orientation toward marketing. Second, the definition stresses tourism research that culminates in the selection of target markets. The concept of market segmentation

---

[1]"Testing the Effectiveness of Promotional Campaigns in International Travel Marketing," World Tourism Organization Seminar, Ottawa, 1975, p. 3.

is useful here. Third, the concepts of positioning and the product life cycle are useful to ensure the proper placement of tourism services on the market and to suggest the appropriate marketing strategies and plans resulting from that decision.

Other definitions of marketing stress the need for a systems approach and recommend a step-by-step process for marketing tourism services. "Marketing is a continuous, sequential process through which management in the tourism industry plans, researches, implements, controls, and evaluates activities designed to satisfy both customers' needs and wants and their own organization's objectives. To be effective, marketing requires the efforts of everyone in an organization and can be made more or less effective by the actions of complementary organizations."[2] This definition indicates that marketing should be an ongoing concern in a tourism organization, not just a one-time effort each year. It also suggests that marketing should involve everyone in the organization, not just the Marketing Department. Five key functions of marketing are identified as planning, research, implementation, control, and evaluation. The interdependency of tourism organizations is also emphasized.

Another important characteristic of marketing is highlighted in this third definition of marketing: "communicating to and giving the target market customers what they want, when they want it, where they want it, at a price they are willing to pay. Any business that does this will fulfill its twofold purpose of creating and keeping customers and, in turn, will produce revenue."[3] This definition emphasizes that it is not enough to attract first-time visitors but that bringing them back for repeat visits is at least equally important for a tourism destination or organization.

MARKETING ORIENTATION

Before embarking on a program to market tourism services, it is necessary to develop an overall philosophy or orientation that will guide the organization's marketing efforts. Such a philosophy will set the tone for every subsequent decision made as part of the overall marketing effort. Although several different orientations are possible, experience has shown that they are not all equally effective.

Some destinations' marketing efforts are guided by a production or product orientation. A *production orientation* suggests that the emphasis is placed on the services or products available. A destination area has many physical, historical, and cultural resources, for example. The extent to which "our" resources are better than those of the competition will determine how many tourists visit our destination. This orientation has been used by the local authorities of a town on the south coast of England who decided in the late 1960's to print brochures only in English. When it was pointed out that a major potential market was the French residents across the English Channel, the reply was given that if the French wanted to visit, then they

---

[2]Alastair M. Morrison, *Hospitality and Travel Marketing.* (Albany, NY, Delmar Publishers, 1989), p. 4.

[3]Robert C. Lewis and Richard E. Chambers, *Marketing Leadership in Hospitality* (New York, Van Nostrand Reinhold, 1989), p. 9.

would be interested enough to learn to read English in order to understand what was available. Although it cannot be denied that the quality of resources is important, a total emphasis on tourism supply fails to take the wishes of the potential tourist into account. A production orientation is only successful if there is a surplus of demand over supply. In this case, the destination or company that offers the best product will get the tourist. The old adage that reflected this said "build a better mousetrap, and the world will beat a path to your door." Often referred to as the "better-mousetrap fallacy," this privileged position or *competitive advantage* is usually short-lived in today's increasingly competitive tourism industries.

When supply exceeds demand, the problem becomes: How can I sell all these mousetraps? The number of destinations actively seeking tourism has increased as has the number of places throughout the world with easy accessibility. The entry into the marketplace of more professional tour wholesalers has increased competition for the tourist dollar and has meant that destination areas can no longer sit back and wait for tourists to come to them. It has become increasingly necessary to convince tourists of the benefits of visiting a particular destination or of purchasing a particular organization's services. The orientation of many has moved from one of emphasizing the product or production to one of intensified selling. The accent is placed on promoting what is available for sale. Yet, this *selling orientation* focuses on the needs of the seller—How can we sell more product? It does not center on the needs of the tourist—What will satisfy them? Obviously, the first priority here is to convince the potential tourist that what is available will please them.

A newer development in orientation is one in which the needs and wants of the tourists are the first priority in the mind of the marketer. This is a *marketing orientation philosophy* that begins with the needs and wants of the tourist and attempts to provide the services to satisfy these needs and wants. It involves being open when the tourist wants the establishment to be, serving breakfast when the tourist wants it rather than when it is convenient for management, and providing the kind of experiences that tourists want rather than what we feel they "should" want. It is realizing that, from the example used above, an individual does not want to buy a mousetrap; rather she wants to kill mice. Some say this is an exercise in "putting yourself in the tourist's shoes," always trying to see things from the customer's viewpoint. If and when a better way is developed of satisfying a need, people will try it. This philosophy was made evident at the beginning of this book when an emphasis was placed on the satisfaction of needs and wants.

Many major organizations outside and within tourism have come to realize that they also have a responsibility to society as well as to their customers. Strictly concentrating on their customers' needs and wants may cause immediate or long-term harm to the customers or society in general. In the developed countries, fast-food companies are beginning to shoulder some social responsibility by improving (or at least providing more information on) the nutritional content of menu items and of using recyclable materials in their packaging. Beer companies and distilleries have joined in the movement against drunk driving by developing advertisements that emphasize the consequences of drinking and driving.

A marketing orientation means—
literally—speaking the language of the
customer

Having a sense of social responsibility is even more important and necessary in tourism. The uniqueness of tourism suggests that a philosophy that concentrates solely on the needs of the market is not the best orientation, even for the tourists themselves. A tourism destination relies on the resources of its community, which both tourists and residents share. To become totally marketing oriented, all aspects of the community would have to be oriented toward satisfying the needs and wants of the tourist. The risk for the community and ultimately for the tourist as well is that by orienting strictly and totally for the tourist's needs, the needs, integrity, and long-term interests of the community and its residents may be harmed. Consider the situations explored in earlier chapters of tourist destination areas that have adapted to the needs of the tourist and have, in the process, lost their uniqueness, their heritage, and their natural resources while getting a relatively poor economic return on their investment. Destination areas that have attempted to adapt their resources to satisfy tourist needs may have lost the very thing that has made them attractive and unique in the first place. The tourist is the ultimate loser, as more and more destinations take on an increasingly similar and familiar appearance.

The erosion of natural, historic, and cultural resources is not the only potential pitfall of tourism development that needs to be considered. The Caribbean, long a favorite destination of North American and European tourists, has begun to realize that tourism contributes to social problems, such as increased prostitution, drug trafficking, and the spread of AIDS. The Barbados Board of Tourism has acted on this problem by airing television commercials that warn against harassing tourists on beachfronts to buy drugs.[4] The Caribbean Tourism Organization (CTO) organized a 28-nation Caribbean conference in 1989 titled "Socially Conscious Tourism." The United Nations Development Programme will provide financial assistance to CTO to prepare further studies on the impact of drugs, prostitution, and other *underground economies* as they relate to Caribbean tourism.

The best solution to these potential problems with tourism is to develop a marketing approach that focuses on the satisfaction of tourist needs and wants while respecting the long-term interests of the community. This orientation is often referred to as a *societal marketing approach.* This philosophy provides for planning, development, and marketing activities that focus on the needs of the tourist, but that also consider the effects of these activities on the long-term interests of the community before any action is taken.

All marketing activities are eventually influenced by the orientations of those directly responsible for marketing. It is essential that these individuals' decisions reflect a predetermined philosophy or *corporate culture* that provides an overall guide for the development and marketing efforts of the destination or organization.

MARKET SEGMENTATION

Another aspect of our first definition of marketing refers to the selection of tourism demand. Market segmentation is a recognized and universally accepted way of analyzing tourism markets and selecting from among them. *Market segmentation* refers to the process by which people with similar needs, wants, and characteristics are grouped together so that an organization can use greater precision in serving and communicating with its chosen customers. Market segmentation, then, is a two-step process of (1) deciding how to group all potential tourists (the *market segments*) and (2) selecting specific groups from among these (the *target markets*) to pursue.

Segmentation is based on four assumptions. First, the market for a service like a vacation, is made up of particular segments whose members have distinctive needs and preferences relative to that vacation. In other words, not all tourists are alike. Second, these potential tourists can be grouped into segments whose members have

---

[4]Cherie Hart, The Caribbean—Caught in a Tourist Trap, World Development, November 1989, pp. 7–9.

similar and identifiable characteristics. Third, a single vacation offering, such as a Mediterranean cruise, appeals to some segments of the market more than others. Fourth, destinations and organizations can make their marketing more effective by developing specific vacation offerings for specific segments of the market. A cruise package may suit one group of potential tourists, while a whitewater rafting trip may appeal more strongly to another.

The process of segmenting the tourism market should be the basis for strategic (long-term) marketing and management decisions. Market segmentation is more than a statistical technique used to analyze demand. It should be utilized as a management tool leading to specific marketing decisions. The development of a marketing strategy should begin with the identification of market segments and their individual characteristics. At one extreme, a firm or destination may maximize its marketing orientation by developing a unique product offering for every potential tourist. Limitations of time and money prevent this. At the other extreme, the firm or destination may save time and money by offering one basic option to everyone. Although that one option will undoubtedly appeal to some potential tourists, it will not to others. The compromise is to separate potential tourists into segments, each segment having similar characteristics, and produce offerings geared to the needs of certain selected segments.

Identifying market segments.   To determine the compromise point between developing a product for everyone and offering one product for all, it is necessary to examine the critieria a segment must meet to determine its viability. A segment must be:

1. *Measurable.* Can the number of potential tourists within this segment be estimated with a reasonable degree of accuracy?
2. *Accessible.* Can these tourists be reached with specific promotional techniques or media? Can they be reached and influenced by existing or potential distribution channels? How easy will this be?
3. *Substantial.* Are there sufficient numbers of tourists in this segment to support a marketing effort tailor-made for them?
4. *Defensible.* Are the segment's characteristics different enough to justify separate marketing activities and expenditures just for them, or can they be grouped with one or more other target markets? If competitors decide to use more of a mass marketing approach, will this have an adverse effect on us?
5. *Durable.* As the market develops, will this segment maintain its uniqueness, or will these differences disappear with time?
6. *Competitive.* Do we have a relative advantage over the competition in serving this market segment?

Market Segmentation Methods

Two overall methods used to segment tourism markets are (1) a priori methods (or *forward segmentation*) and (2) factor-clustering (*backward segmentation*) methods.[5,6] A priori methods have traditionally been the most frequently used in tourism primarily because they are the easier of the two methods to apply. Here, the marketer predetermines the segmentation base or bases to be used for market segmentation, for example, by purpose-of-trip and/or geographic origin. Usually the marketer acts on information such as previous research studies by others that suggest the a priori segmentation base is a key factor in determining tourist behavior. For example, it is a common practice in international tourism to treat the residents of each tourism-generating country as unique target markets. In addition, most practitioners make the a priori decision to address business and pleasure travelers as two separate and distinct groups of target markets.

Factor-clustering methods result in clusters or segments derived from the application of specific statistical analysis techniques. The marketer does not predetermine the segments; the statistical analysis suggests them. In an analysis of Hong Kong residents, five distinct travel segments were identified on the basis of preferred sets of vacation activities: (1) visiting friends and relatives, (2) outdoor sports activity, (3) sightseeing, (4) entertainment, and (5) full-house activity. The study used the factor-analysis technique to maximize the heterogeneity between the clusters and maximize the homogeneity within each individual cluster.[7]

Market Segmentation Bases

Many bases are used to segment the tourism market. Seven general categories are: (a) demographic or socioeconomic, (b) product-related, (c) psychographic, (d) geographic, (e) purpose-of-trip, (f) behavioral, and (g) channel of distribution. (See Table 14.1)

Demographic and Socioeconomic Segmentation.   Early segmentation studies in tourism used demographic and socioeconomic statistics as the basis for forming market segments. These remain the most commonly used today due to the relative ease of acquiring the statistical data, the comparability of the information through Census as well as media-generated data, and the fact that the data are easy to understand and apply. Age and income have, in fact, been very successful predictors of

---

[5]Stephen L. J. Smith, *Tourism Analysis: A Handbook* (Essex, England, Longman Scientific & Technical, 1989), pp. 40–62.

[6]Douglas Pearce, *Tourist Development:* 2nd ed., (Longman Scientific & Technical, 1989), pp. 143–147.

[7]Sheauhsing Hsieh, Joseph T. O'Leary, and Alastair M. Morrison, "Activity Packages for the Hong Kong Pleasure Travel Market." Presentation to the Annual Conference of the Society of Travel and Tourism Educators, Grand Island, New York, October 1990.

TABLE 14.1 RECREATION AND TOURISM
MARKET SEGMENTATION BASES

Socioeconomic and demographic variables

Age
Education
Sex
Income
Family size
Family life cycle
Social class
Home ownership
Second home ownership
Race or ethnic group
Occupation

Product-related variables

Recreation activity
Equipment type
Volume usage
Brand loyalty
Benefit expectations
Length of stay
Transportation mode
Experience preferences
Participation patterns

Psychographic variables

Personality traits
Life-style
Attitudes, interests, options
Motivations

Geographic variables

Region
Market area
Urban, surburban, rural
City size
Population density

---

recreation participation. However, the use of only demographic data to segment markets has come under attack. It has been argued that the rapidly changing nature of society makes it impossible to rely solely on this data as a means of developing a marketing strategy. Just because a segment of people is within a particular age or income group does not necessarily mean the individuals will have similar vacation preferences. Also, socioeconomic information does not give the marketer sufficient information about likes and dislikes to position the tourism destination or organization in the marketplace properly.

Greater success has been found in using demographic criteria that are multivariate (using two or more demographic variables). Status, for example, includes dimensions of income, education, and occupation, and family life cycle is a composite of marital status, age, and the numbers and ages of children at home. Life-cycle segmentation has proven to be an effective way of segmenting in a number of tourism and recreation cases. It is unlikely that segmentation on the basis of demographics will ever be abandoned. Although other segmentation bases provide information useful for strategic decisions on what to offer in the way of tourism services, it is still necessary to communicate with an individual market segment. For all its shortcomings, demographic segmentation offers the best way to access a specific segment of the market.

Product-Related Segmentation.   A major advantage of segmenting by means of product-related variables is that the information gained is directly related to the particular tourism service under consideration. Indeed, a major flaw in some studies is that information is sought from the potential tourist that deals with general benefits sought or, in the case of psychographic segmentation, general attitudes about types of products or services rather than with specific products and services.

Psychographic Segmentation.   Much has been made of this relatively new tool. This technique of segmentation, although expensive to use and difficult to carry out, has been useful for describing segments. It can probably be best used in highly specialized and extensively developed markets to supplement the information gained from simpler analyses. Demographic data may be likened to the bones of a skeleton, and psychographic data may be likened to the flesh. The bones form the basis of the structure, but it is only by covering the form with flesh that the features become recognizable. Information about an individual's attitudes, interests, and opinions give a much closer picture of the segment being described.

In Chapter 3, the VALS (Values and Life Styles) program was described as the most widely recognized application of psychographic segmentation. A 1984 study of travelers to Pennsylvania found that travel selection criteria varied by the nine VALS groupings.[8] There are other psychographic or life-style segmentation methods available including the Prizm Cluster System. The Prizm system identifies forty life-style clusters. One of these, the "Gray Power" cluster, is said to favor cruise ship vacations, while the "Blue Blood Estates" do not like travel by recreation vehicles.

Geographic Segmentation.   Geographic considerations are very important to tourism. Much of the attractiveness of a tourist destination is based on contrasting cultures, climates, or scenery, for example. This implies there is a certain distance between origin and destination. Also, we have already seen the crucial role that accessibility of tourists to a destination plays in tourism. To date, destinations have used geographically-based studies solely to identify primary, secondary, and in some cases, tertiary markets. National and state tourist offices tend to use geographic

[8]Davis Shih, "VALS as a Tool of Tourism Market Research: The Pennsylvania Experience, Journal of Travel Research, Spring 1986, pp. 2–11.

segmentation for the purposes of determining the extent of their promotional efforts. National tourism statistics have traditionally been collected by country of origin and marketing priorities have been set according to the contributions of each country to total arrivals.

Another important aspect of geographical segmentation is that, as with demographics, it provides the means of access to target markets. In marketing, it is essential to know where potential customers live or work in order to communicate with them.

Purpose-of-Trip Segmentation.   Chapter 5 presents a description of travel markets by purpose of trip. This chapter follows the established tradition in tourism of initially dividing the market into two broad purpose-of-trip segments: (1) the business and (2) the pleasure-personal travel markets. These were then further subdivided into the market segments shown in Table 14.2. Another variant of this approach was used in a segmentation study of a hotel located in Singapore. Two broad segments were first defined: (1) the group segment and (2) the individual segment. The group segment was then further subdivided into group tours, conventions, corporate meetings, and airline crews. The individual segment consisted of corporate, full-rate and miscellaneous, frequent travelers, and group inclusive tours (GITs). The

TABLE 14.2 PURPOSE-OF-TRIP SEGMENTATION
OF THE TRAVEL MARKET

Business travel market

1. Regular business travel
   a. Frequent business travelers
   b. Women business travelers
   c. Luxury (executive) business travelers
   d. International business travelers
2. Business travel related to meetings, conventions, and congresses:
   a. International associations
   b. Continental associations
   c. National associations
   d. Regional associations
   e. Corporations
3. Incentive travel

Pleasure personal travel market

1. Visiting friends and relatives
2. Close-to-home leisure trips
3. Touring vacation
4. City trip
5. Outdoors vacation
6. Resort vacation
7. Cruise trip
8. Visit to theme park, exhibition or event

research for this study showed that purpose of trip was a better way of differentiating segments than nationality or income.[9]

Behavioral Segmentation. Behavioral segmentation divides customers by their usage rates, benefits sought, use occasions, usage status and potential, and brand loyalty.[10] It was increasingly used by the tourism industries in the 1970's and 1980's, especially as greater attention became focused on frequent travelers.

Heavy-half segmentation is an example of usage-rate or use-frequency segmentation. Some attempts have been made in recreation and tourism to use this segmentation base. Heavy-half segmentation refers to the idea of segmenting a market on the basis of quantity purchased or consumed. As with other types of products, however, heavy-half segmentation has been found lacking. A major problem is that, in many cases, the characteristics of the heavy half (the major purchases) have been found to be similar to those of the light half. A study of downhill skiers found that preferences and use patterns of both heavy and light skiers are similar, except for such volume-related characteristics as level of skill, incidence of ski vacations, ownership of equipment, and quality of slopes.[11] Similar difficulties have been found with segmentation on the basis of brand loyalty.

Benefit or attribute segmentation is fast becoming a very popular segmentation base in recreation and tourism. This involves segmenting a market according to the relative importance assigned to benefits that consumers expect to realize after purchasing the product. The method entails determining the relative importance of specific product benefits to prospective consumers. Clusters are then formed of people who attach a similar degree of importance to the same product benefits. Although results can have important ramifications for the development of new products and the determination of advertising messages, it is necessary to develop demographic profiles of those identified in the clusters in order to access or reach the market segments.

Use occasion segmentation is also enjoying greater popularity in tourism. Perhaps the best example of this is the growing number of resorts and destinations trying to attract the honeymooner market. Here, the use occasion is obviously a honeymoon. The Japanese honeymooner market has drawn special attention among destinations on the Pacific Rim. Destinations such as Hong Kong and Singapore have been particularly successful in appealing to Japanese honeymooners. Some 8.2% of all Japanese visitors to Singapore in 1988 were on their honeymoons. For all other countries with visitors to Singapore, honeymooners represented just 1.8%.[12]

[9]Subash C. Mehta and Ariel Vera, "Segmentation in Singapore," The Cornell HRA Quarterly, May 1990, pp. 80–87.

[10]Philip Kotler, Marketing Management: Analysis, Planning, Implementation, and Control, 6th ed. (Englewood Cliffs, New Jersey, Prentice-Hall, Inc., 1988).

[11]Daniel J. Stynes and Edward M. Mahoney, "Michigan Downhill Ski Marketing Study: Segmenting Active Skiers" (Michigan State University Agricultural Experiment Station Research Report 391, 1980).

[12]Singapore Tourist Promotion Board, Survey of Overseas Visitors to Singapore 1988, October 1989, p. 42.

Channel-of-Distribution Segmentation. This chapter has already indicated that tourism's distribution channels are unique and play a more powerful role than the middlemen in other industries. While Chapter 16 provides a detailed description of these distribution channels, it is important to recognize that these "intermediaries" can and should be segmented by the other tourism organizations who depend upon them for business. Intermediaries vary according to their principal function (for example, retailing versus wholesaling travel services), area of specialization by travel service, market segment, or destination (for example, cruise-only travel agents, corporate, and ethnic travel agencies), size and structure (such as large franchised travel agency chains versus the small independent retailer), and, of course, geographic location.

While segmentation schemes for distribution channels have received little attention from tourism researchers, the importance of intermediaries in tourism is increasing. Most organizations who target travel intermediaries in their marketing use a two-step process: (1) identify the target market of travelers, and then (2) select the intermediaries who serve or might serve these target markets.

Selecting Target Markets. Once market segments have been identified and profiled, it is necessary to select the *target market* or *markets* that the destination or organization will seek to attract and serve. This decision should be based upon a careful analysis of which market segments will produce the greatest benefits. Such an analysis involves four concerns:

> *Income potential:* What is the current and future potential for income from this segment? Income is a combination of the number of current and potential tourists and their current and potential per-person spending.
> *Competition:* To what extent does competition exist for the segment(s) in question? How strong is our advantage compared to the competitors?
> *Cost:* How much investment is required to develop services to attract this segment and to communicate with its members?
> *Serviceability:* Do we have the financial and managerial capability to design, promote, and distribute the appropriate services and satisfactorily serve the market segments attracted by these services?

The segments chosen become the organization's target markets. Developing marketing programs to meet the needs of these target markets should begin with the use of a technique known as positioning.

Positioning

Positioning is a relatively new concept in marketing and is yet to receive widespread attention in the tourism literature and research. Most experts agree that its origins date back to around 1972 and a series of articles written by advertising executives Al Reis and Jack Trout. These articles were later expanded into a book titled, *Positioning: The Battle for Your Mind.* In these authors' own words, "Positioning is what you do to the mind of the prospect."[13] Other authors have elaborated on this original definition. They include Lewis and Chambers, who say that positioning is "the consumer's mental perception of a product, which may or may not differ from the actual characteristics of a product or brand."[14] Most experts agree that the purpose of positioning is to create a *perception* or *image*—to establish a position—in the targeted customer's mind. Since the object of such an exercise is the individual tourist's perception of the destination or organization, there is a clear linkage to the psychological dimensions of perception discussed earlier in Chapter 2. Effective positioning is expected to grow in importance as the number of tourism destinations and organizations competing for the tourist's dollar continues to increase.

In using positioning, the logical place to start is with the questions: Do we have a position in our potential visitors' minds? and, if so, What is that position? Answering these questions must involve doing some marketing research. Focus group research done in Los Angeles for the Tahiti Tourist Board showed that a variety of misperceptions were hindering further tourism growth from the Southern California market. These were that Tahiti was 14 to 16 hours from Los Angeles (rather than just 8); it was an isolated, single-island nation (it actually has 130 islands); it has limited accommodations; and it is difficult to get there.[15] Another study about India as a travel destination highlighted two significant misperceptions: not many people in India speak English, and it has few first-class hotels.[16] The message from these two examples should be clear; the flow of information to tourists is imperfect, and it would be a major error to assume that they have an accurate image or perception of the destination or organization.

The next step in positioning is to determine whether the visitor's perception or image needs to be established, changed, or reinforced. Here, two forms of positioning can be used: (1) *objective positioning* and (2) *subjective positioning*. With objective positioning, the destination or organization attempts to tailor-make its services and products to match the needs and wants of a selected target market or markets specifically. Some refer to this as *product-market matching*. The emphasis is placed on adding or modifying one or more objective characteristics of the services or facilities being offered. For example, a destination which decides to pursue the scuba diving market will need to add dive shops, dive boats, dive maps, diving guides-instructors, and other services required by this specialized target market. Once the objective attributes have been altered to suit the target market(s), these changes must be communicated to potential tourists through various types of consumer and travel intermediary promotions.

Subjective positioning is an attempt to form, reinforce, or change the potential visitor's image without altering the physical characteristics of the services and prod-

[13]Al Ries and Jack Trout, *Positioning: The Battle for Your Mind,* Warner Books, New York, 1986.

[14]Lewis and Chambers, p. 678.

[15]Claudette Covey, "Tahiti sets out to dispel myths that deter tourists," Travel Agent Magazine, March 31, 1988, pp. 8–9.

[16]Sudhir H. Kale and Katherine M. Weir, "Marketing Third World Countries to the Western Traveler: The Case of India," Journal of Travel Research, Fall 1986, pp. 2–7.

ucts offered by the tourism destination or organization. Subjective positioning normally follows objective positioning. It is often used when research shows that there are misperceptions about a destination or organization, or when a negative image has developed through adverse publicity or for other reasons. This is usually called *repositioning*. When Tahiti discovered its distance misperception, an advertising campaign was launched stating that it was just "Two and a half hours beyond Hawaii and fifty years behind it." Mexico for some time used the *positioning statement* "Feel the Warmth of Mexico" in its promotions to communicate the friendliness of its people.

Once the decision is made to use either or both objective and subjective positioning, the next step is to determine how this will be communicated to potential travelers and/or travel intermediaries. While Chapter 15 deals with communications and promotions in detail, it can be said that there are at least six broad *positioning approaches:* (1) positioning on specific product features; (2) positioning on benefits, problem solution, or needs; (3) positioning for specific usage occasions; (4) positioning for user category; (5) positioning against another product; and (6) positioning by product class dissociation.[17]

Product Life Cycle

The concept of the product life cycle (PLC) is useful as another guideline in choosing, attracting, and serving target markets. The PLC concept suggests that a destination, service, or product moves through four distinct stages: introduction, growth, maturity, and decline. In Chapter 12, the various stages were described from a planning perspective. It is important that the destination or organization examine the PLC concept at two different levels. First, at what stage in the PLC is our part of the tourism industry? Second, at what stage in the PLC is our own destination, service or product? Since the spectacular growth of international tourism in the 1970's and before, year-to-year increases have been much more modest, suggesting a maturing of the industry. In the developed countries, some parts of the industry, such as domestic airline travel, are also in the maturity stage.

It is important to identify the PLC stage situation because the effectiveness of different marketing strategies vary by stage. For example, in the maturity stage, more emphasis must be placed on drawing business away from competitiors or on finding new target markets or uses.

MARKETING PLANNING PROCESS

To summarize what has been said to this point, a tourism destination or organization must segment the market using the most appropriate methods and bases, must select its target market(s); and taking into account the PLC stages of the industry and its own offerings, it must position these markets effectively within the minds

---

[17]Philip Kotler, pp. 274–275.

of the targeted potential customers. Having made these decisions, specific marketing programs using pricing, services and products, promotions, and distribution channels (*marketing mixes*) can now be designed. The process used to develop marketing mixes should be systematic; it should follow a step-by-step procedure known as the *marketing planning process.*

Marketing planning implies a future orientation, It involves identifying suitable marketing objectives as well as determining the most appropriate marketing strategies to achieve these objectives. Marketing planning should take place at two levels: *strategic marketing planning* for three to five years or more in the future, and *tactical marketing planning* for the next year or less. Both levels of planning must be closely integrated with the other. A model of the planning process is suggested in Figure 14.1. As this model shows, marketing objectives should not be set until after an analysis has been completed on the interaction of five factors—external environmental forces, development objectives, services or product, market, and competition.

Figure 14.1 Market planning process

External Environmental Forces

Planning must be accomplished within the framework of the external environment, which is constantly changing, but over which the marketing manager has little or no control. The technique of identifying and analyzing the impact of external environmental forces is known as *environmental scanning.* The basic reason for doing an environmental scan is that it is better to anticipate change before it happens than to react to change after it has happened. This can be accomplished by answering these key questions:

What are the major trends?
Will they affect us and how will they affect us?

How much will they affect us?

How will they affect our closest competitors?

What should we do differently in the future to adapt to these trends and their likely impacts?

The environmental forces to be *scanned* should include (1) legislation and regulation, (2) political situations, (3) sociocultural characteristics, (4) economic conditions, (5) technology, (6) transportation, and (7) competition at a *macro* level. For a tourism organization or destination that attracts visitors from several countries, an environmental scan is needed for each individual tourist-generating country.

The first of the forces to be considered is the legal and regulatory environment. Certain countries in the past have placed legal restrictions on their residents that have hampered the flow of outbound tourism. Residents may be restricted from traveling, or they may be unable to take more than a certain sum of money out of the country. Political factors must also be considered. Tensions or hostilities between the country of origin and a country of destination will affect marketing success. On the sociocultural level, it is important to consider the educational background of residents of the countries being considered for tourism purposes. More international travel is generated from countries exhibiting higher educational standards, from societies regarded as more cultured, and from countries having a higher degree of industrialization.

The pace of technological change within tourism and society in general is accelerating. The industry is experiencing profound changes as a result of the direct and indirect impacts of new technologies. One example is the spectacular growth in the importance of computerized reservations systems, a business dominated by the major airlines. The industry is quickly moving away from being dependent on paper-based information to being more dependent on electronic information. Other technologies that are having a significant impact are videoconferencing and satellite technology, facsimile transmission, and home-entertainment systems.

Another important factor is the technical consideration of transportation and other aspects of accessibility such as documentation requirements. The destination must be accessible to tourists from the generating countries being considered. The current and projected economic conditions in generating countries is also a factor of great importance in tourism. It is essential that there are a sufficient number of people in the country who can afford to travel. Japan's increasing affluence, for example, has attracted much greater attention from destinations around the Pacific Rim and elsewhere. The exchange rate between the host country and the various generating countries is another key economic concern. Past history has shown that major exchange rate shifts have had a direct impact on travel volumes between specific pairs of countries.

Although commonly overlooked, the destination or organization's macro-competition should be analyzed. These are not head-to-head competitors, but they represent the other products and services competing for the same disposble income. For example, the purchase of an expensive home-entertainment system may take the place of a foreign vacation trip. A new car purchase may result in less frequent and shorter vacations being taken. There are potential substitutes for travel, and they should be taken into consideration in marketing planning.

Development Objectives

The marketing plan should be just one part of the overall strategic plan for an individual organization, and just one element in the comprehensive tourism plan for a destination area. Tourism is one, and only one, strategy for development. As was noted in previous chapters, tourism can be used as a political, social, and economic force. Yet, other alternatives are available. The comprehensive tourism plan must itself be consistent with the overall planning and development goals and strategies for the destination area.

Analysis of Markets, Services or Products, and Competition

Many marketing experts refer to this step as a *situation analysis.* One of the principal objectives of such an analysis is to determine the destination's or organization's strengths and weaknesses compared to its closest competitors. Competition is defined as any firm or destination seeking to serve the same target market or markets as your organization serves. A situation analysis considers the organization's own services and products, the target markets, and the competition.

When completing a situation analysis, a tourism destination should compare its destination mix against those of its closest competitors. As indicated in Chapter 8, this would involve an evaluation of the following five destination-mix elements:

Attractions. Natural resources, climate, cultural and historical resources, ethnic attractions, accessibility, manmade attractions

Facilities. Lodging, food and beverage, support industries

Infrastructure. Fresh water supply, sewerage systems, communications systems, road systems, health care facilities, energy systems, security systems

Transportation. Airports, railway systems, cruise ship terminals, bus transporation

Hospitality. Hospitality training programs, friendliness of local residents, overall service levels

It is equally important to analyze the marketing programs, positioning, and overall management of competing destinations or organizations, and to compare this with those of our own destination or organization. What image do competitors have in the minds of our potential customers? How successful have their past marketing programs been? What have been their most successful marketing efforts? Do they have a cohesive, experienced, and marketing-oriented management team?

The culmination of these comparisons between the subject destination and its closest competitors should be an identification of comparative strengths and weaknesses. What do we have that is better than our competition? This information is important by itself, but in keeping with the marketing orientation stated above, it is necessary to place such knowledge in the context of the existing and potential target markets.

Although marketing is not a science and has no scientific laws to guide its actions, there are several useful principles that guide its actions. For an organization or destination developing a marketing plan for the first time, one such principle may be: attract people similar to those you already serve. This involves defining existing target markets and drawing more people with characteristics similar to those of visitors who have previously been attracted from these target markets. The definition and analysis of target markets should address the following questions:

Who are they? How many of them are there? What are their socioeconomic, psychographic, and behavioral characteristics?
Where do they come from and travel to?
How do they make plans and travel to and within the destination?
When do they vacation and for how long? When is the decision made?
Why do they vacation? What are their important motivations?

The crucial task is to determine a picture of the actual tourist then project that picture into the future by considering trends in the country of origin. A second task is to discover potential markets by compiling a picture of the present tourist and seeking to find other markets that meet that profile. For example, if most people in the existing market come from within a 500-mile radius, potential markets may be discovered from areas within 500 miles from which visitors do not yet come.

Part of the market analysis is identifying why people vacation

Tourism Marketing Goals

When the above analysis is complete, it is recommended that the tourism organization or destination prepare a set of broad marketing goals. These need not be as specific as the marketing objectives described later. They should describe the overall purposes and desired outcomes of future marketing programs. These might be stated in terms of the types of:

> *Image* to be created—elite or mass market
>
> *Tourist profile*—low spending or high spending, repeat or new business, and so on
>
> *Income source*—foreign exchange generation or domestic
>
> *Development desired*—high-class hotels or small, locally owned facilities or foreign-owned ones

Once stated these goals should provide overall guidelines for the selection of target markets, the identification of more specific marketing objectives, and the development of marketing mix(es).

Target market selection.   The process of target market selection was discussed earlier in the chapter as part of the discussion on market segmentation. Once a target market is selected, the job then becomes one of positioning and developing a marketing mix that will meet the needs of that market. The very nature of the marketing mix should send out a clear signal to potential travelers about who we want to attract, and perhaps who we do not want. For example, if a high-income, high-status target market is selected, facilities and services will be developed to appeal to high-income, high-status tourists. Prices will be set high, and promotional messages may show pictures of tourists in tuxedos at dinner or older couples dancing cheek to cheek. Thus, the selection of these elements of the marketing mix is done with the expectation that only high-income, high-status tourists can afford to visit.

Market segments should be defined using one or more of the seven segmentation bases discussed earlier: demographic, product-related, psychographic, geographic, purpose of trip, behavioral, or channel of distribution. The segments actually selected as target markets should meet the criteria of being measurable, accessible, substantial, defensible, and durable. The size (substantiality) of the market can be measured in terms of the number of tourists, the number of tourist nights, or the amount of tourist expenditures. Market segments that are large offer less of a risk than ones that are relatively small. As mentioned earlier, other factors that should be considered are the income potential, competition, cost, and serviceability associated with potential target markets. For example, the destination or organization should also have some advantage over one or more competitors in serving the target market.

Positioning.   Next, the positioning of the destination or organization vis-a-vis each selected target market should be developed. Earlier in this chapter, it was mentioned that this should involve answering the following questions:

1. Do we have a position in our potential visitors' minds?

2. If so, what is that position (or image)?

3. Do we need to create, change, or reinforce our positioning (image)?

4. How should we use objective and/or subjective positioning to establish our desired positioning?

5. Which positioning approach or approaches should we use?

Marketing objectives.   The analysis of external environmental factors, development objectives, services and products, competition, and target markets should result in the production of a set of key strengths, weaknesses, opportunities, and threats or problems. This information provides the basis for setting marketing objectives for upcoming periods. The environmental scan and situation analysis address the question: Where are we now? In setting marketing objectives, the question becomes: Where would we like to be?

Marketing objectives should meet four tests. First, they must be capable of being measured. Second, they must address a specific target market or markets? Third, they must be stated in terms of a desired result or outcome that can be related directly to either the environmental scan, situation analysis, or development objectives. Finally, a specific deadline for achievement must be stated. Accountability for actual results should be measured against the degree to which objectives have been achieved.

Marketing mix.   Once the positioning and marketing objectives have been developed for each selected target market, marketing mixes can be designed. Traditional approaches to marketing suggest that a *marketing mix* is comprised of four components—product, price, promotion, and place or distribution. Often these are called *the four P's of marketing*. Various authors in the field of tourism have suggested that there are additional components to the marketing mix in our industry. Because of the uniqueness of tourism marketing, it has been recommended that packaging, programming, people, and partnership be considered as four additional marketing mix components.[18] The traditional *four P's* then expands to eight P's (product, price, promotion, place, packaging, programming, people, and partnership). Whatever components are included, it is important that they be carefully selected to correspond with the particular needs and other specific characteristics of the people in the selected target market.

Product.   It has already been noted that a vacation consists of a number of different services and some products—from transportation and lodging to sightseeing and souvenirs. These services and products are usually offered by a variety of tourism organizations. Each provider organization is dependent on the others to offer an attractive and satisfying overall vacation experience. The marketing orientation philosophy suggests that services and products be carefully designed to match the needs and wants of customers. In addition, the market segmentation concept is

---

[18]Alastair M. Morrison, pp. 37–38.

based on the assumption that a tourism organization cannot possibly provide services and products that will satisfy everyone. An organization must select a target market or markets and provide a variety of services and products to satisfy the targeted customers' needs. Striking the right balance between providing narrow customized services to appeal to one particular target market, while at the same time having enough variety to be attractive to more than one target market, is a difficult decision for tourism marketing managers. The relatively fixed supply of tourism facilities and services, coupled with seasonal fluctuations in demand levels and customer types, makes this task more problematic in tourism.

Crissy has suggested several important criteria that should be met when deciding to provide a service or product.[19] First, there should be a relatively heavy demand for the service or product from at least one important market segment, with the possibility of additional business from other segments of the market. It may be that the product can expect to break even on the basis of business from the major market segment and produce profit from business from the rest of the market. There may, of course, be a period of time before sales for a new attraction or service reach the break-even point.

Second, new products and services should fit in with the positioning or image of the tourism destination area or organization. It should also complement existing offerings. This does not mean that a destination area must appeal only to one segment of the market and that all its services and products must meet the needs of that market segment. A great deal obviously depends upon the size of the destination area. One part of a destination area may appeal to the younger singles and couples, while another part may be more attractive to senior citizens. It is important, however, that each individual part of the destination area develop the services, products, and positioning to fit one or more selected target markets.

Third, new services and products must be in accordance with the available supply of manpower, capital, management expertise, and natural resources. Although new services and products should be based on an identified competitive advantage, they may not be feasible due to a lack of the right quality of human or financial resources. For example, a destination area may have magnificent mountain terrain suitable for skiing but may lack management knowledge in ski-area operations. Experienced management may have to be hired on a permanent or temporary basis before a ski area can be proposed. It is also possible in tourism that certain new services or products may be undesirable for sociocultural or environmental reasons.

Finally, it is necessary that any new services or products contribute to the profit and/or growth of the entire tourism destination or organization. In some cases the new offering may bring in no profit itself, but its provision may contribute to growth. The hotel pool, for example, may cost the operation money while bringing in no direct revenue. However, its availability may bring in additional room business. On the other hand, if the pool is eliminated, this may cause guests to use another

---

[19]W. J. E. Crissy, Robert J. Boewadt, and Dante M. Laudadio, Marketing of Hospitality Services: Food, Lodging, Travel (E. Lansing, MI, Educational Institute of the American Hotel and Motel Association, 1975), pp. 69–70.

hotel or resort. Similarly, a destination may introduce its own airline, not as a revenue-producing venture but as part of a strategy to attract more visitors.

Price.   Many factors influence pricing policy. The price charged in any situation is unique to that situation and is affected by the combination of the factors to be discussed. Nevertheless, some guidelines can be suggested to assist in the pricing decision.

Price is an important part of the marketing mix

In pure economic terms, price is a result of supply and demand. When supply exceeds demand, price will tend to decrease. The reverse is true also. Of greater importance is the extent to which demand changes (as measured by the amount purchased) as price changes—the elasticity of demand. A 5 percent reduction in price may result in a corresponding 10 percent increase in the number of buyers and a subsequent increase in total sales revenue. Demand in this case is elastic. Generally, products aimed at the luxury end of the customer scale are less susceptible to changes in price and, consequently, tend to be price inelastic. For destinations or properties that are open only part of the year, supply is limited and prices will have to be correspondingly higher (everything else being equal) than destinations open year round. Because demand is not often uniform throughout the year, it is common to charge higher prices during the peak season and lower prices when demand slackens.

The expected length of the product life cycle and the destination or organization's position on it also affect pricing decisions. A "fad" item with an expected short life cycle will have to charge high prices to recoup the investment in a relatively short period of time. A product that expects a longer life can be priced lower.

The price charged is influenced by competition. If a destination's facilities and services are very similar to competitors', its prices must be similar to theirs. The extent to which the destination area or other tourism service is unique influences whether it can charge more than the competition. Related to the influence of competition is the management policy regarding *market share.* If the decision is made to increase market share, prices will probably be lower than if we decide to "skim" a small number of tourists from several market segments.

Pricing policy is also influenced by the needs of the selected target market or markets. If a tourism destination or organization is seen as serving the needs and wants of the market and if those needs and wants are perceived as being important to the members of the market segment, those members will be willing to pay a higher price. The price charged must also be perceived by the market as less than or at least equal to the value received. In certain situations the influence of the market seems to go against economic principles. With certain luxury items, demand may increase as price increases. This phenomenon reflects a certain amount of snobbishness on the part of the market. The feeling may be that the higher the price the greater the perceived value and the greater the demand. But the actual value in the minds of the buyers must still equal or exceed the price paid.

The effect of each of these variables cannot be determined exactly in quantitative terms, and the outcome of their interaction is even more difficult to determine. However, the general guidelines stated above can give guidance on pricing decisions for particular tourism destinations or organizations.

Promotion.   The third marketing-mix component is given detailed coverage in Chapter 15. Promotion is the most visible part of the marketing mix, apart from the services or products themselves. Many people fall into the trap of confusing marketing and promotion, thinking of them as being one and the same thing. As should be obvious by now, there is much more to marketing than just promotion. The *promotional mix* is one component of the marketing mix that consists of several elements including advertising, sales promotion, merchandising, personal selling and sales, and public relations and publicity. All the promotional mix elements involve some means of communicating with potential customers.

Place and distribution.   Tourism distribution is unique. In the absence of a physical distribution system, our industry has developed a unique set of distribution channels and travel intermediaries. These intermediaries influence customers' choices of tourism destinations and organizations and require separate attention by the tourism marketer. The choice of specific channels of distribution and intermediaries is influenced by several factors, including the target market, type of tourism service or destination, and the location of the services relative to the customers' residences. Chapter 16 provides detailed information on tourism distribution and individual categories of travel intermediaries.

Packaging and promotion.   Packaging and programming are two additional marketing-mix components that are unique to the tourism industry. They are especially significant because they can be used to help our industry cope with the problems of the immediate perishability of services and the difficulties of matching demand volumes with supply capacities. Another important feature of packaging and programming is that they provide a means of matching services and products with the needs of specific target markets. For example, the tourism industries now offer a multitude of packages for special-interest groups ranging from anthropologists to zoologists.

Packaging is also significant because it brings together many of the elements of the destination mix and combines the services and products of several tourism organizations. The package is more convenient for the customer, since it includes several services and products at an all-inclusive price. Other advantages of packages and programs are listed in Table 14.3. Programming refers to the offering of special activities, events, or other types of programs to increase customer spending or to give added appeal to a package or other tourism service. Many vacation packages include some form of programming, such as escorted ground tours, sports instruction, entertainment events, and so on.

TABLE 14.3 Reasons for the popularity of vacation/holiday packages

a. Customer-related reasons

1. Greater convenience
2. Greater economy
3. Ability to budget for trips
4. Implicit assurance of consistent quality
5. Satisfaction of specialized interests
6. Added dimension to traveling

b. Participant-related reasons

1. Increased business in off-peak periods
2. Enhanced appeal to specific target markets
3. Attraction of new target markets
4. Easier business forecasting and improved efficiency
5. Use of complementary facilities, attractions, and events
6. Flexibility to capitalize on new market trends
7. Stimulation of repeat and more frequent usage
8. Increased per capita spending and lengths of stay
9. Public relations and publicity value of unique packages
10. Increased customer satisfaction

Adapted from *Hospitality and Travel Marketing,* Alastair M. Morrison, Delmar Publishers, 1989, pp. 247–256.

People.   Tourism is a people business! No amount or quality of facilities can make up for poor service. A tourism marketer must ensure that staff are adequately trained in their specific function, and that industry employees and local residents have hospitable attitudes towards tourists.

Partnership-cooperative marketing.   Partnership means cooperative marketing programs involving two or more tourism destinations and/or individual organizations. In an increasingly competitive tourism industry, the pooling of resources with other organizations may provide the added edge necessary for success. Packaging, when it involves two or more organizations, represents one important application of the partnership concept. Cooperative advertising is a second application. For example, the Caribbean Islands of St. Thomas, St. Croix, St. Martin., St. Barthélémy Antigua, Aruba, Curacao, and the Bahamas have joined forces to advertise the "Little Switzerland" concept. This joint advertising campaign promotes the availability of duty-free jewelry, watches, crystal, and perfume in each of these island destinations.

SUMMARY

The marketing of services is different from the marketing of products and, therefore, requires slightly different approaches. Since tourism is a service business and since tourism is itself unique, marketing programs and activities must be formulated accordingly. Marketing in the tourism industries and in most other economic areas has evolved through a series of stages or "eras." The current era of marketing—societal marketing—seems most appropriate for destination tourism marketing, since it goes beyond just pure economic considerations.

Tourism marketing should follow a systematic procedure—the marketing planning process—and it is essential that careful attention be given to market segmentation. It is also important when deciding on marketing programs to consider external forces as well as those factors which the organization can itself control. These controllable factors in tourism consist of product or service, price, place and distribution, promotion, packaging, programming, people, and partnership. Each tourism organization should seek to establish a unique blend or mix of these factors.

REFERENCES

BIGGADIKE. E. RALPH, "The Contribution of Marketing to Strategic Management," Academy of Management Review, vol. 6, no. 4, 1981, pp. 621–32.

DHALIA, NARIMAN K., and SONIA YUSPEH, "Forget the Product Life Cycle Concept," Harvard Business Review, January-February 1976, p. 104.

HOWARD, DENNIS R., and JOHN L. CROMPTON, *Financing, Managing and Marketing Recreation and Park Resources,* (Dubuque, IA, William C. Brown, 1980), ch. 1, p. 314.

MAHONEY, EDWARD MICHAEL, "Two Alternative Approaches to Segmenting Michigan's Downhill Ski Market" (Ph.D. dissertation, Michigan State University, 1979), Appendix A.

PLOG, STANLEY, "Why Destination Areas Rise and Fall in Popularity," Cornell Hotel and Restaurant Administration Quarterly, vol. 12, no. 1, November 1973, pp. 13–16.

REIME, MATT, and CAMERON, HAWKINS. "Planning and Developing Hospitality Facilities That Increase Tourism Demand," in Tourism Marketing and Management Issues, eds. Hawkins, Shafer, and Rovelstad (George Washington University, 1980), pp. 239–48.

SCHMOLL, G. A., "The Planning of Marketing Campaigns in Tourism," in Managerial

Aspects of Tourism: Products, Markets and Plans (Proceedings of an International Seminar, ed. Salah Wahab, Alexandria, Egypt, 1975), pp. 262–65.

SCHMOLL, G. A., *Tourism Promotion* (London, Tourism International Press), pp. 19–21.

STYNES, DANIEL J., "Market Segmentation in Recreation and Tourism" (Michigan State University Agricultural Experiment Station Project NE-137, unpublished paper), p. 11.

WAHAB, SALAH, L. J. CRAMPON, and L. M. ROTHFIELD, *Tourism Marketing* (London, Tourism International Press, 1976), pp. 22–23.

15

TOURISM'S PROMOTIONAL MIX:

Communicating with the Market

"Another thing about Liechtenstein—their road maps are really easy to fold."

Travel agent promoting European travel, quoted in a
cartoon in Travelling Light: Punch Goes Abroad.

The process of promotion is essentially the process of communication—communication between seller and buyer. This chapter discusses the promotional-mix concept. A link is established between the goals of promotion and the customer's buying process stages described in Chapter 4. Appropriate types of promotion are suggested for each of the traveler's buying process stages.

The process of communication is described in detail. Objectives must be established and a target audience identified. Once a budget sufficient to reach the objectives has been drawn up, the content and form of the message (message strategy) can be established. The actual promotional mix is determined at this stage and the appropriate media are selected. At each step of the process, it is essential to have controls to ensure that the promotional campaign remains on track and achieves its ultimate objectives.

Promotional efforts at the federal and state levels in the U.S. are described in some detail to give the reader a picture of what is actually being done to promote tourism destinations.

LEARNING OBJECTIVES

Having read this chapter, you should be able to:

1. Identify and describe which promotional methods are most effective during the various stages of the traveler's buying process.
2. Distinguish between informative promotion, persuasive promotion, and reminder messages, and identify when the use of these techniques is most appropriate.
3. Describe the eight main elements in the communication process.
4. List and describe the five elements of the promotional mix.
5. Identify and explain the procedures involved in selecting and planning media advertising.
6. Describe the typical range of promotional activities of National Tourist Offices (NTOs).
7. Describe the programs operated by the U.S. Travel and Tourism Administration.
8. Compare and contrast the funding and roles of the U.S. Travel and Tourism Administration and Tourism Canada.
9. Describe the programs operated by State Tourism Offices (STOs) in the United States.

PROMOTION IS COMMUNICATION

Goals of Promotion

Developing the promotional mix is essentially an exercise in communication. As suppliers of tourism services or as intermediaries in the distribution channel, our task is to communicate a message to the potential tourist. Through *explicit communication*, language is used in an attempt to promote a common understanding between the sender and the receiver of a message. Only when this common understanding exists is there communication. Communication may also be *implicit* through nonverbal means, such as gestures and facial expressions. For communication to take place, a common understanding must be present or must be developed between the message sender and the message receiver.

The end goal of promotion is *behavior modification*. The task is to initiate a purchase where none has been made before, initiate a change in purchase behavior by having the tourist "buy" a different destination, package, or service, or reinforce existing behavior by having the tourist continue to purchase the services being promoted. This end result is accomplished through messages that seek to inform, persuade, or remind the receiving public. *Informative promotion* is more important during the early stages of the product life cycle when, for example, a new destination is entering the marketplace. Little is known about the destination, and potential visitors must have sufficient knowledge of it before they can be expected to buy. *Persuasive pro-*

motion seeks to get a tourist to buy. This becomes the primary objective of promotion when the growth stage of the life cycle is entered. During the maturity stage of the product life cycle, reminder promotion becomes important. People have already used the services or products at least once. *Reminder promotions* serve to jog the memory and keep the services in the public's mind.

Promotion and the Traveler's Buying Process

The relationship between the goals of promotion and the buying process of the traveler is discussed in Chapter 4. This is further explained in Figure 15.1. To meet the goal of behavior modification, the three types of promotion are used. Informative promotion is important at the attention and comprehension stages of the buying process. Persuasive promotion seeks to change attitudes, to develop intentions to buy, and then to initiate the purchase. Reminder promotions come into play after a purchase has been made. They attempt to stimulate repeat visits or purchases.

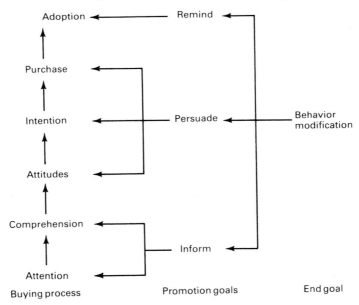

Figure 15.1   Goals of promotion and the traveler's buying process

The Communication Process

The communication process is illustrated in Figure 15.2. The sender (tourism marketer) sets marketing objectives for the target market or markets to be reached. Once a budget is established, the content and form of the message are determined and the appropriate promotional mix and medium are selected and planned. The responses from the receivers (potential customers) are then compared with the sender's objectives to determine the overall effectiveness of the promotional campaign. For example, many state

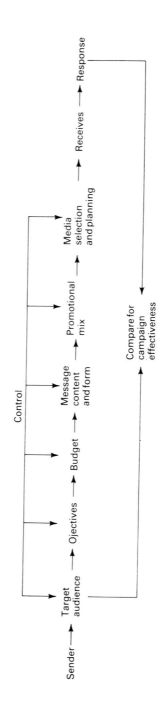

Figure 15.2 Tourism's communication process

government agencies in the U.S. measure advertising response by keeping a tally of the telephone and mail inquiries received following the placement of advertisements. Some agencies go even further and determine, through conversion studies, how many inquirers actually visit the state after being sent the requested information.

Useful as it may be, this form of analysis only goes part of the way in determining promotional effectiveness. If the response does not match the objectives, much time and money will have been wasted. In addition, this final comparison will not indicate where the problem lies; it shows the effects rather than the cause of the problem. Were the objectives too ambitious? Was the message appropriate but for the wrong target audience? Were the right media used to project a message that communicated the wrong information or image? To find out where the problem lies and to find out quickly enough so that a minimum of time and money is wasted, it is necessary to control the communications process at each step of the way. The steps in this process will be explored in fuller detail.

IMPLEMENTATION OF A PROMOTIONAL PROGRAM

Selecting the Target Audience. The process of target market selection was covered in detail in Chapter 14. This process should include an analysis of published market data and primary research results from such things as surveys or focus groups. Any target market selected must be accessible by means of one or more promotional mix elements or through a specific type of media. Accessing a target market in this way means that we have to obtain certain basic information on their demographics (for example, age, income, educational level, household type and size) and their place of residence or business. Through market segmentation analysis, the target audience may be further qualified using one or more of five other segmentation bases: psychographics-lifestyle, purpose of trip, product-related, behavioral, or channel of distribution. The target audience must include people with similar characteristics who, through marketing research and/or past experience, have been shown to be the best prospects for purchasing what is being promoted. This first element of the tourism communication process can be controlled by checking to ensure that a thorough market segmentation analysis has been completed.

Developing promotional objectives. Next, the objectives of a promotional campaign should be established. To be effective, objectives must be target-market specific, be stated in terms of a desired result or outcome, be realistically attainable, and have a deadline for achievement.

When setting promotional objectives, it is important to consider the targeted traveler's buying process stage(s), as well as the destination or service's product life-cycle stage. In order to determine this, we must establish the current level of knowledge of our destination or tourism services. If people in the target market are at the intention stage in the buying process, then informative messages will be a poor use of time and money. Similarly, the promotion of a new package will not be effective if it is assumed that the intention to buy already exists. By conducting an awareness study, either through a survey or focus groups, the buying process stage of the targeted customers can be determined. At the attention (or awareness) stage, the objective may be to expose the message to a specified number of members of the target market within a specific time period. At the intention stage, the objective may be oriented toward increasing purchases. Controlling this second element in the tourism communication process, therefore, involves two steps: (1) ensuring through research that the buying process stage of the target audience has been correctly identified, and (2) ensuring that promotional objectives are target-market specific, measurable, results oriented, time specific, and reasonably attainable.

Establishing the promotional budget.   Unfortunately, there is no widely-accepted or scientific method for setting promotional budgets in tourism. However, some general guidelines can be followed. It is important that objectives be developed before a budget is constructed. Some refer to this as *bottom-up* budgeting or the objective-and-task approach. Only by knowing what is to be achieved can an accurate estimate be made of how much it may cost. All too often a sum of money is obtained, then objectives are set based upon how much one has to spend. This is called *top-down* budgeting or the affordable approach. Obviously, tourism destinations and organizations do not have unlimited funds for marketing and many operate on very limited overall budgets. It must be recognized, however, that setting objectives after the budget is set will probably mean that the objectives will not be achieved.

The development of marketing and promotional budgets should be based on a combination of factors. They should be established in accordance with previously set objectives while taking into account the ability of the destination or organization to support that kind of effort financially. The amount being spent by competitors must also be taken into account. All budgets must be flexible enough to allow for changes due to changing market conditions or competitive actions.

According to Schmoll, the following promotion budgets as a percentage of net sales are typical:[1]

Tour operator	= 10 to 20 percent
Travel agency	= 5 percent
Hotel	= 2.5 to 5 percent
Airline	= 3 to 7 percent
National tourist office	= 50 percent
Total	= 75 percent of total operating budget

Deciding on message content.   Through such things as nondirective interviews, the motives of the target audience can be measured in an attempt to determine what to say. Alternative message concepts can be formulated and shown to a sample of the target audience. Based on its ratings of the various themes, the most effective message concept can be chosen. The control objective at this stage is to develop the appeal that is best suited for the target audience.

---

[1]G.A. Schmoll, *Tourism Promotion* (London, Tourism International Press, 1977), p. 108.

Deciding on message form.   After determining what to say, how to say it is explored. The objective is to develop messages that are understandable, distinctive, and believable. This can be accomplished in a number of ways. Various messages can be shown to sample members of the target audience, and their reactions to the various messages can be compared. Surveys of the target market can be taken after exposure to the message to determine what has been remembered as a test of the message's memorability.

Selecting promotional mix elements.   Many promotional tools exist to convey the message to the audience. The major parts of the promotional mix are:[2]

Advertising. Any paid form of nonpersonal presentation and ideas, goods, or services by an identified sponsor.

Personal selling. Oral conversations, either by telephone or face-to-face, between sales persons and prospective customers.

Sales promotion. Approaches other than personal selling, advertising, and public relations and publicity where customers are given a short-term inducement to make an immediate purchase.

An example of sales promotion

[2]Alastair M. Morrison, *Hospitality and Travel Marketing* (Albany, New York, Delmar Publishers, 1989) pp. 310–318.

Merchandising. Materials used "in-house" to stimulate sales, including brochures on display, signs, posters, displays, tent cards, and other point-of-sale promotional items.

Public relations and publicity. All the activities that a tourism organization engages in to maintain or improve its relationship with other organizations and individuals. Publicity is one public relations technique that involves nonpaid communication of information about an organization's services.

The emphasis on the many parts of the promotional mix will vary with the characteristics of the market, the type of product, and the amount of funds available. The more expensive and complicated the product being sold, the greater the need for some form of personal selling. Although only an advertisement may induce a couple to spend a weekend at a resort, an individual planning a convention for fifty people or a couple thinking of a cruise will tend to require some form of personal selling to solidify the purchase. Within tourism there are actually two markets. Promotional efforts must be directed to the potential tourist as well as to the travel trade intermediaries, including the media. The tools used will be dependent, in part, upon the audience. Sales workshops are very important to the travel trade; advertising is important to the potential tourist. Obviously, the mix is constrained by the amount of money available. A four-color advertisement in a national magazine may cost half of the annual salary of a sales representative. Schmoll has distinguished between the many targets as follows:[3]

To the limited extent that it is possible to generalize about promotional activities, the following conclusions can be made:[4]

- Advertising, especially in newspapers and magazines, accounts for more than half of all promotion expenditures.
- Consumer literature is the basis of sales support; most is published by tour operators.
- Most budgets combine all elements of the promotion mix.
- The percentages allocated to the many elements are relatively stable from year to year.

Selecting promotional media.   In this part of the process the objective is to identify the appropriate media to get the message across to the audience. The media used in the travel and tourism industries are newspapers, magazines, television, radio, and outdoor billboards. Airlines spend more than twice the amount any other tourism and travel supplier spends on advertising. Almost half of their advertising dollars is spent on newspaper advertising; about one-quarter is spent on television. Radio is the next most favored medium, followed by magazines, with outdoor publications receiving a very small percentage of the total. Hotels, motels, and resorts account for about one-fifth of total industry advertising outlay, approximately the same as

[3]G. A. Schmoll, *Tourism Promotion,* p. 121.
[4]G. A. Schmoll, *Tourism Promotion,* p. 125.

PROMOTIONAL ACTIVITIES AND COMMUNICATIONS CHANNELS	
Target: Potential customers	Target: Travel trade
General media advertising (press, television, radio, cinema) Outdoor advertising (posters) Direct mail distribution of catalogs, etc. Showing of travel films Special offers (rebates, etc.) Joint promotion with trade Point-of-sale advertising Participation in travel exhibitions and travel fairs Enquiry and information service	Trade press advertising Newsletters and releases Distribution of publicity materials (catalogs, brochures, audiovisual shows) Information and servicing manuals Schedules and price lists Seminars, workshops for sales staff Familiarization visits Sales contests and premiums
Target: Visitors/actual customers	Target: General and trade media
Welcoming and reception service Local travel information service Visitor surveys Visitor assistance	Press conferences, press releases Editorial material Familiarization visits

is spent by travel services such as travelers' checks companies. Other segments of the industry each account for less than 5 percent of the total media expenditures.

The crucial part of media selection is choosing those which will be seen, read, or heard by the intended audience. Television and radio stations and newspaper and magazine offices will often have market research available on the characteristics of their viewers, listeners, and readers. Also, there are general criteria against which the other media can be compared to determine the most appropriate vehicle for the message. The following criteria are very useful:

Cost per contact

Total Cost

Market selectivity

Geographic selectivity

Source credibility

Visual quality

Noise level

Life span

Pass-along rate

Timing flexibility

Although the cost per contact (cost of reaching one member of the audience) is low for television, the total cost is very high. To a moderate extent, it is possible to select the market we desire by a careful selection of the shows in which we choose to advertise. To a greater extent, it is possible to be geographically selective. Television suffers from a rather low level of credibility or trust among consumers. The visual quality, however, is very high. Noise level refers to the amount of stimuli competing for the viewer's attention. Because of the tendency to watch television with other prople, the noise level tends to be higher than average. Also, because advertising schedules often have to be decided far in advance, the timing flexibility for television is below average.

Radio offes a medium that is low in total cost and in cost per contact. Like television, radio is selective for broad market groups and has a high geographic selectivity. The credibility and noise level are similar to that of television. However, the timing flexibility is far greater.

Newspapers also offer a low total cost and cost per contact. Market selectivity is low, and geographic selectivity is average. It is possible to zero-in on particular cities and towns, for example. The trust factor appears to be low, and the visual quality is less than average. To compensate for a high noise level, low life span, and pass-along rate, newspapers offer a great deal of flexibility in the timing of advertisements.

Magazines have a much higher cost per contact and total cost than do newspapers. Because of the specialized nature of magazines, the market selectivity is above average; regional editions offer some geographic selectivity. The visual quality is much higher than newspapers, and the noise level is lower. Both the life span and pass-along rate are above average, but the timing flexibility is low.

Although the total cost of a direct mail campaign tends to be rather high, the cost per contact varies widely depending upon the quality of the mailing list. Both market selectivity and geographic selectivity are the highest of all media. Source credibility seems to be below average, as is the life span of a direct mail piece. The visual quality can be very high, but the noise level is low. This can make for a high degree of impact. Timing flexibility, however, is rather low due to the need for production lead times.

Although newspapers will continue to dominate as the most-used advertising medium for travel and tourism, their efficiency has been eroding. The travel sections of newspapers tend to be read only after the decision to travel has been made. Because of this, those who do read these sections are highly motivated readers. In order to expand the travel market, the use of other media such as radio and television may be appropriate.

Measuring and evaluating receiver response.   The response to a communication is based upon the way the message is perceived by a receiver (see Chapter 2). It has already been noted that one stimulus can be perceived differently by different people. The problem should be minimized if, in fact, the campaign is controlled and its effectiveness tested at each stage of the way. This, however, appears to be something that is sorely lacking. Many reports indicate that less than half of the organizations, from travel agents to national tourist offices, that have been surveyed measure the effectiveness of their promotional campaigns.

USES OF PROMOTION BY NATIONAL TOURIST OFFICES

A national tourist office (NTO) is the organization officially responsible for the development and marketing of tourism for a country. When the organization is such that the development and marketing functions are split, the body responsible for marketing is usually designated the NTO. The range and importance of the many promotional activities can be seen in Table 15.1. Approximately 14 percent of the total budget is spent on media advertising, with an additional 10 percent being spent on sales promotion and personal selling directed toward the trade. A major amount of the budget goes toward the establishment of offices overseas. Less than 10 percent of the budget is spent on public relations and head office research and administration. Almost a quarter of the budget is spent on producing sales support literature and audiovisuals. The promotional activities of an NTO can be divided into those aimed at the travel trade and those aimed at the consumer.

TABLE 15.1.　TYPICAL BUDGET OF A NATIONAL TOURIST OFFICE

Direct Market Costs		
Media advertising	14%	
Trade seminars and promotions	5	
Regional promotional cooperation	5	24%
Foreign representation:		
Overseas offices	40	
Overseas exhibitions	2	
Subtotal		42
Head Office Costs on Supporting Promotion		
Research and administration	9	
Promotional literature	10	
Publications	4	
Photographs and slides	1	
Films	3	
Public relations	7	
Subtotal		34%
Total		100%

SOURCE:　Salah Wahab, L. J. Crampon, and L. M. Rothfield, *Tourism Marketing* (London, Tourism International Press, 1976), p. 200.

Travel trade promotions.　In order to inform the travel trade about their countries and familiarize it with the tourist product(s) of their area, NTOs organize educational tours for selected tour wholesalers and retail travel agents, who can then sell the countries as tourist destinations more easily. During these tours, the foreign tour wholesalers and retail travel agents inspect tourist facilities, visit tourism attractions, and make contacts with the local travel trade, who may act as their partners in channeling tourist traffic to the country. Such tours may be conducted in small groups, especially for retail travel agents, or individually, especially for wholesalers. Commonly known as familiarization tours or trips, these are also often organized for travel writers.

Educational workshops are normally organized and staged in the tourist-generating markets. They bring together all the main components of the tourism industries, such as hotels, travel agents, airlines, and providers of tourist services, from both the generating and the destination country. The main objectives of these workshops are to promote the tourist product mix of the destination country to the travel trade and other principals of the generating country and to provide a suitable opportunity for the travel principals of the destination and generating countries to establish working relationships.

Like educational tours and tourist workshops, sales seminars are organized by an NTO to familiarize the travel trade with its destination's facilities and services and the latest developments in its tourism industry. They seek to motivate travel trade intermediaries to increase sales of tours and to encourage travel to the destination.

Sales calls are made by NTO staff to retail travel agents and tour wholesalers. The aim of these calls is to assist retail travel agents and wholesalers in selling the country in question by providing them with information, advice, and promotional material.

To keep the travel trade well-stocked with promotional material on the country, an NTO carries out regular direct mailings of its brochures and other literature. The travel trade is, thus, itself in a better position to service inquiries from its clients more adequately and to actually promote and sell the country.

A national tourist office keeps the travel trade well-stocked on travel literature

Many NTOs also establish a permanent channel of communication with the travel trade through the regular issue and distribution of newsletters or bulletins. Through this channel, the NTO may inform the travel trade about all relevant developments at its destination's facilities and services product and other interesting facets of its tourism industry. At the same time, these newsletters or bulletins attempt to promote travel sales to the destination.

In order to increase sales, some NTOs provide incentives or bonuses, usually in the form of free vacations or gifts. These incentives may or may not be linked with so-called retail travel agents' competitions. Incentives and bonuses are usually offered in cooperation with the main tourism principals of the country, that is, hotel and airline companies.

Promotional evenings may be organized exclusively for members of the travel trade and are basically goodwill exercises. They are usually staged in hotels or similar establishments and combine food, drink, and entertainment, often imported from the NTO's country.

Consumer promotions.   Servicing of inquiries from the public can either be done in writing, by telephone, or in person. Brochures and other promotional material are used for servicing the general public's inquiries, but not all inquiries originate from potential or prospective vacationers. A small proportion of inquiries received by an NTO originate from returning tourists and concern the widest possible range of subjects, including complaints and praise. Thus, an NTO abroad has to carry out a kind of *customer relations* or *after-sales service* function.

NTOs abroad offer different kinds of incentives to consumers. These range from free vacations to gas coupons given as prizes and special discounts or concessions for children or family groups.

Participation in consumer travel shows and exhibitions is done with suitably decorated exhibit booths that present the tourist attractions of the country. Here, an NTO aims at contacting large numbers of potential tourists to make them aware of the tourism attractions of its country and to persuade them to travel there. In so doing, the NTO distributes relatively large quantities of brochures and other literature to interested people.

Window display campaigns are specially designed and exhibited in retail travel agencies and in certain other retail outlets (for example, airline sales offices). They provide convenient promotional exposure to the destination's attractions, facilities, and services at the point of sale. This type of promotion is often called merchandising.

Many kinds of promotional events may be organized and staged by an NTO abroad. They aim to convert potential consumer demand into real consumer demand, to create goodwill toward the destination, and to improve its image. Such events are often as much public relations exercises as they are sales promotional activities. Some of the most common events of this kind are promotional evenings, exhibitions of arts and handicrafts, and "national" weeks that are held in department stores and hotels.

Overseas offices.[5]   As was seen earlier, an NTO typically spends approximately 40 percent of its budget for overseas representation. There are several hundred NTOs abroad. Can or should the expenditure be justified? An overseas marketing

[5] "The Role and Functions of a National Tourist Office Abroad," International Tourism Quarterly, no. 3, 1976, pp. 39–58. This section is an abbreviated form of this excellent article.

campaign can certainly be administered from the head office of the destination. The results are unlikely to be effective, however. The effort will probably be more expensive because of the need to hire outside specialists for the marketing effort. Also, the costs of distribution are higher. The effectiveness of a home-based campaign are adversely affected by difficulties in establishing suitable communications channels and in getting enough quality feedback to monitor the campaign.

In an attempt to reduce the costs of marketing, some countries use their embassies or consulates to house those involved in the marketing effort. By and large, this strategy has not worked. The functions of both the political and marketing groups seem to be too dissimilar. The necessary expertise for tourism marketing is lacking in the embassy group, and the necessary contacts in the travel-trade press are different for both the marketing and political groups. It also appears that the travel-trade press in an overseas market prefers to deal with a professionally staffed marketing office. A final point is that embassies, located in a nation's capital, may not necessarily be optimally located for maximizing potential tourist contact. Such would be the case in Canada (Ottawa), Australia (Canberra) and the United States (Washington). Tourist offices would be better placed in larger population centers.

The role of an NTO abroad has changed in many ways in recent decades. In the past, a major function of NTOs was to distribute literature to potential tourists. The increase in potential tourist destinations has meant an increase in NTOs promoting these destinations. This increase in competition has meant that NTOs have been forced to adopt a more professional marketing approach rather than being a relatively passive distributor of information.

Another factor that has caused NTOs to change has been the growth of package and inclusive tours. As tour operators have grown in size and power and vertically integrated distribution systems have been established, tourism destinations have grown increasingly dependent on organized flows of groups of tourists. This growing dependence on tour operators and retail travel agents has caused NTOs to shift their marketing emphasis from appealing to the independent and individual traveler to promoting to and in cooperation with the travel trade. Finally, as both travel trade intermediaries and consumers have become more sophisticated and experienced, NTOs have been forced to adopt a much more professional approach to tourism marketing. Basically, the objectives of an NTO abroad can be identified as follows:

- To increase the availability of the tourist product(s) of the destination by increasing the number of new tour programs and packaged vacations and the capacity of existing ones, or to maintain at targeted levels the number and capacity of such programs.
- To secure maximum promotional exposure for the product-service mix of the destination.
- To promote a favorable image of the country as a tourism destination and to maintain or enhance this image.
- To stimulate and increase demand for the tourist services and products of the destination.

- To familiarize travel-trade distribution channels with the destination's services and products and stimulate them to increase sales.
- To increase and make more effective the supply of information on the tourism services and products of the destination.

Although advertising is very important in achieving these objectives, it is also very costly. Because few, if any, NTOs have enough funds to carry out the kind of advertising campaign necessary to do the job, public relations and publicity have become the most important and cost-effective promotional techniques. Whether aimed at travel-trade intermediaries or the ultimate consumer, effective use must be made of the media. Establishing good relationships with the media or press is a crucial step toward successfully reaching the ultimate objectives of any public relations campaign.

A large amount of literature is produced to support an NTO's marketing efforts. This literature (or collateral) tends to be either general (brief and comprehensive pieces on the destination with information of interest to all potential visitors) or specialized (detailed information on a particular area or theme of interest to fewer travelers). A general piece may ask potential visitors to write for more information on more specialized topics. Because of the large quantity of information requested, and the rising costs of paper, printing, and postage, NTOs have more recently tended to concentrate on producing smaller, standardized brochures or folders, often referred to as *lure* pieces. Others try to subsidize design and printing costs by including advertising, cooperating with the private sector in sharing costs, or charging the consumer for the promotional literature.

NTOs tend to locate their overseas offices where the largest potential markets are thought to exist. The number of offices in a given country depends upon how important the market is to the destination and how large and decentralized the country is. It is doubtful that the United States could be covered by one office, for example. Most NTOs targeting the U.S. have at least two offices—one on the east and one on the west coasts. NTOs traditionally have relied upon street-level offices in prestigious locations. The rationale has been that such locations expose the destination to as many people as possible. This assumption has been questioned with the change in emphasis from the consumer to travel trade intermediaries and due to the rising cost of renting prime retail office locations. Because of this, many NTOs have moved to less expensive locations in the central business district. The preferred location also depends upon the structure of the distribution system. In Germany, where tourists are mainly independent travelers, there is a greater need for consumer access than in the United States, where much travel is done in organized tours. In the latter case, contact with travel-trade intermediaries is more important.

It is better to staff an NTO with its own citizens. This strategy allows destinations to train their staff overseas and, upon transfer, to utilize their firsthand knowledge. It also appears that travel-trade intermediaries prefer dealing with citizens of the country that is being marketed. In reality, most offices are managed by citizens of the destination, assisted by a locally recruited staff.

It is difficult, if not impossible, to determine the effectiveness of an NTO abroad. The number of arrivals from a particular country cannot be directly attributed to the efforts of an NTO. The marketing cost per arrival or per dollar of gross earnings is equally unsatisfactory due to the difficulty of determining the effect of the NTO in achieving the end result. The marketing cost per inquiry can be determined. This figure has to be determined separately for consumer, trade, and media groups, for a contact from each carries different weight. However, the real effectiveness measure is the conversion rate of these contacts. How many of these inquiries result in more arrivals, and how much did these visitors spend in the country? In reality, this is almost impossible to track. The research available indicates that a relatively small percentage of tourists seek information or assistance from NTOs when making travel decisions and when planning trips. However, this should not be used as a condemnation of NTOs. As noted above, the NTO role has changed to involve less contact with consumers and more with travel trade intermediaries. NTOs have become a key source of information for those who package, reserve, and sell destinations to potential travelers.

U.S. TRAVEL AND TOURISM ADMINISTRATION (USTTA)

USTTA's three principal goals, as outlined in the National Tourism Policy Act, are to stimulate U.S. export earnings, to increase U.S. employment, and to promote economic growth through international trade in tourism. To achieve these goals, USTTA established the following six activities for 1990:[6]

1. Stimulating U.S. export earnings by facilitating public- and private-sector travel industry cooperative promotional campaigns abroad.
2. Encouraging and facilitating entry of medium and small-size American travel companies in the international travel market.
3. Collecting, analyzing, and disseminating accurate and timely data on the economic impact of foreign travel to the United States.
4. Conducting a broad range of educational programs designed to increase foreign market awareness of U.S. travel products and improving the ability of the U.S. travel industry to respond to foreign market demands.
5. Identifying and attacking barriers to international trade in tourism.
6. Coordinating Federal policy affecting international tourism trade through the Travel and Tourism Advisory Board and the Tourism Policy Council.

USTTA budget.   The amount of funding provided to the USTTA has been a constant problem and source of friction vis-a-vis the U.S. tourism industries. Most experts and industry participants believe that the agency has been inadequately funded, reflecting a lack of sufficient political commitment to tourism in the United States. For most of the 1980's, the USTTA's total budget was in the range of $11 to $14

---

[6]United States Travel and Tourism Administration, Budget Estimates, Fiscal Year 1990: Congressional Submission, January 1989.

million. The comparable budget for Tourism Canada was about three times greater than this. Many other smaller nations outspend the United States on tourism marketing, including Austria, Ireland, Hong Kong, Singapore, and the United Kingdom. It is also unusual to find that several State Tourism Offices had budgets greater than the NTO's. These include Hawaii, New York, Illinois, Texas, Pennsylvania, and Michigan.

The USTTA's budget for 1990–91 was around $14.1 million. During 1990, the U.S. Congress passed a bill to extend the $5 immigration inspection fee to include air travelers arriving from Canada, Mexico, and the Caribbean. Part of these additional revenues will be channeled to the USTTA and it is expected that the agency's budget will increase to around $19 million.

Regional Office Operations

The many methods used by the USTTA to stimulate travel can be influenced by such external factors as changes in foreign government travel regulations or fluctuations in economic patterns. Thus, it is important that programs be individually tailored to each particular market and constantly refined and updated. USTTA has nine regional offices in Toronto, Mexico City, London, Paris, Frankfurt, Amsterdam, Milan, Sydney, and Tokyo. These nine countries generate 82% of U.S. foreign tourism arrivals and 71% of the country's foreign tourism earnings.[7] In addition, an office in Miami handles travel development in five South American countries (Argentina, Brazil, Colombia, Ecuador, and Venezuela). According to USTTA, "these offices develop and implement USTTA cooperative trade development and marketing support programs which stimulate international trade in tourism to specific areas of the United States." Within each of their countries, VISIT USA Committees consisting of U.S. and foreign travel industry marketing representatives have been established. The nine regional offices also operate cooperative travel development, technical assistance, and educational programs in sixteen other countries. For the 1990 Fiscal Year, these offices were budgeted to cost $5.8 million, about 40% of USTTA's total expenditures. USTTA also maintains a presence in Hong Kong, Taiwan, and South Korea through a contracted representative in each of these countries.

Promotional Programs

Compared to many other countries including Canada, the USTTA's budget for advertising is extremely limited and did not grow much during the 1980's. Because of these budgetary constraints, USTTA's strategy during the 1980's became one of leveraging greater promotional funds through cooperative programs with the private sector and State Tourism Offices and city-area convention and visitors bureaus. In Fiscal 1990, USSTA budgeted $2.044 million for cooperative programs and $1.593 million for cooperative support programs.

---

[7]Zafar U. Ahmed and Franklin B. Krohn, "Reversing The United States' Declining Competitiveness In The Marketing of International Tourism: A Perspective on Future Policy," *Journal of Travel Research*, Fall 1990, pp. 23–29.

The cooperative programs involved approximately 800 private sector firms and state and local tourism agencies. A variety of cooperative promotional techniques were used, including consumer newspaper and magazine advertising, travel-trade newspaper and advertising, travel-trade and consumer shows, familiarization tours, travel missions to the originating countries, and training workshops and seminars.[8] While these USTTA-coordinated promotional programs varied in their execution by country, the greatest emphasis was given to promoting to travel-trade intermediaries (trade shows, travel missions, familiarization trips, trade newspaper and magazine advertising). It is also noticeable that in contrast to many other NTOs, including Tourism Canada, USTTA's advertising only involved the print media (newspapers, magazines, direct mail), and no use was made of the broadcast media (television and radio). In contrast, for just the spring and summer 1990 U.S. Consumer Advertising, Tourism Canada spent an estimated $7.594 million on television advertising in the U.S. (another $2.697 million was earmarked for magazine advertising).[9]

USTTA's cooperative support programs involved the development of travel brochures and displays, consumer and trade information services, maintenance of film and video libraries and reference library materials. These materials are used by market specialists and information counselors in USTTA's regional offices to stimulate travel to the U.S.

Research program.   While not strictly promotion, marketing research studies help to guide promotional programs and measure their effectiveness. A significant portion of USTTA's budget is spent on its research program. In Fiscal 1990, $1.244 million—or approximately 9% of USTTA's total budget—was allocated to the research program, excluding research staff salaries and benefits. The research projects receiving funding were the USTTA Survey of International Air Travelers, Foreign Visitor Arrival Statistics, Cosponsored Consumer Surveys (with Tourism Canada), Surveys of Foreign Travel Trade, and Marketing Program Evaluation Studies.

Other programs.   In addition to the programs mentioned above, USTTA also operates a variety of other programs. These include a Multilingual Receptionist program offered at 12 major U.S. airports and its tourism policy program. Finally, the agency coordinates, organizes, and promotes Federal participation in major world fairs, expositions, and special events that take place in the U.S. These would include such events as the 1992 Winter Olympics and the 1994 World Cup Soccer Championship.

TOURISM CANADA

In contrast with its neighbor to the south, Canada's NTO, Tourism Canada, has tradi-

[8]U.S. Travel and Tourism Administration, Marketing U.S. Tourism Abroad: A Manual of Cooperative Marketing Programs in USTTA MARKETS 1990–91.

[9]Tourism Canada, Tourism Canada Spring/Summer 1990 U.S. Consumer Advertising Plan (undated).

tionally enjoyed much greater Federal Government financial support and an enhanced stature within the political system. With an annual budget almost three times greater than USTTA's, Tourism Canada has been able to, among other things, make greater use of advertising media and to place a larger investment in tourism research. Additionally, Tourism Canada has played a much greater role in domestic tourism and in offering programs to facilitate the development and improvement of Canadian tourism attractions, facilities, and services. As mentioned earlier, USTTA has traditionally had no role or mandate in tourism development and in domestic tourism promotion.

Tourism Canada's advertising campaign "Canada. The World Next Door" provides both a "textbook" example of a well-executed promotional program and a stark contrast to the lackluster "America. Catch the Spirit" advertising programs used by USTTA. For the three years of 1987–88, 1988–89, and 1989–90, Tourism Canada spent a grand total of between $23.6 and $27.1 million (Canadian) on tourism advertising in the United States and overseas. Approximately 84 to 87% of these funds were spent for the U.S. advertising campaign under "The World Next Door" banner. While the USTTA has traditionally emphasized advertising in the print media and travel trade relations, Tourism Canada, with its greater funding has been able to sustain major "image" advertising campaigns aimed at the travel consumer and to make more extensive use of television advertising.

STATE TOURISM OFFICES IN THE UNITED STATES

Several U.S. States, expecting an increase in domestic travel after World War II, established tourism offices at the beginning of the 1940's. By the end of the war, half of the states had established some mechanism to promote tourism. At present, every state has a State Tourism Office (STO). In 43 states, the STO is a component of a state government department or agency.[10] Because of the promotion of tourism for reasons of economic development, most of these STOs are located within their respective Departments of Commerce or Departments of Economic Development. Some STOs are combined with related functions such as parks and recreation, highways, and community and local affairs. Ten STOs, including those in Tennessee and Alabama, are cabinet level, independent agencies or commissions, many of which report directly to their respective Governors. Three states—Alaska, Hawaii, and Texas—each have two organizations responsible for tourism. Texas has two government agencies (Travel and Information Division of the Department of Highways and Public Transportation; Tourism Division of the Department of Commerce). Hawaii has its Hawaii Tourist Office within the Department of Business and Economic Development, plus the independent, nonprofit Hawaii Visitors Bureau. The Alaska Division of Tourism is within the Department of Commerce and Economic Development, and there is also an Alaska Tourism Marketing Council with primary responsibility for conducting domestic marketing programs.

[10]U.S. Travel Data Center, Survey of State Travel Offices 1989–90, March 1990. The statistics quoted in this section are extracted from this annual report.

STO Budgets

The STOs within the United States have assumed a larger role than the Federal Government's NTO (USTTA) in marketing U.S. tourism. This is especially true in the promotion of domestic tourism to U.S. residents, where the USTTA does not have a mandate and plays almost no role.[11] USTTA's total budget represents a small percentage of the combined total spent by the STOs, less than 5% in 1990. STO budgets expanded rapidly during the 1970's and 1980's. The combined STO 1989–90 budgets were estimated at $340.7 million, 7.3 times the figure in 1973–74 and 2.86 times greater than in 1981–82.

STOs have gradually diversified their sources of program funding. While eight out of ten STOs used to receive all of their funding from State Government general revenues, now just 28 of them rely solely on Government allocations. The remaining 22 STOs receive part of their funding from lodging and other tourism-dedicated taxes, membership dues, lottery funds, and private sources. As in the case of the USTTA, STOs have placed increased emphasis on cost-shared, cooperative marketing programs with the private sector and local convention and visitors bureaus.

The largest portion of STO budgets is allocated to media purchases and advertising production costs. Approximately 37% of the combined STO budgets for 1989–90 was dedicated to media advertising, the majority of which was for television, magazine, newspaper, and radio advertising. The other major spending categories are matching funds programs, personnel, welcome center operations, promotion, press, and public relations, printing and production, administration, and inquiry fulfillment.

STO Advertising Programs

All STOs have designated an individual who is responsible for the development of tourism advertising campaigns. In most cases, this is the State Tourism Director or the Assistant Director. All fifty states retain the services of outside advertising agencies. In most states, various groups outside of state government, including convention and visitor bureaus and regional tourism organizations, cooperate in advertising programs. More than thirty STOs have matching funds programs in which grants are given to support promotional and certain other projects on a 50-50 cost-sharing basis. For 1989–90, the average total advertising budget for all STOs was $2.52 million, with a wide range from $150,000 (Delaware) to $11.9 million (New York). STO budgeted expenditures for matching funds programs averaged just under $919,000.

Many STOs also cooperate with USTTA in its efforts to attract foreign visitors. This involvement ranges from cost-sharing newspaper and magazine advertising in foreign countries to assistance with familiarization trips to the U.S. for foreign travel-trade intermediaries and travel writers. Some states also participate in travel-trade and consumer shows and travel missions within foreign countries. Approximately 35 STOs allocate some portion of their advertising budgets for promotions in for-

[11]Alastair M. Morrison, "Selling the USA: Part 2: Tourism promotion by the 50 states," Travel & Tourism Analyst, April 1987, pp. 3–18.

An important part of the state's marketing program is an advertising campaign

eign countries, primarily Canada. In 1989–90, the largest expenditures on foreign advertising were made by Florida, Illinois, Alaska, California, South Carolina, and Texas. The amounts spent on foreign advertising vary considerably from a low of $7,000 to a high of $1,638,013 in 1989–90. The average expenditure for foreign advertising for the thirty-four STOs supplying their budget figures for 1989–90 was $255,161. There was a definite trend in the 1980's for STOs to devote increasing attention to foreign markets.

Almost all STOs direct the majority of their advertising expenditures toward stimulating inquiries. About 90 percent of STOs survey people who inquire to measure the effectiveness of their advertising campaigns through various types of conversion studies. The number of STOs offering one or more toll-free telephone numbers for travel information inquiries grew rapidly during the 1980's. By 1990, almost 90% of the STOs provided this service to potential travelers. A large and growing proportion of information is being requested via these toll-free lines.

All STOs have developed their own tourism advertising slogans or "tag lines"— also sometimes referred to as positioning statements. Among these, some of the best recognized are "I Love New York," "Virginia Is For Lovers," and "Say Yes to Michigan." Some STOs have more than one slogan and direct them at different target markets.

STO public relations and publicity programs.   Almost all STOs have a staff member specifically assigned as a public relations or press information officer. About 90% of STOs publish their own newsletters on a monthly, bimonthly, or quarterly basis. The main focus of media-press relations efforts are out-of-state. Most states are involved in offering familiarization tours for out-of-state travel writers and other media representatives.

Other STO promotional programs.   Most states operate welcome centers or highway information centers. Welcome centers are mostly located along interstate or state highways and perform an important role in the distribution of travel information and STO promotional materials. By 1990, there were over 500 of these centers located in 47 of the states. The majority of these facilities are permanent and are open year-round. In addition to their promotional role, welcome centers are important sources of research information, with most STOs collecting statistics on visitor volumes and characteristics at these centers.

A growing number of STOs are also increasing their out-of-state representation. Ten STOs fund or co-fund information centers in other states, the largest number of these being located in New York City. A larger number of STOs (28 in 1989–90) are represented through information centers outside of the United States. The most popular locations for these foreign information centers are in Canada (Toronto), Japan (Tokyo), United Kingdom (London), and Germany (Frankfurt).

Travel-trade and consumer-travel shows are another important promotional activity for many states. Almost all STOs participate in travel shows, although the number attended ranged in 1989–90 from a low of three (New Hampshire) to a high of 75 (Hawaii). The average number of shows attended in 1989–90 was 14. These shows include both domestic and foreign travel-trade and consumer travel shows. Approximately 40 STOs participate in foreign trade or consumer shows.

STO assistance with package tour promotion and development.   Approximately 80 percent of STOs assist with the promotion and development of package tours. However, only about one third of STOs publish and distribute state package-tour catalogs, although this number seems to be on the increase. Seventy percent of the STOs have a staff member assigned to package tour development. Half of the STOs host familiarization tours, mainly for tour operators and retail travel agents, to promote the packaged tours available in their respective states. Twenty-eight STOs have specific budget allocations for package tour development and/or promotion.

STO Research Programs

During the 1980's, STOs began to place an increasing emphasis on research. Just under 90% of STOs now assign one or more staff members to research, and a growing number of them are making research a full-time staff position. Almost every STO has a continuing travel data-gathering program involving either visitors at welcome centers, motor vehicle counts, travel-related business receipts, or visitation at state-owned and privately operated attractions and facilities. During 1988–89, the most frequently performed types of special research projects were advertising effectiveness-conversion studies, economic impact studies, state visitor profiles, and consumer attitude-awareness-image studies. The projected average total research budget for 1989–90 was just under $129,000, with the largest research commitments being made by the Hawaii Visitors Bureau and the Alaska Tourism Marketing Council.

Other STO programs.   Most states have full-time staff members who devote all or part of their time to encouraging tourism-related development and the improvement of tourism attractions, facilities, and services. The amount of attention being given by STOs to improving and expanding their respective state's tourism has been steadily increasing.

Almost all STOs hold annual state tourism conferences. These conferences serve a variety of purposes. They have definite in-state public relations value for the STOs, but they also often provide education and training sessions for those involved in state tourism and a forum for disseminating information on marketing, research, and other programs.

SUMMARY

Promotion provides the means with which the tourism destination or organization communicates with past and potential travelers. In so doing, the five promotional mix elements of advertising, personal selling, sales promotion, merchandising, and public relations and publicity are used to achieve predetermined objectives. These objectives range from very broad "image" campaigns to promotions geared to increase revenues immediately. Each of the five promotional mix elements and the available communications media has distinct advantages and disadvantages, and it is important to weigh these carefully against a set of evaluation criteria.

National Tourism Offices (NTOs) play a pivotal role in promoting their destinations' tourism attractions, facilities, and services in foreign countries. The role and amount of financial support given to NTOs by their respective governments varies greatly, as can be seen when contrasting USTTA with Tourism Canada. State Tourism Offices (STOs) within the United States have increasingly played a more important role in both domestic and foreign travel promotion.

REFERENCES

DOMMERMUTH, WILLIAM P., *Promotion: Analysis, Creativity, and Strategy,* (Belmont, CA, Kent Publishing Company, 1984).

MORRISON, ALASTAIR M., *Hospitality and Travel Marketing,* (Albany, NY, Delmar Publishers, Inc., 1989).

U.S. TRAVEL DATA CENTER, Survey of State Travel Offices 1989–90, Washington, DC, 1990).

16

THE DISTRIBUTION MIX IN TOURISM

Channeling Messages and Services to the Market

"I imagined that the characteristic independence of Englishmen would revolt against a plan that reduces the traveler to the level of his trunk and obliterates every trace and trait of the individual. I was all wrong. As I write, the cities of Italy are deluged with droves of these creatures."

Charles Lever in Blackwood's Magazine, *mid-nineteenth century, upon hearing of Thomas Cook's plan to package Europe.*

The final link in The Tourism System involves getting messages and services to the market. This is accomplished through the distribution system, which is the subject of this chapter. The purpose of the tourism distribution channel is twofold: (1) to get sufficient information to the right people at the right time and in the right place to allow a purchase decision to be made, and (2) to provide a mechanism whereby travelers can make and pay for their purchases.

The distribution mix is an important component of the overall marketing mix in tourism. Decisions about distribution must be consistent with and complement other marketing mix components.

Chapter 16 describes different types of distribution channels and travel intermediaries. The roles of the tour wholesaler and retail travel agent are explained in depth. The characteristics and functions of both types of intermediaries are outlined. The chapter also discusses the concept of vertical integration within tourism distribution channels.

The chapter concludes with a view toward the future. The implications of changes in travel markets, advances in electronic information systems, and other major industry trends are discussed

---

LEARNING OBJECTIVES

Having read this chapter, you should be able to:

1. Describe the tourism distribution system using a diagram to illustrate the relationship of the various tourism organizations involved.
2. Define direct and indirect distribution, and explain the difference between these two concepts.
3. Explain the concept of vertical integration and discuss three ways of classifying travel distribution channels.
4. Identify and describe the major type of travel intermediaries.
5. Differentiate between escorted, hosted, and package tours.
6. Explain the economics of the tour wholesaling business.
7. Explain the three main business functions of the tour wholesaler.
8. Discuss the development and present-day importance of retail travel agents in tourism.

TOURISM DISTRIBUTION IS UNIQUE

The purpose of distribution is to establish a link between supply and demand, the tourism organization, and the traveler. The distribution system makes services and products available to customers. In tourism, distribution is different than in other industries. There is no physical distribution, since the items sold are usually *intangible*. Unlike in manufacturing, the tourism "product" cannot be physically packaged and shipped to the traveler, nor can it be held in inventory.

While the functions and problems of transportation and warehousing are eliminated, different types of challenges are present in tourism distribution. Tourism services are immediately *perishable*. The hotel room, airline seat, or cruise berth must be sold each and every day, flight, or sailing. A sale lost now is lost forever. More than in other industries, *travel-trade intermediaries*—organizations that operate between the providers of tourism services and travelers—are numerous and have a strong influence on travelers' purchase decisions. A major role of certain travel intermediaries is the "packaging" of complementary travel services and products to provide a more satisfying travel experience for the customer. Retail travel agents, for example, book airline seats, hotel rooms, sightseeing excursions, and rental cars and provide packaged vacations in the form of foreign independent tours (FITs). Tour wholesalers assemble these components into packaged vacations or tours and offer these for sale through retail travel agents. The tourism distribution system is different because it includes these unique intermediaries with unique roles. The system aims to get the promotional messages along with the necessary factual information to the traveler and attempts to make reservations easier for the customer.

DISTRIBUTION'S ROLE IN THE MARKETING MIX

The tourism distribution system or *distribution mix* is just one component of the marketing mix. Distribution-mix decisions must be made as an integrated part of the overall marketing mix. Once target markets have been selected and marketing objectives established, an appropriate marketing mix is chosen. The overall goal of the marketing mix is to reach target markets and achieve the stated objectives for these markets. The distribution system chosen affects other components of the marketing mix and, in turn, is itself affected by these other marketing-mix components. For example, the services offered may have to be modified to meet the specific needs of a travel intermediary. If airline seats are distributed through a tour wholesaler, the schedules and perhaps even the seating configuration of the aircraft may have to be adapted to meet the wholesaler's requirements.

Promotional approaches also need to be adapted to suit the choice of distribution channels and intermediaries. Because retail travel agents do not carry any inventory, there is little or no incentive for them to promote specific destinations. The promotional burden, therefore, falls to the destination marketing organization, transportation companies, and the suppliers of services in the destination. On the other hand, tour wholesalers carry an inventory of airline seats, hotel rooms, and other tourism services. They have a prior investment (in terms of "blocked" reservations) with airlines and individual suppliers in destination areas and are often willing to share the costs of promoting the destination in order to sell the maximum number of tours. For the airlines and suppliers of services, the promotional burden is shared. Often this results in joint advertising or other types of cooperative promotions.

The pricing approaches of the suppliers of tourism services are also influenced by the decision either to distribute directly to the traveler or indirectly through a travel intermediary. When tour wholesalers buy in bulk—such as *blocking* 100 rooms per night for three months—they expect and receive lower room rates.

THE TOURISM DISTRIBUTION SYSTEM

Direct and Indirect Distribution Channels

Carriers (airlines, railroad companies, and other transportation providers), *suppliers* (attractions, lodging, cruise line, and rental car companies), and *destination marketing organizations* face a two-step decision process when selecting their distribution mixes. First, they must make a choice of *distribution channel*, and then (if indirect channels are chosen) they must select specific travel-trade intermediaries. McIntosh defines the tourism channel of distribution as "an operating structure, system or linkage of various combinations of travel organizations through which a producer of travel products describes and confirms travel arrangements to the buyer.[1] This definition indicates that a tourism distribution channel has a twofold purpose—ensuring that

---

[1]Robert W. McIntosh, Definitions, unpublished, 1979.

potential travelers obtain the information they need to make their trip arrangements and, having made that choice, to make the necessary reservations.

Distribution may be direct or indirect. *Direct distribution* occurs when a carrier, supplier, or destination marketing organization sells directly to the traveler; *indirect distribution* is when the sale is made through one or more travel trade intermediaries. This results in a rather complex distribution system as can be seen in Figure 16.1.

Travel-Trade Intermediaries

The tour wholesaler. A *tour wholesaler* is a "business entity which consolidates the services of airlines or other transportation carriers and ground service suppliers into a tour which is sold through a sales channel to the public.[2] The terms *tour wholesaler* and *tour operator* are often used interchangeably. *Wholesaler* is sometimes incorrectly used to describe an organization that strictly handles the operation of a tour—a tour operator. The true tour wholesaler is involved in tour planning, preparation, marketing, and reservations and may or may not also operate the tour. By definition, the tour wholesaler does not sell directly to the public but receives reservations through other travel intermediaries, such as retail travel agents or airline sales offices.

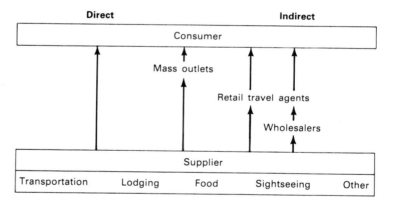

Adapted from: Salah Wahab, L. J. Crampon, and L. M. Rothfield, *Tourism Marketing* (London, Tourism International Press, 1976), p. 101.

Figure 16.1. The tourism distribution system

The retail travel agent. *Retail travel agencies* handle the sale and reservations of tours, vacation packages, airline tickets, hotel rooms, car rentals, cruises, travel insurance, and other related services. There were approximately 30,373 retail travel agencies in the United States in 1989.[3] The retail travel agent is compensated

[2]Tour Wholesaler Industry Study, Touche Ross & Co., 1976, p. 68.

[3]U.S. Travel Agency Survey, Travel Weekly, Vol. 49, No. 52, June 28, 1990.

through commissions from suppliers, carriers, and other intermediaries, such as tour wholesalers; the traveler pays nothing for the travel agent's services. Although some travel agencies in North America have begun to charge fees to the traveler, it will be many years, if ever, before this practice becomes widespread. The principal value of retail travel agents to travelers is the agent's independence and impartiality, coupled with a knowledge of tourism services and access to the inventory of other tourism organizations. Travelers expect that agents can recommend the best services to fit their travel needs. For suppliers, carriers, destination-marketing organizations, and other intermediaries, retail travel agencies represent additional sales outlets for their services and products. For most of them, it would be prohibitively expensive, if not impossible, to establish their own in-house system of nationwide distribution.

Corporate travel agencies and travel departments.   While traditionally considered as just one aspect of the retail travel agent's business, the growth in business travel has led to the emergence of a new breed of specialized travel agency exclusively servicing the corporate traveler. At the same time, an increasing number of companies have seen the wisdom of establishing in-house *corporate travel departments* to get the best prices on travel and to control employee abuses of frequent travel award programs. In the United States, the expansion of corporate travel agencies and departments paralleled the deregulation of the domestic airline industry.

The incentive travel planner.   Another recent newcomer to the tourism industry has been the *incentive travel planning company*, a specialized tour wholesaler who primarily serves corporate clients. The trips they arrange are given to certain of their clients' employees or dealers as a reward for outstanding sales or work performance. Incentive travel is increasing in popularity in North America as a work-related motivational tool. Corporations pay for the incentive travel planners' services either through a mark-up on the incentive package or on a fixed-fee basis.

Other intermediaries.   The number of ways of distributing travel services has increased in recent years and will continue to in the future. Some of these distribution methods will involve new organizations entering tourism (for example, banks and insurance companies) or the creation of new types of service businesses, while others will rely primarily on *electronic distribution* using advances in computer and telecommunications technology.

Three other intermediaries existing at the present time are convention-meeting planners and consultants, travel clubs, and sales representatives. *Convention-meeting planners* are employees of corporations, associations, government agencies, and other nonprofit groups who plan and coordinate meetings, conventions, conferences, or trade shows for their organizations. *Convention-meeting consultants* are specialized firms that assist planners with on-site negotiations and arrangements. *Travel clubs* are groups of individual travelers who use their collective buying power to bargain for discounted prices on tourism services. These include the increasingly popular *last-minute* travel clubs. *Sales representatives* are marketing specialists who represent hotels, resorts, destination areas, and other tourism organizations in foreign countries. This often provides a more economical alternative to having a fully-staffed office in each country.

The mass marketing of travel services has been pioneered in Europe and is gradually gaining ground in North America. In Germany, travel is sold door-to-door, through regional newspapers, and by using other *mass outlets*, such as lottery kiosks, supermarkets, and trade union offices. French trade unions have also become involved in packaging travel as a benefit for their members.[4]

In recent years, technological advances have had the greatest impact on tourism distribution, and the future promises even greater potential for the electronic distribution of tourism information and services. Most retail travel agencies are hooked into an airline computerized reservations system (CRS), giving them instant access to the inventory of the airlines and other tourism suppliers. Computer software programs links to on-line data-base reservations services are now available in most developed countries to allow travelers to make travel reservations in their own homes or offices via personal computers and telephone lines.

INTEGRATION AND CLASSIFICATION OF CHANNELS

Vertical Integration

Subject to the constraints of the legal environment, each carrier, supplier, destination marketing organization, and travel intermediary within the tourism distribution system wants potential travelers to have maximum exposure to information to encourage purchase decisions so that reservations and payments can be received. The more direct control a tourism organization has over the distribution of its services (through *vertical integration*), the greater is the assurance that information will be available and that the traveler can make reservations and payments easily and conveniently. Vertical integration refers to the ownership by one organization of all or part of a tourism distribution channel. For example, in the U.S. and Canada, the Carlson Companies own a hotel chain (Radisson), a full-service incentive company including an incentive travel division, and a chain of retail travel agencies.

Classification of Channels

Distribution channels can be classified in terms of degree of control into three types: (1) consensus channels; (2) vertically integrated channels commanded by suppliers, carriers, tour wholesalers, retail travel agents, or other intermediaries; and (3) vertically coordinated channels led by suppliers, carriers, tour wholesalers, retail travel agents, or other intermediaries.

[4]Lloyd E. Hudman and Donald E. Hawkins, *Tourism in Contemporary Society* (Englewood Cliffs, NJ, Prentice-Hall, Inc., 1989), pp. 158–159.

Consensus channels.   In a consensus channel, no single type of tourism organization exercises control over the entire distribution system. The many participants work together because they see it in their mutual interest to do so. Distribution channels in North America and the United Kingdom tend to be of the consensus type.

Vertically integrated channels.   Vertically integrated channels are those in which the supplier and retail distribution functions are owned or controlled by a single organization. Because tour wholesalers have historically emerged from the retail travel agency field, vertically integrated channels controlled by retail travel agents are commonly found in the United Kingdom (Thomas Cook), Germany (Deutsches Reiseburo), and North America (American Express). In Yugoslavia, Kompas operates a network of domestic travel agencies, acts as a tour wholesaler, and operates its own hotels and resorts. In Australia, the Queensland Tourist & Travel Corporation not only acts as the state's official destination marketing organization, but also operates a series of domestic retail travel agencies.

American Express—an example of a vertically-integrated channel commanded by travel agents

A tour wholesaler may exert control over the entire channel activity through retail outlet ownership and the organization of the channel. This system is commonly found in Germany, where tour wholesalers control not only their own chain of retail outlets, which deal exclusively with the products of one wholesaler, but also their own system of direct mail distribution.

Vertically coordinated channels.   A vertically coordinated channel led by tour wholesalers is one in which the tour wholesaler's power of control over the channel comes from contractual or financial commitments with retail travel agents. Franchising is an obvious example of such a system. In Germany, franchising is a large part of travel distribution. Retail travel agency franchising is also rapidly increasing in popularity in the U.K., U.S.A., and Canada. The franchisor of a particular company agrees to retail only through certain retail outlets (its franchisees) and to promote no other methods of distribution. The retail franchisee benefits from the much larger pool of marketing resources of the franchisor and the *name recognition* it shares with the many other franchised agencies under the same umbrella.

DISTRIBUTION-MIX STRATEGIES

Intensive, Exclusive, and Selective Distribution

Each tourism organization must decide on its distribution-mix strategy or how it will make its services available to potential travelers. With the rapidly expanding number of retail travel agencies and tour wholesalers in the developed countries, these decisions are becoming more complex and difficult. Certain factors, such as costs and getting the maximum exposure to the market (market coverage), suggest using the largest possible number of intermediaries. On the other hand, considerations such as the image of the services or destination and the motivations of individual travel-trade intermediaries favor vertically integrated or coordinated strategies or direct distribution, giving the supplier, carrier, destination marketing organization, or intermediary the greatest control over sales and reservations.

Three different types of strategy options available are intensive, exclusive, or selective distribution. An *intensive distribution* strategy involves maximizing the exposure of travel services by distributing through all available intermediaries (high market coverage). *Exclusive distribution* occurs when a carrier, supplier, tour wholesaler, or destination marketing organization limits the outlets for its services and attempts to have intermediaries sell only its services and not those of the competition. This may be accomplished through franchising or ownership of retail outlets, that is, through a vertically integrated or vertically coordinated approach. *Selective distribution* is a strategy somewhere between intensive and exclusive distribution. More than one but less than all available outlets are used.

Factors Affecting Distribution-Mix Strategy Decisions

For the tourism marketer, the task is to select and design a distribution mix strategy that not only is the most effective in reaching travelers and in taking reservations, but that is also affordable. The following six factors must be considered in making distribution-mix strategy decisions.

Market coverage. If a tour wholesaler, supplier, carrier, or destination marketing organization decides not to use the existing retail travel agency network, an alternative distribution network will have to be developed. In the developed countries, retail travel agencies offer substantial and growing market coverage that would be extremely difficult for one single organization to duplicate.

Cost. The cost of setting up one's own direct distribution channel is largely fixed. Salaries must be paid and offices must be maintained irrespective of the sales volume generated. Although a part of the compensation of sales representatives may be in the form of commissions, few people are willing to work on a commission-only basis. On the other hand, when working through travel-trade intermediaries, only variable costs are incurred. In fact, payments or commissions are made only after sales have been made. Fixed or overhead costs are reduced to a minimum.

Positioning and image. The choice of distribution channel must be consistent with the positioning and image that the supplier, carrier, destination marketing organization, or tour wholesaler is seeking for its services. The marketing of a quality service or destination to an upscale segment of the market must be made through quality intermediaries who themselves cater to upscale customers.

Motivation of travel-trade intermediaries. As shown in Figure 16.2, each type of organization or group within the tourism distribution system has a unique set of objectives and needs. These objectives and needs are not always compatible and often lead to conflicts and stresses in the tourism distribution system.

Tourism Producer	Wholesaler
Sales volume	Sales volume
Loyal repeat business	High margins
High return on investment	Producer reliability
Low-cost channels of distribution	Low risk, little novelty
Maximum channel attention to his or her products	Products that motivate retailers
Retailer	**Client**
Sales volume	Anticipation-creating stimulus
High margins	Product knowledge
Image	Product variety
Regular innovation in products	New products
Good producer service	Help in evaluating product alternatives and coming to a decision
Maximum range of products for his or her attention	Minimum waste of time (including moving from counter to counter or returning to the point of sale)
	Minimum form filling
	Competent staff
	Pleasant service
	Individual identification

SOURCE: Salah Wahab, L. J. Crampon, and L. M. Rothfield, *Tourism Marketing* (London, Tourism International Press, 1976), p. 102.

Figure 16.2 Wants and needs in the channel

Clients (travelers) are looking for a variety of services and products from which to select those that will result in the most satisfying travel or vacation experience. Retail travel agents want a constant variety of destinations and other travel services to offer to their clients, but they need to sell a mix of travel offerings that produce a large enough profit margin. Tour wholesalers want high volume and high margins but are concerned about developing tours and packages that motivate retail travel agents to sell them to their clients while presenting the wholesaler a minimum level of risk. Suppliers, carriers, and destination-marketing organizations want to minimize distribution costs while getting the maximum exposure for their services or destinations. By getting maximum exposure, they hope to generate high traffic volumes and to encourage multiple visits or repeat business. The more integration within the channel, the more customer-contact employees will be motivated to sell particular services or destinations at the expense of others.

Where direct ownership is not feasible or legally permitted, suppliers, carriers, tour wholesalers, and destination-marketing organizations try to increase the motivation of retail travel agents by offering larger commissions (sometimes referred to as *overrides*) for volume business, familiarization trips or training seminars to increase product knowledge, and different types of sales support, ranging from toll-free telephone numbers to in-store displays.

Characteristics of the destination or tourism service.　　The characteristics of the destination or services are a fourth factor to be considered. Where the services are high-priced, where they are purchased infrequently, where services are not subject to discounting, where the customer perceives the services as being distinctive, and when personal selling is required, a tourism organization can be more selective in its choice of retail outlets.

Economic concentration.　　A further consideration is related to the power exerted within the channel. The amount of channel power depends upon the degree of economic concentration among a particular category of tourism organizations. The fewer tour wholesalers serving a destination, the greater is the power those wholesalers have over the destination, and the more profit they can make on that destination. Also, the more wholesalers that are used, the higher the cost will be of selling to and servicing them.

Germany is an example of a country in which travel is exclusively distributed through vertically integrated channels. With the growth in the retail travel agency field in the U.K. and North America, there has been a movement away from distributing through as many retail outlets as possible (intensive distribution) to being more selective in the choice of retail outlets (selective distribution). Carriers, suppliers, and destination-marketing organizations want the maximum sales volumes; for tour wholesalers, volume is even more critical. Although this suggests using the maximum number of retail outlets, many tourism organizations have realized that, while it is more risky to deal with a smaller number of travel agencies, the costs of servicing all retail outlets have become prohibitive. In addition, a small percentage of agencies often produce most of the business for any one supplier, carrier, wholesaler, or destination-marketing organization. By concentrating on those agencies which produce most of the sales, a more efficient and effective distribution system can be achieved.

THE TOUR WHOLESALER

Although tour wholesaling began in the mid-nineteenth century, it was not until the 1960's that the packaging of tours increased dramatically. The increase resulted from development of larger aircraft capable of flying greater distances. Increased capacity led to lower airfares that stimulated demand for low-cost vacations. Although it is true that demand stimulates supply, it is also possible for supply to stimulate demand. To meet this demand, tour wholesalers came into the marketplace to put together low-cost vacation packages.

Roles of the Tour Wholesaler

The principal role of a tour wholesaler is to combine both transportation and ground services into tours or packages that are sold through retail travel agencies to individual or group travelers. This role is performed primarily by independent tour wholesalers who make up about three quarters of all wholesalers. Tour wholesaling is also done by several other types of organizations. Retail travel agents often prepare individual (foreign independent tours or FITs) and group tours (group inclusive tours or GITs) which they market themselves. Many airlines have wholesaling divisions that put together tours. This movement has been slow because of legal restrictions and the possibility of a negative reaction from travel-trade intermediaries that might view an airline's entry into the tour business as competition. Companies specializing in incentive travel, cruise lines, travel clubs, and various nonprofit organizations (unions, religious groups, associations, government and quasi-government agencies) also organize tours.

Many tour wholesalers tailor their tour offerings by target market, destination, mode of transportation, or type of activity or special interest. Some wholesalers cater to specific segments of the market (ethnic groups such as Hispanic or African Americans), while others *mass market* by promoting popular "sun and sand" destinations. Still other wholesalers specialize in developing tours to specific destinations or regions of the world (for example, Classic Hawaii and Pacific Delight Tours). Some wholesalers specialize in one type of transportation. The majority of tours marketed by independent tour wholesalers involve air travel.

Categories of Tours and Packages

Three main categories of tours and packages are offered by tour wholesalers:

1. *Escorted tours:* A type of organized tour that includes the services of a tour escort who accompanies an individual or group throughout the tour.
2. *Hosted tours:* A type of organized tour that includes the services of a tour host who meets an individual or group at each destination to make local arrangements but does not accompany the entire tour.
3. *Package tours:* A type of organized, individual or group tour that includes airfare and some ground transportation arrangements but does not necessarily include the services of anyone meeting the individual or group at the destination.

Economics of Tour Wholesaling

The independent tour wholesaling business is very concentrated, with a small number of companies accounting for a large percentage of the total revenue generated and passengers carried. The tour wholesaling industry is also characterized by relative ease of entry, high velocity of cash flow, low return on sales, and the potential for high return on equity investment.

Ease of entry. Although independent tour wholesalers in some countries are not licensed by government agencies, their activities tend to be constrained by various regulations. To be considered a tour, a vacation offering must meet established guidelines. It must be of a certain minimum duration and priced at a certain minimum, and it may have to include a minimum number of travelers. In the U.S., to be commissionable to travel agents, the domestic air transportation element must conform to standards of the Airlines Reporting Corporation (ARC). For flights on many non-U.S. carriers, the International Airlines Travel Agent Network (IATAN) is the regulating body. To sell charter tours, the tour wholesaler must meet regulations on pricing, advertising, and bonding. Despite the existence of these regulations, it is relatively easy, because of the low "up-front" investment, to become a tour wholesaler.

Cash flow. Cash flow is particularly crucial to a tour wholesaler. The wholesaler contracts for bulk quantities of transportation and ground services (airport transfers, lodging, meals, entertainment, sightseeing, ground transportation, and the like). Deposits have to be made for these services. By contracting in bulk for ground services, the wholesaler receives discounts on regular rates and prices. A wholesaler may, for example, contract for 200 rooms in a hotel every night for three months. The ground portion of a tour, which comprises about half the cost of an average tour, is then marked up by the wholesaler to show a profit. It is then combined with the transportation segment of the tour to arrive at a selling price. The transportation segment of the tour cannot be marked up, since all the commissions usually flow directly to the retail travel agent, since they and not the wholesaler are accredited by the appropriate regulating bodies. Cash flow or "float" is generated when customers' deposits and final payments are received prior to departure. Tour wholesalers do not pay the ground service suppliers until after the tour is over. The resultant cash flow is used to pay the tour wholesalers' operating expenses. Problems arise when the cash flow from one tour has to be used to finance the preparation of another. If demand slows, then even a large tour wholesaler, having little in the way of assets to shield it, can have a significant cash loss.

Return on sales The average return on sales for an independent tour wholesaler is approximately 3 percent, and sales volume is the key to profitability. Usually just under half of total tour revenue is generated from the transportation part of the tour, and over 90 percent of that, on an industrywide basis, goes to the airlines. The tour wholesaler does not receive any of the air ticket revenue. It goes to the airline, with a portion being retained by the retail travel agent as a commission. Just over half of the cost of an average tour is comprised of revenue from ground services, with hotel and meals accounting for almost 60 percent this. The wholesaler, therefore, is left with approximately 50 percent of total revenue from which to pay for the costs of ground services.

The wholesaler's costs are both direct (variable) and indirect (fixed). *Direct costs* represent about 85 percent of total costs and consist of payments made directly to carriers and suppliers, as well as retail travel agent commissions. The retailer receives a commission from both the airline for selling the transportation and from the wholesaler for selling the ground services of the tour. *Indirect costs* are all operating costs that do not involve direct payments to suppliers or retail travel agency commissions. About half of all indirect costs are in employee wages. The major elements of a tour wholesaler's indirect costs are:

Reservations, record keeping, and accounting	25%
Tour preparation	22%
Literature production and printing	15%
Promotion	12%

The economics of a tour are illustrated in Figure 16.3. Although this may not reflect the exact pricing structure of any one tour, the figures shown are indicative of an industry average. Because of the importance of sales volume, a relatively small change in the number of tours sold can mean the difference between a large profit and a large loss. The gross profit is, on the average, 10 percent of the total revenue generated. From this must be paid the indirect or fixed costs of running the tour wholesaling operation. Thus, each 1,000-dollar tour contributes 100 dollars toward payment of the indirect costs. Once these costs have been paid, the contribution goes toward generating new profit.

Return on equity. Because the capital requirements for entering the tour wholesaling business are so low, a substantial return on equity can be realized. The

	Revenue	minus	Direct Costs		equals	Gross Profit
Transportation						
Air	$ 480		$480			
Ground						
Hotels and meals	$ 305		$222			
Sightseeing	65		60			
Car rentals	35		30			
Travel agent commission	78		78			
Miscellaneous	37		30			
Selling price	$1000		$900		$100	
Indirect Costs						
Salaries and wages				$35		
Promotion				14		
Telephone and telegraph				8		
Rent				4		
Miscellaneous				9		
Total					$ 70	
Net profit						$30

Figure 16.3 Economics of a tour

opportunity for a high return on equity (net profit divided by owner's equity) comes about because the equity invested is small, not because the net profit is high.

Business Functions of the Tour Wholesaler

A single tour program consists of three parts: (1) Tour preparation, (2) tour marketing, and (3) tour administration (see Figure 16.4).

Tour preparation.   The preparation of a tour begins with market research. By using the results of research organizations, by analyzing tourist movements, and by surveying retail travel agents and past and potential tour patrons, the wholesaler gets an indication of which tours will sell. This information is combined with past operating results which show which tours have sold well and have been profitable. The policies and tour destinations of competitors are also considered.

When preparing tours for new destinations, tour wholesalers often participate in familiarization trips to determine tour potential, to evaluate ground services, and to solicit government support for tour business. At this point, detailed tour specifications are prepared, such as departure dates, tour length, and modes of transportation and ground services to be used. These activities often take place fourteen to eighteen months before the first tour departure date.

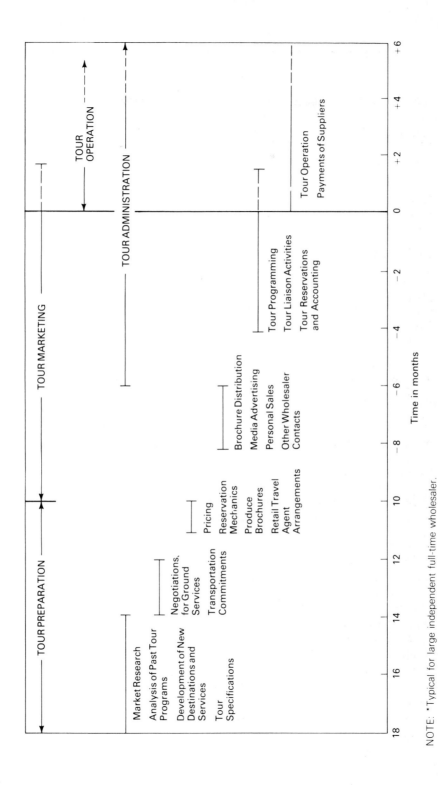

NOTE: *Typical for large independent full-time wholesaler.

SOURCE: Tour Wholesaler Industry Study, Touche Ross & Co., 1976, p. 48.

Figure 16.4 The four wholesaler operating cycle* Single season tour program.

The actual *tour program* is usually confirmed from twelve to fourteen months prior to the first tour departure. Ground services are negotiated and supplier agreements signed. Transportation commitments are made. When these steps are completed, the tour program can be finalized. The tour price is calculated by taking the negotiated costs for ground (or land) services and adding a *mark-up* that, when the expected number of tour patrons is considered, is sufficient to cover indirect (fixed) costs and the tour wholesaler's profit.

A checklist for pricing a tour is illustrated in Figure 16.5. As mentioned earlier, the wholesaler's costs are both fixed (indirect or *overhead*) or variable (direct). A cost is fixed if it must be paid irrespective of the number of travelers on the tour. If a bus is chartered or a tour director engaged, the wholesaler's cost is the same whether five or forty people take the tour. Variable costs are directly related to the number of persons on the tour. Airfare (unless for a charter flight), hotel rooms, or admissions are examples of variable costs.

The three columns in the middle of Figure 16.5 show the cost computations for three different group sizes. The first is the minimum size of group necessary. This would be based upon a specified minimum number of people that the carriers or ground service suppliers require to guarantee their prices to the tour wholesaler. In some cases, the type of airfare used may necessitate that the wholesaler guarantee a certain minimum number of passengers. The third column shows costs based upon the maximum number of travelers possible on the tour, while costs in the middle column should be based on the wholesaler's estimate of the most likely number of tour patrons.

The tour wholesaler's mark-up is expressed as either a percentage of net ground service costs or as a dollar figure. It has to be realistic yet also reflect the time and effort involved in organizing the tour. Airfare is added to total ground services costs and mark-up to arrive at the selling price for the retail travel agent. The final selling price is calculated by adding the retail travel agent's commission.

The mechanics of handling reservations and payment are made and brochure production begun. Brochure production is usually expensive, and often part of the production costs are paid by the transportation company involved in the tour or one or more of the ground service suppliers. Appropriate commission rates and volume incentives are also negotiated with retail travel agents. At this point, there are typically ten months left before the first tour departs.

Tour marketing.   The marketing of a tour is the aspect most crucial to its success. The characteristics of the tour marketing program depend upon the size of the wholesaler and the market segments being targeted. All marketing programs, however, involve brochure distribution, media advertising, personal selling, and contact with other wholesalers.

Brochures are usually distributed to all retail travel agencies. Emphasis may be given to agencies who have worked with the wholesaler before or whose customers have the characteristics of the target market. Tours may also be included in the brochures of the airline providing the transportation and distributed by that airline. The tour brochure may also advertise the airline.

Tour _____   Tour Dates _____

Compiled _____   Cancellation Date _____

Revised _____   Gateway _____

Variable Costs (per person)

1. Air Fare Basis...... _____	7. State/VAT taxes.... _____	13. Package ...... _____
2. Surcharges........ _____	8. Service Charges... _____	based on ( )
3. Airport Taxes ...... _____	9. Meals............ _____	14. Insurance .... _____
4. Transfers........ _____	10. Meal Taxes & Tips.. _____	15. Publications/
5. Baggage Tips...... _____	11. Sightseeing....... _____	· Postage ...... _____
6. Hotel Rooms ...... _____	12 Admissions .... _____	16. Miscellaneous ..... _____

Single Room Supplement _____   Total .... _____

Fixed Costs (Tour Director)

Include only costs not complimented

1. Transportation..... _____	7. Sightseeing/....... _____	12. Passports/Visas .... _____
(home/gateway/home	Admissions	13. Vaccinations .... _____
2. Transportation..... _____	8. Baggage Tips...... _____	14. Currency Conversion _____
(on tour)	9. Insurance _____	15. Miscellaneous ..... _____
3. Airport Taxes...... _____	10. Meals/Hotels...... _____	16. Salary .... _____
4. Hotel Rooms ...... _____	(Day before/	(days @)
5. Meals, Taxes, Tips .. _____	Day after tour)	
6. Transfers .... _____	11. Travelers Checks ... _____	Total .... _____

Fixed Costs (Group)

1. Chartered Vehicles .. _____	7. Programs......... _____	13. Administrative ..... _____
2. Tolls/Ferries ...... _____	8. Speaker Fee....... _____	14. Miscellaneous ..... _____
3. Sightseeing ...... _____	9. Driver Tips....... _____	15. Orientation .... _____
4. Admissions ...... _____	10. Brochures....... _____	16. Fund Raising ...... _____
5. Local Guides ...... _____	11. Promotion....... _____	
6. Transfers .... _____	12. Communications... _____	Total .... _____

Grand Total of all Fixed Costs

Computations Group Size........ _____   _____   _____

Land Costs

  A. Total Variable Costs........ _____   _____   _____

  B. Grand Total of Fixed Costs
    (Divided by Size of Group).. _____   _____   _____

  C. Sum of A and B .... _____   _____   _____

  D. Dollar Markup (%) .... _____   _____   _____

  E. Air Fare .... _____   _____   _____

  F. Sum of C, D, and E .... _____   _____   _____

Selling Price.................. _____   _____   _____

Minimum number of paying passengers. _____   Markup on Land (D) _____

Maximum number of paying passengers. _____   Air Commission _____

     Gross Net _____
     (Per Person)

SOURCE: Rosa Mae Howe, "Analyzing The Trip: Checklist of Steps," The 1980 Travel Agency Guide to Business and Group Travel, *Travel Weekly*, April 1980, p. 110.

Figure 16.5 Price structure sheet

Media advertising consists of advertising to retail travel agencies as well as to potential travelers. The type of messages for each are different. Advertisements in travel-trade publications, such as Travel Weekly or Travel Agent Magazine, are more factual; they describe the tours and give retailers information on how to book them. Toll-free numbers or coupons are often included in ads to encourage travel agents to request tour brochures, posters, and other sales and merchandising aids. The advertising to potential travelers tends to be more at an emotional level. It is often very colorful and glamorous and is designed to create interest in the tours being advertised. The ads are placed in consumer travel magazines such as Travel & Leisure and usually advise travelers to book the tours through their travel agent. Again by either calling a toll-free number or completing and mailing coupons, they may request tour brochures.

Wholesalers also employ sales representatives who concentrate on selling tours to those travel agents regarded as the best prospects. Because of the high cost of distribution, tour wholesalers from one part of the country may, for a fee, use wholesalers from another part of the country to distribute their tours in that region.

Marketing begins up to ten months prior to departure and continues until a few days beforehand. Reservations, deposits, and payments are requested from one to two months in advance of the departure. If insufficient advance bookings are made, tours may be consolidated or promotion increased.

Tour Administration.   The administration of a tour begins six months prior to departure. Detailed schedules or worksheets are prepared describing the tour program, and a reservation system sufficient to detail the documentation and payment status of each tour patron is set up. Liaison procedures are established between the reservation system and the ground service suppliers at each destination.

Reservations are usually received by telephone or via computer from retail travel agencies. They are confirmed, recorded, and filed. Deposits and payments are processed and documentation is sent to the agency for distribution to the traveler. Upon completion of the tour, the suppliers are paid. The tour operation part of the tour may be handled by the tour wholesaler or by ground service operators (for example, motor coach companies) or other destination management companies based in the destinations.

Operating cycle.   The tour wholesaling business is seasonal. At any one time the wholesaler's staff may be preparing the following year's program while marketing and operating the existing year's offering. The operating cycle of a wholesaler is illustrated in Figure 16.6.

THE RETAIL TRAVEL AGENT

Thomas Cook is credited with developing the concept of a travel agent in 1841 when he chartered a train to carry people from Leicester to Loughborough, a distance of twenty-two miles, to attend a temperance convention. In the U.S. in the early 1900s,

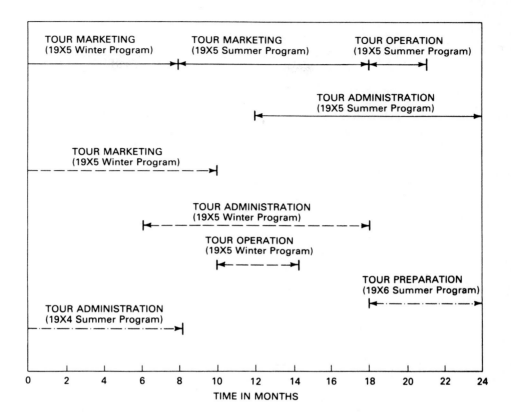

SOURCE: *Tour Wholesaler Industry Study*, Touche Ross & Co., 1976, p. 55.

Figure 16.6   Independent tour wholesaler two-year operating cycle

rail travel was the primary mode of transportation for the business traveler. Little pleasure travel existed. The travel agent of the day was the hotel porter, who would make reservations for the businessman staying at the hotel. The porter received a commission from the railroad and would add a delivery charge for going to the railroad station to purchase the ticket. The airlines, which first purchased planes with seats for passengers in the late 1920s, saw the railroads as their major competitor for the business market. (The pleasure market would not become significant for another ten years.) The airlines approached the hotel porters, equipped them with ticket stock, and offered a 5 percent commission for making the sale. Little expertise was required as most carriers had only one route and the tickets already contained information about fare origin and destination of the flight. The feeling of the carriers was that the porters were providing a ticketing service for business that was already there rather than creating new business. Thus, from the beginning hotel porters and then travel agents were seen as distributors of tickets and entitled to a small commission.

Retail travel agents are an important part of the channel of distribution

As carriers opened their own offices in hotels that provided large enough traffic volume to justify the expense, porters were forced out of business. Also, the carriers restricted the new breed of travel agent from opening an office where it would compete with the airline sales office.

After World War II, two trends resulted in the growth of travel agency business. These were the growth in personal or pleasure travel and the growth in international travel. The airlines continued to exert considerable influence over the birth of an agency. Prior to 1959, when the so-called need clause was abolished by the Civil Aeronautics Board, a U.S. travel agency could be opened only if it was sponsored by an airline and its opening approved by two-thirds of the carriers represented. The sponsoring airline was responsible for checking that the agency was sound from a financial viewpoint, had an acceptable location, and had a staff with sufficient experience. It is now necessary for the agency to be appointed by the appropriate conference to sell tickets and receive commissions. Virtually all U.S. agencies have appointments by the Airlines Reporting Corporation (ARC) to sell domestic air tickets and a somewhat smaller proportion with the International Airlines Travel Agent Network (IATAN), a subsidiary of the International Air Transport Association, for international tickets.

Organization[5]

Sixty-eight percent of U.S. travel agencies are single-location operations, while 19% are branch offices, and 13% are head offices of multi-location operations. Less than

---

[5]Since 1970, Travel Weekly has sponsored a biannual survey, conducted by Louis Harris & Associates, of travel agency operations. This section is largely taken from the reseults of those studies.

10% of agencies are licensees or franchisees of larger companies (such as Uniglobe, Ask Mr. Foster, or Travel Agents International). The percentage of agencies affiliated with marketing consortiums or cooperatives has increased dramatically in recent years, and the trend seems likely to continue. In 1989, 38% of all U.S. agencies were affiliated with vacation and pleasure travel consortiums, while 13% were affiliated with corporate travel consortiums.

Size and volume.   The number of U.S. retail travel agencies has grown substantially in the past two decades, from 6,686 in 1970 to 30,373 in 1989. There was a 105% increase since airline deregulation took effect in the U.S. in 1978. In addition to the 30,373 agencies, there were 4,343 *satellite ticket printer* (STP) locations in the U.S. in 1989. Approved by the Airlines Reporting Corporation in 1986, STPs are used by agencies to print airline tickets at locations remote from the agency, for example, at branch offices of a corporate client.

The total retail revenues of U.S. agencies grew from just over $5 billion in 1970 to $19.4 billion in 1978 and then to $79.4 billion by 1989, placing travel agencies within the top ten retail segments in the country. The average revenue per agency in 1989 was $2.613 million, although 66% of the agencies had sales of less than $2 million. The average was so high because some 34% of the agencies account for 67% of the total industry revenues. Despite these impressive figures, agencies tend to be small businesses in terms of employees, averaging 6.3 employees per agency in 1989.

The most significant trend has been in the distribution of travel agency by size of agency. In 1978, 48% of U.S. agencies had total revenues of less than $1 million; by 1989 there were only 27% in this range. Those agencies producing less than $1 million in bookings have shown a consistent decline in market share while those producing more than $1 million in bookings have shown a corresponding increase. The small agency is declining rapidly. The larger the agency, the more productive the employees, since the sales volume per employee increases as the size of the agency increases.

Sources of Retail Travel Agency Business

U.S. travel agencies operate on relatively small rates of commission. For example, the commission on domestic air and hotel reservations tends to be a standard 10%. Other types of travel offerings produce higher commission rates and are more lucrative to the retail travel agent. These offerings include international air fares, cruises, wholesalers' package tours and vacations, and the sale of travel insurance. International air tickets and tour wholesaler and cruise packages typically earn U.S. travel agents commissions in the range of 12% to 15%. By choosing particular airlines, agencies may also earn *overrides* or additional percentage points of commission. Some 51% of U.S. agencies in 1989 chose this strategy to earn higher commissions on their airline business. The total bookings of U.S. agencies by supplier and carrier in U.S. $ billions are shown below:

U.S. AGENCY BOOKINGS BY SUPPLIER AND CARRIER IN U.S. $ BILLIONS

	1978		1981	1989	
Airline tickets	$11.8	60.9%	$19.5	$45.6	57.4%
Cruises	$ 2.1	10.8%	$ 4.0	$12.1	15.2%
Hotel rooms	$ 2.1	10.8%	$ 3.1	$ 9.0	11.3%
Car rentals	$ 1.4	7.2%	$ 2.2	$ 6.3	8.1%
Rail tickets	n/a	n/a	n/a	$ 3.2	4.0%
Other (including motorcoach tours)	$ 2.0	10.3%	$ 2.2	$ 3.2	4.0%
TOTAL	$19.4	100.0%	$31.0	$79.4	100.0%

About 70% of U.S. travel agency sales in 1989 resulted from domestic travel, and the remaining 30% was from international travel. During the period of 1978 to 1989, domestic volume has increased in importance relative to international travel; domestic travel represented 63% of total agency sales in 1978. This trend is largely due to the increase in corporate travel accounts and business travel bookings since 1970.

About 44% of the total revenues of U.S. travel agencies in 1989 resulted from business-related travel and the remaining 48% from pleasure-personal travel. Business-related travel generated approximately $34.9 billion in total agency revenues, while pleasure-personal travel accounted for $38 billion. An additional $6.4 billion was earned from trips involving a combination of business and pleasure. Approximately $16.4 billion or 43% of the total revenues from pleasure-personal travel resulted from the sale of packaged tours and vacations. The move toward the increased popularity of packaged tours and vacations was a significant trend for U.S. travel agencies during the 1980's. Packages grew in popularity, while foreign independent tours (FITs) lost ground.

The majority of sales volume of U.S. agencies results from individual as opposed to group travel. Only $7.9 billion or 10% of the $79.4 billion in total agency revenues in 1989 came from group travel. Individual travel for business reasons accounted for $37.3 billion and individual pleasure-personal travel for $34.1 billion.

Corporate Travel

In North America, the increased importance of corporate accounts to retail travel agencies is due to a number of factors. First, airline deregulation in the U.S. resulted in the growth of *inplants*—branch offices or additional authorized agency locations of approved agents located at the firm's place of business—as well as more liberal commission policies. In more recent years satellite ticket printers (STPs) have also given agencies more distribution outlets and another convenient method of increasing corporate sales. Second, the use of computerized reservations systems (CRS) has increased agencies' productive capacity and agencies have tried to attract more corporate accounts to make the fullest use of this added capacity. In addition, the combination of deregulation and increased CRS use has led to a situation in which air-

Channel Relationships and Power

A large majority of agents consider familiarization trips as being very important factors in influencing their recommendations of a particular destination. A majority of agents are also concerned with the attractiveness of the price.

In dealing with tour wholesalers, the critical factor is the quality of service received—the dependability, promptness, and efficiency. This is far more important to agents than even prices and customer feedback. Client feedback, however, is important to agents in their selection of package tours for clients. Most agents prefer certain packages over others. The major factor in their selection of a particular package is the reliability and efficiency of the tour operator.

As noted earlier, the alliance among those in the channel of distribution is often an uneasy one. The motivations of the different distribution "partners" are different. Although people at a destination seek tourists, they do not pay a commission to those who produce them. Wholesalers contract for inventory in destinations that they believe will sell, and because of this commitment they actively push the sale of the destination through retail outlets. Retailers carry no inventory and are interested in selling a product that will result in satisfied clients (unhappy clients will probably blame the retailer) while ensuring sufficiently high commission payments.

Who has the power in such a system? Many have thought that control is exerted by the tour wholesalers who can elect whether or not to put a destination on the tourist map. Indeed, the tour wholesaler may have the power in the early stages of destination development. At this point, destinations and other suppliers may be more willing to make concessions to a wholesaler who will take an active role in marketing a new destination to a mass market. Once the destination gains in popularity, however, wholesalers' influence is reduced, and they may even be excluded from the market. Such was the case in London when, with the assistance of tour wholesalers, London became an attractive destination for U.S. travelers. As hotel space became tighter, the balance of power moved to the hotel companies. Tour wholesalers who had helped promote the demand were faced with increased room rates, demands for prepayments, and in some cases, cancellations. The balance of power is very much a balance of supply and demand.

CORPORATE TRAVEL DEPARTMENTS

Many corporations, government agencies, and nonprofits have created their own, in-house corporate travel departments. These have been established for three main reasons: (1) to cut business travel expenses; (2) to provide better service to travelers; and (3) to increase corporate-group purchasing power. More recently, these departments have helped their organizations gain more control over the use (and abuse) of the growing number of frequent-travel reward programs. In North America, the two major associations representing corporate travel managers are the National Business Travel Association (NBTA) and the Association of Corporate Travel Executives (ACTE).

As mentioned earlier, the importance of corporate travel accounts to North American retail travel agents has greatly increased. The streamlining of corporate travel has brought the independent agent more business and has also provided the basis for the establishment of large agencies exclusively serving corporations (often called *outplants*). The growth of *inplants*—travel agent offices located within the physical premises of corporate clients was also highlighted before. Another route followed by some corporations is to become travel agents themselves, operating their own in-house, fully-accredited agencies.

INCENTIVE TRAVEL HOUSES

Incentive travel has enjoyed significant growth in the past two decades. It is used by large and medium-sized corporations to reward company employees, distributors, and sometimes potential customers, typically for outstanding work-related performance. Free travel as a motivational tool is becoming increasingly potent in the developed countries. Historically, incentive travel trips have been used to recognize outstanding sales performance by company employees as well as dealers and distributors. The number of motivational applications of incentive travel have grown, and they are now being used for increasing plant production, encouraging better customer service, improving plant safety, introducing new products, selling new accounts, and enhancing morale and goodwill. The variety of incentive travel offerings has also expanded and now includes more modest weekend vacations as well as the more traditional, once-in-a-lifetime trips to exotic destinations.

The lucrative nature of incentive travel has attracted great interest among all the major parts of the tourism industries, including travel trade intermediaries, suppliers, carriers, and destination marketing organizations. The result has been the emergence of a rather complex distribution system of incentive travel. In North America, the key players are a small number of full-service "motivation houses" and a growing number of smaller, more specialized "incentive travel houses." By the end of the 1980s, there were about 500 of these specialized incentive travel planning companies in the United States. Many of these companies now belong to their own national association called the Society of Incentive Travel Executives (SITE).

The growth of incentive travel has been beneficial for retail travel agents, airlines, hotels, resorts, and other suppliers. It also represents an area of new market potential for national, state, regional, and city tourism marketing agencies. While some travel agents have themselves become involved in planning incentive trips, others simply play a "fulfillment" role by making air and hotel reservations for the incentive travel houses. A new category of firms—sometimes referred to as destination management companies—has also emerged to provide on-site service to incentive groups. Often these on-site arrangements include the staging of special tours and elaborately themed meals and events. Many airlines, hotel companies, NTOs, and convention and visitors bureaus have established special divisions or departments to serve the growing incentive travel market.

Convention, Meeting, and Trade Show Planning

Another part of the tourism business that enjoyed significant growth in the 1970's and 1980's was that related to the staging of conventions, corporate meetings, trade shows, and other similar events. Again, the increased popularity of these events benefited all parts of the tourism industries and, as with incentive travel, provided the foundation for new types of specialists and linkages in the tourism distribution system.

ELECTRONIC DISTRIBUTION SYSTEMS

Technological advances are likely to have an increasing impact on tourism distribution, as they have had in the recent past. The electronic distribution of travel services is now a major factor in most developed countries. One aspect of this has already been mentioned in the form of increased use of computerized reservation systems (CRS) by retail travel agents and within corporate travel departments.

Another innovation are a number of varieties of videotex systems that allow two-way communications on a television monitor. These systems offer exciting possibilities for both the consumer and the tourism industries. The British system, known as Prestel, was the world's first electronic system to be offered on a national scale. It combines television with the telephone and allows a subscriber to call up required information on the telephone and have it displayed on the television screen. The beauty of the system is that information stored in the computer can be continuously updated and that the system is available twenty-four hours a day without busy signals to the subscriber. The updating allows suppliers to pass changes in prices and schedules along instantly. When a particular tour may not be sold out as the departure date approaches, reductions in price can be made and communicated to potential buyers at once. These systems can also cost less for retail travel agents, and they are used extensively by British and other European travel agents.

In the United States, a number of on-line computer systems are now being offered to consumers that allow them to access travel information and make reservations via their own personal computers. These include CompuServe and the Prodigy system. Some airlines, including American, have developed personal-computer based versions of their agent reservation systems, allowing individuals to make their own reservations via the office or home computer.

Some retail travel agents are afraid that advances in electronic distribution and communications systems might cause consumers to bypass them altogether. They fear that eventually, suppliers and wholesalers will be able to transmit their messages directly to consumers who will be able to make travel choices, book tours, and pay for travel in their own homes or offices. It is unlikely, however, that these systems will soon displace retail travel agents. There are two reasons for this. First, the cost of access to these systems will mean that many will not be able to afford them. Much of the so-called mass market will only be able to access such information through intermediaries. Second, some time will pass before anything but the simplest vacations will be sold from a television set. Only if and when wholesalers establish a brand image reputation of quality such that travelers feel secure in buying from them will such sales be made.

Will convenience centers mean that travelers will bypass retail travel agents?

THE FUTURE TOURISM DISTRIBUTION SYSTEM

As the shape of tourism changes, the system of distribution is expected to change. Some changes will occur as tourism continues to develop from a luxury item to a mass-market product. Other changes will be forced upon the distribution system by external forces such as governmental agencies. As tourism shifts from a luxury item to a mass consumer product, there are those who feel that suppliers will exert more control on distribution. Vertical integration, in which transportation and ground suppliers merge and try to control the entire distribution channel, is expected to increase. New selling methods, such as through mail order, department stores, and bookshops, are predicted.

Others feel that the retail agent will continue to be the primary distribution intermediary for future travel services. They cite three reasons for this:[6]

[6]Mary J. Bitner and Bernard H. Booms, "Trends in Travel and Tourism Marketing: The Changing Structure of Distribution Channels," Journal of Travel Research, Spring 1982, pp. 39–44.

1. The industry is growing in terms of agencies and sales volume.

2. Agents will be difficult to replace as they account for a large percentage of bookings.

3. The system works, and it will be too expensive to replace agents with other methods.

There are some indications, however, that the cost of distributing through agents is approaching the point where carriers are questioning its cost effectiveness. At present, the average commission rate paid to agents domestically is around 10 percent, and it is approaching the point at which its cost effectiveness can be studied closely.

REFERENCES

DAVIS, BOB, "How It All Began," Sales Management for Travel Agents (Institute of Certified Travel Agents, 1974), pp. 1-3.

FRIEDHEIM, ERIC, "Who Dominates the Tour Trade?" The Travel Agent, September 3, 1979, pp. 54.

RUBIN, KAREN, "How's Business?" The Travel Agent, August 3, 1981, pp. 60-61.

RUBIN, KAREN, "How's Business?" The Travel Agent, September 6, 1982, pp. 22-23.

SCHMOLL, G. A., *Tourism Promotion* (London, Tourism International Press, 1977), pp. 32.

SIMS, J. TAYLOR, J. ROBERT FOSTER, and ARCH G. WOODSIDE, *Marketing Channels: Systems and Strategies* (New York, Harper & Row, 1977), pp. 138-40.

Tour Wholesaler Industry Study (New York, Touche Ross & Co., 1976), pp. 6, 47.

YACOUMIS, JOHN, Air Inclusive Tour Marketing: The Retail Distribution Channels in the U.K. and West Germany (International Tourism Quarterly Special Report No. 2, November 1975), pp. 35-37, 43.

INDEX